DATE DUE		

NINETEENTH-CENTURY
EUROPEAN CATHOLICISM

GARLAND REFERENCE LIBRARY
OF THE HUMANITIES
(VOL. 965)

NINETEENTH-CENTURY EUROPEAN CATHOLICISM
*An Annotated Bibliography
of
Secondary Works in English*

Eric C. Hansen

GARLAND PUBLISHING, INC. • NEW YORK & LONDON
1989

Library of Congress Cataloging-in-Publication Data

Hansen, Eric C.
 Nineteenth-century European Catholicism : an annotated
 bibliography of secondary works in English / Eric C. Hansen.
  p. cm. — (Garland reference library of the humanities ; vol.
965)
 Includes index.
 ISBN 0–8240–0697–6 (alk. paper)
 1. Catholic Church—Europe—History—19th century—Bibliography.
2. Europe—Church history—19th century—Bibliography. I. Title.
II. Series.
Z7837.7.E85H35 1989
[BX1490]
016.282'4—dc19   88-24746
                                                                    CIP

Printed on acid-free, 250-year-life paper
Manufactured in the United States of America

To
Thomas Michael Loome
Anthony F. Turhollow
and
Roger L. Williams
Scholars, Mentors, and Friends

CONTENTS

vii

ACKNOWLEDGMENTS

Several individuals have played an important role in the
compilation and publication of this bibliography, giving
enthusiastically of their time, talents, and resources.
The staff of the O'Shaughnessy Library of the College of
St. Thomas, St. Paul, Minnesota, fulfilled requests for
books and articles with an incredible efficiency and a
constant good humor; when not processing dozens of inter-
library loan forms, it was proffering valuable advice on
some of the more complex problems of citation. Without
the ongoing assistance of Betty Bigelbach, Jan Orf, Becky
Hagen, Susan Price, Jo Ann Toussaint, and Earl Belisle,
among others, the effort would not have been as enjoyable,
or the final product as comprehensive in its coverage.
A large debt of gratitude is also owed to Dr. John Nemo,
Dean of the College of St. Thomas, for his unstinting
technical support and personal encouragement. Matching
the expertise and generosity of the St. Thomas community,
but on the production side, were two managing editors at
Garland Publishing: Pamela Chergotis, through whose influence the proposal for this bibliography was accepted,
and Paula Ladenburg, a former student become friend and
literary partner, who supervised the final stages of the
work.

INTRODUCTION

The last quarter-century has witnessed an expanding and
deepening interest in the history of the Catholic Church.
Initially propelled by Vatican II's eloquently expressed
concern for ecclesiology, and supported by a parallel and
highly fruitful renewal in theology, this interest can
perhaps best be seen through the ever larger numbers of
individuals, both within and outside of academic institutions, taking courses in ecclesiastical history and
thought. Not limited simply to the traditional clientele
of seminarians and college students, this interest has
led to a proliferation of courses on the secondary level,
in parish adult education programs, in ministry training,
and in diocesan catechetical centers. Moreover, as the
Church, in the continuing spirit of Vatican II, explores
more fully its historical stance as the movement of the
"People of God" through the ages, popular interest will
find a greater sense of identification with a subject
which until rather recently repelled many of its would-
be devotees by concentrating almost exclusively on
prelatial politics and obscure theological disagreements.
    For all this increased interest in Catholic history,
however, there remains a notable dearth of reference works
to which teachers as well as students might turn, whether
for researching a paper or simply looking for further
reading in a given area. This is particularly true of
nineteenth-century European ecclesiastical development.
No substantial bibliography of works in English, either
in annotated form or as a simple listing, currently
exists. While both Catholic and non-Catholic historians
continue to add (and, in many cases, impressively) to the
body of literature, there has been no attempt to assemble
their products, providing for each entry a summary of its
contents, some indication of its critical acceptance or
rejection, and (where appropriate) a cross-listing of
complementary or opposing works in related areas.

Included in this bibliography are books, pamphlets, dissertations, and articles from periodicals and collections, published for the most part since 1900. To qualify for inclusion a work must present Catholic development as its major theme; consequently, no standard histories of nineteenth-century Europe, however useful their ecclesiastical treatment, are found here. At the same time, the listings feature only those materials which can be obtained either at a major college or university library or with relative ease through the national inter-library loan network.

For the purpose of this collection, nineteenth-century European Catholicism is defined in its broadest sense, meaning every aspect of the Catholic experience, from ecclesiastical structure to religious life in the individual countries, during the years 1800-1900. Europe includes not only France, Spain, Portugal, Italy, Germany, Austria, Hungary, the Low Countries, and Switzerland, but also the British Isles (England, Wales, Scotland, and Ireland), Russia, and the Turkish-ruled Balkans.

Each entry, upon its first appearance, is annotated; if reiterated in another section of the bibliography, it may or may not carry another annotation. The annotations offer the major idea or theme of the work as expressed by its author or editor; they are not intended to be mini-reviews by the editor of this collection. Some entries capsulize the work as a whole, while others focus on relevant sections or chapters. The length of an annotation does not reflect the particular work's length or scholarly value. Appended to each new entry and introduced by the word "See," is a listing of specialized journals containing reviews of the work. The listing presents these reviews in their order of appearance; when available, the names of the reviewers are given. These periodical references have been chosen to give the user a reliable idea of not only critical reception, but also of the oftentimes animated controversy among reviewers themselves over the merits or failings of a piece of scholarship.

Though this bibliography does not claim to include every single item written in English on nineteenth-century European Catholicism, it does point unmistakably to an enormous amount of diverse, rich, and challenging sources with which to reconstruct the sometimes triumphant, sometimes tortured course of a Church caught between revolution and reaction, innovation and tradition, and openness and obscurantism. In illustrating the existence of a formidable mine of scholarly resources, may it also

stimulate inquiry into hitherto neglected aspects of belief
and life during an age in which so much of the twentieth-
century Catholic experience is rooted.

ABBREVIATIONS

AAAPSS	Annals of the American Academy of Political and Social Science
AB	Art Bulletin
ABR	American Benedictine Review
ACQR	American Catholic Quarterly Review
AER	American Ecclesiastical Review
AH	Archivium Hibernicum
AHC	Archivium Historiae Conciliorum
AHP	Archivium Historiae Pontificiae
AHR	American Historical Review
AHSI	Archivium Historicum Societatis Iesu
AJIL	American Journal of International Law
AJS	American Journal of Sociology
ALBION	Albion
AM	Ave Maria
AMANTH	American Anthropologist
AMER	America
AMERS	Americas: A Quarterly Review of Inter-American Cultural History

AMLIT	American Literature
AMM	American Mercury
AMPJ	Ampleforth Journal
APSR	American Political Science Review
AR	Antioch Review
AS	Annals of Science
ASEER	American Slavic and East European Review
ASR	American Sociological Review
ATMO	Atlantic Monthly
ATR	Anglican Theological Review
BBN	British Book News
BJS	British Journal of Sociology
BKLST	Booklist
BKMN	Bookman
BLACK	Blackfriars
BM	The Burlington Magazine
BS	Best Sellers
CANHR	Canadian Historical Review
CANLIT	Canadian Literature
CC	Christian Century
CCR	Canadian Catholic Review
CEH	Central European History
CER	Catholic Educational Review
CH	Church History

CHE	The Chronicle of Higher Education
CHOICE	Choice
CHR	Catholic Historical Review
CJH	Canadian Journal of History
CLR	Clergy Review
COMM	Commentary
COMMWL	Commonweal
CONR	Contemporary Review
CQ	Church Quarterly
CR	Christus Rex
CRITIC	Critic
CRITICISM	Criticism
CS	Contemporary Sociology
CSN	Christian Scholar's Newsletter
CSSH	Comparative Studies in Society and History
CW	Catholic World
DALR	Dalhousie Review
DIAL	The Dial
DR	Downside Review
DUBR	Dublin Review
DUNR	Dunwoodie Review
ECHR	Economic History Review
ECON	The Economist
ECR	Ecumenical Review

ECSOR	Economic and Social Review
EEQ	East European Quarterly
EET	Eglise et Théologie
EHR	English Historical Review
ELN	English Language Notes
ENC	Encounter
ENG	English
ER	Edinburgh Review
ES	English Studies
ESR	European Studies Review
ETL	Ephemerides Theologicae Lovanienses
FCSN	Fellowship of Catholic Scholars Newsletter
FHS	French Historical Studies
FORUM	Forum
FR	Fortnightly Review
FRAN	Francia
FREE	Freeman
FRR	French Review
FS	Franciscan Studies
GQ	German Quarterly
GW	Guardian Weekly (Manchester)
HAHR	Hispanic-American Historical Review
HB	Historical Bulletin
HEQ	History of Education Quarterly

HEYJ	Heythrop Journal
HIBJ	Hibbert Journal
HIS	The Historian
HISP	Hispania
HIST	History
HJ	Historical Journal
HMPEC	Historical Magazine of the Protestant Episcopal Church
HPR	Homiletic and Pastoral Review
HR	Historical Reflections
HRNB	History; Reviews of New Books
HRZNS	Horizons
HS	Historical Studies
HT	History Today
IA	International Affairs
IBMR	International Bulletin of Missionary Research
IER	Irish Ecclesiastical Record
IHS	Irish Historical Studies
IJ	International Journal
IJAHS	International Journal of African Historical Studies
INTERP	Interpretation
IQ	Italian Quarterly
IR	Innes Review
ISIS	Isis

ITQ   Irish Theological Quarterly

JAAR   Journal of the American Academy of Religion

JAF   Journal of American Folklore

JAFH   Journal of African History

JAH   Journal of American History

JBR   The Journal of Bible and Religion

JBS   Journal of British Studies

JCEA   Journal of Central European Affairs

JCS   Journal of Church and State

JEH   Journal of Ecclesiastical History

JECH   Journal of Economic History

JECS   Journal of Ecumenical Studies

JES   Journal of European Studies

JHG   Journal of Historical Geography

JHI   Journal of the History of Ideas

JIH   Journal of Interdisciplinary History

JMH   Journal of Modern History

JPE   Journal of Political Economy

JPPSM   Journal of Philosophy, Psychology and
                 Scientific Methods

JQR   Jewish Quarterly Review

JR   Journal of Religion

JRH   Journal of Religious History

JSH   Journal of Social History

JSOH	Journal of Southern History
JSS	Jewish Social Studies
JSSR	Journal for the Scientific Study of Religion
JTS	Journal of Theological Studies
JUR	Jurist
LBIYB	Leo Baeck Institute Year Book
LH	Labor History
LIST	The Listener
LJ	Library Journal
LM	London Mercury
LQHR	London Quarterly and Holborn Review
LQR	London Quarterly Review
LRB	London Review of Books
MA	Modern Age
MEJ	Middle East Journal
MFS	Modern Fiction Studies
MID-AM	Mid-America
MLJ	Modern Language Journal
MLN	Modern Language Notes
MLQ	Modern Language Quarterly
MLR	Modern Language Review
MLS	Marian Library Studies
MODPHILOL	Modern Philology
MONTH	The Month

MQ	Music Quarterly
NAMR	North American Review
NATION	The Nation
NATR	National Review
NB	New Blackfriars
NCF	Nineteenth-Century Fiction
NCW	New Catholic World
NH	Northern History
NJS	Netherlands Journal of Sociology
NOTES	Notes
NR	New Republic
NS	New Scholasticism
NST	New Statesman
NYRB	The New York Review of Books
NYTBR	The New York Times Book Review
OBS	The Observer
OIC	One in Christ
PA	Parliamentary Affairs
PACAF	Pacific Affairs
PARR	Partisan Review
PERS	Personalist
PH	Paedagogica Historica
POPS	Population Studies
P&PR	Philosophical & Phenomenal Resources

PQ	Political Quarterly
PR	Polish Review
PS	Political Studies
PSQ	Political Science Quarterly
PUNCH	Punch
QQ	Queen's Quarterly
QR	Quarterly Review
R&C	Race & Class
RES	Review of English Studies
REVREL	Review for Religious
RH	Recusant History
RM	Review of Metaphysics
RMSSJ	Rocky Mountain Social Science Journal
ROMR	Romanic Review
RP	Review of Politics
RS	Religious Studies
RSCHS	Records of the Scottish Church History Society
RSR	Religious Studies Review
RUSR	Russian Review
SEL	Studies in English Literature
SEWR	Sewanee Review
SF	Social Forces
SHR	Scottish Historical Review
SJR	Social Justice Review

SJT	Scottish Journal of Theology
SOB	Sobornost
SOCAN	Sociological Analysis
SOCED	Social Education
SOCIOL	Sociology
SOCSR	Sociology and Social Research
SOR	Southern Review
SPEC	The Spectator (London)
SPECULUM	Speculum
SR	Slavic Review
SSR	Social Service Review
STUDIES	Studies
TABLET	The Tablet
TC	Twentieth Century
TES	Times Educational Supplement (London)
TESG	Tijdschrift voor Economische en Sociale Geografie
THD	Theology Digest
THEO	Theology
THOUGHT	Thought
THS	Theological Studies
TLS	Times Literary Supplement (London)
TRHS	Transactions of the Royal Historical Society
VPN	Victorian Periodicals Newsletter

VPR	Victorian Periodicals Review
VS	Victorian Studies
WMH	Wisconsin Magazine of History
WMQ	William and Mary Quarterly
WOR	Worship
WPQ	Western Political Quarterly
WR	Wiseman Review
YR	Yale Review
ZYGON	Zygon
OS	Old Series
NS	New Series

Nineteenth-Century
European Catholicism

GENERAL WORKS

Histories of the Church, 1800 - 1900

1. Altholz, Josef L. THE CHURCHES IN THE NINETEENTH
   CENTURY. Indianapolis: Bobbs-Merrill, 1967.

   Situates Catholic developments within the
   larger Christian environment. A reasonably
   comprehensive overview, highlighting the problems of intellectual and spiritual revival and
   structural reform.

   See: CHOICE 5 (March 1968): 68; Alec R. Vidler,
        JTS 19 (October 1968): 719; Patrick
        Collinson, JEH 20 (April 1969): 184; James
        Hennesey, S.J., CHR 56 (October 1970): 574-
        6.

2. Aubert, Roger; Bandmann, Günter; Baumgartner, Jakob;
   Bendiscioli, Mario; Gadille, Jacques; Köhler,
   Oskar; Lill, Rudolf; Stasiewski, Bernhard; and
   Weinzierl, Erika. THE CHURCH IN THE INDUSTRIAL
   AGE. Translated by Margit Resch. History of
   the Church, edited by Hubert Jedin and John
   Dolan, vol. 9. New York: Crossroad, 1981.

   Part One (1878-1903) details the pontificate of
   Leo XIII, the Church's growth or decline within the
   various European countries, its social influence,
   traditional and innovative forms of piety, and the
   impact of religious teaching and theology.

   See: William R. Barnett, AMER 146 (23 January
        1982): 57-8; Francis Schüssler Fiorenza,
        HRZNS 10 (Spring 1983): 151-3; James Healy,
        S.J., MONTH 2nd NS 16 (July 1983): 249-50.

3. Aubert, Roger; Beckmann, Johannes; Corish, Patrick J.;
   and Lill, Rudolf. THE CHURCH BETWEEN REVOLUTION
   AND REACTION. Translated by Peter Becker. History
   of the Church, edited by Hubert Jedin and John
   Dolan, vol. 7. New York: Crossroad, 1981.

   Covers the crucial seven decades from the election
   of Pius VII (1775) to that of Pius IX (1846), an age
   which witnessed both the Church's near-death during
   the revolutionary and Napoleonic period, and its
   spectacular revival in the years after 1815. The
   emphasis here is on the post-Napoleonic recovery,
   incorporating the latest research and rooted in an
   awareness of the interplay between socio-economic
   changes, on the one hand, and the course of theology
   and the institutional Church, on the other.

   See: Francis Schüssler Fiorenza, HRZNS 10 (Spring
        1983): 151-3; Patrick O'Connell, S.J., MONTH
        2nd NS 16 (June 1983): 214-5; Paul Misner,
        CH 52 (December 1983): 516-7.

4. ————. THE CHURCH IN THE AGE OF LIBERALISM.
   Translated by Peter Becker. History of the
   Church, edited by Hubert Jedin and John Dolan,
   vol. 8. New York: Crossroad, 1981.

   Reconstructs the struggle between Catholicism and
   liberalism (1848-1870) by a minute examination of
   several areas: the fortunes of the different national
   churches, missionary activity, religious thought,
   popular devotion, clerical life, and the temporal and
   spiritual status of the Papacy as expressed through
   the Roman Question and the infallibility debate at
   Vatican I.

   See: Francis Schüssler Fiorenza, HRZNS 10 (Spring
        1983): 151-3; Patrick O'Connell, S.J., MONTH
        2nd NS 16 (June 1983): 214-5.

5. Aubert, Roger; Crunican, P.E.; Ellis, John Tracy;
   Pike, F.B.; Bruls, J.; and Hajjar, J. THE
   CHURCH IN A SECULARISED SOCIETY. The Christian
   Centuries: A New History of the Catholic Church,
   vol. 5. New York: Paulist Press/London: Darton,
   Longman and Todd, 1978.

For the most part, a briefer treatment of the
macro-history in volumes 8 and 9 of Jedin (items
4 and 2, respectively). Presents an overview of
developments from 1848 to 1978, and, its specifi-
cally Roman Catholic orientation notwithstanding,
it goes beyond most treatments of similar size and
scope in its sensitivity to the larger non-Roman
context within which the Church operated. Useful
also for its sixty-three pages of illustrations
culled from contemporary sources.

See: James Gaffney, AMER 139 (25 November 1978): 396;
J.H. Crehan, S.J., MONTH 2nd NS 11 (December
1978): 425-6; CHOICE 16 (March 1979): 91;
George G. Higgins, COMMWL 106 (2 March
1979): 122; Donal Kerr, ITQ 46 (no. 4,
1979): 310-3; David P. Effroymson, HRZNS 7
(Spring 1980): 107-8.

6. Bihlmeyer, Karl, and Tüchle, Hermann. CHURCH HISTORY.
Translated by Victor E. Mills, O.F.M., and Francis
J. Muller, O.F.M. Vol. 3: MODERN AND RECENT
TIMES. Westminster, Md.: Newman Press, 1966.

Views nineteenth-century developments within the
framework of triumphant individualism, religious
subjectivism, and the dechristianization of society.
Particularly useful discussions of the inner life of
the Church--organization, legal status, discipline,
cult, art, and piety--and ecclesiastical learning.
An enormous amount of detail.

See: Francis J. Weber, HPR 67 (May 1967): 713-4;
William O. Madden, S.J., THS 28 (June
1967): 419-20; B.J. Blied, SJR 61 (May
1968): 69; John F. Broderick, CHR 55 (April
1969): 95-6.

7. Bokenkotter, Thomas. A CONCISE HISTORY OF THE
CATHOLIC CHURCH. Garden City, N.Y.: Doubleday,
1977.

Chapters 22-28 feature an institution in the
midst of a highly charged spiritual revival and
yet doggedly opposed to the modern world. Thus,
the Catholic dilemma of the nineteenth century,
as seen quintessentially during the reign of

Pius IX: as scores of important European intellectuals converted, religious orders proliferated,
missionaries girdled the globe, and moral theologians
provided valuable ethical insights into the problems
of industrialism, the hierarchy was unconditionally
condemning the secular context in which they all
operated. Critical of the nineteenth-century popes
prior to Leo XIII; for a differing opinion, however,
see item 9.

See: W. Charles Heiser, LJ 102 (15 October
      1977): 2169; Michael M. Dudek, BS 37
      (December 1977): 280-1; Thomas H. Clancy,
      AMER 137 (24 December 1977): 468; Jay P.
      Dolan, CRITIC 36 (Spring 1978): 75-7;
      John Jay Hughes, COMMWL 105 (15 September
      1978): 602-3; Joseph Fitzer, NCW 222 (May/
      June 1979): 138-9.

8. Corrigan, Raymond, S.J. "Before Leo XIII." HB 13
     (November 1934): 3-5.

    Sketches the four major intellectual challenges
faced by the Church during the years 1800-1878: atheism, skepticism, socialism, and secularism.

9. ————. THE CHURCH AND THE NINETEENTH CENTURY.
     Milwaukee: Bruce, 1938.

    Focuses on the relationship between the Church
and European society through the use of vignettes
illustrating either efforts at rapprochement (e.g.,
the encyclicals of Leo XIII) or the recurring
antagonisms (the religious policies of Napoleon,
Bismarck, and the Third French Republic). An in-
troductory chapter establishes the major currents
of the one hundred years following the French
Revolution, all of which posed serious problems
for Rome: the growth of middle-class culture,
capitalism, liberalism, nationalism, and secularism.
Highly sympathetic to the hierarchical structure;
for an opposing view, however, see item 7.

See: Joseph H. Fichter, HB 17 (January 1939): 39;
      Ross J.S. Hoffman, CHR 25 (April 1939): 73-4;
      Gordon Albion, CLR 16 (May 1939): 457-8; John
      M. Lenhart, CH 8 (June 1939): 185-6; P.G.
      Steinbicker, THOUGHT 15 (March 1940): 152-4.

10. Daniel-Rops, Henri. THE CHURCH IN AN AGE OF REVOLU-
    TION, 1789-1870. Translated by John Warrington.
    History of the Church of Christ, vol. 8.
    London: J.M. Dent & Sons/New York: E.P. Dutton,
    1965.

    Chapters 3-5 deal with events and personalities
    from the Bourbon Restoration to Vatican I; emphasized
    are the complexities of Papal politics and the La-
    mennais affair. Chapters 6-8 contain a potpourri of
    widely diverse items: the challenges from science
    and industrialism, missionary progress, the Oxford
    Movement, and the lives and achievements of Möhler,
    Guéranger, and other activists.

    See: Charles Dollen, BS 25 (1 August 1965): 187-8;
        Thomas P. Neill, AMER 113 (2 October 1965): 381;
        CHOICE 2 (January 1966): 780; TLS, 10 February
        1966: 106; Joseph N. Moody, CHR 54 (April
        1968): 175-6.

11. ————. A FIGHT FOR GOD, 1870-1939. Translated by
    John Warrington. History of the Church of Christ,
    vol. 9. London: J.M. Dent & Sons/New York: E.P.
    Dutton, 1966.

    Subsumes all Catholic developments during the
    final three decades of the century under four
    headings: the work of Leo XIII, the advance of
    social Catholicism, the rise of Modernism, and
    the life of St. Teresa of Lisieux. Concludes
    with the apologetical observation that devout
    submission to the Church was the ultimate weapon
    in the struggle against certain political, philo-
    sophical, and religious forms of "atheistic
    humanism."

    See: CHOICE 4 (March 1967): 50; TLS, 16 March
        1967: 224; Evelyn M. Acomb, AHR 73 (October
        1967): 98-9; Thomas P. Neill, CRITIC 25
        (October/November 1966): 96-7.

12. Eberhardt, Newman C., C.M. A SUMMARY OF CATHOLIC
    HISTORY. Vol. 2: MODERN HISTORY. St. Louis
    and London: B. Herder, 1962.

    An encyclopedic treatment meticulously divided

into captions and sub-captions for easy reference.
Moderate tone and balanced judgements, based for
the most part on the findings of standard monographs
in both secular and religious history.

See: Thomas Bokenkotter, CHR 49 (April 1963): 99-
      100; J.J. Dwyer, CLR 51 (June 1966): 494-5.

13. Hales, E.E.Y. THE CATHOLIC CHURCH IN THE MODERN
     WORLD: A SURVEY FROM THE FRENCH REVOLUTION TO
     THE PRESENT. Garden City, N.Y.: Doubleday,
     Hanover House, 1958.

Argues that the nineteenth-century Church confronted two recurring challenges: efforts at
control by the State, and the polarization between
conservative and liberal groups. While ecclesiastical subordination to the political power is
consistently criticized, there is an awareness
that neither of the two internal factions was
either totally right or totally wrong; consequently,
Hales provides a balanced picture of both Gregory
XVI and Lamennais, and of Pius IX and Döllinger,
among others.

See: Joseph N. Moody, AMER 99 (7 June 1958): 315-6;
      Thomas P. Neill, CHR 44 (October 1958): 323-4;
      Denis Mack Smith, SPEC 201 (5 December
      1958): 827; Michael Cook, BLACK 40 (March
      1959): 135-7; Patrick J. Corish, ITQ 26 (no. 2,
      1959): 194-5; J.J. Dwyer, CLR 44 (April
      1959): 246-8; THEO 62 (April 1959): 134-5;
      Neville Masterman, HIST 44 (June 1959): 168-9;
      Edward J. Dunne, S.J., THOUGHT 34 (Winter 1959-
      60): 631-3; Alexander Dru, DR 79 (Summer
      1961): 232-40.

14. ———. REVOLUTION AND PAPACY, 1769-1846. Garden
     City, N.Y.: Doubleday, Hanover House, 1960.

Includes a detailed discussion of Papal fortunes
during the turbulent first half of the nineteenth
century. Sympathetic to Roman policies, and yet the
ten relevant chapters do not overlook Papal shortcomings.

See: Gerard Culkin, DUBR 234 (Winter 1960-1): 378-
      83; Derek Beales, HJ 4 (no. 2, 1961): 234-6;

QR 299 (April 1961): 238-9; Alexander Dru, DR
79 (Summer 1961): 232-40; Guillaume de Bertier
de Sauvigny, CHR 47 (July 1961): 224-6; Esther
de Waal, THEO 64 (July 1961): 295-6; Leonard
Mahoney, S.J., THOUGHT 36 (Autumn 1961): 476-8;
Agatha Ramm, HIST 46 (October 1961): 259;
Charles F. Delzell, JCS 3 (November 1961): 210-
12; John Tracy Ellis, AHR 67 (January
1962): 376-7; H. Hearder, EHR 77 (April
1962): 384.

15. Heyer, Friedrich. THE CATHOLIC CHURCH FROM 1648 TO
    1870. Translated by D.W.D. Shaw. London: A. &
    C. Black, 1969.

    Compresses an enormous amount of solidly documented
    nineteenth-century material into Chapters 5-9. The-
    ology during the romantic period, the Church in the
    British Isles, the Ultramontane movement, and the
    efforts at reunion with the Eastern churches are
    given particularly wide coverage.

    See: Maurus Lunn, DR 87 (April 1969): 234-5; TLS,
    10 April 1969: 393; John McManners, JTS 21
    (April 1970): 251-2; Basil Hall, JEH 24 (July
    1973): 313-4.

16. Holmes, J. Derek, and Bickers, Bernard W. A SHORT
    HISTORY OF THE CATHOLIC CHURCH. New York and
    Ramsey, N.J.: Paulist Press, 1984.

    Chapter 6 ("The Church, Revolution and Reaction,
    1789-1914") highlights fundamental changes within
    the Church brought on by social, economic, and
    political revolution. Discussion centers on the
    position of the pope and his relations with other
    bishops, Church-State tensions, and relations
    between Church and society at large. Interpreta-
    tions are based on the most recent historical re-
    search.

    See: Stephen J. Casey, BS 44 (May 1984): 67; C.H.
    Lawrence, CLR 69 (October 1984): 378-9;
    Michael Richards, MONTH 2nd NS 18 (January
    1985): 35; Joseph A. Varacalli, JSSH 24
    (March 1985): 110; Joseph G. Hubbert, C.M.,
    CHR 71 (April 1985): 310-1; Joseph M.
    McShane, S.J., CH 54 (June 1985): 261-2;

Mary Jo Weaver, HRZNS 12 (Fall 1985): 385-6.

17. Latourette, Kenneth Scott. CHRISTIANITY IN A REVOLU-
     TIONARY AGE: A HISTORY OF CHRISTIANITY IN THE
     NINETEENTH AND TWENTIETH CENTURIES. Vol. 1: THE
     NINETEENTH CENTURY IN EUROPE: BACKGROUND AND THE
     ROMAN CATHOLIC PHASE. New York: Harper &
     Brothers, 1958.

     Illustrates Catholicism in all its dimensions--re-
     ligious, theological, structural, and social--and
     clothes this detailed presentation in an appreciation
     of the seuclar atmosphere, and the ways in which it
     influenced both Catholics and their faith. Beyond
     specific events and influences, however, Latourette
     discerns and accounts for larger and more significant
     spiritual currents.

     See: Winthrop S. Hudson, JBR 27 (July 1959): 247-8;
          Frederick A. Norwood, CH 29 (June 1960): 221-
          3; Roger Aubert, CHR 46 (October 1960): 350-3;
          William Lee Pitts, Jr., WORLD CHRISTIANITY: THE
          CHURCH HISTORY WRITING OF KENNETH SCOTT LA-
          TOURETTE (Ph.D. dissertation, Vanderbilt
          University, 1969); James E. Wood, Jr., "Kenneth
          Scott Latourette (1884-1968): Historian, Ecu-
          menist, and Friend." JCS 11 (Winter 1969): 9-
          15.

18. ———. A HISTORY OF CHRISTIANITY. New York: Harper
     & Brothers, 1953.

     Chapters 45-55 feature a shorter version of item
     17. Offers valuable insights into the structure and
     substance of popular belief.

     See: Edwin E. Aubrey, HIS 16 (Autumn 1953): 87-8;
          Frederick A. Norwood, CH 23 (March 1954): 86-7;
          George H. Williams, AHR 59 (April 1954): 589-
          90; Norman Sykes, THEO 59 (June 1956): 251-2.

19. MacCaffrey, James. HISTORY OF THE CATHOLIC CHURCH IN
     THE NINETEENTH CENTURY (1789-1908). Dublin and
     Waterford: M.H. Gill and Son/St. Louis: B.
     Herder, 1909. 2 vols.

     Volume 1 deals with continental affairs, and

Volume 2 with the Church in the British Isles,
missionary activity, orders and congregations,
theology and religious learning, and social
Catholicism. Analysis revolves around six main
developments: the rise of constitutionalism and
nationalism, Church-State relationships, the
struggle for freedom of religious education, the
conflict between faith and science, tensions
between capital and labor, and the spread of
Catholic teaching by both missionaries and
immigrants.

See: J.F. Hogan, IER 26 (December 1909): 553-70;
      CW 91 (June 1910): 382-4; ACQR 35 (July
      1910): 565-6.

20. Mourret, Fernand, S.S. A HISTORY OF THE CATHOLIC
    CHURCH. Translated by Newton Thompson. Vol.
    8: PERIOD OF THE EARLY NINETEENTH CENTURY
    (1823-1878). St. Louis: B. Herder, 1957.

    A popular account featuring a country-by-country
    survey. Highly suspicious of Lamennais, Mont-
    alembert, and the liberals; enthusiastic about, if
    not completely uncritical of, the activities of
    Pius IX and Veuillot.

    See: B.J. Blied, SJR 50 (November 1957): 242;
          Thomas P. Neill, CHR 44 (July 1958): 190-1;
          J.J. Dwyer, CLR 44 (January 1959): 54-5.

21. ————. A HISTORY OF THE CATHOLIC CHURCH. Trans-
    lated by Newton Thompson. Vol. 7: PERIOD OF
    THE FRENCH REVOLUTION (1775-1823). St. Louis: B.
    Herder, 1955.

    Post-1801 analysis centers on the Concordat of
    1801, Napoleon's abuse of Pius VII, and the re-
    ligious restoration, as exemplified by Chateau-
    briand's literature, de Maistre's political theory,
    and missionary vitality.

    See: Clarence A. Herbst, HB 34 (November 1955): 48-
          9; Harold L. Stansell, CHR 41 (January
          1956): 450-1; James Hennesey, S.J., THOUGHT 31
          (Winter 1956-7): 630.

22. Poulet, Dom Charles. A HISTORY OF THE CATHOLIC
     CHURCH. Translated and adapted by Sidney A.
     Raemers. Vol. 2: THE MODERN PERIOD-CONTEMPORARY
     CHURCH HISTORY. St. Louis and London: B. Herder,
     1945.

     Designed more for reference than for reading; a
     mixture of political narrative, biographical
     sketches, and cultural analysis.

     See: (reviews of the first printing in English) Dom
           Dunstan Pontifex, DR 53 (September 1935): 518;
           IER 46 (September 1935): 328; Raymond Corrigan,
           S.J., HB 13 (November 1935): 17; CLR 11 (April
           1936): 337-9.

23. Vidler, Alec R. THE CHURCH IN AN AGE OF REVOLUTION,
     1789 TO THE PRESENT DAY. The Pelican History of
     the Church, vol. 5. Baltimore: Penguin, 1961.

     Four chapters in this multi-dimensional history
     survey diverse aspects of Catholic political
     activity and thought: Napoleon and Gallicanism,
     liberal Catholicism and Ultramontanism in France,
     the reign of Pius IX, and Modernism.

     See: David Newsome, THEO 65 (January 1962): 33-4;
           Robert T. Handy, CH 34 (December 1965): 474.

                    Collections of Essays

24. Beales, Derek, and Best, Geoffrey, eds. HISTORY,
     SOCIETY AND THE CHURCHES: ESSAYS IN HONOUR OF
     OWEN CHADWICK. Cambridge: Cambridge University
     Press, 1985.

     A *festschrift* for the retiring Regius Professor
     of Modern History at Cambridge, whose lifelong be-
     lief in the centrality of religion within European
     history is reflected in a series of specialized
     essays by former students and friends. Contains
     items 302 and 860.

     See: Conrad Russell, LRB 7 (7 November 1985): 23-4;
           Richard M. Golden, RSR 12 (July/October

1986): 298; Dennis Tamburello, JR 67 (January
1987): 103-4; Albert C. Outler, CHR 74 (April
1988): 293-4.

25. Mews, Stuart, ed. RELIGION AND NATIONAL IDENTI-
TY: PAPERS READ AT THE NINETEENTH SUMMER
MEETING AND THE TWENTIETH WINTER MEETING OF
THE ECCLESIASTICAL HISTORY SOCIETY. Studies
in Church History, vol. 18. Oxford: Published
for the Ecclesiastical History Society by Basil
Blackwell, 1982.

Vignettes illustrative of the tensions caused by
competing religious and political loyalties through
history. However, the picture proffered by the
essays is as much one of cooperation as it is of
contention, for several of the authors indicate how
Christianity, even with its evangelical vision of a
universal Church, has contributed to a feeling of
national identity, and how in turn its own institutional forms have been determined by that national
awareness. Contains items 886, 1004, and 1302.

26. Parsons, Reuben. STUDIES IN CHURCH HISTORY. 3rd
ed. Vol. 5: CENTURY XIX (PART I). Philadelphia: John Joseph McVey, 1898.

Not a narrative, but a series of seventeen
lengthy essays, thirteen of which cover specific
European personalities, policies, and problems.
A wide range of subjects, from the pontificate of
Pius VII to the Old Catholic schism of 1870; always
basically sympathetic to the Church, but not completely uncritical of hierarchical activity. Some
of the selections--e.g., Napoleon's divorce, Polish
Catholicism, and Russian anti-Catholicism--provide
a rich store of data found nowhere else.

See: ACQR 24 (January 1899): 206; CW 68 (February
1899): 707-8.

27. ————. STUDIES IN CHURCH HISTORY. 3rd ed. Vol.
6: CENTURY XIX (PART II). Philadelphia: John
Joseph McVey, 1900.

A continuation of item 26. Seventeen essays
covering the last years of Pius IX (1870-1878)

and the reign of Leo XIII. A highly flattering
portrait of Leo paralleled by a highly critical
evaluation of his "enemies": Bismarck, the Third
Republic, socialists and Freemasons, and Döllinger.
Detailed treatments of Leonine intervention in
fields as far-reaching as education, the rights of
labor, and the slave trade, complete the picture.

See: ACQR 25 (July 1900): 613-4; CW 71 (July
      1900): 562.

28. Sheils, W.J., ed. THE CHURCH AND HEALING: PAPERS
     READ AT THE TWENTIETH SUMMER MEETING AND THE
     TWENTY-FIRST WINTER MEETING OF THE ECCLESIASTICAL
     HISTORY SOCIETY. Studies in Church History, vol.
     19. Oxford: Published for the Ecclesiastical
     History Society by Basil Blackwell, 1982.

     Essays on the relationship between spiritual and
     supernatural healing, on the one hand, and scientific
     medicine, on the other. Certain central assumptions
     underlie the examination of this theme in different
     historical contexts: that the expressions of miracu-
     lous healing are affected by time and place; that
     each example of belief in supernatural cures is
     motivated by a unique thaumaturgical outlook; and
     that attitudes to healing are often a powerful in-
     centive to the formation of popular religious
     feeling. Contains items 1005, 1181, and 1188.

     See: Martin E. Marty, JAAR 52 (March 1984): 178-9;
           George W. Reid, CH 57 (June 1988): 261-2.

29. ———. PERSECUTION AND TOLERATION: PAPERS READ AT
     THE TWENTY-SECOND SUMMER MEETING AND THE TWENTY-
     THIRD WINTER MEETING OF THE ECCLESIASTICAL HISTORY
     SOCIETY, 1983. Studies in Church History, vol.
     21. Oxford: Published for the Ecclesiastical
     History Society by Basil Blackwell, 1984.

     Investigates one of the most prominent interplays
     of forces within the two millennia of ecclesiastical
     history. Beyond traditional considerations of
     clashes between orthodox and heretical elements is a
     recognition by most contributors of the vital part
     played by politics and diplomacy in fostering dog-
     matic unity or in promoting heterodoxy. Contains

items 235, 730, and 1192.

30. ——————, and Wood, Diana, eds. VOLUNTARY RE-
LIGION: PAPERS READ AT THE 1985 SUMMER MEETING
AND THE 1986 WINTER MEETING OF THE ECCLESIASTICAL
HISTORY SOCIETY. Studies in Church History, vol.
23. Oxford: Published for the Ecclesiastical
History Society by Basil Blackwell, 1986.

Focuses on historical examples of those societies
and associations which bring together like-minded
individuals of a "serious minded sociability," in
order to achieve a specific spiritual goal. Selections provide examples of groups operating either
in conjunction with the larger Church, or totally
independent of it. Contains items 309 and 1389.

Collections of Biographies

31. Horgan, John J. GREAT CATHOLIC LAYMEN. New
York: Benziger Brothers, 1906.

Studies of Ozanam, Montalembert, Lucas, Windthorst,
and O'Connell, five lay leaders who served the Church
by throwing themselves fully into the political and
social currents of their time.

See: ACQR 31 (October 1906): 756-60.

32. Kempf, Constantine, S.J. THE HOLINESS OF THE CHURCH
IN THE NINETEENTH CENTURY: SAINTLY MEN AND WOMEN
OF OUR OWN TIMES. New York: Benziger Brothers,
1916.

Features brief biographical sketches of over two
hundred men and women, both clerical and lay, celebrated for their piety. Particulary useful for its
data on founders of nineteenth-century religious
orders.

See: ACQR 42 (January 1917): 175-6; IER 9 (March
1917): 263-4; AMER 16 (24 March 1917): 578.

33. Neill, Thomas P. THEY LIVED THE FAITH.
Milwaukee: Bruce, 1951.

Studies of eleven dynamic laymen and laywomen who, by considering Catholic action a vocation, quickened the pace of the nineteenth-century Church's remarkable revival. Easing the Church's way through the new politics of a revolutionary age were O'Connell, Montalembert, and Windthorst. Adapting Catholic social teaching to modern industrialism were Jaricot, Ozanam, and de Mun. Leading the struggle against deism, utilitarianism, materialism, and atheism were de Maistre, Görres, Donoso Cortés, Veuillot, and Wilfrid Ward.

See: Theodore Maynard, COMMWL 54 (20 April 1951): 45-6; Joseph P. Flynn, C.S.P., CW 173 (August 1951): 397.

34. Steuart, R.H.J., S.J. DIVERSITY IN HOLINESS. New York: Sheed & Ward, 1937.

Establishes the essential unity of mystical experience, expressions of which may be as varied as those of the book's five protagonists: Marie-Eustelle Harpain, Theresa of Lisieux, the abbé Huvelin, Bernadette Soubirous, and the curé of Ars. Concerned more with explaining the extraordinary piety of each of these personalities than with presenting biographical data.

See: AMER 56 (27 March 1937): 598-9; DUBR 201 (July 1937): 182; CW 146 (October 1937): 117-8.

ECCLESIASTICAL STRUCTURES

The Papacy

General Histories

35. Aretin, Karl Otmar von. THE PAPACY AND THE MODERN
    WORLD. Translated by Roland Hill. New
    York: McGraw-Hill, 1970.

    A highly pessimistic assessment of the nineteenth-
    century Popes. Contends that Roman contempt for the
    modern world, manifested during a time in which
    society was by and large not unresponsive to the
    Christian message, not only lost the Church many
    golden opportunities but also threatened to turn
    Catholicism itself into a minor sect.

    See: Alec Randall, AMPJ 76 (Summer 1971): 90-1; J.
    Derek Holmes, CLR 56 (July 1971): 564.

36. Browne-Olf, Lillian. THEIR NAME IS PIUS: PORTRAITS
    OF FIVE GREAT MODERN POPES. Milwaukee: Bruce,
    1941.

    A popular account. Analyzes the nineteenth-
    century Church from the perspective of the turbulent
    lives and controversial activities of its two longest
    reigning Popes: Pius VII and Pius IX.

    See: Raymond Corrigan, S.J., HB 20 (November
    1941): 20; William J. Gauche, CHR 28 (April
    1942): 85-6; E.A. Ryan, THOUGHT 17 (June
    1942): 375.

37. Holmes, J. Derek. THE TRIUMPH OF THE HOLY SEE: A
    SHORT HISTORY OF THE PAPACY IN THE NINETEENTH
    CENTURY. Shepherdstown, W.Va.: Patmos Press,
    1978.

    Traces and explains the astonishing revival of
    papal fortunes, from Pius VI's imprisonment and
    death in revolutionary France to Pius X's autocratic
    policies. The pivotal part in this turnabout was
    played by Pius IX, whose devotional, disciplinary,
    and theological pronouncements centralized power in
    Rome and imposed a hitherto unknown degree of unity
    upon the local churches. Yet this history of success
    contains an element of failure, for through the
    century the Popes proved unable to adapt to the
    changing political climate of Europe.

    See: James Hennesey, CH 48 (September 1979): 352-3;
          CHOICE 16 (December 1979): 1324; Dale A.
          Johnson, RSR 6 (April 1980): 154; Thomas
          Bokenkotter, CHR 67 (April 1981): 315-6.

38. Jalland, Trevor Gervase. THE CHURCH AND THE
    PAPACY: A HISTORICAL STUDY. London: Society
    for Promoting Christian Knowledge, 1944.

    A survey of the relationship between the Papacy
    and its followers. Chapters 7 and 8 examine the
    nineteenth century: the effects of both the French
    Revolution and the emergence of liberalism showed
    the utter hopelessness and even folly of attempting
    to preserve the anachronistic categories of a dead
    social order. Yet such a preservation was exactly
    the goal of Pius VII and Gregory XVI, encouraged by
    the reactionary philosophy of de Maistre and Bonald.
    With Pius IX this desperate adherence to the past
    reached its greatest intensity, until in the long
    run the Pope-King found himself shorn of all temporal
    authority.

    See: Cuthbert Lattey, S.J., HIBJ 43 (no. 1,
          1944): 86-7; R.H. Malden, SPEC 173 (18 August
          1944): 153-4; Norman Sykes, THEO 47 (October
          1944): 227-32; M.L.W. Laistner, JCEA 5 (April
          1945): 64-5; Milton V. Anastos, SPECULUM 23
          (January 1948): 126-8.

39. Moody, Joseph N. "The Papacy: The Church and the
    New Forces in Western Europe and Italy." In
    CHURCH AND SOCIETY: CATHOLIC SOCIAL AND POLITICAL
    THOUGHT AND MOVEMENTS, 1789-1950 (item 308), 23-92.

    Divides the nineteenth-century Papacy's reaction
    to burgeoning political and social developments into
    two periods: a time of almost unqualified resistance
    (1801-1878) and a time of constructive achievement
    (1878-1900). Considers the pontificate of Leo XIII
    the watershed of nineteenth-century Papal history,
    for although he maintained all the principles of his
    predecessors, Leo displayed a softer attitude toward,
    and indeed even a sincere sympathy for, the modern
    world and its problems.

40. Nielsen, Fredrik. THE HISTORY OF THE PAPACY IN THE
    XIXTH CENTURY. Translated by Arthur James Mason.
    London: John Murray, 1906. 2 vols.

    Offers an objective and highly detailed overview
    of Vatican personalities and policies. Volume 1
    concentrates on the eighteenth-century background
    and the years of Pius VII. Volume 2 takes the
    account to the fall of Rome in 1870. Doctrinal
    developments are emphasized, given the strong in-
    fluence of the Grundtvigian revival, with its focus
    on belief, upon the author, the Lutheran Bishop of
    Aarhus, Denmark.

    See: T.A. Lacey, BKMN 31 (November 1906): 83-4;
    R.M. Johnston, AHR 12 (January 1907): 377-9;
    LQR 107 (January 1907): 156-7; DUBR 140 (April
    1907): 395-6; NATION 84 (4 April 1907): 316.

41. Nippold, Frederick. THE PAPACY IN THE 19TH
    CENTURY: A PART OF "THE HISTORY OF CATHOLICISM
    SINCE THE RESTORATION OF THE PAPACY". Trans-
    lated by Lawrence Henry Schwab. New York and
    London: G.P. Putnam's Sons, 1900.

    A highly critical view of Catholic leadership and
    its instruments. Throughout the century Roman
    Catholicism prevented progress by pursuing goals
    directly opposed to those of all European countries.
    Moreover, behind the three insidious additions to

the faith--the dogma of the Immaculate Conception,
the Syllabus of Errors, and the proclamation of
Papal infallibility--lay the Jesuits, who transformed
what had once been solid belief into a centralized
monarchy.

See: NATION 72 (3 January 1901): 16-7; DUBR 129
     (October 1901): 445-8.

42. Woodward, E.L. THREE STUDIES IN EUROPEAN CONSERVA-
    TISM: METTERNICH, GUIZOT, THE CATHOLIC CHURCH IN
    THE NINETEENTH CENTURY. London: Constable, 1929.

    Parallels the arguments made in items 35 and 37.
    Views the Papacy as an institution with a reaction-
    ary program, and therefore incapable of openness or
    progress. Out-of-date temporal power and doctrine
    were simply reaffirmed without any consideration of
    the practical consequences. In the end, extreme
    resistance to the new order led logically to the
    support of the ramshackle Bourbon and Hapsburg
    monarchies, and as their power structure failed, so
    did that of official Catholicism.

    See: G.P. Gooch, HIST 15 (July 1930): 168-9; APSR
          24 (November 1930): 1068-9; C.K. Webster, EHR
          46 (July 1931): 479-80.

        The Popes: Biographies and Spiritual Activity

                    Pius VII (1800 - 1823)

43. Allies, Mary H. PIUS THE SEVENTH, 1800-1823.
    London: Burns & Oates, 1897.

    A straightforward, sympathetic biography. Pro-
    vides a great deal of data and a minimum of inter-
    pretation.

    See: ACQR 22 (July 1897): 672; CW 65 (July
          1897): 551-3; DUBR 122 (January 1898): 185-6.

*   Browne-Olf, Lillian. "Pius VII, 1800-1823." THEIR
    NAME IS PIUS: PORTRAITS OF FIVE GREAT MODERN

POPES (item 36), 59-130.

Details the reign from the viewpoint of the trouble with Napoleon and post-1815 nascent Italian nationalism.

44. Levey, Michael. "Lawrence's Portrait of Pope Pius VII." BM 117 (April 1975): 194-204.

A description of the unusual circumstances surrounding the commission and painting of this masterpiece. Contends that the physically feeble yet strong-willed Pope ultimately became a father-figure for the spiritually hungry artist.

45. Olson, Roberta J.M. "Representations of Pope Pius VII: The First Risorgimento Hero." AB 68 (March 1986): 77-93.

Compares and contrasts major contemporary portraits of Pius VII by both Italian and non-Italian artists. Concludes that whereas the latter saw the Pontiff as either Napoleon's adversary or an enlightened patron of the arts, the former always placed him in a more rhetorical, politically charged context, portraying him as a symbol of Italian national resurgence. Thus, the conservative Pope-King became a catalyst for peninsular unity.

* Parsons, Reuben. "The Pontificate of Pius VII." STUDIES IN CHURCH HISTORY, 5 (item 26), 1-55.

Argues that the Church's policies during the century's first two decades were both vigorous and decided, even if put forth by the gentlest of Popes. Delves deeply into the political subtleties of Pius' election, the Concordat regulations, and Napoleon's abuse of the Church.

Leo XII (1823 - 1829)

46. Lahiff, Bartholomew Patrick, S.J. THE PONTIFICATE OF LEO XII: A STUDY IN CHURCH EMANCIPATION. Ph.D. dissertation. Georgetown University, 1965.

Maintains that the reign of this little-known
Pope witnessed important advances in the Church's
struggle for independence from secular control.
Papal support of emancipation campaigns in England
and the Netherlands displays specific patterns of
Vatican political activity.

Gregory XVI (1830 - 1846)

*   Parsons, Reuben. "The Pontificate of Gregory XVI."
        STUDIES IN CHURCH HISTORY, 5 (item 26), 237-72.

        Highlights the trials of the reign: clerical
        corruption, especially in Italy; nationalist agi-
        tation throughout the Romagna; demands from all
        areas of Europe for Church reform; the challenge
        of Hermesianism, with its "Protestant-like obsti-
        nacy"; persecution of the Church in Prussia; and
        the Spanish Church's decline during a disastrous
        civil war.

Pius IX (1846 - 1878)

*   Browne-Olf, Lillian. "Pius IX, 1846-1878." THEIR
        NAME IS PIUS: PORTRAITS OF FIVE GREAT MODERN
        POPES (item 36), 131-231.

        Centers on the triumphs and failures of the years
        between the declaration of the Immaculate Conception
        and the end of the temporal power. Occasionally
        hagiographical, yet this account contains several
        lengthy citations of important papal allocutions and
        conversations.

47.   Bury, John Bagnell. HISTORY OF THE PAPACY IN THE
        19TH CENTURY (1864-1878). Edited by Rev. R.H.
        Murray. London: Macmillan, 1930.

        Despite its general title, this classical liberal
        view is confined to the final twelve years of Pius'
        reign. Contends that Pius' contest with the modern
        world contained not even one proposition worth
        serious consideration, and that consequently nothing

vital could emerge from a Pope who, without a "gag
rule" and desperate conciliar logrolling, would
have found it impossible to persuade his own bishops
to define the doctrine of infallibility.

See: Outram Evennett, DUBR 186 (July 1930): 1-19;
      QR 255 (July 1930): 202-3; E.C. Butler, DR
      48 (October 1930): 335-6; W.T.M. Gamble, CHR
      18 (October 1932): 352-7; Maurice J.M. Larkin,
      JMH 37 (September 1965): 399.

48. Hales, E.E.Y. PIO NONO: A STUDY IN EUROPEAN
    POLITICS AND RELIGION IN THE NINETEENTH CENTURY.
    New York: P.J. Kenedy & Sons, 1954.

Proffers the picture of a vain, obstinate, and
sometimes even vengeful, leader who intervened re-
peatedly in diplomatic and political affairs, the
subtleties of which he never understood. Makes
extensive use of Italian, French, and English contemporary sources to reconstruct the historical
context.

See: C.C. Plumbe, PUNCH 226 (7 April 1954): 451;
      T. Charles Edwards, HT 4 (May 1954): 357-8;
      DUBR 228 (Summer 1954): 491; QR 292 (July
      1954): 403-4; Leonard Woolf, PQ 25 (July/
      September 1954): 280-1; Thomas P. Neill, HB
      33 (May 1955): 244; A.R. Vidler, THEO 58
      (January 1955): 30-1; Friedrich Engel-Janosi,
      CHR 41 (October 1955): 313-6; Alexander Dru,
      DR 79 (Summer 1961): 232-40.

49. ————. "Pope Pius IX." CLR 44 (May 1959): 270-5.

Mitigates the author's earlier negative evaluation (item 48) by concentrating on Pius' remarkable
personal and spiritual qualities. However, his
celebrated generosity, warm-heartedness, and humor
were not enough to prevent the losses to the Church
caused by his political involvements.

50. Hegarty, W.J., P.P. "A Contrast in Funerals--Pius IX
    and Pius X." IER 82 (October 1954): 256-60.

Details the rioting in Rome during the transfer of
Pius IX's remains to the Church of S. Lorenzo fuori
le mura.

51. Thurston, Herbert, S.J. NO POPERY: CHAPTERS ON
     ANTI-PAPAL PREJUDICE. London: Sheed & Ward,
     1930.

     Chapters 2-4 offer a highly detailed treatment
     of contemporary attacks upon Pius IX's personality
     and activities. Surveys the literary efforts by
     English Protestants and continental Freemasons,
     among which the chronicles of Léo Taxil are singled
     out for their virulence and mendacity.

     See: Joseph Clayton, BLACK 11 (August 1930): 455-
           60; AMER 44 (25 October 1930): 70; Joseph
           McSorley, CW 132 (January 1931): 505-6; D.C.
           Somervell, HIST 16 (April 1931): 67-8.

                    Leo XIII (1878 - 1903)

52. Coleiro, Edward. "Leo XIII--A Modern Humanist."
     DUBR 205 (October/November/December 1939): 344-
     60.

     Discusses Leo's literary tastes and efforts.
     His approximately sixty Latin poems, written main-
     ly during his years as Archbishop of Perugia and
     as Pope, exhibit a strong piety, underwritten by a
     rich imagination and delicate feelings.

53. Corrigan, Raymond, S.J. "Leo the Thirteenth." HB
     15 (November 1936): 12-14.

     Justifies Leo's greatness by highlighting the
     principal trials and achievements of his reign.

54. Fülop-Miller, René. LEO XIII AND OUR TIMES: MIGHT
     OF THE CHURCH--POWER IN THE WORLD. Translated
     by Conrad M.R. Bonacina. London and New
     York: Longmans, Green, 1937.

     Proclaims Leo the first modern Pontiff, and shows
     how the currents and influences emanating from his
     Church interacted with the national, social, and
     political life of late nineteenth-century Europe.

     See: C.W. Hepner, CHR 23 (July 1937): 215-6;

Raymond Corrigan, S.J., HB 16 (November
1937): 13-14; J.P. McGowan, C.M., CH 7
(March 1938): 95-6; IER 51 (April 1938): 440-
1.

55. Gargan, Edward T., ed. LEO XIII AND THE MODERN
WORLD. New York: Sheed & Ward, 1961.

Nine essays on various aspects of Leo's life,
thought, and religious and political outlook.
Contains items 57, 106, 226, 233, 242, 247, and
251.

See: Edwin S. Gaustad, JCS 3 (November 1961): 219-
21; Peter J. Rahill, SJR 54 (November
1961): 246-7; Evelyn M. Acomb, AHR 67 (January
1962): 377-8; Harry C. Koenig, CHR 47 (January
1962): 533-4.

56. Hughes, Philip. "Leo XIII." DUBR 202 (April/May/
June 1938): 249-57.

Hails Leo's freedom of judgement, courage, and
willingness to use new methods to solve old problems.
Urges a reassessment of his reign on the basis of his
overtures to France and Italy.

*   Parsons, Reuben. "The Pontificate of Leo XIII."
STUDIES IN CHURCH HISTORY, 6 (item 27), 139-203.

Parallels the argument made in item 58: Leo's
greatness lay in the intellectual and moral force
of his personality. In his encyclicals he displayed
an openness which surprised even his worst enemies,
the Freemasons.

57. Schmandt, Raymond H. "The Life and Work of Leo
XIII." In LEO XIII AND THE MODERN WORLD (item
55), 15-48.

A sympathetic biographical sketch, along with details of the evolution of the thought behind his
most important encyclicals.

58. Soderini, Eduardo. THE PONTIFICATE OF LEO XIII.
Translated by Barbara Barclay Carter.
London: Burns Oates & Washbourne, 1934.

Part 1 deals with Leo's career as nuncio, bishop, and papal candidate. Part 2 surveys his reign, focusing on his social pronouncements, revival of scholasticism, and encouragement of historical studies. Though a close friend of the Pope, whose private papers form the basis of this work, Soderini candidly admits Leo's shortcomings and limitations.

See: Vincent McNabb, O.P., DUBR 196 (April/May/ June 1935): 338-9; John Tracy Ellis, CHR 21 (January 1936): 461-4.

59. Ward, James E. "In Quest of Leo XIII." DUBR 242 (Spring 1968): 3-15.

Explores the pre-Papal years of Gioacchino Vincenzo Pecci, from the nunciature at Brussels (1843-1846) to the bishopric of Perugia (1847-1878).

The Popes: Temporal Power and Diplomacy

Administration and Finance

60. Cameron, Rondo E. "Papal Finance and the Temporal Power, 1815-1871." CH 26 (June 1957): 132-42.

Concentrates on papal borrowing and debt as the most appropriate reflection of the Vatican's ramshackle internal administration. Asserts that the political difficulties of the 1860s were reinforced by, and to some extent were the result of, financial chaos originating in the early years of the century. Denies, however, the existence of a connection between poor economic planning and doctrinal formulation (i.e., the belief that the Syllabus of Errors, with its condemnation of modern materialism, was prompted by hierarchical bitterness over the ineffectiveness of papal financial policy).

The Pontifical Army and Navy

61. Berkeley, G.F.-H. THE IRISH BATTALION IN THE PAPAL
    ARMY OF 1860. Dublin and Cork: Talbot Press,
    1929.

    An account of the 1100-man Battalion of St.
    Patrick, formed in mid-1860 to prevent an Italian
    takeover of the Papal States. Outlawed by the
    British Government and poorly trained, it fought
    bravely if unsuccessfully.

    See: Leo F. Stock, CHR 19 (January 1934): 478-80;
    Humphrey Johnson, Cong. Orat., DUBR 199
    (July 1936): 14-26.

62. Bouquet, Michael. "The Papal Navy and Its English
    Ships, 1755-1870." DUBR 203 (July/August/
    September 1938): 62-77.

    Describes the tragic neglect of this oldest of
    all European navies. By the mid-nineteenth century
    the papal fleet, which had successfully fought off
    the Barbary pirates a century earlier, was little
    more than a coastguard detachment, relying in-
    creasingly on English naval supplies and expertise
    in its efforts to patrol the Italian coast.

63. Harney, Robert Forest. THE LAST CRUSADE: FRANCE
    AND THE PAPAL ARMY OF 1860. Ph.D. dissertation.
    University of California, Berkeley, 1966.

    Examines the personalities, motivations, and
    activities of those Catholics--French, Irish, and
    Flemish, for the most part--who answered Pius IX's
    appeal for military help against the Italian
    nationalist movement. Points to the Crusade as a
    prime expression of the Papacy's major liability: its
    stubborn refusal to relinquish temporal power.

Diplomacy

64. Ryan, Edwin. "Papal Concordats in Modern Times."

CHR 16 (October 1930): 302-10.

Applies four questions to the seventeen concordats signed during the nineteenth century: (1)
Why were these agreements made? (2) Who made them?
(3) What matters were covered? (4) Who carried out
the provisions?

Pius VII (1800 - 1823)

65. Brady, Joseph H. ROME AND THE NEAPOLITAN REVOLUTION
    OF 1820-1821: A STUDY IN PAPAL NEUTRALITY. New
    York: Columbia University Press, 1937.

    Relates the skillful way in which Pius and his
    Secretary of State, Cardinal Consalvi, struggled
    to remain uncommitted during the revolution in
    southern Italy. Presented as a passing incident
    of major significance in Church history, for it
    underscored the serious challenges which the Pope
    had to face as a temporal leader.

    See: Raymond Corrigan, S.J., HB 16 (March 1938): 56;
         E. Jones Parry, HIST 23 (September 1938): 178-
         9; John Tracy Ellis, CHR 24 (October
         1938): 356-7.

66. Dwyer, J.J. "Cardinal Consalvi." DUBR 176 (April/
    May/June 1925): 211-38.

    An appreciative personality sketch of Ercole
    Consalvi (1757-1824), a staunch defender of the
    Church's right to be free from all State inter-
    ference.

67. ———. "Cardinal Pacca and Napoleon." DUBR 181
    (October/November/December 1927): 247-60.

    Next to Consalvi, Bartolommeo Pacca (1756-1844)
    was the ablest and wisest of Pius' counsellors; but
    unlike Consalvi, he became one of Napoleon's most
    tragic victims. His efforts in both Paris and Rome
    to maintain Papal freedom are the focus here.

68. ———. "Cardinal Pacca and the Temporal Power."

DUBR 183 (October/November/December 1928): 266-81.

A pendant to item 67. Clarifies the part played by Pacca during the restoration of Pius to the Papal States in 1814. Refutes the charge that he vindictively persecuted those who had held office under Napoleon. Portrays him as a conservative who realized that the pre-revolutionary situation in Rome could never be restored in its entirety.

69. Ellis, John Tracy. CARDINAL CONSALVI AND ANGLO-PAPAL RELATIONS, 1814-1824. Washington, D.C.: Catholic University of America Press, 1942.

Traces the hopes and frustrations of Anglo-Papal politics over the decade from Consalvi's London visit to his death. A close friendship between the Cardinal and Foreign Secretary Castlereagh led the two to cooperate at Vienna, but the spirit of cooperation was short-lived, for Consalvi failed to obtain either a concordat or a settlement of the Catholic Question with the British.

See: Raymond Corrigan, S.J., CH 11 (December 1942): 346-7; Donald J. McDougall, CHR 28 (January 1943): 513-5; Joseph S. Brusher, HB 21 (March 1943): 68; James J. Auchmuty, IHS 3 (March 1943): 338-9; Herbert C.F. Bell, AHR 48 (July 1943): 785-6; HIST (September 1943): 226-7; Matthew A. Fitzsimons, RP 6 (January 1944): 128.

70. Francis, Sister M. John, S.H.N. "Cardinal Consalvi and the Concordat of 1801." HB 25 (January 1947): 33-7.

Sets forth Consalvi's role during the extremely difficult negotiations with the French.

71. O'Dwyer, Margaret M. THE PAPACY IN THE AGE OF NAPOLEON AND THE RESTORATION: PIUS VII, 1800-1823. Washington, D.C.: University Press of America, 1985.

Spotlights diplomatic developments by detailing French challenges to the Papal States. Having

himself experienced revolution in the form of the
French occupation of Rome, Pius VII resisted all
new currents and dreamt of reestablishing the pre-
1789 situation.

See: James Muldoon, HRNB 14 (March/April 1986): 113;
      C.T. McIntire, CH 56 (September 1987): 413-4;
      Alan J. Reinerman, CHR 73 (October 1987): 637-
      8; John T. Ford, RSR 13 (October 1987): 355;
      John W. Padberg, S.J., AHR 92 (December
      1987): 1199-1200.

72. O'Rourke, J., P.P. "Cardinal Consalvi: 'Ego et Rex
     Meus.'" IER 73 (February 1950): 148-55.

     Outlines Consalvi's relationship with Napoleon,
     from the negotiations leading to the Concordat of
     1801, to the ways in which the Cardinal helped the
     Allies to defeat the French in the final campaign
     of 1814.

73. Reinerman, Alan. "Metternich and the Papal Condem-
     nation of the *Carbonari*, 1821." CHR 54 (April
     1968): 55-69.

     Illustrates Metternich's manipulation of Pius VII
     and Consalvi to gain their support for Austrian
     domination of the peninsula. Such support was
     crucial to the maintenance of the status quo.

74. Robinson, John Martin. CARDINAL CONSALVI, 1757-1824.
     New York: St. Martin's Press, 1987.

     The only modern biography of the Vatican's leading
     diplomat during the first quarter of the century.
     Renders positive judgements in three areas: (1)
     Consalvi's character, for its faithfulness, kindness,
     courage, wisdom, and honesty; (2) his internal re-
     forms of Papal government and embellishment of the
     city of Rome; and (3) his skillful negotiation of
     concordats with Napoleon and other leaders, along
     with his success in obtaining the restoration of the
     Papal States by the Congress of Vienna.

     See: J.J. Baughman, CHOICE 25 (April 1988): 1298.

Gregory XVI (1830 - 1846)

75. Beck, Andrew, A.A. "Gregory XVI and the Poles."
     CLR 18 (January 1940): 1-12.

     Reveals the Vatican's uneven response to Czar
     Nicholas I's persecution of Catholics in Russia
     and Poland during the 1830s and 40s. During the
     Polish uprising of 1830 Gregory refused Nicholas'
     demand that he order all bishops and priests to
     cease anti-government activity; moreover, he
     complained to the Czar of Catholic hardships in
     Russia, urging (unsuccessfully) that all unlawful
     restrictions on the Roman faith be removed. In
     1832 Gregory retreated from his earlier defiance,
     and the situation continued to deteriorate until
     the Czar's visit to Rome in 1845, and the re-
     sulting Concordat of 1847.

76. Berkeley, G.F.-H. ITALY IN THE MAKING, 1815 TO
     1846. Cambridge: At the University Press,
     1932.

     Offers a variety of insights into the antiquated
     political structure and mechanisms of the Papal
     States during the increasingly feverish years of
     Italian nationalism.

     See: Kent Roberts Greenfield, AHR 38 (July
           1933): 749-50; William Miller, EHR 48
           (October 1933): 668-9; John Van Horne, MLJ
           18 (December 1933): 206-7; Sister Loretta
           Clare, CHR 19 (January 1934): 500; John
           Tracy Ellis, THOUGHT 9 (June 1934): 147-
           50; A.H. Dodd, HIST 19 (December 1934): 271-
           3; M. Mansfield, DUBR 196 (January 1935): 59-
           72; Duane Koenig, JMH 14 (June 1942): 234-6.

77. Broderick, John F., S.J. THE HOLY SEE AND THE IRISH
     MOVEMENT FOR THE REPEAL OF THE UNION WITH ENGLAND,
     1829-1847. Analecta Gregoriana, vol. 55.
     Rome: Pontificia Università Gregoriana, 1951.

     Points to a great dilemma within Papal foreign
     policy: how to cooperate with the British government,

in order to further the process of Catholic emancipation, and yet not alienate Irish Catholic
opinion at the same time.

See: Denis Gwynn, CLR 36 (July 1951): 58-61; Denis
      Gwynn, IER 76 (October 1951): 257-73; D.J.
      McDougall, AHR 57 (January 1952): 434-5; James
      A. Reynolds, CHR 37 (January 1952): 459-61;
      R.B. McCallum, JEH 3 (January/April 1952): 120-
      2; D.J. McDougall, HB 30 (March 1952): 178-80;
      R. Dudley Edwards, IHS 8 (September 1952): 178-
      81; R.B. McDowell, EHR 68 (January 1953): 153-
      4; D.J. McDougall, JMH 25 (March 1953): 77-8;
      HIST 38 (June 1953): 180-1.

Pius IX (1846 - 1878)

78. Beck, Andrew, A.A. "Pius IX, Russia and Poland."
    CLR 18 (May 1940): 399-418.

    Details Pius' intervention on behalf of the Poles
    as revolutionary fervor intensified during the early
    1860s. The Pope repeatedly pleaded for greater
    understanding on the part of Czar Alexander II,
    whose only response was to heighten Catholic per-
    secution, and thus hasten the outbreak of the
    revolution of 1863.

79. Case, Lynn M. "Anticipating the Death of Pius IX in
    1861." CHR 43 (October 1957): 309-23.

    In the wake of Pius' seemingly fatal epileptic
    seizure in April 1861, French and Italian political
    leaders speculated about the succession, and what
    each group could do to assure the election of a
    candidate congenial to their mutual interests.

80. Coppa, Frank J. POPE PIUS IX: CRUSADER IN A
    SECULAR AGE. Twayne's World Leaders Series,
    vol. 81. Boston: Twayne, 1979.

    A broad sketch of the chief architect of the pre-
    Vatican II Church, along with his impact upon the
    Risorgimento, Italy, and the Church. Emphasizes
    political rather than religious developments.

Balances sympathy for the man with criticism of many of his decisions.

See: CHOICE 17 (July/August 1980): 686; Paul Misner, CH 50 (June 1981): 223-4; Egidio Papa, CHR 68 (October 1982): 666-7; Richard Camp, AHR 90 (February 1985): 175-6.

81. George, Robert Esmonde Gordon [Sencourt, Robert]. "Rosmini and Pius IX." CONR 188 (December 1955): 387-9.

Evaluates Rosmini's attempt of 1848 to persuade Pius IX to support the growing Italian nationalist movement. Though Rosmini was greeted warmly by Pius, his hopes for a Papacy which would mediate between the Italians and the Austrian government were destroyed by the Roman Revolution of 1848 and the Pope's flight to Gaeta.

82. Lalli, Anthony B., S.X., and O'Connor, Thomas H. "Roman Views on the American Civil War." CHR 57 (April 1971): 21-41.

Measures the extent of the gap between official Vatican neutrality and private sympathy for the North. Pius' rebuffed offers of mediation are also considered.

*   Parsons, Reuben. "The Pontificate of Pius IX." STUDIES IN CHURCH HISTORY, 5 (item 26), 505-71.

Rebuts the image presented in items 47 and 48. Sees Pius as an unwilling but decisive participant in the political affairs of post-1848 Italy. Suggests that the preponderant Masonic and atheist influence within the nationalist movement explains Italian hostility to the Vatican.

83. Wallace, Lillian Parker. "Pius IX and Lord Palmerston, 1846-1849." In POWER, PUBLIC OPINION, AND DIPLOMACY: ESSAYS IN HONOR OF EBER MALCOLM CARROLL BY HIS FORMER STUDENTS, edited by Lillian Parker Wallace and William C. Askew, 3-46. Durham, N.C.: Duke University Press, 1959.

An in-depth investigation of the Anglo-Papal

rapprochement of 1846-1848, based on the personal
friendship between the Pontiff and the Foreign
Secretary. Though Pius qualified his liberalism
as early as August 1846, Palmerston continued to
consider him the best hope of Italian nationalists,
and proposed the establishment of diplomatic relations through Lord Minto (see item 84). With
Pius' abandonment of liberalism after 1848,
English enthusiasm waned, killing all further
thought of a diplomatic link.

See: G. Bernard Noble, AHR 65 (January 1960): 359-
      60; J.E. Tyler, HIST 45 (June 1960): 169-70.

84. Williams, H. Russell. "Pius IX and a Visitor in
     Plaid Trousers." CHR 50 (July 1964): 208-10.

Examines Anglo-Papal relations during the first
months of the reign. In the summer of 1846 Prime
Minister Russell dispatched Lord Minto to Rome,
with the aim of encouraging the new Pontiff's
liberalism. Though he appeared at the Quirinal in
incorrect attire, Minto was quite perspicacious,
sending back to Whitehall a number of valuable
reports on the major ecclesiastical personalities
and motivations during the period.

The Unification of Italy

85. Berkeley, G.F.-H. and J. ITALY IN THE MAKING,
     JANUARY 1ST 1848 TO NOVEMBER 16TH 1848.
     Cambridge: At the University Press, 1940.

A more detailed continuation of items 76 and 86.
Focuses sympathetically on Pius' dilemma: how to
be both liberal and head of the Church at the same
time.

See: Sister Loretta Clare, CHR 27 (April 1941): 123-
      4; Kent Roberts Greenfield, AHR 47 (January
      1942): 332; Duane Koenig, JMH 14 (June
      1942): 234-6; EHR 57 (July 1942): 406-7.

86. ————. ITALY IN THE MAKING, JUNE 1846 TO 1 JANUARY
     1848. Cambridge: At the University Press, 1936.

In the same series as items 76 and 85. Explores the diplomatic machinery of Pius' first eighteen months, contending that the virtually unanimous esteem in which the Pope was held masked a poor understanding of the real and necessary limits of his liberalism.

See: C. Foligno, HIST 21 (June 1936): 80-1; Hans Kohn, AAAPSS 186 (July 1936): 208-10; Humphrey Johnson, Cong. Orat., DUBR 199 (July 1936): 14-26; Sister Loretta Clare, CHR 22 (October 1936): 320-1; Kent Roberts Greenfield, AHR 42 (January 1937): 326-8; EHR 52 (April 1937): 376-7; Duane Koenig, JMH 14 (June 1942): 234-6.

87. Coppa, Frank J. "Cardinal Antonelli, the Papal States, and the Counter-*Risorgimento*." JCS 16 (Autumn 1974): 453-71.

Studies the role played by Giacomo Cardinal Antonelli (1806-1876) in the spectacular turnabout which transformed Pius from the venerated leader of Italy in 1846-1848 to the unpopular opponent of national aspirations in 1849. Antonelli's influence during the final days of temporal power is also assessed.

88. ————. "From Cholera to Earthquake: The Transition from *Destra* to *Sinistra* Viewed from the Vatican." IQ 23 (Fall 1982): 81-90.

An analysis of Pius IX's view of the two major Italian political parties of his day. In 1873 the Pope compared the *Destra* and *Sinistra* to the two great natural catastrophes of that year, cholera and earthquake; though different in degree, they were, he believed, motivated by the same Masonic and Satanic personalities and ideas. Consequently, the Church could never reach an understanding with them.

89. Engel-Janosi, Friedrich. "The Return of Pius IX in 1850." CHR 36 (July 1950): 129-62.

Enumerates the reasons for the Papal flight of 1848. Maintains that with Pius' restoration in 1850

the conflict between political nationalism and
ecclesiastical conservatism could no longer be
confined to the peninsula. Antonelli's failure
to appreciate the much changed nature of the
situation made the Church's final defeat inevitable.

90. Guerrieri, Dora. "The Attitude of the *Civiltà
     Cattolica* on the Italian Question, 1866-
     1870." CHR 34 (July 1948): 154-74.

     Explains the newspaper's fundamental and
     unvarying opposition to the new Italian govern-
     ment, which it denounced as illegal and immoral.
     Provides background on its founding, aims, and
     early personnel.

91. Johnston, R.M. THE ROMAN THEOCRACY AND THE REPUBLIC,
     1846-1849. London: Macmillan, 1901.

     Condemns Papal temporal power as administratively,
     financially, and judicially antiquated; those who
     wielded it are portrayed as ignorant and unscrupu-
     lous.

     See: NATION 74 (23 January 1902): 78; William Roscoe
           Thayer, AHR 7 (April 1902): 576-7; W. Miller,
           EHR 18 (January 1903): 188-9.

92. Lynch, Sister Clare, O.S.B. "Abbot Tosti, the Last
     of the Neo-Guelphs." HB 27 (November 1948): 7-8,
     14-18.

     A brief biography of Luigi Tosti (1811-1897),
     historian and last surviving representative of
     those liberals of 1848 who sought to unite Italy
     under Papal control. Insights into the zealous
     but oftentimes impetuous neo-Guelph mentality are
     provided by constant references to Tosti's own
     ever youthful personality.

93. Patterson, Lawrence K. "Papacy and the Unification
     of Italy." HB 15 (March 1937): 43-4.

     A broad survey of the interaction between Italian
     nationalists and the Papacy during the first half of
     the nineteenth century. Continued in item 94.

94.   ————. "Papacy and the Unification of Italy (II)."
      HB 15 (May 1937): 73-5.

      A continuation of item 93, tracing developments
      from 1850 to 1870. Contrasts Papal "statesmanship"
      with Cavour's "machinations."

95.   Randall, Sir Alec. "Italy and the Papacy in 1864."
      WR 238 (Autumn 1964): 208-18.

      A reassessment of the Franco-Italian Convention of
      September 1864, the penultimate scene in the drama of
      Papal temporal power. Analyzes the character and
      motivations of each of the parties with a stake in
      the agreement.

The Roman Question

96.   Andrieux, Maurice. ROME. Translated by Charles Lam
      Markmann. New York: Funk & Wagnalls, 1968.

      Chapter 31 features Pius' relationship with his
      city during the last two decades of the temporal
      power.

      See: BS 28 (15 May 1968): 81.

97.   Blakiston, Noel, ed. THE ROMAN QUESTION: EXTRACTS
      FROM THE DESPATCHES OF ODO RUSSELL FROM ROME,
      1858-1870. London: Chapman & Hall, 1962.

      Essentially a comparison of two very different
      views of a highly complex situation. Russell, a
      devout Protestant and ardent pro-nationalist, under-
      stood Papal intransigence, but recognized that Pius
      would have to accept the inevitable and surrender
      Rome. Against this broad-mindedness is posed Pius'
      strange delusions, which led him to believe that
      Queen Victoria, after her imminent conversion to
      Roman Catholicism, would support the Papal retention
      of Rome. Also contains valuable descriptions of
      many lesser known churchmen.

      See: Patrick J. Corish, IER 99 (January 1963): 63-4;
           Shane Leslie, QR 301 (January 1963): 102-9;

Philip Hengist, PUNCH 244 (23 January
1963): 139; Elizabeth Wiskemann, HT 13 (March
1963): 209-13; Dom Wilfrid Passmore, DR 81
(July 1963): 294-6; Winifred Taffs, JEH 14
(October 1963): 246-7; Agatha Ramm, HIST 49
(February 1964): 102-3; Derek Beales, EHR 79
(October 1964): 876; Joseph N. Moody, CHR 50
(January 1965): 594-5; Gwendolyn E. Jensen,
CH 50 (December 1981): 478.

98. Bolton, Glorney. ROMAN CENTURY, 1870-1970.
    London: Hamish Hamilton, 1970.

    Chapters 1-8 offer a detailed, anecdotal look at
    everyday life in Pius IX's diocese. For a similar
    approach, see item 100.

    See: TLS, 12 March 1971: 290; Richard L. Blanco, LJ
          96 (15 March 1971): 957; George E. Snow, BS 31
          (15 July 1971): 182-3; C.H. Church, ESR 4
          (January 1974): 96.

99. Case, Lynn M. FRANCO-ITALIAN RELATIONS, 1860-
    1865: THE ROMAN QUESTION AND THE CONVENTION OF
    SEPTEMBER. Philadelphia: University of Pennsyl-
    vania Press, 1932.

    Investigates joint Franco-Italian efforts to
    produce a comprehensive settlement of the Roman
    problem. Details the intricate negotiations leading
    up to the Convention of 1864, with heavy emphasis on
    the Italian government's mercurial mentality.

    See: Graham H. Stuart, APSR 26 (June 1932): 568-9;
          Kent Roberts Greenfield, AHR 37 (July
          1932): 751-2; HIST 18 (April 1933): 95-6.

100. De Cesare, R. THE LAST DAYS OF PAPAL ROME, 1850-1870.
     Abridged and translated by Helen Zimmern. Boston
     and New York: Houghton Mifflin, 1909.

     Complements item 98. A narrative of social life,
     with occasional incursions of political turmoil.
     Thus, alongside discussions of theatres, newspapers,
     and religious devotion are examinations of the
     uprisings in the Papal States, the September Con-
     vention, and Mentana.

See: William Roscoe Thayer, AHR 15 (January 1910): 388-9; DIAL 48 (16 January 1910): 56.

101. Engel-Janosi, Friedrich. "The Roman Question in the Diplomatic Negotiations of 1869-1870." RP 3 (July 1941): 319-49.

Uncovers secret efforts by France, Austria, and Italy, starting in mid-1868, to form an alliance based on a mutually acceptable resolution of the Italo-Papal conflict. Sharp differences among the protagonists, as well as with Pius on the outside, brought the talks to an end in 1870.

102. Halperin, S. William. ITALY AND THE VATICAN AT WAR: A STUDY OF THEIR RELATIONS FROM THE OUTBREAK OF THE FRANCO-PRUSSIAN WAR TO THE DEATH OF PIUS IX. Chicago: University of Chicago Press, 1939.

A minutely detailed account of relations between the governments of Pius IX and Victor Emmanuel II, together with their impact on Europe as a whole and on each nation in particular. Focus of this study is the post-1870 controversy surrounding control of Rome, as expressed through the conflict over clericalism between the Italian left and right, as well as through the aging Pontiff's futile diplomatic efforts to secure continental support for his claims.

See: R.L. Porter, HB 17 (May 1939): 90; John Brown Mason, APSR 33 (June 1939): 537; Andrew Beck, A.A., CLR 17 (July 1939): 61-2; Herbert W. Schneider, CH 8 (September 1939): 297-8; Willis D. Nutting, RP 1 (October 1939): 505-6; IA 18 (November/December 1939): 807-8; Kent Roberts Greenfield, PSQ 55 (March 1940): 146-8; G. LaPiana, AHR 45 (April 1940): 646-7; Gordon Ireland, AJIL 34 (July 1940): 547-8.

103. Randall, Sir Alec. "Rome--or Death." DUBR 234 (Autumn 1960): 195-205.

Summarizes Pius IX's reactions to the progress of the "Roman idea," that is, the conviction that Rome must become the capital of a united Italy, during the last years of Cavour's life (1856-1861).

104. Scott, Ivan. THE ROMAN QUESTION AND THE POWERS,
      1848-1865. The Hague: Martinus Nijhoff, 1969.

      Sees the Roman Question as part of the larger
      nineteenth-century conflict between revolution
      and the Church. In formulating its views on Rome,
      therefore, each power was in fact making a larger
      choice than simply that between Italy and the
      Vatican. Provides particularly insightful cover-
      age of the mechanics of Papal diplomacy.

      See: N.W. Passmore, DR 89 (January 1971): 107-9;
            John W. Bush, S.J., CHR 59 (April 1973): 105-7.

105. Wallace, Lillian Parker. THE PAPACY AND EUROPEAN
      DIPLOMACY, 1869-1878. Chapel Hill: University
      of North Carolina Press, 1948.

      A detailed account of relations between the
      Vatican and the major European powers during the
      final years of Pius IX. Places Bismarck, as well
      as the Pope, at the center of activity, as it
      focuses on German reactions to Vatican I and the
      Kulturkampf.

      See: George Huntston Williams, CH 17 (December
            1948): 350-2; W.N. Medlicott, EHR 64 (October
            1949): 564-5; C. Grove Haines, THOUGHT 25
            (September 1950): 557-9; Friedrich Engel-
            Janosi, CHR 36 (January 1951): 461-4.

                    Leo XIII (1878 - 1903)

106. Halperin, S. William. "Leo XIII and the Roman
      Question." In LEO XIII AND THE MODERN WORLD
      (item 55), 99-124.

      Contrasts Leo's moderate attitude toward the
      Roman Question with the intransigence of his
      predecessor, Pius IX. Shows clearly how, through
      the prolongation of the *non expedit* and active
      Papal diplomacy, the issue of Rome played a con-
      tinuous and decisive role during the entire twenty-
      five years of Leo's reign.

107. Larkin, Maurice. "The Vatican, France and the Roman
     Question, 1898-1903: New Archival Evidence." HJ
     27 (March 1984): 177-97.

     Sheds light on the motivations behind Leo's
     benevolence toward the French government during
     the height of its anticlerical campaign. Using
     newly released Vatican and Jesuit archival material
     on Leo's pontificate, Larkin outlines the unreal-
     istic efforts by the nuncio, Msgr. Benedetto
     Lorenzelli, to enlist French support for the
     removal of the Italian government from Rome and
     its transfer to Florence.

108. Soderini, Eduardo. LEO XIII, ITALY AND FRANCE.
     Translated by Barbara Barclay Carter.
     London: Burns Oates & Washbourne, 1935.

     Examines Leo's stormy relationship with the two
     major Catholic powers of Western Europe. Elements
     covered within the Italian connection include the
     governments' decrees against Catholic education,
     the secularization of charitable institutions, and
     the strong influence of the Masonic lodges. Sub-
     jects within the French context include the
     politics of papal nuncios (the impotent Meglia
     versus the dynamic Czacki), the link between
     political legitimism and the Church, and the
     anticlerical campaign in the wake of the Dreyfus
     Affair.

     See: John Tracy Ellis, CHR 22 (April 1936): 84-6;
           Humphrey Johnson, Cong. Orat., DUBR 198 (April/
           May/June 1936): 322-4; R. Butcher, CLR 11 (June
           1936): 424-5; S. William Halperin, CH 5
           (September 1936): 297.

109. Ward, James E. "Leo XIII and Bismarck: The Kaiser's
     Vatican Visit of 1888." RP 24 (July 1962): 392-
     414.

     Shows that the visit was prompted by Leo's hope of
     persuading the German government to help him retrieve
     Rome.

110. ————. "Leo XIII: 'The Diplomat Pope.'" RP 28
     (January 1966): 47-61.

Measures Leo's skill and success in dealing with
the governments of Europe. Evaluates his abilities
as professional negotiator and as formulator of
foreign policy, concluding that, though perhaps an
outstanding political leader, the Pope was not a
particularly impressive diplomat.

The First Vatican Council (1869 - 1870)

111. Ahern, Eugene J., S.J. "The Ecumenical Spirit of the
First Vatican Council." IER 106 (November
1966): 265-84.

With selected passages of the first schema as his
starting point, Ahern describes the various expressions of the Council's openness both toward the
world at large, and toward non-Catholics in particular. However, significantly absent within the
document is any elaboration of the layman's place
in the Church, beyond simply that of obedience to the
hierarchy.

112. Butler, Dom Cuthbert. THE VATICAN COUNCIL: THE
STORY TOLD FROM INSIDE IN BISHOP ULLATHORNE'S
LETTERS. London: Longmans, Green, 1930. 2
vols.

The fullest account of the subject in English,
using conciliar acts and documents, letters and
diaries written by many of the protagonists, and
the standard general histories in German and
French. Views the official endorsement of ultramontanism as a logical and desirable development
of Catholic history. Treatment of anti-infallibilist positions and activities is consequently
minimal.

See: F.F. Urquhart, DR 48 (May 1930): 114-21; QR
255 (July 1930): 203; Outram Evennett, DUBR
186 (July/August/September 1930): 1-19; John
Telford, LQR 154 (October 1930): 230-40; M.
Browne, IER 36 (November 1930): 555-7; Canon
George, CLR 1 (January 1931): 101-6; Francis
Augustine Walsh, O.S.B., CHR 17 (April
1931): 75-8; E.L. Woodward, EHR 46

(April 1931): 312-4; D.C. Somervell, HIST 16
(January 1932): 365-7; DUBR 200 (January/
February/March 1937): 168-9; Philip Hengist,
PUNCH 244 (23 January 1963): 139.

113. Caffrey, Thomas A., S.J. "Consensus and Infallibility: The Mind of Vatican I." DR 88 (April
   1970): 107-31.

   Studies the phrasing of the Council's decree on
   infallibility, so as to discover whether the bishops
   really intended to give the Pope that exclusive
   privilege of error-free pronouncement to which they
   overwhelmingly assented on 18 July 1870.

114. Conzemius, Victor. "Acton, Döllinger and
   Gladstone: A Strange Variety of Anti-Infalli-
   bilists." In NEWMAN AND GLADSTONE: CENTENNIAL
   ESSAYS (item 1248), 39-55.

   Indicates that anti-infallibilist sentiment
   during the years immediately preceding and following
   Vatican I was not as monolithic as supposed; within
   the general opposition to the declaration were highly
   individual viewpoints, as seen in the attitudes of
   Acton, Döllinger, and Gladstone.

115. Dewan, Wilfrid F., C.S.P. "Preparation of the
   Vatican Council's Schema on the Power and Nature
   of the Primacy." ETL 36 (1960): 23-56.

   Lays out the process by which Chapter 3 of the
   first Dogmatic Constitution of the Church of Christ
   was prepared. Among the diverse aspects considered
   are the choice of theologians for the draft committee, the selection and editing of materials, and
   the patterns of friction between factions.

116. Ellis, John Tracy. "The Church Faces the Modern
   World: The First Vatican Council." In THE
   GENERAL COUNCIL: SPECIAL STUDIES IN DOCTRINAL
   AND HISTORICAL BACKGROUND, edited by William J.
   McDonald, 113-45. Washington, D.C.: Catholic
   University of America Press, 1962.

   Considers four significant aspects of the
   Council: (1) the intellectual climate in which

it met and worked; (2) its preparatory stages, presented from the viewpoint of theologians, bishops,
and statesmen; (3) the controversy over the definition of papal infallibility; and (4) its impact
on the Curia, the worldwide Church, and various
politicians and diplomats.

117. Fenton, Joseph Clifford. "The Necessity for the
      Definition of Papal Infallibility by the Vatican
      Council." AER 115 (December 1946): 439-57.

      Justifies the mentality and activities of the
      infallibilists at Vatican I, claiming that their
      main concern in voting for the Papal prerogative
      was the defense of doctrine.

118. ————. "The Requisites for an Infallible Pontifical
      Definition According to the Commission of Pope
      Pius IX." AER 115 (November 1946): 376-84.

      Analyzes the findings of the special theological
      commission of 1852 concerning the qualities which a
      doctrine need not have, on the one hand, and must
      have, on the other, to be defined as revealed
      Catholic dogma. Indicates that Pius IX was guided
      by these criteria in deciding to define the dogma of
      the Immaculate Conception.

119. Hales, E.E.Y. THE FIRST VATICAN COUNCIL; THE SMITH
      HISTORY LECTURE, 1962. Houston: University of
      Saint Thomas, 1962.

      A general introduction to the subject, with some
      insights into the difficulties encountered while
      trying to consult the original sources in the
      Vatican Archives.

120. ————. "The First Vatican Council." In COUNCILS
      AND ASSEMBLIES: PAPERS READ AT THE EIGHTH
      SUMMER MEETING AND THE NINTH WINTER MEETING OF
      THE ECCLESIASTICAL HISTORY SOCIETY, edited by
      G.J. Cuming and Derek Baker, 329-44. Studies in
      Church History, vol. 7. Cambridge: At the
      University Press, 1971.

      A fully documented presentation of the strengths
      and weaknesses of the Council. Agrees with Newman

that the declaration of infallibility was inop-
portune, for it antagonized many Catholics and
non-Catholics needlessly. Denies the assertion
that the bishops were bullied or tricked by Pius
IX into doing what they had not intended to do.
The atmosphere of fear, suspicion, and half-truths
surrounding the meeting still haunts its histori-
ography, concludes Hales, who urges a return by
scholars to the original transcriptions of the
full proceedings.

See: Donald G. Vincent, JAAR 41 (June 1973): 307-8.

121. Hasler, August Bernhard. HOW THE POPE BECAME
      INFALLIBLE: PIUS IX AND THE POLITICS OF
      PERSUASION. Translated by Peter Heinegg.
      Garden City, N.Y.: Doubleday, 1981.

      Contrasts sharply with items 112 and 120, while
      relying on many of the same primary sources.
      Vigorously upholds the thesis that Pius IX and a
      small but determined group of his creatures con-
      spired to force the dogma of papal infallibility
      upon a reticent Church. The hierarchy was cowed
      by a skillfully manipulated Council as well as by
      a mentally unbalanced Pontiff who was not against
      using heavy-handed methods against anyone perceived
      as standing in his way. Features a wide and unique
      array of contemporary photographs of all the
      leading personalities.

      See: John T. Ford, AMER 144 (7 February 1981): 106-
            7; Susan Jacoby, NYTBR, 22 March 1981: 15;
            Thomas F. Benestad, BS 41 (May 1981): 70;
            CHOICE 18 (June 1981): 1431; Kaye Ashe, O.P.,
            CRITIC 39 (15 June 1981): 5; James Heft,
            COMMWL 108 (3 July 1981): 412-3; A.N. Wilson,
            SPEC 249 (3 July 1982): 20-1; John T. Ford,
            RSR 8 (October 1982): 342-4; Peter Raedts,
            S.J., CLR 68 (February 1983): 71-3; Donald J.
            Grimes, C.S.C., CH 52 (March 1983): 96-7;
            James Hitchcock, REVREL 42 (March/April
            1983): 318-9; Gabriel Daly, O.S.A., STUDIES
            72 (Spring 1983): 102-6; J.K.S. Reid, SJT 37
            (March 1984): 131-4.

122. Hayward, Fernand. THE VATICAN COUNCIL: A SHORT

HISTORY. Translated by the Earl of Wicklow.
Dublin: Clonmore and Reynolds, 1951.

A fragment of Hayward's otherwise untranslated
PIE IX ET SON TEMPS (1948). Sets the Council within
the contemporary scene. Chapter 1 investigates the
highly charged political atmosphere in Rome as the
bishops prepared to meet. Chapter 2 details the
ecclesiastical tensions and personality conflicts
manifested during the proceedings.

See: IER 77 (March 1952): 237-8.

123. Hill, Edmund, O.P. "The Vatican Dogma." BLACK 41
      (September 1960): 324-30.

      Maintains that the divisions over the infalli-
      bility issue were far more subtle than the tra-
      ditional "Opportunist-versus-Inopportunist"
      accounts indicate. Identifies four major factions
      at work during the proceedings: the Gallicans,
      "Bellarmine Ultramontanists," Neo-Ultramontanists,
      and Inopportunists. Of these it was the Inoppor-
      tunists, and not the Gallicans, who most strenuously
      opposed the passage of the dogma.

124. Hoffmann, Joseph. "Theology and the Magisterium: A
      'Model' Deriving from Vatican I." Translated by
      Dom Frederick Hockey, O.S.B. CLR 68 (January
      1983): 3-18.

      Assesses the extent to which the decrees on papal
      teaching were influenced by the historical and
      ecclesiastical situation in which the Council was
      held.

125. Hughes, John Jay. "Catholic Anti-Infallibilism."
      AMPJ 76 (Summer 1971): 44-54.

      Investigates in detail the negative reactions of
      Acton and Newman, among other thoughtful contempo-
      raries, to the Council's official endorsement of
      papal infallibility.

126. Hughes, Philip. "The First General Council of the
      Vatican, 1869-70." THE CHURCH IN CRISIS: A
      HISTORY OF THE GENERAL COUNCILS, 325-1870, 333-65.

Garden City, N.Y.: Doubleday, Hanover House,
1961.

Emphasizes questions of procedure and debates over
dogma. Clarifies the levels of opposition to the
declaration of papal infallibility.

See: John B. Morrall, HT 11 (July 1961): 511-2;
Lawrence J. Shehan, CHR 47 (October 1961): 356-
8; R.E. McNally, S.J., THOUGHT 37 (Spring
1962): 130-1.

127. Jedin, Hubert. "The Vatican Council." ECUMENICAL
COUNCILS OF THE CATHOLIC CHURCH: AN HISTORICAL
OUTLINE, 187-239. Translated by Ernest Graf,
O.S.B. New York: Herder and Herder, 1960.

A summary of the arguments in item 112. Dismisses
the fears of anti-infallibilists by underscoring
post-1870 Papal restraint.

See: Martin R.P. McGuire, AHR 66 (April 1961): 768-
9; Edward Day, C.SS.R., SJR 53 (May 1960): 65-
6; J.J. Dwyer, CLR 45 (July 1960): 437-9;
Albert J. Loomie, CHR 46 (October 1960): 329;
Dom Dunstan Pontifex, DR 79 (Winter 1960-
1): 69-70; E.F. Jacob, HIST 46 (February
1961): 77-8; C.M.D. Crowder, EHR 76 (July
1961): 520-1.

128. Lucas, Herbert, S.J. "The Council of the
Vatican: After Fifty Years." DUBR 167
(October/November/December 1920): 161-82.

Corrects some of the leading misapprehensions
concerning the Council. Vatican I's main purpose
was *not* to proclaim papal infallibility; nor was
there ever any serious intention of declaring
Pius' Syllabus of Errors infallible. Moreover,
the Inopportunists were in fact strident anti-
infallibilists, as their obstructionist tactics
so clearly proved. (However, for a widely
differing view of the Inopportunists, see item
123.)

129. MacGregor, Geddes. THE VATICAN REVOLUTION.
Boston: Beacon Press, 1957.

A study of the Council's public proceedings, with
constant reference to the behind-the-scenes intrigue
and dealing. Though the narrative relies heavily on
item 112, this account differs widely from Butler on
two crucial points. First, the Council was never
free in its deliberations; had it been, it would
have never accepted either papal primacy or infallibility. Consequently, neither of these two decrees
can be considered legitimate pronouncements of the
Catholic Church. Secondly, the existence of an
"Inopportunist" minority was a Vatican-fostered
fabrication, which tried to prove that hierarchical
opposition to the decree concerned only its timeli-
ness, and not its substance.

See: Gerard Culkin, DUBR 232 (Spring 1958): 89-93;
      Gustave Weigel, CHR 44 (January 1959): 468-9.

130. McNamara, Kevin. "The First Vatican Council." IER
      100 (October 1963): 201-20.

      Looks at the emotional context of the public
      debate over infallibility.

131. MacSuibhne, Peadar, P.P. "Ireland at the Vatican
      Council--I." IER 93 (April 1960): 209-22.

      Describes the personalities and activities of the
      twenty-eight Irish bishops in Rome, with special
      reference to their positions on infallibility.
      Continued in item 132.

132. ———. "Ireland at the Vatican Council--II." IER
      93 (May 1960): 295-307.

      A continuation of item 131. Outlines both pro-
      and anti-infallibility intrigues and debate activity
      by Irish bishops between late April and 18 July 1870.

133. Moss, C.B. THE OLD CATHOLIC MOVEMENT, ITS ORIGINS
      AND HISTORY. London: Society for Promoting
      Christian Knowledge, 1948.

      Chapters 15-17 detail the anti-infallibilists'
      mentality and tactics during the Council, and the
      post-1870 disillusionment which prompted many of
      them, including well-known laymen like Döllinger

and Johann Friedrich von Schulte, to break with Rome
and join the Old Catholic Church.

See: Eric J. Patterson, IA 25 (July 1949): 333;
       Henry R.T. Brandreth, THEO 52 (September
       1949): 347-9; John H.S. Burleigh, SJT 3
       (December 1950): 436-7.

134.   Noether, Emiliana P. "Vatican Council I: Its
       Political and Religious Setting." JMH 40
       (June 1968): 218-33.

       Explores the connection between conciliar actions
       and larger developments. The boost to Rome's
       spiritual power, as a result of the infallibility
       decree, was balanced by the Italian takeover of Rome,
       which sealed once and for all the end of the Church's
       temporal power.

135.   O'Neill, John. "Archbishop Leahy at the First
       Vatican Council." IER 100 (November 1963): 284-
       92.

       Evaluates the role of the Archbishop of Cashel as
       one of the two most vigorous Irish Ultramontanists
       in Rome. (The other was Cullen of Dublin.) High-
       lights his address of 21 May 1870 to the Council
       Fathers, in which he clearly and forcefully tackled
       each of the objections to infallibility.

*   Parsons, Reuben. "The Council of the Vatican
       (Nineteenth General)." STUDIES IN CHURCH
       HISTORY, 5 (item 26), 571-607.

       A highly pro-Papal narrative. Regards the defi-
       nition of infallibility as not only opportune but
       also desirable, for ecclesiastical vitality required
       doctrinal certainty as its base. Objections to the
       doctrine, along with those presenting them, are
       dismissed rather summarily.

*   ————. "The 'Old Catholics' or Neo-Protestants."
       STUDIES IN CHURCH HISTORY, 5 (item 26), 607-29.

       Presents the rift as an inevitable consequence of
       the infallibility decree, and instigated by a con-
       spiracy of ill-willed "religious freaks."

136.   Ryan, Thomas R., C.PP.S.   "Environment of Hostility
        to Vatican Council I."   HPR 62 (August
        1962): 949-59.

        Analyzes the diversity of negative reactions,
        Catholic and non-Catholic, and institutional as
        well as individual, both to Pius' announcement of
        the Council, and to the Council proceedings them-
        selves. Among the critical responses presented
        are the fears of European governments, the cynicism
        of "Janus," the ridicule by the British press, and
        Bishop Strossmayer's conciliar address expressing
        concern over the Orthodox opinion of infallibility.

137.   Simpson, W.J. Sparrow.   ROMAN CATHOLIC OPPOSITION TO
        PAPAL INFALLIBILITY.   London: John Murray, 1909.

        An in-depth treatment of both clerical and lay
        anti-infallibilist sentiment throughout Europe
        before, during, and after Vatican I. Focus of the
        discussion of the post-infallibility period is the
        process by which recalcitrant bishops, priests, and
        laity were pressured to accept the new teaching.
        Against those who refused to submit Simpson presents
        the theological perception of the majority of
        average Roman Catholics who embraced the dogma
        without any hesitation whatsoever.

138.   Sivrič, Ivo, O.F.M.   BISHOP J.G. STROSSMAYER: NEW
        LIGHT ON VATICAN I.   Chicago: Franciscan Herald
        Press, 1975.

        Examines the efforts by the pan-Slavist Bishop of
        Djakovo (Bosnia and Sirmium) to direct the Council's
        attention toward reunion with the Eastern churches.
        Secondary consideration is given to his anti-
        infallibilist activities.

        See: James Hennesey, S.J., CHR 64 (October
              1978): 694-5.

139.   Sweeney, Garrett.   "The Forgotten Council."   CLR 56
        (October 1971): 738-54.

        Dispels some commonly held misconceptions about
        Vatican I's declaration of papal infallibility.
        Clarifies the Council Fathers' understanding of an

ex cathedra pronouncement.

140. ———. "The Primacy: The Small Print of Vatican
I." CLR 59 (February 1974): 96-121.

Presents views of the Primacy as expressed by the
Council's majority and minority. Concludes that if
the dogma is properly restated, it need not be an
obstacle to Christian unity.

The Hierarchy

141. ———. "The 'Wound in the Right Foot': Unhealed?"
CLR 60 (September 1975): 574-93.

Shows how and why the nineteenth-century Papacy,
after much reluctance, accepted the unprecedented
responsibility of nominating bishops for sees
throughout the world. Stresses the fact that
although Article 329 of the Canon Law Code of 1917
formalized this so-called *jus patronatus*, there is
nothing sacrosanct or immutable about it.

142. Viton, Philip A. "'Obligatory' Cardinalatial
Appointments, 1851-1929." AHP 21 (1983): 275-
94.

Offers insights into the give-and-take of Curial
politics, by studying one aspect of papal power in
which there was neither discretion nor freedom.
Certain dioceses—between thirteen and twenty-four
in the years 1851-1929—could not be denied the
cardinalate; consequently, and because of canonical
limitations on the size of the Sacred College of
Cardinals, nineteenth-century Popes had at most
between forty-six and fifty-seven unfettered
selections.

Diocesan Clergy

143. Shahan, Thomas J. "Higher Education of the Catholic
Clergy." CHR 14 (April 1928): 38-54.

Discusses the origins and nineteenth-century
progress of advanced programs of study for
priests. Among the European institutions surveyed
are the Catholic University of Louvain, Oxford and
Cambridge, and the Catholic Institutes of Paris,
Lyons, Angers, Lille, and Toulouse.

Orders and Congregations: Male

The Jesuits

144. Corrigan, Raymond, S.J. "The Jesuits and Liberalism
      a Century Ago." HB 20 (November 1941): 5-6, 17-
      19.

      Investigates the liberal hatred of the Jesuits
      as it crystallized and intensified in the decade
      after 1840. Contends that the dispute over control
      of education, as in France, was superficial, and
      that the real cause of the conflict between the two
      groups was their diametrically opposed views of
      humanity's origins, nature, and final destiny.

145. Delehaye, Hippolyte, S.J. THE WORK OF THE BOLLAND-
      ISTS THROUGH THREE CENTURIES, 1615-1915.
      Princeton: Princeton University Press, 1922.

      Divides the Bollandists' nineteenth-century
      development into two phases. From 1773, the year
      of the Jesuits' suppression, until 1794, they
      continued the publication of the ACTA SANCTORUM
      under Norbertine auspices. With the French occu-
      pation of Belgium, however, their property was
      confiscated, and they themselves were dispersed.
      Only in 1837, with a new foundation in Brussels,
      did the group resume its scholarship. The first
      volume of a new series on the saints appeared in
      1887, reinvigorating the old criticism that they
      were promoting superstition.

146. Dinnis, Enid. "The Centenary of the Restoration of
      the Society of Jesus." MONTH OS 123 (January
      1914): 56-76.

Highlights the issues confronting the Order during
the fifteen years following its resurrection in
August 1814: Should it reactivate its old, pre-
suppression identity? In what areas should it
concentrate its activities?

147. Garraghan, Gilbert J. "John Anthony Grassi, S.J.,
      1775-1849." CHR 23 (October 1937): 273-92.

A biography of one of the most dynamic clerics of
the century. After studying at houses in Italy and
Russia, Grassi served as Jesuit agent in pre-
Emancipation England, President of Georgetown
University, and confessor to the House of Savoy.
Few careers were richer in personal contacts, both
political and social, and yet his work for the
Order always remained his priority.

148. Harney, Martin P., S.J. THE JESUITS IN HISTORY: THE
      SOCIETY OF JESUS THROUGH FOUR CENTURIES. New
      York: America Press, 1941.

Surveys in the final four chapters the myriad
careers and activities of administrators, educators,
preachers, missionaries, theologians, and scholars
during the century following the Order's restoration. Presents and answers nineteenth-century
accusations against the Jesuits, maintaining that
their motivation lay either in deficient thinking
or in malice.

See: Theodore E. Treutlein, MID-AM 24 (April
      1942): 146-7; J. Cribbin, HB 21 (November
      1942): 21; Wallace K. Ferguson, AHR 48
      (April 1943): 537-8; William J. Schlaerth,
      THOUGHT 44 (December 1944): 714-6.

149. Hollis, Christopher. THE JESUITS: A HISTORY. New
      York: Macmillan, 1968.

Emphasizes the problems of the post-1815 restored
Society in dealing with a significantly changed
continent and Church. Balances the Order's financial
and educational successes against its alignment with
reactionary forces and widespread bad press.

See: John Bossy, NST 76 (6 September 1968): 288;

TLS, 17 October 1968: 1182; E.E.Y. Hales, HT
18 (December 1968): 886-7; James Finn, NYTBR,
2 February 1969: 12; Aloysius A. Jacobsmeyer,
S.J., REVREL 28 (March 1969): 337-8; Dunstan
Pontifex, DR 87 (April 1969): 236; Lubomir
Gleiman, HIS 31 (August 1969): 622-4; Eric
McDermott, CHR 58 (January 1973): 641-2.

150. Mitchell, David. THE JESUITS: A HISTORY. New
     York: Franklin Watts, 1981.

     Expands Harney's treatment of anti-Jesuit
     propaganda (item 148) within a larger framework
     sympathetic to the Order's sophisticated spiritual
     and moral teaching, but critical of its close
     identification with political reaction and
     ecclesiastical triumphalism.

     See: John W. Padberg, S.J., MONTH 2nd NS 13
           (September 1980): 320; C.R. Boxer, HT 31
           (January 1981): 57; William V. Bangert,
           AMER 144 (9 May 1981): 392; CHOICE 18
           (July/August 1981): 1559; James Hennesey,
           S.J., NCW 224 (July/August 1981): 187;
           Francine du Plessix Gray, NR 185 (22
           August 1981): 30-3; J. Derek Holmes, CLR
           66 (November 1981): 417; John Endres, RSR
           8 (April 1982): 192-3.

151. North, Robert G., S.J. THE GENERAL WHO REBUILT THE
     JESUITS. Milwaukee: Bruce, 1944.

     A detailed biography of Johann Philipp Roothan
     (1785-1853), focusing on the final twenty-four
     years of his life, during which he served as the
     Society's Superior-General. Almost singlehandedly
     and in the face of persistent political opposition
     he reestablished the Order throughout Restoration
     Europe by promoting missionary activity and updating
     Loyola's RATIO STUDIORUM and SPIRITUAL EXERCISES.

     See: Stephen McKenna, CHR 30 (January 1945): 458-9;
           Thomas O'B. Hanley, HB 23 (January 1945): 45;
           CLR 25 (March 1945): 138-9; IER 65 (March
           1945): 211-2.

152. Odell, Walter Tomkins. THE POLITICAL THEORY OF

CIVILTA CATTOLICA FROM 1850 TO 1870. Ph.D. dissertation. Georgetown University, 1969.

Points to the critical role in Catholic political thought played by the Jesuit journal during its first twenty years. Attributes its campaign against contemporary liberalism to its Thomist perspective on human nature and its conviction that the Protestant Reformation, with its emphasis on human independence, caused most of the nineteenth century's troubles. Details the editors' stance on particular issues of the day, including the temporal power, Church-State relations, and the place of science in society.

* Parsons, Reuben. "The Vagaries of Father Curci, S.J." STUDIES IN CHURCH HISTORY, 6 (item 27), 400-13.

Traces the passage of this Neapolitan intellectual from a stubborn defender of reaction, appointed by Superior-General Roothan to answer Gioberti's anti-Jesuit PROLEGOMENI, to one of the leading liberal critics of mid-century Vatican policy. Though his anti-Papal, pro-Italian works were publicly condemned by the Holy Office, and he himself excommunicated in 1884, he relented shortly before his death in 1891, reconciled with Rome, and was readmitted to the Order.

The Christian Brothers

153. Battersby, W.J. HISTORY OF THE INSTITUTE OF THE BROTHERS OF THE CHRISTIAN SCHOOLS. Vol. 2: THE INSTITUTE DURING THE NINETEENTH CENTURY, 1800-1850 (PART ONE); 1850-1900 (PART TWO). London: Waldegrave, 1961-3.

Situates the development of the Institute within the context of a century of rapid change. Attributes the threefold increase in membership between 1800 and 1870 to the demand by the middle class for more sophisticated educational facilities staffed by highly trained personnel. After several structural and spiritual reforms, inspired by the Concordat of 1801, and despite numerous obstacles, the Brothers met this demand admirably and effectively.

See: Charles F. Donovan, AMER 105 (8 April 1961): 86-
7 (for Part One); A.F. Kuhn, CHR 50 (January
1965): 597-8 (for Part Two).

The Spiritans

154. Hogan, Edmund M. "The Congregation of the Holy Ghost
and the Evolution of the Modern Irish Missionary
Movement." CHR 70 (January 1984): 1-13.

Outlines the role played by the Holy Ghost Fathers
in introducing the continental missionary impulse
into Ireland. Because of this instigation, which
began in the 1860s, the Irish were at the forefront
of the Church's apostolate by the beginning of the
twentieth century.

155. Koren, Henry J., C.S.Sp. THE SPIRITANS: A HISTORY
OF THE CONGREGATION OF THE HOLY GHOST. Duquesne
Studies, Spiritan Series, vol. 1.
Pittsburgh: Duquesne University Press, 1958.

Chapters 4-9 deal with nineteenth-century developments, of which the critical event was the reinvigoration of the 150-year-old Congregation by its
eleventh Superior-General, Francis Libermann (1802-
1852). Under Libermann's equally dynamic successors,
the Congregation grew spectacularly, absorbing
several nearly defunct orders along the way.

See: Raphael M. Wiltgen, CHR 44 (October 1958): 322-
3.

156. Moore-Rinvolucri, Mina. "François-Marie Paul
Libermann." IER 91 (April 1959): 242-7.

Focuses on the years after his conversion from
Judaism (1826), during which both as seminarian and
as head of a major religious order he displayed an
amazing spiritual stamina.

157. Van Kaam, Adrian L., C.S.Sp. A LIGHT TO THE
GENTILES: THE LIFE STORY OF THE VENERABLE

FRANCIS LIBERMANN. Pittsburgh: Duquesne
University, 1959.

Approaches the Congregation not on an institutional
level, as in item 155, but through the private life
of its renovator. Adds much to the portrait presented
in item 156, including background on the contemporary
French Church, Libermann's upbringing as the son of a
rabbi, and his reaction to the Congregation's initial
setbacks in the missionary field.

See: Hermes Kreilkamp, CHR 46 (July 1960): 201-2.

The Salesians

158. Auffray, Augustin Fernand, S.C. BLESSED JOHN BOSCO
       (1815-1888). Translated by W.H. Mitchell.
       London: Burns Oates & Washbourne, 1930.

       Presents a highly sympathetic character sketch,
       based on records gathered during the beatification
       process. Concentrates on his activity as dispenser
       of charity, seer, and miracle-worker.

       See: DR 49 (January 1931): 186-7; DUBR 188
             (January 1931): 165-7.

159. Fitzsimons, John. "Don Bosco, Apostle of Youth."
       CLR 31 (February 1949): 91-9.

       Analyzes his work with wayward boys, its
       theoretical foundations and failures.

160. Mich, Mario A., S.D.B. "Don Bosco, Apostle of the
       Papacy." AER 147 (August 1962): 96-105.

       Outlines Bosco's passionate devotion to the
       Papacy, as shown through his personal relationship
       with both Pius IX and Leo XIII, his LIVES OF THE
       POPES (1857) and pamphlets celebrating Vatican I,
       and his efforts to persuade his students to share
       his attitude.

161. Sheppard, Lancelot C. DON BOSCO. London: Burns &
       Oates, 1957.

Sees Bosco as a realist, sustained by an acute
sense of vocation, impressive natural abilities,
and a deep faith. Places his establishment of the
Salesians within both the Italian and Papal contexts, as expressed during the final years of the
Risorgimento. Large portions of this work are also
devoted to his achievements in education, spiritual
practice, and literature.

See: Dom Charles Hallinan, DR 76 (Summer 1958): 321.

162. Stella, Pietro. DON BOSCO IN THE HISTORY OF CATHOLIC
RELIGIOUS THOUGHT AND PRACTICE. Vol. 1: DON
BOSCO: LIFE AND WORK. 2nd ed. rev. Translated
by John Drury. New Rochelle, N.Y.: Don Bosco
Publications, 1985.

Not strictly a biography, but rather a psychological interpretation of his life. Explores his
religious motivations as priest, educator, and
clerical leader, with special reference to the
initial formulation and occasional frustration of
these motivations. To be followed by two (as of
yet untranslated) volumes, dealing with his religious
outlook and spirituality, and later influence and
continuing significance, respectively.

See: James W. Connell, O.F.M., BS 46 (June
1986): 101; Kevin J. Kirley, C.S.B., CCR 5
(January 1987): 31-2; Stephen M. Di Giovanni,
CHR 73 (October 1987): 664-5.

The White Fathers

163. Arteche, José de. THE CARDINAL OF AFRICA: CHARLES
LAVIGERIE, FOUNDER OF THE WHITE FATHERS.
Translated by Mairin Mitchell. London: Catholic
Book Club, 1964.

A brief but complete biography, interspersed with
character analysis and descriptions of the political
and ecclesiastical milieu. Full of praise for its
subject.

164. Burridge, William. DESTINY AFRICA: CARDINAL
     LAVIGERIE AND THE MAKING OF THE WHITE FATHERS.
     London and Dublin: G. Chapman, 1966.

     Describes the White Fathers' daily work in
     Africa, based on Lavigerie's letters and
     memoranda sent to Church officials and friends.
     Against the vivid descriptions of poverty, ex-
     treme heat, hunger, fatigue, and personal danger
     is posed an in-depth examination of the Cardinal's
     ideas of missionary activity and of the community
     life and sincere adaptation to the local environ-
     ment which he considered absolutely necessary for
     success.

     See: DR 84 (October 1966): 452-4.

                    The Society of Mary

165. Burton, Katherine. CHAMINADE, APOSTLE OF MARY,
     FOUNDER OF THE SOCIETY OF MARY.
     Milwaukee: Bruce, 1949.

     An account of the personal, political, and social
     considerations which prompted William Joseph
     Chaminade (1761-1850) to establish the Society of
     Mary in 1817. Buttressed by his conviction that the
     Virgin Mary had directed him to found an order which
     would revitalize French Catholicism, Chaminade chose
     an exuberant apostolicity as the only appropriate
     counterpoise to what he considered the militant
     revolutionary sentiment of his day.

     See: Francis L. Filas, S.J., AMER 82 (3 December
          1949): 286-7; James E. Donnelly, THOUGHT 25
          (December 1950): 732-3.

             The Oblates of St. Francis de Sales

166. ———. SO MUCH, SO SOON: FATHER BRISSON, FOUNDER
     OF THE OBLATES OF ST. FRANCIS DE SALES. New
     York: Benziger Brothers, 1953.

A sketch of Louis Brisson (1817-1908), his
character and work, based heavily on his own
writings and on the recollections of associates
and friends. As founder of a community dedicated
to the schooling of youth, he was responsible for
several major innovations in the Catholic educational system, rooted in a profound understanding
of adolescent psychology.

See: Francis L. Ryan, CHR 39 (January 1954): 486-7.

The Dominicans

167. Devas, Raymond, O.P. THE DOMINICAN REVIVAL IN THE
      NINETEENTH CENTURY; BEING SOME ACCOUNT OF THE
      RESTORATION OF THE ORDER OF PREACHERS THROUGHOUT
      THE WORLD UNDER FR. JANDEL, THE SEVENTY-THIRD
      MASTER-GENERAL. London: Longmans, Green, 1913.

      Details the return to the primitive purity of
      Dominic and his companions, mainly through the
      efforts of Alexander Vincent Jandel (1810-1872).
      Chosen by Pius IX in 1850 to restore long-forgotten
      discipline and religious observance, and against
      enormous opposition, Jandel successfully reinstated
      the fact of poverty, the practice of night prayer,
      and abstinence from meat. Frequent visitations of
      the provinces by the Master-General himself assured
      scrupulous obedience, and Jandel's new edition of
      the Order's Constitution, published the year before
      his death, received unanimous approval by his fellow
      Dominicans.

      See: AMER 9 (3 May 1913): 91; CW 97 (September
            1913): 831-2.

The Oblates of Mary Immaculate

168. Leflon, Jean. EUGENE DE MAZENOD, BISHOP OF
      MARSEILLES, FOUNDER OF THE OBLATES OF MARY
      IMMACULATE, 1782-1861. Translated by Francis
      D. Flanagan, O.M.I. New York: Fordham
      University Press, 1961-70. 4 vols.

Combines a detailed narrative of Mazenod's life
with a presentation of the larger political and
intellectual currents within French and European
Catholicism. Sees the establishment of the Order,
with its wide-ranging activities, as a logical
development within a Church beset by recurring
crises since the outbreak of the French Revolution.

See: Walter D. Gray, CHR 48 (July 1962): 258-9;
Helene Magaret, THOUGHT 38 (Spring 1963): 154-
5 (both for vol. 1); Walter D. Gray, CHR 47
(January 1962): 528-9 (for vol. 2); Walter D.
Gray, CHR 54 (April 1968): 187-8 (for vol. 3).

The Claretians

169. Sargent, Daniel. THE ASSIGNMENTS OF ANTONIO CLARET.
New York: Declan X. McMullen, 1948.

Follows the life of Anthony Mary Claret (1807-
1870), from parochial work in Catalonia to the
Archbishopric of Santiago, Cuba. Within the
context of a declining Carlist Spain this restless
cleric also served as missionary, royal confessor,
participant in Vatican I, and, most importantly,
founder (in 1849) of the Sons of the Immaculate
Heart of Mary.

See: Sister Natalie Kennedy, CHR 35 (July 1949): 230.

Orders and Congregations: Female

The Society of the Sacred Heart

170. Monahan, Maud. LIFE AND LETTERS OF JANET ERSKINE
STUART, SUPERIOR-GENERAL OF THE SOCIETY OF THE
SACRED HEART, 1857 TO 1914. London and New
York: Longmans, Green, 1922.

An account of Mother Stuart's numerous talents
and activities, both religious and secular. In
addition to her worldwide travels, she wrote books,

short stories, plays, poems, and hundreds of letters.
Large portions from her correspondence form the basis
for the sections describing her experiences on the
continent and in the Americas, the South Pacific, and
the Far East.

See: DR 41 (January 1923): 82-3; Bernard Holland,
      DUBR 172 (January/February/March 1923): 50-60.

171. ———. SAINT MADELEINE SOPHIE, FOUNDRESS OF THE
      SOCIETY OF THE SACRED HEART, 1779 TO 1865.
      New York: Longmans, Green, 1925.

      Makes extensive use of her correspondence to
      reveal her cosmopolitanism, clarity of judgement,
      kindness, simplicity, and humor. In the face of
      strong opposition, she refused to abandon either
      her newly-founded order or her commitment to that
      variety of austere religious education from which
      she herself had profited.

      See: CW 122 (October 1925): 140; DR 44 (May
            1926): 222.

172. Smith-Steinmetz, Pauline. THE LIFE OF MOTHER JANET
      STUART. Dublin: Clonmore and Reynolds, 1948.

      Similar in content to item 170, with the addition
      of some new material and the citation of different
      letters.

      See: CLR 33 (February 1950): 136.

173. Williams, Margaret, R.S.C.J. SAINT MADELEINE
      SOPHIE: HER LIFE AND LETTERS. New York: Herder
      and Herder, 1965.

      Describes the sixty-four years of service by
      Madeleine Sophie Barat, after her foundation of the
      Society of the Sacred Heart in 1801. During that
      time this far-seeing Burgundian opened 111 houses
      and accepted 4768 followers.

      See: Sister M. Linnea Welter, CHR 54 (April
            1968): 190-1.

174. ———. THE SOCIETY OF THE SACRED HEART: HISTORY

OF A SPIRIT, 1800-1975. London: Darton, Longman and Todd, 1978.

Follows the progress of Barat's Order as it confronted contemporary religious trends, producing a form of spirituality specially suited to its ministry and community life.

See: Alice Marie Welch, C.S.J., CHR 67 (April 1981): 314-5.

The Irish Sisters of Charity

175. Father Hilary, O.F.M. Cap. "Mother Mary Aikenhead: *The Charity of Christ Presseth Us.*" IER 90 (July 1958): 28-37.

A biography of the foundress of the Irish Sisters of Charity (1787-1858). Though bedridden for twenty-seven years due to spinal problems, Mother Aikenhead governed like a general, rigorously supervising her Order's work among the poor in schools, asylums, and hospitals.

176. THE LIFE AND WORK OF MARY AIKENHEAD, FOUNDRESS OF THE CONGREGATION OF IRISH SISTERS OF CHARITY, 1787-1858, BY A MEMBER OF THE CONGREGATION. London: Longmans, Green, 1924.

Elaborates upon the general points raised in item 175. Singles out Aikenhead's personal and professional obstacles, which ranged from her family's initial opposition to her conversion to Catholicism in 1802, to the threats posed to her newly founded Order by typhus, cholera, and unfriendly churchmen.

See: DR 43 (January 1925): 73-4.

The Good Shepherd Sisters

177. Bernouville, Gaetan. ST. MARY EUPHRASIA PELLETIER, FOUNDRESS OF THE GOOD SHEPHERD SISTERS. Dublin: Clonmore and Reynolds, 1959.

Less a biography than a chronicle of the battles
waged by Pelletier (1796-1868) to organize and keep
alive her Congregation. Against the opposition of
the French government, on the one hand, and her own
Bishop of Angers, on the other, she devoted herself
to the moral regeneration of young girls.

See: IER 93 (January 1959): 130-1.

178. BLESSED MARY OF ST. EUPHRASIA PELLETIER, FIRST
     SUPERIOR-GENERAL OF THE CONGREGATION OF OUR
     LADY OF CHARITY OF THE GOOD SHEPHERD OF ANGERS,
     BY A RELIGIOUS OF THE CONGREGATION.
     London: Burns Oates & Washbourne, 1933.

Describes in painstaking detail the birth and
growth of the Congregation, with tangential short
biographies of her early co-workers.

See: DR 51 (October 1933): 756.

The Sisters of Mercy

179. Bauman, Sister Mary Beata. A WAY OF MERCY: CATHERINE
     MC AULEY'S CONTRIBUTION TO NURSING. New
     York: Vantage Press, 1958.

Explains how McAuley (1781-1841) prepared her
first Sisters of Mercy for the profession of
nursing. Her devotion to the sick is placed
within the historical background of a British
Isles racked by social problems caused by industrialization and religious persecution inspired
by the harsh penal code.

See: Sister Mary Augustine Kwitchen, CHR 45
     (January 1960): 503-4.

180. Bolster, Evelyn. THE SISTERS OF MERCY IN THE CRIMEAN
     WAR. Cork: Mercier Press, 1964.

Relates the experiences of the fifteen Sisters who
were part of the second group of nurses dispatched by
the British government to care for wounded soldiers.
Against the backdrop of their thorough professionalism

and high efficiency, which earned them unanimous
admiration, is presented the recurrent clash
between two extremely strong and naturally in-
compatible personalities--Mother Bridgeman, the
leader of the Sisters, and Florence Nightingale.

See: DR 84 (April 1966): 238-40; R.A. Lewis, HIST
      52 (February 1967): 102-3.

181. Burke-Savage, Roland, S.J. CATHERINE MC AULEY,
      THE FIRST SISTER OF MERCY. Dublin: M.H. Gill
      and Son, 1950.

      The most complete biography. Attributes her
      success with uneducated girls, wayward young
      women, and the ill to the attractiveness of her
      personality and the strength of her commitment.

See: CLR 35 (June 1951): 426-7; James A. Reynolds,
      CHR 37 (January 1952): 461-2.

182. Degnan, Sister M. Bertrand, R.S.M. MERCY UNTO
      THOUSANDS: LIFE OF MOTHER MARY CATHERINE
      MC AULEY, FOUNDRESS OF THE SISTERS OF MERCY.
      Westminster, Md.: Newman Press, 1957.

      Balances sympathetic accounts of her life and of
      the early years of her Order. Provides the fullest
      information on her own youth, spent in a virulently
      anti-Catholic household, in which the ideals of
      religious life, as she would later come to embrace
      them, were seen as the antithesis of true spiritu-
      ality.

See: Edward A. Ryan, CHR 44 (July 1958): 194-6;
      CLR 44 (August 1959): 508-9.

                 The Little Sisters of the Poor

183. Helleu, Arsène. JEANNE JUGAN, FOUNDRESS OF THE
      LITTLE SISTERS OF THE POOR. Translated by Mary
      Agatha Gray. St. Louis and London: B. Herder,
      1940.

      A hagiographical account, written by the

Vice-Postulator for her canonization. Concentrates
on the troubled years both immediately before and
after her foundation of the Sisters in 1839.

See: Laurence P. Emery, CLR 20 (January 1941): 68-9.

184. Trochu, Francis. JEANNE JUGAN: SISTER MARIE OF THE
      CROSS, FOUNDRESS OF THE INSTITUTE OF THE LITTLE
      SISTERS OF THE POOR, 1792-1879. 2nd ed.
      Translated by Hugh Montgomery. London: Burns
      Oates, 1960.

      Extends the concentration in item 183 by adding
      new details concerning the slander, humiliation,
      and other tactics used by Jugan's opponents.

      See: CLR 37 (June 1952): 372.

              The Society of the Holy Child Jesus

185. Bisgood, Mother Marie Thérèse, S.H.C.J. CORNELIA
      CONNELLY: A STUDY IN FIDELITY. Westminster,
      Md.: Newman Press, 1963.

      Tackles some of the most distressing and tragic
      aspects of her life, including the delicate and
      bewildering problem of her relationship with her
      husband and children.

      See: IER 100 (November 1963): 340-1; Hugh J. Nolan,
           CHR 50 (January 1965): 617-9.

186. THE LIFE OF CORNELIA CONNELLY, 1809-1879, FOUNDRESS
      OF THE SOCIETY OF THE HOLY CHILD JESUS, BY A
      MEMBER OF THE SOCIETY OF THE HOLY CHILD JESUS.
      London: Longmans, Green, 1922.

      A factual treatment, emphasizing her noble
      character, strong faith, and deep piety.

      See: DR 41 (January 1923): 80-2; DUBR 172 (January/
           February/March 1923): 138-43; CLR 34 (November
           1950): 355-6.

187. McCarthy, Caritas, S.H.C.J. THE SPIRITUALITY OF
      CORNELIA CONNELLY: IN GOD, FOR GOD, WITH GOD.
      Studies in Women and Religion, vol. 19.
      Lewiston, N.Y., and Queenston, Ont.: The
      Edwin Mellen Press, 1986.

      Studies Connelly's spiritual development within
      the context of a stubbornly misogynistic establish-
      ment which severely limited her religious and moral
      options. Though women's issues are central to this
      story, this is not specifically feminist history;
      it is rather a detailed investigation of one durable
      individual's inner journey as it experienced both
      fulfillment and frustration at the same time.

188. Marmion, John P. CORNELIA CONNELLY'S WORK IN
      EDUCATION, 1848-1879. Ph.D. dissertation.
      2 vols. University of Manchester, 1984.

      Regards Connelly's educational activity--both
      theoretical and practical--as a major and effective
      effort to raise Victorian standards of teaching and
      classroom discipline. Inspired by the Jesuit
      tradition and by her own experiences as a mother of
      five, her BOOK OF STUDIES proffered numerous
      distinctive insights into the schooling process.
      Asked by Cardinal Wiseman in 1846 to found a system
      of schools in England, she established the tradition
      of quality education for females of all social
      classes.

189. Wadham, Juliana. THE CASE OF CORNELIA CONNELLY.
      New York: Pantheon, 1957.

      The most recent and fullest biography, set against
      the background of the Catholic revival in mid-
      nineteenth-century England.

      See: Mother Mary Peter Carthy, CHR 43 (January
      1958): 493-4.

                  The Congregation of the Assumption

190. Lovat, Alice Mary. LIFE OF MÈRE MARIE EUGÉNIE
      MILLERET DE BROU, FOUNDRESS OF THE

ASSUMPTION NUNS. London and Edinburgh: Sands, 1925.

Sets the story of Mother de Brou (1817-1898) within the larger picture of the nineteenth-century French Church, the main celebrities of which--including Lamennais, Lacordaire, Mont-alembert, and Dupanloup--she knew well. Her fame, however, was due as much to her role as educational pioneer as to that of foundress. For after establishing the Congregation, to which she gave the priority of faithful reci-tation of Divine Office, she devoted herself to the teaching of women in fields as diverse as philosophy and industrial techniques.

See: DR 44 (May 1926): 223; Agnes Repplier, FORUM 76 (August 1926): 316-7; CHR 12 (October 1926): 495-6.

191.   Reilly, A.J. CATHERINE O'NEILL: MOTHER THERESE EMMANUEL, CO-FOUNDRESS OF THE CONGREGATION OF THE ASSUMPTION. Dublin: Clonmore and Reynolds, 1959.

A pendant to item 190. As Mother de Brou's assistant, the Irish-born O'Neill exerted so great an influence over the Congregation during its first forty years that she is often regarded as a co-foundress. Most of the material here deals with her four decades as mistress of novices rather than with the richness and complexity of her inner life.

See: IER 92 (July 1950): 70.

The Little Company of Mary

192.   Dougherty, Patrick. MOTHER MARY POTTER, FOUNDRESS OF THE LITTLE COMPANY OF MARY. London and Glasgow: Sands, 1963.

Focuses on her struggles to retain the mission and spirit of the "Blue Nuns" as she first formulated them at Nottingham in 1877. In pursuit of her aim she challenged first her local bishop, and then the

Vatican itself; in the end, she won, for Leo XIII approved of her ideals in 1893. Presents Potter as indomitable and occasionally even abrasive, but always under Divine guidance.

See: IER 101 (February 1964): 139-40.

193. Johnson, Vernon. "Mother Mary Potter." DUBR 196 (January/February/March 1935): 124-33.

A survey of her stormy life and activity, seen from the viewpoint of a double paradox: though a lover of home life, she had no home of her own, and though a follower of authority, she opposed high churchmen.

Other Female Orders and Congregations

194. Devas, Dominic, O.F.M. MOTHER MARY OF THE PASSION, FOUNDRESS OF THE FRANCISCAN MISSIONARIES OF MARY (1839-1904). New York: Longmans, Green, 1924.

Traces the career of Helen de Chappotin from her missionary work in India (1866-1876) through her establishment of the Order (1877) and its initial apostolate in the Far East, North Africa, and Canada (1882-1885).

195. Devas, Francis C., S.J. MOTHER MARY MAGDALEN OF THE SACRED HEART, FOUNDRESS OF THE POOR SERVANTS OF THE MOTHER OF GOD. New York: Benziger Brothers, 1927.

Considers Mother Mary Magdalen (née Frances Margaret Taylor, 1832-1900) one of the prime restorers of Catholic religious life in Victorian England. The daughter of an Anglican curate, she converted in 1855, while serving as a nurse in the Crimea. The rest of her life was spent seeking out colleagues who would share her ministry to the poor and suffering.

See: DUBR 182 (January/February/March 1928): 155-6; James Healy, COMMWL 7 (29 February 1928): 1132; CW 126 (March 1928): 861.

196. Sister Francis de Chantal, S.N.D. JULIE BILLIART AND
      HER INSTITUTE. London and New York: Longmans,
      Green, 1938.

      A detailed biography of the foundress (1751-1816),
      followed by a brief history of the Institute of the
      Sisters of Notre Dame. Clarifies many of the reasons
      for the misconceptions which surrounded Billiart's
      image and work after the Institute's founding in
      1804. For a fuller picture, item 201 should be read
      at the same time.

      See: CLR 15 (December 1938): 554; IER 53 (February
            1939): 221; DR 57 (July 1939): 404-5.

197. Graf, Dom Ernest, O.S.B. FOUNDRESS AND
      MYSTIC: MOTHER DU BOURG. Buckfast: Buckfast
      Abbey Publications, 1949.

      Highlights the life and character formation of
      Josephe du Bourg (1782-1862) up to her founding of
      the Congregation of the Saviour and Our Lady in
      1834. Though a staunch believer in the priority
      of the inner life, she spent most of her time
      working as a friend of the poor, nurse to the sick,
      and teacher of youth.

      See: CLR 33 (March 1950): 213.

198. Laplace, Abbé Louis. IMMOLATION: LIFE OF MOTHER
      MARY OF JESUS (MARIE DELUIL-MARTINY). Trans-
      lated and adapted by J.F. Newcomb. New York
      and Cincinnati: Benziger Brothers, 1926.

      Covers the forty-three austere and tragic years
      of the woman who in 1873 founded the Daughters of
      the Heart of Jesus. The Order sought to make
      reparation to the Sacred Heart for clerical in-
      difference and for outrages committed against the
      clergy; personal immolation--i.e., severe personal
      sacrifice on a day-to-day basis--was practiced not
      only to mitigate Divine wrath but also to obtain
      large numbers of zealous priests. In 1884, at the
      height of her apostolate, Mother Mary was killed by
      an anarchist as she walked in her convent garden.

      See: AMER 36 (27 November 1926): 165;

CW 125 (April 1927): 141.

199. Lechner, Sister Cecile, S.C.C. AT THE RIGHT TIME SHE
CAME: PAULINE VON MALLINCKRODT, PIONEER SOCIAL
WORKER. 2nd ed. Mendham, N.J.: Mallinckrodt
Convent of the Sisters of Christian Charity, 1970.

A largely panegyrical treatment of the foundress
of the Sisters of Christian Charity (1817-1881), who
chose as the special object of her activity the
blind, orphans, and homeless living in the streets
of Europe's rapidly industrializing urban centers.

See: Ramon J. Betanzos, CHR 60 (July 1974): 316-7.

200. LIFE AND WORK OF MOTHER MARY ST. IGNATIUS (CLAUDINE
THEVENET) (1774-1837), FOUNDRESS OF THE
CONGREGATION OF JESUS AND MARY, WITH AN ACCOUNT
OF THE DEVELOPMENT OF THE CONGREGATION, BY A
RELIGIOUS OF JESUS AND MARY. Dublin: Clonmore
and Reynolds, 1953.

Details the motivations which inspired the heroic
Thévenet to devote her future and that of her congregation to works of charity and education. Includes
several experiences common to a large number of
nineteenth-century foundresses, e.g., a youth shaped
by the excesses of the French Revolution, and the
opposition of a misinformed clergy.

See: CLR 39 (October 1954): 635-6.

201. THE LIFE OF MERE ST. JOSEPH (MARIE LOUISE FRANCOISE
BLIN DE BOURDON), CO-FOUNDRESS AND SECOND SUPERIOR
GENERAL OF THE INSTITUTE OF SISTERS OF NOTRE DAME
OF NAMUR, BY A MEMBER OF THE INSTITUTE OF SISTERS
OF NOTRE DAME OF NAMUR. Translated by Sister
Francis de Chantal, S.N.D. London: Longmans,
Green, 1923.

Complements item 196 by examining the role played
by Mère St. Joseph (1756-1838), first, in helping
the frail Julie Billiart through the establishment
and early years of the Institute, and then in
succeeding her as Superior General.

See: DR 41 (July 1923): 173-4;

AMER 30 (9 February 1924): 405-6.

202. THE LIFE OF THE VERY REVEREND MOTHER MARY PHILOMENA
     JULIANA MOREL, BY A SERVITE NUN. London: Sands,
     1942.

     A biography of the first Prioress-General of the
     Anglo-French branch of the Servite Mantellate.
     Examines the steps by which she introduced her
     Congregation into England after 1850. As the first
     religious in England to wear their habits publicly
     since the Reformation, Morel's followers were
     actually applauded by passers-by.

     See: J. Cartmell, CLR 22 (November 1942): 513;
           Gerald M. Corr, O.S.M., BLACK 24 (May
           1943): 200.

203. Sister M. Liguori, O.S.F. MOTHER MAGDALEN DAEMEN
     AND HER CONGREGATION, SISTERS OF ST. FRANCIS OF
     PENANCE AND CHRISTIAN CHARITY. Buffalo: Rauch
     and Stoeckl, 1935.

     Recounts the life and activities of Mother
     Daemen (1787-1858), along with the work of her
     group as it spread from Holland throughout
     Europe, Asia, and the Americas.

     See: Joseph B. Code, CHR 24 (July 1938): 213.

204. Martindale, C.C., S.J. THE LIFE OF ST. ANNE-MARIE
     JAVOUHEY. London: Longmans, Green, 1953.

     Presents the life and efforts of Javouhey (1809-
     1880) as the best expression of the spirit of her
     Congregation of St. Joseph of Cluny. Despite
     constant opposition by unreasonable clerics, her
     heroic ministry among the mentally distressed and
     the poor both in Europe and French Guiana was
     enormously successful and won her wide popular
     acclaim.

     See: CLR 39 (October 1954): 636-7.

205. Moore-Rinvolucri, Mina J. "Madame Carré de Malberg,
     Foundress of the Daughters of St. Francis of
     Sales." IER 104 (October/November 1965): 295-8.

Features the process whereby Caroline-Barbe Colchen (1829-1891) became acquainted with the writings of St. Francis de Sales and established in 1870 an organization of lay women committed to Francis' ideals of a Gospel-based life and constant charitable activity.

206. Watterott, Ignaz. THE LIFE OF MOTHER CLARE FEY, FOUNDRESS OF THE CONGREGATION OF THE POOR CHILD JESUS, 1815-1894. Translated by a Member of the Congregation. St. Louis: B. Herder, 1923.

Contrasts Fey's quiet years in Aachen, prior to the establishment of the Congregation in 1844, with her relentless activity on behalf of poor children through religious houses based in Bonn, Derendorf, Dusseldorf, and Coblenz. Highly appreciated by the German people--the Emperor awarded it the Cross of Merit for its attention to sick and wounded soldiers during the War of 1870-1871--the Congregation was expelled during the *Kulturkampf*, resettling in the Low Countries and France.

See: IER 25 (March 1925): 334.

207. Whitehead, Elizabeth. A FORM OF CATHOLIC ACTION (THE LITTLE SISTERS OF THE ASSUMPTION). London: Sands, 1947.

An account of the collaboration between Father Pernet and Mother Mary of Jesus, leading to the establishment of the Congregation in 1867. In 1880 the Little Sisters embarked upon their first foreign, i.e., non-French, foundation; their work of caring for the sick and poor thereafter spread throughout England.

See: CLR 33 (June 1950): 431.

The Ecumenical Movement

Relations with the Eastern Churches

208. Asher, Richard E. "Vladimir Solovyev, Ecumenist and
        Mystic." ABR 33 (June 1982): 214-21.

        A sketch of Solovyev's efforts to bring together
        the Roman and Orthodox Churches, based on his
        conviction that the West had maintained true ortho-
        doxy while the East had become immersed in numerous
        doctrinal errors. Though he himself never converted,
        he held several conversations with Jesuits in Paris
        during 1888, and in the following year he published
        his most important work, RUSSIA AND THE UNIVERSAL
        CHURCH, in which he accepted the Pope as earthly head
        of Christianity.

209. D'Herbigny, Michael. VLADIMIR SOLOVIEV: A RUSSIAN
        NEWMAN (1853-1900). Translated by A.M. Buchanan.
        London: R. & T. Washbourne, 1918.

        Justifies the comparison to the English churchman
        by concentrating on Soloviev's equally sophisticated
        religious outlook, which boldly upheld the valid
        claims of the universal (i.e., Roman) Church before
        a stubbornly antagonistic nation. A Catholic
        Russia, Soloviev contended, would undoubtedly be a
        prelude to a spiritual transformation of the entire
        world.

        See: IER 11 (June 1918): 526-8.

210. Everitt, Mark. "Vladimir Solov'ev: A Russian
        Newman?" SOB 1 (no. 1, 1979): 23-38.

        Supplements item 209, by providing a more detailed
        comparison of the Russian's and Englishman's works on
        the development of doctrine. Resolves the contro-
        versial issue of Solov'ev's conversion, arguing that
        his acceptance of the Roman faith did not mean his
        renunciation of Orthodoxy; as a good ecumenist, he
        hoped to unite the two faiths first in his own
        person ("a prophetic sign") and then in the world.

211. Kadic, Ante. "Vladimir Soloviev and Bishop
     Strossmayer." ASEER 20 (April 1961): 163-88.

     Outlines the enthusiastic reception of Soloviev's
     ecumenical ideas among enlightened Catholic Slavic
     circles in eastern Europe. Leader of those whose
     deep emotional attachment to "Mother Russia" led
     them to embrace Soloviev's vision was Strossmayer,
     who hoped to bridge the religious gap between the
     Slavic peoples, but without a diminution of spiritual
     vitality on either side. For more on Strossmayer in
     this context, see item 138.

212. Munzer, Egbert. SOLOVYEV: PROPHET OF RUSSIAN-
     WESTERN UNITY. London: Hollis and Carter,
     1956.

     Summarizes Solovyev's ideas on ecumenism and
     his relations with Rome. Maintains that he was
     the inspiration for Dostoyevsky's Alyosha
     Karamazov.

     See: CLR 41 (October 1956): 630-1; Burton Rubin,
           SR 16 (1957): 211-3; John Sommerville, P&PR
           17 (June 1957): 563-5; Tatiana Nennsberg,
           JCEA 17 (July 1957): 192-3; Helene Iswolsky,
           RUSR 16 (July 1957): 65-6; Ralph Tyler
           Flewelling, PERS 38 (Autumn 1957): 402;
           Eugene S. Tanner, JBR 25 (October 1957): 391-
           2; John L. Groom, WPQ 10 (December 1957): 950.

213. Raybould, A.N. "Solovieff: The Great Russian's
     Plea for the Union of the Churches." CLR 15
     (October 1938): 283-94.

     An introduction to his activity and thought,
     using arguments culled from items 209 (the com-
     parison with Newman) and 214 (the image of
     visionary and dreamer). Asserts, contrary to
     item 208, that Solovieff declared his allegiance
     to Rome in February 1896, though his decision
     caused him nothing but anxiety.

214. Ronan, Myles V. "Vladimir Soloviev: A Russian
     Newman (I)." IER 8 (October 1916): 310-24.

     Covers the first twenty-eight years of Soloviev's

life. At the age of twenty, after years of religious
anguish caused by studying German philosophy, he
accepted Christianity, under the influence of Spinoza
and other thinkers who had convinced him of the
reality of the spirit. His travels to Western
Europe, taken after becoming Professor of Philosophy
at Moscow University, gave him his first ideas about
Christian reunion. In the wake of Alexander II's
assassination in 1881, he was dismissed from his
teaching post, and turned to writing on religious
subjects. Continued in item 215.

215.   ————. "Vladimir Soloviev: A Russian Newman (II)."
        IER 8 (November 1916): 388-400.

A continuation of item 214. Centers on Soloviev's
personal and literary relationship with Catholicism,
as cultivated during the final two decades of his
life. Extends the comparison with Newman beyond
that found in items 213 and 214, to speak of their
personal similarities. Of his diverse religious
writings the emphasis is placed on the three-volume
HISTORY AND THE FUTURE OF THEOCRACY, which praised
such Catholic doctrinal formulations as Papal infallibility, the Immaculate Conception, and the
Filioque clause of the Nicene Creed. Concludes in
item 216.

216.   ————. "Vladimir Soloviev: A Russian Newman (III)."
        IER 8 (December 1916): 484-95.

Continued from item 215. A brief examination of
some of Soloviev's more significant philosophical
and theological works dealing with Rome, along with
the Russian political, educational, and religious
context within which they were produced.

217.   Zernov, Nicolas. THREE RUSSIAN PROPHETS: KHOMIAKOV,
        DOSTOEVSKY, SOLOVIEV. London: S.C.M. Press,
        1944.

Chapter 4 reconstructs the events and outlook
which led Soloviev ever closer to Rome. Against
item 213, Zernov submits that he died in the faith
of his fathers, though some of his statements from
the years 1886-1888 indicate that he had at least
considered the possibility of conversion.

See: W.S. Urquhart, HIBJ 42 (July 1944): 374-6;
B.H.G. Wormald, THEO 48 (July 1945): 162-3.

Relations with the Church of England

218. Echlin, Edward P., S.J. "Towards a Contemporary
Appropriation of *Apostolicae Curae*." AMPJ 77
(Summer 1972): 8-30.

Reassembles and analyzes the data and arguments
(both for and against) placed at Leo XIII's disposal
in 1896, and on the basis of which he decided to
declare Anglican orders invalid.

219. Halifax, [Charles Lindley Wood, 2nd] Viscount.
LEO XIII AND ANGLICAN ORDERS. London and
New York: Longmans, Green, 1912.

A detailed, non-interpretive account of the ill-
fated ecumenical dialogue of 1894-1896 between
Halifax, leader of the High Church party interested
in reunion with Rome, and the abbé Portal. For the
basis of the discussions the two men chose the
question of Anglican orders. Prominent Catholic
clerics and laymen—among them, Gasquet and
Bishop—tried to discourage these contacts; and in
1894 Cardinal Vaughan declared the Church of England
schismatic and heretical, and in need of total sub-
mission to Rome. But Vaughan's address at Preston
only damaged the cause of ecumenism; Leo XIII's
Apostolicae curae, issued two years later, killed it.

220. Hawks, Edward F. "The Anglican Reunion Movement and
the Catholic Church." CHR 24 (July 1938): 129-
40.

Examines the various efforts by both Anglicans
and Roman Catholics to draw closer together.
Spotlights the mechanics, hopes, and impact of the
Oxford Movement, Ambrose Phillipps de Lisle's
Association for the Promotion of the Unity of
Christendom, the Lambeth Conference of 1880, and
Halifax's Anglo-Catholic Party. Stresses Roman
reactions to each of these, ranging from suspicion
(as with Keble's Tractarians) to outright

condemnation (as with de Lisle's and Halifax's
initiatives).

221. Hemmer, H. FERNAND PORTAL (1855-1926), APOSTLE OF
     UNITY. Translated and edited by Arthur T.
     Macmillan. New York: St. Martin's Press, 1961.

     Describes Portal's pioneering activity in favor
     of a greater understanding between Rome and
     Canterbury. A French Lazarist, whose ecumenical
     drive was instigated by a chance meeting with
     Halifax in 1889, Portal seized upon the issue of
     Anglican orders as an area of negotiation and
     possible rapprochement. He never received the
     official support of the Roman hierarchy in England,
     and the publication in 1896 of *Apostolicae curae*
     killed the entire venture.

     See: IER 95 (June 1961): 425-6; Robert W. Hovda,
           CHR 48 (July 1962): 273-4.

222. Holmes, J. Derek. "Archbishops of Westminster and
     the Reunion Movement during the Nineteenth
     Century." OIC 8 (1972): 55-68.

     Spells out the positions of Cardinals Wiseman,
     Manning, and Vaughan toward both Roman and Anglican
     ecumenical initiatives. Illustrates the intransi-
     gence of Wiseman and Manning by referring to their
     undermining of de Lisle's Association for the
     Promotion of the Unity of Christendom. Shows the
     ill-concealed contempt expressed by Vaughan, for
     whom true reunion meant Canterbury's complete sub-
     mission, and at whose repeated urging Leo XIII
     delved into the question of Anglican orders.

223. Hughes, John Jay. ABSOLUTELY NULL AND UTTERLY
     VOID: THE PAPAL CONDEMNATION OF ANGLICAN
     ORDERS, 1896. Washington, D.C.: Corpus
     Books, 1968.

     The most complete account of the complex
     circumstances leading to the issuance of
     Apostolicae curae. Concludes that although
     Leo XIII justified his condemnation by the
     existence of defects in the form of the 1552
     Church of England ordinal, as well as in the
     intention with which that ordinal was used,

the real motive behind the Papal action was a
tragic absence of goodwill within the
hierarchies of both sides.

See: Columba Cary-Elwes, DR 86 (October 1968): 424-
       6; Titus Cranny, AMER 119 (12 October
       1968): 333-4; E.L. Mascall, THEO 71 (November
       1968): 513-4; Carl J. Armbruster, COMMWL 89
       (28 February 1969): 680; Henry Chadwick, JTS
       20 (April 1969): 362-3; Rudolf J. Ehrlich,
       SJT 22 (June 1969): 245-6; David Milburn, CLR
       55 (March 1970): 241-4; J.S. Nurser, HIST 55
       (June 1970): 285-6; Frans Jozef van Beeck,
       S.J., JEH 21 (July 1970): 278-9; Martin E.
       Marty, JMH 43 (June 1971): 329-30; Martin
       Molyneux, CHR 58 (April 1972): 94-5; Andrew
       Kurzyna, DUBR 13 (Fall 1973): 57-9.

224.   ————. STEWARDS OF THE LORD: A REAPPRAISAL OF
       ANGLICAN ORDERS. London and Sydney: Sheed &
       Ward, 1970.

       Chapter 1 dissects the theology of *Apostolicae
       curae* and gauges its impact on both supporters and
       critics.

See: Patrick J. Corish, ITQ 38 (January 1971): 79-
       80; Anthony A. Stephenson, AMPJ 76 (Spring
       1971): 98-100; Michael Moreton, THEO 74
       (April 1971): 173-4.

225.   McClelland, Vincent Alan.   "Corporate Reunion: A
       Nineteenth-Century Dilemma." THS 43 (March
       1982):   3-29.

       Investigates reunion proposals originating from
       the Roman side during the first half of the century.
       Passes from the initial suggestion of Anglican-
       Catholic dialogue by Bishop Doyle of Kildare (1824)
       to de Lisle's Association for the Promotion of the
       Unity of Christendom (1857), with a number of other
       idealistic--and equally futile--steps in-between.

226.   McDermott, Eric, S.J.   "Leo XIII and England."   In
       LEO XIII AND THE MODERN WORLD (item 55), 127-56.

       Details the process whereby Leo decided upon the

invalidity of Anglican orders. Emphasizes the
role played by the anti-ecumenical Cardinals
Vaughan and Gasquet in the formulation of the
Papal position.

*   Parsons, Reuben. "Pope Leo XIII and the English
       People: The Decision on Anglican 'Orders.'"
       STUDIES IN CHURCH HISTORY, 6 (item 27), 225-36.

       A straightforward, non-analytical, and sympathetic
       explanation of the motives behind the Papal
       declaration of nullity.

227. Pawley, Bernard and Margaret. ROME AND CANTERBURY
       THROUGH FOUR CENTURIES: A STUDY OF THE RELATIONS
       BETWEEN THE CHURCH OF ROME AND THE ANGLICAN
       CHURCHES, 1530-1973. New York: Seabury Press,
       1975.

       Assesses the nineteenth-century relationship in
       Chapters 6-12, with the reunion initiatives by both
       sides as pivot. Among the pre-1850 themes
       considered: each church's view of the other's
       hierarchy, clergy, and claims; the Oxford Movement;
       and the earliest (and ridiculously unrealistic)
       proposals to bring Anglicans and Romans together.
       Post-1850 material includes the changing definition
       of "reunion"; the opposing hopes and activities of
       de Lisle and Wiseman; English reactions to such
       Catholic formulations as the Immaculate Conception,
       the Syllabus of Errors, and Papal infallibility; and
       the deathblow to ecumenism administered by
       Apostolicae curae.

       See: Herbert J. Ryan, AMER 133 (20 September
             1975): 151-2; CHOICE 12 (December 1975): 1323;
             J.C. Dickinson, ECR 28 (January 1976): 119;
             Norris Merchant, COMMWL 103 (9 April 1976): 249-
             50; William A. Johnson, CH 45 (September
             1976): 403-5; R.F. Smith, S.J., REVREL 36
             (January 1977): 159; Gerald P. Fogarty, S.J.,
             JAAR 46 (December 1978): 597.

228. Stuart, Elizabeth. "The Condemnation of Anglican
       Orders in the Light of the Roman Catholic
       Reaction to the Oxford Movement." HEYJ 29
       (January 1988): 86-98.

Sees *Apostolicae curae* as the inevitable result
of the English ultramontane disappointment over the
failure of the Oxford Movement to lead to Roman
Catholicism. Acting on their belief that they
had been deliberately deceived by the Movement,
which was interested only in getting its orders
recognized by Rome, the ultramontanes reacted
angrily, and had no other choice but to support
the invalidity of Anglican orders at all costs.

Anticlericalism

229. Sánchez, José. ANTICLERICALISM: A BRIEF HISTORY.
Notre Dame and London: University of Notre
Dame Press, 1972.

Divides nineteenth-century anticlericals into
two major groups, indicating the specific thrust
and long-term impact of each. The political
anticlericals, led by the Freemasons, sought to
diminish both the clergy's vast landholdings and
its influence over education. Usually moderate
in their activity, they could become violent in
times of crisis. The social anticlericals
directed their more often than not violent
attacks not so much against clerical property
and power as against the clerics themselves.
Four successive chapters apply this analysis to
France, Spain, Italy, and Portugal.

See: CHOICE 10 (July/August 1973): 790; Francis N.
Korth, S.J., REVREL 32 (September 1973): 1191-
2; Henry G.J. BECK, AHR 79 (February 1974): 112.

230. Schapiro, J. Salwyn. ANTICLERICALISM: CONFLICT
BETWEEN CHURCH AND STATE IN FRANCE, ITALY, AND
SPAIN. Princeton: D. Van Nostrand, 1967.

A survey of the conflict over the powers and
privileges enjoyed by the Catholic Church in France,
Italy, and Spain, from the close of the eighteenth
century to the middle of the twentieth. Incorporates
almost one hundred pages of significant primary
sources (e.g., Lamennais, Veuillot, Cavour, Leo
XIII) to illustrate points made in the text.

THEOLOGY, SPIRITUALITY, AND APOSTOLIC ACTIVITY

Papal Teaching

231. Aubert, Roger. "Religious Liberty from 'Mirari vos'
to the 'Syllabus.'" Translated by Eileen
O'Gorman, R.S.C.J. In HISTORICAL PROBLEMS OF
CHURCH RENEWAL, edited by Roger Aubert, 89-105.
Concilium: Theology in the Age of Renewal, vol.
7. Glen Rock, N.J.: Paulist Press, 1965.

Places two key nineteenth-century Papal documents
on religious liberty in their historical context, so
as to ascertain their true impact and lasting
doctrinal significance. Gregory XVI's *Mirari vos*
(1832) must be read in light of the agitation caused
within the Church by Lamennais and *l'Avenir*, and
outside the Church by the proponents of Italian
unity. Pius IX's Syllabus of Errors (1864) should
be seen not as a series of fanatical innovations,
but as a reinforcement of his predecessor's teachings.
(But for a diametrically opposed view of the latter
document, see item 235.)

232. Camp, Richard L. THE PAPAL IDEOLOGY OF SOCIAL
REFORM: A STUDY IN HISTORICAL DEVELOPMENT,
1878-1967. Leiden: E.J. Brill, 1969.

Analyzes the body of Leo XIII's social teaching,
its roots, and the activities which it inspired.

See: John M. Krumm, AHR 75 (October 1970): 1713;
Thomas E. Morrissey, CH 39 (December 1970): 565-
6; Maurice J.M. Larkin, HIST 56 (February
1971): 154; Joseph N. Moody, CHR 59 (April
1973): 116-7.

233.   Collins, James.   "Leo XIII and the Philosophical
          Approach to Modernity."   In LEO XIII AND THE
          MODERN WORLD (item 55), 181-209.

          An appreciation of Leo's philosophical outlook,
          as it developed during his pre-Papal years and
          reached full maturity in his encyclical of 1879,
          Aeterni Patris, which encouraged the revival of
          Thomistic thought within the Church.

234.   De Freitas, José Cursino.   CITIZENSHIP EDUCATION IN
          THE THOUGHT OF LEO XIII.   Ph.D. dissertation.
          Fordham University, 1964.

          Sets forth Leo's ideas on the subject, explaining
          how the Pope expected the principles broadly
          enunciated in his writings to be applied by Catholics
          on a day-to-day basis.   Predicates Leo's concern
          with citizenship on his belief that only as good
          citizens could Catholics bring real truth and lasting
          peace to increasingly secularized modern societies.

235.   Doyle, Peter.   "Pope Pius IX and Religious Freedom."
          In PERSECUTION AND TOLERATION: PAPERS READ AT
          THE TWENTY-SECOND SUMMER MEETING AND THE TWENTY-
          THIRD WINTER MEETING OF THE ECCLESIASTICAL
          HISTORY SOCIETY, 1983 (item 29), 329-41.

          Rebuts item 231.   Sees the Syllabus of Errors not
          as a carefully considered theological pronouncement,
          but as proof of a simplistic outlook which painted
          the world in harsh blacks and whites, with no
          allowance whatsoever for shadings.   Attributes Pius'
          religious intolerance to a number of different but
          interrelated motivations, including fear of intel-
          lectual diversity, a psychological need for that
          kind of certainty and security provided by the
          medieval world-view, and the conviction that
          Catholicism alone had truth.

236.   Ellis, John Tracy.   "From the Enlightenment to the
          Present: Papal Policy Seen Through the
          Encyclicals."   CHR 69 (January 1983):   51-8.

          Describes the place of encyclicals in Papal
          history, with special reference to those issued
          by Pius IX and Leo XIII.

237. Elsbernd, Mary. PAPAL STATEMENTS ON RIGHTS: A
     HISTORICAL CONTEXTUAL STUDY OF ENCYCLICAL
     TEACHING FROM PIUS VI TO PIUS XI (1791-1939).
     Ph.D. dissertation. Catholic University of
     Louvain, 1985.

     An examination of both the historical context
     within which Papal statements on rights were made
     and the evolution of the vocabulary used to refer
     to those rights. Concludes that the Papacy's
     recognition of rights as natural and individual
     was a gradual process, determined by historical
     realities; as such, the statements are not only
     important in themselves, but serve as a valuable
     insight into the evolutionary nature of modern
     magisterial activity.

238. Fenton, Joseph Clifford. "The Teaching of the
     Testem Benevolentiae." AER 129 (August
     1953): 124-33.

     Claims that Leo XIII's famous letter to Cardinal
     Gibbons, 22 January 1899, did not, as often mistaken-
     ly believed, condemn any heresies. No specific
     individual or group opinions were stigmatized, nor
     in fact was the word "heretical" mentioned anywhere
     in its text. Rather, the thrust of *Testem
     Benevolentiae* was against those Catholic intel-
     lectuals who maintained that the Church should
     change its *depositum fidei* to meet modern tastes.

239. Husslein, Joseph, S.J. THE CHRISTIAN SOCIAL
     MANIFESTO: AN INTERPRETIVE STUDY OF THE
     ENCYCLICALS *RERUM NOVARUM* AND *QUADRAGESIMO
     ANNO* OF POPE LEO XIII AND POPE PIUS XI.
     Milwaukee: Bruce, 1931.

     Reorganizes the ideas of *Rerum Novarum* under a
     wide variety of subject headings, including
     individualism, socialism, private property, the
     proper use of wealth, government's duties toward
     labor, human rights, the issue of a just wage,
     the equitable distribution of wealth, labor
     unions, and social reconstruction.

     See: Philip H. Burkett, S.J., AAAPSS 163 (September
     1932): 242; C. Bruehl, SJR 25

(September 1932): 181; SOCSR 17 (November/
December 1932): 188.

240. Laurentin, René. "The Role of the Papal Magisterium
      in the Development of the Dogma of the Immaculate
      Conception." Translated by Charles E. Sheedy,
      C.S.C., and Edward S. Shea, C.S.C. In THE DOGMA
      OF THE IMMACULATE CONCEPTION: HISTORY AND
      SIGNIFICANCE, edited by Edward Dennis O'Connor,
      271-324. Notre Dame: University of Notre Dame
      Press, 1958.

      Lists the steps taken by nineteenth-century Popes
      to encourage devotion to the doctrine of the Immacu-
      late Conception. Whereas Pius VII and Gregory XVI
      moved slowly and cautiously in extending permission
      to orders and dioceses which petitioned to celebrate
      the Marian privilege on 8 December, Pius IX laid the
      groundwork for its official definition as early as
      1847. After almost seven years of discussion, the
      bull *Ineffabilis Deus* (1854) declared the Immaculate
      Conception an integral part of Roman Catholic belief.

      See: IER 92 (September 1959): 209-13; E.L. Mascall,
            JTS 11 (April 1960): 223-5; Donal Flanagan,
            ITQ 28 (no. 3, 1961): 246-7.

241. McKevitt, Peter. "Pope Leo XIII and Social Reform."
      IER 57 (May 1941): 438-51.

      Refutes the claim that *Rerum Novarum* dramatically
      reversed the Papal attitude toward liberalism, as
      established three decades earlier by Pius IX. In
      fact, by pointing out specific evils in the social
      sphere and indicating remedies to them, Leo
      reaffirmed the thrust of his predecessor.

242. Moody, Joseph N. "Leo XIII and the Social Crisis."
      In LEO XIII AND THE MODERN WORLD (item 55), 65-86.

      Discusses Leo's outlook on social issues, with
      emphasis on the background and ideas of *Rerum
      Novarum*. Simultaneously provides several insights
      into the complex process by which an encyclical is
      put together.

243. Murray, John Courtney, S.J. "Leo XIII on Church and

State: The General Structure of the Controversy."
THS 14 (March 1953): 1-30.

Follows the development of Leo's thought on the
relationship between government and religion, as
seen in twenty major pronouncements. Within the
development Murray looks for the most frequently
reiterated themes and the historical circumstances
which may have inspired them.

244. ———. "Leo XIII: Separation of Church and State."
THS 14 (June 1953): 145-214.

Clarifies Papal intentions in condemning the
separation of Church and State. Leo was not
condemning the American concept of separation;
rather, his indictment was aimed at a situation
in which neither politics nor society recognized
Christian values as being the foundation of their
entire structure.

245. ———. "Leo XIII: Two Concepts of Government."
THS 14 (December 1953): 551-67.

Extrapolates three central ideas from Leo's
writings on the nature of civil authority: (1)
governments must play a strictly political role
with regard to the socio-economic order; (2) in
religious and cultural affairs, governments must
exercise much more than simply a political influence; and (3) the reasons for the wide divergence
between governmental responsibilities in the
different areas are rooted in the historical
situation with which this particular Pope was
confronted.

246. O'Rahilly, Alfred. "The Syllabus." IER 41 (January
1933): 13-26.

A defense of Pius IX's controversial statement,
based on the contention that it did not condemn
anything specific, nor was it meant to be a positive
and systematic exposition of Catholic teaching. Unravels some of the most common misrepresentations of
individual propositions.

* Parsons, Reuben. "Pope Leo XIII and Socialism."
  STUDIES IN CHURCH HISTORY, 6 (item 27), 354-
  82.

  A detailed examination of *Rerum Novarum*, issued
  by the Pope as a wise and moderate response to the
  challenge posed by socialism, a movement born of
  the Protestant spirit and perpetuated by Freemasonry.

247. Vagnozzi, Egidio. "Leo XIII and the Problem of
     Human Liberty." In LEO XIII AND THE MODERN
     WORLD (item 55), 89-97.

     Analyzes Leo's concept of true liberty, as
     enunciated in his *Libertas Praestantissimum*
     (1888). Ironically, the essence of this liberty
     was conformity to all divine and just human laws.

248. Wallace, Lillian Parker. LEO XIII AND THE RISE OF
     SOCIALISM. Durham, N.C.: Duke University
     Press, 1966.

     Studies the pontificate within the framework of
     late nineteenth-century thought and activity.
     Views *Rerum Novarum* as an effort to counter Marxism
     by a more intelligent approach to the major social
     problems of the day. By such action Leo refuted
     once and for all the Marxist claim that religion
     diverted attention away from pressing social
     concerns by emphasizing a future paradise.

     See: CHOICE 3 (December 1966): 896; Edward T. Gargan,
          AHR 72 (January 1967): 529-30; Raymond Grew,
          AAAPSS 370 (March 1967): 214-5; Vernon L.
          Lidtke, CJH 3 (March 1968): 121-2; James E.
          Ward, RP 30 (July 1968): 363-70; John Ratté,
          JMH 40 (September 1968): 436-7; Joseph N.
          Moody, CHR 55 (July 1969): 217-8.

249. Watt, Lewis, S.J. LEO XIII AND THE SOCIAL
     MOVEMENT: THE BACKGROUND TO *RERUM NOVARUM*.
     London: Catholic Truth Society/Oxford: Catholic
     Social Guild, 1941.

     Praises *Rerum Novarum* for having given birth to
     the social Catholicism of the late nineteenth century.
     Reconstructs the political, social, and economic

atmosphere in which Leo, both as Bishop of Perugia
and as Pope, denounced the exploitation of workers
and the false hopes given those workers by misguided socialists and liberals. Presents a wealth
of information on the ten years of Vatican
preparation leading up to the pronouncement, along
with an appreciation of the crucial but usually
neglected roles played by Bishops Mermillod
(Geneva) and Ketteler (Mainz) during that
decade.

250.   ———. "Leo XIII as Sociologist." CLR 8 (November
        1934): 345-56.

A survey of Leo's great social encyclicals: *In-
scrutabili Dei* (1878), on the evils of modern society;
Quod Apostolici muneris (1878), on socialism,
rationalism, and naturalism; *Diuturnum* (1881), on
civil sovereignty; *Immortale Dei* (1885), on the
relationship between Church and State; and *Rerum
Novarum* (1891). Uses the vigor of their arguments
to show that Leo was far from being the timid,
irresolute, and naive character portrayed by his
opponents in the Belgian government during his
nunciature in Brussels.

251.   Weigel, Gustave, S.J.   "Leo XIII and Contemporary
        Theology." In LEO XIII AND THE MODERN WORLD
        (item 55), 213-26.

Concludes that although Leo did not define any
new dogma or explore any new lives of doctrinal
inquiry, he did open the door to a new spirit in
theology which has done much to invigorate Catholic
thinking in the twentieth century.

252.   Woollen, C.J. *"Divinum Illud."* DR 58 (January
        1940): 77-87.

Places Leo XIII's encyclical on the Holy Spirit
(1897) in the context of his reign. Suggests that
Cardinal Manning, well-known for his special
devotion to the Holy Spirit, was at least partially
responsible for the Pope's decision to issue the
statement.

Religious Thought and Its Development

General Works

253. Chadwick, Owen. THE SECULARIZATION OF THE EUROPEAN
MIND IN THE NINETEENTH CENTURY; THE GIFFORD
LECTURES IN THE UNIVERSITY OF EDINBURGH, 1973-
1974. Cambridge: Cambridge University Press,
1975.

Disputes the view that industrialization, science,
Darwinism, and Marxism, among other nineteenth-
century products, led Europeans naturally away from
religion and toward atheism. Sketches the views of
Renan, Taine, Michelet, and Brunetière on the role
which Catholicism should have in a time when belief
was still respected but ecclesiastical organization
was scorned.

See: ECON 258 (31 January 1976): 97; Alasdair
McIntyre, NST 91 (6 February 1976): 160;
Philip Toynbee, OBS, 22 February 1976: 27;
Michael Richards, CLR 61 (July 1976): 290-1;
Martin E. Marty, RSR 2 (July 1976): 55;
CHOICE 13 (July/August 1976): 650; Alan Ryan,
HJ 19 (September 1976): 801-2; Vernon L.
Lidtke, HRNB 4 (September 1976): 230-1;
Gertrude Himmelfarb, COMM 62 (October
1976): 87-92; Joseph N. Moody, AHR 81
(December 1976): 1098; TLS, 11 February
1977: 148; A.O. Dyson, THEO 80 (March
1977): 137-9; James McMillan, AMPJ 82
(Spring 1977): 56-7; Hugh McLeod, JEH 28
(April 1977): 222-3; Bernard Norling, RP
39 (July 1977): 418-20; Eric C. Rust, JCS
19 (Autumn 1977): 567-70; Geoffrey Rowell,
EHR 93 (January 1978): 210-1; John D. Root,
JMH 50 (March 1978): 131-2; Daniel Pals, CH
47 (June 1978): 241-2; Frederick Gregory,
CSN 8 (no. 3, 1978): 266-8; R.E. Dreher,
JRH 11 (June 1980): 156-7.

254. McCool, Gerald A. CATHOLIC THEOLOGY IN THE
NINETEENTH CENTURY; THE QUEST FOR A UNITARY
METHOD. New York: Seabury Press, 1977.

Part 1 details the Catholic intellectual encounter with the early nineteenth-century idealists, resulting in the attempt by French, German, and Italian theologians--Bonald, Lamennais, Bautain, Drey, Hermes, Günther, Gioberti, and Rosmini, among them--to develop a program of faith and historical revelation in line with the findings of Fichte, Schelling, Kant, and Hegel. Part 2 highlights the post-1840 neoscholastic revival presented by the Papacy and Jesuits as a vibrant alternative to moribund idealism. Emphasizes Joseph Kleutgen's key role in the revival.

See: Thomas Franklin O'Meara, AMER 138 (7-14 January 1978): 22-4; Francis Schüssler Fiorenza, HRZNS 5 (Spring 1978): 106-7; Ronald Burke, JAAR 46 (December 1978): 600-1; Joseph A. Komonchak, RSR 6 (October 1980): 311-2.

255. Reardon, Bernard M.G. RELIGION IN THE AGE OF ROMANTICISM: STUDIES IN EARLY NINETEENTH-CENTURY THOUGHT. Cambridge: Cambridge University Press, 1985.

Explores the religious aspects of the romantic movement. Most of the Catholics to whom space is given ultimately found themselves under ecclesiastical censure (e.g., Rosmini, Lamennais, Renan).

See: W.R. Ward, JEH 37 (July 1986): 477-8; David Jasper, JTS 37 (October 1986): 649-52; Harry J. Ausmus, AHR 91 (December 1986): 1185-6; James C. Livingston, RSR 13 (January 1987): 82; Darrell Jodock, CH 56 (June 1987): 265-6; Theodore Ziolkowski, JR 67 (July 1987): 340-7; Thomas O'Meara, O.P., CHR 73 (October 1987): 650.

256. ———. RELIGIOUS THOUGHT IN THE NINETEENTH CENTURY ILLUSTRATED FROM THE WRITERS OF THE PERIOD. New York: Cambridge University Press, 1966.

A lengthy introduction places Catholic religious thought within the larger context of nineteenth-century Christian theology and philosophy. Spotlights the contributions of Lamennais and Newman.

See: TLS, 21 July 1966: 626; I.M. Davies, THEO 69

(November 1966): 514-5; M.G. Wiebe, QQ 73
(Winter 1966): 613-4; J.B. Hibbitts, DALR
46 (Winter 1966-7): 521-2; W.R. Ward, VS 10
(March 1967): 312-3; CHOICE 4 (April
1967): 176; John Kent, JEH 18 (April
1967): 125-6; Owen Chadwick, HJ 10 (no. 3,
1967): 476-8; A.E. Firth, EHR 82 (October
1967): 856-7; N.C. Masterman, HIST 53
(February 1968): 141; CH 37 (September
1968): 348; James Hennesey, CHR 55 (July
1969): 198.

257. Schoof, Mark, O.P. A SURVEY OF CATHOLIC THEOLOGY,
      1800-1970. Translated by N.D. Smith. Glen
      Rock, N.J.: Paulist Newman Press, 1970.

      A chronological analysis of the diverse currents
      which enlivened nineteenth-century Catholic theology.
      Positions individual thinkers solidly within the
      larger political, religious, and intellectual picture,
      as it follows the shifts in thought brought about by
      the Tübingen academics, Newman, the neo-scholastic
      revival of the 1860s, and the modernist episode.

      See: Gary MacEoin, CW 213 (May 1971): 97-8; William
            H. Petersen, CH 41 (December 1972): 553-5.

258. Smart, Ninian; Clayton, John; Sherry, Patrick; and
      Katz, Steven T., eds. NINETEENTH CENTURY
      RELIGIOUS THOUGHT IN THE WEST. Cambridge: Cam-
      bridge University Press, 1985. 3 vols.

      A collection of twenty-seven essays by twenty-
      nine British, American, and German specialists.
      Looks at the ideas, intellectual background, and
      impact of thinkers whose writings dealt directly
      or indirectly with one or more of the century's
      three major and interrelated themes: (1) the
      limits of reason and the essence of rationality;
      (2) the question of human nature and the definition
      of "true humanity"; and (3) the problem of history
      and historicism. Contains items 281, 663, and 953.

      See: John E. Thiel, THS 47 (March 1986): 168-9 (for
            vol. 1); Colin Gunton, MONTH 2nd NS 19 (April
            1986): 140 (for vol. 3); P.L. Urban, Jr.,
            CHOICE 23 (May 1986): 1405-6; Daniel W. Hardy,

THEO 89 (July 1986): 320-3; R.H. Roberts, SJT
39 (August 1986): 413-8 (for vol. 1); John E.
Thiel, THS 47 (September 1986): 544-6 (for
vols. 2-3); W.R. Ward, JEH 37 (October
1986): 640-1; Nicholas Lash, JTS 37 (October
1986): 654-62; Joseph Fitzer, JR 67 (July
1987): 378-9 (for vol. 2); Walter E. Wyman,
Jr., JR 67 (July 1987): 379-80 (for vol. 3);
Gerald A. McCool, S.J., CHR 73 (October
1987): 636-7; James W. McClendon, Jr., RSR 13
(October 1987): 308-11; R.H. Roberts, SJT 40
(December 1987): 621-3 (for vol. 2); R.H.
Roberts, SJT 41 (May 1988): 130-5 (for vol. 3).

259. Sykes, Stephen. THE IDENTITY OF CHRISTIANITY: THEO-
LOGIANS AND THE ESSENCE OF CHRISTIANITY FROM
SCHLEIERMACHER TO BARTH. Philadelphia: Fortress
Press, 1984.

Includes an account of the nineteenth-century
debate between Catholic and Protestant theologians
over the intellectual essence of Christianity.
Compares the ideas of Newman (Chapter 5) and
Schleiermacher (Chapter 4), and the works of
Loisy and Harnack (Chapter 6).

See: John Heywood Thomas, BBN, November 1984: 659;
Dennis Nineham, TLS, 28 December 1984: 1510;
Robert Webber, CC 102 (1 May 1985): 451-2;
Maurice Wiles, THEO 88 (May 1985): 233-4;
Bernard M.G. Reardon, JEH 36 (July 1985): 506-
7; Ruth Page, SJT 38 (September 1985): 426-8;
John Clayton, RS 21 (December 1985): 591-4;
Michael Vertin, HRZNS 14 (Fall 1987): 388-9;
John E. Thiel, HEYJ 29 (January 1988): 105-7.

260. Trevor, Meriol. PROPHETS AND GUARDIANS: RENEWAL AND
TRADITION IN THE CHURCH. London/Sydney/
Toronto: Hollis and Carter, 1969.

Sees the movement of nineteenth-century Catholic
theology in terms of the recurring tensions between
liberals and conservatives. Dramatizes those
tensions by presenting biographical sketches of the
leading reformers and traditionalists in each battle,
from Lamennais in the 1830s to the Modernists in the
1890s.

See: Wilfrid Passmore, DR 88 (January 1970): 85-8;
      TLS, 29 January 1970: 114; David O'Brien,
      COMMWL 91 (27 February 1970): 589-90; Michael
      J. Zeps, S.J., REVREL 29 (May 1970): 465-6;
      Raymond Pelly, THEO 73 (August 1970): 377-8;
      Alec R. Vidler, JEH 22 (April 1971): 172-3.

                    Scriptural Studies

261. Burtchaell, James Tunstead, C.S.C. CATHOLIC THEORIES
      OF BIBLICAL INSPIRATION SINCE 1810: A REVIEW AND
      CRITIQUE. Cambridge: At the University Press,
      1969.

      Illustrates the rich diversity of the nineteenth-
      century literature dealing with the problem of
      inspiration. Highlights the exegetical contributions
      of the Tübingen school, the Oxford Movement, the
      Syllabus of Errors, and the Modernists, leaving the
      impression of a much higher level of Biblical
      scholarship than was previously thought to be the
      case.

      See: CHOICE 6 (January 1970): 1589; Raymond Pelly,
            THEO 73 (March 1970): 138; Bernard M.G.
            Reardon, AMPJ 75 (Spring 1970): 85-6; Frederick
            C. Moriarty, S.J., THOUGHT 45 (Spring
            1970): 148-50; Bernard M.G. Reardon, JTS 21
            (April 1970): 253-5; John R. Donahue, S.J., CH
            39 (June 1970): 260-1; John L. McKenzie,
            INTERP 24 (July 1970): 405-6; E.L. Mascall,
            JEH 21 (July 1970): 274-6; H. Butterfield, EHR
            86 (October 1971): 807-10; Roland E. Murphy,
            JR 51 (October 1971): 301-5.

262. Johnson, H.J.T. "Leo XIII, Cardinal Newman and the
      Inerrancy of Scripture." DR 69 (Autumn
      1951): 411-27.

      Compares the answers of the Pope and his Cardinal
      to the highly controversial question of the late
      1880s and early 1890s, namely, how were Catholics to
      consider the creation account in Genesis? Demon-
      strates that their responses in *Providentissimus Deus*
      (1893) and "Inspiration in its relation to revelation"

(1884), respectively, were much less significant than usually assumed.

Ecclesiology

263. Costigan, Richard F., S.J. ROHRBACHER AND THE
      ECCLESIOLOGY OF ULTRAMONTANISM. Miscellanea
      Historiae Pontificiae, vol. 47. Rome: Ponti-
      ficia Università Gregoriana, 1980.

      Describes how René-François Rohrbacher (1789-
      1856), a one-time follower of Lamennais, used his
      writings in Church history to further the cause of
      Papal supremacy. His major work, the bitterly
      anti-Gallican *Histoire universelle de l'Eglise
      Catholique* (1842-1849), exalted the Roman position
      at every possible opportunity.

      See: T. Corbett, ITQ 48 (nos. 1-2, 1981): 146-9;
            Bernard M.G. Reardon, JEH 32 (July 1981): 387-
            8; Dale A. Johnson, CH 51 (June 1982): 232-3;
            Thomas Franklin O'Meara, O.P., CHR 68 (October
            1982): 663-4.

Historical Studies

264. Chadwick, Owen. CATHOLICISM AND HISTORY: THE
      OPENING OF THE VATICAN ARCHIVES.
      Cambridge: Cambridge University Press, 1978.

      Recounts in great detail the behind-the-scenes
      motivations and maneuvers which resulted in Leo
      XIII's decision to grant scholars access to what
      had been up to that time one of the most carefully
      guarded collections of documents in the world.
      Links the progress of the story to the fate of two
      specific and very important sets of sources, the
      minutes of the Council of Trent and the records of
      the trial of Galileo.

      See: James Muldoon, HRNB 6 (September 1978): 189;
            J.H. Crehan, S.J., MONTH 2nd NS 11 (October
            1978): 356-7; John Tracy Ellis, AMER 139 (4

November 1978): 315-7; Denys Hay, TLS, 17
November 1978: 1344; CHOICE 15 (February
1979): 1679; Richard Camp, AHR 84 (April
1979): 425-6; Alec R. Vidler, JTS 30 (April
1979): 380; Hugh R. Trevor-Roper, NYRB 26
(31 May 1979): 3; Gailfred Boller Sweetland,
JAAR 47 (June 1979): 339; John N. Molong,
JRH 10 (June 1979): 337-8; H.C.G. Matthew,
EHR 94 (October 1979): 900-1; Godfrey
Anstruther, O.P., CLR 64 (November 1979): 419;
Leonard E. Boyle, O.P., JEH 31 (April
1980): 265; John D. Root, CHR 66 (July
1980): 430-2; Peter Iver Kaufman, CH 49
(September 1980): 344-5.

265. Faherty, W. Barby. "Leo XIII and Historical Studies."
      HB 17 (November 1938): 9-10.

      Summarizes the reasons behind Leo's decision of
      1881 to open the Vatican Archives to scholars.

266. Guilday, Peter, ed. CHURCH HISTORIANS, INCLUDING
      PAPERS ON EUSEBIUS, OROSIUS, ST. BEDE THE
      VENERABLE, ORDERICUS VITALIS, LAS CASAS,
      BARONIUS, BOLLANDUS, MURATORI, MOEHLER, LINGARD,
      HERGENROETHER, JANSSEN, DENIFLE, LUDWIG VON
      PASTOR. New York: P.J. Kenedy & Sons, 1926.

      Features fourteen papers on eminent ecclesiastical
      historians, first presented at the annual meeting of
      the American Catholic Historical Association at Ann
      Arbor, Michigan, in December 1925. Of the fourteen,
      six deal with nineteenth-century figures. Contains
      items 669, 672, 676, 732, and 1112.

      See: AHR 32 (January 1927): 296-7.

                        The Scholastic Revival

267. Bonansea, Bernardino M., O.F.M. "Pioneers of the
      Nineteenth-Century Scholastic Revival in Italy."
      NS 28 (January 1954): 1-37.

      A chronological account of the work done by
      pioneer Italian neo-scholastics. Considers

Vincenzo Buzzetti (1777-1824) the forerunner of the movement; his INSTITUTIONES SANAE PHILOSOPHIAE (3 vols., c. 1800) was the first textbook of neo-Thomism to appear in the nineteenth century. Discusses the achievements and weaknesses of Buzzetti's leading students, among whom are singled out Domenico and Serafino Sordi, Luigi Taparelli, Matteo Liberatore, and Gaetano San-severino.

268. Harris, Abram L. "The Scholastic Revival: The Economics of Heinrich Pesch." JPE 54 (February 1946): 38-59.

Introduces the work of Heinrich Pesch, S.J. (1854-1926), who epitomized the Leonine revival of scholastic teaching in the economic field. Evaluates his ideas on production and value.

269. Holmes, J. Derek. "Some English Reactions to the Publication of *Aeterni Patris*." DR 93 (October 1975): 269-80.

Assesses the reception of the Leonine scholastic revival among Catholics and non-Catholics alike. Despite the fact that the revival paralleled the rise of Ultramontanism, and was itself an Ultra-montanist movement, English liberal Catholics regarded it as liberal and enlightened, and received it enthusiastically. Non-Catholics, on the other hand, attacked it as another sign of nineteenth-century Roman stagnation.

270. Manzo, Marcellus, O.F.M. Cap. "Capuchin-Franciscan Response to the Revival of Scholastic Studies." FS 6 (September 1946): 332-49.

Attributes the late nineteenth-century Capuchin and Franciscan revival of scholasticism to the encouragement of Leo XIII (*Aeterni Patris*, 1879) and to the intense efforts of the Minister-General of each order. Out of this revival came impressive advances not only in theology and philosophy, but also in jurisprudence, hagiography, missionary science, literature, and the arts.

271. Perrier, Joseph Louis. THE REVIVAL OF SCHOLASTIC

PHILOSOPHY IN THE NINETEENTH CENTURY. New
York: Columbia University Press, 1909.

Chapters 9-14 tally the achievements of the
leading neo-scholastics in each European country.
Extended treatment is given to Italy (Pecci, Mari,
and Liberatore), Spain and Portugal (Balmes,
Urráburu), Germany and Austria (Kleutgen), France
(the Sulpicians and Dominicans), and Belgium
(de San, Mercier, and the Institute of Philosophy
at Louvain). Developments in Hungary, Bohemia,
the Netherlands, and England are mentioned briefly.

See: ACQR 34 (April 1909): 375-6.

Science

272. Dauben, Joseph W.   "Georg Cantor and Pope Leo
          XIII: Mathematics, Theology, and the Infinite."
          JHI 38 (January/March 1977):   85-108.

Shows how mathematics, philosophy, and theology
interacted during the late nineteenth century.
Cantor (1845-1918), the creator of transfinite set
theory, was convinced that his discovery would
prevent Catholic thinkers from misinterpreting the
nature of infinity; in an effort to further the
spirit of Leo's *Aeterni Patris*, he undertook an
extensive correspondence with a number of theologians and addressed several pamphlets to the
Pope.

273. Dorlodot, Henri de. DARWINISM AND CATHOLIC THOUGHT.
          Vol. 1: THE ORIGIN OF SPECIES. Translated by
          Ernest Messenger. New York: Benziger Brothers,
          1923.

Analyzes Leo XIII's *Providentissimus Deus* (1893),
which encouraged Catholic scholars to devote human
learning to the study of such controversial Biblical
texts as the creation account in Genesis. Dorlodot
was Director of the Geological Institute at the
University of Louvain.

274. Johnson, Humphrey J.T.   "Catholics and Evolution."

DR 67 (Autumn 1949):   375-94.

Surveys the diversity of mid-century reactions to
Darwinism, from the not unsympathetic Newman and the
cynical Ullathorne in England to the hostile Cardinal
von Giessel in Germany.

Modernism

General Works

275. Daly, Gabriel, O.S.A. TRANSCENDENCE AND
      IMMANENCE: A STUDY IN CATHOLIC MODERNISM
      AND INTEGRALISM. Oxford: Clarendon Press,
      1980.

      Traces the stages of the conflict between Roman
      fundamental theology and the challenges to it by
      Blondel, Laberthonnière, Loisy, von Hügel, Tyrrell,
      Le Roy, and their Italian colleagues. Details the
      official campaign launched against these thinkers
      by the "integralists," who, with complete papal
      backing, accused them of preaching a perverse
      philosophy. Points to the narrowness of the Roman
      theological outlook as the main cause of the
      tension; had the Vatican been able to overcome its
      neo-scholastic bias, it might have been able to
      accept the legitimacy of the modernists' concerns.

      See: John Coventry, S.J., ITQ 48 (nos. 1-2,
            1981): 140-2; Alec R. Vidler, JEH 32 (April
            1981): 248-9; Ronald Burke, RSR 7 (October
            1981): 296-7; Roger Haight, S.J., JR 62
            (January 1982): 90-2; John D. Root, CHR 68
            (October 1982): 694-5; Terry L. Miethe, JAAR
            51 (March 1983): 146; David G. Schultenover,
            S.J., CH 52 (June 1983): 228-9.

276. Kurtz, Lester R. THE POLITICS OF HERESY: THE
      MODERNIST CRISIS IN ROMAN CATHOLICISM. Berkeley
      and Los Angeles: University of California Press,
      1986.

      A sociological interpretation of the modernist

conflict, contending that as tensions mounted during
the last decade of the nineteenth century, the issue
of doctrinal orthodoxy was superseded by the question
of the relationship between intellectual freedom and
hierarchical authority.

See: Alec Vidler, THEO 90 (May 1987): 234; Kevin J.
       Christiano, AJS 93 (September 1987): 470-2;
       David G. Schultenover, S.J., CHR 73 (October
       1987): 670-1.

277.   Loome, Thomas Michael. LIBERAL CATHOLICISM, REFORM
       CATHOLICISM, MODERNISM: A CONTRIBUTION TO A
       NEW ORIENTATION IN MODERNIST RESEARCH.
       Tübinger Theologische Studien, vol. 14.
       Mainz: Matthias-Grünewald-Verlag, 1979.

       Not a history of modernism, but a reexamination of
       the debate over modernism, in an effort to clear the
       way for subsequent research in the field. Positions
       modernism within the older tradition of liberal
       Catholicism, the origins of which are fixed as early
       as the seventeenth century.

       See: J. Derek Holmes, TABLET 233 (3 November
              1979): 1076; George A. Kelly, FCSN 3 (December
              1979): 11-15; THD 27 (Winter 1979): 380; Ronald
              Burke, THS 41 (March 1980): 218-20; CHOICE 17
              (April 1980): 235; Gabriel Daly, O.S.A., ITQ
              47 (no. 2, 1980): 152-5; Alec R. Vidler, JEH
              31 (April 1980): 245-6; Michael J. Kerlin, JR
              60 (April 1980): 228-9; Mary Jo Weaver, RP 42
              (April 1980): 270-2; James Hitchcock, HPR 80
              (July 1980): 75-7; John Coulson, CLR 65
              (August 1980): 303-4; Ronald Burke, JECS 17
              (Fall 1980): 670-6; Normand Provencher, O.M.I.,
              EET 11 (October 1980): 464-6; Bernard M.G.
              Reardon, JTS 31 (October 1980): 669-72; Eamon
              Duffy, HEYJ 22 (January 1981): 49-55; Lawrence
              F. Barmann, CH 50 (June 1981): 227; Francis
              Schüssler Fiorenza, HRZNS 8 (Fall 1981): 381-2;
              James C. Livingston, AHR 86 (October 1981): 831-
              2; Ronald Burke, RSR 7 (October 1981): 293-4;
              Ronald Burke, RSR 8 (January 1982): 58-9; Hans
              Rollmann and Ronald Burke, DR 100 (July
              1982): 157-61; Daniel Donovan, DR 100 (July
              1982): 162-8; Darrell Jodock, DR 100 (July

1982): 169-76; James C. Livingston, DR 100
(July 1982): 177-82; David Schultenover, DR
100 (July 1982): 183-92; Hans Rollmann, DR
100 (July 1982): 193-200; John D. Root, CHR
68 (October 1982): 696-7; James C. Livingston,
ATR 65 (January 1983): 83-7.

278. Ranchetti, Michele. THE CATHOLIC MODERNISTS: A
STUDY OF THE RELIGIOUS REFORM MOVEMENT, 1864-
1907. Translated by Isabel Quigly. New
York: Oxford University Press, 1969.

Offers in Part 2 the only in-depth consideration
of the Italian modernists--Minocchi, Bonaiuti, Murri,
Fogazzaro, and their followers--in the English
language. Part 1 covers the work of Loisy, Blondel,
Tyrrell, and von Hügel. Situates the movement within
the general historicist crisis of the late nineteenth
century, for it sought to restore the pure truth of
Catholic doctrine by appealing to past theological
developments.

See: TLS, 12 March 1970: 286; J. Derek Holmes, CLR
55 (May 1970): 410-2; Bernard M.G. Reardon,
AMPJ 75 (Summer 1970): 213-9; Raymond Pelly,
THEO 73 (August 1970): 377-8; Alec R. Vidler,
JEH 22 (April 1971): 172-3; Mary Jo Weaver, RP
34 (January 1972): 115-6; James Hennesey, S.J.,
CHR 59 (April 1973): 120-1.

279. Ratté, John. THREE MODERNISTS: ALFRED LOISY, GEORGE
TYRRELL, WILLIAM L. SULLIVAN. New York: Sheed &
Ward, 1967.

Focuses on the theological aspects of modernism
by an analysis of the personalities, beliefs, and
impact of the enigmatic Loisy, the attractive yet
tragic Tyrrell, and the ambitious but intellectually
limited American, William L. Sullivan.

See: Alice Mayhew, COMMWL 87 (1 December 1967): 313;
Michael Morrison, AMER 118 (17 February
1968): 234, 236; John W. Padberg, S.J., REVREL
27 (March 1968): 345-6; Edward H. Peters, CW
207 (April 1968): 39-40; John P. Duffell, DUNR
8 (May 1968): 181-4; Robert Coles, NR 158
(8 June 1968): 35-6; CHOICE 5 (July/August

1968): 639; Edward A. Reno, Jr., RM 22
(September 1968): 153; Meriol Trevor, DR 86
(October 1968): 423-4; P. McKevitt, ITQ 35
(October 1968): 401-3; Anne Louis-David,
THEO 71 (December 1968): 558-60; J. Derek
Holmes, CLR 54 (September 1969): 736-7;
Thomas E. Morrissey, CHR 56 (January
1971): 671-2.

280.   Reardon, Bernard M.G., ed. ROMAN CATHOLIC MODERNISM.
       Stanford: Stanford University Press, 1970.

The sixty-seven-page Introduction to this
collection of modernist writings is more concerned
with the philosophical and historical sides of the
movement than with its theology or leading
personalities.

See: JES 1 (March 1971): 94; Maryellen Muckenhirn,
       COMMWL 94 (11 June 1971): 316-7; Thomas
       Michael Loome, DR 89 (July 1971): 254-8;
       Jean-Jacques D'Aoust, CH 40 (December
       1971): 502; Mary Jo Weaver, RP 34 (January
       1972): 116-7; Lawrence F. Barmann, JMH 44
       (March 1972): 126-8; H. Cunliffe-Jones, AMPJ
       77 (Spring 1972): 103; Thomas E. Morrissey,
       CHR 59 (April 1973): 121-2; Norman Pittenger,
       JR 53 (July 1973): 390-3.

281.   ————. "Roman Catholic Modernism." In NINETEENTH
       CENTURY RELIGIOUS THOUGHT IN THE WEST (item 258),
       II, 141-77.

An overview of the key issues at stake in the
modernist struggle. Selects Loisy and Tyrrell as
the major spokesmen; to their efforts Reardon adds
brief treatments of their not as celebrated French,
Italian, and German colleagues.

282.   Richards, Michael. "The Historical Background to the
       Rise of Modernism." CLR 70 (June 1985): 204-11.

Asks the question, What exactly was condemned by
Pius X's *Pascendi Dominici gregis* (1907)? Maintains
that the encyclical's condemnation fell upon
traditionalists as well as modernists, though for
different reasons and in different ways.

283. Schoenl, William J. THE INTELLECTUAL CRISIS IN
     ENGLISH CATHOLICISM: LIBERAL CATHOLICS,
     MODERNISTS, AND THE VATICAN IN THE LATE
     NINETEENTH AND EARLY TWENTIETH CENTURIES.
     New York: Garland, 1982.

     Sees modernism as the logical outgrowth of a more
     broadly based and older liberal Catholic tradition,
     referring to the beliefs of Tyrrell, von Hügel,
     Wilfrid Ward, Gasquet, and Bishop as the link
     between the two movements. Balances the modernist
     hope of Catholic renewal with the intransigence of
     Vatican traditionalism, with sympathy for the
     former.

     See: CHOICE 20 (April 1983): 1155; John D. Root,
          CH 53 (March 1984): 118; Frank M. Turner,
          AHR 89 (April 1984): 441-2; Nicholas Sagovsky,
          JEH 35 (April 1984): 328; Alec R. Vidler, JTS
          35 (April 1984): 273-4; Lawrence F. Barmann,
          CHR 70 (October 1984): 623-4; Sheridan Gilley,
          EHR 100 (October 1985): 923-4; Josef L.
          Altholz, VS 29 (Winter 1986): 321.

284. Vidler, Alec R. THE MODERNIST MOVEMENT IN THE ROMAN
     CHURCH: ITS ORIGINS & OUTCOME. Cambridge: At
     the University Press, 1934.

     Challenges Pius X's view of modernism as a homo-
     geneous whole, contending that the "movement" to
     which *Pascendi Dominici gregis* referred was in
     reality composed of widely varying schools in many
     different fields. Traces modernism's origins to the
     growing disparity between modern knowledge and Roman
     Catholic orthodoxy, one which began with Chateau-
     briand and the liberals during the early decades of
     the nineteenth century. Highly sympathetic to the
     modernists and their ideas.

     See: W.F. Lofthouse, LQHR 159 (October 1934): 530-3;
          A.L. Lilley, THEO 29 (November 1934): 306-10;
          DUBR 196 (January/February/March 1935): 163-7;
          W.E. Garrison, AHR 41 (April 1936): 578-9.

285. ————. A VARIETY OF CATHOLIC MODERNISTS.
     Cambridge: Cambridge University Press, 1970.

Profiles of the leaders and some of the "lesser lights" of modernism. Although they shared a common vision, their personalities and ideas differed greatly, as shown by the large number of anecdotes dispersed throughout the text.

See: Bernard M.G. Reardon, AMPJ 75 (Summer 1970): 219-21; Lawrence F. Barmann, REVREL 29 (July 1970): 594; TLS, 2 July 1970: 730; Thomas Michael Loome, DR 88 (October 1970): 431-8; Owen Chadwick, JEH 22 (April 1971): 163-4; Norman Pittenger, JR 51 (April 1971): 137-41; Marcel Simon, JTS 22 (April 1971): 295-8; Jean-Jacques D'Aoust, CH 40 (June 1971): 237; Bernard Brandon Scott, JAAR 39 (September 1971): 395-6; A.E. Firth, EHR 86 (October 1971): 875; Mary Jo Weaver, RP 34 (January 1972): 114-5; P. Joseph Cahill, INTERP 27 (October 1973): 498; John J. Heaney, CHR 59 (January 1974): 708-9.

Alfred Loisy

286.   Petre, M.D.   ALFRED LOISY: HIS RELIGIOUS SIGNIFICANCE. Cambridge: At the University Press, 1944.

Not a biography, but an appreciation of a deeply spiritual man and the work he produced after 1893. Identifies three major contributions to religious thought: his concept of the New Testament as catechetical rather than historical, his repudiation of all artificial mythologizing, and his belief in the historical experience of Christ, though he refused to accept the accompanying claims of divinity.

See: John M.T. Barton, CLR 24 (July 1944): 298-305; A.L. Lilley, HIBJ 42 (July 1944): 372-3; C. Ryder Smith, LQHR 169 (July 1944): 285; Alec R. Vidler, JTS 45 (July/October 1944): 234-7; Louis A. Arand, CHR 30 (October 1944): 305-7; L.J. Collins, THEO 47 (November 1944): 258-9.

*   Ratté, John. "Alfred Loisy." THREE

MODERNISTS: ALFRED LOISY, GEORGE TYRRELL, WILLIAM
L. SULLIVAN (item 279), 43-141.

Maneuvers through the ambiguities of his character
and creed to distinguish three major aspects of his
activity as a "philosophical historian": his innovative and controversial insistence on a Catholicism
without Christianity, his negative view of human
nature, and his idea of doctrinal development.

George Tyrrell

287. Chapman, Ronald. "The Thought of George Tyrrell."
In ESSAYS & POEMS PRESENTED TO LORD DAVID CECIL,
edited by W.W. Robson, 140-68. London: Constable,
1970.

Hails Tyrrell as a man of our time, curious about
everything and eager to pursue the truth wherever it
might lead him. Committed to the examination of the
most controversial issues of his day, he was "a
religious Burke."

See: Thomas Michael Loome, DR 89 (July 1971): 258-
61.

288. Leonard, Ellen, C.S.J. GEORGE TYRRELL AND THE
CATHOLIC TRADITION. New York: Paulist Press,
1982.

A study of Tyrrell's theological options,
methodology, and themes, with emphasis on his
ecclesiology. Compares his religious ideas to
those of his contemporaries. Admiring, but at
the same time aware of his personal and professional flaws, including snobbishness,
parochialism, and doctrinal relativism.

See: Ronald Burke, HRZNS 10 (Spring 1983): 155-6;
Robert Butterworth, S.J., MONTH 2nd NS 9 (May
1983): 175; Norman Pittenger, THEO 86 (May
1983): 237-8; M.E. Williams, CLR 68 (June
1983): 226; Paul Misner, COMMWL 110 (16
December 1983): 694-6; Ronald Burke, JAAR 52
(June 1984): 397; Clyde F. Crews, CHR 70
(October 1984): 627-8.

*   Ratté, John. "George Tyrrell." THREE
        MODERNISTS: ALFRED LOISY, GEORGE TYRRELL,
        WILLIAM L. SULLIVAN (item 279), 143-256.

        Portrays Tyrrell as a propagator of others' ideas
        rather than as an original thinker himself. Sees
        his life as motivated by a search to free his faith
        from traditional images of God and Christ; in the
        face of Catholic rationalism he flung a non-rational
        apologetic, which he hoped others would follow.
        That his hope, like his entire journey, foundered
        and ultimately failed, was a foregone conclusion,
        given the atmosphere of the late nineteenth-century
        Church.

289.   Sagovsky, Nicholas. "'Frustration, Disillusion and
        Enduring Filial Respect': George Tyrrell's Debt
        to John Henry Newman." In NEWMAN AND THE
        MODERNISTS (item 971), 97-115.

        Chronicles Tyrrell's love-hate relationship with
        Newman, one which inevitably affected his relation-
        ships with other intellectuals of the time. For
        Tyrrell, initial infatuation with "Newmanism" turned
        to desertion, as he concluded that it could no longer
        assist him in his work.

290.   Schultenover, David G., S.J. GEORGE TYRRELL: IN
        SEARCH OF CATHOLICISM. Shepherdstown,
        W.Va.: Patmos Press, 1981.

        Follows Tyrrell's intellectual evolution from
        militant orthodoxy through a mediating liberalism,
        inspired by Newman, to stubborn modernism. Gauges
        the mechanics of these transitions by studying the
        progress of his apologetics. Of Tyrrell's numerous
        writings, both published and unpublished, two loom
        larger than the rest: RELIGION AS A FACTOR OF LIFE
        (1902) and THE CHURCH AND THE FUTURE (1903).

        See: CHOICE 19 (February 1982): 778; Ronald Burke,
               AMER 146 (27 March 1982): 246; Sheridan Gilley,
               MONTH 2nd NS 15 (June 1982): 210-1; Ronald
               Burke, RSR 8 (July 1982): 265; William J.
               Schoenl, AHR 87 (October 1982): 1101; Nicholas
               Sagovsky, JEH 33 (October 1982): 662-3; Mary Jo
               Weaver, JAAR 51 (March 1983): 137;

Ellen Leonard, C.S.J., HRZNS 10 (Spring
1983): 154-5; Josef L. Altholz, CH 52
(June 1983): 229-30; Paul Misner, COMMWL
110 (16 December 1983): 694-6; Michael J.
Kerlin, JR 64 (July 1984): 390-1; Charles
J. Healey, S.J., CHR 70 (October 1984): 626-7.

Friedrich von Hügel

291. Barmann, Lawrence F. BARON FRIEDRICH VON HÜGEL AND
      THE MODERNIST CRISIS IN ENGLAND. New York: Cam-
      bridge University Press, 1972.

      Reassesses von Hügel's role in the modernist
      movement between 1890 and 1910, with the conclusion
      that the Baron was in fact far more active than has
      been previously suggested. Explains how he managed
      to stay in the Church, despite the fact that he was
      for his fellow intellectuals a symbol of unity and
      strength, one who never compromised his belief in
      the necessity of Catholic renewal.

      See: John Jay Hughes, AMPJ 77 (Summer 1972): 40-7;
            CHOICE 9 (November 1972): 1142; William Beatie,
            F.S.C., REVREL 31 (November 1972): 1064; Noel
            D. O'Donoghue, SJT 25 (November 1972): 466-7;
            John Coulson, THEO 75 (November 1972): 600-2;
            Bernard M.G. Reardon, JEH 24 (January
            1973): 101-2; J. Derek Holmes, CLR 58 (February
            1973): 154-5; Josef L. Altholz, CH 42 (March
            1973): 137-8; Gabriel Daly, O.S.A., ITQ 40
            (no. 2, 1973): 186-8; William J. Schoenl, AHR
            78 (April 1973): 447-8; John J. Heaney, CHR 59
            (April 1973): 122-4; Peter Hinchliff, JTS 24
            (April 1973): 325-6; Sheldon Rothblatt, JMH 45
            (June 1973): 331-2; Mary Jo Weaver, RP 35
            (July 1973): 415-6; James C. Livingston, JAAR
            41 (December 1973): 606-9; Emiliana P. Noether,
            THOUGHT 49 (March 1974): 109-10.

292. Bedoyere, Michel de la. THE LIFE OF BARON VON HÜGEL.
      London: J.M. Dent & Sons, 1951.

      Unravels some of the enigmas surrounding this
      self-appointed go-between for the leading modernists

in England and France. A devout son of the Church,
he championed the modernist cause; without regular
schooling, he authored a number of insightful works
on Scripture and mysticism. Simultaneously recreates
the atmosphere in which von Hügel's celebrated
friends devised and shared their progressive concepts.

See: Humphrey J.T. Johnson, DR 69 (Autumn 1951): 500-
      3; J.D. Crichton, CLR 36 (September 1951): 151-
      7; W. Longden Oakes, LQHR 176 (October
      1951): 347-9; Clement C.J. Webb, JTS 3 (April
      1952): 143-8; William R. O'Connor, CHR 38
      (October 1952): 328-30.

293. Eigelsbach, Jo Ann. "The Intellectual Dialogue of
      Friedrich von Hügel and Wilfrid Ward." DR 104
      (April 1986): 144-57.

      On one level, shows the extent to which these two
      longtime friends agreed and disagreed on certain
      issues raised at critical junctures of the
      modernist controversy. On another level, presents
      their dialogue as a microcosm of the dilemma felt by
      all loyal and thoughtful Catholics during the last
      years of the nineteenth century.

294. Heaney, John J. THE MODERNIST CRISIS: VON HÜGEL.
      Washington, D.C., and Cleveland: Corpus Books,
      1968.

      Situates von Hügel at the eye of the storm which
      modernism unleashed. In him one finds a perfect
      symbol of the centuries-old problem of authority
      versus liberty within the Catholic tradition.

See: Meriol Trevor, DR 87 (July 1969): 322-3;
      CHOICE 6 (September 1969): 832, 834; Alec
      Vidler, THEO 72 (September 1969): 419-20;
      Patrick J. Corish, ITQ 38 (January 1970): 85-
      6; John W. Padberg, S.J., REVREL 29 (January
      1970): 172; Charles J. Mehok, CHR 58 (April
      1972): 95-7.

295. Kelly, James J. BARON FRIEDRICH VON HÜGEL'S
      PHILOSOPHY OF RELIGION. Bibliotheca
      Ephemeridum Theologicarum Lovaniensium, vol.
      62. Leuven: Leuven University Press, 1983.

A presentation of his ideas on the structure and meaning of belief, prefaced by a consideration of the thinkers who inspired him and a description of his own writings on the philosophy of religion.

See: Nicholas Lash, JTS 36 (April 1985): 285; Gabriel Daly, O.S.A., ITQ 51 (no. 4, 1985): 325-7; Lawrence F. Barmann, CHR 72 (July 1986): 446.

296. Nédoncelle, Maurice. BARON FRIEDRICH VON HÜGEL: A STUDY OF HIS LIFE AND THOUGHT. Translated by Marjorie Vernon. London: Longmans, Green, 1937.

Finds some extraordinary juxtapositions in his personality and ideas: liberal thought combined with fidelity to Roman Catholic dogma, and an insistence on the application of the scientific method to the study of religion balanced by an equally strong respect for the mystery of super-natural belief.

See: Edwyn E. Bevan, SPEC 158 (26 March 1937): 588-9; Dom Christopher Butler, DR 55 (April 1937): 259-62; Edwin E. Aubrey, CH 6 (June 1937): 191; DUBR 201 (July/August/September 1937): 163-5.

297. Whelan, Joseph P., S.J. THE SPIRITUALITY OF FRIEDRICH VON HÜGEL. New York/Paramus/Toronto: Newman Press, 1971.

A synthesis of his ideas on various aspects of the spiritual life, including the nature of sanctity; one's relationship with Christ, God, and the ecclesial community; and the production of a personality that is at once deeply theocentric and joyfully open to the world.

See: TLS, 25 February 1972: 225; Martin Hancock, CLR 57 (July 1972): 563-4; Sydney Evans, THEO 75 (July 1972): 375-6; Lawrence F. Barmann, AMPJ 77 (Autumn 1972): 64-8; Noel D. O'Donoghue, SJT 25 (November 1972): 465-7; Doris Donnelly, AMER 127 (25 November 1972): 454-5; Lawrence F. Barmann, JTS 24 (April 1973): 326-9; Mary Jo Weaver, RP

35 (July 1973): 417-8.

Maude Petre

298. Crews, Clyde F. ENGLISH CATHOLIC MODERNISM: MAUDE
      PETRE'S WAY OF FAITH. Notre Dame: University of
      Notre Dame Press/Tunbridge Wells: Burns & Oates,
      1984.

      The first full-length study of the only woman
      among the leading modernists. Dissects her ideas
      within the chronological framework of her life,
      which was marked by valor in the midst of recurrent
      tragedy, and criticisms of Rome even as she
      professed unswerving adherence to the Catholic
      faith.

      See: William J. Schoenl, AHR 90 (February 1985): 136;
            Robert Butterworth, S.J., MONTH 2nd NS 18
            (March 1985): 106-7; Ellen Leonard, C.S.J.,
            HRZNS 12 (Spring 1985): 174-5; Nicholas
            Sagovsky, JTS 36 (October 1985): 567-8; John D.
            Root, CHR 72 (July 1986): 450-1.

299. Hamilton, Robert. "Faith and Knowledge: The
      Autobiography of Maude Petre." DR 85 (April
      1967): 148-59.

      Shows how in MY WAY OF FAITH (1937) Petre
      succeeded in creating a subtle blend of auto-
      biographical and psychological elements, i.e.,
      of the intensely personal and the abstract.
      Enhancing this blend was the three-dimensional
      quality of the writing, attributed by Hamilton
      to the depth, wide range, and richness of her
      mind.

300. Healey, Charles J., S.J. "Maude Petre: Her Life
      and Significance." RH 15 (May 1979): 23-42.

      A factual account of her life, based on her
      writings and on the Petre Papers in the British
      Library. Claims that she was significant for
      two reasons: she knew Tyrrell better than anyone
      else, and shared that knowledge; and, more

importantly, she was a woman of unwavering faith,
independence, courage, and generosity.

Maurice Blondel

301. Dru, Alexander. "The Importance of Maurice Blondel."
      DR 81 (April 1962): 118-29.

      Declares that of all his colleagues, Blondel
      provided the most accurate explanation of the
      modernist movement, because he did it from his
      vantage point in the center of the controversy.
      His view of modernism as a reformation from
      within (or, variously, as a revolution, and the
      final stage of the Protestant Reformation)
      therefore makes him of interest to historians
      as well as to theologians and philosophers.

Political Thought and Influence

302. Blanning, T.C.W. "The Role of Religion in European
      Counter-Revolution, 1789-1815." In HISTORY,
      SOCIETY AND THE CHURCHES: ESSAYS IN HONOUR OF
      OWEN CHADWICK (item 24), 195-214.

      Challenges the often repeated view that religion
      played an inconsequential role in the dynamics of
      early nineteenth-century counter-revolution. Claims
      that Catholicism was perceived by the French as a
      potent feature of anti-revolutionary activity, a
      feature which was constant and everywhere. Points
      to the prominence of counter-revolutionary sentiment
      in the emergence of popular religiosity, confra-
      ternities, processions, pilgrimages, and cults during
      the Napoleonic era.

303. Corrigan, Raymond, S.J. "Catholic Liberalism." HB
      14 (January 1936): 32-4.

      Explains its philosophical foundations and aims
      within their historical setting. Turns to the
      activity of Lamennais as the prime example of how
      Catholic liberals attempted to influence the question

of Church-State relations.

304. Droz, Jacques. "Religious Aspects of the Revolutions
     of 1848 in Europe." In FRENCH SOCIETY AND CULTURE
     SINCE THE OLD REGIME; THE ELEUTHERIAN MILLS
     COLLOQUIUM, 1964, OF THE SOCIETY FOR FRENCH
     HISTORICAL STUDIES AND THE SOCIETE D'HISTOIRE
     MODERNE (item 371), 133-49.

     Analyzes Catholic reactions to the French, German,
     and Italian revolutions of 1848. Looks at the two
     major movements--religious liberalism and social
     Catholicism--used by Catholics to meet the dangers
     to the faith posed by the emergence of democracy and
     socialism, concluding that in the long run neither
     could reawaken traditional Christian values within
     European society.

305. Fogarty, Michael P. CHRISTIAN DEMOCRACY IN WESTERN
     EUROPE, 1820-1953. Notre Dame: University of
     Notre Dame Press, 1957.

     Divides the evolution of nineteenth-century
     Christian Democracy into two phases: 1820-1880
     (Chapters 11 and 12) and 1880-1950 (Chapter 13).
     Within each phase two generations worked
     simultaneously, the first feeling its way through
     discovery and discussion of elementary political
     models, and the second elaborating upon and
     publicizing these models, until an attempt could
     be made to put them into practice. Fitted into
     this analysis are the ideas and activities of
     Lamennais, Montalembert, Lacordaire, Ketteler,
     and de Mun; beyond the references to individuals
     is the treatment of the impact made by liberal
     groups in Belgium, Bavaria, the Rhineland, and
     Italy.

     See: Ferdinand A. Hermens, RP 19 (July 1957): 393-4;
           David Harris, AHR 63 (October 1957): 96-7;
           Bernard Wall, IA 33 (October 1957): 489-90;
           Thomas P. Peardon, PSQ 72 (December 1957): 621-
           2; James Edward Gillespie, AAAPSS 315 (January
           1958): 183-4; CLR 43 (June 1958): 379-81;
           Aidan C. McMullen, CHR 44 (July 1958): 193-4.

306. Maier, Hans. REVOLUTION AND CHURCH: THE EARLY HISTORY
      OF CHRISTIAN DEMOCRACY, 1789-1901. Translated by
      Emily M. Schossberger. Notre Dame: University of
      Notre Dame Press, 1969.

      A broad treatment of the ideas and aims of
      Christian Democracy. Selects specific
      personalities--e.g., de Maistre, Lamennais,
      Buchez, Léon Harmel, and Leo XIII--to clarify
      the relationship between Christian Democracy,
      on the one side, and liberal Catholicism and
      social Catholicism, on the other.

      See: Joseph L. Walsh, COMMWL 92 (10 July 1970): 348-
            9; Guenter Lewy, APSR 64 (September 1970): 929-
            30; Serge Hughes, CW 213 (June 1971): 153; R.
            William Rauch, Jr., CHR 57 (January 1972): 676-
            7; Rocco Caporale, PSQ 87 (June 1972): 299-301.

307. Menczer, Béla, ed. CATHOLIC POLITICAL THOUGHT,
      1789-1848. London: Burns Oates and Washbourne,
      1952.

      A series of selections from the writings of de
      Maistre, Chateaubriand, Schlegel, Cortés, Balmes,
      and Veuillot, among others. Menczer's fifty-seven-
      page Introduction addresses the problem of liberty
      versus authority within the early nineteenth-century
      Church.

      See: IER 78 (August 1952): 153-4; Thomas P. Neill,
            CHR 38 (October 1952): 335-7; J.M. Cameron,
            DUBR 226 (Winter 1952): 30-40.

308. Moody, Joseph N., ed. CHURCH AND SOCIETY: CATHOLIC
      SOCIAL AND POLITICAL THOUGHT AND MOVEMENTS, 1789-
      1950. New York: Arts, 1953.

      Presents the enormous variety and depth of
      nineteenth-century Catholic political thought
      and activity. The essays, written by thirteen
      specialists, are arranged on a national basis,
      and of sufficient length as to permit a detailed
      examination of oftentimes complex and intricate
      problems. Contains items 39, 554, 662, 740, 742,
      750, 767, and 1602.

See: Gordon Wright, PSQ 69 (June 1954): 303-4; Paul
       Hanly Furfey, AAAPSS 294 (July 1954): 213-4;
       Robert F. Byrnes, CHR 40 (July 1954): 203-4;
       Blahoslav S. Hrubỹ, JCEA 14 (October 1954): 277-
       9; R.J. McNamara, S.J., THOUGHT 29 (Winter 1954-
       5): 600-1; Peter Viereck, AHR 61 (January
       1956): 358-9; JSS 18 (July 1956): 234.

Social Thought and Influence

309.   McLeod, Hugh. "Building the 'Catholic
       Ghetto': Catholic Organisations, 1870-
       1914." In VOLUNTARY RELIGION: PAPERS
       READ AT THE 1985 SUMMER MEETING AND THE
       1986 WINTER MEETING OF THE ECCLESIASTICAL
       HISTORY SOCIETY (item 30), 411-44.

       An overview of Catholic subcultures in the
       relatively industrialized countries of central
       and northwestern Europe. Assesses the extent
       and forms of that phenomenon which the Germans
       called *Vereinskatholizismus*, the network of
       organizations, ranging from political and
       economic to social and recreational, intended
       to protect the interests of Catholics as a
       group. Looks at motives behind the formation
       of these groups and the impact upon individual
       members.

310.   ————. RELIGION AND THE PEOPLE OF WESTERN EUROPE,
       1789-1970. Oxford: Oxford University Press,
       1981.

       Measures the effect of developments such as
       socialism, urbanization, and social conflict on
       Catholicism. Along the way McLeod looks into
       French anti-clericalism, Catholic-Protestant
       tensions in Germany during the 1880s, the growing
       gap between the beliefs of the middle classes and
       those of the workers, and the appeal of Ultra-
       montanism, in the light of this crisis-filled
       atmosphere.

       See: J.M. Taylor, BBN, April 1982: 217; CHOICE 19
              (July/August 1982): 1623-4; Judith F. Champ,

CLR 67 (August 1982): 300; Bernard M.G.
Reardon, ESR 13 (January 1983): 110-2;
C.T. McIntire, CH 53 (March 1984): 147-8;
John M. Roberts, EHR 99 (April 1984): 446-7.

* Moody, Joseph N., ed. CHURCH AND SOCIETY: CATHOLIC
SOCIAL AND POLITICAL THOUGHT AND MOVEMENTS, 1789-
1950. Cited above as item 308.

Includes within each of the thirteen essays a
sociological analysis of the Catholic community in
the particular country under consideration. In
addition to providing data on the social character
and status of Catholics throughout Europe, the
authors list many of the major social initiatives,
both theoretical and practical, coming out of the
different geographical areas.

311. Phayer, J. Michael. SEXUAL LIBERATION AND RELIGION
IN NINETEENTH CENTURY EUROPE. Totowa, N.J.: Row-
man and Littlefield, 1977.

Inquires into the effects of the new sexual
freedom on Catholic society. Concludes that
sexual behavior was not a deterrent to the
faithful practice of religion; especially in
the rural areas, where the inhabitants stubbornly
resisted the efforts by civil and ecclesiastical
leaders to curb their behavior, popular piety
continued to flourish, at least until mid-century.

See: CHOICE 14 (October 1977): 1102; Robert P.
Neuman, AHR 83 (February 1978): 153; Howard
J. Happ, CS 7 (March 1978): 176-7; Joseph
N. Moody, CHR 64 (October 1978): 679-80.

Social Catholicism

312. Cronin, John F., S.S., and Flannery, Harry W.
THE CHURCH AND THE WORKINGMAN. Twentieth
Century Encyclopedia of Catholicism, vol.
104. New York: Hawthorn Books, 1965.

Chapters 1-6 assemble Papal teaching on labor
issues, climaxing with Leo XIII's views on a

living wage, the right to organize, labor-management
relations, decent housing, and social security.
Chapters 7-8 are a chronological account of the
progress of social Catholicism in England, Germany,
and France. After commenting on the Catholic
reaction to the Industrial Revolution, the authors
examine the activities of Wiseman and Manning in
England, von Baader, Ketteler, Kolping, Lassalle,
and Hitze in Germany, and Villeneuve-Bargemont, de
Melun, Ozanam, and de Mun in France.

See: BKLST 62 (1 June 1966): 929.

313. Newman, Jeremiah. "The Catholic Social Movement."
        IER 83 (February 1955): 96-107.

Details the origins of the movement, both negative
(opposition to socialism) and positive (a dynamic
response to the physical and spiritual misery caused
by the French and Industrial Revolutions).

314. Nitti, Francesco S. CATHOLIC SOCIALISM. Translated
        by Mary Mackintosh. London: Swan Sonnenschein/
        New York: Macmillan, 1895.

Compares the goals, techniques, and effects of
nineteenth-century social Catholicism as practiced
in eight European countries. Germany receives the
greatest amount of coverage (Chapters 5-7); the
sections on Switzerland (Chapter 9) and on Spain
and Italy (Chapter 11) are the only in-depth
accounts in English.

See: ACQR 33 (October 1908): 753-4.

315. Vidler, Alec R. A CENTURY OF SOCIAL CATHOLICISM,
        1820-1920. London: Society for Promoting
        Christian Knowledge, 1964.

Essays of various lengths on the movement's place
in France, Belgium, Germany, and Italy. Emphasizes
the wide spectrum of opinion within social
Catholicism, ranging from the conservatives, for
whom private charity was the answer to the ills
caused by industrialism and perpetuated by *laissez-
faire* economics, to the socialists, who advocated a
radical change in the social structure.

See: Michael Jackson, THEO 67 (June 1964): 270-1;
Neville Masterman, HIST 49 (October 1964): 378;
Mauricio Lopez, ECR 17 (January 1965): 81-2;
Gerard C. Thormann, CHR 51 (July 1965): 274-5;
Irene Collins, EHR 81 (January 1966): 191-2;
Wilfrid Passmore, DR 88 (January 1970): 88-90.

Piety and Devotion

Liturgy and Spirituality

316. Bouyer, Louis. LITURGICAL PIETY. Notre Dame: University of Notre Dame Press, 1955.

Chapter 2 describes and assesses the liturgical movement in France and Germany during the romantic period. Highly critical of its stultifying systematization of tradition, naive adherence to medievalism, and incredibly weak scholarship.

See: Charles J. Corcoran, AM 81 (7 May 1955): 23-4;
H.A. Reinhold, COMMWL 62 (26 August 1955): 521-3; J. Quasten, CER 53 (September 1955): 421-2;
Cornelius Hurley, THOUGHT 30 (Autumn 1955): 469-70; James Carmody, AMER 94 (15 October 1955): 74; Dom Bede Scholz, O.S.B., SJR 48 (November 1955): 290-1; Thomas T. McAvoy, C.S.C., RP 18 (January 1956): 106.

317. Franklin, R.W. NINETEENTH-CENTURY CHURCHES: THE HISTORY OF A NEW CATHOLICISM IN WÜRTTEMBERG, ENGLAND, AND FRANCE. New York and London: Garland Publishing, 1987.

A panoramic view of the nineteenth-century liturgical revival inspired by Guéranger and the Benedictines in France and Möhler and the Tübingen School in Germany. Sees both of these groups motivated by a desire to revitalize a creed beset by the liberalism and skepticism of an increasingly secular civilization. Points to the importance of their efforts in the overall restoration of nineteenth-century Catholicism, while at the same time finding within them the

seeds of that twentieth-century Roman revival which
led to the reforms of Vatican II.

318.   _____. "The Nineteenth Century Liturgical Movement."
        WOR 53 (January 1979): 12-39.

    Details the post-1833 campaign for the restoration
    of worship by Benedictine monks at Solesmes (France),
    Beuron and Maria Laach (Germany), and Maredsous
    (Belgium).

319.   Pourrat, Pierre, S.S. CHRISTIAN SPIRITUALITY.
        Translated by Donald Attwater. Vol. 4: FROM
        JANSENISM TO MODERN TIMES. Westminster,
        Md.: Newman Press, 1955.

    Chapters 18, 19, and 20 group nineteenth-century
    teachers of spirituality according to nationality
    (i.e., German, England, and French), lines of
    thought, and method. Emphasizes French developments
    as reaching a new peak both in the spiritual life
    and in the formulation of spiritual doctrine.

    See: John Jolin, S.J., SJR 49 (November 1956): 244-5.

                Marian Apparitions and Devotion

                        General Works

320.   Carroll, Michael P. THE CULT OF THE VIRGIN MARY.
        Princeton: Princeton University Press, 1986.

    Explores the sociological, psychological, and
    historical processes which gave rise to today's
    Marian devotion. Central to Carroll's argument
    is the issue of apparitions, which he dissects
    psychoanalytically, but not without sympathy for
    those to whom they occurred. Concludes, along
    with item 322, that from the century's five
    appearances emerge certain patterns in the
    background and behavior of the visionaries which
    hold the key to the proper understanding of those
    appearances.

    See: CHE 33 (22 October 1986): 10; D.S. Ferguson,

CHOICE 24 (March 1987): 1084-5; W.W. Meissner,
S.J., THS 48 (June 1987): 362-5; Marina Werner,
TLS, 12 June 1987: 638; John Boswell, NR 196
(15 June 1987): 37-9; Lawrence S. Cunningham,
COMMWL 114 (9 October 1987): 569-70.

321. Delaney, John J., ed. A WOMAN CLOTHED WITH THE
      SUN: EIGHT GREAT APPEARANCES OF OUR LADY IN
      MODERN TIMES. Garden City, N.Y.: Doubleday,
      Hanover House, 1960.

Eight essays, four of which deal with nineteenth-
century apparitions; each is written by a recognized
authority in that visitation about which he or she
writes. Each article provides the same basic
material: the background; a sketch of those
involved, along with their family, education, and
faith; a description of the appearance; the messages
given (if any); and public reaction to the
announcement of the vision. Contains items 324, 327,
331, and 343.

322. Graef, Hilda. MARY: A HISTORY OF DOCTRINE AND
      DEVOTION. Vol. 1: FROM THE REFORMATION TO
      THE PRESENT DAY. New York: Sheed & Ward,
      1965.

A comprehensive treatment of all aspects of
nineteenth-century Marian belief and activity.
Details the progress of the doctrine of the
Immaculate Conception, from Anna Katharine
Emmerich's visions, first made public in 1833,
to the Papal pronouncement of 1854. Investigates
the four apparitions in France, arguing (as does
item 320) that their true explanation may well
lie not in authenticity, deceit, or hallucination,
but in simple child psychology. Analyzes the
growth of Mariology after 1850, particularly
through Papal teaching, the practices of religious
orders, and the efforts of distinguished thinkers,
such as Matthias Joseph Scheeben.

See: TLS, 17 March 1966: 227; Charles V. Liggio,
      DUNR 6 (May 1966): 316-7; Wilfrid Passmore,
      DR 84 (July 1966): 312-4; CHOICE 3 (September
      1966): 532; Donald P. Gray, COMMWL 84 (16
      September 1966): 590-1.

Paris (1830)

323.   Carr, John F., C.M. "The Miraculous Medal and the
       Dogma of the Immaculate Conception." IER 40
       (September 1952): 240-51.

       Details the visions of St. Catherine Labouré and
       their impact on the Church over the following twenty-
       five years, which culminated with Pius IX's decla-
       ration of the Immaculate Conception.

324.   Dirvin, Joseph I., C.M. "The Lady of the Miraculous
       Medal, Paris, 1830." In A WOMAN CLOTHED WITH THE
       SUN: EIGHT GREAT APPEARANCES OF OUR LADY IN
       MODERN TIMES (item 321), 57-77.

       Combines a biography of St. Catherine Labouré with
       a factual treatment and theological interpretation of
       her vision.

325.   ————. SAINT CATHERINE LABOURE OF THE MIRACULOUS
       MEDAL. New York: Farrar, Straus and Cudahy,
       1958.

       The most complete biography in English, based on
       previously inaccessible archival materials.
       Emphasizes the frustration and suffering of a life
       which, unlike Bernadette's, was lived in complete
       anonymity; in fact, not until a few months before
       her death, and then only because of extreme
       circumstances, did she reveal to her Superior that
       she was the mysterious sister to whom the Virgin
       Mary had appeared some forty-six years earlier.

       See: Sister Ritamary, C.H.M., CW 188 (January
             1959): 342-3; Norbert F. Gris, C.M., AER
             140 (February 1959): 139-40.

La Salette (1846)

326.   Carroll, Michael P. "The Virgin Mary at La Salette
       and Lourdes: Whom Did the Children See?" JSSR
       24 (March 1985): 56-74.

       Develops a psychodynamic explanation for many of

the more baffling features at La Salette. Explains
why the vision appeared to certain children only,
why the "lady" was not initially identified as the
Virgin Mary, and why she cried during the visitation.
Suggests, in dismissing any supernatural dimension,
that the apparition was inspired by some parental
figure in the children's background. For a fuller
development of these theories, see item 320.

327. Kennedy, John S. "The Lady in Tears: La Salette,
        1846." In A WOMAN CLOTHED WITH THE SUN: EIGHT
        GREAT APPEARANCES OF OUR LADY IN MODERN TIMES
        (item 321), 81-101.

    Subjects the appearance to serious questioning,
    as it considers St. John Vianney's reservations
    and the post-apparition lives of Maximin and
    Mélanie.

Lourdes (1858)

328. Blanton, Margaret Mary. BERNADETTE OF LOURDES.
        New York: Longmans, Green, 1939.

    A sympathetic biography, with additional material
    on the history of the Grotto of the Apparitions
    after Bernadette's death. Based primarily on the
    three volumes of inquiry produced by the episcopal
    commission appointed to pronounce on the supernatural
    character of the appearances.

    See: Louis A. Arand, CHR 26 (July 1940): 261-2;
         Jean Lyle, NATION 151 (7 September 1940): 197.

329. Buckley, Michael F., O.M.I. "One Hundred Years of
        Miracles." IER 91 (February 1959): 89-102.

    Reconstructs the first miracles at Lourdes and
    the consequent establishment of a permanent medical
    bureau to validate the supernatural basis of cures.

  * Carroll, Michael P. "The Virgin Mary at La Salette
        and Lourdes: Whom Did the Children See?" Cited
        above as item 326.

Offers a psychological explanation as to why only
Bernadette could see the lady, and why that lady, not
initially identified as the Virgin Mary, referred to
herself as the Immaculate Conception.

330. Deery, Joseph, P.P. OUR LADY OF LOURDES.
      Dublin: Browne and Nolan, 1958.

      Describes the complex of churches, shrines, and
      hospitals built around the Grotto during the late
      nineteenth century.

      See: IER 89 (May 1958): 387.

331. Keyes, Frances Parkinson. "Bernadette and the
      Beautiful Lady: Lourdes, 1858." In A WOMAN
      CLOTHED WITH THE SUN: EIGHT GREAT APPEARANCES
      OF OUR LADY IN MODERN TIMES (item 321), 105-28.

      Stresses the ordinary atmosphere in which the
      apparitions occurred.

332. McGreevy, John J. "The Lourdes Miracles." IER 89
      (February 1958): 106-23.

      Gives detailed examples of early cures, emphasizing
      their rarity, immediacy, and very natural form.

333. Matt, Leonard von, and Trochu, Francis. ST.
      BERNADETTE: A PICTORIAL BIOGRAPHY.
      Translated by Herbert Rees. Chicago: Henry
      Regnery, 1957.

      Combines 183 photographs by von Matt and a
      brief sympathetic account of Bernadette's life
      by Trochu.

      See: BS 17 (15 July 1957): 135; Sister M. David
            Cameron, S.S.N.D., CRITIC 16 (August/
            September 1957): 31-2; Kieran Mulvey, O.P.,
            BLACK 38 (September 1957): 395; CLR 42
            (November 1957): 695.

334. Neame, Alan. THE HAPPENING AT LOURDES, OR THE
      SOCIOLOGY OF THE GROTTO. London: Hodder and
      Stoughton, 1968.

Sees the Lourdes story as a combination of three phenomena: the town itself, in which ordinary lives were abruptly shaken by an extraordinary event; the apparitions of 1858; and the political, social, and religious climate of the outside world. Deals with aspects of the "happening" which are often glossed over or misinterpreted, such as Bernadette's everyday activities--why was she gathering bones beside a mountain torrent?--and the dynamics of the provincial culture in which she lived.

See: Phoebe Adams, ATMO 221 (March 1968): 134; Bernard Hrico, BS 27 (15 March 1968): 480.

335. Petitot, Henri, O.P. SAINT BERNADETTE. Chicago: Henry Regnery, 1955.

Concentrates heavily on Bernadette's post-apparition life in the convent at Nevers. A sympathetic treatment of her spiritual loneliness and physical problems.

336. ————. THE TRUE STORY OF SAINT BERNADETTE. Translated by a Benedictine of Stanbrook Abbey. Westminster, Md.: Newman Press, 1950.

Explores her pre- and post-apparition personality, its weaknesses as well as its strengths. As a child she was too affectionate; as a Sister of Charity of Nevers she had to struggle against a hot temper, which had plagued her since her youth.

See: IER 73 (June 1950): 569-70.

337. Saint-Pierre, Michel de. BERNADETTE AND LOURDES. New York: Farrar, Straus and Young, 1954.

Concentrates on the religious, political, and scientific implications of the apparitions. Shows how Lourdes and all it represented became part of the anticlerical struggle during the early years of the Third Republic. The Epilogue features a scientific account of the cures, with documentation supporting their supernatural origin.

See: Sister M. Evangeline Steinmann, CHR

41 (October 1955): 370.

338.   Stafford, Ann.   BERNADETTE AND LOURDES.
       London: Hodder and Stoughton, 1967.

       Places the apparitions against the background of
       government opposition, clerical indifference, and
       popular acclamation.

       See: TLS, 17 August 1967: 748.

*   Steuart, R.H.J., S.J.   "St. Bernadette Soubirous."
       DIVERSITY IN HOLINESS (item 34), 165-82.

       Admires her heroism in the face of numerous
       enemies, not the least dangerous of which were
       her own impatience and lack of self-control.

339.   Trochu, Francis.   SAINT BERNADETTE SOUBIROUS, 1844-
       1879.   Translated by John Joyce, S.J.   New
       York: Pantheon, 1958.

       Focuses on the impact of the apparitions on
       Bernadette's life and personality.   Her family,
       already a victim of extreme poverty, was deeply
       concerned about the humiliation to which she was
       subjected by atheists and others.   Nor did the
       skepticism end during her days in the convent at
       Nevers.

       See: John Jolin, S.J., SJR 51 (April 1958): 29-30;
              Mother Mary Alice Gallin, CHR 44 (July
              1958): 196-7; CLR 43 (November 1958): 697.

340.   Trouncer, Margaret.   SAINT BERNADETTE: THE CHILD
       AND THE NUN.   New York: Sheed & Ward, 1958.

       Published in England as A GRAIN OF WHEAT: THE
       STORY OF ST. BERNADETTE OF LOURDES, 1844-1879.
       A popular treatment, emphasizing Bernadette's
       as a nun at Nevers.   Salutes her sense of humor,
       vigorous honesty, and great courage in the face of
       numerous obstacles.

       See: Sister Mary Faith Schuster, ABR 8 (September
              1957): 282; Sister Mary Cornelius, S.S.N.D.,
              CRITIC 16 (March 1958): 31-2;

Philip Devlin, C.S.C., AM 88 (4 October 1958): 27.

Pontmain (1871)

341. Galvin, Navin. "Pontmain and Marian Apparitions." MLS 2 (December 1970): 95-8.

A brief account of the events of 17 January 1871.

Knock (1879)

342. O'Keeffe, Daniel. THE STORY OF KNOCK. Cork and Liverpool: Mercier Press, 1949.

Presents the vision as both a religious and a socio-cultural phenomenon, since it was rooted in faith and in the background and perception of the eyewitnesses. Maintains that the evidence in favor of authenticity is arresting and stronger than that of any of its contemporary counterparts in France.

343. Purcell, Mary. "Our Lady of Silence: Knock, 1879." In A WOMAN CLOTHED WITH THE SUN: EIGHT GREAT APPEARANCES OF OUR LADY IN MODERN TIMES (item 321), 131-51.

Offers a variety of natural explanations for the vision, none of which are deemed plausible. Emphasizes the unique characteristics of the apparition: it was witnessed by adults as well as children, no one experienced ecstasy, and the heavenly visitors neither spoke nor left a message.

344. Walsh, Michael. THE APPARITION AT KNOCK: A SURVEY OF FACTS AND EVIDENCES. Leinster: Leinster Leader, 1955.

A straightforward evaluation of the eyewitness testimony, with the conclusion that a supernatural cause should be admitted as a "probable explanation."

       See: CLR 41 (May 1956): 311-2; S. O'Riordan, C.SS.R.,
              IER 89 (February 1958): 141-7.

                        Missionary Activity

                          General Works

345.   Delavignette, Robert. CHRISTIANITY AND COLONIALISM.
       Translated by J.R. Foster. Twentieth Century
       Encyclopedia of Catholicism, vol. 97. New
       York: Hawthorn Books, 1964.

       Chapter 6 examines the role of the Catholic Church
       in nineteenth-century colonial situations. Contends
       that every case in which the Church came into contact
       or conflict with colonialism can be fitted into one
       of three categories: (1) Catholicism was favored by
       the colonial authorities; (2) Catholicism, though not
       persecuted, was rejected by the authorities, in favor
       of another religion; and (3) Christianity was seen by
       the authorities as having the right to the same
       treatment as other religions.

       See: CHOICE 2 (May 1965): 165.

346.   De Vaulx, Bernard. HISTORY OF THE MISSIONS.
       Translated by Reginald F. Trevett. Twentieth
       Century Encyclopedia of Catholicism, vol. 99.
       New York: Hawthorn Books, 1961.

       A listing, both chronological and geographical, of
       the areas of the world in which nineteenth-century
       European missionaries ministered. Within each of the
       chapters dealing with ecclesiastical foundations in
       Africa, Asia, America, Oceania, and the Near East
       (Chapters 9-17) are references to changing ex-
       pressions of hierarchical support, and to the
       enormous obstacles (including illness and martyrdom)
       faced by individual clergymen.

347.   Latourette, Kenneth Scott. "The Christian Missionary
       Movement of the Nineteenth and Twentieth
       Centuries: Some Peculiar and General
       Characteristics." CHR 23 (July 1937): 153-9.

Calls attention to some features which made
nineteenth-century Catholic missionary activity
unique in the annals of religious expansion.
Besides its unprecedented worldwide scope, the
activity sprung mainly from industrialized areas,
depended upon the generosity of millions of
individual donors, and profited from the services
of women in a number of important roles.

348.   ————. A HISTORY OF THE EXPANSION OF CHRISTIANITY.
       Vol. 4: THE GREAT CENTURY, A.D. 1800-A.D.
       1914: EUROPE AND THE UNITED STATES OF AMERICA.
       New York and London: Harper & Brothers, 1941.

Chapters 1-4 present the secular and religious
context within which nineteenth-century European
missionary activity operated, and the process by
which the faith was spread through the other
continents. Underscores the extraordinary vigor
and huge scale of the effort, from the training
schools for missionaries and support societies
to the daily work of the priests and nuns in the
overseas establishments.

See: Charles S. Braden, JBR 4 (August 1941): 188-9;
      Robert Hastings Nichols, CH 10 (September
      1941): 292-4; John Tracy Ellis, CHR 27
      (January 1942): 457-9; William W. Sweet, JMH
      14 (March 1942): 106-7; Ralph T. Flewelling,
      PERS 23 (Summer 1942): 321; David S. Muzzey,
      AHR 48 (October 1942): 66-8; Thomas T. McAvoy,
      C.S.C., RP 5 (April 1943): 260-1; Willard L.
      Sperry, YR 35 (September 1945): 158-61; Ernest
      A. Payne, JTS 47 (July/October 1946): 143-5.

349. Neill, Stephen. A HISTORY OF CHRISTIAN MISSIONS.
      The Pelican History of the Church, vol. 6.
      New York: Penguin, 1964.

Characterizes the nineteenth-century missionary
picture as one of abounding vitality and heroism in
all areas of the world, but especially in Asia and
Africa. Criticizes the missionaries' distrust of
their Protestant counterparts and their insistence
on complete westernization as an adjunct to the
conversion process.

See: Desmond Gregory, DR 82 (July 1964): 269-71;
       H.A. Dammers, THEO 67 (September 1964): 416-7;
       Gerald H. Anderson, CH 34 (March 1965): 112;
       RM 19 (March 1966): 595-6; Henry McKennie
       Goodpasture, INTERP 20 (July 1966): 362-3;
       Matthias Braun, CHR 53 (January 1968): 667-9.

350. Nemer, Lawrence, S.V.D. ANGLICAN AND ROMAN CATHOLIC
      ATTITUDES ON MISSIONS: AN HISTORICAL STUDY OF TWO
      ENGLISH MISSIONARY SOCIETIES IN THE LATE NINETEENTH
      CENTURY (1865-1885). Studia Instituti Missiologici
      Societatis Verbi Divini, vol. 29. St. Augustin/
      Washington, D.C./Buenos Aires: Steyler Verlag,
      1981.

      A comparison of two diverse approaches to mid-
      century missionary activity. Against the committee-
      run Evangelical C.M.S. is placed the authoritarian
      Mill Hill Society. Contends that differences in
      outlook and operation explain key differences between
      their overseas establishments, including the degree
      to which each fostered the development of an
      indigenous church.

      See: C.P. Williams, JEH 34 (January 1983): 145;
             Thomas J. Jonas, CH 52 (September 1983): 392-3;
             William D. McCarthy, M.M., CHR 70 (October
             1984): 617-8.

351. Schmidlin, Joseph. CATHOLIC MISSION HISTORY. Edited
      by Matthias Braun, S.V.D. Translated by T.J.
      Kennedy and W.H. Robertson. Techny, Ill.: Mission
      Press, 1933.

      A country-by-country narrative of where the
      missionaries came from, and where they went. A
      lengthy introduction to the nineteenth-century
      achievements highlights the internal and external
      factors behind the renewal of European missionary
      activity: better transportation, Pius XII's
      reestablishment of *Propaganda Fidei* in 1817, the
      founding of new orders dedicated to overseas work,
      a vast increase in financial contributions, and
      the campaign by Catholic periodicals to stimulate
      vocations.

      See: AMER 50 (31 March 1934): 621-2;

Joseph McSorley, CW 139 (May 1934): 248-9;
George J. Willmann, S.J., THOUGHT 9 (September
1934): 333-9.

352. Sullivan, Thomas A. "Fifty Years of Missionary
      Labour." IER 8 (September 1916): 233-43.

Describes the origins, program, and apostolate of
St. Joseph's Foreign Missionary Society of Mill Hill.
Founded in 1866 by Herbert Vaughan, it trained
priests for ministry in areas as diverse as the
United States, India, the Upper Nile, and the
Philippines.

Africa

353. Crummey, Donald. PRIESTS AND POLITICIANS: PROTES-
      TANT AND CATHOLIC MISSIONS IN ORTHODOX ETHIOPIA,
      1830-1868. Oxford: Clarendon Press, 1972.

Unravels the complex Ethiopian political, social,
and religious atmosphere within which Catholics,
represented by the Lazarists and Capuchins, and the
Protestant C.M.S. vied for control of the missionary
field. Shows that the spread of Catholicism in
colonial areas was often obstructed by a Protestantism
enjoying the full support of an imperialist power--in
this case, Britain--or by the opposition of a native
clergy which saw the Church as just one more symbol
of hated Western aggression.

See: TLS, 1 June 1973: 609; CHOICE 10 (October
      1973): 1262; Tadesse Tamrat, JAFH 15 (no. 1,
      1974): 156-8; Donald N. Levine, CH 44
      (December 1975): 553-4.

354. Hogan, Edmund M. CATHOLIC MISSIONARIES AND
      LIBERIA: A STUDY OF CHRISTIAN ENTERPRISE IN
      WEST AFRICA, 1842-1950. Cork: Cork University
      Press, 1981.

Recounts the struggle to penetrate Africa's most
intractable missionary field. Confronted by an
unfriendly government headed by Protestants and
Freemasons, and an unhealthy climate, which caused

many deaths, two nineteenth-century ventures failed
to establish a permanent base.

See: John Iliffe, JEH 33 (July 1982): 509; Svend E.
       Holsoe, CHR 69 (April 1983): 315-6; Lawrence
       Nemer, S.V.D., CH 52 (June 1983): 274-5.

                              Asia

355.   Ronan, M.V. "The Holy See and the Protectorate of
       the Chinese Missions." IER 15 (June 1920):   468-
       81.

       Investigates the twenty-five-year process (1844-
       1869) by which the Chinese government granted the
       French the right of protecting Catholic missions in
       China. Adds, as a postscript, a sketch of Leo
       XIII's futile overtures to Peking in 1885-1886, in
       the hope of establishing diplomatic relations.

                            Oceania

356.   Laracy, Hugh. MARISTS AND MELANESIANS: A HISTORY OF
       CATHOLIC MISSIONS IN THE SOLOMON ISLANDS.
       Honolulu: University Press of Hawaii, 1976.

       Part 1, spanning the years 1845-1855, details the
       failure of the French missionaries to gain a foothold
       among the strongly resistant native population.

       See: William E. Tagupa, CH 45 (December 1976): 546-
              7; CHOICE 14 (March 1977): 81; George Woodcock,
              PACAF 50 (Spring 1977): 180-1.

357.   ————. "Roman Catholic 'Martyrs' in the South
       Pacific, 1841-55." JRH 9 (December 1976):   189-
       202.

       Reconstructs the gruesome deaths of seven
       missionaries--six of whom were French Marists--at
       the hands of Pacific islanders, between 1841 and
       1855. Attributes this defeat to faulty techniques
       and recklessness by the victims, who failed to

understand either the difficulties of survival in the
southwestern Pacific, or the virtual impossibility of
communicating Christianity to a people whose
traditional religious values remained intact. For a
detailed look at the larger context within which this
event occurred, see item 356.

358. Thornley, A.W. "'Heretics' and 'Papists': Wesleyan-
         Roman Catholic Rivalry in Fiji, 1844-1903." JRH
         10 (June 1979): 294-312.

         Similar in theme and tone to items 350 and 353.
         Denounces the conflict between the French Marists
         and the Methodists, arguing that it unnecessarily
         disturbed the natives' way of life and, after 1870,
         discredited the message of Christianity. Whatever
         evangelization occurred, occurred for the wrong
         reasons: it was stimulated by an increasingly
         intense rivalry.

359. Wiltgen, Ralph M. THE FOUNDING OF THE ROMAN CATHOLIC
         CHURCH IN OCEANIA, 1825 TO 1850. Canberra: Aus-
         tralian National University Press, 1979.

         Focuses not on the everyday side of missionary
         life, but on the hierarchical strategies behind the
         introduction of Catholicism to the Pacific islands.
         Relies heavily on the archives of *Propaganda Fidei*
         and various religious orders, without losing sight
         of the political aspect of this enterprise, namely,
         the maneuvering by the Great Powers.

         See: James A. Scherer, RSR 7 (January 1981): 94;
                 James Waldersee, JRH 11 (June 1981): 487-9;
                 Hugh Laracy, CHR 67 (October 1981): 668-70.

                     The Arts and Literature

                 Painting, Sculpture, and Architecture

360. Addison, Agnes. ROMANTICISM AND THE GOTHIC REVIVAL.
         New York: Richard R. Smith, 1938.

         Chapters 4 and 5 survey the evolution of the

Gothic in nineteenth-century France, Germany, and
Austria. The Orleans Chapel at Dreux (1816-1847),
Ste-Clotilde in Paris (1846), and the restoration
work of Viollet-le-Duc show the impact of
Chateaubriand's and Madame de Staël's writings on
the Middle Ages. In the German-speaking areas it
was the brothers Boisserée, the Nazarenes, and the
nationalists who, in extolling medieval culture,
provided the impetus for the completion of Cologne
Cathedral (1823-1880) and the construction of St.
Nicholas in Hamburg (1844) and the Votivkirche,
Vienna (1853-1879).

See: Ernest Bernbaum, AMLIT 11 (November 1939): 316.

361. Clark, Kenneth. THE GOTHIC REVIVAL: AN ESSAY IN THE
      HISTORY OF TASTE. London: Constable, 1928.

      Traces the beginning of the revival in Catholic
      ecclesiastical architecture to Bishop John Milner,
      Vicar Apostolic of the Western District, who in
      1792 built St. Peter's Chapel, Winchester, in the
      new style.

      See: W.H. Godfrey, HIST 15 (April 1930): 72-3.

362. Germann, Georg. GOTHIC REVIVAL IN EUROPE AND
      BRITAIN: SOURCES, INFLUENCES AND IDEAS.
      Translated by Gerald Onn. Cambridge: M.I.T.
      Press, 1972.

      Goes beyond a discussion of stylistic techniques
      and themes to assess the degree to which the
      revivalists themselves--most notably, Pugin in
      England, Görres in Germany, and Viollet-le-Duc in
      France--were influenced by non-architectural
      considerations, such as the equation of the Gothic
      and the sublime, and nationalism.

363. Wilson, Winefride. MODERN CHRISTIAN ART. Twentieth
      Century Encyclopedia of Catholicism, vol. 123.
      New York: Hawthorn Books, 1965.

      Contains sections on nineteenth-century religious
      painting (David, Ingres, Millet, Puvis de Chavannes,
      Gauguin, and the Pont-Aven group), sculpture (Canova,
      Thorwaldsen, Carpeaux, Rude, and Rodin), architecture

(Pugin, Gaudi, iron churches, and the popular
Byzantine style), and minor arts (work in
precious metals, stained glass, textiles,
mosaics, and ceramics).

See: Sister Blanche Marie, B.V.M., CER 65 (November
       1967): 559-60.

Music

364. Dannreuther, Edward. THE ROMANTIC PERIOD. The
      Oxford History of Music, vol. 6.
      Oxford: Clarendon Press, 1905.

      Chapter 9 proffers a lengthy analysis of the
      religious music of Berlioz, Liszt, Rossini, and
      Verdi. Berlioz's sacred compositions were con-
      ceived on a large scale, though often too long
      and ambitious to achieve the dramatic effect
      originally intended. Liszt considered the Mass
      a theatrical production, and composed accordingly;
      his *Missa solemnis* (1855) makes enormous demands
      on the senses, in its effort to touch the soul.
      Rossini and Verdi both sought dramatic impact,
      but without the histrionics of their French and
      Hungarian colleagues.

      See: NATION 82 (17 May 1906): 413-4.

365. Donakowski, Conrad L. A MUSE FOR THE MASSES: RITUAL
      AND MUSIC IN AN AGE OF DEMOCRATIC REVOLUTION,
      1770-1870. Chicago and London: University of
      Chicago Press, 1977.

      Part 2, Chapter 5 investigates the resurrection of
      plain chant through the efforts of Lamennais,
      Guéranger, and Joseph d'Ortigues. Chapter 6 de-
      scribes the campaign in France and Germany to restore
      classical polyphony to the liturgy.

      See: Carl Schalk, CC 95 (17 May 1978): 548-9; CHOICE
             15 (October 1978): 1064; Paul Westermeyer, JR
             58 (October 1978): 445-7; William Weber, AHR 83
             (December 1978): 1248-9; Hans Lenneberg, NOTES
             35 (December 1978): 306-8; Robert M. Isherwood,

JMH 51 (June 1979): 338-40; Calvin R. Stapert,
CSN 9 (no. 4, 1980): 367-9; John Richard Orens,
CH 50 (September 1981): 353-4.

366. Fellerer, Karl Gustav. THE HISTORY OF CATHOLIC
      CHURCH MUSIC. Translated by Francis A. Brunner,
      C.SS.R. Baltimore: Helicon Press, 1961.

Includes an overview of nineteenth-century
developments, as they were guided by the vagaries
of taste and the requirements of churchmen.
Emphasis is placed on specific attempts at reform
in Italy, France, Germany, and Belgium, attempts
which led logically to a recultivation of the
stile antico, that is, medieval chant and ancient
classical polyphony. Among the composers whose
contributions are analyzed, are Michael Haydn,
Donizetti, Rossini, Cherubini, Berlioz, Gounod,
Liszt, Bruckner, and Verdi.

367. Hutchings, Arthur. CHURCH MUSIC IN THE NINETEENTH
      CENTURY. London: Herbert Jenkins, 1967.

A series of personal observations rather than a
comprehensive history. Looks into particular
aspects of musical development, along with the
intellectual and cultural atmosphere which
propelled or retarded them. Divides church music
into the great compositions (Masses from Schubert
to Bruckner), choral work, and congregation
pieces.

See: TLS, 2 November 1967: 1042; Michael Dawney,
      NOTES 24 (March 1968): 486-7; CHOICE 5 (May
      1968): 352.

368. Lewis, Anthony. "Choral Music." In THE AGE OF
      BEETHOVEN, 1790-1830, edited by Gerald Abraham,
      593-657. The New Oxford History of Music, vol.
      8. London: Oxford University Press, 1982.

Oriented toward individual accomplishments in
liturgical music. A detailed analysis, with
illustrative sections from scores, of the best work
of Cherubini, Schubert, Beethoven, Michael Haydn,
and a host of lesser-known composers (Bellini,
Hummel, von Weber, and Le Sueur).

See: David Matthews, TES, 31 December 1982: 22;
William S. Newman, NOTES 40 (September
1983): 47-9; CHOICE 21 (October 1983): 291;
Leon Botstein, MQ 70 (Winter 1984): 146-52.

Literature

369. Jennings, Elizabeth. CHRISTIAN POETRY. Twentieth
Century Encyclopedia of Catholicism, vol. 118.
New York: Hawthorn Books, 1965.

Chapter 7 displays the rich variety of Catholic
poets and poetry throughout the nineteenth century.
Most, with the exception of Hopkins, may have been
minor; but the attitudes toward religion expressed
in the verses of Patmore, Wilde, and Thompson show
the unmistakable vitality of the Catholic influence
upon them.

370. Kranz, Gilbert. MODERN CHRISTIAN LITERATURE.
Translated by J.R. Foster. Twentieth Century
Encyclopedia of Catholicism, vol. 119. New
York: Hawthorn Books, 1961.

Distinguishes, in Part 3, three major currents in
nineteenth-century Catholic literature. Common to
all three were practitioners who came to belief from
the realm of unbelief, but only after a mental and
spiritual struggle. Treatment of the romantics, who
revealed the strongest Catholic bias among the
century's writers, covers de Maistre, Chateaubriand,
Manzoni, Novalis, Görres, Brentano, Eichendorff, and
Annette von Droste-Hülshoff. Gezelle, Hopkins, and
Thompson represent the school of nature mysticism,
which preached a heartfelt trust in the God who was
best found in nature. The sketch of the current of
prophecy evaluates Newman and Soloviev not as a
theologian and ecumenist, respectively, but as
Catholic-inspired writers.

THE CHURCH IN INDIVIDUAL COUNTRIES

France

General Works and Collections

371. Acomb, Evelyn M., and Brown, Marvin L., Jr., eds.
      FRENCH SOCIETY AND CULTURE SINCE THE OLD REGIME;
      THE ELEUTHERIAN MILLS COLLOQUIUM, 1964, OF THE
      SOCIETY FOR FRENCH HISTORICAL STUDIES AND THE
      SOCIETE D'HISTOIRE MODERNE. New York: Holt,
      Rinehart and Winston, 1966.

   A series of twelve essays. Part 2 covers
   aspects of nineteenth-century French Catholicism.
   Contains items 304 and 582.

   See: Jean T. Joughin, AHR 73 (April 1968): 1166;
         Irene Collins, EHR 83 (July 1968): 624;
         Donald R. Penn, CHR 55 (October 1969): 484-6.

372. Dansette, Adrien. RELIGIOUS HISTORY OF MODERN
      FRANCE. Translated by John Dingle. New
      York: Herder and Herder, 1961. 2 vols.

   Written by a devout liberal Catholic, who does not
   hesitate to point out weaknesses and criticize
   ecclesiastical decisions. Presents as the central
   theme the conflict between the Church and modern
   society caused by the French and Industrial Revolutions. Lists four major problems faced by
   nineteenth-century churchmen: post-Napoleonic
   reconstruction, the alienation of political forces
   on the right, the backwardness of Catholic philosophy,
   and the steady deterioration of relations with the
   working classes. Though three major efforts were

made to reconcile the Church with the new forces, the
first two--liberal Catholicism (1830-1847) and
Christian Democracy (1848)--failed miserably, while
the third, the *Ralliement*, occurred only at the end
of the century, by which time the Church had already
lost much of its former prestige and authority.

See: Nigel J. Abercrombie, DR 81 (April 1962): 183-5;
      J.J. Dwyer, CLR 47 (May 1962): 308-10; Patrick
      J. Corish, IER 97 (May 1962): 349-50; Robert A.
      Graham, CHR 48 (July 1962): 260-2; Evelyn M.
      Acomb, AHR 68 (October 1962): 121-2; John
      McManners, JRH 2 (December 1963): 342-6.

373. Gooch, G.P. FRENCH PROFILES: PROPHETS AND PIONEERS.
      London: Longmans, Green, 1961.

      Part 2 follows the fortunes of the nineteenth-
      century Catholic revival in France through a series
      of eight brief sketches of its leading personalities
      (Chateaubriand, de Maistre, Lamennais, Montalembert,
      Lacordaire, Ozanam, Veuillot, and Dupanloup). All
      draw on memoirs, letters, and formal works; all are
      judged from a liberal viewpoint.

      See: QR 300 (January 1962): 111; John C. Cairns,
            AHR 68 (January 1963): 518.

374. Phillips, C.S. THE CHURCH IN FRANCE, 1848-1907.
      London: Society for Promoting Christian
      Knowledge, 1936.

      Cites the French Church's ultramontanism and
      stubborn opposition to the principles of 1789 as
      the two main reasons for the rise of anticlericalism.
      The shift in the meaning of ultramontanism--from the
      outlook of an institution free from temporal threats,
      to an advocacy of extreme papal claims--is singled
      out for its contribution to the growing disillusion-
      ment with religion among all classes.

      See: Philip Hughes, CLR 12 (July 1936): 78-80;
            Joseph McSorley, CW 143 (September 1936): 755-
            6; H.A. Moreton, THEO 33 (December 1936): 373-
            5; Gerald Hurst, EHR 52 (April 1937): 377-8;
            HIST 22 (September 1937): 188-9.

375. ————. THE CHURCH IN FRANCE, 1789–1848: A STUDY IN REVIVAL. London and Oxford: A.R. Mowbray, 1929.

     Analyzes the reawakening of ecclesiastical organization and life in France under Napoleon, the Bourbon Restoration, and the July Monarchy. Interweaves religious and political developments, demonstrating the large extent to which the latter inspired the former: Napoleon's Concordat healed the schism caused by the Revolution, while Bourbon reaction and Orleanist indifference left the Church free to do its work. Measures the depth of contemporary religious feeling as evidenced by the reestablishment of religious orders, the rising number and increasingly better quality of ordinands, the growth of the Marian cult, and the exaltation of Roman authority.

     See: TABLET 155 (8 February 1930): 170; Elizabeth S. Kite, CHR 16 (October 1930): 344–5; John Keating Cartwright, AHR 36 (January 1931): 437–8; E.L. Woodward, EHR 46 (January 1931): 168–9; Martin P. Harney, S.J., THOUGHT 13 (June 1938): 339–40.

376. Simpson, W.J. Sparrow. FRENCH CATHOLICS IN THE NINETEENTH CENTURY. London: Society for Promoting Christian Knowledge/New York: Macmillan, 1918.

     Detailed portraits of Catholic political, social, and religious thinkers, both clerical and lay, and progressive and traditional. Shows a decided preference for the liberals (Lamennais, Lacordaire, Montalembert, Ollivier, and Loisy).

     See: LQR 130 (July 1918): 130; A.J. Grant, HIST 5 (July 1920): 113–4.

377. Zeldin, Theodore, ed. CONFLICTS IN FRENCH SOCIETY: ANTICLERICALISM, EDUCATION AND MORALS IN THE NINETEENTH CENTURY. St. Antony's Papers, vol. 1. London: George Allen and Unwin, 1970.

     Analyzes diverse aspects of hostility to Catholicism in France throughout the century,

but particularly during the period of the Second
Empire (1852-1870). Submits that the causes and
expressions of this hostility were far more complex
than previously thought. Explodes several myths
about anticlericalism, including that of a Church
solidly united against opposition.

See: Richard Cobb, SPEC 226 (16 January 1971): 85;
       TLS, 14 May 1971: 563; A.R. Vidler, THEO 74
       (July 1971): 333; Donald Nicholl, CLR 56
       (August 1971): 640-1; Wilfrid Passmore, DR 89
       (October 1971): 345-7; CHOICE 8 (November
       1971): 1240; H.L. Robinson, JCS 14 (Spring
       1972): 351-2; R.B. Rose, HS 15 (April
       1972): 317-8; W.M. Simon, HIST 57 (June
       1972): 301-2; Edward T. Gargan, AHR 77
       (October 1972): 1134-5; John McManners, JRH 7
       (December 1973): 365-7; Joseph N. Moody, CHR
       59 (January 1974): 705-7; Phyllis H. Stock,
       HEQ 14 (Spring 1974): 143-6; Ralph Gibson, ESR
       8 (April 1978): 280.

                  Relations with the Papacy

378.   Costigan, Richard F., S.J. "Tradition and the
       Beginning of the Ultramontane Movement." ITQ
       48 (nos. 1-2, 1981): 27-46.

       Explores the lives and writings of three of the
most significant leaders of the early ultramontane
movement in France: Philippe-Olympe Gerbet (1798-
1864), the most forceful exponent of the Mennaisian
critique of Gallicanism; René-François Rohrbacher
(1789-1856), whose multi-volume Church history
weaned many away from Gallicanism; and Thomas
Gousset (1792-1866), the major critic of traditional
French moral theory.

379.   Gough, Austin. PARIS AND ROME: THE GALLICAN CHURCH
       AND THE ULTRAMONTANE CAMPAIGN, 1848-1853.
       Oxford: Clarendon Press, 1986.

       Details the intense five-year feud between the
Gallicans, headed by Archbishop Sibour of Paris,
and the Ultramontanists, represented by Louis

Veuillot, the fanatical editor of *L'Univers*. Shows, in Chapters 1 to 5, why and how the idea of papal supremacy was eagerly embraced by an ignorant and poor lower clergy. Reconstructs, in Chapters 6 to 13, the step-by-step sabotage of Gallicanism, as its political, social, and ecclesiastical underpinnings were weakened by a series of measures culminating in the year 1870.

See: John McManners, TLS, 30 January 1987: 117;
      W.L. Pitts, Jr., CHOICE 24 (March 1987): 1086;
      Richard F. Costigan, S.J., CHR 73 (October
      1987): 657-8; Sandra Horvath-Peterson, AHR 93
      (February 1988): 163-4.

380. —————. "The Roman Liturgy, Gregorian Plain-chant
      and the Gallican Church." JRH 11 (December
      1981): 536-57.

Illustrates how the liturgy became a battleground during the mid-nineteenth-century conflict between Ultramontanists and Gallicans for the control of the French Church. Emphasizes Guéranger's role in pressing for nationwide use of the Roman rite and Gregorian chant, and the dogged but futile resistance to his campaign.

381. Hassett, Sister Mary Barat, C.S.J. DUPANLOUP ON THE
      "ROMAN QUESTION." Ph.D. dissertation. St. Louis
      University, 1967.

Follows the evolution of Dupanloup's attitude toward the Roman Question, from his inflexible pro-papal stance of the 1860s, to his acceptance in 1874 of the possibility of negotiations between the Holy See and the Italian government.

382. O'Connell, Marvin R. "Ultramontanism and
      Dupanloup: The Compromise of 1865." CH 53
      (June 1984): 200-17.

Maintains that the high tide of nineteenth-century Ultramontanism occurred not at Vatican I, as often thought,--the declaration of infallibility was an anticlimax,--but rather with Dupanloup's skillful interpretation of the Syllabus of Errors, some five years earlier.

383. Shelley, Thomas J. "The Politics of the French
      Ultramontanes in the Nineteenth Century." DUNR
      2 (January 1962): 53-62.

      Sketches the development of Ultramontanism, from
      its origins as a rallying cry against the anti-
      clericalism of 1789, to its emergence after 1850 as
      the dominant ecclesiology in France. Argues that
      differences latent in the movement from its
      beginning made the eventual split between moderates
      and intransigents inevitable.

                          The Hierarchy

                            General

384. May, Anita Rasi. "Is *Les Deux France* a Valid
      Framework for Interpreting the Nineteenth-
      Century Church? The French Episcopate as a
      Case Study." CHR 73 (October 1987): 541-61.

      Sees a fundamental transformation occurring
      within the French episcopate around the middle
      of the nineteenth century. Through the use of
      data relating to the hierarchy's social back-
      ground, training, and response to political
      change, May suggests that the bishops of France
      may not have been involved in the strife between
      Church and State, born of the Revolution of 1789.
      On the contrary, ecclesiastical leaders were
      careful to avoid political and ideological
      conflicts which would only hinder their
      administrative and spiritual work.

                            Sibour

385. Gabbert, Mark A. "Bishop *Avant Tout*: Archbishop
      Sibour's Betrayal of the Second Republic."
      CHR 64 (July 1978): 337-56.

      Tracks Sibour's passage from a sincere liberalism
      in 1848, to the support of Louis Napoleon's coup,

three years later. Traces the Archbishop's "treason" to a fear of revolution, with its attendant growth of ultramontanism.

386. ————. THE ECCLESIASTICAL AND SECULAR POLITICS OF MONSIGNOR MARIE-DOMINIQUE-AUGUSTE SIBOUR, 1847-1852. Ph.D. dissertation. University of California, Santa Barbara, 1973.

Argues that the contradictions within Sibour's religious and political attitudes were less the result of personal inconsistencies than of religious and political developments beyond his control. Notwithstanding an element of opportunism, his shift from Ultramontanism to Gallicanism was prompted by changes in the Papacy and in the character of French Ultramontanism; his support of Louis Napoleon's coup of 1851, coming only three years after his warm endorsement of the newly established Second Republic, was the result of his growing fear of social turmoil.

387. ————. "The Limits of French Catholic Liberalism: Mgr. Sibour and the Question of Ecclesiology." FHS 10 (Fall 1978): 641-63.

Uses Sibour's ecclesiology and political outlook to highlight the problem experienced by French Catholic liberals in attempting to reconcile two diverse views of the origin and nature of authority, one stemming from 1789, and the other rooted solidly in the distant feudal past. Asks whether Catholics were justified in demanding greater civil freedom for the Church, as long as its internal atmosphere was not very free.

388. Williams, Roger L. MANNERS AND MURDERS IN THE WORLD OF LOUIS-NAPOLEON. Seattle and London: University of Washington Press, 1975.

Chapter 2 recreates the assassination of Archbishop Sibour by a deranged priest, Jean-Louis Verger, on 3 January 1857. Places the event within the polemical religious atmosphere of the day, in which popular misconceptions concerning the Immaculate Conception vied with the true meaning, liberal and conservative Catholics denounced each other, and Gallican and

Ultramontane forces sought to destroy each other's power base.

See: Rayner Heppenstall, TLS, 11 June 1976: 687;
       CHOICE 13 (September 1976): 879; Spencer C.
       Tucker, HRNB 5 (January 1977): 75; Benjamin
       F. Martin, Jr., AHR 82 (February 1977): 118-9;
       Frederick Busi, FRR 50 (May 1977): 940.

Darboy

389.   Horvath-Peterson, Sandra. "Abbé Georges Darboy's
       Statistique Religieuse du Diocèse de Paris
       (1856)." CHR 68 (July 1982): 401-50.

       Analyzes the most important and complete diocesan
       study produced in nineteenth-century France. In
       addition to reproducing, for the first time, the
       entire report, Horvath-Peterson discusses its
       background and conclusions, accounting for its
       optimism about the future of religion in the
       capital.

390.   Price, Lewis C. ARCHBISHOP DARBOY AND SOME FRENCH
       TRAGEDIES, 1813-1871. London: George Allen
       and Unwin, 1915.

       A sympathetic portrait of Darboy, placed within
       the larger context of the Second Empire and the
       Commune. Sketches a number of other ecclesiastical
       dignitaries along the way, including the other two
       Archbishops of Paris who died by violence, Affre
       and Sibour.

Richard

391.   La Vergne, Yvonne de. GOOD CARDINAL RICHARD,
       ARCHBISHOP OF PARIS. Translated by Newton
       Thompson. St. Louis: B. Herder, 1942.

       A character study of the leading French
       ecclesiastic during the last decade of the
       century. Contains little political and social

background, beyond noting that the royalist Richard found it difficult to live under the Third Republic. Emphasizes his personal goodness and commitment to priestly service.

See: Felix Fellner, CHR 28 (April 1942): 90-1; Frederic Eckhoff, SJR 35 (January 1943): 317-8.

Dupanloup

392. Belloc, Elizabeth. "Monsignor Félix Dupanloup." AER 152 (April 1965): 249-59.

A succinct biography, stressing his efforts on behalf of Papal temporal power and primary education.

* Gooch, G.P. "Bishop Dupanloup, Friend of Children." FRENCH PROFILES: PROPHETS AND PROFILES (item 373), 244-8.

Describes some of the various expressions of his lifelong commitment to youth: his first clerical assignment as a catechist at the Madeleine, Paris, preparing children for their first communion; his years of teaching at the Seminary of St. Nicholas and the Sorbonne; his crucial role in the passage of the Falloux Law; and his three-volume treatise on Christian education, produced during his time as Bishop of Orleans.

393. Lagrange, Abbé F. LIFE OF MONSEIGNEUR DUPANLOUP, BISHOP OF ORLEANS. Translated by Lady Herbert. London: Chapman and Hall, 1885. 2 vols.

An abridgement of the three-volume work in French. Volume 1 follows Dupanloup's rather quiet pre-1855 life, and Volume 2 the turbulence of his final two decades. Offers an enormous amount of data on his personality and private life, as well as his political struggles. Above all else, however, Lagrange sees his subject as the quintessential pastor of souls, a multi-dimensional cleric whose life was dedicated to the service of his people, for whom he was priest, bishop, catechist, homilist, writer, and educator. A highly flattering portrait,

enhanced by the English edition's omission of some of
the more unpleasant aspects of his life, such as his
running feud with Veuillot.

* Parsons, Reuben. "Dupanloup." STUDIES IN CHURCH
    HISTORY, 5 (item 26), 349-63.

    Focuses on the high points of his distinguished
    clerical career; three successive Popes issued a
    total of forty-six briefs commending him for his
    work on behalf of religion and in defense of the
    Papacy.

Pie

394. Gough, Austin. "The Conflict in Politics: Bishop
     Pie's Campaign against the Nineteenth Century."
     In CONFLICTS IN FRENCH SOCIETY: ANTICLERICALISM,
     EDUCATION AND MORALS IN THE NINETEENTH CENTURY
     (item 377), 94-168.

     Details the twelve-year struggle waged by the
     Bishop of Poitiers against Bonapartism, a struggle
     which brought him into conflict with every level of
     imperial authority, from the local *procureur-général*
     to the Emperor himself. Concludes that his crusade
     against a society which hailed Napoleon III and
     scorned legitimism was doomed to failure.

Bellot des Minières

395. Woodall, John Burwell. "Henri Bellot des Minières,
     Republican Bishop of Poitiers, 1881-1888." CHR
     38 (October 1952): 257-84.

     An appreciation of the difficulties encountered
     by the successor to the reactionary Pie (see item
     394). As the only true republican in the French
     hierarchy of the 1880s, he was constantly at odds
     with his monarchist constituency; despite his short
     tenure and numerous opponents, he prefigured the
     Ralliement, in his desire to reconcile Church and
     Republic.

Lavigerie

396. O'Donnell, J. Dean, Jr. "Cardinal Charles
      Lavigerie: The Politics of Getting a Red Hat."
      CHR 63 (April 1977): 185-203.

      Reconstructs Lavigerie's campaign for the
      cardinalate, starting with the repeated failures
      of the 1870s, and concluding with the success of
      1882. Shows that the recognition came about only
      after anticlerical political leaders like Ferry
      and Gambetta, grateful for Lavigerie's pro-
      imperialist stance, joined with him in exerting
      pressure on Leo XIII.

Diocesan Clergy and Pastoral Activity

General

397. Baisnée, Jules A. "The French Clergy in the
      Nineteenth Century." CHR 23 (July 1937): 185-
      204.

      Speculates as to why and how most French priests
      became alienated from their society. Attributes the
      rift to clerical anxiety caused by political, social,
      and intellectual challenges of unprecedented magni-
      tude.

398. Gargan, Edward T. "The Priestly Culture in Modern
      France." CHR 57 (April 1971): 1-20.

      Identifies efforts by nineteenth-century priests
      to clarify their social status, and thus overcome
      their alienation from the culture within which they
      ministered.

399. ————, and Hanneman, Robert A. "Recruitment to the
      Clergy in Nineteenth-Century France: 'Moderni-
      zation' and 'Decline'?" JIH 9 (Autumn 1978): 275-
      95.

      Speculates as to whether those features of

modernization most often identified by nineteenth-
century French clerics as contributing to their
numerical gains and losses showed any correlation
to the actual levels and rates of ordination.
Approaches the question from two directions: (1)
by examining the clergy's views on those
nineteenth-century social changes which it
perceived as threatening to its future; and (2)
by selecting indicators based on these perceptions,
and noting whether they reveal any relationship
with ordination rates throughout the century.

400. Singer, Barnett. VILLAGE NOTABLES IN NINETEENTH-
        CENTURY FRANCE: PRIESTS, MAYORS, SCHOOLMASTERS.
        SUNY Series in European Social History.
        Albany: State University of New York Press,
        1983.

        Profiles the rural priest in nineteenth-century
        France, his social background, character, outlook,
        financial position, daily life, and challenges.
        Stresses his (usually negative) interaction with
        the two other village notables, the mayor and the
        schoolmaster. Sees as the result of this inter-
        action, as well as of the average priest's
        character flaws, deficient training, and intolerance
        of popular recreations, a gradual but marked decline
        in clerical prestige, especially after 1830.

        See: Clive Emsley, HT 33 (August 1983): 55; CHOICE
              21 (September 1983): 176; Robert T. Denommé,
              FR 57 (December 1983): 289; Eric A. Johnson,
              JIH 14 (Spring 1984): 861-3; Robert R. Locke,
              AHR 89 (April 1984): 454-5; Ted W. Margadant,
              JMH 56 (December 1984): 681-2; Roger Magraw,
              EHR 101 (January 1986): 278-9.

                        St. John Vianney

401. Fourrey, René. THE CURE D'ARS: A PICTORIAL
        BIOGRAPHY. New York: P.J. Kenedy & Sons,
        1959.

        Combines photographs with text, to provide
        various insights into Vianney's character and

spirituality. Features lengthy commentaries on
simple sentences or phrases by him.

See: CLR 46 (January 1960): 63-4; Joseph B. Coyne,
      CHR 46 (April 1960): 109-10.

402. Hamilton, Robert. "The Temptation of the Curé d'Ars."
      IER 68 (July 1946): 35-41.

      Isolates his weaknesses and failures, as
      expressed through his temperament and ministry.
      Includes considerations of his deep morbidity,
      excessive sense of sinfulness, and three
      abortive flights from Ars.

403. La Varende, Jean de. THE CURE OF ARS AND HIS CROSS.
      Translated by Jane Wynne Saul, R.S.C.J. New York
      and Tournai: Desclée, 1959.

      An elaboration of the problems raised by item
      402. Looks for the personal flaws which led
      Vianney to desert his army post, condemn dancing
      in excessive terms, and consider fleeing from his
      duties at Ars on several occasions.

See: IER 93 (April 1960): 272-3.

404. Sheppard, Lancelot C. PORTRAIT OF A PARISH
      PRIEST: ST. JOHN VIANNEY, THE CURE D'ARS.
      London: Catholic Book Club, 1958.

      A study of the man as well as the saint, with the
      time and moral ambience in which he lived and
      operated. Takes special interest in his self-imposed
      rigors, inspired by the precepts of Bishop Joly de
      Choin's RITUEL DE TOULON (1738-1759), the only
      theological manual he ever read.

See: Renée Haynes, DUBR 232 (Winter 1958): 380-3.

  *   Steuart, R.H.J., S.J. "The Curé d'Ars." DIVERSITY
      IN HOLINESS (item 34), 183-201.

      Examines his daily routine as a parish priest.

405. Trochu, Francis. THE CURE D'ARS; A SHORTER
      BIOGRAPHY. Translated by Ronald Matthews.

Westminster, Md.: Newman Press, 1955.

An abridgement of item 406.

See: CLR 42 (January 1957): 60-1.

406.   ————. THE CURE D'ARS: ST. JEAN-MARIE-BAPTISTE
        VIANNEY (1786-1859). Translated by Dom Ernest
        Graf, O.S.B. London: Burns Oates & Washbourne,
        1927.

The classic study, based on the documents gathered
for the canonization process. Balances analysis with
narrative, and Vianney's virtue with his excessive
austerity. Belittles the traditional view of his
poor intellect, noting that such an image should not
be accepted too literally. For an abridgement of
this work, see item 405.

See: IER 72 (July 1949): 92.

Abbé Huvelin

*   Steuart, R.H.J., S.J. "The Abbé Huvelin." DIVERSITY
    IN HOLINESS (item 34), 147-63.

Sketches the life of a parish priest (1838-1910)
whose undistinguished and quiet life concealed a
rich spirituality and complete dedication to charity.

Orders and Congregations

General

407.   Herbst, Clarence A., S.J. "The French Decree of
        March 29, 1880." HB 26 (March 1948): 51-2, 60-1.

Analyzes the mechanics and impact of the law
ordering the dissolution of the Jesuit order in
France by 31 August 1880. Provides background
material on relations between the Jesuits and
the State since 1790.

408. Kessler, Sister Veronica, O.S.B. "French Benedictines
          under Stress." ABR 17 (Autumn 1966): 314-35.

      Evaluates the reaction of the community at Solesmes
      to attempts by the Third Republic to annihilate
      religious orders. Even after their exile (1880) and
      the consequent sale of their monastic lands, the
      Benedictines remained devoted to their traditional
      concepts and continued to grow in membership.

409. Warrilow, Dom Joseph. "The Congregation of
          Solesmes: A Centenary, 1837-1937." DR 55
          (July 1937): 297-308.

      Describes the uneven development of Solesmes,
      from its probationary years (1833-1837), to its
      elevation to full abbey status (1837), and then
      through the next four decades of Guéranger's
      dynamic leadership.

St. Thérèse of Lisieux

410. Balthasar, Hans Urs von. THERESE OF LISIEUX.
          Translated by Donald Nicholl. London: Sheed &
          Ward, 1954.

      An existential look, which considers her life
      under three aspects: the essential, the vocation,
      and the doctrine. Finds a dynamic tension between
      her role as a divine instrument totally devoid of
      self, and her personality, operating on an everyday
      level as an end in itself. Combines theological
      constructs and traditional historiography to detail
      this tension.

      See: Gerard Brady, IER 82 (August 1954): 138-9;
          H.W. Lawton, THEO 57 (November 1954): 436-7;
          CLR 40 (November 1955): 698-9.

411. Beevers, John. STORM OF GLORY: THE STORY OF ST.
          THERESE OF LISIEUX, New York: Sheed & Ward,
          1950.

      Offers a reverent but honest analysis of her
      life, character, beatification and canonization

proceedings, and spiritual teachings.

See: D.H. Moseley, COMMWL 51 (31 March 1950): 661-2;
       William A. Botzum, AM 72 (1 July 1950): 27-8.

412.   Furlong, Monica. THERESE OF LISIEUX. New
       York: Pantheon, 1987.

       Portrays Thérèse's life in terms of her inner
       spiritual struggle, seeing this struggle as her
       way of dealing with energies which as a woman
       she was not permitted to expend in the world.
       Written by an admirer, but with a clear recognition
       of Thérèse's weaknesses and failings.

       See: GW 137 (5 July 1987): 19; CONR 251 (August
              1987): 111-2.

413.   Gaucher, Guy. THE STORY OF A LIFE: ST. THERESE OF
       LISIEUX. Translated by Sister Anne Marie
       Brennan, O.D.C. San Francisco: Harper & Row,
       1987.

       Published in England as THE SPIRITUAL JOURNEY OF
       ST. THERESE OF LISIEUX. Decries attempts by admirers
       to whitewash Thérèse's life, opting instead for a
       portrait of her all too human side. Traces her
       evolution from a psychologically fragile adolescent
       into a strong-willed saint who detested "old wives'"
       devotions and longed to be a missionary and martyr.
       Contains numerous well-reproduced photographs.

414.   Görres, Ida Frederike. THE HIDDEN FACE: A STUDY OF
       ST. THERESE OF LISIEUX. Translated by Richard
       and Clara Winston. New York: Pantheon, 1959.

       Dispenses with the image of the "Little Flower,"
       in order to display an overly sensitive and
       extremely temperamental Thérèse. Explains how the
       reality of the sister became the myth of the saint,
       including the process whereby her original manu-
       scripts were edited to the point of insipidity.

415.   Keyes, Frances Parkinson. ST. TERESA OF LISIEUX.
       London: Eyre & Spottiswoode, 1951.

       Highlights, using photographs as well as text,

the various locations in which Thérèse spent her life.
Highly sympathetic, bordering on hagiography.

416. Norbury, James. WARRIOR IN CHAINS: ST. THERESE OF
    LISIEUX. London: Catholic Book Club, 1966.

    Refutes those critics who claim that Thérèse's
    canonization was a strategem devised by her sister
    Pauline. Grounds her saintliness in the reality
    of her triumph over a restrictive environment, and
    not in her popular but misleading image as passive
    and meek.

    See: TLS, 2 March 1967: 170.

417. Petitot, Henry. SAINT THERESA OF LISIEUX: A
    SPIRITUAL RENASCENCE. Translated by the
    Benedictines of Stanbrook. London: Burns
    Oates & Washbourne, 1948.

    Balances four negative characteristics of her
    ascetic life against three positive expressions
    of her sanctity. Against the absence of the key
    elements of the mystical life--extreme mortifi-
    cation, a fixed method of meditation, evidence of
    extraordinary favors, and diverse spiritual
    activity--Petitot poses the presence of three
    crucial attributes of holiness, i.e., wisdom,
    fortitude, and love.

418. Robo, Etienne. TWO PORTRAITS OF ST. TERESA OF
    LISIEUX. London and Glasgow: Sands, 1955.

    A rigorously scientific study of the saint.
    Criticizes her saccharine image, based on touched-
    up photographs and perpetuated by sentimentality.
    Presents, by applying the rules of historical
    criticism to the facts of her life, a far more
    realistic, human, and womanly figure than is
    usually seen.

    See: Dom Raphael Appleby, DR 74 (Winter 1955-
        6): 89-91; CLR 41 (January 1956): 62-3;
        IER 85 (January 1956): 77-9.

419. Rohrbach, Peter-Thomas, O.C.D. THE SEARCH FOR
    SAINT-THERESE. Garden City, N.Y.: Doubleday,

Hanover House, 1961.

De-mythologizes Thérèse's early life, using
testimony gathered during her canonization process.
Profiles a shy, timid girl, inconsolable at her
mother's death, and afflicted by illnesses which
produced convulsions, comas, and hallucinations.

420. Sainte-Marie, François de, O.C.D. THE PHOTO ALBUM
      OF ST. THERESE OF LISIEUX. Translated by Peter-
      Thomas Rohrbach, O.C.D. New York: P.J. Kenedy &
      Sons, 1962.

Features unretouched photographs of Thérèse,
taken mostly by her natural sister, Céline (also
known as Sister Geneviève of the Holy Face). A
visual complement to the text of item 418.

  *   Steuart, R.H.J., S.J. "St. Theresa of Lisieux."
      DIVERSITY IN HOLINESS (item 34), 133-46.

Explains her "Little Way," the process by which
she sought to achieve holiness through the performance of routine duties.

421. Ulanov, Barry. THE MAKING OF A MODERN SAINT: A
      BIOGRAPHICAL STUDY OF THERESE OF LISIEUX.
      Garden City, N.Y.: Doubleday, 1966.

Points to Thérèse as the great Christian realist
of modern times, a latter-day Pascal, for whom even
the most ordinary event or thing assumed a cosmic
significance. Hails her ability to evoke supernatural images, using only middle-class rhetoric.

See: Sister Claire Lynch, CHR 55 (January
      1970): 709-10.

                        The Laity

422. Moody, Joseph N. "The Dechristianization of the
      French Working Class." RP 20 (January
      1958): 46-69.

Cites a large body of statistics to prove the

increasing religious alienation of French industrial
workers through the nineteenth century. Attributes
the growth of indifference to the Church's hostility
to modern times, the lingering anti-religious spirit
of 1789, an inadequately trained clergy, and the
workers' perception that churchmen were not really
concerned with social issues.

Missionary Activity

423. Attwater, Donald. THE WHITE FATHERS IN AFRICA.
London: Burns Oates & Washbourne, 1937.

A brief treatment of the organization and
activity of the Order, with emphasis on contributions by individual missionaries.

See: George Telford, CLR 14 (March 1938): 281;
DR 56 (April 1938): 254; G.M. Durnford,
DUBR 203 (December 1938): 392.

424. Clarke, Richard F., S.J. CARDINAL LAVIGERIE AND
THE AFRICAN SLAVE TRADE. London and New
York: Longmans, Green, 1889.

Describes and evaluates Lavigerie's campaign after
1870 to suppress the slave traffic. Introduces as
part of the complex background to this issue a look
at the relationship between French missionaries and
the Islamic societies of Africa.

See: DUBR 106 (January 1890): 205-6; ACQR 15 (April
1890): 380-1.

425. Kittler, Glenn D. THE WHITE FATHERS. New
York: Harper & Brothers, 1957.

More the history of one man--Lavigerie--and his
efforts to convert African Moslems, than an
examination of the work of his Order. Presents his
life as a series of steps leading inevitably to his
special apostolate, one which he believed was as
crucial to French imperial policy as it was to the
Church's spiritual outreach. Highlights the
Cardinal's ideal of complete assimilation: success

could only come when his missionaries learned how to
think, act, and live like Moslems.

See: John J. Daly, CHR 44 (July 1958): 205-6.

426. O'Donnell, J. Dean, Jr.   LAVIGERIE IN TUNISIA: THE
      INTERPLAY OF IMPERIALIST AND MISSIONARY.
      Athens: University of Georgia Press, 1979.

Examines the skillful blend of apostolic zeal and
patriotism behind Lavigerie's two decades of activity
in Tunisia (1873-1892).   Shows how the founder of the
White Fathers used his influence as apostolic
administrator of the vicariate of Tunis (1881) and
Archbishop of Carthage (1884) to extend French
control in north Africa.   Through his cooperation
with the anticlerical leaders of the Third Republic,
he not only played a key role in the establishment of
the protectorate over Tunisia, but succeeded, in
1890, in his campaign to abolish slavery in the newly
acquired area.

See: Garland Downum, HIST 8 (January 1980): 66;
      Dwight L. Ling, AHR 85 (February 1980): 182-3;
      Patrick W. Carey, CH 49 (December 1980): 470-1;
      Kenneth J. Perkins, MEJ 34 (Winter 1980): 92;
      David E. Gardinier, CHR 67 (July 1981): 435-7;
      Oscar L. Arnal, JEH 32 (July 1981): 376-7.

 *   Parsons, Reuben.   "Pope Leo XIII and the African
      Slave Trade: The Apostolate of Cardinal
      Lavigerie."   STUDIES IN CHURCH HISTORY, 6
      (item 27), 291-310.

Places the Cardinal's crusade against slavery
within the context of Leo XIII's two encyclicals,
In Plurimis (1888) and *Catholicae Ecclesiae* (1890).
Sees his intellectual opposition to trafficking in
humans as important as his practical agitation on
behalf of abolition.

427. Tudesco, James Patrick.   MISSIONARIES AND FRENCH
      IMPERIALISM: THE ROLE OF CATHOLIC MISSIONARIES
      IN FRENCH COLONIAL EXPANSION, 1880-1905.   Ph.D.
      dissertation.   University of Connecticut, 1980.

Focuses on the role played by French missionaries

in their country's late nineteenth-century colonial
expansion. Presents the paradox of a large number of
priests, supported and protected by an anticlerical
Third Republic, which considered them the best
representatives of French civilization and culture in
foreign lands. Details the synchronization of
religious and political goals, the structure and size
of what was the Catholic world's largest and most
dynamic missionary organization, and the fate of the
system in the wake of the legislation of 1901-1905.

Ecumenical Activity

428. Caron, Vicki, and Hyman, Paula. "The Failed
Alliance: Jewish-Catholic Reactions in
Alsace-Lorraine, 1871-1914." LBIYB 26
(1981): 3-21.

Enumerates the ideological, social, and religious
obstacles to cooperation between the pro-French Jews
of Alsace-Lorraine and their Catholic neighbors who
refused to accept the German annexation of 1871.

429. Klein, Charlotte. "From Conversion to Dialogue--The
Sisters of Sion and the Jews: A Paradigm of
Catholic-Jewish Relations?" JES 18 (Summer
1981): 388-400.

Details the origins of the Congregation of Our
Lady of Sion, founded in 1843 by two converts from
Judaism, Theodore and Alphonse Ratisbonne, with the
avowed aim of Christianizing their former
coreligionists.

Religious Thought

General

430. Guérard, Albert Leon. FRENCH PROPHETS OF YESTER-
DAY: A STUDY OF RELIGIOUS THOUGHT UNDER THE
SECOND EMPIRE. New York: D. Appleton, 1913.

A study of progressive Catholicism in mid-
nineteenth-century France, as seen through the
ideas and activities of the liberal Catholics,
Maret, Gratry, and, most notably, Renan. Offers
a positive assessment of these individuals' contributions, while supporting their effort to end
the Church's war on modern civilization.

See: LQR 119 (April 1913): 353-4; Irving Babbitt,
      NATION 97 (25 September 1913): 288-9; J.W.
      Cunliffe, JPPSM 11 (12 March 1914): 218-20;
      DIAL 55 (1 October 1914): 266; George L.
      Hamilton, MLN 29 (December 1914): 258-61.

431. Reardon, Bernard. LIBERALISM AND TRADITION: ASPECTS
      OF CATHOLIC THOUGHT IN NINETEENTH-CENTURY FRANCE.
      New York: Cambridge University Press, 1975.

      Surveys the development of such major religious
      issues as traditionalism versus change, liberal
      Catholicism, fideism, positivism, scholasticism,
      the philosophy of action, and modernism, by
      presenting thinkers, both well-known and not so
      well-known, who were intimately involved with
      them. Situates each intellectual, including
      Chateaubriand, de Maistre, Bonald, Lamennais,
      Bautain, Maret, Gratry, Blondel, and Loisy,
      within his time; his ideas are explained, and
      his impact upon contemporaries is measured.
      Offers at the same time a discussion of less
      familiar concepts and their leading partisans
      (e.g., Branchereau's ontologism, Maine de Biran's
      voluntarism, and Ballanche's palingenesis).

      See: Alec Vidler, JEH 27 (April 1976): 219-20;
            CHOICE 13 (May 1976): 386; J.M. Cameron,
            TLS, 14 May 1976: 574; Joseph N. Moody,
            AHR 81 (December 1976): 1129-30; James
            McMillan, AMPJ 82 (Spring 1977): 57; JR
            57 (April 1977): 208; Bernard Aspinwall,
            SJT 30 (April 1977): 177-80; John W.
            Padberg, S.J., CHR 64 (October 1978): 676-
            7; Austin Gough, JRH 10 (June 1979): 336-7;
            Richard M. Golden, JCS 21 (Autumn 1979): 584-
            5; Ronald Burke, RSR 7 (October 1981): 292.

432. Simpson, W.J. Sparrow. RELIGIOUS THOUGHT IN FRANCE

IN THE NINETEENTH CENTURY. London: George Allen
and Unwin, 1935.

Defines "religious thought" broadly, investigating
not only modernist scholarship, exegesis, Church
history, and dogmatics, but also preaching and
Catholic literature.

See: H. Watkin-Jones, LQHR 160 (October 1935): 542-
3; HIST 21 (June 1936): 95.

433.   Spencer, Philip. POLITICS OF BELIEF IN NINETEENTH-
       CENTURY FRANCE: LACORDAIRE, MICHON, VEUILLOT.
       New York: Grove Press, 1954.

Maintains that the nineteenth-century French Church
committed a tragic mistake in ultimately submitting to
papal authoritarianism. Uses the varied careers of
three prominent Catholics to illustrate the rejection
of liberal Catholicism, Gallicanism, and the freedom
of theological inquiry, in favor of religious
reaction, ultramontanism, and a rigid dogmatism.
Castigates Pius IX for his vanity, obstinacy, and
vengefulness.

See: DUBR 228 (Summer 1954): 490; CLR 39 (July
       1954): 436-8; C.W. Crawley, JTS 5 (October
       1954): 319; Paul Farmer, AAAPSS 297 (January
       1955): 172-3; Russell E. Planck, CHR 41
       (April 1955): 170-2; H.J. Hunt, MLR 50
       (April 1955): 217-9; Robert Rouquette, S.J.,
       THOUGHT 30 (Autumn 1955): 440-2.

434.   Stunkel, Kenneth R. "India and the Idea of a
       Primitive Revelation in French Neo-Catholic
       Thought." JRH 8 (June 1975): 228-39.

Assesses the impact of Indian religious thought
on Catholic intellectuals from Baron Ferdinand
d'Eckstein to Frédéric Ozanam, that is, during the
first half of the nineteenth century. Contends
that Eastern ideals reinforced their contempt for
eighteenth-century rationalism, broadened their
religious outlook, and deepened their commitment
to a historical analysis of dogma.

De Maistre

435. Cecil, Algernon. "Joseph de Maistre." DUBR 203
      (October/November/December 1938): 286-301.

      Traces the early years and intellectual develop-
      ment of "the Catholic Voltaire." Considers him the
      most influential layman since Thomas More, saluting
      his ideas as a prelude to the solemn pronouncements
      of Vatican I. Continues in item 436.

436. ————. "Joseph de Maistre (Continued)." DUBR 204
      (January/February/March 1939): 20-31.

      A continuation of item 435. Analyzes de Maistre's
      DU PAPE (1819) and the role it played in the Papal
      recovery during the decade after Waterloo.

437. Corrigan, Raymond, S.J. "De Maistre: Freemason and
      Ultramontane." HB 17 (March 1939): 47-8, 57-9.

      Looks into the circumstances which transformed the
      Freemason of 1788 into the Ultramontane of 1819.
      Accounts for the latter stance by pointing to de
      Maistre's passionate belief in the divinely guaran-
      teed infallibility of the Pope, which no other
      sovereign could rightfully claim; dismisses the
      former position as a sign of immaturity, without any
      intentional malice against the Church.

  *   Gooch, G.P. "Joseph de Maistre and the Vatican."
      FRENCH PROFILES: PROPHETS AND PIONEERS (item
      373), 171-89.

      A brief intellectual biography, highly sympathetic.
      Emphasizes the contentions found in DU PAPE and in his
      massive apology for Christianity, LES SOIREES DE
      SAINT-PETERSBOURG (1821).

438. Lebrun, Richard A. THRONE AND ALTAR: THE POLITICAL
      AND RELIGIOUS THOUGHT OF JOSEPH DE MAISTRE.
      Ottawa: University of Ottawa Press, 1965.

      Displays de Maistre's coupling of religion and
      politics, a fusion which led him to consider all
      political problems as essentially religious problems,

requiring nothing more than the guiding force of an
infallible Papacy for their solution.

See: G.S. Couse, CJH 1 (March 1966): 101-2; J.W.
       Gough, EHR 82 (January 1967): 182-3; Edward
       T. Gargan, JMH 40 (March 1968): 140-1;
       Francis G. Wilson, CHR 54 (April 1968): 183-
       4; Douglas Johnson, HIST 54 (February
       1969): 112.

*   Neill, Thomas P.   "Joseph de Maistre." THEY LIVED
      THE FAITH (item 33), 198-221.

      Presents de Maistre as the prime theorist of
      nineteenth-century ultramontanism, whose writings
      not only crippled Gallicanism but also prompted a
      Catholic revival, by emphasizing orthodoxy and a
      Romeward orientation. Maintains that to varying
      degrees, Montalembert, Cortés, de Mun, and
      Veuillot were all inspired by him.

Migne

439. Cotter, Anthony C., S.J.   "Abbé Migne and Catholic
      Tradition." THS 7 (March 1946):   46-71.

      An in-depth treatment of Migne's compilation of
      the patrologies and his simultaneous publication
      of religious periodicals, theological encyclopedias,
      Scriptural studies, and the writings of the saints.

440. Hamell, Patrick J.   "Jacques Paul Migne."   IER 67
      (January 1946):   23-31.

      Discusses Migne's compilation of the patrologies,
      both Latin (in 217 volumes, 1844-1855) and Greek (in
      161 volumes, 1857-1866), along with several dozen
      other series of documents vital to historians of
      early and medieval Christianity.

441. Hillgarth, J.N.   "The Revival of Catholic Patristic
      Studies: The Old and the New Migne." DR 78
      (Spring 1960):   108-16.

      Examines Migne's work, its motivations, and its

impact upon twentieth-century Catholic scholarship.

Renan

442. Bierer, Dora. "Renan and His Interpreters: A Study
     in French Intellectual Warfare." JMH 25
     (December 1953): 375-89.

     Defends Renan against those of his contemporaries
     who, after distorting the ideas of his VIE DE JESUS,
     accused him of blasphemy. Maintains that the Renan
     who passed into the twentieth century is more often
     a caricature drawn by critics--for example, the
     Bishops of Paris, Orleans, Nimes, Grenoble, and
     Algiers--and then magnified and perpetuated by public
     opinion.

*   Guérard, Albert Leon. "Ernest Renan." FRENCH
     PROPHETS OF YESTERDAY: A STUDY OF RELIGIOUS
     THOUGHT UNDER THE SECOND EMPIRE (item 430),
     224-55.

     Looks sympathetically at Renan's life, work, and
     religious philosophy during the years 1848-1870.
     Contrasts his reputedly anti-religious Biblical and
     ecclesiastical studies with his strictly Catholic
     youth in Brittany and Paris.

443. Kaufmann, Alfred, S.J. "Renan--The Man." CHR 10
     (October 1924): 388-98.

     Details Renan's crisis of faith as expressed
     through his personality and in his writings.
     Balances a deep respect for his intellect with a
     criticism of his irresolution and indifference.

444. Mott, Lewis Freeman. ERNEST RENAN. New York and
     London: D. Appleton, 1921.

     Chapter 1 explains Renan's early religious
     training, his life at the seminary of Saint-
     Sulpice, and his later rejection of the Church.
     Chapter 7 surveys popular and academic reactions
     to his VIE DE JESUS, with special reference to
     the review by Sainte-Beuve.

See: E. Preston Dargan, MODPHILOL 19 (May 1921): 429;
Felix Grendon, NATION 113 (17 August 1921): 180-
1; James F. Mason, MLN 37 (November 1922): 428;
James Main Dixon, PERS 4 (July 1923): 213.

* Reardon, Bernard M.G. "Ernest Renan and the Religion
of Science." RELIGION IN THE AGE OF
ROMANTICISM: STUDIES IN EARLY NINETEENTH-CENTURY
THOUGHT (item 255), 237-66.

Describes Renan's lifelong vacillation between the
tenets of religious faith and the certainties of
Comtian science.

445. Wardman, H.W. ERNEST RENAN: A CRITICAL BIOGRAPHY.
London: Athlone Press, 1964.

A reconstruction of Renan's life and work, set
closely against the background of his time. Chapter
4 summarizes the VIE DE JESUS and the critical reactions which it inspired.

See: Richard M. Chadbourne, ROMR 57 (April
1966): 145-6; James J. Hennesey, CHR 53
(April 1967): 113.

Ozanam

446. Klaas, A.C., S.J. "Frederick Ozanam--Historian."
HB 10 (May 1932): 65-6.

A portrait of the social reformer as religious
historian, with a brief comment on each of his
major literary efforts, from the doctoral thesis
on Dante and thirteenth-century Catholic philosophy,
to the volumes on the Christianization of northern
Europe. See also item 447.

447. Souvay, Charles L. "Ozanam as Historian." CHR 19
(April 1933): 1-16.

Complements item 446. Maintains that Ozanam's
greatest contribution to Church history was not his
social activity, but rather his efforts to prove
the truth of Catholicism by pointing to the

antiquity of its beliefs. Praises the versatility
and refinement of his historical writings.

Other Thinkers

* Guérard, Albert Leon. "Philosophers: Mgr. Maret and
Father Gratry." FRENCH PROPHETS OF YESTERDAY: A
STUDY OF RELIGIOUS THOUGHT UNDER THE SECOND EMPIRE
(item 430), 56-63.

Sketches Maret's speculations concerning the
evolution of dogma, and Gratry's application of
inductive rationalism to matters of faith.

448. Reardon, Michael F. "Pierre Ballanche as a French
Traditionalist." CHR 53 (January 1968): 573-99.

Examines Ballanche's complex theological outlook,
from its belief in a divinely ordained plan in
history, to its representation of Catholicism as the
truest form of religious sentiment.

449. Roberts, M.J.D. "The Religious Thought of Charles de
Rémusat during the Second Empire." JRH 7
(December 1972): 129-43.

Attributes his interest in theology, as evidenced
by three books and fifteen articles on either
religious questions or Church-State relations, to
his political frustration after being displaced,
along with Guizot and other Orleanist leaders, by
the events of 1848-1851.

* Simpson, W.J. Sparrow. "Gratry." FRENCH CATHOLICS
IN THE NINETEENTH CENTURY (item 376), 122-42.

Reviews Gratry's campaign to reconcile nineteenth-
century science, philosophy, and religion. Attributes
his failure to his attempt to do too much in too short
a time.

Scientific Thought

450. Paul, Harry W. "The Crucifix and the Cruci-
        ble: Catholic Scientists in the Third
        Republic." CHR 58 (July 1972): 195-219.

        Measures the impact of the Third Republic's
        anticlerical values and policies on Catholic
        scientists working within France's higher in-
        stitutions of learning.

451. ————. THE EDGE OF CONTINGENCY: FRENCH CATHOLIC
        REACTION TO SCIENTIFIC CHANGE FROM DARWIN TO
        DUHEM. Gainesville: University Presses of
        Florida, 1979.

        Commends the courage and persistence of those
        French Catholic intellectuals who, during the
        final four decades of the nineteenth century,
        strove to reconcile Darwinism and other scientific
        concepts with traditional Church teaching on
        creation and human nature. Illustrates the slow,
        tortuous, and obstacle-ridden route taken by these
        thinkers as they sought to adapt their oftentimes
        brilliant insights to the demands of orthodoxy.

        See: Ronald Burke, RSR 7 (January 1981): 80-1;
              Frank M. Turner, AHR 86 (February 1981): 148-9;
              Dale A. Johnson, CH 50 (June 1981): 224-5;
              James F. McCue, JAAR 49 (September 1981): 527-
              8; Roy Porter, JEH 33 (January 1982): 152-3;
              John Lyon, RP 44 (January 1982): 154-5;
              Maurice Larkin, EHR 97 (April 1982): 450-1;
              Raymond Grew, CHR 68 (October 1982): 682-3;
              John D. Root, ZYGON 18 (March 1983): 104-6;
              Gary C. Hatfield, HIS 45 (May 1983): 410-1.

  *   Spencer, Philip. "Michon's Dilemma." POLITICS OF
        BELIEF IN NINETEENTH-CENTURY FRANCE: LACORDAIRE,
        MICHON, VEUILLOT (item 433), 117-97.

        Presents a cleric tormented by the nineteenth
        century's ever widening discrepancy between the
        faith he professed and the analytical sciences to
        which he was so passionately attached. Shows how
        Michon tried to retain both, by denying their

contradictory positions, and how he slipped increasingly farther from the Church as he judged
its structure, beliefs, and practices by the same
rational perspective used in his botanical and
graphological studies.

Education

452. Anderson, Robert. "The Conflict in Education: Catho-
      lic Secondary Schools (1850-70): A Reappraisal."
      In CONFLICTS IN FRENCH SOCIETY: ANTICLERICALISM,
      EDUCATION AND MORALS IN THE NINETEENTH CENTURY
      (item 377), 51-93.

      Investigates the effects over a two-decade span of
      the Falloux Law (1850), which authorized private
      religious schools. Emphasizes the oftentimes
      backward nature of these institutions vis-à-vis
      their public counterparts.

453. Bush, John W. "Education and Social Status: The
      Jesuit *Collège* in the Early Third Republic."
      FHS 9 (Spring 1975): 125-40.

      Measures the degree to which Jesuit schools were
      able, through their curriculum, to enhance or
      improve the social position of their clientele.

454. Elwell, Clarence Edward. THE INFLUENCE OF THE
      ENLIGHTENMENT ON THE CATHOLIC THEORY OF RELIGIOUS
      EDUCATION IN FRANCE, 1750-1850. Harvard Studies
      in Education, vol. 29. Cambridge: Harvard
      University Press, 1944.

      Discusses the impact of the rationalist and
      empirical spirit of the French Enlightenment upon
      the aims, content, and methods of Catholic religious
      education during the first half of the nineteenth
      century.

      See: Abraham J. Brachman, JSS 6 (October 1944): 407-
            8; Paul Schrecker, AHR 50 (January 1945): 323-
            4; Timothy F. O'Leary, CHR 31 (July 1945): 206-
            7; M.M. Thompson, PERS 26 (Winter 1945): 107-8.

455. Grew, Raymond, and Harrigan, Patrick J.   "The
      Catholic Contribution to Universal Schooling
      in France, 1850-1906."   JMH 57 (June
      1985):   211-47.

      Explains how Catholic schools helped to make
      elementary instruction universal. Contends that
      these schools attracted the kind of students
      (e.g., girls) who otherwise might not have been
      attracted by their lay counterparts.

456. Harrigan, Patrick Joseph. CATHOLIC SECONDARY
      EDUCATION IN FRANCE, 1851-1882. Ph.D.
      dissertation. University of Michigan, 1970.

      Analyzes the aims, appeal, and social impact
      of Catholic secondary schools in France over
      the thirty years following the passage of the
      Falloux Law.

457. ————. "The Church and Pluralistic Education: The
      Development of and Teaching in French Catholic
      Secondary Schools, 1850-1870."   CHR 64 (April
      1978):   185-213.

      Focuses on the overall evolution and everyday
      operation of Catholic secondary institutions as
      they attempted to adjust to the ever changing
      needs of a highly diverse society.

458. ————. "French Catholics and Classical Education
      after the Falloux Law."   FHS 8 (Fall 1973):   255-
      78.

      Shows how the Falloux Law, by placing religious
      schools squarely in competition with state establish-
      ments, challenged the Church to devise a modern
      curriculum rooted in classical humanism.

459. ————. "The Social Appeals of Catholic Secondary
      Education in France in the 1870s."   JSH 8 (Spring
      1975):   122-41.

      Examines how and why Catholic schools attracted an
      ever larger upper-class clientele, along with the
      impact which this attraction would have upon the
      later political evolution of the Third Republic.

460. Huckaby, John K.   "Roman Catholic Reaction to the
        Falloux Law." FHS 4 (Fall 1965): 203-13.

        Qualifies the traditional view that the Falloux
        Law was enthusiastically greeted by the French
        clergy; since the legislation did not give the
        Church complete independence in educational
        affairs, it received at best a lukewarm reception
        from most clergy and a contemptuous one from many.

461. Langdon, John William.   SOCIAL IMPLICATIONS OF JESUIT
        EDUCATION IN FRANCE: THE SCHOOLS OF VAUGIRARD AND
        SAINTE-GENEVIEVE. Ph.D. dissertation. Syracuse
        University, 1973.

        Tests the claim of the French Jesuits that their
        secondary schools, by providing Christian training
        and a superior curriculum, produced superior students.
        Uses two of the Order's establishments as test cases,
        combining a consideration of their different
        backgrounds with a statistical analysis of the
        careers of their alumni. Concludes that although the
        Jesuit schools did provide an excellent education,
        they did not guarantee their graduates an influential
        political, military, or social position.

462. Padberg, John W., S.J. COLLEGES IN CONTROVERSY: THE
        JESUIT SCHOOLS IN FRANCE FROM REVIVAL TO
        SUPPRESSION, 1815-1880. Cambridge: Harvard
        University Press, 1969.

        Charts the uneven fortunes of Jesuit education in
        France through much of the nineteenth century,
        showing two periods of growth and promise (1814-1828,
        1850-1880), separated by a time in which the Order
        was prohibited by law from all academic activity.
        Details the development of curricula and the
        encouragement of patriotism in the schools. Declares
        the government's suppression of these schools in 1880
        a blessing in disguise, since it released the Order
        from an enormous financial and human drain.

        See: CHOICE 6 (February 1970): 1808; Lynn Osen, CH
              39 (March 1970): 125; George E. Ganss, S.J.,
              REVREL 29 (March 1970): 332-3; Evelyn Acomb
              Walker, AHR 75 (June 1970): 1464-5; A.C.F.
              Beales, JEH 22 (April 1971): 171;

John McManners, JTS 22 (April 1971): 292-3;
Joseph N. Moody, CHR 59 (April 1973): 94-6;
Richard M. Golden, JCS 21 (Spring 1979): 370-1.

* Parsons, Reuben. "Montalembert and the Struggle for
  Freedom of Education in France." STUDIES IN
  CHURCH HISTORY, 5 (item 26), 320-48.

A highly sympathetic account of Montalembert's
twenty-two-year campaign to promote independent
religious education in France.

463. Schuster, Alice. THE STRUGGLE BETWEEN CLERICALS AND
     ANTICLERICALS FOR CONTROL OF FRENCH SCHOOLS
     (1789-1879). Ph.D. dissertation. Columbia
     University, 1967.

Surveys the seesaw-like contest between Church and
State over control of education. Napoleon made all
instruction subject to ecclesiastical supervision,
while during the Restoration the Church regained even
more of the power it had lost in the time of the
Revolution. Liberal Catholic efforts under the July
Monarchy to establish "freedom of teaching" were
rewarded by the passage of the Falloux Law in 1850;
however, the Ferry laws of 1879 returned educational
control to the State.

464. Washington, Eric Steven. A STUDY OF THE STRUGGLE IN
     FRANCE BETWEEN CHURCH AND STATE FOR CONTROL OF
     SECONDARY EDUCATION, 1789-1850. Ph.D. disser-
     tation. University of Mississippi, 1979.

Follows the course of the conflict between the
Church, with its insistence on widespread religious
instruction, and the advocates of a "neutral
education," from the clerical reverses of the
Revolution to the clerical triumph, however
temporary, of the Second Republic's Falloux Law.

The Press

General

465. May, Anita Marie Rasi. THE CHALLENGE OF THE FRENCH
      CATHOLIC PRESS TO EPISCOPAL AUTHORITY, 1842-
      1860: A CRISIS OF MODERNIZATION. Ph.D.
      dissertation. University of Pittsburgh,
      1970.

      Details the French hierarchy's resistance to
      efforts by journalists to become involved in
      ecclesiastical decision-making. Dismisses the
      portrayal of the conflict as one of liberals
      versus conservatives, or Gallicans versus ultra-
      montanists.

466. ————. "The Falloux Law, the Catholic Press, and
      the Bishops: Crisis of Authority in the French
      Church." FHS 8 (Spring 1973): 77-94.

      Pinpoints the origins of a significant structural
      and ideological change within the French Church; as
      the episcopate discovered after 1850 that it could
      no longer strictly control lay journalists, it
      decided to allow them a role in the ecclesiastical
      decision-making process, one which would ultimately
      accrue to the bishops' benefit.

467. Moody, Joseph N. "The French Catholic Press in the
      Education Conflict of the 1840's." FHS 7 (Spring
      1972): 394-415.

      Maintains that true Catholic journalism in France
      during the nineteenth century was impossible; despite
      its zeal, the religious press was too uncertain, both
      methodologically and ideologically, as seen in its
      attitudes toward educational issues of the 1840s.

468. ————. "The French Catholic Press of the 1840's on
      American Catholicism." CHR 60 (July 1974): 185-
      214.

      Describes the treatment of the American Church in
      four prominent Catholic journals: *L'Ami de la*

religion (moderate royalist), *L'Univers* (imminently intransigent), *Le Correspondant* (liberal), and *L'Atelier* (socialist).

L'Ami de la religion

469. Dougherty, Mary Patricia. *L'AMI DE LA RELIGION* AND THE EARLY JULY MONARCHY: A CATHOLIC VIEW OF POLITICS, RELIGION, AND SOCIETY, Ph.D. dissertation. Georgetown University, 1984.

A study of the most important Catholic newspaper during the first ten years of the July Monarchy. Details its founding, early development, outlook, and relationship with the hierarchy. Emphasizes its rather cautious, even defensive, posture, given its fear of reawakening the violent anticlericalism of the past; yet, while considered wise by its editors, this posture only resulted in isolating the newspaper from the new forces at work within French society, including those which during the 1830s were attempting to reconcile Catholicism with the religiously neutral state of Louis-Philippe.

Le Correspondant

470. Augustine, Mother Flavia, R.C.S.J. *LE CORRESPONDANT*, FRENCH LIBERAL JOURNAL, 1843-1870. Ph.D. dissertation. The Catholic University of America, 1958.

Presents the editors' views concerning freedom of teaching, the relationship between the Church and modern society, deference to ecclesiastical authority, Napoleon III, and Pius IX.

471. Gimpl, Sister M. Caroline Ann. *THE CORRESPONDANT* AND THE FOUNDING OF THE FRENCH THIRD REPUBLIC. Washington, D.C.: Catholic University of America Press, 1959.

Details the attitudes of the review toward the major constitutional and political problems

confronting France between 1871 and 1875. Points to
its unoriginal program and lack of forceful leadership as a reflection of the inherent weaknesses of
liberal Catholicism, which it attempted to keep alive,
but in vain.

See: Evelyn M. Acomb, AHR 65 (January 1960): 416-7;
      Leon Bernard, CHR 46 (July 1960): 230-1; William
      Savage, JMH 32 (September 1960): 304-5; J.P.T.
      Bury, EHR 75 (October 1960): 738; Walter D.
      Gray, RP 24 (April 1962): 299.

472. Kenny, Mary Elizabeth. "The *Correspondant*: Catholic
      Liberalism in the Cultural Press in Nineteenth-
      Century France." ABR 38 (September 1987): 243-60.

      Focuses on the literary critics who contributed
      over the course of the century to a journal which
      sought to reconcile Catholicism and the modern world.
      Includes biographical sketches of Father Félix Klein,
      François-Adolphe Mathurin de Lescure, Edmond Biré,
      René Doumic, Armand de Pontmartin, and Victor Fournel.

473. McElrath, Damian, O.F.M. "Richard Simpson and Count
      de Montalembert, the *Rambler* and the *Correspon-
      dant*." DR 84 (April 1966): 150-70.

      Compares Montalembert's work on the *Correspondant*
      with that of his counterpart, Richard Simpson of the
      Rambler, across the Channel. Delineates, using their
      unpublished correspondence of 1859, their respective
      positions on a number of issues which were of concern
      to liberal Catholics.

                          L'Ere nouvelle

474. Smith, Sister Mary Avila, C.S.J. *L'ERE NOUVELLE*,
      ORGAN OF CATHOLIC POLITICAL AND SOCIAL THOUGHT,
      1848-1849. Ph.D. dissertation. St. Louis
      University, 1965.

      Follows in detail the twelve months of a joint
      clerical and lay enterprise, designed to persuade
      French Catholics to adapt their political and
      social attitudes to the contemporary revolutionary

situation in Europe. Attributes its short life to
internal dissension and attacks not only from the
hierarchy and other Catholic journals, but also
from such prominent liberal laymen as Montalembert.

L'Univers

475. Brown, Marvin L., Jr. LOUIS VEUILLOT: FRENCH
ULTRAMONTANE CATHOLIC JOURNALIST AND LAYMAN,
1813-1883. Durham, N.C.: Moore Publishing,
1977.

Recounts his life and work, using wherever possible
his own words, and placing him solidly within the
larger political, intellectual, and religious scene.
Neither laudatory nor condemnatory; an objective study
of a personality too often obscured by partisanship.

See: George D. Balsama, AHR 83 (October 1978): 1026-
7; Joseph N. Moody, CHR 65 (October 1979): 665-
7.

476. Ghezzi, Bertil William. *L'UNIVERS* AND THE DEFINITION
OF PAPAL INFALLIBILITY. Ph.D. dissertation.
University of Notre Dame, 1969.

Illustrates how Veuillot's *L'Univers* exerted
considerable influence upon Vatican I's decision to
declare papal infallibility, by helping to create
the circumstances within which it was thought
proper to make the declaration, and by strongly
opposing both the power and the arguments of anti-
infallibilists as expressed during the Council's
daily sessions.

* Gooch, G.P. "Louis Veuillot and the Press." FRENCH
PROFILES: PROPHETS AND PIONEERS (item 373), 235-
43.

Accounts for his intellectual hold upon a large
segment of French Catholics.

477. Gurian, Waldemar. "Louis Veuillot." CHR 36
(January 1951): 385-414.

Portrays Veuillot as a lifelong crusader for truth
and salvation, whose shortcomings must be understood
against the background of a time in which polemics
and politics were more important than the subtleties
of theology and Christian philosophy.

478. Jules-Bois, H.A. "Veuillot of *L'Univers*." COMMWL
          27 (8 April 1938): 655-6.

Excuses his acerbity as the fanaticism of an
over-generous soul. Mitigates accusations of
coldness by pointing to his faithfulness to family
and friends.

479. ————. "Veuillot, Master of Obedience." COMMWL 27
          (1 April 1938): 623-4.

Distinguishes three major causes to which he
showed fanatical devotion throughout his life as a
Catholic: freedom of teaching, papal infallibility,
and the restoration of the temporal power; he considered their promotion a religious duty.

480. Myers, E. "Louis Veuillot." CW 77 (August
          1903): 597-610.

Discusses the political and social conditions
which formed the background for Veuillot's career.

  *   Neill, Thomas P. "Louis Veuillot." THEY LIVED THE
          FAITH (item 33), 299-324.

Traces his controversial personality to a refusal
to compromise with his age. Evaluates the images he
earned during his lifetime: "more Catholic than the
pope," and "more Ultramontane than the General of
the Jesuit Order."

481. ————. "Louis Veuillot and the February Revolution."
          HB 28 (May 1950): 75-6, 82-7.

Argues that Veuillot never opposed republicanism
or democracy in theory, but only in practice, after
witnessing the disintegration of the Second Republic.
Faults him, however, for not giving the republicans
a sufficient trial period before declaring his
opposition to them.

* Parsons, Reuben. "Louis Veuillot." STUDIES IN
     CHURCH HISTORY, 6 (item 27), 427-40.

  A highly positive view of a journalist who
  sought no other pleasures but the service of
  God and the mastery of grandeur.

* Simpson, W.J. Sparrow. "Louis Veuillot." FRENCH
     CATHOLICS IN THE NINETEENTH CENTURY (item 376),
     107-21.

  Focuses on his newspaper campaign in favor of
  papal infallibility.

* Spencer, Philip. "Veuillot's Triumph." POLITICS
     OF BELIEF IN NINETEENTH-CENTURY FRANCE: LA-
     CORDAIRE, MICHON, VEUILLOT (item 433), 199-260.

  An unflattering treatment. Stresses Veuillot's
  strenuous and oftentimes uncharitable efforts on
  behalf of ultramontanism. Leaves the vivid
  impression of a true believer, rigid philosopher,
  and passionate absolutist, living in a world in
  which few shared his belief, most rejected his
  philosophy, and democracy was on the move.

482. Stuart, Henry Longan. "Louis Veuillot (I)." COMMWL
     1 (12 November 1924): 15-16.

  Attributes Veuillot's unpopularity to the volatile
  interaction between his temperament and the events of
  his time. Continues in item 483.

483. ————. "Louis Veuillot (II)." COMMWL 1 (19
     November 1924): 44-5.

  Continued from item 482. Addresses the oft-
  repeated charge that Veuillot was simply a muckraker.

La Croix

484. Arnal, Oscar. "The Ambivalent *Ralliement* of *La
     Croix*." JEH 31 (January 1980): 89-106.

  Uses statements found in *La Croix*, the press

voice of Catholic leaders in Third Republic France,
to suggest that the *Ralliement* of the 1890s, with
its public acceptance of modern democracy and social
change, was much slower and more uncertain than
traditional scholarship has implied.

485. Grenier, Joseph A. "An Apostolate of Battle: *La
      Croix*, 1883-1890." CHR 67 (April 1981): 214-35.

      An abridgement of item 486. Inquires into the
      intellectual position of the Assumptionist newspaper
      during its first seven years of publication.
      Concludes that, its originality and fervor notwith-
      standing, *La Croix* exercised no real influence upon
      the political or religious situation of the late
      nineteenth-century French Church.

486. ————. TO REACH THE PEOPLE: *LA CROIX*, 1883-1890.
      Ph.D. dissertation. Fordham University, 1976.

      Examines the newspaper's goals during its early
      years, and the way in which its editors, anxious
      to bring their message to common people, handled
      various subjects in the light of their goals.
      Attributes its limited impact to the somewhat
      constricting Christian mentality which guided its
      editors from the first. For a shorter version of
      this analysis, see item 485.

487. Marion, Raymond Joseph. *LA CROIX* AND THE *RALLIEMENT*.
      Ph.D. dissertation. Clark University, 1957.

      Shows how the Assumptionists, working through *La
      Croix*, their newspaper, played a significant part in
      the failure of the *Ralliement*. While the Order
      sincerely if unenthusiastically accepted the Leonine
      policy of reconciliation, it nevertheless continued
      throughout the 1890s to condemn much of the Third
      Republic's religious legislation. Blind zeal and
      short-sighted anti-Semitism, found in every issue of
      La Croix, discredited Rome's position and pushed the
      Assumptionists into the Dreyfus Affair, which
      ultimately proved their undoing.

488. Mather, Judson. "The Assumptionist Response to
      Secularization, 1870-1900." In MODERN EUROPEAN
      SOCIAL HISTORY, edited by Robert J. Bezucha,

59-89. Lexington, Mass.: D.C. Heath, 1972.

A summary of item 489.

See: CHOICE 9 (December 1972): 1344; William H.
Sewell, Jr., JMH 45 (September 1973): 467-8.

489. ————. *LA CROIX* AND THE ASSUMPTIONIST RESPONSE TO
SECULARIZATION IN FRANCE, 1870-1900. Ph.D.
dissertation. University of Michigan, 1971.

Describes how one of the Church's most conservative
orders used a modern medium to propagate its
reactionary views. Studies the ways in which the
Assumptionists popularized their belief in the demonic
character of modern society.

Piety and Devotion

490. Kselman, Thomas A. MIRACLES AND PROPHECIES IN
NINETEENTH-CENTURY FRANCE. New Brunswick,
N.J.: Rutgers University Press, 1983.

Documents the wave of religious fervor in France
as expressed through Marian apparitions, healings,
and millenarian prophecies. Uses archival material
as well as published devotional and prophetic
literature to analyze the dynamics of popular piety
and the manner in which these were adopted and used
by the Church to create a national community of
belief. Establishes at the same time the relationship between the manifestations of religious revival
and an increasingly secularized society characterized
by industrialization, urbanization, and political
turmoil.

See: Hillel Schwartz, RSR 10 (April 1984): 185;
Charles Rearick, AHR 89 (June 1984): 782-3;
Michael Phayer, CHR 70 (July 1984): 484-5;
John W. Padberg, S.J., CH 53 (September
1984): 414-5; Gregor Dallas, JSH 18 (Spring
1985): 507-9; David Higgs, JMH 57 (September
1985): 564-7; Maurice Larkin, EHR 101 (April
1986): 531-2.

491. Phayer, J. Michael. "Politics and Popular
        Religion: The Cult of the Cross in France,
        1815-1840." JSH 11 (Spring 1978): 346-65.

        Asserts that instead of being a milestone in
        the ongoing process of dechristianization, the
        removal, defacement, or destruction of mission
        crosses throughout France during the years 1830-
        1833 actually signalled a strengthening of
        popular faith, for now it was shorn of all
        political associations and could thus provide
        a sound basis from which French society could
        continue to modernize. Contains much data on
        the rise and mechanics of the cult of the cross.

*   Pourrat, Pierre, S.S. "The Nineteenth Century in
        France." CHRISTIAN SPIRITUALITY. Vol. 4: FROM
        JANSENISM TO MODERN TIMES (item 319), 469-527.

        Balances the activists who contributed to the
        rebuilding of the French Church during the first
        half of the century against the writers. Included
        among the former are John Joseph Allemand (1772-
        1836), who originated the *Oeuvres de jeunesse*; St.
        John Baptist Vianney; John Claud Colin (1790-1875),
        founder of the Society of Mary; Pauline Jaricot;
        Antony Chevrier (1826-1879), a model of clerical
        poverty; Francis Paul Libermann; and Leo Papin
        Dupont (1797-1876), who popularized the devotion
        to the Holy Face. Among the latter are Ozanam,
        Lacordaire, and Charles Gay (1815-1892).

*   Steuart, R.H.J., S.J. "Marie-Eustelle Harpain."
        DIVERSITY IN HOLINESS (item 34), 115-32.

        Sketches the life and personality of a provincial
        woman whose fame rested upon her absolute devotion
        to the Eucharist and selfless service to others.

                    The Liturgical Movement

492. Franklin, R.W. "Guéranger: A View on the Centenary
        of His Death." WOR 49 (June/July 1975): 318-28.

        Places Guéranger's liturgical renewal within an

international context, paralleling its main features
and aims with those of Keble at Oxford and Möhler at
Tübingen. Disputes the traditional image of
Guéranger as a fanatical ultramontane, arguing that
he was in fact a far-reaching reformer who revived
the Church not through ecclesiastical or political
parties, but through an international network of
liturgically aware parishes and monasteries.

493. ————. "Guéranger and Pastoral Liturgy: A
      Nineteenth Century Context." WOR 50 (March
      1976): 146-62.

      Discusses the applications of Guéranger's liturgic-
      al vision to various nineteenth-century parochial
      situations.

494. ————. "Guéranger and Variety in Unity." WOR 51
      (September 1977): 378-99.

      Explains Guéranger's view of the proper balance
      between the Roman liturgy as the Church's one model
      of worship and the variant liturgies of the national,
      and especially French, churches.

495. Johnson, Dom Cuthbert. "Dom Prosper Guéranger, Abbot
      of Solesmes, 1805-1875." CLR 60 (February
      1975): 95-102.

      An account of his life and work. Contends that
      he understood the Church better than any of his
      contemporaries. Fixes his place in ecclesiastical
      history as father of the nineteenth-century liturgic-
      al movement and restorer of Benedictine life in post-
      revolutionary France.

Social Catholicism

General

496. Moon, Parker Thomas. THE LABOR PROBLEM AND THE
      SOCIAL CATHOLIC MOVEMENT IN FRANCE. New
      York: Macmillan, 1921.

Highlights the motivations of the leading agents
of social Catholicism. Sympathizes with the pleas
of Lamennais, Lacordaire, Montalembert, Ozanam, and
de Mun. Views the post-1848 interplay of clerical
and political forces on behalf of the poor less
admiringly.

See: R.S. Meriam, APSR 15 (November 1921): 600-2;
      DUBR 170 (January/February/March 1922): 147-
      50; CHR 8 (April 1922): 89-91; R.A. McGowan,
      JPE 30 (June 1922): 594-5.

497. ————. "The Social Catholic Movement in France
      under the Third Republic." CHR 7 (April
      1921): 24-34.

A continuation, in significantly briefer form,
of the historical sketch found in item 496.
Considers de Mun's Workingmen's Clubs the prime
example of a force which ranks as one of the three
or four most important efforts aimed at a radical
modification of the capitalist system.

498. Moser, Mary Theresa. THE EVOLUTION OF THE OPTION
      FOR THE POOR IN FRANCE, 1880-1965. Washington,
      D.C.: University Press of America, 1985.

Analyzes the late nineteenth-century Church's
perception of the needs of the poor, using both
historical narrative and sociological theory.

See: Leonard J. Weber, HRZNS 13 (Fall 1986): 425-6.

499. Schwartz, Sister M. Christina. THE CATHOLIC CHURCH
      WORKING THROUGH ITS INDIVIDUAL MEMBERS IN ANY AGE
      AND NATION MAKES A POSITIVE SOCIAL CONTRIBUTION
      AS SEEN IN FRANCE, 1815-1870. Washington,
      D.C.: Catholic University of America Press,
      1939.

Provides sketches of forty-one men and women, both
religious and lay, who distinguished themselves in
one or more of the following activities: relief of
the poor, service to the sick, care of the homeless
and downtrodden, education, and spiritual minis-
trations (e.g., parish missions, retreats, individual
direction).

* Vidler, Alec R. "France." A CENTURY OF SOCIAL
  CATHOLICISM, 1820-1920 (item 315), 3-78, 112-
  40.

  An extended survey of the rich variety of French
  social Catholicism through most of the nineteenth
  century. Examines in turn the programs and impact
  of Lamennais and the *Avenir* circle, Villeneuve-
  Bargemont, the Christian socialists of the 1830s
  and 40s (Buchez and Fourier), Armand de Melun and
  his fellow conservatives under the July Monarchy,
  the Christian democrats of 1848 (Maret, Ozanam, and
  the staff of *L'Ere nouvelle*), the conservative
  social theoreticians of the Second Empire (Le Play
  and Périn), and the post-1870 conservatives, both
  lay and clerical (de Mun, La Tour du Pin, and
  Harmel).

Jaricot

500. Burton, Katherine. DIFFICULT STAR: THE LIFE OF
     PAULINE JARICOT. New York: Longmans, Green,
     1947.

     Follows her passage from being the daughter of a
     wealthy silk-merchant in Lyons, to becoming a model
     of Catholic Action, involved in projects as diverse
     as the "Living Rosary," the Society for the Propa-
     gation of the Faith, and, fifty years before *Rerum
     Novarum*, programs for the material betterment of
     workers.

     See: Joseph P. Ryan, CHR 33 (January 1948): 466-8.

501. Canning, Bernard J. "Pauline Jaricot (1862-1962),
     Foundress of the Association for the Propagation
     of the Faith." IER 98 (December 1962): 303-6.

     A short account of her spiritual transformation
     at eighteen, and the activities which it inspired
     during the rest of her life.

502. Corrigan, Raymond, S.J. "A Catholic Lay
     Leader: Pauline Jaricot." CW 150 (January
     1940): 414-9.

Touches upon the high points of her intensely active career, including the physical and mental suffering, prayer and action, dreams and dis-illusionments, and triumphs and defeats.

503. Hickey, Edward John. THE SOCIETY FOR THE PROPAGATION OF THE FAITH: ITS FOUNDATION, ORGANIZATION AND SUCCESS (1822-1922). Washington, D.C.: Catholic University of America Press, 1922.

Chapter 2 details the establishment of the Society by Jaricot, Mme. Petit, and Benoît Coste; Chapter 3 examines the deliberations of the organizational meetings at Lyons (3-25 May 1822), which resulted in a definite structure and a rule.

504. Moore, Mina J. "Pauline Jaricot: A Daughter of Lyons." IER 59 (February 1942): 172-84.

Concentrates on her roles as foundress of the Society for the Propagation of the Faith (1818) and initiator of the "Living Rosary" (1826).

*   Neill, Thomas P. "Pauline Marie Jaricot." THEY LIVED THE FAITH (item 33), 123-44.

Discusses her diverse apostolic activity, going beyond the standard treatment of her two celebrated achievements (item 504), to comment upon those which are not as well-known.

Ozanam

505. Cadwallader, Raymond, S.J. "Ozanam: Christian Teacher." AMER 49 (24 June 1933): 278-9.

Illustrates Ozanam's deep devotion to teaching and research; though exacting in his demands for creative thinking and precision, he was loved by his students.

506. Fitzsimons, John. "Pioneers of Social Work: I. Frédéric Ozanam, Apostle of Charity and Truth." CLR 29 (January 1948): 36-43.

Measures his deepening involvement with social
problems over the years, leading to the foundation
of the Society of Saint Vincent de Paul.

* Gooch, G.P. "Ozanam and the Claims of Charity."
   FRENCH PROFILES: PROPHETS AND PIONEERS (item
   373), 226-34.

   A brief biography, emphasizing his activity as
   friend of the friendless.

* Horgan, John J. "Frédéric Ozanam: Founder of the
   Society of St. Vincent de Paul." GREAT CATHOLIC
   LAYMEN (item 31), 95-158.

   Offers several examples of Ozanam's life of
   service to the poor and homeless.

507. Husslein, Joseph, S.J. "Ozanam on Employers and
     Employed." AMER 10 (18 October 1913): 29-30.

     Stresses Ozanam's belief that justice and charity
     must regulate all employer-employee dealings, and
     that the government must intervene, when necessary,
     to prevent exploitation of the workers.

508. ———. "Ozanam on Labor and Wages." AMER 10
     (11 October 1913): 8-10.

     Summarizes the two leading aspects of Ozanam's
     economic philosophy: his categories of labor
     (physical, intellectual, and moral) and his criteria
     for determining a proper wage (faithful service,
     educational background, and strength).

509. ———. "Ozanam on Liberalism and Socialism." AMER
     9 (4 October 1913): 609-11.

     Explains Ozanam's rejection of both liberalism and
     socialism as proper solutions to the social question
     of his day; each in its own way robbed humanity of
     its religious dimension.

510. ———. "Ozanam on Poverty and Wealth." AMER 10
     (25 October 1913): 55-7.

     Discovers Ozanam's solution to the social problem

in the ideal of charity, which the rich must be
encouraged to practice, so as to diminish the
vast inequities between classes.

511. Klaas, Augustine, S.J. "Frederick Ozanam, Pioneer of
      Catholic Action." AMER 49 (20 May 1933): 150-1.

      Describes how a History club for students at the
      Sorbonne, founded under Ozanam's direction in 1832,
      was transformed into the Society of Saint Vincent de
      Paul.

  *   Neill, Thomas P. "Frédéric Ozanam." THEY LIVED THE
      FAITH (item 33), 145-65.

      An overview of Ozanam's life and religious
      activity; sees him as the ideal combination of
      Christian scholarship and activism.

  *   Parsons, Reuben. "Ozanam." STUDIES IN CHURCH
      HISTORY, 5 (item 26), 303-19.

      Sketches Ozanam's character and achievements.
      Salutes him as *the* great layman of the nineteenth
      century.

512. Schimberg, Albert Paul. THE GREAT FRIEND: FREDERICK
      OZANAM. Milwaukee: Bruce, 1946.

      Spotlights the contributions to Catholic thought
      made by a man who at one time or another had been
      closely associated with Lamennais, Lacordaire, Mont-
      alembert, Veuillot, Gerbet, Migne, and other
      intellectual luminaries of the day.

      See: Theodore Roemer, CHR 32 (April 1946): 72-4;
            C. Bruehl, SJR 39 (November 1946): 247;
            Raymond W. Schouten, THOUGHT 21 (December
            1946): 754-5.

                        De Mun

513. Lynch, Sister Miriam. THE ORGANIZED SOCIAL
      APOSTOLATE OF ALBERT DE MUN. The Catholic
      University of America Studies in Sociology,

vol. 36. Washington, D.C.: Catholic University
of America Press, 1952.

Looks into de Mun's work with formal humanitarian
associations on behalf of workers. Describes the
origins, nature and purpose, membership, structure
and function of each group with which de Mun was
connected, his role within that group, and the long-
term influence he may have exerted over it.

See: Liam Brophy, SJR 45 (September 1952): 156;
CLR 38 (April 1953): 253; Robert F. Byrnes,
CHR 39 (July 1953): 203-4.

514. Martin, Benjamin F. COUNT ALBERT DE MUN: PALADIN
OF THE THIRD REPUBLIC. Chapel Hill: University
of North Carolina Press, 1978.

A detailed portrait of an intellectual anomaly: a
political conservative whose social outlook, rooted
in Christian precepts, often found favor solely among
the extreme left. Balances his absolute devotion to
the Church with the Vatican's frequent reservations
concerning his social idealism and hearty acceptance
of the Third Republic.

See: James J. Cooke, HRNB 7 (February 1979): 86;
CHOICE 16 (April 1979): 283; John Rothney,
AHR 84 (October 1979): 1067-8; Alexander
Sedgwick, JMH 51 (December 1979): 820-1;
Maurice Larkin, EHR 95 (July 1980): 666-7;
Marvin L. Brown, Jr., CHR 67 (April 1981): 336-
7.

* Neill, Thomas P. "Albert de Mun." THEY LIVED THE
FAITH (item 33), 166-89.

Compresses de Mun's intense activity into a
battle for three causes: poor workers, the Church,
and France; these three were inextricably bound
together in his mind. Claims that his outlook,
though never fully embodied in French law, prepared
the way for such progressive papal pronouncements as
Rerum Novarum.

515. Porter, Richard L., S.J. "Albert De Mun and Social
Catholicism." HB 18 (January 1940): 29-30, 41-2.

Enumerates the obstacles faced by de Mun both from inside and from outside the Church.

Others

516. Griffiths, Gordon. "The Vicomte Armand de Melun and the Catholic Social Movement in France, 1848-1851." In STUDIES IN MODERN EUROPEAN HISTORY IN HONOR OF FRANKLIN CHARLES PALM, edited by Frederick Cox, Bernerd C. Weber, Richard M. Brace, and John F. Ramsey, 141-56. New York: Bookman, 1956.

Reconstructs Melun's efforts to bring charity into the politics of the Second Republic. After his election to the Assembly in 1849 he instigated a large amount of social legislation, but realized that class conflict could only be avoided through massive government intervention in everyday life. With Louis Napoleon's coup in 1851, and the subsequent resurgence of Le Play's *laissez-faire* economics, Melun turned social Catholicism away from republicanism and toward royalism.

See: Huntley Dupre, AHR 62 (July 1957): 891-2.

517. Necheles, Ruth F. THE ABBE GREGOIRE, 1787-1831: THE ODYSSEY OF AN EGALITARIAN. Contributions in Afro-American and African Studies, vol. 9. Westport, Conn.: Greenwood, 1971.

Reviews Grégoire's egalitarian campaign on behalf of blacks and Jews, a campaign no doubt weakened by his own association with the schismatic revolutionary Church, but nevertheless representative of all that was best in the enlightened tradition of nineteenth-century liberal Catholicism.

See: CHOICE 9 (April 1972): 270; Joseph N. Moody, CHR 58 (April 1972): 89-91; Joan Brace, IJAHS 5 (no. 3, 1972): 485-7; John W. Padberg, S.J., CH 41 (December 1972): 548; Isser Woloch, JMH 45 (March 1973): 138-40; Peter N. Stearns, AHR 78 (October 1973): 1074-5; Eric A. Arnold, RMSSJ 11 (April 1974): 120-1.

518. Ring, Sister Mary Ignatius, S.N.D. VILLENEUVE-
      BARGEMONT: PRECURSOR OF MODERN SOCIAL
      CATHOLICISM, 1784-1850. Milwaukee: Bruce,
      1935.

      Details the intellectual struggles and social
      apostolate of one of the earliest, most passionate,
      and most gifted champions of workers' rights in
      nineteenth-century France. Follows his shift away
      from the classical economics of Adam Smith and
      Jean Baptiste Say and toward a belief in the
      necessity of government activity on behalf of
      labor. Points to his devout Catholicism as the
      motive force behind his revised economic outlook;
      his insistence that human beings and their welfare
      should take precedence over the production of
      wealth, repeated several times in his ECONOMIE
      POLITIQUE CHRETIENNE (1834), makes him one of Leo
      XIII's leading precursors.

      See: Herbert C. Noonan, AMER 53 (22 June 1935): 257-
            8; William G. Welk, AAAPSS 183 (January
            1936): 280-1.

                       Art and Literature

                           Painting

519. Spector, Jack J. THE MURALS OF EUGENE DELACROIX AT
      SAINT-SULPICE. New York: College Art Association
      of America, 1967.

      A study of what is widely considered the finest
      religious art produced in nineteenth-century France.
      Examines every major aspect of the process underlying
      the creation of the three paintings in the Chapelle
      des Saints-Anges (1849-1861): the circumstances
      under which the skeptical artist accepted the
      commission and worked, the evolution of his compo-
      sitional ideas, the influence of older masters
      (Raphael, Titian, and Rubens) upon his style and
      technique, and the long-term influence of the entire
      work.

See: CHOICE 6 (June 1969): 504; TLS, 31 July
       1969: 850.

Music

520.   Shebbeare, Dom Alphege.   "Dom Mocquereau."   DR 48
          (May 1930):   122-39.

       Describes and evaluates Mocquereau's campaign
    to restore Gregorian chant to its rightful place
    within Catholic worship.   Emphasizes the diversity
    of his efforts, from his research into, and
    classification of, ancient manuscripts, to his
    writings on the beauties of medieval technique, to
    his establishment of the internationally famous
    monastic choir at Solesmes in 1889.

Literature

521.   Brophy, Liam.   "J.K. Huysmans, Aesthete Turned
          Ascetic."   IER 86 (July 1956):   43-51.

       Clarifies Huysmans' view of Lourdes, as expressed
    in LES FOULES DE LOURDES (1906).   Argues, against
    the claim that he was attacking the shrine, that he
    was denouncing only the shoddy ecclesiastical art
    which he found surrounding the Grotto.   Places this
    controversy within his larger spiritual journey.

*   Gooch, G.P.   "Chateaubriand and the Charms of
          Christianity."   FRENCH PROFILES: PROPHETS AND
          PIONEERS (item 373), 157-70.

       Presents Chateaubriand's belief in the inter-
    penetration of great literature and Christianity
    through the ages.

522.   Griffiths, Richard.   "The Catholic Revival: Reaction
          Then and Now."   CLR 57 (October 1972):   765-73.

       Accounts for the reactionary nature of the
    Catholic resurgence in late nineteenth-century
    French literature.   Roots it in the authors'

extreme anguish over dangerous changes in what they
considered traditional doctrine.

523.   ————. THE REACTIONARY REVOLUTION: THE CATHOLIC
         REVIVAL IN FRENCH LITERATURE, 1870-1914.
         New York: Frederick Ungar, 1965.

         Documents the dynamic growth of a strongly
         Catholic literature, represented by Barbey
         d'Aurevilly, Villiers de l'Isle-Adam, Bloy,
         Bourget, Claudel, Huysmans, Péguy, and a host
         of lesser lights. Traces the process by which
         pre-1870 writers--for the most part, anti-
         Catholic, rationalistic, deistic, and
         positivistic--became after 1870 deeply involved
         in significant religious thought and stubbornly
         attached to the Church.

         See: Martin Turnell, SPEC 216 (14 January 1966): 46;
               F.W.J. Hemmings, NST 71 (11 February 1966): 196-
               7; Louis Allen, COMMWL 85 (28 October
               1966): 100-2; TLS, 22 December 1966: 1188;
               Bernard Bergonzi, ENC 28 (February 1967): 78-81;
               Douglas Johnson, EHR 82 (April 1967): 424; D.G.
               Charlton, MLR 62 (July 1967): 535-7.

524.   Master-Karnik, Paul Joseph. LEON BLOY AND LITERARY
         DISCOURSE: A STRUCTURAL APPROACH TO CATHOLICISM,
         LETTERS AND SOCIETY IN NINETEENTH CENTURY FRANCE.
         Ph.D. dissertation. Rutgers University, 1978.

         Uses the works of Bloy (1846-1917), an extremely
         conservative journalist, pamphleteer, and novelist,
         to challenge the traditional interpretation of the
         late nineteenth-century Catholic literary revival in
         France. Demonstrates that far from retreating into
         an aesthetic medievalism, Bloy and his colleagues
         proffered in their literary discourse a notably
         modern critique of contemporary society, politics,
         and economics.

525.   Moody, Joseph N. "Religion on the Parisian Stage in
         the 1840's." CHR 59 (July 1973): 245-63.

         Gauges the theatrical view of religion during a
         time of growing debate over the proper extent of
         Catholic influence in French public life. Finds a

mixed outlook, with playwrights either lauding
religion or presenting clerical foibles in a
gentle way; Catholicism had ceased to be the
polarizing issue it was during the Revolutionary
period a half-century earlier.

Special Challenges

Church and State

General

526.   Hegarty, W.J., C.C.   "Will the Napoleonic Concordat
       Survive?   III. The Concordat in Action, 1801-
       1905."   IER 65 (January 1945):   35-42.

       Argues that although the Concordat was flawed
    from the beginning, it at least brought religious
    peace to France and presided over a Church which
    made extraordinary progress throughout the century.

527.   McManners, John.   CHURCH AND STATE IN FRANCE, 1870-
       1914.   New York: Harper & Row, 1972.

       Follows the fortunes of the Church in its continu-
    ing struggle with the Third Republic.   Dismisses as
    absurd the anticlericals' perception of the Church's
    great strength, given the loss of the centralized
    ecclesiastical structures of the old order.   Focuses
    on the education issue as the main battleground
    between Church and State.

       See: John M. Roberts, EHR 88 (July 1973): 658-9;
              Maurice Larkin, JEH 24 (July 1973): 330-1;
              J.P.T. Bury, HIST 59 (February 1974): 137-8;
              C.R. Day, CHR 60 (July 1974): 296-7; Richard
              J. Schiefen, JCS 17 (Spring 1975): 316-8;
              Ralph Gibson, ESR 8 (April 1978): 278.

The Napoleonic Era

528. Sister M. Barbara, S.S.J. "Napoleon Bonaparte and
      the Restoration of Catholicism in France." CHR
      12 (July 1926): 241-57.

      Surveys the confused and confusing Church-State
      relations on the eve of the Concordat.

529. Barton, John M.T. "Napoleon's 'Divorce' from
      Josephine in 1810." CLR 43 (June 1958): 321-33.

      Recounts the circumstances surrounding the annul-
      ment of Napoleon's first marriage.

530. Hegarty, W.J., C.C. "Will the Napoleonic Concordat
      Survive? II. The Revolution, the Schism and the
      Making of the Concordat." IER 64 (December
      1944): 392-401.

      Details the negotiations leading up to the
      Concordat. Maintains that the reconciliation
      between Church and State was of far greater
      advantage to the latter.

531. Noakes, Robert. "Cardinal Erskine and Napoleon."
      DUBR 206 (January/February/March 1940): 102-14.

      Describes the difficulties of the Concordat-
      making process, as seen through the eyes of one
      of the leading ecclesiastical negotiators.

532. Plongeron, Bernard. "Napoleon I and Political
      Ethics." Translated by John Griffiths. In
      POWER, DOMINATION, SERVICE, edited by Franz
      Böckle and Jacques-Marie Pohier, 66-76.
      Concilium: Theology in the Age of Renewal,
      New Series, vol. 10, no. 9. London: Burns &
      Oates, 1973.

      Delineates the relationship between Napoleon and
      the Church, from the perspective of political
      morality. Shows that the imperial government
      attempted to defuse royalist-inspired clerical
      opposition by the careful appointment of Bonapartist
      bishops and by an emphasis on the Imperial Catechism

of 1806, which distorted Scripture by equating
opposition to the Emperor with opposition to
God.

533.   Grant, Hugh. "Napoleon and the Papacy." IER 79
       (June 1953): 422-8.

       Condemns Napoleon's harsh treatment of Pius VII.

534.   Hales, E.E.Y. THE EMPEROR AND THE POPE: THE STORY
       OF NAPOLEON AND PIUS VII. Garden City,
       N.Y.: Doubleday, 1961.

       Contrasts, through the events of 1799-1814, the
       arrogance of the powerful political ruler with the
       diffidence of the victimized spiritual leader.

       See: Helene Magaret, QR 300 (July 1962): 357-8;
             Alexander Dru, DR 81 (October 1962): 385-6;
             Joseph S. Brusher, CHR 48 (January 1963): 520-1.

  *   Parsons, Reuben. "The Pretended Divorces of Napoleon
       and Jerome Bonaparte." STUDIES IN CHURCH HISTORY,
       5 (item 26), 56-71.

       Illustrates Napoleon's heavy-handed campaign to
       pressure the Church into granting an annulment of
       the marriage of his brother Jerome, and then of his
       own marriage to Josephine.

535.   Patterson, Laurence K., S.J. "The Religion of
       Napoleon." HB 14 (May 1936): 71-2.

       Denies that Napoleon was a sincere believer; for
       him, religion was nothing more than a necessary
       social force. Continues in item 536.

536.   ————. "The Religion of Napoleon: II." HB 15
       (November 1936): 5-6.

       Continued from item 535. Speculates on the
       reasons behind Napoleon's apparent return to sincere
       belief during his time on St. Helena.

537.   Rose, J. Holland. NAPOLEONIC STUDIES. 3rd ed.
       London: G. Bell and Sons, 1914.

Doubts that Napoleon was a sincere Catholic,
adding that his attitudes toward religion were
determined by political, and not spiritual,
considerations. Asserts that at most he may
have wavered between a cynical materialism and
a vague theism, with the latter growing stronger
as the years went on.

See: E.D. Adams, DIAL 38 (16 January 1905): 41-3;
H. Nelson Gay, AHR 10 (April 1905): 658-61;
C.T. Atkinson, EHR 20 (April 1905): 388-90;
SHR 3 (July 1906): 513.

538. Walsh, Henry H. THE CONCORDAT OF 1801: A STUDY OF
THE PROBLEM OF NATIONALISM IN THE RELATIONS OF
CHURCH AND STATE. New York: Columbia University
Press, 1933.

Places heavy emphasis on the oftentimes diametrically opposed backgrounds and attitudes of the leading
lay and clerical personalities involved in the
Concordat negotiations.

See: G.E. Wilson, DALR 14 (April 1934): 128-9;
Eneas B. Goodwin, MID-AM 16 (April 1934): 253-
6; Louis Gottschalk, CH 3 (June 1934): 156-8.

The Second Empire

* Simpson, W.J. Sparrow. "Emile Ollivier." FRENCH
CATHOLICS IN THE NINETEENTH CENTURY (item 376),
143-63.

Reviews the masterful survey of Church-State
relations found in Ollivier's sixteen-volume
L'EMPIRE LIBERAL.

539. Wheeler, Lawrence Jefferson. THE CONFLICT BETWEEN
THE GOVERNMENT OF NAPOLEON III AND THE SOCIETY OF
SAINT VINCENT DE PAUL, 1860-1862. Ph.D.
dissertation. University of Georgia, 1972.

Reviews the circumstances leading up to the dis-
mantling of the Saint Vincent de Paul Society by the
Duc de Persigny, Napoleon III's Minister of the

Interior, in April 1862. Aware of the royalists' use
(or, more accurately, misuse) of the Society to
inspire resistance to the increasingly pro-Italian
position of France, Persigny charged its leadership
with having violated the Association Law of the Penal
Code of 1834, which prohibited religious or political
assemblies of more than twenty persons without
official authorization.

The Third Republic

540. Acomb, Evelyn M. THE FRENCH LAIC LAWS (1879-
      1889): THE FIRST ANTI-CLERICAL CAMPAIGN OF
      THE THIRD FRENCH REPUBLIC. New York: Columbia
      University Press, 1941.

      Traces the origins, development, and final victory
      of the political campaign against the Church during
      the first years of the Third Republic. Establishes
      the strengths and weaknesses of each of the protago-
      nists in the battle for control of education, while
      at the same time offering the key insight that the
      anticlerical fervor exhibited by positivists,
      materialists, deists, and other anti-Catholic
      elements was not unlike the missionary zeal of the
      institution against which they fought.

      See: Raymond Corrigan, S.J., HB 20 (November
            1941): 23; Emile Benoît-Smullyan, ASR 7
            (February 1942): 128; A. Paul Levack,
            THOUGHT 17 (March 1942): 172-3; John B.
            Wolf, AHR 47 (April 1942): 604-5; Leo L.
            Rummel, CHR 28 (April 1942): 91-3; F.W.
            Buckler, CH 11 (June 1942): 157-8; Thomas
            F. Power, RP 4 (July 1942): 356-7; Ralph
            T. Flewelling, PERS 23 (Autumn 1942): 437-8.

541. Bertocci, Philip A. JULES SIMON: REPUBLICAN ANTI-
      CLERICALISM AND CULTURAL POLITICS IN FRANCE, 1848-
      1866. Columbia: University of Missouri Press,
      1978.

      Distinguishes between Voltairean and political
      anticlericalism by presenting the early life and
      career of one unbeliever who opposed, but did not

hate, the Church, believing that hatred would in the long run lead to a prohibition of religious freedom.

See: CHOICE 15 (February 1979): 1711; Peter H. Amann, AHR 84 (April 1979): 468-9; Stuart L. Campbell, JMH 52 (March 1980): 152-3; R.D. Anderson, EHR 95 (April 1980): 441-2; Alexander Sedgwick, JCS 22 (Autumn 1980): 525-7; Joseph N. Moody, CHR 67 (April 1981): 329-30.

542. Jacob, James E. "Ethnic Identity and the Crisis of Separation of Church and State: The Case of the Basques of France, 1870-1914." JCS 24 (Spring 1982): 303-20.

Demonstrates how a deep sense of ethnicity helped mobilize Basque political support for the Church in its struggle against the anticlerical Third Republic.

543. Larkin, Maurice J.M. "The Church and the French Concordat, 1891 to 1902." EHR 81 (October 1966): 717-39.

Gauges the effects of the last decade of the concordatory regime upon the Church, concluding, contrary to the view of most ecclesiastics during that period, that Catholicism gained much more from the arrangement than it lost.

544. ————. CHURCH AND STATE AFTER THE DREYFUS AFFAIR; THE SEPARATION ISSUE IN FRANCE. New York: Barnes & Noble, 1973.

The most complete general survey currently available. Like Partin (item 546), Larkin considers the Dreyfus Affair the prime motivation behind the anticlericals' demands for the separation of Church and State. Refines traditional interpretations, however, by closer inspection of the mentalities of the leading figures in the conflict (e.g., the reluctant anticlericalism of Combes, the fearfulness of Pius X and Merry del Val) and the impact of the political measures both in the short and long term.

See: ECON 250 (16-22 February 1974): 110; Theodore Zeldin, NST 87 (22 February 1974): 261-2; James F. McMillan, AMPJ 79 (Summer 1974): 93;

CHOICE 11 (September 1974): 1011; TLS, 22
November 1974: 1322; John W. Padberg, S.J.,
CH 44 (March 1975): 125-6; Alec R. Vidler,
JEH 26 (April 1975): 203; Wallace Sokolsky,
AAAPSS 419 (May 1975): 170-1; J.P.T. Bury,
EHR 90 (July 1975): 677-8; Alexander
Sedgwick, AHR 80 (December 1975): 1347-8;
Joseph N. Moody, CHR 62 (October 1976): 643-
5; Ralph L. Lynn, JCS 18 (Winter 1976): 127-
9; Jack Hayward, APSR 71 (June 1977): 779-80;
Ralph Gibson, ESR 8 (April 1978): 279-80;
Ronald Burke, RSR 7 (October 1981): 292.

545. Lugan, Abbé Alphonse. "How Politics Has Injured
Religion in France." Translated by Leo Ward.
DUBR 184 (January/February/March 1929): 95-109.

Contends that the course of nineteenth-century
French politics forced the Church into a partner-
ship with intransigent royalism; and as the fortunes
of royalism declined, so also did those of
Catholicism.

* Parsons, Reuben. "A Fighting Clergy and the
Ecclesiastical Canons." STUDIES IN CHURCH
HISTORY, 6 (item 27), 132-8.

Outlines the Church's reaction to the government's
decision in 1889 to draft priests.

* ————. "Pope Leo XIII and the Third French
Republic." STUDIES IN CHURCH HISTORY, 6
(item 27), 203-16.

Discusses Papal efforts to solve the political and
religious conflict between Church and State in
France; contrasts the humanitarianism of de Mun,
aimed at restoring national peace, with the Masonic
promotion of continuing discord.

* ————. "The Third French Republic as a Persecutor
of the Church." STUDIES IN CHURCH HISTORY, 6
(item 27), 111-32.

Points to Freemasonry as the source of anticlerical
initiatives in the fields of education and compulsory
military service.

546. Partin, Malcolm O. WALDECK-ROUSSEAU, COMBES, AND
      THE CHURCH: THE POLITICS OF ANTICLERICALISM,
      1899-1905. Durham, N.C.: Duke University
      Press, 1969.

      A detailed treatment of the only period in post-
      1800 French history when moderate anticlericals
      were willing to follow the lead of their radical
      colleagues in establishing an officially anti-
      Catholic religious policy. Sees the Church's
      attitude during the Dreyfus Affair as the crucial
      element in forging the moderate-radical alliance.

      See: CHOICE 6 (November 1969): 1290; Maurice J.M.
            Larkin, HIST 55 (June 1970): 296; David L.
            Schalk, JMH 42 (September 1970): 442-4;
            Joseph N. Moody, CHR 59 (April 1973): 117-
            8; Ralph Gibson, ESR 8 (April 1978): 278-9.

  *   Schapiro, J. Salwyn. "Triumph of Anticlericalism in
        the Third French Republic." ANTICLERICALISM: CON-
        FLICT BETWEEN CHURCH AND STATE IN FRANCE, ITALY,
        AND SPAIN (item 230), 57-71.

      A brief account of republican legislation aimed at
      breaking the power of the Church over French society.

                Catholic Political Activity

547. Brown, Marvin L., Jr. "Catholic-Legitimist Militancy
        in the Early Years of the Third French Republic."
        CHR 60 (July 1974): 233-54.

      Examines the structure and activities of the
      alliance between traditionalist Catholics and the
      followers of the Comte de Chambord, the legitimist
      pretender, up to 1883. Indicates that their
      cooperation was based more on negative than on
      positive motivations, that is, more on a shared
      resentment over political and social developments
      than on a common enthusiasm for a specific program.

548. Byrnes, Robert F. "The French Christian Democrats in
        the 1890's: Their Appearance and Their Failure."
        CHR 36 (October 1950): 286-306.

A portrait of the Party's origins, major personalities, leaders, and program. Attributes its failure
to two decisive factors: (1) the absence of a true
understanding of political and social democracy by
the members themselves; and (2) the inability to
attract either the Catholic masses, who were repelled
by the group's radical ideas and anti-Semitism, or
the republicans, who normally supported radicals or
socialists.

549.   Cobban, Alfred. "The Influence of the Clergy and the
       'Institeurs Primaires' in the Election of the
       French Constituent Assembly, April 1848." EHR 57
       (July 1942): 334-44.

       Details the clergy's determined intervention in
       the political affairs of the nascent Second Republic,
       in an effort to assure the election of representatives
       who would attempt to incorporate the Church's stands
       on education, divorce, and the freedom of religious
       orders into the new constitution.

550.   Collins, Ross William. CATHOLICISM AND THE SECOND
       FRENCH REPUBLIC, 1848-1852. New York: Published
       by Longmans, Green for Columbia University, 1923.

       Uses contemporary religious journals and pamphlets,
       supplemented by the memoirs and correspondence of
       leading political figures, to show the diversity of
       Catholic reaction to the establishment and development
       of the Second Republic. Includes lengthy discussions
       of the impact of the June Days upon liberal Catho-
       licism, the debate over the Falloux Law, the Church's
       support of Louis Napoleon Bonaparte, and the French
       restoration of Pius IX to Rome.

       See: Robert H. Lord, APSR 18 (May 1924): 416-7;
              David Baird Smith, SHR 21 (July 1924): 310;
              E.L. Woodward, EHR 39 (October 1924): 638-9;
              Clyde L. Grose, JAH 11 (December 1924): 429-
              30.

551.   Detert, Sister Mary Xavier, C.S.J. CATHOLIC POLITICAL
       ACTIVITY IN FRANCE, 1892-1914. Ph.D. dissertation.
       The Catholic University of America, 1963.

       Investigates the structure, aims, activities, and

interrelationships of various Catholic political
groups, including the *ralliés*, the Christian
Democrats, and the Electoral Federation of 1898.
Attributes their disappointing performance to
their inability to work together, and to the
repugnance which most French showed for
confessional politics.

552. Ducattillon, J.V., O.P. "The Church in the Third
  Republic." RP 6 (January 1944): 74-93.

  Spells out the reasons for the hostility between
  post-1870 republicanism and Catholicism, tracing
  each to its antecedents as found in the political
  and religious crisis begun in 1789 by the Revolution.

553. Fitzpatrick, Brian. CATHOLIC ROYALISM IN THE
  DEPARTMENT OF THE GARD, 1814-1852. New
  York: Cambridge University Press, 1983.

  Illustrates how the strong religious basis of
  politics in the Gard inspired loyalties which
  transcended class and survived through three
  different political regimes.

  See: Roger Bullen, BBN, September 1983: 549-50;
  R.D. Anderson, JEH 35 (January 1984): 172;
  Alan B. Spitzer, AHR 89 (June 1984): 783-4;
  David Higgs, JMH 57 (September 1985): 564-
  5; David Longfellow, JCS 27 (Winter 1985): 144-
  5; Robert Gildea, EHR 101 (January 1986): 267-8;
  Guillaume de Bertier de Sauvigny, CHR 72
  (April 1986): 299-300.

554. Moody, Joseph N. "Catholicism and Society in
  France: Catholic Social and Political
  Movements, 1789-1950. I. From Old Regime to
  Democratic Society." In CHURCH AND
  SOCIETY: CATHOLIC SOCIAL AND POLITICAL THOUGHT
  AND MOVEMENTS, 1789-1950 (item 308), 95-186.

  Presents in some detail the evolution, expecta-
  tions, successes and failures of Catholic political
  thought and involvement through the course of the
  nineteenth century.

555. Pickersgill, J.W. "The French Plebiscite of 1870

and the Catholics." EHR 52 (April 1937): 254-66.

Distinguishes three major viewpoints among Catholic
voters: (1) the legitimist, which opposed the Second
Empire in principle, and therefore urged either
abstention or a negative vote; (2) the liberal, which
refused to commit itself, out of fear that the
plebiscite might in the long run lead to a revival of
Bonapartist authoritarianism, despite the recent
restoration of true parliamentary government; and (3)
the ultramontanist, which cared little for principle,
and was willing to sell its vote in return for a more
favorable imperial attitude toward Vatican I.
Underscores the fact that in all three cases the
controlling factor was fear, and not enthusiasm.

556. Sutton, Michael. NATIONALISM, POSITIVISM AND
      CATHOLICISM: THE POLITICS OF CHARLES MAURRAS
      AND FRENCH CATHOLICS, 1890-1914. Cambridge
      Studies in the History and Theory of Politics.
      Cambridge: Cambridge University Press, 1982.

      Charts the impact of Maurras' ideas upon the
      political activity of those French Catholics who,
      while ignoring his unconcealed agnosticism, eagerly
      embraced his devotion to authority and hostility to
      individualism.

      See: R.K. Browne, MONTH 2nd NS 16 (April 1983): 143;
            Vincent Wright, BBN, June 1983: 397; Alec R.
            Vidler, JTS 34 (October 1983): 687-8; John
            Hellman, AHR 89 (February 1984): 140; R.P.
            Tombs, JEH 35 (October 1984): 652-3; R.D.
            Anderson, EHR 100 (October 1985): 927-8;
            Jean-Marie Mayeur, JMH 58 (March 1986): 332;
            Robert E. Sullivan, CHR 72 (April 1986): 334-5.

                    The Ralliement

557. Sedgwick, Alexander. THE RALLIEMENT IN FRENCH
      POLITICS, 1890-1898. Harvard Historical
      Studies, vol. 74. Cambridge: Harvard
      University Press, 1965.

Highlights the role of Etienne Lamy, hand-picked
in 1896 by Leo XIII to mobilize pro-republican
sentiment among his fellow Catholics. Describes
Lamy's creation of a political organization, in
anticipation of the general elections of 1898, and
the numerous obstacles encountered during the
process, particularly from his conservative
coreligionists.

See: CHOICE 2 (May 1965): 187; Evelyn M. Acomb, AHR
      71 (January 1966): 580-1; Eugen Weber, CJH 1
      (March 1966): 118-20; Maurice J.M. Larkin, JMH
      38 (March 1966): 103-4; John C. Cairns, IJ 21
      (Spring 1966): 256-7; J.P.T. Bury, EHR 81
      (October 1966): 866; Douglas Johnson, HIST 52
      (June 1967): 235-6; John Q.C. Mackrell, CHR 53
      (October 1967): 456-7.

558. Shapiro, David. "The *Ralliement* in the Politics of
      the 1890's." In THE RIGHT IN FRANCE, 1890-
      1919: THREE STUDIES, edited by David Shapiro,
      13-48. St. Antony's Papers, vol. 13.
      London: Chatto & Windus, 1962.

Looks into the interaction between Leo XIII's
acceptance of the Republic in 1890 and the course
of French domestic politics. Focuses on the role
of the Right in the Chamber of Deputies between
1893 and 1898, and the degree to which its attitudes,
whether positive or negative, toward the *Ralliement*
changed as the years, with their many changes of
government, proceeded.

See: D.W. Brogan, SPEC 209 (27 July 1962): 120;
      David Thomson, HJ 6 (no. 1, 1963): 147-9;
      Eugen Weber, AHR 68 (April 1963): 794;
      Edward R. Tannenbaum, JMH 35 (December
      1963): 441-2; Charles A. Micaud, PSQ 79
      (September 1964): 450-2.

559. Ward, James E. "The Algiers Toast: Lavigerie's
      Work or Leo XIII's?" CHR 51 (July 1965): 173-
      91.

Examines Lavigerie's role as herald of the
Ralliement, asking whether it was something he
actively sought or something for which he was

selected by Leo XIII. Surveys the conflicting
accounts of the major figures themselves,
supplementing them with unpublished evidence.

560.   ————. "Cardinal Place and Leo XIII's *Ralliement*
         Policy." CHR 57 (January 1972): 606-28.

Considers the successful resistance of Philippe
Place, Cardinal-Archbishop of Rennes, to Leo XIII's
efforts to make him the prime instrument through
which France and the Church would reconcile.

561.   ————. "Cardinal Richard versus Cardinal
         Lavigerie: Episcopal Resistance to the
         Ralliement." CHR 53 (October 1967): 346-
         71.

Outlines the alternative proposal for Church-
State reconciliation offered by Cardinal Richard
of Paris in 1891, and quickly accepted by most of
his episcopal colleagues. Agrees with Sedgwick
(item 557) that most of the hierarchy reacted
quite negatively to the Algiers toast, and sees
Richard's maneuver as an opportunity for them to
express their pent-up feelings.

562.   ————. FRANCO-VATICAN RELATIONS, 1878-1892: THE
         DIPLOMATIC ORIGINS OF THE *RALLIEMENT*. Ph.D.
         dissertation. Cornell University, 1962.

Analyzes the reasons for the shift in Franco-
Vatican relations from the tensions of 1878-1885
to the cordiality of 1887-1892.

563.   ————. "The French Cardinals and Leo XIII's
         Ralliement Policy." CH 33 (March 1964): 60-73.

Spells out Leo XIII's abortive campaign, several
months before the Algiers toast, to persuade six
French cardinals to initiate the *Ralliement*.

564.   Woodall, John Burwell. THE *RALLIEMENT* IN
         FRANCE: ORIGINS AND EARLY HISTORY, 1876-1894.
         Ph.D. dissertation. Columbia University, 1964.

Concentrates on the attitudes of the vast majority
of Catholic conservatives who remained royalist or

Bonapartist after Thiers and the Left Center had
already accepted the Republic. Details their
stubborn resistance to any display of pro-
republican sentiment by Church leaders, from that
of Bishop Guilbert of Gap in 1876, to that of
Leo XIII during the first decade of his pontificate.

Anticlericalism and Anticatholicism

565. Gadille, Jacques. "On French Anticlericalism: Some
     Reflections." ESR 13 (April 1983): 127-44.

     General observations on the origins, meaning,
     varieties, and direction of nineteenth-century
     anticlericalism. Locates its greatest strength
     and influence in the cities during the 1860s,
     and traces the roots of its decline to the later
     1870s, with the impact of Leo XIII's progressive
     outlook.

566. Hartman, Mary S. "The Sacrilege Law of 1825 in
     France: A Study in Anticlericalism and
     Mythmaking." JMH 44 (March 1972): 21-37.

     Shows how the debate over the law which made it
     a capital offense to attack the consecrated host
     prompted the rise of a clerical myth among opponents
     of both Throne and Altar, a view of inordinate
     ecclesiastical influence which helped to bring
     down the Bourbons in 1830.

567. Headings, Mildred J. FRENCH FREEMASONRY UNDER THE
     THIRD REPUBLIC. Baltimore: The Johns Hopkins
     Press, 1949.

     Chapter 5 recounts the Masonic campaign to mitigate
     the influence of Catholicism in post-1870 France.
     Strategies studied include the agitation for
     compulsory non-religious education (1869-1872) and
     the legalization of civil divorce (1884).

     See: J.P.T. Bury, EHR 65 (April 1950): 286.

568. Hogue, Leo A., S.J. "The Jesuit Martyrs of the
     Commune Uprising in Paris, April-May 1871."

HB 9 (May 1931): 63-6, 77.

Describes the imprisonment and execution of six
Jesuits, including Père Ducoudray, Rector of the
Ecole Sainte-Geneviève, and Père Olivaint, Rector
of the Jesuit headquarters in Paris.

569. Holley, John Bostwick. THE RELIGIOUS IDEAS OF
      PROSPER MERIMEE. Ph.D. dissertation. The
      Catholic University of America, 1971.

      Fixes Mérimée's anti-Catholicism in his anti-
      clericalism rather than in his liberal ideology.
      Shows, however, that his antipathy toward the
      clergy was not constant; in 1848 and 1851, he
      was grateful for clerical assistance in keeping
      public order. Concludes that his view of priests
      as promoters of superstition and credulity was
      shared by many of his countrymen; their feelings
      would play an important role in the evolution of
      the Third Republic.

570. Hughes, Sister Barbara Ann, C.S.J. ANTICLERICALISM
      IN THE WRITINGS OF PIERRE-JOSEPH PROUDHON. Ph.D.
      dissertation. St. Louis University, 1972.

      Analyzes the theoretical and practical bases of
      one of the most important nineteenth-century anti-
      clericals. Central to his hatred of the clergy was
      his passionate attachment to justice, which he saw
      defiled by a reactionary Church.

571. Jones, W.R. "Palladism and the Papacy: An Episode
      of French Anticlericalism in the Nineteenth
      Century." JCS 12 (Autumn 1970): 453-73.

      Investigates one of the most extraordinary and
      entertaining episodes in the history of the conflict
      between Catholics and anticlericals. Relates the
      efforts of Léo Taxil, a noted Parisian journalist,
      to prove the existence of a high-grade Masonic plot
      against the Church and public order; after twelve
      years of intensifying the hatred on both sides, it
      was revealed in 1897 that no such plot existed, and
      that the ostensibly Catholic Taxil was himself an
      anticlerical, out to expose by his hoax the credulity
      of both the Pope and the French clergy.

572. McMillan, James F.   "Clericals, Anticlericals and
         the Women's Movement in France under the Third
         Republic." HJ 24 (June 1981): 361-76.

         Challenges the thesis that French feminism
         received its most strenuous support from among
         anticlericals, who believed that the "masculinist
         system" of the Church, in addition to its other
         faults, oppressed women. Proves that Catholic
         attitudes to women's issues did not differ
         considerably from those of anticlericals.

573. Magraw, Roger. "The Conflict in the Villages: Popu-
         lar Anticlericalism in the Isère (1852-70)." In
         CONFLICTS IN FRENCH SOCIETY: ANTICLERICALISM,
         EDUCATION AND MORALS IN THE NINETEENTH CENTURY
         (item 377), 169-227.

         Qualifies the traditional contention that the
         rural population of France was unshakably devout
         by nature, by reconstructing within one specific
         area the clashes among clergy, mayors, and
         teachers, along with the workers' and peasants'
         indifference to them.

574. Mitchell, Allan. "Crucible of French Anti-
         clericalism: The Conseil Municipal de Paris,
         1871-1885." FRAN 8 (1980): 395-405.

         Presents the Municipal Council of Paris as a
         microcosm of the growing anticlericalism of the
         nascent Third Republic; long before the passage
         of the Ferry laws, radicals on the Council were
         urging the secularization of public education and
         the complete separation of Church and State.

575. Moody, Joseph N. THE CHURCH AS ENEMY: ANTICLERICALISM
         IN NINETEENTH CENTURY FRENCH LITERATURE.
         Washington, D.C.: Corpus Books, 1968.

         Features an author-by-author analysis of the image
         of the priest, from Stendhal to Anatole France, and
         concludes that in every case the perception of the
         clergy and its influence was at least partially
         positive.

         See: H.L. Robinson, JCS 11 (Spring 1969): 334-5;

Thomas P. Anderson, COMMWL 90 (25 July
1969): 469; CHOICE 6 (November 1969): 1230;
James D. Flanagan, DUNR 10 (January 1970): 75-
7; Edward T. Gargan, AHR 75 (April 1970): 1133-
4; Robert M. Healey, CH 40 (June 1971): 235;
Jean T. Joughin, CHR 57 (January 1972): 678-80.

576.   ————. "French Anticlericalism: Image and Reality."
        CHR 56 (January 1971): 630-48.

        Charts the origins and evolution of nineteenth-
        century anticlericalism, citing the important
        contributions of Michelet, Zola, the Ultramontanists,
        and the Utopians to the myth of the cleric as the
        embodiment of social ills.

577.   ————. "The Third Republic and the Church: A Case
        History of Three French Historians." CHR 66
        (January 1980): 1-15.

        Illustrates the subtle varieties of nineteenth-
        century anticlericalism by examining the attitudes
        of three major historians--Ernest Lavisse, Alphonse
        Aulard, and Charles Seignobos--toward the Church.

   *   Parsons, Reuben. "The Clerical Victims of the
        Commune of 1871." STUDIES IN CHURCH HISTORY, 6
        (item 27), 85-110.

        A sympathetic treatment of the imprisonment,
        humiliation, and execution of Archbishop Darboy,
        the Dominicans of Arcueil, and eleven other priests.

   *   Sánchez, José. "France." ANTICLERICALISM: A BRIEF
        HISTORY (item 229), 95-121.

        Stresses the posture of nineteenth-century anti-
        clericals, given their constant self-awareness and
        decidedly intellectual approach to life.

578.   Strumhinger, Laura S. "'A bas les Prêtres! A bas
        les couvents!': The Church and the Workers in
        Nineteenth-Century Lyon." JSH 11 (Summer
        1978): 546-53.

        Assesses the Church's spiritual and moral regimen-
        tation of factory workers in Louis-Philippe's France,

and the workers' hostile response to it during the
Revolution of 1848. In schools, workshops, and
clubs, as well as in church itself, men, women,
and children were urged to lead less spontaneous,
more productive lives, while at the same time
accepting their humble status, in the hope of
salvation. Upon Louis-Philippe's fall appeared a
tremendous worker backlash against a patronizing
clergy.

579.   Zeldin, Theodore.   "The Conflict of Moralities: Con-
        fession, Sin and Pleasure in the Nineteenth
        Century."   In CONFLICTS IN FRENCH SOCIETY: ANTI-
        CLERICALISM, EDUCATION AND MORALS IN THE
        NINETEENTH CENTURY (item 377), 13-50.

        Indicates how the practice of confession was used
        by the Church's enemies to bolster their critique of
        an immoral and obscurantist clergy.

580.   ————.   "Religion and Anticlericalism."   FRANCE,
        1848-1945. Vol. 2:   INTELLECT, TASTE AND ANXIETY,
        983-1039. Oxford: Clarendon Press, 1977.

        Goes beyond the idea of persecution, legislation,
        and abuse, to speak of anticlericalism as a crisis of
        communication, that is, the Church's inability to
        relate to its time. Views various aspects of French
        Catholicism--parish clergy, bishops, monks and nuns,
        and lay organizations--in the light of this inability.

        See: Roderick Kedward, LIST 98 (8 September
               1977): 314-5; Gordon Wright, TLS, 14 October
               1977: 1195-6; Eugen Weber, SPEC 239 (22 October
               1977): 17-8; David Caute, NST 94 (28 October
               1977): 589-90; Malcolm Anderson, TES, 11
               November 1977: 21; Joanna Richardson, HT 27
               (December 1977): 822-3; R.F. Mullen, CONR 232
               (January 1978): 52-3; Leonard Bushkoff, NYTBR,
               12 February 1978: 1, 24; CHOICE 15 (March
               1978): 132; Elisabeth Israels Perry, HRNB 6
               (March 1978): 106-7; Edward T. Gargan, CHE 16
               (17 April 1978): 21-2; Robert A. Nye, AHR 83
               (June 1978): 738-9; Katherine Auspitz, NR 179
               (8-15 July 1978): 42-3; Eugen Weber, JMH 50
               (September 1978): 538-40; Robert O. Paxton,
               NYRB 25 (28 September 1978): 16-8; Edward

Rossmann, FRR 52 (October 1978): 192-3; F.W.J.
Hemmings, MLR 74 (January 1979): 215-6; Maurice
Larkin, EHR 94 (April 1979): 417-22; Peter
Alexis Gourevitch, APSR 73 (June 1979): 671-2.

Liberal Catholicism

General

*   Guérard, Albert Leon. "The Liberal Catholics."
FRENCH PROPHETS OF YESTERDAY: A STUDY OF
RELIGIOUS THOUGHT UNDER THE SECOND EMPIRE
(item 430), 49-56.

Outlines the program and status of liberal
Catholicism during the 1840s; though politically
insignificant, it was socially prominent and, in
its ecclesiastical outlook, highly diverse.

581.   Huckaby, John Keith. LIBERAL CATHOLICISM IN FRANCE,
1843-1870. Ph.D. dissertation. Ohio State
University, 1957.

Concentrates on the efforts of Montalembert,
Lacordaire, Dupanloup, and Ozanam to reconcile
the Church with post-revolutionary liberalism.
Points to their insistence on the freedom of
conscience and religion as the reason for the
loss of Vatican support, which they had enjoyed
after such early successes as the passage of the
Falloux Law. Skepticism, and ultimately
defeatism, took the place of idealism.

582.   Moody, Joseph N. "French Liberal Catholics, 1840-
1875." In FRENCH SOCIETY AND CULTURE SINCE THE
OLD REGIME; THE ELEUTHERIAN MILLS COLLOQUIUM,
1964, OF THE SOCIETY FOR FRENCH HISTORICAL STUDIES
AND THE SOCIETE D'HISTOIRE MODERNE (item 371),
150-71.

Clarifies the French liberal Catholic program,
showing that it was neither a static body of
doctrine nor a challenge to ecclesiastical
authority. Attributes its failure to a gross

misreading of the basic trends of public opinion,
ultramontanism, and the Second Empire. Credits
the liberals, however, with providing an
atmosphere for the sensitive and intelligent
political training which would later form the
foundation for the anti-infallibilism of Vatican
I.

Lamennais

583. Ages, Arnold. "Lamennais and the Jews." JQR 63
     (October 1972): 158-70.

     Contends that Lamennais' liberalism did not
     preclude a deep, almost racist anti-Semitism.
     Analyzes his use of rabbinic writings to condemn
     the alleged failings of both ancient and modern
     Judaism. Though he questioned many of the
     Church's key teachings, Lamennais simply accepted
     the traditional Roman attitude toward the Jews.

584. Gibson, W. THE ABBE DE LAMENNAIS AND THE LIBERAL
     CATHOLIC MOVEMENT IN FRANCE. London: Longmans,
     Green, 1896.

     Considers Lamennais the most forceful spiritual
     figure of the first half of the nineteenth century.
     Highly sympathetic, but without hiding weaknesses,
     of which his stormy temperament and lengthy bouts
     of deep depression are underscored.

     See: John J. O'Shea, CW 64 (February 1897): 634-41;
           ACQR 22 (April 1897): 447-8; W.S. Lilly, FR
           72 (1 July 1899): 73-84.

  *   Gooch, G.P. "Lamennais and Christian Democracy."
      FRENCH PROFILES: PROPHETS AND PIONEERS (item
      373), 190-203.

      Comments on the importance of Lamennais' ESSAI SUR
      L'INDIFFERENCE (1818-1823) in his early intellectual
      and religious development.

585. Gurian, Waldemar. "Lamennais." RP 9 (April
     1947): 205-29.

Deals exclusively with his life, ideas, and
activity before the break with Rome. Sees him
as a stimulator of movements rather than as a
creative thinker, a figure whose inability to
live comfortably in either the world of the
spirit or the world of the senses left him
eternally restless and unhappy.

586. Kitchin, William P.H. "The Story of Lamennais."
CHR 8 (July 1922): 198-211.

Complements item 585; details the final, tragedy-
ridden years of Lamennais, after his split with Rome.

587. Oldfield, John J. THE PROBLEM OF TOLERANCE AND
SOCIAL EXISTENCE IN THE WRITINGS OF FELICITE
LAMENNAIS, 1809-1831. Leiden: E.J. Brill,
1973.

Examines and evaluates the two main intellectual
preoccupations of Lamennais' Catholic phase, the
problems of order and authority in post-revolutionary
France. To account for the ever shifting assessment
of these problems in Lamennais' own mind, Oldfield
situates him within the political, religious, and
philosophical currents of the early nineteenth
century. Full of admiration for the man and his
ideas, but aware of such intellectual flaws as his
imprecise language and propensity to oversimplifi-
cation and utopianism.

See: Guillaume de Bertier de Sauvigny, CHR 62
(April 1976): 313-4.

    *   Reardon, Bernard M.G. "Lamennais and *Paroles d'un
Croyant*." RELIGION IN THE AGE OF
ROMANTICISM: STUDIES IN EARLY NINETEENTH-CENTURY
THOUGHT (item 255), 176-206.

Contends that Lamennais' lifelong goal, as seen
in his PAROLES D'UN CROYANT (1834) and LE LIVRE DU
PEUPLE (1837), was the realization of a type of
"religionless" Christianity, identified with the
cause of liberty, democracy, and social renewal.

588. Ryan, John A. "Condemnation of 'L'Avenir'." CHR 23
(April 1937): 31-9.

Argues that his journalistic excesses notwithstanding, Lamennais achieved that reconciliation
of Catholicism and popular liberty for which he
yearned. Provides a large amount of data on the
foundation, operation, and Papal rejection of
L'Avenir.

* Schapiro, J. Salwyn. "Lamennais and the Rise of
Liberal Catholicism." ANTICLERICALISM: CONFLICT
BETWEEN CHURCH AND STATE IN FRANCE, ITALY, AND
SPAIN (item 230), 38-47.

A useful introduction to Lamennais' principal
ideas and activities.

* Simpson, W.J. Sparrow. "Lamennais." FRENCH
CATHOLICS IN THE NINETEENTH CENTURY (item
376), 9-40.

Focuses on Lamennais the journalist. Criticizes
his excessively harsh treatment at the hands of
most contemporaries and some historians, while at
the same time admitting his lack of intellectual
depth. Discovers in Lamennais' failure the workings
of nineteenth-century Catholicism's greatest
weakness: its overly centralized authority.

589. Stearns, Peter N. "The Nature of the *Avenir*
Movement (1830-1831)." AHR 65 (July 1960): 837-
47.

Distinguishes three fairly clear currents of
liberal Catholic thought within *L'Avenir*, correcting
the traditional interpretation of a united group
under Lamennais' aegis.

590. ————. PRIEST AND REVOLUTIONARY: LAMENNAIS AND
THE DILEMMA OF FRENCH CATHOLICISM. New
York: Harper & Row, 1967.

An intricate reconstruction of Lamennais' dramatic
conflict with the Papacy, its origins and results,
placed within the larger context of a Catholicism
trying to find its rightful place in a post-revolutionary world.

See: Charles P. Bruderle, AMER 116 (13 May

1967): 735; Judah Adelson, LJ 92 (15 June
1967): 2418; John Ratté, COMMWL 87 (6 October
1967): 26-7; Evelyn M. Acomb, AHR 73 (December
1967): 493-4; CHOICE 4 (December 1967): 1128;
Guillaume de Bertier de Sauvigny, CHR 56
(October 1970): 577-8.

591. Vidler, A.R.   PROPHECY AND PAPACY: A STUDY OF
        LAMENNAIS, THE CHURCH, AND THE REVOLUTION.
        New York: Charles Scribner's Sons, 1954.

Presents the origins and consequences of
traditionalism, ultramontanism, and liberal
Catholicism within the context of Lamennais'
struggle with the Papacy.

See: CLR 39 (May 1954): 306-9; J.P.T. Bury, THEO 57
        (May 1954): 186-8; DUBR 228 (Summer 1954): 490;
        W.J. Hegarty, IER 82 (July 1954): 64-5;
        Waldemar Gurian, RP 16 (July 1954): 376-7;
        Charles Breunig, AHR 60 (October 1954): 88-9;
        C.W. Crawley, JTS 5 (October 1954): 291-3;
        Joseph S. Brusher, CHR 40 (January 1955): 454-
        5; D.E. Easson, SJT 8 (March 1955): 83-4; A.
        Goodwin, JEH 6 (April 1955): 114-5; H.J. Hunt,
        MLR 50 (July 1955): 344-5; Thomas P. Neill, HB
        34 (November 1955): 39-40; A. Davies, HIST 41
        (February/October 1956): 314-5.

Montalembert

592. Aspinwall, Bernard.   "Charles de Montalembert and
        England." DR 88 (April 1970):   132-49.

Attributes Montalembert's love of England to his
enthusiasm for the dynamic Catholicism he found
there. English Catholics, secure in their religious
freedom, were intellectually awake, and definitely
far less parochial in outlook than their French
counterparts; moreover, as evidenced by the "Second
Spring" phenomenon, laymen could find adequate
service for their talents within the Church.

593. ————. "Montalembert and 'Idolatry.'" DR 89
        (April 1971):   158-64.

Discusses Montalembert's parting shot against the
ultramontanists, penned a few weeks before his death.
Rates his denunciation of those who worship "the idol
they raised up for themselves in the Vatican" a
seemingly hopeless gesture of defiance in support of
a noble cause.

594.   Daley, Joseph Gordian.   "Montalembert and His Visit
       to O'Connell."   CW 71 (June 1900):   331-9.

       Maintains that much of Montalembert's ecclesi-
       astical program, including, most importantly, the
       desideratum of a free Church in a free State, was
       inspired by his visit of 1829 to O'Connell's home
       at Derrynane.

595.   Finlay, James C., S.J.   THE LIBERAL WHO FAILED.
       Washington, D.C., and Cleveland: Corpus
       Books, 1968.

       Studies Montalembert's efforts to reconcile
       Catholicism and the post-revolutionary order,
       after Lamennais' departure from the Church.
       Traces his failure to his identification of the
       Church with the bourgeois establishment.

       See: Joseph N. Moody, THOUGHT 44 (Summer 1969): 317-
              8; Guillaume de Bertier de Sauvigny, CHR 56
              (October 1970): 576-7.

  *   Gooch, G.P.   "Montalembert and Church Schools."
       FRENCH PROFILES: PROPHETS AND PIONEERS (item
       373), 204-15.

       Despite its title, a sketch of Montalembert's
       work with Lamennais.

  *   Horgan, John J.   "Montalembert: Peer of France."
       GREAT CATHOLIC LAYMEN (item 31), 159-202.

       Explores Montalembert's interaction with the four
       great passions of his life: God, the Church, France,
       and liberty.   Highlights his relationship with
       Lamennais and the *Avenir* movement.

  *   Neill, Thomas P.   "Count Charles Montalembert."
       THEY LIVED THE FAITH (item 33), 47-70.

Praises Montalembert as a pioneer model layman
who roused Catholics not only to a consciousness
of their Catholicity but also to an acceptance of
the ideals of democracy and liberty.

596. O'Connell, Marvin R.   "Montalembert at Mechlin: A
        Reprise of 1830." JCS 26 (Autumn 1984): 515-36.

Lists the major personalities, beliefs, and events
in Montalembert's life which inspired his famous
speech of August 1863 before the International
Congress of Belgian Catholics. Emphasizes the
prominence of Lamennais in his overall formation.

  *   Simpson, W.J. Sparrow. "Montalembert." FRENCH
        CATHOLICS IN THE NINETEENTH CENTURY (item 376),
        77-106.

An intellectual biography, underscoring his
commitment to freedom and Catholicism. Describes
in detail his relationship with Lamennais and
Lacordaire.

597. Williams, Roger L.   "Montalembert and Liberal
        Catholicism." GASLIGHT AND SHADOW: THE WORLD
        OF NAPOLEON III, 65-95. New York: Macmillan,
        1957.

Highlights Montalembert's connections with
L'Avenir, the campaign for freedom of education,
and the proponents of papal temporal power.

See: John C. Cairns, CANHR 38 (December 1957): 334;
      Lynn M. Case, AHR 63 (January 1958): 486;
      John Roberts, HT 8 (January 1958): 67-9;
      Raymond J. Maras, CHR 44 (April 1958): 49-51;
      Bernerd C. Weber, SOCED 22 (December
      1958): 411-2.

Lacordaire

598. Abercrombie, Nigel J. "Lacordaire." WR 235
        (Autumn 1961): 251-64.

A character study. Hails Lacordaire as a man of

principle and self-consistency, a reasonable and
realistic ultramontanist, and a supporter of a
Catholicism open to the contemporary world.

*   Gooch, G.P. "Lacordaire in the Pulpit." FRENCH
      PROFILES: PROPHETS AND PIONEERS (item 373),
      216-25.

      Justifies Lacordaire's universal reputation as
the greatest French preacher of the nineteenth
century.

599.   Grant, Hugh. "Lacordaire." IER 96 (October
      1961): 276-82.

      An appreciation of Lacordaire's early years, from
his days with his parents through his connection
with Lamennais and Montalembert.

*   Parsons, Reuben. "Lacordaire and Lamennais."
      STUDIES IN CHURCH HISTORY, 5 (item 26),
      272-303.

      Outlines their collaboration on *L'Avenir* and
the reasons behind their later separation.

600.   Sheppard, Lancelot R. LACORDAIRE: A BIOGRAPHICAL
      ESSAY. New York: Macmillan, 1964.

      The only full-scale biography in English.
Reconstructs Lacordaire's life within the larger
political, religious, and intellectual atmosphere
of nineteenth-century France, showing his interaction with such prominent issues as Church-State
relations, freedom of conscience, religious
education, and the nature of democracy.

      See: Nigel Abercrombie, DR 82 (October 1964): 376-7;
         J.J. Dwyer, CLR 49 (December 1964): 788-90;
         IER 103 (January 1965): 71; Evelyn M. Acomb,
         AHR 70 (April 1965): 862-3; CHOICE 2 (July/
         August 1965): 308; J.N. Moody, JMH 37
         (September 1965): 388; Edward T. Gargan, CHR
         53 (January 1968): 740.

*   Simpson, W.J. Sparrow. "Lacordaire." FRENCH
      CATHOLICS IN THE NINETEENTH CENTURY

(item 376), 41-76.

Unravels his curious mixture of ultramontanism
and liberalism, indicating how he promoted each of
them through his unrivalled preaching.

*   Spencer, Philip.   "Lacordaire's Hour."   POLITICS OF
        BELIEF IN NINETEENTH-CENTURY FRANCE: LACORDAIRE,
        MICHON, VEUILLOT (item 433), 15-115.

Not a biography, but a series of vignettes
illustrating momentous steps in Lacordaire's
career: the years with Lamennais and *L'Avenir*,
the *conférences* at Notre-Dame, his propagation
of ultramontanism, and his entry into the newly
reconstituted Dominican order.

601. Woodgate, M.V.   PERE LACORDAIRE: LEADER OF YOUTH.
        St. Louis: B. Herder, 1939.

A brief treatment of Lacordaire's life and times,
with particular reference to his religious work
among young men.

See: IER 54 (November 1939): 549-50; DR 58
        (January 1940): 126-7.

Spain and Portugal

General Works

602. Callahan, William J.   CHURCH, POLITICS, AND SOCIETY
        IN SPAIN, 1750-1874.   Harvard Historical Mono-
        graphs, vol. 73.   Cambridge: Harvard University
        Press, 1984.

Chapters 3-8 detail the long nineteenth-century
conflict between the Spanish Church and liberalism,
along with its tragic effect upon the Church's
position in society.   By the end of the century,
Catholicism's social base was largely confined to
the northern peasantry and the conservative middle
classes of the cities.

See: M.A. Burkholder, CHOICE 22 (December 1984): 604;
José M. Sanchez, HRNB 13 (January 1985): 65;
Frances Lannon, TLS, 8 February 1985: 152;
Richard Herr, AHR 90 (June 1985): 705-6; Stanley
G. Payne, AMERS 42 (October 1985): 254-7; David
R. Ringrose, RSR 11 (October 1985): 410; Carol
O'Brien English, CHR 72 (April 1986): 287-8;
David R. Ringrose, RSR 12 (April 1986): 173;
R.A.H. Robinson, HAHR 66 (May 1986): 359-60;
James S. Amelang, CH 55 (June 1986): 238-9;
Charles C. Noel, EHR 101 (July 1986): 698-702;
Joan C. Ullman, JIH 17 (Autumn 1986): 457-8;
Marvin Lunenfeld, HIS 49 (November 1986): 100-
1; Raymond Carr, JMH 58 (December 1986): 971-3.

603. ———. "Two Spains and Two Churches, 1760-1835."
HR 2 (Winter 1976): 157-81.

Traces the conflict between traditionalists and
reformers for control of the Spanish Church. Ties
the outcome of this conflict at any one time to the
results of the simultaneous political contest
between conservatives and liberals for control of
the Spanish State. Illustrates the seesaw nature
of the ecclesiastical struggle. From 1780 to 1808
the reformers dictated the Church's policies; with
the Napoleonic invasion and the restoration of 1814,
however, the traditionalists returned to power,
staying there until 1835.

604. Parker, A.A. "The Catholic Church in Spain from
1800 to the Present (I)." TABLET 171 (5 March
1938): 293-4.

A survey of developments from 1800 to 1814.
Presents an institution deeply divided between
Gallicans (court, government, and intellectuals)
and traditionalists (the people), and seriously
weakened by intellectual forces (deism, skepticism,
and materialism) and the persecution during the
Napoleonic occupation. Continued in item 605.

605. ———. "The Catholic Church in Spain from 1800 to
the Present (II)." TABLET 171 (12 March
1938): 325-6.

Continues from item 604. Discusses the liberal

assault upon ecclesiastical possessions and preroga-
tives, following the successful revolution of 1820.
Carries the attack through to 1844, when religious
peace returned, as a result of the electoral victory
of the moderates. Continued in item 606.

606. ————. "The Catholic Church in Spain from 1800 to
       the Present (III)." TABLET 171 (19 March
       1938): 359-60.

       Continues from item 605. Assesses the spiritual
       status and economic position of the Church in the
       wake of two decades of liberal persecution. Displays
       the wisdom of the moderate policy of the late 1840s,
       in its determination to reform ecclesiastical
       structure and the religious orders in cooperation
       with, and not in defiance of, the hierarchy.
       Continued in item 607.

607. ————. "The Catholic Church in Spain from 1800 to
       the Present (IV)." TABLET 171 (26 March
       1938): 391-2.

       Continues from item 606. Examines the making,
       provisions, and effects of the Concordat of 1851.
       Criticizes the drastic changes made in the Church-
       State relationship by the anticlericals following
       their successful revolution of 1868. Continued in
       item 608.

608. ————. "The Catholic Church in Spain from 1800 to
       the Present (V)." TABLET 171 (2 April
       1938): 434-6.

       Continues from item 607. Covers the evolution of
       the Spanish Church from 1874, the year in which both
       the monarchy and the original Concordat were
       reinstated, to the end of the century. Notes with
       satisfaction that after 1875 no anticlerical legis-
       lation of any importance was passed, though the
       Constitution of 1876 did grant freedom of religion
       to all faiths.

609. Payne, Stanley G. SPANISH CATHOLICISM: AN
       HISTORICAL OVERVIEW. Madison: University of
       Wisconsin Press, 1984.

Chapters 3 and 4 review the mechanics and
consequences of two major phenomena within the
nineteenth-century Spanish Church: (1) the
increasingly stronger liberal challenge to the
ecclesiastical structure; and (2) the vibrant
post-1874 revival, reflected in such disparate
areas as culture, philosophy, education,
spirituality, clerical activity, and regional
identity.

See: W.L. Pitts, Jr., CHOICE 22 (January 1985): 700;
Frances Lannon, TLS, 8 February 1985: 152; Paul
Merritt Bassett, RSR 12 (April 1986): 173-4;
Raymond Carr, JMH 58 (December 1986): 971-3;
William J. Callahan, CHR 73 (January 1987): 102.

610.   Peers, E. Allison. THE CHURCH IN SPAIN, 1737-1937.
London: Burns Oates & Washbourne, 1938.

Devoted almost entirely to the nineteenth-century
situation, within which are distinguished three
continuing threats to the Church's well-being: anticlericalism, atheism, and government control.

611.   ————. SPAIN, THE CHURCH AND THE ORDERS.
London: Eyre & Spottiswoode, 1939.

Follows the evolution of nineteenth-century Spanish
Catholicism from the perspective of the religious
orders, whose history during the period is
characterized as one of unabated persecution and
spoliation. Chapters 2 and 3 offer an in-depth
analysis of anti-Catholic motives and strategies,
while Appendices 2 and 3 provide, respectively, a
chronological listing of significant events, and
statistics on membership in the different orders.

See: William C. Atkinson, IA 18 (September/October
1939): 703.

Religious Thought

General

612. Schumacher, John N. "Integrism: A Study in
      Nineteenth-Century Spanish Politico-Religious
      Thought." CHR 48 (October 1962): 343-64.

      Traces the rise and evolution of the most
      fanatical of all anti-liberal religious movements,
      that of the *Integristas*, whose war against every
      aspect of modern life could not be ended even
      through the personal intercession of Leo XIII.
      Their refusal to come to terms with their time
      was all the more tragic since, ironically, their
      creed contained much that was urgently needed by
      nineteenth-century Spain.

Donoso Cortés

613. Briefs, Goetz. A CHRISTIAN STATESMAN AND POLITICAL
      PHILOSOPHER: DONOSO CORTES. St. Louis: Central
      Bureau Press, 1938.

      An introduction to Cortés' religious and social
      philosophy. Enthusiastic about many of his ideas,
      but highly critical of his excessive pessimism,
      Manicheanism, and overemphasis on the creation of
      a "Catholic" civilization as the answer to the
      disorder and immorality of his time.

614. Cossio, Alphonse de. "Donoso Cortés: A Prophet of
      Our Times." DUBR 220 (Spring 1947): 30-49.

      Focuses on his polemics against liberalism and
      socialism. Admires his dedication to truth and
      lack of sympathy for his opponents.

615. Graham, John T. DONOSO CORTES: UTOPIAN ROMANTICIST
      AND POLITICAL REALIST. Columbia: University of
      Missouri Press, 1974.

      Offers insights into the mentality of conservative

Catholics in mid-nineteenth-century Spain. Highlights Cortés' belief that Catholicism alone could effectively check the spread of liberalism, socialism, and materialism; such a conclusion more than justified the establishment of an ecclesiastical dictatorship. Places these views within a European context, comparing them with the philosophy of other counter-revolutionaries of the day, including Metternich, Guizot, Schelling, Comte, and Bismarck.

> See: CHOICE 11 (October 1974): 1198-9; J. Lee Shneidman, HRNB 3 (November/December 1974): 28; Iris M. Zavala, AHR 82 (April 1977): 375-6.

616. Mayer, J.P. "Donoso Cortés' *De Civitate Dei*." DUBR 225 (Spring 1951): 76-88.

Analyzes his ENSAYO SOBRE EL CATOLOCISMO, EL LIBERALISMO Y EL SOCIALISMO, CONSIDERADOS EN SUS PRINCIPIOS FUNDAMENTALES (1851). Its effort to solve the problem of social disorder, combined with its emphatic style and deep sense of humanitarianism, make this work one of the great documents of modern Catholic history.

617. Menczer, Béla. "Donoso Cortés, 1809-53: A Centenary Appraisal." TABLET 201 (2 May 1953): 365-6.

Sees him as a visionary and prophet rather than as a philosopher or theologian. Fixes his belief in the futility of all intellectual systems at the center of his outlook.

618. ————. "Metternich and Donoso Cortés: Christian and Conservative Thought in the European Revolution." DUBR 221 (Winter 1948): 19-51.

Explains the friendship between two men of entirely different backgrounds, careers, and temperaments, locating it in their shared conviction that without a recognition of the supernatural, barbarism--in the form of revolution--would once again sweep through Europe.

619. Neill, Thomas P. "Juan Donoso Cortés: History and
          'Prophecy.'" CHR 40 (January 1955): 385-410.

      Points to his religious and historical writings as
      his major contribution to nineteenth-century
      Catholicism. Emphasizes his in-depth criticism of
      liberalism, for its attempt to adapt faith to the
      needs of the age, and of socialism, for its godless-
      ness.

*   ————. "Donoso Cortés." THEY LIVED THE FAITH
          (item 33), 242-66.

      Presents him as a counterbalance to liberal
      Catholic thinkers like Montalembert and Ozanam.
      Sympathetic to his refinement of de Maistre's
      thought, seeing in it an accurate prediction of
      such twentieth-century European phenomena as
      dictatorship and war.

620. ————. "Juan Donoso Cortés: Prophet of Our Time."
          CW 170 (November 1949): 121-7.

      Praises his courage in denouncing theologically
      what he perceived as the widespread decadence of
      European civilization in his day.

621. ————. "Juan Donoso Cortés: Spanish Catholic
          Layman." HB 27 (May 1949): 77-8, 83-7.

      Examines the position he held in nineteenth-century
      Spanish politics, European intellectual affairs, and
      Catholicism.

                              Balmes

622. George, Robert Esmonde Gordon [Sencourt, Robert].
          "Jaime Balmes, 1810-1848." DUBR 221 (Autumn
          1948): 29-43.

      Finds the core of Balmes' thought in his
      exaltation of Catholicism and condemnation of
      Protestantism, democracy, and socialism. Like
      Cortés, Balmes sought to vindicate the Church in
      the face of modern civilization; without

Catholicism, which gives true authority and culture, society degenerates into the absolutism of the masses and ignorance.

Special Challenges

Church and State

623. Callahan, William J. "The Origins of the Conservative Church in Spain, 1793-1823." ESR 10 (April 1980): 199-223.

     Divides the growth of conservative Catholicism into three distinct phases: (1) 1793-1813, which witnessed a vigorous reform movement within the Church, led by clerics tied to the major secular currents of the day; (2) 1814-1820, in which the restored Ferdinand VII brought Throne and Altar closely together, so as to use the latter for the benefit of the former; and (3) 1820-1823, which saw the Church's initial support of the successful revolution of 1820 fade as ecclesiastical property was destroyed and priests were executed. With the second restoration of Ferdinand in 1823, the Church had no choice but to side with absolute monarchy.

624. ————. "The Spanish Church and the Restoration State, 1874-1900." JCS 26 (Spring 1984): 313-32.

     Outlines the Church's efforts to establish a harmonious relationship with the government, despite a highly unstable political situation. Follows the process by which Catholicism, favored by the Concordat of 1851 and the Constitution of 1876, became the object of anticlerical abuse after 1899.

625. Hughey, John David, Jr. RELIGIOUS FREEDOM IN SPAIN, ITS EBB AND FLOW. Nashville: Broadman Press, 1955.

     Decries, in Chapters 2-6, the Church's role in

creating an atmosphere of religious intolerance in
nineteenth-century Spain. Colored by the author's
deeply held Protestantism.

See: C. Ryder Smith, LQHR 181 (January 1956): 78.

626. Lannon, Frances. PRIVILEGE, PERSECUTION, AND
        PROPHECY: THE CATHOLIC CHURCH IN SPAIN,
        1875-1975. Oxford: Clarendon Press, 1987.

Discusses the evolution of popular cults,
religious communities, clergy, ecclesiastical
organizations, and hierarchical politics within
the larger national experience. Draws heavily
on material from regional archives, as it
describes the Catholic impact upon politics,
society, and culture.

See: Denis Smyth, TLS, 26 June 1987: 685.

627. Picó, Fernando A., S.J. "Emilio Castelar and the
        Spanish Church." CHR 52 (January 1967): 534-48.

Evaluates the religious policy of one of
nineteenth-century Spain's greatest political
figures. Though President of the First Republic
for less than four months (September 1873 - January
1874), his belief in the compatibility between
Catholicism and democracy provided a valuable
middle ground between the traditionalists, for whom
faith and reaction were identical, and the anticlericals, who advised him never to trust the
religious establishment.

628. Rosenblatt, Nancy A. "Church and State in Spain: A
        Study of Moderate Liberal Politics in 1845."
        CHR 62 (October 1976): 589-603.

Describes the *moderado* campaign to end the rupture
between Church and State which began during the civil
war of 1833-1839. Explains why the attempt at a
concordat in 1845 failed, when six years later it
succeeded with relative ease.

629. ————. "The Spanish *Moderados* and the Church,
        1834-1835." CHR 57 (October 1971): 401-20.

Investigates the ecclesiastical policy of the
moderate liberals during the early years of the
First Carlist War, providing insights into their
view of the Church's proper role in Spanish
society. Concludes that their anticlericalism
never disputed the idea of an established religion
per se.

Anticlericalism and Anticatholicism

630. Devlin, John. SPANISH ANTICLERICALISM: A STUDY IN
     MODERN ALIENATION. New York: Las Americas,
     1966.

     Chapter 1 looks at the main currents of anti-
     clericalism in pre-1900 Spanish literature, with
     emphasis on the novels of Benito Pérez Galdos
     (1843-1920) and Vicente Blasco Ibáñez (1867-
     1928).

     See: Walter Patterson, HISP 51 (March 1968): 201-2.

631. O'Connell, James Robert. THE SPANISH PARLIAMENT
     AND THE CLERICAL QUESTION, 1868-1936. Ph.D.
     dissertation. Columbia University, 1966.

     Reconstructs the late nineteenth-century parlia-
     mentary struggles between clerical and anticlerical
     forces over the twin issues of religious toleration
     and "free," i.e., secular, university and secondary
     education. Details the critical role played by the
     political philosophy of Antonio Cánovas del Castillo,
     the "Architect of the Restoration," in these
     struggles.

 *   Sánchez, José. "Portugal." ANTICLERICALISM: A
     BRIEF HISTORY (item 229), 161-8.

     Underscores the absence of a strong social anti-
     clericalism in nineteenth-century Portugal.

 *   ———. "Spain." ANTICLERICALISM: A BRIEF HISTORY
     (item 229), 123-41.

     Offers reasons as to why nineteenth-century Spain

was the only European country in which social anticlericalism was more powerful than its political
counterpart.

*   Schapiro, J. Salwyn. "Spain, a Church-State Nation."
     ANTICLERICALISM: CONFLICT BETWEEN CHURCH AND
     STATE IN FRANCE, ITALY, AND SPAIN (item 230), 86-
     96.

     A useful introduction to the evolution of
     nineteenth-century Spanish anticlericalism.

632. Ullman, J.C. THE TRAGIC WEEK: A STUDY OF ANTI-
      CLERICALISM IN SPAIN, 1875-1912.
      Cambridge: Harvard University Press, 1968.

      Analyzes the function and importance of anti-
      clericalism in Spanish politics through much of
      the nineteenth century. Sketches the image and
      reality of clerical domination of such areas as
      education and finance. Follows the waxing and
      waning of anticlerical feeling from 1833 to 1875,
      finding that after the latter date churchmen lost
      most of their popular support as they turned a
      deaf ear to the workers' campaign for justice.

      See: CHOICE 5 (May 1968): 399; Martin E. Marty,
            CH 37 (September 1968): 340-1; Gabriel
            Jackson, AHR 74 (October 1968): 194-5;
            Stanley G. Payne, JSH 3 (Fall 1969): 86-9;
            Gerald H. Meaker, LH 10 (Fall 1969): 695-7;
            V.G. Kiernan, EHR 84 (October 1969): 877-8;
            Wilfrid Passmore, DR 88 (April 1970): 226-
            9; James R. O'Connell, CHR 57 (January
            1972): 700-2.

633. ————. "The Warp and Woof of Parliamentary Politics
      in Spain, 1808-1939: Anticlericalism versus
      'Neo-Catholicism.'" ESR 13 (April 1983): 145-76.

      Studies the degree to which religion in nineteenth-
      century Spain served as a divisive rather than a
      unifying force. Reviews the parliamentary interplay
      between supporters and opponents of the Church, and
      its reflection in the relationship between Catho-
      licism and the State, on the one hand, and Catho-
      licism and society, on the other.

Italy

General Works

634. Hughes, H.L. THE CATHOLIC REVIVAL IN ITALY, 1815-
      1915. London: Burns Oates & Washbourne, 1935.

      Contrasts the activities and ideas of pro- and
      anti-Catholic leaders on the peninsula. Among
      those discussed are Alessandro Manzoni, Pius IX,
      Don Bosco, Giuseppe Toniolo, Camillo Cavour, and
      Giuseppe Mazzini.

      See: DR 54 (January 1936): 133-4; Richard L. Smith,
            CLR 11 (April 1936): 335-6; Humphrey Johnson,
            Cong. Orat., DUBR 198 (April/May/June
            1936): 322-4; S. William Halperin, CH 5 (June
            1936): 196-7; John Tracy Ellis, CHR 22 (July
            1936): 199-200.

The Hierarchy

635. Caliaro, Marco, and Francesconi, Mario. JOHN BAPTIST
      SCALABRINI, APOSTLE TO EMIGRANTS. Translated by
      A. Zizzamia. New York: Center for Migration
      Studies, 1977.

      A portrait of one of the most dynamic Italian
      churchmen of the nineteenth century. Scalabrini
      (1839-1905), named Bishop of Piacenza at the age
      of thirty-six, not only founded the Congregation
      of St. Charles, for the purpose of bringing spiritual
      and social assistance to Italian immigrants in the
      United States and Brazil; within his diocese he
      encouraged education and catechetical innovation,
      and urged clergy and laity alike to greater devotion
      to the Eucharist.

      See: Salvatore J. La Gumina, CHR 67 (July 1981): 444-
            6.

636. Felici, Icilio. FATHER TO THE IMMIGRANTS: THE LIFE
      OF JOHN BAPTIST SCALABRINI. Translated by

Carol della Chiesa. New York: P.J. Kenedy & Sons, 1955.

Presents the diverse achievements of the Bishop of Piacenza, including the foundation of the Pious Society of the Missionaries of Saint Charles (also known as the Scalabrinian Fathers) and the pioneering social outlook which inspired him to tackle some of the major problems faced by Italian immigrants around the turn of the century.

See: Sister Dolorita Marie, C.S.J., SJR 48 (February 1956): 398-9; John E. Wrigley, CHR 42 (April 1956): 115-6; IER 87 (May 1957): 397-8.

The Press

637.   Halperin, S. William. "Catholic Journalism in Italy and the Italo-Papal Conflict of the 1870's." CHR 59 (January 1974): 587-601.

Demonstrates how the highly partisan, oftentimes inflammatory, and always determined Catholic press in Italy during the last eight years of Pius IX's reign reinforced that segment of public opinion which hoped to regain the Papal States. Deals at the same time with the question of how much effective control the Papacy exercised over these journals.

Piety and Devotion

638.   Williamson, Benedict. BLESSED GEMMA GALGANI. 2nd ed. London: Alexander Ouseley/St. Louis: B. Herder, 1932.

Places Galgani's extraordinary spirituality within the framework of her rather ordinary life. Her short life (1878-1903), spent entirely at Lucca, was devoted to the Passion of Christ and was crowded with both trials and visions, culminating in her reception of the stigmata. Includes large extracts from her letters.

See: AMER 48 (1 April 1933): 632.

Social Catholicism

*   Vidler, A.R. "Italy." A CENTURY OF SOCIAL
        CATHOLICISM, 1820-1920 (item 315), 152-63.

    Discusses the origins and early years of "Catholic
    Action," as practiced by the *Opera dei Congressi*, and
    the Christian democrat movement, as formulated and
    spread by Giuseppe Toniolo and Romolo Murri.

Special Challenges

Church and State

639. Coppa, Frank J. "*Realpolitik* and Conviction in the
        Conflict between Piedmont and the Papacy during
        the *Risorgimento*." CHR 54 (January 1969): 579-
        612.

    Reevaluates the contention that the Church was
    entirely at fault in its conflict with the emerging
    Italian state. Maintains that blame must be borne
    as much by Cavour's commitment to *realpolitik* as by
    Pius IX's religious convictions, which demanded that
    he ignore the new political reality.

640. Cummings, Raymond L. "Francis II of Naples--Shield
        for Pio Nono?" CHR 60 (April 1974): 41-54.

    Details the diplomatic and military relationship
    between the Pope and his highly sympathetic southern
    neighbor in 1859-1860. Attributes Francis' refusal
    to protect the Papal States to his own political
    insecurity.

641. Halperin, S. William. "Church and State in Italy
        during the Last Years of Pius IX." CH 5 (March
        1936): 71-84.

    Explains why no compromise between the Church and

the Italian government was possible between 1871 and
1878.   Divides the intransigence equally between an
aging Pontiff dominated by a fanatical entourage and
a group of politicians bent on a policy of secularization.

642.   ———. THE SEPARATION OF CHURCH AND STATE IN
        ITALIAN THOUGHT FROM CAVOUR TO MUSSOLINI.
        Chicago: University of Chicago Press, 1937.

        Considers and appraises the various currents
        within Italian thought on Church-State relations.
        Features an in-depth look at the political and
        philosophical bases of Cavour's "free Church in a
        free State" idea, along with its implementation in
        the Law of Guarantees (1871). Poses against the
        moderate Cavourian stance the programs of the
        radicals (complete separation) and the ultramontane
        reactionaries (anti-separation).

        See: Raymond Corrigan, S.J., HB 16 (November
              1937): 18; Carl Conrad Eckhardt, JMH 9
              (December 1937): 560; William G. Welk,
              AAAPSS 195 (January 1938): 230; Herbert
              W. Schneider, CH 7 (March 1938): 96-7;
              Lynn M. Case, PSQ 53 (June 1938): 314-5;
              Sister Loretta Clare, CHR 24 (July
              1938): 205-6; Andrew Beck, A.A., CLR 15
              (October 1938): 352-3.

643.   Jemolo, A.C. CHURCH AND STATE IN ITALY, 1850-1950.
        Translated by David Moore. Oxford: Basil
        Blackwell, 1960.

        A survey by a liberal historian, for whom even
        the slightest encroachment by one upon the freedom
        of the other is intolerable. Highlights the views
        of several major thinkers--Gioberti, Rosmini, and
        Ricasoli, among them--on the problem of the
        connection between politics and religion.

        See: Alec Randall, DUBR 234 (Summer 1960): 188-90;
              Joseph N. Moody, CHR 46 (January 1961): 463-5;
              Agatha Ramm, HIST 46 (February 1961): 71-2;
              Roy Pryce, PS 9 (February 1961): 82-3; L.C.
              Webb, JRH 1 (June 1961): 189-91; S. William
              Halperin, PSQ 76 (June 1961): 319-20;

Richard A. Webster, AAAPSS 343 (September 1962): 152-3.

Catholic Political Activity

644. Drake, Richard. "Giulio Salvadori and the Catholic Political Tradition in Italy." RP 44 (July 1982): 386-412.

   Uses Salvadori's sometime liberal, sometime conservative career to show the multiplicity of acceptable yet conflicting currents within political Catholicism. Provides, within a larger context, insights into the workings of Italian Catholic culture during the last quarter of the nineteenth century.

645. Hall, Basil. "Alessandro Gavazzi: A Barnabite Friar and the Risorgimento (Presidential Address)." In CHURCH, SOCIETY AND POLITICS: PAPERS READ AT THE THIRTEENTH SUMMER MEETING AND THE FOURTEENTH WINTER MEETING OF THE ECCLESIASTICAL HISTORY SOCIETY, edited by Derek Baker, 303-56. Studies in Church History, vol. 12. Oxford: Published for the Ecclesiastical History Society by Basil Blackwell, 1975.

   Recounts the life and work of one of a large group of Italian priests who, finding it impossible to follow both Pius IX and the *Risorgimento*, left the Church and became passionately involved in the creation of the new peninsular order. Highly favorable to Gavazzi. Illustrates the dynamics of the inner conflict felt by those who sought to be sincere Christians and Italian patriots at one and the same time.

   See: Helen Forshaw, S.H.C.J., CLR 62 (May 1977): 211-2; John Van Engen, RSR 7 (October 1981): 354.

646. Hundelt, Sister M. Martine, C.S.F. ROMOLO MURRI AND THE FIRST CHRISTIAN DEMOCRATIC MOVEMENT IN ITALY. Ph.D. dissertation. St. Louis University, 1964.

Recreates Murri's campaign to build an independent
Catholic political party during the late 1890s.
Finds the inspiration for the party in Murri's desire
to concretize the social teachings of Leo XIII.

647. Orlando, Francis Peter. THE POLICY OF CATHOLIC
        ABSTENTION FROM ITALIAN PARLIAMENTARY AFFAIRS,
        1861-1919. Ph.D. dissertation. University of
        Notre Dame, 1970.

A chronological account and evaluation of the
policy adopted by the Vatican in reaction to its
loss of temporal power to the Italian government.
Deems the entire effort useless, for it neither
demoralized the government nor restored the Papal
States.

648. Webster, Richard A. CHRISTIAN DEMOCRACY IN ITALY,
        1860-1900. London: Hollis and Carter, 1961.

Reviews the structure and activity of lay
democratic organizations; based to a large
extent on Italian historical scholarship not
otherwise available in English.

See: Alec Randall, WR 235 (Summer 1961): 189-90;
       Dom Daniel Rees, DR 79 (Autumn 1961): 376-8;
       L.C. Webb, JRH 1 (December 1961): 254-6;
       J.J. Dwyer, CLR 47 (May 1962): 310-2.

Anticlericalism and Anticatholicism

649. Halperin, William. "Italian Anticlericalism, 1871-
        1914." JMH 19 (March 1947): 18-34.

Identifies the desire to reduce the influence of
the Catholic Church and laicize daily life as rapidly
as possible, as the one common denominator uniting
followers of such widely disparate movements as
socialism, republicanism, and militant liberalism.

650. Lyttelton, Adrian. "An Old Church and a New
        State: Italian Anticlericalism, 1876-1915."
        ESR 13 (April 1983): 225-48.

Looks into the social background of Italian anticlericalism, raising questions such as the motivations
behind rural religious attitudes, the ambivalent
stance of the lower middle class vis-à-vis the
Church, and the relationship between anticlericalism
and a concern with the position of women.

* Sánchez, José. "Italy." ANTICLERICALISM: A BRIEF
  HISTORY (item 229), 143-60.

  Compares Italian anticlericalism to its French
  and Spanish counterparts, finding it more moderate
  and more discerning in separating the reality from
  the myth of clerical domination.

* Schapiro, J. Salwyn. "Unification and the Temporal
  Power in Italy." ANTICLERICALISM: CONFLICT
  BETWEEN CHURCH AND STATE IN FRANCE, ITALY, AND
  SPAIN (item 230), 72-8.

  A brief discussion of the factors leading to the
  rise of an anticlerical mentality in nineteenth-
  century Italy.

Liberal Catholicism

651. Casella, M.C. RELIGIOUS LIBERALISM IN MODERN ITALY.
     London: Faith Press, 1965-6. 2 vols.

     Volume 1 studies the oftentimes stormy evolution
     of nineteenth-century Catholic liberal movements,
     with emphasis on the years of the *Risorgimento*.
     Offers a balanced account of the main issues at
     stake in the Papal-liberal conflict.

     See: E.E.Y. Hales, JEH 17 (October 1966): 278-80;
          A.R. Vidler, THEO 70 (May 1967): 234-5.

652. Leetham, Claude. ROSMINI: PRIEST, PHILOSOPHER AND
     PATRIOT. Baltimore: Helicon Press, 1958.

     Describes his personality and justifies his ideas
     and activity. Emphasizes, along with Rosmini's
     foundation of the Institute of Charity, his complex
     political relationship with both Pius IX and Manzoni.

Sees his lack of intellectual concern over the
temporal power as the most logical response to
the *Risorgimento* by a devout Italian Catholic.

See: IER 88 (November 1957): 369-70; Norman St.
        John-Stevas, TC 163 (January 1958): 82-3;
        Roland Hill, DUBR 232 (Spring 1958): 93-6;
        James Collins, CHR 45 (January 1960): 459-
        61.

653.   Pagani, G.B.   THE LIFE OF ANTONIO ROSMINI-SERBATI.
       London: George Routledge and Sons, 1906.

       A highly positive portrait.   Points to his
       virtuous and indomitable spirit as his greatest
       asset.

  *   Reardon, Bernard M.G.   "Italian Ontologism: Gioberti
       and Rosmini."   RELIGION IN THE AGE OF
       ROMANTICISM: STUDIES IN EARLY NINETEENTH-CENTURY
       THOUGHT (item 255), 146-75.

       Traces the attempt by Gioberti and Rosmini to
       formulate a philosophy which would assist the
       Church in speaking more effectively to the radically
       changing world of the nineteenth century.

                          Germany

                       General Works

654.   Dru, Alexander.   THE CONTRIBUTION OF GERMAN
       CATHOLICISM.   The Twentieth Century
       Encyclopedia of Catholicism, vol. 101.
       New York: Hawthorn Books, 1964.

       Focuses on the cultural side of nineteenth-century
       German Catholicism, and the way it affected history,
       philosophy, science, art, and popular customs.
       Carries the survey from the romantics in Münster
       through the scholastic circle at Mainz and
       Döllinger's scholarship, to the political and social
       programs of Görres and Ketteler.

See: E.E.Y. Hales, CLR 49 (February 1964): 122-3;
       Desmond Gregory, DR 82 (April 1964): 178-80;
       N.A. Weber, CHR 50 (October 1964): 427-8;
       CW 200 (March 1965): 381-2.

655.   ————. "The Reformation of the Nineteenth
       Century: Christianity in Germany from 1800
       to 1848." DUBR 226 (Autumn 1952): 34-45.

An introduction to the main developments within
German Catholicism during the first half of the
nineteenth century.

The Hierarchy

656. Logan, F. Donald. "The 1875 Statement of the German
      Bishops on Episcopal Powers." JUR 21 (July
      1961): 285-95.

Contends that the bishops' reassertion of their
own powers came about because of (1) Vatican I's
failure to clarify the role of residential bishops
within the structure of the Church; and (2)
Bismarck's campaign to misrepresent the Council's
decrees on papal infallibility and jurisdiction
as the first steps in a new age of papal absolutism.

657. Marschke, Paul Otto. THE PRUSSIAN EPISCOPATE AND
      THE STATE, 1878-1890. Ph.D. dissertation.
      University of Minnesota, Minneapolis, 1971.

Clarifies the crucial role played by the Prussian
bishops during the last stages of the *Kulturkampf*.
Contrasts Bismarck's efforts to end the war against
the Church with the hierarchy's continuing
resistance to his exercise of the right of clerical
appointment.

Orders and Congregations

658. Kohler, Sister Mary Hortense, O.P. LIFE AND WORK
      OF MOTHER BENEDICTA BAUER. Milwaukee: Bruce,
      1937-62. 2 vols.

An in-depth study of the personality of Mother
Bauer (1803-1865), along with her accomplishments,
first as Prioress of the Dominican convent of the
Holy Cross, Regensburg, and then, during the
final decade of her life, as foundress of the
community of St. Catherine of Siena at Racine,
Wisconsin.

See: AMER 57 (28 August 1937): 503; WMH 21
      (September 1937): 112-3; Bernard J. Monks,
      HB 16 (May 1938): 79.

Missionary Activity

659. Rivinius, Karl Josef, S.V.D. "Efforts of the
      Imperial German Government to Establish a
      Protectorate over the German Catholic Missions
      in South Shantung." IBMR 9 (April 1985): 71-4.

      Maintains that the Divine Word Fathers entered
      into a contractual agreement with the German
      government during the 1880s and 90s, not only to
      advance the imperial regime's interests in China
      but also to assure the Church a greater amount of
      religious freedom within Germany.

660. Schabert, Joseph A. "The Ludwig-Missionsverein."
      CHR 8 (April 1922): 23-41.

      Examines the Bavarian government's financial
      support of worldwide missionary activity during
      the years 1838-1914.

Religious Thought

661. Acton, [John Emerich Edward Dalberg, 1st] Lord.
      "Doellinger's Historical Work." EHR 5
      (October 1890): 700-44.

      A lengthy, appreciative study of Döllinger's
      writings on ecclesiastical history. Considers
      Christianity the essence of his historical outlook,
      which Acton finds best expressed in his four-volume

CHURCH HISTORY (1833-1838).

662. Alexander, Edgar. "Church and Society in
     Germany: Social and Political Movements and
     Ideas in German and Austrian Catholicism
     (1789-1950). III. Catholicism and German
     Romanticism." In CHURCH AND SOCIETY: CATHOLIC
     SOCIAL AND POLITICAL THOUGHT AND MOVEMENTS,
     1789-1950 (item 308), 366-406.

     Pinpoints the nature and significance of Catholic
     romanticism in Germany through an analysis of the
     philosophy and activities of its three leading
     representatives, Joseph von Eichendorff, Joseph
     Görres, and Franz von Baader.

663. Burtchaell, James Tunstead, C.S.C. "Drey, Möhler
     and the Catholic School of Tübingen." In
     NINETEENTH CENTURY RELIGIOUS THOUGHT IN THE WEST
     (item 258), II, 111-39.

     An overview of the historical theology produced
     by the Catholic faculty at Tübingen from 1817 to
     1869. Takes the scholarship of Drey and Möhler as
     typical of the commitment to serve the Church
     through serious academic research, a research which
     often led to their censorship by the very authorities
     for whose intellectual benefit they were writing.

664. Conzemius, Victor. "Ignaz v. Dollinger: The
     Development of a XIXth-Century Ecumenist." In
     HUNDERT JAHRE CHRISTKATHOLISCH-THEOLOGISCHE
     FAKULTÄT DER UNIVERSITÄT BERN, edited by Kurt
     Stalder, 110-27. Berne: Internationalen
     Kirchlichen Zeitschrift, 1974.

     Traces Döllinger's long and difficult development
     as an ecumenical theologian and activist. Attributes
     his changing outlook, which replaced a militant
     Catholicism with a belief in dialogue with
     Protestants, to a combination of personal experiences
     and the political, social, and cultural climate of
     his time.

665. Detzler, Wayne. "Protest and Schism in Nineteenth-
     Century German Catholicism: The Ronge-Czerski
     Movement, 1844-5." In SCHISM, HERESY AND

RELIGIOUS PROTEST: PAPERS READ AT THE TENTH
SUMMER MEETING AND THE ELEVENTH WINTER MEETING
OF THE ECCLESIASTICAL HISTORY SOCIETY, edited
by Derek Baker, 341-9. Studies in Church
History, vol. 9. Cambridge: At the University
Press, 1972.

Looks at the origins of the two currents of
religious revolt which merged in 1845 to form the
German Catholic Church. The first originated in
upper Silesia, where Father Johannes Ronge was
excommunicated in 1844 for accusing Bishop
Wilhelm Arnoldi of Trier of exploiting his people
by an exhibition of Christ's robe; after his
excommunication, he rejected the sacrament of
penance and clerical celibacy. Led by Father
Johann Czerski, the second movement started in
Schneidemuehe (northeast of Poznan); in 1845,
Czerski declared his independence from Rome,
married, and introduced a vernacular Mass. The
merger of these movements foundered after 1848,
due to internal disputes and weak leadership.

See: John W. O'Malley, S.J., REVREL 32 (January
      1973): 186; CHOICE 10 (April 1973): 305;
      Roland H. Bainton, CH 42 (June 1973): 275-
      6; Scott H. Hendrix, JAAR 41 (December
      1973): 636-7.

666. Dietrich, Donald J. THE GOETHEZEIT AND THE
      METAMORPHOSIS OF CATHOLIC THEOLOGY IN THE
      AGE OF IDEALISM. European University
      Studies, Series 23, vol. 128. Berne and
      Frankfurt/Main: Peter Lang, 1979.

      Argues that romanticism and idealism provided the
      context and categories for the various creative
      currents within German theology during the first
      half of the nineteenth century. Includes detailed
      treatments of Georg Hermes, Johann Michael Sailer,
      Drey, Möhler, Franz Anton Staudenmaier, and
      Johannes von Kuhn.

      See: Francis S. Fiorenza, CHR 68 (October
            1982): 661-2.

667. ———. "Priests and Political Thought: Theology

and Reform in Central Europe, 1845-1855." CHR 71
(October 1985): 519-46.

Details the attempts of two priests, Johann
Baptist Hirscher and Anton Günther, to combine
theology and philosophy with serious reflection
on social and political reform, in order to
integrate the Church into the rapidly changing
world of the nineteenth century. Attributes
their total failure to their lack of influence
among the hierarchy, which feared the challenges
of the time.

668. Fehr, Wayne L. THE BIRTH OF THE CATHOLIC TÜBINGEN
SCHOOL: THE DOGMATICS OF JOHANN SEBASTIAN DREY.
American Academy of Religion Academy Series,
vol. 37. Chico, Calif: Scholars Press, 1981.

A historical study of the founder of the Catholic
faculty at Tübingen. Interprets his work as an
effort to counter the Enlightenment's historicism by
a synthesis based heavily upon the philosophical
idealism of the early Schelling.

See: Gerald A. McCool, S.J., RSR 9 (April
1983): 148-9; Michael J. Himes, JR 64
(April 1984): 250-1; Gerald A. McCool,
S.J., CHR 70 (July 1984): 492-3; R.H.
Roberts, JTS 36 (April 1985): 285.

669. Fischer, Herman C. "Hergenroether (1824-1890)." In
CHURCH HISTORIANS, INCLUDING PAPERS ON EUSEBIUS,
OROSIUS, ST. BEDE THE VENERABLE, ORDERICUS
VITALIS, LAS CASAS, BARONIUS, BOLLANDUS, MURATORI,
MOEHLER, LINGARD, HERGENROETHER, JANSSEN, DENIFLE,
LUDWIG VON PASTOR (item 266), 289-320.

A sketch of the passionately anti-liberal
historian of the medieval Church and foremost
academic opponent of Döllinger in the years
after Vatican I. In 1879 he was appointed
Cardinal-Prefect of the Vatican Archives, the
first after Leo XIII's decision to open them
to scholars.

670. Gottfried, Paul. CONSERVATIVE MILLENARIANS: THE
ROMANTIC EXPERIENCE IN BAVARIA.

New York: Fordham University Press, 1979.

Details the intellectual dimension of the Catholic
revival in Munich at the beginning of the nineteenth
century. Analyzes the ideas of the romantic conservatives, with special reference to their historical
sense, eschatology, and campaign against the secular
liberal state, the Enlightenment, and the exaltation
of reason. Singles out the contributions of Baader,
Döllinger, Görres, Novalis, and Schlegel.

See: Virgil Nemoianu, MA 24 (Fall 1980): 424-7;
       Theodore S. Hamerow, AHR 85 (December
       1980): 1217-8.

671.   Gwatkin, Jean Bowes.   "Döllinger, the Renoufs and
       Rome." TABLET 222 (20 January 1968):   54-5.

Brings to light a new aspect of Döllinger's
relationship with the Vatican after his excommunication. Outlines the efforts made by Peter
Le Page Renouf, Professor of Ancient History at
the Irish University, and his wife to reconcile
their longtime friend and the Pope. Döllinger's
death in 1890 ended the maneuvering.

672.   Miller, Leo F.   "Moehler (1796-18380." In CHURCH
       HISTORIANS, INCLUDING PAPERS ON EUSEBIUS,
       OROSIUS, ST. BEDE THE VENERABLE, ORDERICUS
       VITALIS, LAS CASAS, BARONIUS, BOLLANDUS,
       MURATORI, MOEHLER, LINGARD, HERGENROETHER,
       JANSSEN, DENIFLE, LUDWIG VON PASTOR (item
       266), 240-76.

Balances a discussion of his well-known theological and political views with an analysis of
his often neglected historical work.

673.   O'Donnell, Terrence F.   "The Dry Bones of
       Knowledge: Augustin Theiner, 1804-1874."
       DUNR 3 (January 1963):   66-89.

Rescues Theiner from the oblivion into which he
sank after his dismissal as Prefect of the Vatican
Archives in 1870. Emphasizes his vital contributions
to nineteenth-century Catholicism: his historical
studies of canon law, behind-the-scenes activity at

Vatican I, and publication of much primary material
from the Archives during his fifteen-year tenure.

674. O'Meara, Thomas Franklin, O.P. ROMANTIC IDEALISM
     AND ROMAN CATHOLICISM: SCHELLING AND THE
     THEOLOGIANS. Notre Dame: University of Notre
     Dame Press, 1982.

     Assesses the impact of the German romantics, and
     particularly Schelling, upon early nineteenth-century
     Catholic theologians. Maintains that romanticism's
     emphasis on feeling, intuition, and the discovery of
     God within the historical process found a ready-made
     audience within the Church.

     See: John C. Moore, HRNB 11 (November/December
          1982): 57; Peter C. Hodgson, RSR 9 (October
          1983): 362; Darrell Jodock, CH 52 (December
          1983): 517-8; John E. Toews, JMH 55 (December
          1983): 688-90; John Coulson, JTS 35 (April
          1984): 266-7; Donald J. Dietrich, CHR 70
          (July 1984): 495-6; Ronald Burke, JAAR 52
          (September 1984): 623.

675. O'Sullivan, J.M. "Heinrich Suso Denifle, O.P.,
     Historian." IER 5 (May 1915): 460-74.

     An appreciation of the foremost Catholic
     historian of his time. Praises his insistence
     on full and proper documentation as well as his
     debunking of several medieval legends.

*   Parsons, Reuben. "The Apostasy of Doellinger."
     STUDIES IN CHURCH HISTORY, 6 (item 27), 413-26.

     Claims that Döllinger abandoned Rome long before
     the decrees of Vatican I, pointing to his writings
     of the 1860s as proof.

*   Reardon, Bernard M.G. "German Catholic Theology in
     the Romantic Era." RELIGION IN THE AGE OF
     ROMANTICISM: STUDIES IN EARLY NINETEENTH-CENTURY
     THOUGHT (item 255), 117-45.

     Divides the theological revival of the romantic
     period in Germany into two currents: the "semi-
     rationalism" of Hermes and Günther, and the

romanticist thought of the Munich and Tübingen
schools, the former represented by Baader and
Görres, and the latter by Drey and Möhler.

676. Stratemeier, Boniface. "Denifle (1844-1905)."
      In CHURCH HISTORIANS, INCLUDING PAPERS ON
      EUSEBIUS, OROSIUS, ST. BEDE THE VENERABLE,
      ORDERICUS VITALIS, LAS CASAS, BARONIUS,
      BOLLANDUS, MURATORI, MOEHLER, LINGARD,
      HERGENROETHER, JANSSEN, DENIFLE, LUDWIG VON
      PASTOR (item 266), 354-72.

      Discusses his histories of medieval universities,
      the Hundred Years War, and Martin Luther.

677. Swidler, Leonard. AUFKLÄRUNG CATHOLICISM, 1780-
      1850: LITURGICAL AND OTHER REFORMS IN THE
      CATHOLIC AUFKLÄRUNG. American Academy of
      Religion Studies in Religion, vol. 17.
      Missoula, Mont.: Scholars Press, 1978.

      A concise treatment of the intellectual forces
      behind liturgical reform in the German Catholic
      states. Casts the Enlightenment liturgists as
      well-intentioned men who sought to reform the
      Church along Scriptural lines, and wanted to use
      the liturgy to teach basic doctrine and improve
      public morality.

      See: John F. Broderick, CH 49 (March 1980): 103;
             T.C.W. Blanning, JEH 31 (April 1980): 241-
             2; Conrad L. Donakowski, CHR 67 (October
             1981): 629-30.

678. Tonsor, Stephen John. IGNAZ VON DÖLLINGER: A STUDY
      IN CATHOLIC HISTORICISM. Ph.D. dissertation.
      University of Illinois, 1955.

      Deals with Döllinger's pre-schismatic career.
      Underscores both the revolutionary techniques he
      introduced into the study of the past and the
      enormous respect with which his interpretation of
      the Church's development was greeted by academics
      and the public alike.

Education

679. Helmreich, Ernst Christian. RELIGIOUS EDUCATION IN
      GERMAN SCHOOLS: AN HISTORICAL APPROACH.
      Cambridge: Harvard University Press, 1959.

      Chapters 3-6 investigate religious instruction in
      nineteenth-century elementary and secondary schools,
      with special reference to its content, methods,
      supervision by the state, impact on school adminis-
      tration, and general political effects.

      See: Robert La Follette, AHR 60 (October 1960): 215-
            6; George W. Forell, JCEA 20 (January
            1961): 479; Eric H. Boehm, AAAPSS 338 (November
            1961): 163.

680. Lamberti, Marjorie. "State, Church and the Politics
      of School Reform during the Kulturkampf." CEH 19
      (March 1986): 63-81.

      Proposes a new perspective and methodology for
      ascertaining the specific impact of the *Kulturkampf*
      on Catholic elementary education.

                     Piety and Devotion

681. Ponet, Marthe Bordeaux [Danemarie, Jeanne]. THE
      MYSTERY OF STIGMATA FROM CATHERINE EMMERICH TO
      THERESA NEUMANN. Translated by Warre B. Wells.
      London: Burns Oates & Washbourne, 1934.

      Devotes the first five chapters to the century's
      most famous stigmatist, Catherine Emmerich of
      Dülmen (1774-1824), who received the mark of the
      cross on her breast in 1812. Thoroughly examined
      by political as well as ecclesiastical authorities,
      and constantly besieged by pilgrims from all over
      Europe, she enhanced the popular image of her
      saintliness by admitting that she had experienced
      supernatural visions since the age of four.

      See: IER 44 (August 1934): 213-7.

*   Pourrat, Pierre, S.S. "Germany." CHRISTIAN
      SPIRITUALITY, vol. 4: FROM JANSENISM TO
      MODERN TIMES (item 319), 412-22.

      Surveys the spiritual writings of John Joseph
      Görres, Anne Catherine Emmerich, and Clement
      Brentano.

682. Schmöger, K.E., C.SS.R.   LIFE OF ANNE CATHERINE
      EMMERICH. New York: Pustet, 1885. 2 vols.

      The standard life of the most celebrated
      European mystic of the nineteenth century.
      Emmerich, an Augustinian nun, received the
      stigmata in 1812-1813; through the next decade
      came a succession of ecstasies, visions, and
      messages, which were collected and published
      by her secretary, Clement Brentano.

      See: AMER 51 (29 September 1934): 595.

683. Sperber, Jonathan. POPULAR CATHOLICISM IN NINETEENTH-
      CENTURY GERMANY. Princeton: Princeton University
      Press, 1984.

      Focuses on the revival of popular Catholic
      religiosity in the middle Rhineland between 1850
      and 1880, along with its political implications.
      Contrasts the post-1850 renewal, as expressed
      through a dramatic rise in Mass attendance, parish
      missions, pilgrimages, and new religious associ-
      ations, with the clerical laxity and lay indiffer-
      ence of the *Vormärz*, seeing in the vitality of the
      former the basis for a coherent political Catholicism
      which would become an important force in Westphalia
      and the northern Rhineland during the years
      immediately preceding the *Kulturkampf*.

      See: Ronald J. Ross, AHR 90 (October 1985): 955-6;
            Nicholas Hope, JEH 37 (January 1986): 134-6;
            Gary Lease, RSR 12 (January 1986): 78-9; Ann
            Taves, CH 55 (March 1986): 124-5; Nadia M.
            Lahutsky, JAAR 54 (Spring 1986): 195-6;
            Michael Phayer, CHR 72 (April 1986): 295-6;
            Walter D. Kamphoefner, JSH 20 (Fall 1986): 214-
            6.

684. ————. "The Transformation of Catholic Associations
in the Northern Rhineland and Westphalia, 1830-
1870." JSH 15 (Winter 1981): 253-63.

Describes in a particularly dynamic regional
setting the formative stages of the development
of Catholic organizations--e.g., brotherhoods
and sodalities--founded by clergy, with the
purpose of thwarting the century's growing
secular tendencies. Outlines, at the same time,
the political and social contours of the formation
process.

The Liturgical Movement

685. Franklin, R.W. "Response: Humanism and
Transcendence in the Nineteenth Century
Liturgical Movement." WOR 59 (July
1985): 342-53.

A reply to item 686. Measures the degree to which
the romantic notion of community influenced the
nineteenth-century liturgical movement's emphasis on
the Eucharist, lay participation, and humanism.
Highlights the work of the Wolter brothers at Beuron.

686. O'Meara, Thomas F. "The Origins of the Liturgical
Movement and German Romanticism." WOR 59 (July
1985): 326-42.

Finds within German romanticism's concern with
time, revelation, mysticism, and community the
seeds, promise, and limitations of the nineteenth-
century liturgical movement. Focuses on developments in Ludwig I's Munich (1826-1848), looking at
the religious revival sparked by Schelling, Görres,
and the Abbey of Saint Boniface. For a reply to
these arguments, see item 685.

Social Catholicism

General

687. Brauer, T. THE CATHOLIC SOCIAL MOVEMENT IN GERMANY.
      Oxford: The Catholic Social Guild, 1932.

      Traces the origins of the movement in the years
      immediately before 1850, as Catholics sought to
      counter the growing popularity of socialism and
      communism. Spotlights three leading personalities
      within the movement: Adolf Kolping (1813-1864),
      Wilhelm Emmanuel von Ketteler (1811-1877), and
      Franz Hitze (1851-1921).

688. Brose, Eric Dorn. CHRISTIAN LABOR AND THE POLITICS
      OF FRUSTRATION IN IMPERIAL GERMANY. Washington,
      D.C.: Catholic University of America Press, 1985.

      Details the origins, program, and social
      philosophy of Catholic and Protestant trade
      unions. Illustrates the degree to which their
      leaders were thwarted in their political aims
      by their own clergy as well as by the government
      and traditional elites.

      See: Ellen L. Evans, AHR 90 (December 1985): 1219-
            20; Robert W. Lougee, HRNB 14 (March/April
            1986): 115; Thomas A. Knapp, CHR 72 (April
            1986): 329-30; Spencer C. Tucker, RSR 12
            (July/October 1986): 305; William L. Patch,
            Jr., JMH 58 (December 1986): 985-7.

689. Christie, Francis A. "Aspects of the Catholic Social
      Movement." CHR 9 (April 1923): 48-56.

      Sees Bishop Ketteler's demands for reform,
      expressed through the Center Party, as one of the
      main motivations behind Bismarck's social legislation.

690. Kraus, Ingrid Marianne. THE BERLIN CATHOLIC CHURCH,
      1871-1918: ITS SOCIAL AND POLITICAL ENDEAVORS.
      Ph.D. dissertation. University of Nebraska,
      Lincoln, 1981.

Measures the response of the Berlin Church to both
national and local political and social problems of
the Wilhelmine era. Lists, among other activities,
its support of workers' associations and sponsorship
of numerous charitable and social programs.

691. Schneider, Michael. "Religion and Labour Organization: The Christian Trade Unions in the
Wilhelmine Empire." ESR 12 (July 1982): 345-69.

Reexamines traditional views of the nature of
Catholic trade unionism in late nineteenth-century
Germany. Gauges the degree of religious influence
over the organization of a workforce usually seen
as alienated from the Church and therefore impervious
to contemporary Catholic social teaching.

* Vidler, Alec R. "Germany." A CENTURY OF SOCIAL
CATHOLICISM, 1820-1920 (item 315), 99-111.

Concentrates on the achievements of Ketteler,
who is declared the greatest figure in nineteenth-
century social Catholicism.

Ketteler

692. Bock, Edward Cornelius. WILHELM EMMANUEL VON
KETTELER: HIS SOCIAL AND POLITICAL PHILOSOPHY.
Ph.D. dissertation. University of Oklahoma,
1967.

Focuses on his program to Christianize German
society and politics, along with his work with
the Center Party, which made him the undisputed
leader of the Church in Germany between 1848 and
1871.

693. Hogan, William Edward. THE DEVELOPMENT OF BISHOP
WILHELM EMMANUEL VON KETTELER'S INTERPRETATION
OF THE SOCIAL PROBLEM. The Catholic University
of America Studies in Sociology, vol. 22.
Washington, D.C.: Catholic University of
America Press, 1946.

Follows Ketteler's odyssey from his early reforms,

undertaken as a parish priest, to his demands for
national social legislation. Details the variety
of experiments through which he sought to eradicate
the "social problem," i.e., the widespread existence
of poverty. Mitigates his attractive image by
noting that he never pursued a project long enough
for it to be effective, and in all of his writings
he rarely exhibited a profound or original thought.

694. Laux, John Joseph [Metlake, George]. CHRISTIAN
      SOCIAL REFORM: PROGRAM OUTLINED BY ITS PIONEER,
      WILLIAM EMMANUEL BARON VON KETTELER, BISHOP OF
      MAINZ. Philadelphia: Dolphin Press, 1912.

      Concentrates on various aspects of Ketteler's
      treatment of the contemporary labor problem,
      including his criticism of liberalism and socialism,
      his view of the relationship between the Church and
      the worker, and his vital role during the *Kultur-
      kampf*.

      See: AMER 7 (28 September 1912): 594-5; CW 96
            (October 1912): 103-4.

695. Schmidt, Hunter, and Bock, Edward C. "Wilhelm von
      Ketteler: The 'Social Bishop.'" SJR 76 (July/
      August 1985): 99-103, 106.

      A brief biography. Declares Ketteler the father
      of social Catholicism in Germany and the most
      important leader in the nineteenth-century German
      Church.

                        Special Challenges

                        Church and State

696. Anderson, Margaret Lavinia. "The Kulturkampf and
      the Course of German History." CEH 19 (March
      1986): 82-115.

      Maintains that the *Kulturkampf* caused a massive
      realignment of the Catholic political structure; as
      Bismarck's campaign against the Church succeeded in

removing, compromising, or isolating an increasingly
larger number of bishops, the Catholic political
milieu, now bereft of its episcopal leadership,
became democratized and laicized. But for a response
to this argument, see item 703.

697. Grant, Hugh. "Bismarck and the Papacy." IER 88
(July 1957): 35-40.

Sketches the origins, course, and results of the
Kulturkampf from 1864 to 1888. Gives Bismarck the
entire responsibility for the conflict.

698. Hatfield, Douglas W. "Kulturkampf: The Relationship
of Church and State and the Failure of German
Political Reform." JCS 23 (Autumn 1981): 465-84.

Examines the motives and activities of the
bureaucrats, National Liberals, Progressives, and
other factions supporting Bismarck in his fight
against the Church. Shows that while the *Kulturkampf* tended to bring the Catholic laity and
hierarchy closer together, it only highlighted how
the causes of political liberalism and secularization worked at cross-purposes with one another,
thereby preventing any true reform of the traditional
political structure.

699. Herbst, Clarence A., S.J. "The Beginnings of the
Kulturkampf." HB 27 (March 1949): 55-9.

Lists, among the reasons for the campaign against
the Church, Bismarck's own dislike of Catholicism,
general hostility throughout Germany against
religious orders, and resentment over the decree on
papal infallibility.

700. ————. "The 'Catholic Fraction.'" HB 29 (March
1951): 121-34.

Describes the Catholic side of the most serious
case of pre-*Kulturkampf* Church-State conflict. The
"Catholic Fraction" was founded in 1852 to combat
the growing number of government encroachments on
the Church's freedom. Its vigorous and frequently
successful activity continued until 1858, when it
was abandoned by the liberals.

701. Higby, Chester Penn. THE RELIGIOUS POLICY OF THE
      BAVARIAN GOVERNMENT DURING THE NAPOLEONIC PERIOD.
      Studies in History, Economics and Public Law,
      vol. 85, no. 1. New York: Published for
      Columbia University by Longmans, Green, 1919.

      Analyzes the four main aspects of the Bavarian
      government's religious policy between 1799 and
      1815: official toleration of Protestants and
      Jews; secularization of all monastic, cathedral,
      and collegiate property; subjection of hierarchy
      and clergy to State control; and political regu-
      lation of popular religious practice. Of the
      four the first two are judged new, revolutionary,
      and successful; while the third is considered
      only partially successful, and the fourth neither
      wise nor successful.

702. Kent, George O. ARNIM AND BISMARCK.
      Oxford: Clarendon Press, 1968.

      Unravels the intrigues of Bismarck and Harry
      von Arnim, his Minister to the Holy See, aimed
      against an ever more forceful Papacy. Clarifies
      their efforts to influence or at least minimize
      Papal power during the late 1860s and early
      1870s. Considers their policy an ill-conceived
      foretaste of the *Kulturkampf.*

      See: TLS, 29 May 1969: 587; CHOICE 6 (September
            1969): 894; James J. Sheehan, AHR 75 (October
            1969): 149-50; Frank Eyck, HIST 55 (February
            1970): 147-8; Otto Pflanze, JMH 42 (September
            1970): 423-4; Norman Rich, CHR 57 (April
            1971): 141-2; A.J. Nicholls, EHR 86 (July
            1971): 637-8.

703. Lidtke, Vernon L. "Catholics and Politics in
      Nineteenth-Century Germany: A Comment." CEH
      19 (March 1986): 116-22.

      A response to item 696.

704. Lougee, Robert W. "The *Kulturkampf* and Historical
      Positivism." CH 23 (September 1954): 219-35.

      Locates the intellectual roots of the *Kulturkampf*

within a group of Berlin scholars who, by helping to
draft and then defend the May Laws, were aiming not
at a secular society or an absolute state, but at
achieving a Church-State balance built on historical
custom, positive law, and contemporary realities,
and therefore a good in itself.

* Parsons, Reuben. "The Bismarckian So-Called 'War for
    Civilization.'" STUDIES IN CHURCH HISTORY, 6
    (item 27), 1-44.

    Condemns Bismarck's policy as the counter-
    productive work of Protestants, Freemasons, Old
    Catholics, and, most importantly, those for whom
    the State was omnipotent.

* ————. "Pope Leo XIII and the German Empire."
    STUDIES IN CHURCH HISTORY, 6 (item 27), 265-83.

    An overview of post-*Kulturkampf* relations between
    the Vatican and Berlin, centering on William II's
    visits to Leo XIII in 1888 and 1893.

705. Prill, Felician. IRELAND, BRITAIN AND GERMANY, 1870-
    1914: PROBLEMS OF NATIONALISM AND RELIGION IN
    NINETEENTH CENTURY EUROPE. Dublin: Gill and
    Macmillan, 1975.

    Compares, within a discussion of official and
    unofficial German attitudes toward the Irish
    Question, German and British relations with the
    Holy See.

    See: CHOICE 12 (January 1976): 1492; J.C. Beckett,
    TLS, 16 January 1976: 61; Joseph M. Hernon,
    Jr., AHR 81 (October 1976): 846-7; Paul M.
    Kennedy, EHR 91 (October 1976): 928.

706. Ross, Ronald J. "Enforcing the Kulturkampf in the
    Bismarckian State and the Limits of Coercion in
    Imperial Germany." JMH 56 (September 1984): 456-
    82.

    Explains the reasons behind the failure of
    Bismarck's campaign against the Catholic Church
    between 1871 and 1887: Imperial Germany never
    developed suitable institutions and procedures

with which to coerce its Catholic population.
Moreover, Catholic resistance to the new
ecclesiastical regulations and restrictions
remained strong, fueled by a consistently
high morale.

707.   Southern, Gilbert Edwin, Jr.   THE BAVARIAN *KULTUR-
        KAMPF*:   A CHAPTER IN GOVERNMENT, CHURCH AND
        SOCIETY IN THE EARLY *BISMARCKREICH*.   Ph.D.
        dissertation.   University of Massachusetts,
        1977.

        Examines the programs, leadership, and membership
        of the approximately 170 regional and local Catholic
        political associations involved in the Bavarian
        clerical movement during the years 1871-1875.

708.   Windell, George G.   THE CATHOLICS AND GERMAN UNITY,
        1866-1871.   Minneapolis: University of Minnesota
        Press, 1954.

        Delineates the varying reactions of German
        Catholics to the national unification movement
        during the period between the Prussian defeat
        of the Hapsburgs and the establishment of the
        Empire.   Catholic bewilderment in 1866 led to
        a wide fragmentation of opinion, seen in the
        conflicts between pro- and anti-Bismarck forces,
        conservatives and liberals, and centralizers and
        federalists.

        See: Garland Downum, AAAPSS 300 (July 1955): 172-3;
                B.J. Blied, SJR 48 (July/August 1955): 163-4;
                Carlton J.H. Hayes, AHR 61 (October 1955): 126-
                7; William O. Shanahan, JMH 28 (March
                1956): 71-2; A.J.P. Taylor, EHR 71 (April
                1956): 344-5; John K. Zeender, CHR 42 (July
                1956): 205-7; George N. Shuster, JCEA 16
                (October 1956): 313-4.

Catholic Political Activity

709.   Anderson, Margaret Lavinia.   WINDTHORST: A POLITICAL
        BIOGRAPHY.   New York: Oxford University Press,
        1981.

Reconstructs the process by which Windthorst
created a Catholic parliamentary opposition party
after 1871. Offers a new perspective on the
workings of the *Kulturkampf*, interpreting it from
the viewpoint of German Catholics rather than from
that of either Bismarck or Rome.

See: James Joll, TLS, 9 October 1981: 1151; James C.
Hunt, RP 44 (July 1982): 464-6; Ronald J. Ross,
AHR 87 (October 1982): 1118; J.R.C. Wright,
JEH 33 (October 1982): 640-2; Theodore S.
Hamerow, GQ 56 (March 1983): 354-5; Jonathan
Sperber, JMH 55 (March 1983): 168-70; Klaus P.
Fischer, MA 27 (Spring 1983): 220-1; Gwendolyn
E. Jensen, CH 52 (June 1983): 227-8; Juergen
Doerr, DALR 63 (Summer 1983): 341-4; Martin
Kitchen, HIS 46 (November 1983): 108-9; David
W. Hendon, JCS 25 (Winter 1983): 165-6; Agatha
Ramm, EHR 99 (April 1984): 458-9; Eric C.
Kohler, CHR 70 (October 1984): 599-600.

710. "Bishop Ketteler and the Prussian Programme." TABLET
179 (28 March 1942): 158.

Summarizes Ketteler's GERMANY AFTER THE WAR OF
1866, in which he denounced the deification of the
modern state which he found so apparent in Prussian
thought and political activity.

711. Blackbourn, David. CLASS, RELIGION AND LOCAL
POLITICS IN WILHELMINE GERMANY: THE CENTER
PARTY IN WÜRTTEMBERG BEFORE 1914. New
Haven: Yale University Press, 1980.

Explains the changing political and social
contours of the Catholic Center Party during the
1890s, by examining its activities in the
culturally and economically isolated area of
Württemberg. With the decline of elite-controlled
politics, Center leaders turned to mass mobili-
zation of the urban and rural lower middle class,
traditionally shunned as a "backward" constituency,
and one which changed the party's direction from
left to right. For a briefer treatment of these
developments by the same author, see item 712.

See: CHOICE 18 (December 1980): 574;

Shelley Baranowski, RSR 7 (January 1981): 80;
Robert W. Lougee, HRNB 9 (February 1981): 101;
Jill Stephenson, TLS, 20 March 1981: 319; David
J. Diephouse, JCS 23 (Spring 1981): 354-5;
Ronald J. Ross, AHR 86 (June 1981): 607; Peter
Pulzer, EHR 96 (July 1981): 632-4; David C.
Smith, JAAR 49 (December 1981): 694-5; Lamar
Cecil, JMH 53 (December 1981): 750-2; Robert
P. Grathwol, HIS 44 (February 1982): 265; John
C. Fout, CH 51 (June 1982): 237-8; Juergen
Doerr, DALR 63 (Summer 1983): 344-6; John K.
Zeender, CHR 70 (July 1984): 431-3.

712. ————. "The Political Alignment of the Centre Party
in Wilhelmine Germany: A Study of the Party's
Emergence in Nineteenth-Century Württemberg." HJ
18 (December 1975): 821-50.

A summary of item 711.

713. Blackburn, John Glenn, Jr. FRANZ VON BAADER: A
LIBERAL CATHOLIC. Ph.D. dissertation. University
of North Carolina, Chapel Hill, 1974.

Evaluates his political thought, its origins and
impact. Of special importance is the discussion of
his theory of Church government, which led him to
espouse ecumenism and propose that the hierarchy
help the German proletariat to form corporate bodies
in support of workers' rights.

714. Corrigan, Raymond, S.J. "Görres: Battler for
Liberty." HB 16 (November 1937): 9-11.

Praises Görres' lifelong commitment to political
and religious freedom, both for individuals and for
the Church.

715. Curran, Francis X., S.J. "Ludwig von Windthorst."
HB 17 (January 1939): 25-6.

Deals with his role as the first leader of the
Center Party.

716. Evans, Ellen L. "Catholic Political Movements in
Germany, Switzerland, and the Netherlands: Notes
for a Comparative Approach." CEH 17

(June/September 1984): 91-119.

Finds significant similarities between the Center Party in Germany, on the one hand, and contemporary Catholic political parties in Switzerland and the Netherlands, on the other. Especially noteworthy, according to Evans, is the common pattern behind their origins: each developed in the first place as the defensive reaction of a national minority, branded as less than patriotic by the majority.

717. ————. THE GERMAN CENTER PARTY, 1870-1933: A STUDY IN POLITICAL CATHOLICISM. Carbondale: Southern Illinois University Press, 1981.

A survey of the Party's development. Emphasizes its continuing image of itself as a persecuted minority with little choice but to follow a democratic line. Provides along the way discussions of Bismarck's provocations and the mechanics of *Kulturpolitik* (state policy on such religious issues as clerical appointments and church-building).

See: CHOICE 19 (March 1982): 976; Gordon C. Zahn, AMER 146 (8 May 1982): 367-8; David Blackbourn, AHR 87 (December 1982): 1411-2; Juergen Doerr, DALR 63 (Summer 1983): 346-8; David W. Hendon, JCS 25 (Autumn 1983): 566; John E. Groh, CH 52 (December 1983): 518-9; Roger Chickering, HIS 46 (May 1984): 447-8; John K. Zeender, CHR 70 (July 1984): 431-3.

718. Farr, Ian. "From Anti-Catholicism to Anti-clericalism: Catholic Politics and the Peasantry in Bavaria, 1860-1900." ESR 13 (April 1983): 249-69.

Attributes the intense anticlericalism of the Bavarian peasants during the late nineteenth century to their disillusionment with the Center Party. The Party was castigated by the small farmers as backward and inactive; inevitably, its main supporters, the hierarchy and clergy, were incriminated.

719. Hendon, David Warren. THE CENTER PARTY AND THE AGRARIAN INTEREST IN GERMANY, 1890-1914.

Ph.D. dissertation. Emory University, 1976.

Illustrates the close working relationship between
small landholding areas, represented by Christian
Farmers Associations, and the Center Party.

*   Horgan, John J.   "Windthorst: The German 'Liberator.'"
      GREAT CATHOLIC LAYMEN (item 31), 247-88.

Focuses on Windthorst's political career. Against
Bismarck, who symbolized power, Windthorst stood for
principle and the inseparability of faith and
patriotism.

720.   Johnson, Humphrey J.T.   "Ludwig Windthorst and the
       German Centre Party." CLR 31 (January 1949): 23-
       35.

A brief introduction to the development of the
Center Party from the foundation of the Empire to
the close of the *Kulturkampf*. Stresses the crucial
role played by Windthorst in protecting Catholic
interests.

*   Neill, Thomas P.   "Joseph Görres." THEY LIVED THE
      FAITH (item 33), 222-41.

Labels Görres "the O'Connell of the Rhineland,"
in recognition of his commitment to the freedom of
the German Church. Out of the liberal tradition
which he fostered, and which he found best represented through history by Roman Catholicism, came
the politically dynamic Catholics of Ketteler's and
Windthorst's day.

*   ————.   "Ludwig Windthorst." THEY LIVED THE FAITH
      (item 33), 71-93.

Presents Windthorst the political organizer and
parliamentary strategist, whose Center Party was the
realization of the ideas of O'Connell and Montalembert.

721.   Newman, E.J.   "Politics and Religion: Robert Blum
       and the German Catholic Movement, 1844-6." JRH
       8 (June 1975): 217-27.

Details how German radicalism politicized Catholic
popular devotion during the mid-1840s. Robert Blum's
republican movement achieved national recognition
after attaching itself to the German Catholic Movement, a revivalist group formed in 1842 by a
schismatic priest, Johannes Ronge (see item 665).

722. Ross, Ronald J. BELEAGUERED TOWER: THE DILEMMA OF
      POLITICAL CATHOLICISM IN WILHELMINE GERMANY.
      Notre Dame: University of Notre Dame Press, 1976.

      Describes the campaign of Julius Bachem, a
      Centrist leader in the Rhineland, to redefine his
      party along nonsectarian lines, so as to prevent
      Catholic political isolation and impotence.
      Examines the strategy of the campaign and the
      angry controversy it caused in Catholic circles.

      See: CHOICE 13 (July/August 1976): 714; Robert E.
            Neil, HRNB 4 (August 1976): 204; John E. Groh,
            CH 45 (December 1976): 538-9; Jonathan Sperber,
            JMH 49 (June 1977): 333-5; John K. Zeender,
            CHR 46 (October 1978): 708-9; Ellen L. Evans,
            AHR 84 (June 1979): 785-6.

723. ————. "Critic of the Bismarckian Consti-
      tution: Ludwig Windthorst and the Relationship
      between Church and State in Imperial Germany."
      JCS 21 (Autumn 1979): 483-506.

      Goes beyond Windthorst's formidable parliamentary
      tactics to discuss his three political ideals: re-
      ligious freedom, which outranked even self-government
      in importance; limited government, since political
      authority was not the remedy for every problem; and
      the German Empire, which served as a bulwark against
      those groups and ideologies most dangerous to the
      Church.

724. Silverman, Dan P. "Political Catholicism and Social
      Democracy in Alsace-Lorraine, 1871-1914." CHR 52
      (April 1966): 39-65.

      Discusses the German government's exploitation of
      the inability of Catholics in Alsace-Lorraine to
      organize politically. Only during the 1890s, with
      the rising threat of social democracy in the recently

annexed areas, did Catholics feel the need to form
regular organizations which might compete with the
socialist parties.

725. Sperber, Jonathan. "Competing Counterrevo-
           lutions: Prussian State and Catholic Church in
           Westphalia during the 1850's." CEH 19 (March
           1986): 45-62.

      Disputes the usual picture of unrelieved hostility
      between Prussia and the Church, by showing how, at
      least in Prussian Westphalia during the 1850s, the
      two were counterrevolutionary allies, each accepting
      the political legitimacy of the other, and each
      prepared to cooperate with the other in checking
      radicalism.

726. ————. "The Shaping of Political Catholicism in the
           Ruhr Basin, 1848-1881." CEH 16 (December
           1983): 347-67.

      Maintains that the development of political
      Catholicism in the Ruhr Basin was shaped by a
      subtle interaction of national events and the
      regional social structure.

727. Stehlin, Stewart A. BISMARCK AND THE GUELPH PROBLEM,
           1866-1890: A STUDY IN PARTICULARIST OPPOSITION TO
           NATIONAL UNITY. The Hague: Martinus Nijhoff,
           1973.

      Places Bismarck's fear of the Center Party within
      the context of his broader fear of the resurgence of
      particularism after 1871. Though the DHP, or
      Guelphs, never openly joined the Center, for fear of
      losing its own special identity, it cooperated with
      Windthorst's group, finding in it a similar
      commitment to political decentralization and local
      autonomy.

      See: G.P. Bassler, CJH 9 (August 1974): 231-3;
            James Joll, EHR 90 (October 1975): 927-8.

728. Zeender, John K. THE GERMAN CENTER PARTY, 1890-1906.
           Philadelphia: The American Philosophical Society,
           1976.

Concentrates on the party's parliamentary programs
and strategies in the years after Windthorst's death.
Establishes the continuity of the defensive mentality
under Ernst Lieber, Windthorst's successor, a
mentality which made the art of political maneuvering
more important for the Center than for any other
party in imperial Germany.

See: James C. Hunt, AHR 82 (February 1977): 127-8;
       Vernon Lidtke, CHR 64 (October 1978): 707-8.

729. Zucker, Stanley. "Philipp Wasserburg and Political
      Catholicism in Nineteenth-Century Germany." CHR
      70 (January 1984): 14-27.

Assigns Wasserburg (1827-1897) an important place
in the development of political Catholicism in
Germany: not only was he an outspoken defender of
Church interests, but played a key role in helping
the Center Party to retain the loyalty of large
numbers of working-class voters.

Anticlericalism and Anticatholicism

730. Stone, Norman. "The Religious Background to Max
      Weber." In PERSECUTION AND TOLERATION: PAPERS
      READ AT THE TWENTY-SECOND SUMMER MEETING AND THE
      TWENTY-THIRD WINTER MEETING OF THE ECCLESIASTICAL
      HISTORY SOCIETY, 1983 (item 29), 393-407.

Contends that Weber admirably summarizes the
typical German Protestant view of Catholics during
the last twenty years of the century: the Church
was a dangerous institution, hostile to both modern
capitalism and education, indulgent toward peasants'
superstititons and fantasies, and anxious only to
increase its power and financial reserves.

Austria and Hungary

Orders and Congregations

731. Reinerman, Alan. "The Return of the Jesuits to the
      Austrian Empire and the Decline of Josephinism."
      CHR 52 (October 1966): 372-90.

      Describes the obstacle-ridden process by which
      the Society of Jesus was restored within the Empire.
      Though the government's religious policy was
      dominated as of 1820 by the Josephinists, who
      disapproved of the Jesuits' return, Emperor Francis
      I allowed the reestablishment of the Order in 1822.
      This alteration in imperial strategy, motivated by
      an alarming shortage of trained priests, was the
      beginning of Josephinism's death-knell.

Religious Thought

732. Fellner, Felix, O.S.B. "Ludwig von Pastor (1854-)."
      In CHURCH HISTORIANS, INCLUDING PAPERS ON
      EUSEBIUS, OROSIUS, ST. BEDE THE VENERABLE,
      ORDERICUS VITALIS, LAS CASAS, BARONIUS, BOLLANDUS,
      MURATORI, MOEHLER, LINGARD, HERGENROETHER,
      JANSSEN, DENIFLE, LUDWIG VON PASTOR (item 266),
      373-415.

      Sketches his family background, character, and
      academic training. Analyzes in detail his HISTORY
      OF THE POPES FROM THE CLOSE OF THE MIDDLE AGES, the
      first volume of which appeared in 1886.

733. ————. "Ludwig von Pastor, the Historian of the
      Popes." CHR 15 (July 1929): 154-70.

      Covers in less detail the points raised in item
      732, but adds a consideration of the critical
      reception of his HISTORY OF THE POPES FROM THE CLOSE
      OF THE MIDDLE AGES.

Social Thought

734. Gordon, Bertram Martin. CATHOLIC SOCIAL THOUGHT IN
AUSTRIA, 1815-1848. Ph.D. dissertation. Rutgers
University, 1969.

Studies the social thought of Catholic clergy and
and lay Catholic romantics, with emphasis on the
Church's response to the new economic and urban
situation ushered in by the Industrial Revolution.

Special Challenges

Church and State

735. Engel-Janosi, Friedrich. "Austria and the Conclave
of 1878." CHR 39 (July 1953): 142-66.

Probes the speculation of the Austrian government,
as early as 1871, over the location and outcome of
the next Conclave, given the tense relationship
between the Vatican and the Italian government.
Investigates, on a secondary level, the imperial
administration's evaluation of the last years of
Pius IX and its strategy to influence the election
of his successor.

736. ————. "French and Austrian Political Advice to
Pius IX, 1846-1848." CHR 38 (April 1952): 1-20.

Places Austrian and French efforts to advise the
newly elected Pius IX within the context of the
centuries-old rivalry between the two countries for
hegemony over the peninsula. Attributes the polite
Papal rebuff in both cases to Pius' dislike of
Austrian Josephinism and French Orleanism.

737. ————. "Two Austrian Ambassadors Discuss the
Successor of Pius IX." CHR 30 (April 1944): 1-
27.

Compares the reports of Baron Bach (1861) and
Count Trautmannsdorff-Weinsberg (1869) concerning

possible successors to the physically declining Pius
IX. Shows that the differences between the reports,
both in tone and content, reflected important changes
in the European political picture over the eight-year
interval.

738. Lukács, Lajos. THE VATICAN AND HUNGARY, 1846-
       1878: REPORTS AND CORRESPONDENCE ON HUNGARY
       OF THE APOSTOLIC NUNCIOS IN VIENNA. Translated
       by Zsófia Kormos. Budapest: Akadémiai Kiadó,
       1981.

       A lengthy introduction presents the Vatican's
       perception of Hungarian political affairs--e.g.,
       Kossuth and revolutionary agitation--during the
       reign of Pius IX.

       See: Frank J. Coppa, HRNB 11 (September 1983): 232;
             Bertram M. Gordon, AHR 88 (December
             1983): 1295; Andrew Harsanyi, CH 52 (December
             1983): 519-20; Alfons Lengyel, RSR 10 (January
             1984): 78; Owen Chadwick, EHR 99 (April
             1984): 457; John Lukacs, CHR 70 (July
             1984): 496-7.

  *   Parsons, Reuben. "Pope Leo XIII and the Austrian
       Empire: The Questions of Mixed and Civil
       Marriages in Hungary." STUDIES IN CHURCH HISTORY,
       6 (item 27), 236-65.

       Refutes the charge that the pro-French Leo XIII
       was also anti-Austrian. Reviews Papal resistance
       to the Hungarian *Kulturkampf* and its legalization
       of civil marriage.

739. Reinerman, Alan J. AUSTRIA AND THE PAPACY IN THE AGE
       OF METTERNICH. Vol. 1: BETWEEN CONFLICT AND
       COOPERATION, 1809-1830. Washington, D.C.: Catho-
       lic University of America Press, 1979.

       Views Church-State relations through the eyes of
       Metternich rather than through those of the Pope.
       Uses a diversity of archival sources to illustrate
       Metternich's dilemma, as Austria became the pro-
       tector and master of papal policy in the years after
       Waterloo. Though a true eighteenth-century Catholic,
       Metternich felt constrained to control the Church

insofar as the Popes themselves did not enforce peace,
order, and obedience. Yet he knew that control of the
Church, however necessary, became counter-productive
as soon as it became obvious to the public. Highly
favorable to Cardinal Consalvi, who is seen as the
only Church leader who was able to modernize an
anachronistic papal structure. Volume 2, AUSTRIA,
ENGLAND, AND THE ROMAN QUESTION, 1830-1848, is
forthcoming.

See: Arthur G. Haas, AHR 86 (June 1981): 616-7;
      T.C.W. Blanning, JEH 32 (July 1981): 371-2;
      Owen Chadwick, JMH 53 (September 1981): 583-4;
      Guillaume de Bertier de Sauvigny, CHR 67
      (October 1981): 630-2; Gwendolyn E. Jensen,
      CH 51 (March 1982): 105-6; Derek Beales, HJ
      25 (March 1982): 235-6.

Catholic Political Activity

740. Alexander, Edgar. "Church and Society in
      Germany: Social and Political Movements and
      Ideas in German and Austrian Catholicism (1789-
      1950). V. Political Catholicism. The
      Christian Socialists in Austria." In CHURCH
      AND SOCIETY: CATHOLIC SOCIAL AND POLITICAL
      THOUGHT AND MOVEMENTS, 1789-1950 (item 308),
      477-86.

      A survey of the Christian Social Party, its
      religious and intellectual origins, program, and
      impact on Austrian political life.

741. Dietrich, Donald J. "Anton Günther: Catholic
      Liberal in the Hapsburg Empire." JCS 23
      (Autumn 1981): 497-517.

      A politicotheological analysis of Günther's
      solutions to problems faced by the Church in an
      era of rapid modernization. Breaks down his
      political program to a hatred of absolutism,
      whether religious or secular, and a deep commitment
      to democratic or, at least, participatory government.
      Balances Günther's condemnation by Rome in 1857 with
      Leo XIII's acceptance of much of his outlook a few

decades later.

742. Juhasz, William. "The Development of Catholicism in
      Hungary in Modern Times." In CHURCH AND
      SOCIETY: CATHOLIC SOCIAL AND POLITICAL THOUGHT
      AND MOVEMENTS, 1789-1950 (item 308), 659-719.

      Features discussions of clerical participation in
      mid-century political life, the Church's post-1848
      status as a privileged ward of the State, and the
      formation of Catholic political parties during the
      1890s.

743. Lewis, Gavin. THE CATHOLIC CHURCH AND THE CHRISTIAN
      SOCIAL PARTY IN LOWER AUSTRIA, 1885-1907. Ph.D.
      dissertation. Princeton University, 1972.

      Follows the early development of the leading right-
      wing and Catholic party in nineteenth-century German
      Austria. Highlights three significant phenomena
      within the development: (1) the Church's success in
      adapting its political strategy to changes in
      political institutions; (2) the conflicts within the
      hierarchy over the decision to engage in mass
      politics; and (3) the contradiction between the
      Church's primary spiritual status and its active
      involvement in secular politics.

744. Neitzel, Sarah C. "The Salzburg Catholic Gisellen-
      verein: An Alternative to Socialism." JRH 12
      (June 1982): 62-73.

      Delineates the workings of the Journeymen's
      Association, founded in 1847 by Father Adolph
      Kolping as part of the Austrian Church's effort
      to provide a Catholic alternative to the socialism
      and secularism of the day.

745. Simons, Thomas W., Jr. "Vienna's First Catholic
      Political Movement: The Güntherians, 1848-1857.
      Part I." CHR 55 (July 1969): 173-94.

      Discusses the formation of a group around Anton
      Günther during the years 1820-1848. Composed of
      laymen and priests, this group sought to take the
      lead in organizing Catholics for social action.
      For its post-1848 activity and impact, see items

746 and 747.

746.   ————. "Vienna's First Catholic Political
        Movement: The Güntherians, 1848-1857.
        Part II." CHR 55 (October 1969): 377-93.

        Continues from item 745. Details the Güntherians'
        "finest hour," that is, their activities during the
        Viennese revolution of March-October 1848. Commends
        their mobilization of clerical and lay forces on
        behalf of Church interests, as well as their willing-
        ness to attack their German counterparts for their
        contemptible theology and ambivalence toward Church
        authority. For the Güntherians' post-1848 situation,
        see item 747.

747.   ————. "Vienna's First Catholic Political
        Movement: The Güntherians, 1848-1857.
        Part III." CHR 55 (January 1970): 610-26.

        Continues from item 746. Traces the nine-year
        breakdown of the Güntherians, in the wake of the
        defeat of the 1848 Revolution. Points to two major
        factors behind their demise: (1) the dilution of
        the original program's aims; after 1850 Güntherianism
        became more a matter of personal piety than of
        philosophy and theology; and (2) the placing of
        Günther's works on the Index in 1857. Credits the
        group with having made the first and only attempt
        during the nineteenth century to mobilize the
        educated Catholic middle class of Vienna in the
        interests of the Church.

The Low Countries and Switzerland

Belgium

748.   Bittel, Ronald Denis. BELGIAN 'LIBERAL CATHOLICISM'
        AND THE PAPACY, 1863-1879. Ph.D. dissertation.
        Washington University, 1973.

        Describes the relationship between Belgian liberal
        politicians, loyal both to the Church and to the
        Revolution of 1830, and a conservative, if not

reactionary, Papacy, whose condemnation of liberalism
did not prevent it from supporting those politicians.
Such paradoxical cooperation was made possible by the
fact that the liberals forswore any attachment to the
separation of Church and State, or to "modern"
liberties.

749.   Denis, Valentin.   CATHOLIC UNIVERSITY OF LOUVAIN,
       1425-1958.   Translated by Bartholomew Egan,
       O.F.M.   Louvain: Catholic University of
       Louvain, 1958.

       Emphasizes, in the Introduction, the University's
       expansion during the half-century following its
       reestablishment in 1833.   Originally founded in
       1425, it had been suppressed by the French in 1797.

750.   Haag, Henri.   "The Catholic Movement in Belgium,
       1789-1950.   I. The Political Ideas of Belgian
       Catholics (1789-1914)."   In CHURCH AND
       SOCIETY: CATHOLIC SOCIAL AND POLITICAL THOUGHT
       AND MOVEMENTS, 1789-1950 (item 308), 281-98.

       Presents Belgian Catholic political thought and
       activity in terms of the struggle within the Church
       between the traditionalists, supported by Veuillot
       and the Ultramontanists, and the liberals, inspired
       by Lamennais, Montalembert, and the social Catholicism
       which made its debut during the early 1860s.

751.   Herbst, Clarence A., S.J.   "Belgian Elections of
       1884."   HB 23 (January 1945):   27-8, 41-3.

       Demonstrates how Catholic political organization
       in the national elections of June and October 1884
       succeeded in throwing out of office the liberals,
       who had cut aid to schools and teachers of religion.

752.   Lord, Robert H.   "Belgium: A Study in Catholic
       Democracy."   CHR 9 (April 1923):   30-47.

       Traces the mixed fortunes of the Catholic Party,
       founded in 1830 to protect the Church's freedom.
       Praises its major role in the passage of the
       universal suffrage legislation of 1893.

  *   Parsons, Reuben.   "Pope Leo XIII and the Educational

Question in Belgium." STUDIES IN CHURCH HISTORY,
6 (item 27), 310-19.

Looks at the provocation behind the events treated
in item 751. Summarizes an ugly episode in the
history of Church-State relations in Belgium. In
1879 Minister of the Interior Van Humbeeck introduced
a bill to establish a national system of lay
education; the project was immediately denounced by
the Belgian bishops, with Leo XIII's approval. To
discredit the hierarchy, the government declared that
the Pope had actually disapproved of the episcopal
protest; when the nuncio attempted to expose the lie,
he was blocked.

* Vidler, Alec R. "Belgium." A CENTURY OF SOCIAL
CATHOLICISM, 1820-1920 (item 315), 79-95, 141-51.

Details the relatively late and slow emergence,
leading personalities, initial paternalism, and
later corporate character of Belgian social
Catholicism.

The Netherlands

753. Bax, Mart, and Nieuwenhuis, Aad. "Peasant
Emancipation in the Roman Catholic South of
the Netherlands: The Shattering of a Tableau-
Vivant." NJS 18 (April 1982): 25-45.

Revises the traditional interpretation of the
impact of the emancipation movement promoted by
the North Brabant Christian Farmers' Union during
the late 1890s. Rather than bettering social and
economic conditions for all peasants in the sandy
moorlands of the South, it actually made it
increasingly possible for a new inequality to
develop within the ranks of the peasants themselves.

* Evans, Ellen L. "Catholic Political Movements in
Germany, Switzerland, and the Netherlands: Notes
for a Comparative Approach." Cited above as item
716.

Finds significant similarities in the nineteenth-century origins of Dutch Catholic political parties, on the one side, and those of their German and Swiss counterparts, on the other.

754. Homan, Gerlof D. "Catholic Emancipation in the Netherlands." CHR 52 (July 1966): 201-11.

Looks into the major obstacles to the legal emancipation of Dutch Catholics, and the strategies by which they were overcome in the years before 1848. Points to the necessity of a certain combination of factors before William II's emancipation decree of October 1848 could be passed; crucial among these were a deep Catholic discontent over social and economic discrimination, and the Church's willingness to join with the liberals to press for thorough constitutional reform.

755. Saueressig-Schreuder, Yda. "Dutch Catholic Emigration in the Mid-Nineteenth Century: Noord-Brabant, 1847-1871." JHG 11 (January 1985): 48-69.

Establishes that Catholic emigration from the southern provinces of Noord-Brabant was determined by a decline in rural industry, and that the social and economic background of the emigrants was more varied than usually thought.

756. Swierenga, Robert P., and Saueressig-Schreuder, Yda. "Catholic and Protestant Emigration from the Netherlands in the 19th Century: A Comparative Social Structural Analysis." TESG 74 (no. 1, 1983): 25-40.

Develops the idea that nineteenth-century Catholics, centered in Noord-Brabant, Limburg, and Gelderland, were reluctant emigrants at best, leaving after the main Protestant outflow, and over a briefer period of time. Occupationally, Catholic emigrants contained proportionally more skilled workers and fewer agriculturalists than their Protestant counterparts; socially, however, both groups were of middle- and lower class origin, predominantly male, young, and looking for a better economic life beyond the Netherlands.

Switzerland

* Evans, Ellen L. "Catholic Political Movements in Germany, Switzerland, and the Netherlands: Notes for a Comparative Approach." Cited above as item 716.

Sketches the process whereby Catholic political organizations were established in nineteenth-century Switzerland, in an effort to defend the interests of the Catholic minority against the Protestant majority, and to combat the image of Catholics as less nationalistic than their Protestant countrymen.

England and Wales

General Works and Collections

757. Anstruther, G. Elliot. A HUNDRED YEARS OF CATHOLIC PROGRESS; BEING A SHORT ACCOUNT OF THE CHURCH'S FORTUNES IN GREAT BRITAIN SINCE THE TIME OF THE EMANCIPATION ACT. London: Burns Oates & Washbourne, 1929.

Chapters 1 to 8 trace the progress of nineteenth-century Catholicism, from the Emancipation of 1829 through the Oxford Movement, the vigorous growth of the 1840s, the "Papal Aggression," the "Second Spring," and the effects of Vatican I. Goes beyond hierarchical developments to look at religious orders, missions, converts, education, and the press.

See: BLACK 10 (October 1929): 1410.

758. Attwater, Donald. THE CATHOLIC CHURCH IN MODERN WALES: A RECORD OF THE PAST CENTURY. London: Burns Oates & Washbourne, 1935.

Focuses on diocesan affairs and on the various activities of religious orders.

See: Ivor Daniel, DUBR 197 (July/August/September 1935): 163-8; J.R. Meagher, CLR 11

(January 1936): 68-9; L.L. McVay, CHR 22 (July
1936): 230.

759. Beck, George Andrew, A.A., ed. THE ENGLISH CATHOLICS,
      1850-1950: CENTENARY ESSAYS TO COMMEMORATE THE
      RESTORATION OF THE HIERARCHY. London: Burns
      Oates, 1950.

      Presents nineteen lengthy essays, each written by
      a recognized authority, on various dimensions of the
      nineteenth-century English Catholic experience.
      Contains items 764, 771, 799, 801, 803, 805, 809,
      919, 1011, 1056, 1070, 1086, 1144, 1145, 1156, 1172,
      1189, and 1223.

      See: TABLET 196 (23 September 1950): 262-4;
            Christopher Dawson, DUBR 224 (Winter 1950): 1-
            12; Michael Derrick, CLR 35 (January 1951): 49-
            53; John Brady, IER 75 (January 1951): 88-89;
            Nathaniel Micklem, QQ 58 (Summer 1951): 282-3;
            Herbert C.F. Bell, CHR 37 (October 1951): 309-
            10; Thomas P. Neill, HB 31 (March 1953): 174.

760. Carson, Robert L. "Multiplication Tables: The
      Progress of Catholicism in England and Wales,
      1702-1949." CLR 32 (July 1949): 21-30.

      A statistical breakdown of Catholics, priests,
      and church buildings, for the years 1800, 1851,
      and 1900. Shows that the increase of Catholics
      (70,000 in 1800; 1,000,000 in 1851; 2,000,000 in
      1900) compares favorably with the growth of the
      total population (10,000,000 in 1800; 17,927,609
      in 1851; 32,527,843 in 1900).

761. CATHOLIC EMANCIPATION, 1829 TO 1929: ESSAYS BY
      VARIOUS WRITERS. London and New York: Longmans,
      Green, 1929.

      Contributions by specialists in spirituality,
      education, literature and science, music, religious
      orders, and the development of Catholic life.
      Contains items 778, 1010, 1060, 1064, 1065, 1100,
      1142, 1184, 1191, 1219, and 1221.

      See: AMER 41 (27 April 1929): 69; DR 47 (May
            1929): 172-3; IER 33 (May 1929): 552;

LQR 152 (July 1929): 124; George D. Meadows,
CW 129 (August 1929): 590-2; Georgiana Putnam
McEntee, COMMWL 10 (16 October 1929): 623-4;
A.H. Dodd, HIST 18 (October 1933): 272-3.

762. Chadwick, Owen. THE VICTORIAN CHURCH. An
Ecclesiastical History of England, vols. 7-8.
New York: Oxford University Press, 1966-70.
2 vols.

Volume 7 includes considerations of Catholic
emancipation, the Oxford Movement, and the "Papal
Aggression." Volume 8 concentrates on the dynamism
and growing importance of the post-1860 Church, as
seen through Manning's work and influence, the
proliferation of religious communities and
Catholic scholarship, and the serious impact of
Vatican I on the British government.

See: (for both volumes) Josef L. Altholz, AHR 78
(April 1973): 438-9
(for vol. 7) A.O.J. Cockshut, OBS, 5 June
1966: 26; R.G.G. Price, PUNCH 250 (15 June
1966): 891; TLS, 21 July 1966: 625-6; ECON
220 (23 July 1966): 361; John Kent, THEO 69
(August 1966): 459-61; John Vincent, NST 72
(5 August 1966): 201; HIBJ 64 (Midsummer
1966): 173; Dorothy Sinclair, LJ 91 (15
September 1966): 4122; CHOICE 3 (January
1967): 1027; Wilfrid Passmore, DR 85 (January
1967): 111-4; Martin E. Marty, JR 47 (April
1967): 157; Winthrop S. Hudson, CH 36 (June
1967): 233; Esther de Waal, VS 10 (June
1967): 435-9; J.A. Ross Mackenzie, INTERP 21
(July 1967): 367-8; F.C. Mather, EHR 83
(January 1968): 133-5; Neville C. Masterman,
HIST 53 (February 1968): 140-1.
(for vol. 8) A.O.J. Cockshut, OBS, 1 March
1970: 34; TLS, 19 March 1970: 318; Albert
Hourani, SPEC 224 (30 May 1970): 715-6; John
Kent, DR 88 (July 1970): 318-21; John Kent,
THEO 73 (September 1970): 413-4; K.S. Inglis,
VS 14 (March 1971): 340-2; Frederick V. Mills,
CC 88 (24 March 1971): 387-9; P.T. Marsh, EHR
86 (April 1971): 370-3; Bernard M.G. Reardon,
AMPJ 76 (Summer 1971): 103-5; Winthrop S.
Hudson, CH 40 (September 1971): 332;

Horton Davies, JR 51 (October 1971): 306-7.

763. Connolly, Gerard. "The Transubstantiation of
        Myth: Towards a New Popular History of
        Nineteenth-Century Catholicism in England."
        JEH 35 (January 1984): 78-104.

        Dismisses as mythical the traditional Catholic
        claim that the Church's reestablishment in nineteenth-
        century England was providential, coming as it did
        at the eleventh hour, in the wake of centuries of
        persecution and uncertainty, and yet giving birth to
        an institution which came to rival not only the
        Established Religion but the English Protestant
        State itself.

764. Gwynn, Denis. "Growth of the Catholic Community."
        In THE ENGLISH CATHOLICS, 1850-1950: CENTENARY
        ESSAYS TO COMMEMORATE THE RESTORATION OF THE
        HIERARCHY (item 759), 410-41.

        A statistical examination of the unbroken progress
        of all phases of nineteenth-century Catholic life.

765. ————. A HUNDRED YEARS OF CATHOLIC EMANCIPATION
        (1829-1929). London and New York: Longmans,
        Green, 1929.

        Recounts the principal episodes in the development
        of nineteenth-century English Catholicism, with an
        emphasis on the extraordinary impact of each in
        helping to transform the small, uncertain body of
        believers which obtained its political rights in
        1829, into a vigorous national force by 1900.

        See: IER 33 (May 1929): 552; LQR 152 (July 1929): 123-
              4; A.H. Dodd, HIST 18 (October 1933): 272.

766. ————. THE SECOND SPRING, 1818-1852: A STUDY OF
        THE CATHOLIC REVIVAL IN ENGLAND. London: Burns
        Oates, 1942.

        Follows the renascence of English Catholicism
        from the young Wiseman's arrival at the English
        College in Rome, to the opening of the First
        Provincial Synod of Westminster, chaired by
        Cardinal Wiseman. Emphasizes the contributions

of the Cambridge converts (Ambrose Phillipps de Lisle
and George Spencer), the Oxford Movement, Pugin, Lord
Shrewsbury, and Dominic Barberi.

See: David Mathew, TABLET 181 (2 January 1943): 8;
Robert Bracey, O.P., BLACK 24 (Book Supplement,
February 1943): i; Joseph P. Bradley, CHR 30
(October 1944): 359-60.

767. Hollis, Christopher. "The Second Spring in English
Catholicism." In CHURCH AND SOCIETY: CATHOLIC
SOCIAL AND POLITICAL THOUGHT AND MOVEMENTS, 1789-
1950 (item 308), 811-34.

A survey which emphasizes the increasingly
important role played by Roman Catholicism in
nineteenth-century British life.

768. Holmes, J. Derek. "English Catholicism from Wiseman
to Bourne (I)." CLR 61 (February 1976): 57-69.

An overview of developments from the restoration
of the hierarchy to 1875, based on recent research.
Continues in item 769.

769. ————. "English Catholicism from Wiseman to Bourne
(II)." CLR 61 (March 1976): 107-16.

A continuation of item 768. Describes the
Church's growth during the last twenty-five years
of the century.

770. ————. MORE ROMAN THAN ROME: ENGLISH CATHOLICISM
IN THE NINETEENTH CENTURY. London: Burns & Oates/
Shepherdstown, W.Va.: Patmos Press, 1978.

Balances a hierarchy-oriented narrative with a
treatment of Catholic Emancipation, ultramontanism,
liberal Catholicism, and Modernism, on the one hand,
and an analysis of usually ignored or inadequately
covered social and spiritual patterns, on the other.
Sees through all of this the slow but definite
triumph of ultramontane opinion among all levels of
the Church.

See: Auberon Waugh, SPEC 240 (25 March 1978): 22-3;
Meriol Trevor, MONTH 2nd NS 11 (June

1978): 212; CHOICE 15 (January 1979): 1538;
Vincent Alan McClelland, VS 22 (Spring
1979): 365-7; R.W. Linker, AHR 84 (April
1979): 461; Godfrey Anstruther, O.P., CLR
64 (June 1979): 225-6; James Hennesey, CH 48
(September 1979): 352-3; Joseph A. Komonchak,
RSR 7 (January 1981): 48; R.J. Schiefen, CHR
67 (April 1981): 317-8.

771. Hughes, Philip. "The Coming Century." In THE
     ENGLISH CATHOLICS, 1850-1950: CENTENARY ESSAYS
     TO COMMEMORATE THE RESTORATION OF THE HIERARCHY
     (item 759), 1-41.

     Places the diverse achievements of nineteenth-
     century Catholicism within the context of national
     progress.

772. Mathew, David. CATHOLICISM IN ENGLAND, 1535-1935;
     PORTRAIT OF A MINORITY, ITS CULTURE AND
     TRADITION. London: Longmans, Green, 1936.

     Details the major social and economic changes
     affecting the Catholic community during the
     nineteenth century.

     See: T.E. Flynn, CLR 11 (June 1936): 422-4; DR 54
          (July 1936): 456-9; Shane Leslie, DUBR 199
          (July/August/September 1936): 89-104; Henry
          Watts, AMER 55 (15 August 1936): 453; Patrick
          J. Barry, COMMWL 25 (13 November 1936): 80-1;
          Joseph McSorley, C.S.P., CW 144 (February
          1937): 624-5; Michael Tynan, IER 55 (March
          1940): 260-73; Richard S. McMonigal, CHR 35
          (October 1949): 359-60; William Gordon Wheeler,
          "Archbishop David Mathew, M.A., Litt.D., F.S.A.,
          F.R.S.L., 1902-1975." AMPJ 81 (Spring
          1976): 5-8.

773. Norman, Edward. THE ENGLISH CATHOLIC CHURCH IN THE
     NINETEENTH CENTURY. Oxford: Clarendon Press,
     1984.

     Deals primarily with developments at the "top end"
     of the Church, that is, with structural, administra-
     tive, and constitutional affairs. Views the course
     of nineteenth-century English Catholicism as one

formed largely by a few leading clerics and laymen.
Contains little material on the evolution of theology
and learning, and nothing on social patterns.

See: Gerald Priestland, LIST 111 (8 March 1984): 25;
       ECON 291 (21 April 1984): 86; John Bossy, TLS,
       11 May 1984: 513; John Kent, BBN, July
       1984: 400; J. Derek Holmes, MONTH 2nd NS 17
       (August 1984): 277; Keith Robbins, JEH 35
       (October 1984): 643-4; René Kollar, ALBION 17
       (Spring 1985): 95-6; John D. Root, CH 54
       (September 1985): 422-3; Josef L. Altholz, AHR
       91 (February 1986): 111-2; Norman Gash, JMH 58
       (March 1986): 305-7; Richard J. Schiefen, CHR
       72 (April 1986): 293-5; William L. Pitts, JCS
       28 (Winter 1986): 137-8; G.I.T. Machin, EHR 102
       (January 1987): 244-5.

774.   ————. ROMAN CATHOLICISM IN ENGLAND FROM THE
       ELIZABETHAN SETTLEMENT TO THE SECOND VATICAN
       COUNCIL. Oxford: Oxford University Press,
       1985.

       Chapters 4 to 6 feature a synthesis of the most
       recent secondary sources on the nineteenth century,
       interspersed with the author's own interpretation.

       See: Walter L. Arnstein, HRNB 14 (January/February
              1986): 75-6; Lawrence F. Barmann, CH 55 (March
              1986): 108-9; James C. Holland, ALBION 18
              (Spring 1986): 97-8; Nadia M. Lahutsky, RSR 13
              (January 1987): 81.

775.   O'Connor, John J. THE CATHOLIC REVIVAL IN ENGLAND.
       New York: Macmillan, 1942.

       Introduces the landmarks of nineteenth-century
       Catholic growth: the Emancipation Act, the Oxford
       Movement, Irish immigration, the restoration of the
       hierarchy and the Synod of 1852, Wiseman's activity,
       the relationship between Manning and Newman, the
       University Question, and the infallibility
       controversy.

       See: Florence D. Cohalan, AMER 66 (21 March
              1942): 664; R.J. Imbs, HB 20 (May 1942): 86-7;
              Frederick E. Welfle, CHR 28 (July 1942): 296;

Michael Williams, COMMWL 36 (7 August 1942): 372-3; Joseph McSorley, C.S.P., CW 155 (September 1942): 762-3; Robert Wilberforce, THOUGHT 17 (September 1942): 521-2; J.A. Muller, CH 11 (December 1942): 345-6.

776. Reynolds, E.E. THE ROMAN CATHOLIC CHURCH IN ENGLAND AND WALES: A SHORT HISTORY. Wheathampstead, Herts.: Anthony Clarke, 1973.

A brief account intended for the general reader. Alongside the account of official developments is a running commentary on spirituality, religious practice, clerical education and activity, construction of ecclesiastical buildings, and the political and social position of Catholics within the context of national life.

See: Albert C. Outler, ECR 26 (July 1974): 521-2; TLS, 14 September 1973: 1065; Helen Forshaw, S.H.C.J., CLR 59 (October 1974): 700-1; John Charles-Roux, AMPJ 80 (Spring 1975): 103-4.

777. Thureau-Dangin, Paul. THE ENGLISH CATHOLIC REVIVAL IN THE NINETEENTH CENTURY. Translated by Wilfrid Wilberforce. New York: E.P. Dutton, 1919. 2 vols.

A translation of Thureau-Dangin's classic three-volume work in French (1899-1906). Presents nineteenth-century English Catholic progress within the framework of the Oxford Movement, credited by the sympathetic author with not only the betterment of Anglicanism but also the reawakening of the Roman faith.

See: CW 102 (February 1916): 695-7; AMER 15 (27 May 1916): 162; AHR 21 (July 1916): 802-4; Charles H.A. Wager, DIAL 61 (16 November 1916): 393-4; Edward Porritt, PSQ 32 (September 1917): 501-2; CW 112 (November 1920): 249-50; Joseph M. Egan, CHR 7 (January 1922): 511-3.

778. Thurston, Herbert, S.J. "Statistical Progress of the Catholic Church." In CATHOLIC EMANCIPATION, 1829 TO 1929: ESSAYS BY VARIOUS WRITERS (item 761), 243-64.

Charts English Catholic growth through the nineteenth century, using as a yardstick the ongoing increases in baptisms, marriages, ordinations, and church-building.

779. Ward, Bernard. THE EVE OF CATHOLIC EMANCIPATION; BEING THE HISTORY OF THE ENGLISH CATHOLICS DURING THE FIRST THIRTY YEARS OF THE NINETEENTH CENTURY. London: Longmans, Green, 1911-2. 3 vols.

Volumes 1 and 2 examine the mentality and activities of English Catholics from 1803 to 1820. In addition to the faltering campaign for equality, the Church suffered from numerous internal disputes, including, most notably, the Blanchardist schism and the highly suspect miracles of St. Winefrid at Holywell. Volume 3 studies the nine years leading up to the Emancipation Act, during which Catholic agitation reached a new level. Discussion of the political victory of 1829 is supplemented by an investigation of less familiar events of the time: the full reestablishment of the Jesuits in England, the Douai College's presentation of claims against the French government, and the controversy surrounding a Catholic scheme to reunite the churches of England. Several appendices proffer supporting documentation, drawn from Roman and English episcopal archives, and speculation of specific points of interest (e.g., was Lingard the famous cardinal *in petto* of Leo XII?).

See: (for all volumes) ACQR 37 (October 1912): 759-60; DR 33 (December 1914): 263-5. (for vols. 1 and 2) William Barry, BKMN 41 (March 1912): 293-5; NATION 94 (25 April 1912): 416; CW 95 (May 1912): 245-6; EHR 27 (July 1912): 609-10; William F. Dennehy, ACQR 38 (January 1913): 100-9. (for vol. 3) M. Kenny, S.J., AMER 7 (20 April 1912): 29-30; CW 96 (January 1913): 545-8; EHR 28 (January 1913): 200-1; William Barry, BKMN 44 (April 1913): 43-4.

780. ————. THE SEQUEL TO CATHOLIC EMANCIPATION: THE STORY OF THE ENGLISH CATHOLICS CONTINUED DOWN TO

THE RE-ESTABLISHMENT OF THEIR HIERARCHY IN 1850.
London: Longmans, Green, 1915. 2 vols.

Pinpoints personalities, ideas, and events which
made the restoration of the hierarchy not only
necessary but inevitable. Includes detailed considerations of the dispute between Bishop Baines
and the Benedictines at Downside, which led to
the Bishop's foundation of a college at Prior Park;
the enormous influence of Pugin's Gothic revival on
religious thought and practice; the Oxford Movement's
effect upon the "Old Catholics"; and Wiseman's
efforts to rid the English Church of its insularity.

See: ACQR 40 (October 1915): 702-8; AMER 14 (18
      December 1915): 234; DR 35 (January 1916): 36-
      9; William Barry, DUBR 158 (January 1916): 136-
      56; CW 102 (February 1916): 697-8; EHR 31
      (April 1916): 341-2; Ephraim Emerton, NATION
      103 (24 August 1916): 180-1.

781. Warre Cornish, Francis. THE ENGLISH CHURCH IN THE
      NINETEENTH CENTURY. A History of the English
      Church, edited by W.R.W. Stephens, vol. 8 (in
      two parts). London: Macmillan, 1910. 2 vols.

      Considers the "Papal Aggression" of 1850 the
      central fact of nineteenth-century English
      Catholicism. Outlines its antecedents and impact,
      both on the government and the public.

      See: LQR 115 (January 1911): 161-2; DUBR 149 (July
            1911): 191-3; G. McN. Rushforth, EHR 26 (July
            1911): 605-8.

782. Watkin, E.I. ROMAN CATHOLICISM IN ENGLAND FROM THE
      REFORMATION TO 1950. London: Oxford University
      Press, 1957.

      A useful introduction, written from a liberal
      Catholic viewpoint. Intersperses the narrative of
      events with sketches of the leading ecclesiastical
      players, among whom Newman is favored.

      See: Gaetano L. Vincitorio, CHR 44 (July 1958): 186-
            8; Owen Chadwick, JEH 9 (October 1958): 276;
            William Kolbourn, JMH 30 (December 1958): 393-4;

R.W. Greaves, HIST 44 (June 1959): 191.

Relations with the Papacy

783. Clark, Eugene V. CATHOLIC LIBERALISM AND ULTRA-
MONTANISM, FREEDOM AND DUTY: A STUDY OF THE
QUARREL OVER THE CONTROL OF CATHOLIC AFFAIRS
IN ENGLAND, 1855-1866. Ph.D. dissertation.
University of Notre Dame, 1965.

Maintains that the conflict over the liberal
policies and articles of the *Rambler* reflected
a deeper and more significant dispute over the
degree of papal authority over the English
Church.

784. Clonmore, Lord. "Anglo-Catholics and the Holy See."
CLR 16 (June 1939): 471-84.

Inquires into the opinions of the Papacy expressed
by nineteenth-century converts from Anglicanism.

785. Hastings, Adrian, ed. BISHOPS AND WRITERS: ASPECTS
OF THE EVOLUTION OF MODERN ENGLISH CATHOLICISM.
Wheathampstead, Herts.: Anthony Clarke, 1977.

Assesses the degree to which nineteenth-century
English Catholics were preoccupied with Rome and the
Papacy. Contains items 995 and 1341.

See: Alec R. Vidler, AMPJ 83 (Summer 1978): 72;
Alan M.G. Stephenson, THEO 81 (November
1978): 455-6; Gavin D. White, SJT 32 (August
1979): 394-5.

786. McElrath, Damian, O.F.M. THE SYLLABUS OF PIUS
IX: SOME REACTIONS IN ENGLAND. Bibliothèque
de la Revue d'Histoire Ecclésiastique, vol. 39.
Louvain: Publications Universitaires de Louvain,
1964.

Illustrates the strength and complexity of the
controversy surrounding the publication of the
Syllabus in England. Concentrates on the argument
between William George Ward and Ignatius Ryder, an

Oratorian serving as Newman's mouthpiece, over the
former's claim that the document was an infallible
pronouncement. Goes beyond the fight over the
Syllabus to re-create the mixed emotions felt by
Catholics and non-Catholics alike at the opening
of Vatican I.

See: Gilbert A. Cahill, AHR 71 (October 1965): 188-
      9; Owen Chadwick, EHR 81 (April 1966): 418;
      Dunstan Pontifex, DR 84 (October 1966): 459-60.

787. Schiefen, Richard J. "'Anglo-Gallicanism' in
      Nineteenth-Century England." CHR 63 (January
      1977): 14-44.

      Reveals a certain mistrust of Roman authority
among nineteenth-century English Catholics. Gauges
its depth by studying its origins and comparing it
with its oftentimes virulent French counterpart.

788. Supple, Jennifer F. "Ultramontanism in Yorkshire,
      1850-1900." RH 17 (May 1985): 274-86.

      Shows that although the Church in Yorkshire, as in
the rest of England, was undeniably ultramontane
during the second half of the nineteenth century,
there was also evidence of a persistent attachment to
"Old Catholic" attitudes and practices. Thus, Yorkshire experienced not an unqualified triumph of
ultramontanism, but rather the gradual assimilation
of two different types of English Catholicism, as the
old clergy and laity came to terms with the
ultramontane bishops and priests.

            The Hierarchy and Diocesan Organization

                         General

789. Connell, Joan. THE ROMAN CATHOLIC CHURCH IN ENGLAND,
      1750-1850: A STUDY IN INTERNAL POLITICS.
      Philadelphia: The American Philosophical Society,
      1984.

      Probes the status, activities, and

interrelationships of the English Vicars Apostolic,
from the easing of religious and political
restrictions on Catholics to the restoration of the
hierarchy. Criticizes their constant inability to
work together, which often caused serious in-fighting
over such issues as support for the restored Jesuits
after 1814, the division of district boundaries, and
church governance. Compounds this negative portrait
by asserting that several of these churchmen clearly
suffered from psychological problems.

See: Dale A. Johnson, CH 54 (December 1985): 534-5;
Josef L. Altholz, AHR 91 (February 1986): 111-2;
Joseph P. Chinnici, O.F.M., CHR 72 (April
1986): 288-9; F. Ellen Weaver, RSR 13 (July
1987): 269.

790. Coyne, John J. "The First Westminster Synod." CLR
38 (May 1953): 269-80.

Provides details concerning the ceremonies and
decisions of an event which marked the end of one
era in English Catholic history, ruled by the
vicariate system, and the beginning of another,
characterized by diocesan and parochial organization. Contrasts the two attitudes within the
Church to the Synod's results: the satisfaction
of the bishops against the discontent of the clergy,
who were given no part in the choice of future
members of the hierarchy.

791. Cwiekowski, Frederick J., S.S. THE ENGLISH BISHOPS
AND THE FIRST VATICAN COUNCIL. Bibliothèque de
la Revue d'Histoire Ecclésiastique, vol. 52.
Louvain: Publications Universitaires de Louvain,
1971.

Describes the mentality and participation of the
English hierarchy during the proceedings in Rome,
using new material drawn from Cardinal Manning's
own notes on the daily debates and committee meetings.
Touches briefly upon the reactions of Acton, Newman,
and Gladstone to conciliar developments.

See: Josef L. Altholz, CH 43 (June 1974): 274;
Richard J. Schiefen, JEH 25 (October
1974): 432-3; Garrett Sweeney, CLR 59

(November 1974): 776-9; William J. Schoenl, AHR
80 (February 1975): 111-12; Thomas Joyce, C.M.F.,
CHR 61 (April 1975): 305-7; Owen Chadwick, EHR
90 (October 1975): 931.

792. Hemphill, Basil, O.S.B. "The Vicars Apostolic of
England: VII. England Divided Into Eight
Vicariates." CLR 32 (September 1949): 180-7.

Brief biographies of the Vicars Apostolic of the
London, Yorkshire, Lancashire, and Welsh Districts
during the years 1840-1850, along with an evaluation
of the spiritual state of each vicariate. For the
other districts of England during the same decade,
see item 793.

793. ————. "The Vicars Apostolic of England: VIII.
England Divided Into Eight Vicariates (Continued)." CLR 32 (October 1949): 249-56.

Continued from item 792. Brief biographies of the
Vicars Apostolic of the Western, Eastern, Northern,
and Central Districts during the years 1840-1850,
supplemented by an evaluation of the spiritual state
of each vicariate.

794. ————. "The Vicars Apostolic of England: III.
England Divided Into Four Vicariates." CLR 31
(March 1949): 165-73.

Includes sketches of the four Vicars Apostolic of
the London District during the years 1800-1847. See
also items 792, 793, 795, and 796.

795. ————. "The Vicars Apostolic of England: IV.
England Divided Into Four Vicariates." CLR 31
(April 1949): 247-54.

Brief biographies of the three Vicars Apostolic of
the Midland District during the first half of the
century. See also items 792, 793, 794, and 796.

796. ————. "The Vicars Apostolic of England: V.
England Divided Into Four Vicariates (Continued)."
CLR 31 (June 1949): 394-400.

Features sketches of the four Vicars Apostolic of

the Northern District during the years 1800-1861.
See also items 792-795.

797.   —————. "The Vicars Apostolic of England: IX.
Miscellanea." CLR 32 (November 1949): 323-30.

Analyzes the Vicars Apostolic as a whole, pointing
out strengths and weaknesses, and important similarities and differences among the individual churchmen.
An overview of the material detailed in items 792-796.

798.   Hogan, David C. "The Four Westminster Provincial
Synods." CLR 69 (December 1984): 444-50.

Discusses the aims and achievements of the
meetings of 1852, 1855, 1859, and 1873. Reaches
beyond the data to give the flavor of each gathering.

799.   Hughes, Philip. "The Bishops of the Century." In
THE ENGLISH CATHOLICS, 1850-1950: CENTENARY
ESSAYS TO COMMEMORATE THE RESTORATION OF THE
HIERARCHY (item 759), 187-222.

An overview of the nineteenth-century hierarchy.
Singles out certain members on the basis of
personality or achievement. Praises the English
episcopate's activity at Vatican I as its finest
hour.

800.   Schiefen, R.J. "The First Provincial Synod of
Westminster (1852)." AHC 4 (1972): 188-213.

Hails the achievements of the gathering at Oscott
College: a striking demonstration of episcopal
unity; the establishment of a diocesan structure, with
the rights and responsibilities of authority clari-
fied; a recognition of the distinctly English
situation within which the recently restored
hierarchy had to operate; the implementation of
uniform discipline involving worship and sacraments;
and an emphasis on the necessity of religious
education, and especially for the poor.

801.   Sweeney, Morgan V. "Diocesan Organisation and
Administration." In THE ENGLISH CATHOLICS, 1850-
1950: CENTENARY ESSAYS TO COMMEMORATE THE
RESTORATION OF THE HIERARCHY (item 759), 116-50.

Qualifies the traditional historical view that the
reestablishment of the hierarchy in 1850 regularized
ecclesiastical structure and administration, leaving
nothing for the new ordinaries to do except rule
their dioceses. Stresses the problems raised by the
restoration,--internal diocesan organization, the
role of religious orders, relations among the bishops
themselves, canonical legislation, and financial
support,--many of which would not be satisfactorily
solved until after the turn of the century.

802. Van der Heydt, Odo, O.S.B. "Monsignor Talbot de
     Malahide." WR 238 (Winter 1964): 290-308.

     A biography and character study of the link
between the English bishops and Rome during the
crucial years 1850-1870. Talbot, a tough cleric
who showed no sympathy whatsoever for the modern
world, was involved in all the problems faced by
the newly restored hierarchy and shared in their
solution.

803. Wheeler, Gordon. "The Archdiocese of Westminster."
     In THE ENGLISH CATHOLICS, 1850-1950: CENTENARY
     ESSAYS TO COMMEMORATE THE RESTORATION OF THE
     HIERARCHY (item 759), 151-86.

     Traces the development of the Metropolitanate
through the careers of Cardinals Wiseman, Manning,
and Vaughan.

804. Whelan, Horace, S.J. "Blanchardism and the English
     Vicars-Apostolic." IER 44 (September 1934): 241-
     53.

     Details the feud between Bishop Milner, Vicar
Apostolic of the Midland District, and the abbé
Blanchard during the first decade of the century.
Milner criticized what he considered the slackness
of his colleagues who believed that the French
bishops in English exile should resign their sees,
as requested by the Pope, but who refused to put
pressure on them to do so. Blanchard responded to
Milner with a vigor which propelled him into schism;
by 1810 the Vicars Apostolic were expressing concern
over the growing impact of the Blanchardist movement
upon their own priests.

The Restoration of the Hierarchy

805. Albion, Gordon. "The Restoration of the Hierarchy, 1850." In THE ENGLISH CATHOLICS, 1850-1950: CENTENARY ESSAYS TO COMMEMORATE THE RESTORATION OF THE HIERARCHY (item 759), 86-115.

Surveys the complex ecclesiastical politics leading up to the restoration, and the anti-Catholic feelings generated by it. Concludes with an English translation of the Papal letters reestablishing the hierarchy.

806. Corish, Patrick J. "The Restoration of the English Catholic Hierarchy." IER 74 (October 1950): 289-307.

Lists the reasons for, and major personalities behind, the events of 1850. Brands the restoration inevitable, in light of the increasing strains on the vicariate system, due to the growing number of converts and immigrants entering the English Church. Singles out the ideas and activities of Wiseman and Ullathorne as crucial to the success of a step which public opinion called "Papal Aggression."

807. Doran, Patrick. "The Restoration of the Hierarchy." CLR 34 (September 1950): 161-78.

Fixes on the canonical and political questions raised by the prospect of the restoration.

808. Holmes, J. Derek. "Church Government in England: Past, Present and Future." CLR 60 (July 1975): 420-8.

Sees the controversy surrounding the restoration of the hierarchy as the result of a combination of Protestant prejudice and Catholic blunders. Underscores the fact that there were several good reasons for not reestablishing the old system in 1850, including a lack of serious bishops, the dissatisfaction of the lower clergy over the diocesan structure announced by Wiseman, and the realization that some areas of England were simply not ready for a more sophisticated ecclesiastical organization.

809.   Hughes, Philip.   "The English Catholics in 1850."   In
       THE ENGLISH CATHOLICS, 1850-1950:   CENTENARY
       ESSAYS TO COMMEMORATE THE RESTORATION OF THE
       HIERARCHY (item 759), 42-85.

       Describes the social and economic status of mid-
       nineteenth-century Catholics, as reflected in the
       Census of 1851 and other official government reports.
       Pays special attention to figures of Mass attendance
       and to the five bishops created to fill the new sees
       established by Pius IX.

810.   Johnson, Humphrey J.T.   "Parliament and the Restored
       Hierarchy: A Centenary and Its Lesson."   DUBR
       224 (Summer 1950):   1-16.

       Dissects the British government's response to the
       restoration; though it had not inspired the "No
       Popery" agitation of 1850, it realized that it could
       not survive unless it did something to placate
       Protestant indignation.   Russell's Ecclesiastical
       Titles Act of 1851, however, was stillborn, for
       during the twenty years of its existence,--it was
       repealed in 1871,--not a single prosecution arose
       from its provisions.

811.   Joyce, Thomas P., C.M.F.   THE RESTORATION OF THE
       CATHOLIC HIERARCHY IN ENGLAND AND WALES, 1850:   A
       STUDY OF CERTAIN PUBLIC REACTIONS.
       Rome: Officium Libri Catholici, 1966.

       Evaluates the public response to the "Papal
       Aggression" of 1850, as presented in periodicals,
       pamphlets, speeches, meetings, and parliamentary
       debates.   Attributes the anti-Catholicism to more
       than simple bigotry, seeing it as fueled by the
       equation of Protestantism and the national identity.
       Relates, at the same time, the anti-Roman movement
       to the reaction against the Tractarians.

       See: Josef L. Altholz, CHR 55 (January 1970):   687-
       8.

812.   McReavy, Lawrence L.   "The Hierarchy and Canon Law."
       CLR 34 (September 1950):   179-87.

Enumerates the real gains made as a result of the
restoration of 1850: (1) no longer mere delegates of
the Pope, the ordinaries now acted in their own name;
(2) diocesan chapters of canons were formed; (3)
quasi-parochial organization among the pastoral
clergy was established; (4) the custom of regular
episcopal visitation was revived; (5) relations
between bishops and regulars were normalized; and
(6) synodal deliberation and action became a common-
place of English Catholic governance.

Wiseman

813. Fothergill, Brian. NICHOLAS WISEMAN. New
     York: Doubleday, 1963.

     A short, popular account of Wiseman's life and
     work. Adds little to Ward's much earlier two-
     volume biography (item 828), except for some new
     evidence concerning the Cardinal's relationship
     with Pius IX during the period immediately following
     the restoration of the English hierarchy.

     See: Adam Sargent, PUNCH 244 (24 April 1963): 611;
          J.H. Whyte, IHS 14 (March 1964): 93; Sister
          Albertus Magnus, CHR 50 (April 1964): 103;
          Edward I. Watkin, VS 8 (December 1964): 189-90.

814. ————. "Wiseman: The Man and His Mission." WR
     236 (Autumn 1962): 236-46.

     Presents a highly complex personality: generous,
     overly emotional, deeply creative, amazingly
     tolerant, and, as a result of these traits, extremely
     controversial.

815. Gwynn, Denis. CARDINAL WISEMAN. New York: P.J.
     Kenedy & Sons, 1929.

     Goes beyond biographical data to establish the
     difficult ecclesiastical situation within which
     Wiseman had to work. Details his problems with
     the "Old Catholics" as he attempted to initiate a
     dialogue with the Oxford Movement. Paints a
     favorable portrait of Archbishop Errington during

his awkward tenure as Wiseman's coadjutor.

See: DR 48 (January 1930): 59-63; Edwin Ryan, CHR 16
       (April 1930): 81-2; J.J. Dwyer, CLR 35 (January
       1951): 58-9; Patrick J. Corish, IER 76 (July
       1951): 90-1.

816.   ————. "Cardinal Wiseman and Ireland." IER 74
       (October 1950): 308-20.

       Follows Wiseman's constant awareness of his Irish
origins, along with the impact it had upon his life
and career. Maintains that he was never entirely
comfortable with either the English or the cautious
conservatism of English Catholics; his own Irish
impulsiveness and generosity of outlook were a
source of frequent apprehension among "Old Catholics,"
who were not pleased by their leader's triumphal tour
of Ireland in 1858, or by his readiness to entrust
major ecclesiastical responsibilities to converts
like Manning.

817.   ————. "The Paradox of Wiseman." CLR 34 (September
       1950): 187-202.

       Defines the paradox as that of a Roman-trained
prelate incapable of understanding the English over
whom he served as Primate. Challenges the
nineteenth-century image of Wiseman as an incompetent
administrator and a leader not to be trusted.

818.   ————. "Wiseman and Daniel O'Connell." CLR 28
       (December 1947): 361-73.

       Sees the Wiseman-O'Connell relationship as an
important factor in promoting the earliest phase of
the Catholic revival in England. Despite Newman's
negative feelings toward the Irish leader, Wiseman
cultivated a friendship, on the correct assumption
that it would bring English and Irish Catholics
closer together.

819.   ————. "Wiseman's Return to England in 1840."
       CLR 19 (September 1940): 189-204.

       Relates the circumstances under which Wiseman was
appointed President of Oscott College and coadjutor

to Dr. Walsh, Vicar Apostolic of the Midland District. His presence in England was immediately darkened when he announced his plans for the College, disagreeing with Pugin over the style of the new buildings to be erected, and made his first contacts with the Tractarians.

820. Jackman, S.W. NICHOLAS CARDINAL WISEMAN: A VICTORIAN PRELATE AND HIS WRITINGS. Charlottesville: University Press of Virginia, 1977.

Positions Wiseman within the milieu of the embattled Victorian Catholicism which he led. His status as a Victorian is derived from his ability to respond discreetly and successfully to the diverse interests and tastes of his day.

See: T. Patrick Hill, AMER 137 (29 October 1977): 291-2; E.R. Norman, TLS, 3 February 1978: 131; M.E. Williams, AMPJ 83 (Summer 1978): 71; Mary G. Holland, CHR 65 (October 1979): 657-8.

821. Kerns, Vincent M., S.F.S. "Wiseman and the 'Second Spring'--A Centenary." IER 74 (October 1950): 321-37.

Describes Wiseman's friendship with the Tractarians during the early 1840s, a friendship brought about by Ambrose Phillipps, in the hope of bringing Oscott and Oxford together, but frowned upon by the rest of the English episcopate. Sketches the first steps taken by Wiseman toward the restoration of the hierarchy (1847-1850).

822. McNabb, Vincent, O.P. "Cardinal Wiseman and Cardinal Mercier on Reunion." DUBR 204 (January/February/March 1939): 160-73.

Discusses Wiseman's enlightened ecumenical outlook, as expressed in a letter of 1841 to the Earl of Shrewsbury. Wiseman advised Catholics to refrain from all harsh language, bitterness, and sarcasm against Protestants.

823. Markus, Julia. "Bishop Blougram and the Literary
        Men." VS 21 (Winter 1978): 171-95.

        Demonstrates that the title character of Robert
        Browning's "Bishop Blougram's Apology" was modeled
        rather closely after the Wiseman of the "Papal
        Aggression" years. Yet, though the work was a
        parody of the Roman hierarchy's reestablishment in
        England, Wiseman, in the guise of Blougram, was
        treated, according to the author himself, "not
        ungenerously."

824. Messenger, E.C. "Wiseman, the Donatists, and
        Newman: A 'Dublin' Centenary." DUBR 205
        (July/August/September 1939): 110-19.

        Commemorates the centenary of the last of three
        articles on the Tractarians, written for the *Dublin
        Review* by Wiseman. In a carefully researched and
        skillfully crafted effort Wiseman compared the
        Anglican break from Rome with the early Church's
        Donatist schism. Newman challenged the parallel in
        a response of 1840, one so weak that it led him to
        rethink the question of where exactly true
        Catholicity lay.

  *   Norman, Edward. "Cardinal Wiseman: Catholic
        Consolidation." THE ENGLISH CATHOLIC CHURCH IN
        THE NINETEENTH CENTURY (item 773), 110-57.

        Surveys Wiseman's attempts to bring English
        Catholic spirituality and ecclesiastical style into
        line with the continental Catholicism of the first
        half of the nineteenth century. Speculates, however,
        as to whether the implementation of Roman centralism
        in England really required the presence of a
        Wiseman, in the first place.

825. Reynolds, E.E. THREE CARDINALS: NEWMAN--WISEMAN--
        MANNING. London: Burns & Oates, 1958.

        Interweaves the careers of the three prelates,
        looking at how as individuals and as a group they
        were the prime agents of the nineteenth-century
        Catholic revival in England. Offers a positive
        portrait of Wiseman, the prelate who led English
        Catholics into a new era. Praises his personal

abilities, great learning, aura of authority, and
perpetual optimism. Considers him a classic
example of the right man at the right time.

See: J.J. Dwyer, CLR 44 (January 1959): 50-3; J.M.
Cameron, VS 2 (March 1959): 282-3; B.E.
Kenworthy-Browne, DR 77 (Summer/Autumn
1959): 321-35; Patrick J. Brophy, IER 92
(July 1959): 67-8; Josef L. Altholz, JMH 31
(December 1959): 373-4; Eric McDermott, S.J.,
THOUGHT 35 (Spring 1960): 151-2.

826. Schiefen, Richard J. NICHOLAS WISEMAN AND THE
TRANSFORMATION OF ENGLISH CATHOLICISM.
Shepherdstown, W.Va.: Patmos Press, 1984.

Disputes the tendency by posterity to condemn
Wiseman to obscurity or caricature. Details his
personal and public life, with special reference
to the many battles he fought in his campaign to
introduce continental Catholicism into England.
Proclaims the Cardinal's career the epitome of
the burgeoning Catholic life during the post-
Emancipation period.

See: John T. Ford, RSR 11 (July 1985): 305;
Lawrence F. Barmann, CH 54 (September
1985): 423-4; Edward Norman, ALBION 17
(Spring 1985): 100-1; Vincent Alan
McClelland, MONTH 2nd NS 18 (September
1985): 314; Aidan Bellenger, DR 104
(January 1986): 48-50; J. Derek Holmes,
CHR 72 (April 1986): 306-7; Peter Doyle,
JEH 37 (July 1986): 478-9; Sheridan
Gilley, HEYJ 29 (January 1988): 136-8.

827. ————. "Some Aspects of the Controversy between
Cardinal Wiseman and the Westminster Chapter."
JEH 21 (April 1970): 125-48.

Identifies the fundamental issue at stake as the
right of the Archdiocesan Chapter to intervene in
matters which Wiseman perceived as being clearly
within the sole jurisdiction of the Archbishop.
Shows how, in the decade following the restoration
of the hierarchy, the controversy became so
contentious that the Cardinal was plagued by

litigation in both England and Rome.

828. Ward, Wilfrid. THE LIFE AND TIMES OF CARDINAL
        WISEMAN. London: Longmans, Green, 1897.
        2 vols.

        A sympathetic treatment of a leader who, by dint
        of talent and will, turned a persecuted sect into a
        Church. Volume 1 covers developments up to the
        restoration of the English hierarchy in 1850;
        volume 2 completes the study. Goes beyond the
        achievements and mistakes of the prelate, to probe
        the complexity of the man, at once pompous and shy,
        grandiose and childlike, and cultured and boyish.
        Throws much sidelight on European Catholicism during
        Wiseman's time.

        See: W.S. Lilly, FR 69 (1 February 1898): 287-307;
              PUNCH 114 (19 February 1898): 77; St. George
              Mivart, ACQR 23 (April 1898): 358-81; NATION
              66 (23 June 1898): 481-3; LQR 95 (January
              1901): 183.

Manning

829. Albion, Gordon. "Manning and the See of Westminster,
        1865-1892." In MANNING: ANGLICAN AND CATHOLIC
        (item 839), 57-65.

        Summarizes the practical effects of Manning's
        preoccupation with widows, orphans, and religious
        education.

830. Altholz, Josef L. "Some Observations on Victorian
        Religious Biography: Newman and Manning." WOR
        43 (August/September 1969): 407-15.

        Lists the three stages through which all
        Victorian religious biography passed: (1) the multi-
        volume "Life and Letters," authorized, highly
        selective in the choice of data, and with little or
        no interpretation; (2) the one-volume treatment,
        still amateurish in approach; and (3) the well-
        researched, well-written work produced by
        professional historians and biographers. Applies

these three phases to several biographies of Newman
and Manning.

831. Arnstein, Walter L.   THE BRADLAUGH CASE: A STUDY IN
      LATE VICTORIAN OPINION AND POLITICS.
      Oxford: Clarendon Press, 1965.

      Chapter 17 delineates Manning's significant role
      in one of the most serious problems of Gladstone's
      Second Ministry (1880-1885), the refusal of Charles
      Bradlaugh, a well-known atheist, to take the
      parliamentary oath, and his five subsequent ex-
      pulsions from the Commons. Considers the churchman
      one of the villains in the case, for he used his
      influence behind the scenes to pressure Roman
      Catholic members of Parliament to vote for the
      expulsions. Labels Manning "a politician by
      instinct," who loved the fray, and whose efforts
      within Parliament were paralleled by a more open
      literary campaign against what he perceived as the
      encroachment of blatant atheism.

      See: A.J.P. Taylor, NST 70 (27 August 1965): 288;
            CHOICE 3 (June 1966): 352-4; Joseph O. Baylen,
            AHR 71 (July 1966): 1350-1; John Clive, JMH 40
            (March 1968): 143-4.

832. Beck, George Andrew. "English Spiritual
      Writers: XXI. Cardinal Manning." CLR 45
      (September 1960): 513-24.

      Points to a relatively unknown aspect of
      Manning's work, that is, his spiritual teaching, as
      found in his sermons, public addresses, theological
      statements, and other works. Most fruitful of all
      his pronouncements on personal conduct and religious
      ideals were those he placed in the journals kept
      throughout his life.

833. Bodley, John Edward Courtney. CARDINAL MANNING.
      THE DECAY OF IDEALISM IN FRANCE. THE INSTITUTE
      OF FRANCE. London: Longmans, Green, 1912.

      A tribute from a close friend. Concerned more
      with the man and his humble simplicity than with
      his rank or precedence.

See: LQR 119 (April 1913): 358-9; NAMR 197 (April
      1913): 568-9; Shane Leslie, QR 301 (January
      1963): 102-9.

834. Chapeau, Alphonse. "Manning the Anglican." In
      MANNING: ANGLICAN AND CATHOLIC (item 839),
      1-39.

      Follows Manning's slow and painful progress from
      Anglicanism to Roman Catholicism. Displays the
      Archdeacon's efforts to present the Church of
      England as a pure branch of the Catholic Church,
      along with his eventual bewilderment and indecision,
      as his study of the Fathers showed him the enormous
      difficulties of such a task.

835. Davis, H. Francis. "Manning the Spiritual Writer."
      In MANNING: ANGLICAN AND CATHOLIC (item 839),
      149-60.

      Presents examples of Manning's religious works,
      arguing that their cumulative impact may have been
      as important as that of his social involvement or
      any other of his achievements. Contends that
      books like THE INTERNAL MISSION OF THE HOLY GHOST
      or THE GLORIES OF THE SACRED HEART were designed
      to combat the growing naturalism of the day.

836. Dingle, A.E., and Harrison, B.H. "Cardinal Manning
      as Temperance Reformer." HJ 12 (September
      1969): 485-510.

      As with item 832, concentrates on an almost
      completely ignored but highly significant part of
      Manning's career. Manning was a strongly committed
      temperance leader who believed that intemperance,
      though evil in itself, was more importantly the
      cause of many other vices and crimes. Consequently,
      no solution for Irish political problems would be
      found until the problems of excessive drinking among
      the Irish were first solved.

837. Fitzgerald, Edward, S.D.B. "Priesthood: Manning and
      Kierkegaard." CLR 58 (September 1973): 671-9.

      A pendant to item 843. Stresses Manning's lofty
      view of the priesthood, as opposed to Kierkegaard's

more down-to-earth image.

838. Fitzsimons, John. "Cardinal Manning: Friend of the
     People." CLR 32 (September 1949): 145-56.

     Speaks of Manning's constant and active interest
     in social justice. His firmly intellectual approach
     to the problems of workers was rooted in his
     recognition of both the individual value of human
     beings and the dignity of labor. His interventions
     on behalf of workers' rights were numerous, varied,
     and usually successful.

839. ————, ed. MANNING: ANGLICAN AND CATHOLIC.
     London: Burns Oates & Washbourne, 1951.

     Ten essays, written by specialists, in commemo-
     ration of Manning's conversion to Roman Catholicism.
     Each essay is a synopsis of a particular aspect of
     his rich and active life, from his Anglican period
     to his intense activity on behalf of workers during
     his later years. Contains items 829, 834, 835, 840,
     842, 844, 851, 852, 864, and 867.

     See: Christopher Sykes, DUBR 225 (Autumn 1951): 81-
          3; CLR 36 (October 1951): 265-7; IER 77 (March
          1952): 230; John Edmund O'Brien, CHR 38 (July
          1952): 231-2.

840. ————. "Manning and the Workers." In
     MANNING: ANGLICAN AND CATHOLIC (item 839), 136-
     48.

     Enumerates the various expressions of Manning's
     concern for the working poor: his membership on the
     Royal Commission on the Housing of the Working Class,
     his support of trade and agricultural unions, his
     mediation of the London Dock Strike of 1889, and his
     public addresses and articles on the social question,
     produced mainly during the last twenty years of his
     life.

841. Gray, Robert. CARDINAL MANNING: A BIOGRAPHY. New
     York: St. Martin's Press, 1985.

     The most recent full biography, broadly
     sympathetic. Explains the public side of the man

by delving into his private motivations, including
the strengths and weaknesses which have made him so
controversial a figure for so many years.

See: Kenneth Ballhatchet, BBN, January 1986: 19-20;
       Robert Blake, LRB 8 (23 January 1986): 17;
       Ian Ker, TLS, 7 February 1986: 136; John W.
       Padberg, S.J., AMER 154 (17 May 1986): 405-6;
       J.R. Griffin, CHOICE 23 (July/August
       1986): 1690; Alberic Stacpoole, O.S.B., MONTH
       2nd NS 19 (October 1986): 275-6; Sheridan
       Gilley, CCR 5 (February 1987): 69-71; Walter L.
       Arnstein, AHR 92 (June 1987): 668-9; Robert P.
       Rooney, NATR 39 (28 August 1987): 54-6.

842.   Gwynn, Denis.   "Manning and Ireland."   In
       MANNING: ANGLICAN AND CATHOLIC (item 839),
       111-35.

       Links Manning's awareness of the growing Irish
       presence in England with his campaign for political
       and religious liberty and his commitment to social
       justice.

843.   Hay, Jerome, C.SS.R.   "Manning and the Priesthood."
       CLR 58 (March 1973):   184-92.

       An analysis of Manning's ETERNAL PRIESTHOOD
       (1883), in which the priest is seen as an *alter
       Christus*, the visible sign of Christ in the world.
       For a comparison of Manning's view with that of
       Kierkegaard, his contemporary, see item 837.

844.   Howard, Christopher.   "Manning and Education."   In
       MANNING: ANGLICAN AND CATHOLIC (item 839), 101-
       10.

       Concentrates on Manning's work in primary
       education, conceding the fact that his effect on
       the development of Catholic higher and secondary
       institutions was far from praiseworthy.

845.   Ippolito, Robert F.   "Archbishop Manning's Champion-
       ship of Papal Infallibility, 1867-1872."   AMPJ 77
       (Summer 1972):   31-9.

       A detailed consideration of Manning's

pro-infallibilist activity at Vatican I and his pre-
conciliar literary activity on behalf of the definition. During the years immediately preceding the
Council, he not only made a considerable study of the
Petrine office and its claims, but also issued three
pastorals--in 1867, 1869, and 1870--on the validity of
the magisterial privilege granted the Papacy.

846. Leslie, Shane. CARDINAL MANNING. New York: P.J.
Kenedy & Sons, 1954.

An abstract, with some new material, of item 848.

See: Alban Baer, COMMWL 61 (31 December 1954): 364;
Gerald Ellard, HB 33 (March 1955): 180-1;
George A. Kelly, CHR 41 (April 1955): 172-4.

847. ————. "Cardinal Manning & the London Strike of
1889." DUBR 167 (October/November/December
1920): 219-31.

Details Manning's patient and skilled mediation,
based on his belief that while capital enjoyed many
supporters, labor had none. Beyond being the most
signal victory in the churchman's life, this
intervention also inspired Leo XIII's encyclical on
labor, *Rerum Novarum* (see items 242, 249, and 312).
For a much lengthier study of Manning's activity
during the strike, see item 868.

848. ————. HENRY EDWARD MANNING, HIS LIFE AND LABOURS.
London: Burns Oates & Washbourne, 1921.

Written as a response to the highly negative
portraits presented by Purcell (item 863) and
Strachey (item 866). Uses many of Manning's
personal papers now either lost or unavailable
to researchers. Focuses on his personal,
theological, and administrative controversies,
his relationship with Newman, and his efforts on
behalf of democracy and labor. For a revised
edition of this work, with some new material, see
item 846.

See: William Barry, BKMN 60 (May 1921): 90-2; AMER
25 (2 July 1921): 261-2; R. Ellis Roberts, LM
4 (September 1921): 551-2; Henry A. Lappin,

CW 114 (October 1921): 25-33; William Hamilton
Drummond, HIBJ 20 (no. 3, 1922): 606-8.

849.   ———. "Irish Pages from the Postbags of Manning,
        Cullen and Gladstone." DUBR 165 (October/November/
        December 1919): 161-91.

        Outlines the role played by Manning and Cullen in
        advising Gladstone as to how to secure Parliamentary
        approval for the disestablishment of the Irish
        Church. Includes generous excerpts from the letters
        passed among the three leaders.

850.   ———. "Manning, America and Democracy." DUBR 165
        (July/August/September 1919): 1-20.

        Portrays Manning as an inveterate patron of
        democracy, which he sought to win back to the
        Church. He admired the union of democracy and
        Christianity achieved in America, and consequently
        supported the efforts of Cardinal Gibbons of
        Baltimore to obtain papal approval of the American
        labor movement. Without that approval, Manning
        believed, the alliance of democrats and Christians
        in America would die, as it had in France during
        the later stages of the Revolution of 1789.

851.   ———. "Manning and His Friends." In
        MANNING: ANGLICAN AND CATHOLIC (item 839), 66-72.

        Reviews Manning's relationships with Gladstone,
        Florence Nightingale, Sir Charles Dilke, and other
        Victorian luminaries.

852.   ———. "Manning and Newman." In MANNING: ANGLICAN
        AND CATHOLIC (item 839), 73-83.

        Compares the personalities and philosophies of the
        two Cardinals; Manning was part of the Petrine rock,
        while Newman was as variable as the ocean surrounding
        that rock.

853.   ———. "Some Birmingham Bygones, Illustrated by
        Letters from the Postbags of Ullathorne and
        Manning." DUBR 166 (April/May/June 1920): 203-21.

        Refutes the charge that Manning never sought or

took the advice of his fellow bishops, by pointing to
his close, cordial, and sometimes even humorous
relationship with Bishop Ullathorne of Birmingham.

854. ————. "Virginia Crawford, Sir Charles Dilke, and
Cardinal Manning." DUBR 241 (Autumn 1967): 177-
205.

Examines Manning's attempts to rehabilitate the
reputation of the repentant Virginia Crawford, who
in 1886 had been convicted of adultery with Dilke,
a member of Gladstone's cabinet.

855. McClelland, Vincent Alan. CARDINAL MANNING: HIS
PUBLIC LIFE AND INFLUENCE, 1865-1892.
London: Oxford University Press, 1962.

Praises Manning's transformation of Roman
Catholicism in England from a narrow, unruly,
conservative faith to a democratic, open
community which became an important part of
the national scene.

See: David Lodge, SPEC 209 (21 December 1962): 967;
Dom Daniel Rees, DR 81 (January 1963): 83-4;
Shane Leslie, QR 301 (January 1963): 102-9;
Ronald Chapman, CLR 48 (March 1963): 194-6;
Thomas P. Joyce, CHR 49 (April 1963): 124-5;
John Tracy Ellis, CH 32 (June 1963): 220-1;
Walter L. Arnstein, VS 6 (June 1963): 365-7;
A. Chapeau, EHR 79 (October 1964): 880-1;
Christopher Howard, JEH 15 (October 1964): 267-
8.

856. ————. "The Irish Clergy and Archbishop Manning's
Apostolic Visitation of the Western District of
Scotland, 1867. Part I: The Coming of the Irish."
CHR 53 (April 1967): 1-27.

Describes the troubled ecclesiastical situation
which led to Manning's tour of October 1867. In-
fighting between Scottish and immigrant Irish
Catholics, evident as early as 1827, grew increasingly worse, until Manning, Vicar Apostolic of the
Western District, agreed to hear the grievances of
all concerned and proffer a just and unbiased
settlement. Continues in item 857.

857.   ———. "The Irish Clergy and Archbishop Manning's
        Apostolic Visitation of the Western District of
        Scotland, 1867. Part II: A Final Solution."
        CHR 53 (July 1967): 229-50.

        Continued from item 856. Reconstructs Manning's
        five-day stay in Glasgow, during which he spoke with
        both Scots and Irish, and after which he was more
        convinced than ever that a speedy solution was
        necessary. His recommendations to Rome were adopted
        and proved effective; at the same time, Manning
        deliberately delayed the reestablishment of the
        Scottish hierarchy until the Western District was
        pacified and its ecclesiastical life normalized.

858.   ———. "Manning and the Universities: A Reappraisal
        of the Background to the Kensington Venture."
        TABLET 217 (30 March 1963): 335-7.

        Sketches the circumstances of 1864-1872 which
        persuaded Manning to impose a ban on Catholic
        attendance at Oxford and Cambridge. With the two
        major universities forbidden to Catholic pro-
        fessionals, the Cardinal realized that he bore the
        responsibility of establishing his own institution
        of higher learning, and thus the Kensington scheme
        was born.

859.   Newsome, David. THE PARTING OF FRIENDS: A STUDY OF
        THE WILBERFORCES AND HENRY MANNING. London: John
        Murray, 1966.

        The American edition (Cambridge: Harvard
        University Press, Belknap Press, 1966) reverses the
        title. Demonstrates how Manning's secession from
        Anglicanism, itself the result of much painful soul-
        searching, was accompanied by an equally painful loss
        of Samuel Wilberforce's friendship.

        See: ECON 221 (12 November 1966): 706; A. Dwight
              Culler, YR 56 (Spring 1967): 458-61; Martin E.
              Marty, CH 36 (June 1967): 232-3; John Kent,
              NST 74 (11 August 1967): 178; R.W. Greaves,
              HIST 52 (October 1967): 353-4; F.R. Salter,
              EHR 83 (April 1968): 415-6; Josef L. Altholz,
              CHR 55 (July 1969): 205-6; Geoffrey Best, HJ
              12 (December 1969): 707-10.

860. Norman, Edward. "Cardinal Manning and the Temporal
      Power." In HISTORY, SOCIETY AND THE
      CHURCHES: ESSAYS IN HONOUR OF OWEN CHADWICK
      (item 24), 235-56.

      Evaluates Manning's complex reasons for defending
      the continued existence of the Papal States during
      the period of their dismemberment by Italian
      liberals. Sees within the tangle of his motivations
      a clear interpenetration of the sacred and secular,
      that is, a mixture of religious, historical, utili-
      tarian, and pragmatic considerations, which showed an
      affinity to his other opinions concerning English
      political and social issues of his day.

*   ————. "Cardinal Manning: Ultramontanist
      Confidence." THE ENGLISH CATHOLIC CHURCH IN THE
      NINETEENTH CENTURY (item 773), 244-86.

      Presents a leader of great strengths and weak-
      nesses, dedicated to the extension of the Roman
      spirit brought to England by Wiseman, and to social
      reform.

861. O'Rourke, James. "Manning and Newman." IER 52
      (November 1938): 459-69.

      Compares the two men, their personalities and
      talents. Maintains that their relationship
      ultimately ruptured precisely because they were so
      very dissimilar: Newman was a perpetual student
      and dreamer; Manning was a man of action and a
      realist. The things about which Newman only dreamt,
      Manning achieved.

862. Pressensé, Francis de. PURCELL'S 'MANNING' REFUTED;
      LIFE OF CARDINAL MANNING, WITH A CRITICAL
      EXAMINATION OF E.S. PURCELL'S MISTAKES.
      Translated by Francis T. Furey.
      Philadelphia: John Joseph McVey, 1897.

      A direct response to item 863, written by a
      French Protestant. Criticizes Purcell's unethically
      selective use of Manning's diaries and letters,
      along with the resulting portrait of an ambitious
      schemer.

See: ACQR 22 (July 1897): 664-5; DUBR 121 (October
       1897): 424-6.

863.   Purcell, Edmund Sheridan.   LIFE OF CARDINAL MANNING,
       ARCHBISHOP OF WESTMINSTER.   London: Macmillan,
       1896.   2 vols.

       The first full-length biography.   A devastating
       assessment of Manning's personality, based on
       oftentimes inaccurate transcriptions of the prelate's
       own private papers.   Beneath a veneer of flattery the
       author draws a picture of a fanatically ambitious
       churchman, inordinately attached to honors and
       distinctions, consumed by the will to power, and
       prepared to take any step, however unscrupulous, to
       gain that power.   Inspired Strachey's view (item
       866).   For a refutation of Purcell, see item 862.

       See: NATION 62 (20 February 1896): 161-2; A.F. Hewit,
              CW 62 (March 1896): 836-41; Tuley Francis
              Huntington, DIAL 20 (16 March 1896): 169-71;
              Thomas F. Galwey, ACQR 21 (April 1896): 374-89;
              LQR 86 (April 1896): 137-54; C.C. Tiffany,
              FORUM 21 (July 1896): 577-94; Shane Leslie, QR
              301 (January 1963): 102-9.

864.   Purdy, William.   "Manning and the Vatican Council."
       In MANNING: ANGLICAN AND CATHOLIC (item 839),
       84-100.

       Exhibits Manning's unswerving ultramontanism and
       his successful prevention of the British government's
       intervention in conciliar affairs, an intervention
       urged upon Gladstone by Acton.

  *   Reynolds, E.E.   THREE CARDINALS: NEWMAN--WISEMAN--
       MANNING.   Cited above as item 825.

       A mixed portrait of Manning.   Beyond his indomi-
       table will, which towered well above his other
       characteristics, he displayed little of Wiseman's
       or Newman's intellectual distinction or imagination.
       Moreover, his intransigence led to some unfortunate
       behavior, including his failure to appreciate the
       purpose of much of Newman's work.

865.   Selby, D.E.   "Cardinal Manning, Campaigner for

Children's Rights."   JEH 27 (October 1976):   403-
12.

Publicizes the little-known role played by the
aging prelate in helping to secure children's rights.
Not only did he work to ensure the successful passage
of two major pieces of legislation during the 1880s,
protecting children against neglect, cruelty, and
exploitation; he was also highly influential in the
formation of the National Society for the Prevention
of Cruelty to Children.

866.   Strachey, Lytton. EMINENT VICTORIANS: CARDINAL
         MANNING, FLORENCE NIGHTINGALE, DR. ARNOLD,
         GENERAL GORDON. London: Chatto & Windus,
         1918.

Uses Purcell (item 863) as the basis for its
lengthy treatment of Manning, who is portrayed as
self-absorbed, manipulative, overly ambitious, and
power-hungry.

See: DUBR 163 (July/August/September 1918): 110-13;
         LQR 130 (July 1918): 126; Edward Shanks, DIAL
         65 (18 July 1918): 54-5; J. Moffatt, BKMN 54
         (August 1918): 153-4; Randolph Bourne, DIAL
         65 (28 December 1918): 603-4; Maurice Francis
         Egan, YR 8 (April 1919): 640-6; Joseph Wood
         Krutch, NATION 134 (17 February 1932): 199-200.

867.   Ward, Denis, O.S.C. "Manning and His Oblates." In
         MANNING: ANGLICAN AND CATHOLIC (item 839), 40-56.

Recalls Manning's foundation of the Oblates of St.
Charles at Bayswater (1856), a congregation of
missionary priests directed by Wiseman to give
retreats and lectures throughout England.

868.   Wheeler, Arthur Francis. CARDINAL MANNING AND THE
         LONDON DOCK STRIKE OF 1889. Ph.D. dissertation.
         University of Notre Dame, 1979.

Combines an account of the strike, an explanation
of Manning's involvement, and an evaluation of the
impact of the eighty-two-year-old prelate's intervention upon Roman Catholicism in England, the non-
Catholic churches, and the general public.

Vaughan

869. Bolton, C.A. "Cardinal Vaughan as Educator." CLR
      28 (October 1947): 237-45.

      Echoes the treatment of Vaughan's educational
      theory and activity found in Snead-Cox (item 874).
      Emphasizes the grand scale of his educational
      plans, his willingness to experiment, his belief
      in the necessity of forming a student's character,
      and his efforts to persuade Rome to rescind the
      ban on Catholic attendance at Oxford and Cambridge.

870. Hanrahan, Noel. "Cardinal Vaughan and Priestly
      Devotion to the Eucharist." IER 102 (August
      1964): 101-7.

      Illustrates Vaughan's personal devotion to the
      Eucharist, as seen especially during his twenty
      years as Bishop of Salford.

871. ————. "Cardinal Vaughan and the Secular Clergy."
      CLR 46 (December 1961): 715-33.

      Highlights Vaughan's lifetime efforts to improve
      the benighted image of the secular priest: the
      establishment of an innovative diocesan seminary at
      Salford; the foundation of the Mill Hill Missionaries,
      intended specifically for secular clergy; and the
      promotion of the concept of perfection achieved
      through working in the world.

872. McCormack, Arthur. "Cardinal Vaughan: The Fourth
      Cardinal." DUBR 239 (Winter 1965-6): 295-336.

      An abridgement of item 873. Argues that Vaughan,
      though overshadowed by Wiseman, Manning, and Newman,
      played an important role in the English Church during
      the last three decades of the nineteenth century, and
      thus deserves a secure place among the ecclesiastical
      giants of his time.

873. ————. CARDINAL VAUGHAN; THE LIFE OF THE THIRD
      ARCHBISHOP OF WESTMINSTER, FOUNDER OF ST.
      JOSEPH'S MISSIONARY SOCIETY, MILL HILL.
      London: Burns & Oates, 1966.

A general introduction to Vaughan's character and career. Highly flattering.

See: TLS, 26 May 1966: 478; Wilfrid Passmore, DR 84 (October 1966): 449-52; Dudley W.R. Bahlman, VS 10 (March 1967): 314-5; John Tracy Ellis, CHR 55 (July 1969): 206-8.

*   Norman, Edward. "Cardinal Vaughan: End of an Era." THE ENGLISH CATHOLIC CHURCH IN THE NINETEENTH CENTURY (item 773), 345-73.

Contrasts Vaughan's unimpressive showing as a religious leader with his achievements as an ecclesiastical administrator and the richness of his spiritual life. Compares his goals, methods, and results with those of his predecessor, Manning.

874.   Snead-Cox, J.G. THE LIFE OF CARDINAL VAUGHAN. London: Herbert & Daniel/St. Louis: B. Herder, 1910. 2 vols.

Balances biographical data with a more general treatment of Catholic life in England during the second half of the nineteenth century. Makes extensive use of Vaughan's diaries, to which during crises in his life he always turned, pouring out his most intimate thoughts and feelings. Leaves the impression of a saintly yet practical man, overflowing with vitality, and propelled by a deep sense of humility.

See: BKMN 38 (August 1910): 215-6; John Telford, LQR 114 (October 1910): 246-58; J.F. Scholfield, ACQR 36 (January 1911): 1-17; R.L. Gales, HIBJ 9 (April 1911): 683-5; John Mann, BKMN 86 (June 1934): 174.

Ullathorne

875.   Butler, Dom Cuthbert. THE LIFE AND TIMES OF BISHOP ULLATHORNE, 1806-1889. London: Burns Oates & Washbourne, 1926. 2 vols.

Details the career of William Ullathorne, who

began life as a Yorkshire cabin-boy, and died Bishop
of Birmingham and titular Archbishop of Cabasa in
lower Egypt. Assesses the role he played in the
expansion and internal policies of Victorian
Catholicism. Credits him with a powerful and
critical influence on the character of the Roman
revival in England.

See: Bertram C.A. Windle, COMMWL 3 (10 March
1926): 499-501; Egerton Beck, DUBR 178
(April/May/June 1926): 172-82; William F.
Brown, DUBR 178 (April/May/June 1926): 161-
71; Algar Thorold, DR 44 (May 1926): 133-45;
AMER 35 (29 May 1926): 163; Gerald B. Hurst,
EHR 41 (July 1926): 472-3; Henry Harrington,
THOUGHT 1 (December 1926): 549-54; IER 29
(February 1927): 214-18; R.E. Gordon George,
THEO 15 (July 1927): 52-4.

876. Dunne, Joseph W. "The Letters of Archbishop
Ullathorne." CLR 25 (July 1945): 298-303.

Finds in Ullathorne's correspondence a good deal
of pastoral wisdom; a flexible and easy prose; a
high regard for Newman, whom he often advised; lively
character sketches of foreign churchmen, such as St.
John Vianney, visited by the Bishop in 1854; and
various observations on art, literature, politics,
and personal affairs.

877. Gwynn, Denis. "Heralds of the Second Spring: IX.
Bishop Ullathorne." CLR 30 (December 1948): 389-
406.

Covers Ullathorne's two years as Vicar Apostolic
of the Western District (1846-1848), during which he
restored financial solvency and set a remarkable
example of clerical piety.

878. Lamb, J.C. "English Spiritual Writers: XVI. William
Bernard Ullathorne, O.S.B." CLR 45 (April
1960): 193-206.

Focuses on Ullathorne's work as a spiritual
director who maintained that true holiness was
achieved through a mixture of prayer and activity.

* Leslie, Shane. "Some Birmingham Bygones, Illustrated
  by Letters from the Postbags of Ullathorne and
  Manning." Cited above as item 853.

Hedley

879. Cummins, J.I., O.S.B. "Bishop Hedley." DUBR 188
     (April/May/June 1931): 241-53.

     Sketches the varied ecclesiastical career of John
     Cuthbert Hedley, Second Bishop of Newport (1881-
     1915). In addition to his pastoral duties, he
     contributed to a large number of Catholic periodic-
     als--*The Tablet* and *Ampleforth Journal*, among
     others--for over fifty years; from 1879 to 1884 he
     served as editor of the *Dublin Review*. His wide
     intellectual background was complemented by his
     oratorical skills and deep faith in what he preached.

880. Matthews, J.E., O.S.B. "Bishop Hedley as Editor."
     DUBR 198 (April/May/June 1936): 253-66.

     Praises Hedley's establishment of the "Third
     Series" of the *Dublin Review*. Anxious to preserve
     the high standards set for the periodical by
     Wiseman and Ward, he succeeded in obtaining
     articles--and for little pay--from such distinguished
     contributors as Manning, Vaughan, Gasquet, Mivart,
     and Lilly; to their work he added over the years
     fifteen scholarly efforts of his own.

881. Wilson, J. Anselm. THE LIFE OF BISHOP HEDLEY.
     London: Burns Oates & Washbourne, 1930.

     A detailed study of a bishop whose personal
     influence among his colleagues was second only to
     that of the Archbishop of Westminster. Attributes
     his powerful reputation to his charismatic
     personality, erudition, and position as unofficial
     spokesman for the hierarchy, in which capacity he
     often voiced the hopes and ideals of English
     Catholicism.

     See: Dom Basil Whelan, DUBR 186 (July/August/
          September 1930): 167-70; G.R. Huddleston,

DR 48 (October 1930): 336-9.

Baines

882. The Abbot of Downside. "The Controversy with Bishop
      Baines." DR 33 (June 1914): 91-117.

      Looks into Baines' establishment in 1830 of a
      college at Prior Park, after the Downside Benedictines
      refused to let him take over their educational facili-
      ties. Enrollment at Downside dropped greatly, as
      students flocked to the newer and more attractive
      school.

883. Roche, J.S. A HISTORY OF PRIOR PARK COLLEGE AND ITS
      FOUNDER, BISHOP BAINES. London: Burns Oates &
      Washbourne, 1931.

      Attempts to rehabilitate the controversial bishop.
      Sees Baines as the ablest and most far-sighted
      English prelate of his time. Against Baines' repu-
      tation for contentiousness and financial irrespon-
      sibility, Roche balances his vision of and commitment
      to Prior Park, which he opened in 1830.

      See: IER 39 (January 1932): 107-9; R.H. Willson,
            O.S.B., DUBR 190 (January/February/March
            1932): 155-60; Dom Cuthbert Butler, DR 50
            (October 1932): 333-49.

884. Stuart, E.B. "Bishop Baines and His 1840 Lenten
      Pastoral: The Last Full-Scale Manifesto of
      Traditional English Catholicism?" DR 105
      (January 1987): 40-59.

      Reexamines the role of Peter Augustine Baines
      (1787-1843), Vicar Apostolic of the Western District
      (1829-1843), in promoting the "Second Spring."
      Demonstrates that far from being the archetypal
      "Old Catholic," alarmed and revolted by Wiseman's
      introduction of foreign devotions, he was quite
      sympathetic with the aims of the ultramontanist
      party in England. Places his pastoral of 1840,
      calling for prayers for the conversion of England,
      within the context of these sympathies.

Other Bishops

885. Coyne, John J. "Anglo-Irish Hierarchy." IER 60
     (September 1942): 229-38.

   Presents biographies of Irishmen who became leaders
   of the nineteenth-century English episcopate.
   Discusses the lives and activities of Wiseman, James
   Chadwick (1813-1882, Second Bishop of Hexham and
   Newcastle), William Cotter (1866-1940, Third Bishop
   of Portsmouth), Bernard O'Reilly (1824-1894, Bishop
   of Liverpool), John Carroll (1838-1897, Bishop of
   Shrewsbury), and John Keily (1854-1928, Bishop of
   Plymouth). Stresses the commitment by the latter
   three to Catholic education.

886. Doyle, Peter. "Bishop Goss of Liverpool (1856-1872)
     and the Importance of Being English." In RELIGION
     AND NATIONAL IDENTITY: PAPERS READ AT THE
     NINETEENTH SUMMER MEETING AND THE TWENTIETH WINTER
     MEETING OF THE ECCLESIASTICAL HISTORY SOCIETY
     (item 25), 433-47.

   Neither a biography nor a character analysis, but
   a consideration of one aspect of Goss' career,
   namely, his fierce and steadfast opposition to undue
   Papal interference in English diocesan affairs.
   This opposition, which made him an anti-infallibilist
   in 1870, was based on two convictions: (1) that
   excessive Curial authority in England injured the
   dignity of the local episcopate and failed to take
   local conditions into account; and (2) that English
   Catholics were citizens only of England, and thus the
   Pope could not expect to receive their political
   obedience. In his campaign to destroy the old
   English image of Roman Catholicism as something
   foreign and un-English, Goss was attacked by many,
   including Wiseman, who branded him anti-Roman and
   pro-Anglican.

887. Edwards, Francis. "An English Bishop and the Other
     Council." MONTH 1st NS 28 (December 1962): 325-
     35.

   Reconstructs the experiences of Francis Kerril
   Amherst, Bishop of Northampton (1858-1879), during

Vatican I. Uses excerpts from his previously unpublished diary to show his lack of concern with
the day-to-day business of the Council, a lack
which was more than counterbalanced by his anger
at the British press for what he considered its
anti-papal stance.

888. Gwynn, Denis. "Heralds of the Second Spring: V.
        Bishop Walsh." CLR 30 (August 1948): 100-18.

        Recalls the crucial role played by Bishop Thomas
Walsh during his tenure as Vicar Apostolic of the
Midland District (1826-1848). His deep personal
holiness and sense of charity, combined with
outstanding organizational skills, enabled him to
restore discipline among his restless clergy. At
the same time he enthusiastically supported Pugin's
Gothic extravagances as an appropriate symbol of
the Catholic revival.

889. O'Meara, Kathleen. THOMAS GRANT, FIRST BISHOP OF
        SOUTHWARK. 2nd ed. London: Catholic Truth
        Society, 1886.

        A detailed and highly favorable biography of a
churchman who served as Rector of the English
College in Rome and agent for the Vicars Apostolic
(1844-1851), and then as First Bishop of Southwark
(1851-1870). Underscores his extraordinary holiness,
as reflected in his numerous acts of self-mortifi-
cation, protection of orphans, and concern over the
welfare of Catholic soldiers during the Crimean War.

        See: DUBR 101 (July 1887): 215.

890. Supple, Jennifer F. "Robert Cornthwaite: A
        Neglected Nineteenth Century Bishop." RH 17
        (October 1985): 399-412.

        Resurrects the career of the Bishop of Beverley
(1861-1890). Cornthwaite, the most ultramontane of
English bishops, was Manning's chief supporter at
Vatican I; moreover, as an able and energetic
administrator, he laid the foundations for the
modern dioceses of Middlesbrough, Leeds, and Hallam.

<u>Newman</u>

Bibliographies and General Works

* Altholz, Josef L. "Some Observations on Victorian Religious Biography: Newman and Manning." Cited above as item 830.

891. Blehl, Vincent Ferrer, S.J. JOHN HENRY NEWMAN: A BIBLIOGRAPHICAL CATALOGUE OF HIS WRITINGS. Charlottesville: University Press of Virginia, 1978.

   Lists the various editions of Newman's books, his articles in periodicals and newspapers, edited and translated works, and assorted items published posthumously.

   See: Owen Chadwick, JTS 30 (April 1979): 406; John Tracy Ellis, CHR 67 (April 1981): 321-2.

892. Earnest, J.D., and Tracey, G. JOHN HENRY NEWMAN: AN ANNOTATED BIBLIOGRAPHY OF HIS TRACT AND PAMPHLET COLLECTION. New York: Garland, 1984.

   An annotated bibliography of the eight collections of tracts and pamphlets from Newman's library at the Birmingham Oratory. The 2,178 items, many of which are filled with Newman's marginalia, are grouped chronologically.

   See: Nicholas Lash, JEH 37 (April 1986): 357; John R. Griffin, CH 55 (September 1986): 402.

893. Griffin, John R. NEWMAN: A BIBLIOGRAPHY OF SECONDARY SOURCES. Front Royal, Va.: Christendom Publications, 1980.

   A large collection of general studies, monographs, articles, and doctoral dissertations covering such areas as Newman's life and personality, theology and philosophy, and religious thought. Includes works published in France, Germany, Belgium, and the Netherlands, as well as in the English-speaking countries.

See: CHOICE 19 (March 1982): 891; John Richard Orens,
CH 51 (September 1982): 376-7; Michael D.
Moore, RSR 9 (April 1983): 170.

894. Haight, Roger. "Bremond's Newman." In NEWMAN AND
THE MODERNISTS (item 971), 119-37.

Evaluates Bremond's portrait of Newman as an
existentialist.

895. Lahutsky, Nadia M. "Ward's Newman: The Struggle to
Be Faithful and Fair." In NEWMAN AND THE
MODERNISTS (item 971), 47-67.

Examines the technical problems and personal
intrigues surrounding Ward's writing of the
"official" biography of Newman (item 930).

896. Nédoncelle, Maurice. "The Revival of Newman
Studies: Some Reflections." DR 86 (October
1968): 385-94.

Suggests some new avenues of inquiry for future
Newman scholars, while listing the merits and
shortcomings of several recently published pieces
of Newmaniana.

897. Weaver, Mary Jo. "Wilfrid Ward's Interpretation and
Application of Newman." In NEWMAN AND THE
MODERNISTS (item 971), 27-46.

Tests the validity of Ward's claim (item 930) that
of all his generation he was the only one who ever
really understood Newman.

898. Wright, T.R., ed. JOHN HENRY NEWMAN: A MAN FOR OUR
TIME? Newcastle upon Tyne: Grevatt & Grevatt,
1983.

Approaches Newman's complex personality and life
from various angles, but always with the presumption
that the reader already has some knowledge of the
subject. To the question posed by the title, the
six contributors, who discuss topics as diverse as
Newman's Anglican years, novels, educational views,
and theology, offer no conclusive reply; they all
agree, however, on Newman's intense interest in the

problems confronting the Catholicism of his day.
Contains items 943 and 996.

See: Roderick Strange, MONTH 2nd NS 17 (February
       1984): 69; Joseph A. Komonchak, RSR 10 (July
       1984): 270; Josef L. Altholz, VS 29 (Winter
       1986): 320-2.

899. Father Zeno, O.F.M. Cap. "The Reliability of
      Newman's Autobiographical Writings (I)."
      IER 86 (November 1956): 297-305.

Attempts to prove as far as possible the objec-
tivity of Newman's early journals (1816-1847) and
other autobiographical works, against those who
find their discussion of his inner life incredible
or, at the very least, problematic. Evaluates not
only his honesty, but also his reliability; that
is, his capacity to understand and formulate
adequately the hidden workings of his emotional
side. Offers conclusions in item 900.

900. ————. "The Reliability of Newman's Autobiographical
      Writings (II)." IER 87 (January 1957): 25-37.

Continues from item 899. Finds no dishonesty or
insincerity in Newman's writings, even with all
their internal contradictions.

Biographies

901. Bouyer, Louis. NEWMAN: HIS LIFE AND SPIRITUALITY.
      Translated by J. Lewis May. New York: P.J.
      Kenedy & Sons, 1958.

Less a conventional biography than a study of a
soul's progress. Selective in its coverage, emphasizing the manifestations of Newman's spirituality
and their impact on the rest of his life. Hagiographical, but based on a large amount of Newmaniana,
some of it from the Birmingham Oratory, to which the
author, a converted Calvinist, belonged.

See: Rose Macaulay, SPEC 200 (31 January 1958): 137;
      H. Francis Davis, CLR 43 (March 1958): 182-4;

John M. Todd, DR 76 (Spring 1958): 200-4;
D.J.B. Hawkins, DUBR 232 (Spring 1958): 81-8;
IER 89 (June 1958): 463-5; Louis A. Arand,
CHR 44 (July 1958): 197-205; Martin J.
Svaglic, VS 2 (December 1958): 162-4.

902. Campion, Edmund. JOHN HENRY NEWMAN: FRIENDS, ALLIES,
      BISHOPS, CATHOLICS. Melbourne: Dove Communi-
      cations, 1980.

Based on a careful sifting of the twenty-one
volumes of Newman's letters and diaries published
between 1962 and 1977. Identifies Newman's friends
and supporters, on the one hand, and his opponents,
on the other. Among those placed in the latter
group, on the basis of their treatment of Newman
via letter, are Wiseman, Cullen, Manning, Talbot,
and Ward.

See: John Tracy Ellis, CHR 67 (October 1981): 678-9;
      M.D. Stephen, JRH 11 (December 1981): 613-6.

903. Chadwick, Owen. NEWMAN. Oxford and New York: Oxford
      University Press, 1983.

A brief psychological and intellectual portrait.
Assesses Newman's place both in the general history
of the Church and in the history of theology.
Singles out his idea of development as his most
important contribution to Christianity; his views on
the nature of faith are labeled some of the most
interesting put forth by any nineteenth-century
religious author. Hails Newman as one of the most
significant influences on twentieth-century thought.

See: CHOICE 21 (October 1983): 296; John Coventry,
      THEO 87 (January 1984): 75-6; Roderick Strange,
      MONTH 2nd NS 17 (February 1984): 69; John T.
      Ford, C.S.C., THS 45 (March 1984): 185; Vincent
      Ferrer Blehl, S.J., NCW 227 (March/April
      1984): 95; Edward Royle, HT 34 (May 1984): 56;
      John R. Griffin, CH 53 (September 1984): 410;
      Gerald Fitzgibbon, S.J., SJT 37 (September
      1984): 412-3; Keith Robbins, JEH 35 (October
      1984): 648-50; Thomas Bokenkotter, CHR 71
      (April 1985): 306; Gabriel Daly, O.S.A., ITQ
      51 (no. 3, 1985): 248.

904. Coulson, John. "John Henry Newman: His Genius for Friendship." CLR 62 (January 1977): 18-21.

Explores Newman's relationship with his Oratorian colleagues. Though the recognized head at Birmingham, Newman stressed the familial, informal, and non-assertive nature of his Order; his men were bound not by a rule, but by friendship. If from time to time he himself collided with authority, it was because he always said what he thought, and all too often what he thought and said--as in the case of his insistence on an enthusiastic and educated laity--was not shared by his superiors.

905. ————, and Allchin, A.M., eds. THE REDISCOVERY OF NEWMAN. London: Sheed & Ward/S.P.C.K., 1967.

A series of papers delivered at the Newman Symposium, Oxford University, March-April 1966. Measures Newman's role in English history, his contributions to the intellectual development of nineteenth-century Europe, and his place in the two-thousand-year span of the Christian inheritance.

See: Colin Cross, OBS, 14 January 1968: 30; Meriol Trevor, DR 86 (April 1968): 203-7; P. McKevitt, ITQ 35 (April 1968): 206-8; Alan G. Hill, SJT 21 (June 1968): 227-8; TLS, 27 June 1968: 672; W.D. White, JAAR 36 (December 1968): 385-6, 388-9; Owen Chadwick, JTS 20 (April 1969): 357-60; Bernard M.G. Reardon, CLR 54 (May 1969): 398-400.

906. ————, ————, and Trevor, Meriol. NEWMAN: A PORTRAIT RESTORED. London: Sheed & Ward, 1965.

Argues that Newman's hitherto ignored or under-stated place in English history must be revised, in light of his strong ecumenical posture. Includes a survey of his life and a full bibliography of his literary output.

See: Maurice Nédoncelle, DR 83 (October 1965): 392-4; John Challenor, CLR 51 (March 1966): 245-7.

907. Cross, Frank Leslie. JOHN HENRY NEWMAN. London· Philip Allan, 1933.

Of special importance in this biography is Chapter 9, dealing with the intellectual, theological, and psychological reasons for Newman's conversion to Roman Catholicism.

See: DR 51 (July 1933): 556-7; Nigel J. Abercrombie, DUBR 193 (September 1933): 307-8.

908.   Culler, A. Dwight.   "Newman: The Remembrance of Things Past." In A NEWMAN SYMPOSIUM: REPORT ON THE TENTH ANNUAL MEETING OF THE CATHOLIC RENASCENCE SOCIETY AT THE COLLEGE OF THE HOLY CROSS, WORCESTER, MASS., APRIL 1952 (item 931), 59-70.

A tally of Newman's personal effects, as found at the Birmingham Oratory after his death. Uses the items on the list to reconstruct Newman's mental habits.

909.   Dessain, Charles Stephen.   JOHN HENRY NEWMAN. London: Thomas Nelson and Sons, 1966.

A brief but profound study by the editor of Newman's letters and diaries. Covers all the major facets of the churchman's eventful career. Stresses the innovative thinker rather than the man.

See: Thomas Vargish, VS 10 (June 1967): 446-7; Dunstan Pontifex, DR 85 (July 1967): 364-5; John T. Wilkinson, LQHR 192 (July 1967): 253; D.C. Duivesteijn, CLR 52 (October 1967): 834-5; John Pick, AMER 117 (7 October 1967): 388, 390; W.D. White, JAAR 36 (December 1968): 385; John Tracy Ellis, CHR 55 (July 1969): 201-3; Donald Capps, JR 53 (January 1973): 136-8; William Myers, SEWR 91 (Spring 1983): 279-80; Meriol Trevor, "Father C.S. Dessain, Cong. Orat., 1907-76." AMPJ 82 (Spring 1977): 30-2.

910.   George, Robert Esmonde Gordon [Sencourt, Robert]. THE LIFE OF NEWMAN. Westminster: Dacre Press, 1948.

Focuses on Newman's achievements as Tractarian reformer, convert, Roman Catholic apologist,

educational theorist, writer, and prophet. Places
his success within the context of his oftentimes
high-strung, combative, and overly sensitive
personality.

See: D.V. Henry, DR 66 (Summer 1948): 347-9; Denis
Gwynn, CLR 30 (October 1948): 285; H. Francis
Davis, DUBR 221 (Winter 1948): 144-9.

911. Gornall, Thomas, S.J. "The Newman Problem (I)."
CLR 62 (April 1977): 137-42.

A psychobiographical sketch. The "problem" to
which the title refers, is Newman's lifelong over-
intensity, which oftentimes led to severe stress
and an excessive self-protectiveness. Traces this
weakness to a hidden genetic cause. Concludes in
item 912.

912. ————. "The Newman Problem (II)." CLR 62 (October
1977): 410-13.

Develops the argument introduced in item 911.
Highlights some of Newman's "occasional aberrations,"
including his decision to lead a dangerous intellectual life and his inability or unwillingness,
especially in later years, to account for his
failures and disappointments.

913. Gwynn, Denis. "John Henry Newman, 1801-1890." In
JOHN HENRY NEWMAN: CENTENARY ESSAYS (item 918),
16-35.

A useful introduction to Newman's life and work.

914. ————. "Was Newman Badly Treated?" CLR 25
(October 1945): 433-44.

Denies the contention that Newman's post-conversion
life was frustrating because his fellow Catholics
never really trusted him, and were thus unable and
unwilling to tap his genius and desire to serve.
Traces the origins of Newman's obvious frustration to
sources other than the attitude of his coreligionists.

915. Harrold, Charles F. JOHN HENRY NEWMAN: AN EXPOSITORY
AND CRITICAL STUDY OF HIS MIND, THOUGHT AND ART.

Reconstructs Newman's life in terms of his intellectual development and achievements. Analyzes the
personal and historical situations which inspired his
"three great labours," AN ESSAY ON THE DEVELOPMENT OF
CHRISTIAN DOCTRINE (1845), THE IDEA OF A UNIVERSITY
(1852-1859), and AN ESSAY IN AID OF A GRAMMAR OF
ASSENT (1870).

See: George Simpson, SF 24 (March 1946): 363-4;
       William O. Aydelotte, AHR 51 (April 1946): 498-
       9; J.F. Leddy, CHR 32 (April 1946): 74-5; Alvan
       S. Ryan, MLQ 7 (September 1946): 367-8; Philip
       Hallett, MLR 41 (October 1946): 435-6; Carl E.
       Purinton, JBR 14 (November 1946): 221.

916.   Hodge, Robert, O.C.S.O. "Was Newman a Saint?"   CLR
       62 (January 1977): 9-18.

       Counters the image of a hyper-sensitive, humorless,
       reclusive Newman presented in items 910 and 911.
       Speaks enthusiastically in favor of his canonization
       by the Church.

917.   Hughes, Philip. "Newman and His Age." DUBR 217
       (October/November/December 1945): 111-36.

       Scans Newman's life, in a search for an underlying
       central commitment. Proclaims him the great
       Christian prophet of a liberal age, one whose
       devotion to the Church was both unbroken and deep.

918.   JOHN HENRY NEWMAN: CENTENARY ESSAYS. London: Burns
       Oates & Washbourne, 1945.

       Contains twelve essays by specialists on aspects
       of Newman's life to which little attention is usually
       paid. Underscores the churchman's solutions to the
       major problems confronting nineteenth-century
       Catholicism. Contains items 913 and 956.

       See: DR 64 (January 1946): 49-50; Andrew Beck, A.A.,
              CLR 26 (March 1946): 162-3.

919.   Johnson, Humphrey J.T. "Cardinal Newman." In THE
       ENGLISH CATHOLICS, 1850-1950: CENTENARY ESSAYS
       TO COMMEMORATE THE RESTORATION OF THE HIERARCHY
       (item 759), 243-64.

Highlights the problem-solver, who devoted almost
forty-five years of his life as a Catholic to the
study of a surprisingly large number of obstacles to
religious progress. Driven to defend the claims of
revealed religion as embodied in the Catholic Church,
Newman touched on everything from the development of
doctrine and the relationship of faith and science,
to Biblical inspiration, the Church in modern society,
and the limits of civil and ecclesiastical power; if
his contributions in all these areas were not always
of prime quality, they always shed at least some
light on the subject.

920.   Lease, Gary. "Newman: The Roman View." In NEWMAN
       AND THE MODERNISTS (item 971), 161-82.

       Describes and accounts for the Vatican's
       ambiguous opinion of the "controversial Cardinal."

921.   Martin, Brian. JOHN HENRY NEWMAN: HIS LIFE AND WORK.
       New York: Oxford University Press, 1982.

       Introduces Newman's life and achievements to the
       general reader. A sympathetic portrait, based on a
       thorough reading of Newman's own writings. Lavishly
       illustrated with drawings, paintings, and photo-
       graphs.

       See: Richard Deveson, NST 104 (6 August 1982): 23;
             Renée Haynes, BBN, September 1982: 539; John
             C. Hawley, AMER 147 (4-11 September 1982): 115,
             117; Maureen Sullivan-Drury, BS 42 (November
             1982): 306-7; Roderick Strange, CLR 67
             (November 1982): 413-4; Peter Hebblethwaite,
             TLS, 5 November 1982: 1224; Clyde F. Crews,
             COMMWL 110 (11 February 1983): 90-1; CHOICE 20
             (March 1983): 1006; Daniel Costello, S.J.,
             REVREL 42 (May/June 1983): 471-2; Gerald T.
             Dunne, NATR 35 (10 June 1983): 709; Nicholas
             Lash, VS 27 (Autumn 1983): 110; David R. Boone,
             RSR 9 (October 1983): 386-7; John T. Ford,
             C.S.C., THS 45 (March 1984): 184-5.

922.   May, J. Lewis. CARDINAL NEWMAN. New York: Dial
       Press, 1930.

       Looks at Newman's achievements as a whole rather

than as compartmentalized reflections of a complex
personality.

See: NATION 130 (26 March 1930): 373; Edwin Ryan,
       CHR 17 (April 1931): 97-9; A.C. Sculpholm,
       THEO 48 (October 1945): 236.

923.   Moody, John. JOHN HENRY NEWMAN. New York: Sheed &
       Ward, 1945.

       A popular biography, balancing Newman's person-
ality and work.   Sympathetic to its subject.

See: Charles Frederick Harrold, MODPHILOL 43
       (February 1946): 213-4; John Sparrow, SPEC
       176 (29 March 1946): 328; William O. Aydelotte,
       AHR 51 (April 1946): 498-9; DR 64 (April
       1946): 118-9; Gaius Glenn Atkins, CH 15
       (June 1946): 142-3; CLR 26 (July 1946): 387-8;
       C. Ryder Smith, LQHR 171 (October 1946): 377-8.

924.   Newman, Bertram. CARDINAL NEWMAN: A BIOGRAPHICAL
       AND LITERARY STUDY.   New York and London: Century,
       1925.

       Designed for the general reader with little or no
background in religious history.   Presents a multi-
dimensional personality: the Tractarian leader,
Roman Catholic orator, writer, churchman, philosopher, theologian, and historian.

See: R. Ellis Roberts, BKMN 68 (April 1925): 33-4;
       DUBR 176 (April/May/June 1925): 302-3; LQR
       144 (July 1925): 124-5; DR 43 (October
       1925): 279; CHR 12 (April 1926): 145.

925.   O'Faolin, Sean. NEWMAN'S WAY: THE ODYSSEY OF JOHN
       HENRY NEWMAN.   New York: Devin-Adair, 1952.

       Explores the background to Newman's conversion by
detailing both his ancestry and his relationship with
his immediate family.   Admiring and critical at the
same time.

See: Frank Getlein, AMM 75 (October 1952): 107-9;
       Helen Woodward, FREE 3 (6 October 1952): 32;
       Lawrence J. Shehan, CHR 38 (January

1953): 422-4; J. Lewis May, CLR 38 (January
1953): 49-51; TC 153 (January 1953): 78;
IER 79 (June 1953): 477-8.

* Reynolds, E.E. THREE CARDINALS: NEWMAN--WISEMAN--
MANNING. Cited above as item 825.

Gives priority not to Newman the churchman, but
to Newman the intellectual, whose only true home
was the Oratory, and who was unable to treat a
subject without getting down to fundamental
principles still relevant today.

926. Ross, J. Elliot. JOHN HENRY NEWMAN: ANGLICAN
MINISTER, CATHOLIC PRIEST, ROMAN CARDINAL.
New York: W.W. Norton, 1933.

Concentrates on the five great failures of a
personality too far ahead of its time. Admires
Newman, while deprecating those whose excessive
admiration hides his limitations and weaknesses.
Includes extensive quotations from both published
works and private letters.

See: NATION 137 (29 September 1933): 630; Gaius
Glenn Atkins, CH 2 (December 1933): 246-7;
BKMN 86 (April 1934): 76; Edwin Ryan, CHR
20 (April 1934): 56-8; LQHR 159 (April
1934): 268; Gerald G. Walsh, S.J., THOUGHT
9 (March 1935): 684-5.

927. Sugg, Joyce. "Did Newman Have a Sense of Humor?"
CLR 68 (March 1983): 100-4.

Refutes Strachey's image of the sad spider
sequestered in his room at the Oratory (item 866).
Maintains that his high seriousness notwithstanding,
Newman showed a light and joyous touch throughout his
life.

928. Tierney, Michael, ed. A TRIBUTE TO NEWMAN: ESSAYS
ON ASPECTS OF HIS LIFE AND THOUGHT.
Dublin: Browne and Nolan, 1945.

Sketches significant events and activities in
Newman's life and career. Contains items 939,
974, 984, and 985.

    See: Denis Meehan, IER 68 (February 1946): 73-82;
           DR 64 (April 1946): 119-21.

929. Trevor, Meriol. NEWMAN. London: Macmillan, 1962.
      2 vols.

         Focuses on Newman the man. Evaluates his person-
      ality, reputation, and personal relationships.
      Volume 1 deals with his Anglican period and first
      years as a Catholic, concluding in 1853, the year
      in which his future as a member of his new Church
      was at its ebb. Volume 2 follows a "reverse curve,"
      covering his place within the Catholic revival and
      the many controversies with which he became embroiled,
      and in which he always clearly demonstrated his
      superiority over his adversaries. Meticulously
      researched, based on some 20,000 letters, and
      extremely detailed. An uncritical treatment. For
      the background to this work, see item 930.

      See: (for both volumes) Frederick T. Wood, ES 44
            (August 1963): 303; Edward E. Kelly, S.J.,
            THOUGHT 38 (Autumn 1963): 476-8; David
            Newsome, JTS 14 (October 1963): 420-9; J.M.
            Cameron, VS 7 (December 1963): 200-2; James R.
            Bennett, MODPHILOL 61 (May 1964): 318-20; John
            K. Cartwright, CHR 50 (January 1965): 592-3;
            J. Heywood Thomas, SJT 18 (December 1965): 435-
            43.
            (for vol. 1, THE PILLAR OF THE CLOUD) David
            Lodge, SPEC 208 (13 April 1962): 484-5; Patrick
            J. Corish, IER 97 (May 1962): 345-6; Christopher
            Hollis, WR 236 (Summer 1962): 182-90; H. Francis
            Davis, CLR 47 (October 1962): 629-32; A. Dwight
            Culler, YR 52 (December 1962): 283-6.
            (for vol. 2, LIGHT IN WINTER) David Lodge, SPEC
            209 (21 December 1962): 967; Patrick J. Corish,
            IER 99 (January 1963): 70; Shane Leslie, QR 301
            (January 1963): 102-9; Christopher Hollis, WR
            237 (Spring 1963): 78-86.

930. Ward, Wilfrid. THE LIFE OF JOHN HENRY CARDINAL
      NEWMAN. New York: Longmans, Green, 1912.
      2 vols.

         Considers Newman the great treasure of nineteenth-
      century English Catholicism; more than a source of

controversy or a defender of the Church, he was a
thinker of the first order, who understood, as no
one else could and did, why the English were so
opposed to the Roman faith. Volume 1 follows Newman
through 1864, the year in which he published his
APOLOGIA PRO VITA SUA; Volume 2 details the last
three decades of his life. Though commissioned by
the Oratorians, who gave Ward free access to their
archives, the result was not to their liking. The
portrait seemed to them too cold and impersonal,
showing none of the natural, dynamic, and humorous
man with whom they had lived. Four decades later,
they commissioned Meriol Trevor (item 929) to
produce a more human Newman. See also items 895
and 897.

See: NATION 94 (28 March 1912): 314-5; William
Barry, BKMN 42 (April 1912): 22-6; ER 215
(April 1912): 263-90; John Telford, LQR 117
(April 1912): 291-317; H.C. Corrance, HIBJ
10 (no. 3, 1912): 746-7; Michael Tynan, IER
55 (March 1940): 260-73.

931. Yanitelli, Victor R., S.J., ed. A NEWMAN
SYMPOSIUM: REPORT ON THE TENTH ANNUAL MEETING OF
THE CATHOLIC RENASCENCE SOCIETY AT THE COLLEGE OF
THE HOLY CROSS, WORCESTER, MASS., APRIL 1952.
New York: Fordham University, n.d.

Features eighteen papers presented at a convo-
cation commemorating the centenary of Newman's IDEA
OF A UNIVERSITY. Subjects covered range from
Newman's personal habits to his educational views
and his influence in the twentieth century. Contains
items 908, 978, 979, and 1043.

See: Lawrence J. Shehan, CHR 39 (January 1954): 495.

932. Yao-shan, Ching, S.J. "Newman Looks Backward and
Forward." CLR 62 (September 1977): 347-61.

Studies the interplay of two opposite tendencies
in Newman's life and thought. Simultaneously
backward-looking and forward-looking, as evident
through his use of such literary images as "home"
and "light," he unified the two outlooks in a
skillful way.

Early Years and Conversion

933. Brent, Allen. "Newman's Moral Conversion." DR 104
      (April 1986): 79-93.

      Compares and contrasts Newman's attitudes toward
      Catholicism, as expressed during his visit to Rome
      in 1833 as an Anglican, with those set forth during
      visits subsequent to his conversion.

934. Dessain, Charles Stephen. "Newman and Oxford." WR
      237 (Autumn 1963): 295-302.

      Studies the interaction between the University
      and the young Newman, who arrived there in 1817.
      Offers insights into the origins of Tractarianism,
      as well as a glimpse into Newman's lifelong affection
      for "the sacred city of Anglicanism."

935. Gornall, Thomas, S.J. "Newman: The Tutorship
      Quarrel." CLR 64 (June 1979): 205-9.

      Reconstructs the dispute between the disagreeable
      Provost Hawkins of Oriel College, Oxford, and Newman
      over the latter's changes in the lecture system.
      Sees the episode of 1829-1830 as a major step in the
      development of Newman's religious outlook and his
      first challenge to high and dry Anglicanism.

936. ————. "Newman's 'Failure in the Schools.'" CLR
      63 (February 1978): 65-8.

      Lists the reasons for Newman's poor showing in his
      examinations of November-December 1820. His second
      in classics and failure in mathematics gave him the
      shock he needed, and he not only recovered but won a
      fellowship to Oriel College, Oxford.

937. Gwynn, Denis. "Dominic Barberi and Newman's
      Conversion." CLR 25 (February 1945): 49-58.

      Emphasizes the often overlooked subtleties behind
      Newman's submission to Barberi and the Roman Church.

938. ————. "Newman, Wiseman and Dr. Russell." IER 58
      (September 1941): 275-86.

Outlines the collaborative efforts of Wiseman and
Russell, admirers of the Oxford Movement, to bring
Newman into the Church.

939. McGrath, Fergal, S.J. "The Conversion." In A
      TRIBUTE TO NEWMAN: ESSAYS ON ASPECTS OF HIS
      LIFE AND THOUGHT (item 928), 57-83.

      Retraces Newman's complicated path to Roman
      Catholicism. Points to his search for the true
      Church of Christ as the crucial element pushing
      him forward on his journey.

940. Merrigan, Terrence. "Newman's Progress toward
      Rome: A Psychological Consideration of His
      Conversion to Catholicism." DR 104 (April
      1986): 95-112.

      Applies Jung's theory of psychological types to
      Newman's decision to join the Roman Church, in an
      effort to break through what has often been called
      "the mystery of Newman."

941. Middleton, R.D. NEWMAN AT OXFORD: HIS RELIGIOUS
      DEVELOPMENT. New York: Oxford University Press,
      1950.

      Traces the evolution of Newman's theology up to
      the time he left the Anglican Church. Believes that
      the Tractarian leader might have been kept within
      the Anglican fold if only the religious authorities
      at Oxford had possessed broader vision and greater
      sensitivity.

      See: Louis Bouyer, THEO 54 (January 1951): 29-31;
            Alfred Noyes, ENG 8 (no. 46, 1951): 206-7;
            Lawrence J. Shehan, CHR 37 (January 1952): 459-
            61; Martin J. Svaglic, MODPHILOL 49 (February
            1952): 213-6.

942. O'Hare, Charles M. "John Henry Newman in Rome, 1833."
      IER 36 (November 1930): 449-58.

      Describes Newman's impressions of both the city
      and the Church. Though enchanted by the former, he
      was repulsed by the latter.

943. Ramsey, Michael. "Newman the Anglican." In JOHN
      HENRY NEWMAN: A MAN FOR OUR TIME? (item 898),
      3-6.

      Discusses Newman's relatively unknown role as a
      revitalizer of Anglicanism.

944. Thirlwall, John C. "John Henry Newman: His Poetry
      and Conversion." DUBR 242 (Spring 1968): 75-88.

      Explores the connection between Newman's
      inveterate love of poetry, on the one side, and
      his progress within Tractarianism, and then
      toward Roman Catholicism, on the other.

945. Tristram, Henry, Cong. Orat. "Dr. Russell and
      Newman's Conversion." IER 66 (September
      1945): 189-200.

      Details the understated campaign of Charles
      Russell, Professor of Humanities at Maynooth, to
      win Newman over to Rome. Cites large sections of
      their correspondence (1841-1842), which began with
      Russell's letter to Newman, congratulating him on
      the publication of Tract 90. Underscores the fact,
      however, that Russell's chief contribution to
      Newman's decision of 1845--and Newman once said
      that no one had more to do with his conversion
      than Russell--was his virtual inactivity.

946. Ward, Maisie. YOUNG MR. NEWMAN. New York: Sheed &
      Ward, 1948.

      Supplements her father's account of Newman's early
      years, as found in item 930. Discusses Newman's
      family life, childhood activities, anti-Catholicism
      at Oxford, travels, and early efforts on behalf of
      the Tractarians.

      See: IER 70 (October 1948): 953-5; H. Francis Davis,
            DUBR 221 (Winter 1948): 144-9; Georgiana P.
            McEntee, CHR 34 (January 1949): 451-2; Michael
            A. O'Connor, THOUGHT 24 (March 1949): 129-31;
            Charles H. Lyttle, CH 19 (June 1950): 140-1.

Political Thought

947. Holmes, J. Derek. "Cardinal Newman and the Affirmation Bill." HMPEC 36 (March 1967): 87-97.

Explains Newman's position in the Bradlaugh
case (item 831). Newman, in the name of freedom
of conscience, took his own line on the Affirmation
Bill, one directly against the hierarchy's official
policy and the general attitude of his fellow
Catholics. Though his views had no significance
nationally and did not influence the course of
events, they did demonstrate that English Catholic
opinion was not as monolithic as Manning and others
would have liked to believe.

948. ————. "Factors in the Development of Newman's
Political Attitudes." In NEWMAN AND
GLADSTONE: CENTENNIAL ESSAYS (item 1248), 57-
87.

Salutes Newman's LETTER TO THE DUKE OF NORFOLK
within the context of his approach to politics as
a whole. Highlights his opposition to political
liberalism and emphasis on the role of reason in
political affairs.

949. Johnson, Humphrey J.T. "The Controversy between
Newman and Gladstone over the Question of Civil
Allegiance." DUBR 217 (October/November/
December 1945): 173-82.

Asserts that of the three major Catholic responses
to Gladstone's VATICAN DECREES IN THEIR BEARING ON
CIVIL ALLEGIANCE (1874),--Acton's, Manning's, and
Newman's,--Gladstone was most impressed by Newman's,
which had been framed as an open letter to the Duke
of Norfolk. To defeat the charge of divided loyalty,
according to Newman, it was necessary for Catholics
to cultivate a sober and deeply Christian patriotism.

950. Kenny, Terence. THE POLITICAL THOUGHT OF JOHN HENRY
NEWMAN. London: Longmans, Green, 1957.

Challenges any effort to identify Newman as a
conservative or a liberal. Indicates that Newman

used political labels and concepts in his own unique
way, and thus even his self-professed Toryism and
repeated denunciations of liberalism do not provide
an accurate picture of his political stance.

See: H. Francis Davis, CLR 42 (December 1957): 759-
       61; Thomas H. Parker, JEH 9 (April 1958): 118-
       9; James Kavanagh, IER 91 (February 1959): 149-
       50; A. Dwight Culler, YR 48 (June 1959): 506-7;
       Alvan S. Ryan, CHR 45 (January 1960): 461-3;
       Kenneth F. Lewalski, CH 30 (March 1961): 119-
       21.

Religious Thought

951.   Bouyer, Louis. "Newman's Influence on France."
       DUBR 217 (October/November/December 1945): 182-8.

       Measures the enormous breadth and depth of his
       influence, which Bouyer considers the result of
       both the power of his thought and the otherworldli-
       ness of his personality.

952.   Burke, Ronald. "Was Loisy Newman's Modern Disciple?"
       In NEWMAN AND THE MODERNISTS (item 971), 139-57.

       Inquires into the connection between Newman's
       ESSAY ON THE DEVELOPMENT OF CHRISTIAN DOCTRINE and
       Loisy's exegetical works.

953.   Cameron, J.H. "John Henry Newman and the Tractarian
       Movement." In NINETEENTH CENTURY RELIGIOUS
       THOUGHT IN THE WEST (item 258), II, 69-109.

       A summary of Newman's Anglican theology and
       activity as a member of the Oxford Movement.

954.   Chadwick, Owen. FROM BOSSUET TO NEWMAN: THE IDEA OF
       DOCTRINAL DEVELOPMENT. 2nd ed.
       Cambridge: Cambridge University Press, 1987.

       Relates the main ideas of Newman's ESSAY ON THE
       DEVELOPMENT OF CHRISTIAN DOCTRINE (1845) to the
       theological tradition of Bossuet, the seventeenth-
       century Spanish Jesuits, the eighteenth-century

Anglicans,--notably Bishop Butler,--and the
nineteenth-century German Catholic historians.
Comments on the reception given the ESSAY by
Catholics and non-Catholics alike.

See: (for the first edition) F.W. Dillistone, THEO
61 (February 1958): 75-6; Maurice Nédoncelle,
JEH 9 (April 1958): 116-8; H. Francis Davis,
DR 76 (Summer 1958): 294-6; Vincent T. O'Keefe,
S.J., THOUGHT 33 (Summer 1958): 313-5; Stephen
J. Tonsor, AHR 63 (July 1958): 1043; C.
Stephen Dessain, CHR 44 (July 1958): 188-90;
Martin J. Svaglic, VS 2 (December 1958): 164-5.

955. Davies, Horton. WORSHIP AND THEOLOGY IN ENGLAND.
Vol. 4: FROM NEWMAN TO MARTINEAU, 1850-1900.
Princeton: Princeton University Press, 1962.

Places the Catholics, represented by Newman's
strongly traditional outlook, at one end of the
liturgical and theological spectrum of Victorian
England, and the vigorously radical Martineau and
his Unitarians at the other. Concentrates on
Newman's thought as expressed through his preaching,
which presented complex philosophical and theological
points in a highly theatrical way.

See: Damian McElrath, CHR 48 (July 1962): 268-9;
Josef L. Altholz, AHR 68 (October 1962): 197-8;
Olive J. Brose, VS 6 (December 1962): 187-8;
Leonard W. Cowie, HIST 48 (February 1963): 99;
John T. Wilkinson, LQHR 188 (April 1963): 166;
Roland H. Bainton, CH 33 (March 1964): 107-8.

956. Davis, H.F. "The Catholicism of Cardinal Newman."
In JOHN HENRY NEWMAN: CENTENARY ESSAYS (item
918), 36-54.

Corrects several misconceptions concerning
Newman's relationship with the Church, showing that
his integral Catholicism colored every aspect of his
intellectual life.

957. Hegarty, W.J., C.C. "Cardinal Newman's 'Second
Spring': A Sermon Which Made History." IER 78
(July 1952): 34-43.

Claims that Newman's eloquent and spellbinding
preaching at the Provincial Synod of Oscott (1852)
proved that English, if still not a Catholic
language, was nevertheless a language through
which Catholic beliefs could be expressed with a
force and beauty which few non-Catholics could
equal or excel.

958. Holmes, J. Derek. "Newman and Mivart: Two Attitudes
      to a Nineteenth-Century Problem." CLR 50
      (November 1965): 852-67.

      Shows, through a consideration of their personal
      and intellectual relationship, their similar visions
      and varied fates. Both sought to prepare English
      Catholics to confront the challenges of the time in
      which they lived; however, Newman's and Mivart's
      routes to this goal were quite different, the extent
      of their divergence being as wide as that between
      Newman's greatness and Mivart's limitations.

959. Huneke, Anne Marie. RELIGIOUS CONTROVERSY IN THE
      CATHOLIC LETTERS OF JOHN HENRY CARDINAL NEWMAN.
      Ph.D. dissertation. St. Louis University, 1980.

      Presents a Newman as eager to enter into theo-
      logical disputes by letter as by book and conver-
      sation, a committed controversialist who used
      rational, historical, and ecclesiological arguments
      to convince his correspondents of the truth of the
      Catholic faith. Focuses on the religious disputes
      following his conversion, the publication of his
      APOLOGIA PRO VITA SUA, and his decision to try to
      bring William Froude, a noted agnostic, to the
      Church.

960. Lash, Nicholas. NEWMAN ON DEVELOPMENT: THE SEARCH
      FOR AN EXPLANATION IN HISTORY. Shepherdstown,
      W.Va.: Patmos Press, 1975.

      Shows the strengths and weaknesses of Newman's
      theology, both within the context of the century in
      which it was formed, and in the estimation of the
      twentieth century, upon which it has exerted so
      wide an influence.

      See: Brian Martin, TLS, 2 April 1976: 405;

Josef L. Altholz, CH 45 (June 1976): 261-2;
Edward E. Kelly, CHR 63 (October 1977): 602-3.

961. MacDougall, Hugh A., O.M.I. THE ACTON-NEWMAN
      RELATIONS: THE DILEMMA OF CHRISTIAN LIBERALISM.
      New York: Fordham University Press, 1962.

      Examines, within the setting of their longtime
      friendship, the concern shared by Acton and Newman
      over how, as educated Catholic Englishmen, they
      could at the same time obey and yet seek to restrain
      the impetuous authority of a Pope who seemed to have
      no awareness of the modern world.

      See: Edward E. Kelley, S.J., THOUGHT 38 (Summer
            1963): 289-90; G.D. Gregory, DR 81 (July
            1963): 296-7; Patrick J. Corish, IER 100
            (August 1963): 133-5; Brian Heeney, DALR
            43 (Autumn 1963): 420-1; Stephen J. Tonsor,
            VS 7 (December 1963): 199-200; Josef L.
            Altholz, CHR 50 (July 1964): 228-9; J.S.
            Nurser, EHR 80 (January 1965): 196-7; R.B.
            McDowell, IHS 15 (September 1966): 207-9.

962. McElrath, Damian, O.F.M. "Richard Simpson and John
      Henry Newman: The *Rambler*, Laymen, and Theology."
      CHR 52 (January 1967): 509-33.

      Assesses the extent of Newman's influence upon
      Simpson's view of the relationship between the
      hierarchy and laity, as spelled out during the
      year 1859 in the *Rambler*.

963. Misner, Paul. "The 'Liberal' Legacy of John Henry
      Newman." In NEWMAN AND THE MODERNISTS (item
      971), 3-24.

      Explains why and how Newman was used both as a
      source of ideas and a model by a number of the
      modernists.

964. Reardon, Bernard M.G. "John Henry Newman." FROM
      COLERIDGE TO GORE: A CENTURY OF RELIGIOUS THOUGHT
      IN BRITAIN, 122-57. London: Longmans, 1971.

      Analyzes Newman's ideas on belief and doctrine in
      the light of his personality. Labels his religious

vision retrogressive and reactionary.

See: TLS, 25 June 1971: 742; Hamish F.G. Swanston,
       AMPJ 77 (Spring 1972): 99-102; Geoffrey Rowell,
       JTS 23 (April 1972): 296-8; David M. Thompson,
       HIST 57 (October 1972): 448-9; CHOICE 10
       (October 1973): 1174; P.B. Clarke, RS 18 (June
       1982): 244; William L. Sachs, CH 52 (June
       1983): 270.

965. ————. "Newman and the Catholic Modernist Movement."
       CQ 4 (July 1971): 50-60.

       Submits that while Newman anticipated and would
       have probably endorsed Blondel's and Laberthonnière's
       view of dogma as an expression and interpretation of
       existence, he would have been appalled by the
       theology and Biblical scholarship of Loisy and
       Tyrrell. Thus, to see Newman as the forerunner of
       Modernism, as some have done, is not entirely
       accurate.

966. Robbins, William. THE NEWMAN BROTHERS: AN ESSAY IN
       COMPARATIVE INTELLECTUAL BIOGRAPHY.
       Cambridge: Harvard University Press, 1966.

       Contrasts and accounts for the strikingly
       different lives and outlooks of John Henry and
       Francis, despite their common evangelical roots
       and similar fortunes at Oxford. Francis became
       the apostle of the liberal and rationalist creed
       which his more celebrated older brother repeatedly
       denounced.

       See: Dunstan Pontifex, DR 84 (October 1966): 458;
              Wayne Burns, CANLIT 32 (Spring 1967): 68-70;
              J.B. Hibbitts, DALR 47 (Spring 1967): 121, 123;
              Norman Brown, QQ 74 (Spring 1967): 186-7;
              CHOICE 4 (April 1967): 176; William S. Morris,
              CH 36 (June 1967): 233-4; J.M. Cameron, VS 10
              (June 1967): 442-3; J.R. Bennett, VS 10 (June
              1967): 443-6; Standish Meacham, JMH 40
              (September 1968): 433-4; Gilbert A. Cahill,
              AHR 74 (February 1969): 993-4; James C.
              Holland, CHR 55 (July 1969): 203-4.

967. Simon, Paul. "Newman and German Catholicism."

DUBR 219 (July/August/September 1946): 75-84.

Develops the position that Newman's hour in
Germany only came some ten years after his death,
during the modernist controversy. With the
Vatican's condemnation of modernism, many Germans
questioned the Church's ability to affect the
modern world; Newman, however, proved to them that
Catholics could adapt to the times.

968. Strange, Roderick. NEWMAN AND THE GOSPEL OF CHRIST.
New York: Oxford University Press, 1981.

Reconstructs Newman's understanding of Christ, as
expressed in passages scattered throughout his
sermons, lectures, essays, tracts, notes, and
letters. Shows a remarkably complete Christology
already in place by the 1830s and remaining consistent
through the next sixty years. Traces this consistency
to Newman's detailed patristic studies, and
particularly to his interest in St. Athanasius and
fourth-century Arianism.

See: Alberic Stacpoole, TLS, 24 July 1981: 854;
David Watson, CLR 67 (February 1982): 72-3;
I.M. Davies, JTS 33 (April 1982): 325-6;
Paul Misner, RSR 8 (October 1982): 388;
William Myers, SR 91 (Spring 1983): 279-80;
Lawrence F. Barmann, CH 52 (June 1983): 226-7;
Joseph A. Komonchak, JR 63 (July 1983): 307-8;
Gabriel Daly, JEH 35 (April 1984): 288-91.

969. Tristram, Henry. "Cardinal Newman and Baron von
Hügel." DUBR 240 (Autumn 1966): 295-302.

Investigates von Hügel's enormous intellectual
debt to Newman, one based on a certain degree of
personal intimacy.

970. Weatherby, Harold L. CARDINAL NEWMAN IN HIS
AGE: HIS PLACE IN ENGLISH THEOLOGY AND
LITERATURE. Nashville: Vanderbilt University
Press, 1973.

Demonstrates Newman's radical divergence from the
thought of St. Thomas Aquinas and the realist school.
Places him with Wordsworth, Coleridge, Carlyle,

Arnold, and others who repudiated Aristotelianism and
opted for an updated Platonism. Analyzes Newman's
ideas of conscience, certitude, and doctrinal
development in the light of his Platonism.

See: CHOICE 10 (May 1973): 441; J.A. Appleyard,
      COMMWL 98 (18 May 1973): 266-8; TLS, 18 May
      1973: 565; M.E. Bradford, MA 17 (Summer
      1973): 308-10; Mary Louise Fitzpatrick, RM
      27 (September 1973): 164-5; Thomas Vargish,
      VS 17 (September 1973): 124-6; Gerhard Joseph,
      SEL 13 (Autumn 1973): 728; Edward E. Kelley,
      S.J., REVREL 33 (January 1974): 215-6; J.M.
      Cameron, ELN 11 (March 1974): 227-30; W.D.
      White, JAAR 42 (March 1974): 156-7, 160;
      Herbert Sussman, MODPHILOL 72 (November
      1974): 212-14; E.D. Mackerniss, MLR 70
      (January 1975): 166-7; A.O.J. Cockshut, JTS
      26 (April 1975): 260; Marvin R. O'Connell,
      CHR 62 (October 1976): 630-1.

971. Weaver, Mary Jo, ed. NEWMAN AND THE MODERNISTS.
      College Theology Society Resources in Religion,
      vol. 1. Lanham, Md.: University Press of
      America, 1986.

      Dissects the complex portrait of Newman drawn by
      the Modernists and their opponents. Contains nine
      essays, written by theologians and historians,
      considering various aspects of Newman's thought as
      viewed and used by some of the leading thinkers of
      his time, including Wilfrid Ward, Tyrrell, Bremond,
      and Loisy. Contains items 289, 894, 895, 897, 920,
      952, and 963.

See: John R. Griffin, THS 47 (December 1986): 749-
      50; Jo Ann Eigelsbach, RSR 13 (July 1987): 244;
      Edward E. Kelly, VS 31 (Autumn 1987): 124-5;
      C.T. McIntire, AHR 92 (October 1987): 958-9;
      Lawrence F. Barmann, CHR 73 (October
      1987): 669-70.

Historical Thought

972. Altholz, Josef L. "Newman and History."

VS 7 (March 1964): 285-94.

Agrees with Bokenkotter (item 973) that although
Newman cannot be included among the great scientific
historians, he does deserve a place of honor within
the ranks of nineteenth-century historians of
Christian antiquity. Examines the strengths and
weaknesses of his work on the Age of the Fathers.

973. Bokenkotter, Thomas S. CARDINAL NEWMAN AS AN
        HISTORIAN. Louvain: Bibliothèque de l'Université,
        Bureaux de Recueil, 1959.

Details various aspects of Newman's work as an
historian: on the one side, his profound love of
history, the important place given history in his
general intellectual outlook, his matchless library,
and the depth of his historical comprehension; and
on the other, his ignorance of contemporary German
scholarship, and his sometimes less than scientific
attitude toward such phenomena as legends and
miracles.

See: Meriol Trevor, DUBR 234 (Summer 1960): 190-2;
        Florence D. Cohalan, CHR 46 (October 1960): 357-
        9; Owen Chadwick, EHR 76 (January 1961): 172-3;
        Josef L. Altholz, VS 4 (March 1961): 278-9.

974. Gwynn, Aubrey, S.J. "Newman and the Catholic
        Historian." In A TRIBUTE TO NEWMAN: ESSAYS ON
        ASPECTS OF HIS LIFE AND THOUGHT (item 928), 279-
        306.

Examines the bases of Newman's historical scholarship and the influences which shaped them.

975. Holmes, J. Derek. "Cardinal Newman and the Study of
        History." DUBR 239 (Spring 1965): 17-31.

Examines Newman's approach to history within three
contexts: (1) his self-education in historical
technique; (2) his broad view of the nature of
historical development; and (3) his attitude toward
the process by which knowledge is acquired. Displays
his limitations in each of these areas, limitations
which he himself felt deeply, despite the opinion of
some of the greatest of his contemporaries--Acton,

Döllinger, and Duchesne--that he was one of the
century's best historians.

976. Leibell, J.F. "Newman as an Ecclesiastical
        Historian." CHR 11 (January 1926): 645-52.

      Places Newman among the weightiest of English
      ecclesiastical historians. Shows how even his
      non-historical products--e.g., PLAIN AND PAROCHIAL
      SERMONS--were deeply informed by a historical sense.
      Discusses the significance of his ESSAYS CRITICAL
      AND HISTORICAL (1828-1846); ESSAYS ON THE MIRACLES
      OF EARLY ECCLESIASTICAL HISTORY (1842-1843);
      translation of the SECRET TREATISE OF ST. ATHANASIUS
      (1841-1844); PRESENT POSITION OF CATHOLICS IN ENGLAND
      (1851); CALLISTA (1856), his only historical novel;
      and APOLOGIA PRO VITA SUA (1964).

Educational Thought and Activity

977. Beales, A.C.F. "John Henry Newman." In PIONEERS OF
        ENGLISH EDUCATION, edited by A.V. Judges, 128-59.
        London: Faber and Faber, n.d.

      Describes Newman's approach, both theoretical and
      practical, to the field of education. As a theorist
      Newman reminded his contemporaries of ends, which had
      been obscured by the emphasis on the machinery of the
      learning process. At the same time he grappled
      throughout his life with the major problem con-
      fronting Catholic education: how the traditional
      Christian inheritance could be maintained and yet
      adapt to the new outlook inspired by science. The
      answer, Newman discovered, lay in the acceptance of
      religious truth as not just another subject, but as
      a condition of general knowledge; theology would have
      to become the basis of all disciplines, lest they
      descend into total anthropocentrism.

      See: QR 291 (January 1953): 134-5; Margaret Cole,
            PQ 24 (January/March 1953): 118-9; H.C.
            Barnard, EHR 68 (April 1953): 335-6; A.S.
            Mowat, DALR 34 (Summer 1954): 187, 189.

978. Bernard, Edmond Darvil. "The Background and Theory

of the *Idea*." In A NEWMAN SYMPOSIUM: REPORT ON
THE TENTH ANNUAL MEETING OF THE CATHOLIC RENASCENCE
SOCIETY AT THE COLLEGE OF THE HOLY CROSS, WORCESTER,
MASS., APRIL 1952 (item 931), 1-13.

Provides the historical context for THE IDEA OF A
UNIVERSITY, with treatments of Newman's own experiences and interests at Oxford, his intellectual
development and orientation, and the "mixed education"
issue in Ireland.

979. Donovan, Charles F., S.J. "Newman's University: The
Actuality." In A NEWMAN SYMPOSIUM: REPORT ON THE
TENTH ANNUAL MEETING OF THE CATHOLIC RENASCENCE
SOCIETY AT THE COLLEGE OF THE HOLY CROSS, WORCESTER,
MASS., APRIL 1952 (item 931), 14-20.

Presents Newman as the founder, builder, energetic
administrator, and harassed rector of the Catholic
University, who struggled vigorously but in vain to
make his vision work.

980. Hegarty, W.J., C.C. "Ireland's Debt to Newman." IER
65 (March 1945): 150-60.

Outlines Newman's six troubled years in Ireland
(1852-1858), during which he served as head of the
ill-fated Catholic University in Dublin. Out of
this failure, however, came his literary masterpiece,
THE IDEA OF A UNIVERSITY.

981. Holmes, J. Derek. "Newman and the Kensington
Scheme." MONTH 1st NS 33 (January 1965): 12-23.

Discusses Newman's opposition to Manning's
proposal of 1871 to establish a Catholic college
attached to London University. Yet Newman's lack
of support did not prevent Manning from using
Newman's reputation as an educator to gain popular
backing for the scheme.

982. La Ferrière, Frank Vincent. A DOCUMENTARY HISTORY OF
JOHN HENRY NEWMAN'S RECTORSHIP OF THE CATHOLIC
UNIVERSITY OF IRELAND, 1851-1858. Ph.D.
dissertation. University of California, Los
Angeles, 1965.

Focuses on 1854-1858, the years of Newman's active rectorship and the gestation period for THE IDEA OF A UNIVERSITY. Uses Catholic University and Birmingham Oratory archival materials to measure the extent to which Newman implemented his own educational theories.

983. McGrath, Fergal. NEWMAN'S UNIVERSITY: IDEA AND REALITY, London: Longmans, 1951.

Emphasizes the problems faced by Newman during his rectorship in Dublin. Sets these problems against the background of the general situation in Ireland, and especially the highly charged "mixed education" controversy. Reinforces Ward's view (item 930) that Newman's own difficult personality played a major role in the failure of the enterprise.

See: TC 149 (March 1951): 242; T.S. Gregory, DUBR 225 (Summer 1951): 119-23; Denis Gwynn, CLR 36 (July 1951): 61-4; T.W. Moody, IHS 7 (September 1951): 305-7; A.H. Armstrong, DR 69 (Autumn 1951): 496-9; IER 76 (November 1951): 441-4; Bernard J. Kohlbrenner, CHR 37 (January 1952): 462-3; R.W. Greaves, EHR 67 (January 1952): 147-8; T. Charles Edwards, HT 2 (February 1952): 146-7; John E. Wise, THOUGHT 27 (Autumn 1952): 474-5.

984. McHugh, Roger. "The Years in Ireland." In A TRIBUTE TO NEWMAN: ESSAYS ON ASPECTS OF HIS LIFE AND THOUGHT (item 928), 144-71.

Sets Newman's personal success in Ireland against the inevitable failure of the university scheme.

985. Tierney, Michael. "Catholic University." In A TRIBUTE TO NEWMAN: ESSAYS ON ASPECTS OF HIS LIFE AND THOUGHT (item 928), 172-206.

Qualifies the view that Newman's academic work in Ireland was a complete failure. Contends that his involvement with university organization, as seen in his writings and in his activities as Rector of the Catholic University, should not be condemned or dismissed summarily.

986. Trevor, Meriol. "Manning's University and Newman's

Aloofness." TABLET 217 (5 January 1963): 7-8.

Supplements the material on the Kensington scheme
found in Trevor's second volume on Newman (item 929).
Identifies Newman's main reason for opposing Manning's
plan: the proposed college would not expose students
to a challenging intellectual life, as at Oxford.
Without such challenge, there was no true higher
education. Moreover, he could not see the logic of
isolating Catholics in clerical colleges; so rarefied
an atmosphere hardly deserved the title of university.

987. Whyte, J.H. "Newman in Dublin: Fresh Light from the
       Archives of Propaganda." DUBR 234 (Spring
       1960): 31-9.

Sheds light on the relationship between Newman and
Paul Cullen, Archbishop of Dublin. Using Cullen's
letters of 1853 to Rome, Whyte paints a highly
strained association, one which led the Archbishop
to dissuade the Vatican from raising the Rector of
the Catholic University to the episcopate. Presents,
for the first time, Cullen's side of the argument.

Ecumenical Activity

988. Dessain, Charles Stephen. "Cardinal Newman and
       Ecumenism." CLR 50 (February 1965): 119-37.

Contends that Newman's lifelong dream of a return
to Christian unity made him one of the chief promoters
of ecumenism during the not very tolerant nineteenth
century. Traces his ecumenical work from the early
days of the Oxford Movement to 1864, the year in which
the Vatican forbade Catholics to join the Association
for the Promotion of the Union of Christendom.
Emphasizes Newman's acknowledgement and realistic
assessment of the truth and value in non-Catholic
Christianity. For his post-1865 efforts, see item
989.

989. ———. "Cardinal Newman and Ecumenism (Concluded)."
       CLR 50 (March 1965): 189-206.

Continued from item 988. Studies Newman's

post-1865 correspondence with Ambrose Phillipps de
Lisle on the notion of corporate reunion of the
churches. However, the major prerequisite to unity,
according to Newman, was the removal of all
hindrances to charity within the individual
communions.

990. Ellis, John Tracy. "John Henry Newman: A Bridge for
      Men of Good Will." CHR 56 (April 1970): 1-24.

      Sees Newman as the perfect mediator between
      Protestant and Catholic, as they seek mutual
      understanding and reconciliation. Bases this
      view on three considerations: (1) he was both
      Protestant and Catholic, and for approximately
      equal amounts of time; (2) even after his con-
      version, he cherished his Protestant friends;
      and (3) his profound historical sense has
      continued to inspire both Protestant and Catholic
      historians in the twentieth century.

                    Newman *and* *Vatican* *I*

991. Dessain, C.S. "What Newman Taught in Manning's
      Church." In INFALLIBILITY IN THE CHURCH: AN
      ANGLICAN-CATHOLIC DIALOGUE, 59-80.
      London: Darton, Longman and Todd, 1968.

      Highlights Newman's discreet but very real efforts
      to minimize the impact of Vatican I's definition of
      papal infallibility, which he saw as scandalous in
      its method of passage, unsettling for many Catholics
      and non-Catholics alike, dangerous in the hands of
      churchmen like Manning, and an unnecessary addition
      to the Church's statements concerning its teaching
      authority.

      See: TLS, 17 October 1968: 1182.

992. Holmes, J. Derek. "Liberal Catholicism and Newman's
      Letter to the Duke of Norfolk." CLR 60 (August
      1975): 498-511.

      Focuses on the motivations behind, and arguments
      of, Newman's expostulation of 1874, published as a

rejoinder to Gladstone's VATICAN DECREES. The anti-Erastian Newman believed that a state with an established religion was undesirable, if not also impractical. Closely related to this view was his dislike of Ultramontanism, which denied the primacy of conscience and sought to maintain a ramshackle, hopelessly outdated temporal power.

993.   ————. "Cardinal Newman and the First Vatican Council." AHC 1 (1969): 374-98.

Looks into the reasons for Newman's uneasiness over the definition of papal infallibility. Though an ardent pro-infallibilist in the early 1860s, he changed his mind by the decade's end, seeing the idea as a theological opinion, and not a dogmatic certainty, but one which would nevertheless alienate non-Catholics and hinder freedom of discussion within Catholicism.

994.   ————. "How Newman Blunted the Edge of Ultramontanism." CLR 53 (May 1968): 353-62.

Demonstrates Newman's use of history, in the form of his theory of development, to expose the weaknesses of Ultramontanism.

995.   ————. "Newman's Attitude to Ultramontanism and Liberal Catholicism on the Eve of the First Vatican Council." In BISHOPS AND WRITERS; ASPECTS OF THE EVOLUTION OF MODERN ENGLISH CATHOLICISM (item 785), 15-33.

Details Newman's association with liberal Catholics through his work with the *Rambler*. By the end of the 1860s, Newman was already expressing reservations about the validity of the projected infallibility decree; as early as 1860 itself, he had shown outright opposition to the idea of papal temporal power. Positions such as these naturally earned him the enmity of the ultramontanists, including Herbert Vaughan, future Archbishop of Westminster, and H.J. Coleridge, future editor of *The Month*.

996.   ————. "Newman's Reaction to the Definition of Papal Infallibility." In JOHN HENRY NEWMAN: A MAN FOR OUR TIME? (item 898), 37-44.

Asserts that Newman expressed his opposition to
the definition by interpreting it in a sense quite
different from that intended by the Council Fathers
and understood by the ultramontanists.

997. Misner, Paul. PAPACY AND DEVELOPMENT: NEWMAN AND
      THE PRIMACY OF ROME. Leiden and New York: E.J.
      Brill, 1976.

Investigates Newman's presuppositions, aims,
conclusions, and weaknesses in dealing with the
idea of Papal primacy as expressed in his time.
Examines his thought in this area during the
three religious phases of his life: the Anglican,
the transitional (during which appeared AN ESSAY
ON THE DEVELOPMENT OF DOCTRINE), and the Roman
Catholic.

See: John F. Broderick, S.J., CH 46 (March
       1977): 123-4; H.A. MacDougall, AHR 82
       (June 1977): 639; Roderick Strange,
       AMPJ 83 (Autumn 1978): 56; J. Derek
       Holmes, CHR 64 (October 1978): 697-8.

The Cardinalate

998. Blehl, Vincent F. "Newman and the Missing Miter."
      THOUGHT 35 (Spring 1960): 111-23.

Blames Cardinal Cullen for Newman's failure to be
named a bishop, despite Wiseman's promise to him in
1854 that he would be awarded a diocese *in partibus*.
Proffers a previously unpublished letter from Cullen
to the Pope, giving reasons against Newman's elevation
to the episcopate; this letter persuaded the Pope to
postpone the honor.

999. Boyce, Philip, O.C.D. "John Henry Newman a
      Cardinal: One Hundred Years Ago." CLR 64
      (December 1979): 425-31.

Describes the circumstances surrounding the
elevation to the cardinalate: Leo XIII's reasons
for his choice; Newman's initial rejection, followed
by his acceptance of the honor; the reaction of the

English people; and Newman's trip to Rome to receive
the red hat.

1000. Snider, Carlo. "The Cardinalate of John Henry
        Newman." In JOHN HENRY NEWMAN: COMMEMORATIVE
        ESSAYS ON THE OCCASION OF THE CENTENARY OF HIS
        CARDINALATE, 1879-1979, edited by M.K. Strolz,
        61-94. Rome: The Centre of Newman-Friends,
        n.d.

        An in-depth treatment of the process leading to
        Newman's reception into the College of Cardinals.
        Concentrates on Manning's efforts against the
        proposed elevation. Sees the honor as a vindication
        of Newman's theology, a recognition by the Holy See
        of his constant devotion to the Church, and a
        significant step in nineteenth-century Catholicism's
        intellectual development.

                    Diocesan Clergy and Pastoral Activity

1001. Bellenger, Dominic Aidan. "The Emigré Clergy and the
        English Church, 1789-1815." JEH 34 (July
        1983): 392-410.

        Indicates that anti-Catholicism within the Anglican
        community was merely concealed, and not forgotten,
        during the twenty-five years of the exiled French
        clergy's presence in England. Though accepted into
        the country as the victims of infidel attacks, the
        priests were never granted either equality or a
        guarantee of permanent residence; toleration did not
        mean freedom.

1002. ————. "The English Catholics and the French Exiled
        Clergy." RH 15 (October 1981): 433-51.

        Charts the progress of the French clergy in
        England, from their initial welcome, through the
        signs of growing problems, to their extreme
        unpopularity. Indicates that in education, theology,
        literature, devotion, and spirituality, the French
        clerical influence was minimal, since the exiles
        were preoccupied with simple survival and the
        thought of returning to France, while the English

resented their strange language, customs, and Gallican arrogance.

1003.   ————. THE FRENCH EXILED CLERGY IN THE BRITISH ISLES
          AFTER 1789: AN HISTORICAL INTRODUCTION AND
          WORKING LIST. Bath: Downside Abbey, 1986.

          Chapters 1-4 describe the interplay between the
          exiles and their hosts, noting that although the
          French were initially welcomed by both the government
          and the Roman Catholic community in England, they
          rarely sought an active role in the affairs of their
          adopted country. Chapters 5-8 detail the three main
          forms of exile life: religious communities, the
          King's House at Winchester, and London. Shows how
          the leaders of the emigration emphasized detachment
          and "self-help," in an effort to preserve their own
          identity, an identity most formidably expressed in
          the Blanchardist schism. Concludes that many of the
          exiles, despite their alienation and frustration,
          found the challenge of life in England a source of
          personal growth.

1004.   ————. "The French Exiled Clergy in England and
          National Identity, 1790-1815." In RELIGION AND
          NATIONAL IDENTITY: PAPERS READ AT THE NINETEENTH
          SUMMER MEETING AND THE TWENTIETH WINTER MEETING OF
          THE ECCLESIASTICAL HISTORY SOCIETY (item 25), 397-
          407.

          Shows how internal and external influences upon
          the exiles combined to create a deeply introverted
          mentality. Sketches the effects of the separation
          between the English and their guests, who were a
          source of embarrassment to His Majesty's Government,
          which had invited them in the first place, and an
          object of suspicion to a people for whom Englishness
          and Protestantism were one and the same thing.

1005.   Connolly, G.P. "Little Brother Be At Peace: The
          Priest as Holy Man in the Nineteenth-Century
          Ghetto." In THE CHURCH AND HEALING: PAPERS
          READ AT THE TWENTIETH SUMMER MEETING AND THE
          TWENTY-FIRST WINTER MEETING OF THE ECCLESIASTICAL
          HISTORY SOCIETY (item 28), 191-206.

Highlights the mechanics of clerical power in the Irish ghettos of England. Situates the priest's prestige within his image as a bearer of holiness, to whom was entrusted both thaumaturgic powers and important social functions.

1006. Doyle, Peter. "The Education and Training of Roman Catholic Priests in Nineteenth-Century England." JEH 35 (April 1984): 208-19.

Evaluates the educational standards and ideals which bishops set down for their seminaries, showing that in most cases seminaries were isolated from all contemporary secular developments and thus became highly suspicious of the world. Moreover, theological studies were narrow and required no thought whatsoever, either before or after ordination.

1007. Holmes, J. Derek. "English Ultramontanism and Clerical Education." CLR 62 (July 1977): 266-78.

Illustrates how the training and education of the nineteenth-century English clergy reflected the spread and development of ultramontanism, from Wiseman's years as President of Oscott (1840-1847) to Vaughan's campaign to establish Tridentine seminaries throughout the country.

1008. Supple, Jennifer F. "The Catholic Clergy of Yorkshire, 1850-1900: A Profile." NH 21 (1985): 212-35.

Probes the personal background, changing role, and social status of northern English priests during a period of transition. Finds a highly diverse racial, social, and educational composition, along with a growing clerical concern for the social welfare of the faithful.

1009. Warren, L. "Hard Times in Catholic Preston." In CATHOLIC ENGLISHMEN: ESSAYS PRESENTED TO THE RT. REV. BRIAN CHARLES FOLEY, BISHOP OF LANCASTER (item 1077), 45-51.

A sequel to item 1025. Outlines clerical activity in Preston between 1831 and 1861, a period during which the town's population nearly tripled, resulting

in serious social unrest. Evaluates the ways in which
the need for new ecclesiastical buildings, religious
instruction, and parish organizations was met.

Orders and Congregations: Male

General

1010.   Butler, Cuthbert, O.S.B. "Religious Orders of Men."
        In CATHOLIC EMANCIPATION, 1829 TO 1929: ESSAYS BY
        VARIOUS WRITERS (item 761), 177-99.

        Sketches the nineteenth-century activities of a
        wide variety of teaching, charitable, and missionary
        orders, including the Black, Grey, and White Friars,
        Jesuits, Passionists, Redemptorists, Oratorians,
        Vincentians, Mill Hill Missionaries, Josephites, and
        Christian Brothers.

1011.   Cruise, Dom Edward. "Development of the Religious
        Orders." In THE ENGLISH CATHOLICS, 1850-
        1950: CENTENARY ESSAYS TO COMMEMORATE THE
        RESTORATION OF THE HIERARCHY (item 759), 442-74.

        Charts the immense growth in numbers, religious
        facilities, and influence of the orders, both
        traditional and new.

The Benedictines

1012.   The Abbot of Downside. "Abbot Gregory Gregory (1813-
        1877)." DR 89 (July 1971): 191-5.

        A tribute to Henry Gregory Gregory, first (and
        last) Abbot of St. Mary's Abbey, Sydney; Vicar-
        General of the Archdiocese of Sydney; and after
        his return to England in 1861, Abbot of St.
        Gregory's Abbey, Downside.

1013.   The Abbot of Downside. "The Record of the Century."
        DR 33 (June 1914): 18-90.

Narrates the history of the Benedictines of St.
Gregory's Abbey, from their expulsion from Douai in
1794, to their years at Acton Burnell (1795-1814)
and final installation at Downside. Pays special
attention to the leadership--the priors, abbots,
and bishops associated with the establishment--and
to the monastic school and its numerous achievements.

1014. Almond, Dom Cuthbert, O.S.B. THE HISTORY OF
AMPLEFORTH ABBEY FROM THE FOUNDATION OF ST.
LAWRENCE'S AT DIEULOUARD TO THE PRESENT TIME.
London: R. & T. Washbourne, 1903.

Chapters 28 to 35 cover nineteenth-century
developments. After being forced by the French
revolutionaries to flee their two-hundred-year-
old establishment at Dieulouard (Lorraine), the
Benedictines of St. Lawrence's Priory settled at
Ampleforth in 1802. Through the next century,
and because of their talented leadership and
excellent educational facilities, they flourished,
though not without numerous disputes among the
Benedictines themselves, and between the Benedictines and outsiders.

See: DUBR 135 (July 1904): 213-6.

1015. Birt, Henry Norbert, O.S.B. DOWNSIDE: THE HISTORY OF
ST. GREGORY'S SCHOOL FROM ITS COMMENCEMENT AT DOUAY
TO THE PRESENT TIME. London: K. Paul, Trench,
Trübner, 1902.

Chapters 5 to 9 interweave a detailed treatment of
the major nineteenth-century developments with an informal look at daily life (e.g., recreation days,
cricket rivalries, theatrical activity, student clubs,
and the fire-brigade) and lists of "Gregorian
Worthies," i.e., prominent alumni of the monastic
school.

See: DUBR 135 (July 1904): 177-9.

1016. Campbell, W.E. "The First Abbot of Downside." DUBR
189 (October/November/December 1931): 237-54.

Sketches the personality and accomplishments of
Hugh Edmund Ford, whose clear sense of justice, keen

mind, and outstanding leadership as sub-prior, prior,
and Abbot of Downside made him one of the greatest
lights of late nineteenth-century English Catholicism.

1017.   Hicks, Dom Bruno.   HUGH EDMUND FORD (FIRST ABBOT OF
             DOWNSIDE).   London: Sands, 1947.

         Displays the innumerable controversies, disap-
pointments, and reverses faced by Ford as he sought
to reinstate full observance of the Benedictine rule
in all of the English Congregation's houses.
Includes a detailed personality study, emphasizing
his strong sense of charity and deep holiness.

         See: IER 71 (February 1949): 169-70.

The Cistercians

1018.   Elliott, Bernard.   "The Return of the Cistercians to
             the Midlands."   RH 16 (May 1982):   99-104.

         Describes Cistercian efforts to gain a foothold in
central England during the first half of the
nineteenth century.   Though their initial foundation
of 1795 at Lulworth (Dorset), composed of monks
exiled from La Trappe, was disbanded by government
decree in 1817, the Cistercians, with the help of
Ambrose Phillipps de Lisle and Father Norbert
Woolfrey, were able to erect a permanent house at
Mount St. Bernard's, in Derbyshire, in 1835.

1019.   Lacey, Andrew.   THE SECOND SPRING IN CHARNWOOD FOREST.
             Loughborough, Leics.:   Loughborough University
             Press, 1985.

         A study of Mount St. Bernard's, the first
Cistercian community established in England since
the Dissolution, and the center of the Catholic
revival in Leicestershire.   Founded in 1835, with
the help of Ambrose Phillipps de Lisle, the Earl
of Shrewsbury, and Pugin, the monastery was em-
broiled in a number of conflicts through the rest
of the century; it fought with Shrewsbury over the
parochial duties of its priests, and with de Lisle
over his introduction of Rosminian missionaries

into the Loughborough area.

See: Vincent Alan McClelland, MONTH 2nd NS 19 (June 1986): 216.

The Franciscans

1020. Docherty, Howard, O.F.M. "The Friars Minor in England: Their Historical Continuity." CLR 37 (June 1952): 332-51.

Challenges the traditional belief that all three branches of the First Order of Franciscans died out in England before 1850. Establishes the continuity, however shaky, of the English Province during the period between the French Revolution and the restoration of the hierarchy.

The Dominicans

1021. Jarrett, Bede, O.P. THE ENGLISH DOMINICANS. London: Burns Oates & Washbourne, 1921.

Chapter 10 outlines the resurrection and impressive growth of the English Province after 1822, under the leadership of Provincial Ambrose Woods.

See: AMER 26 (29 October 1921): 42; BKMN 61 (Christmas Supplement 1921): 64; DR 40 (January 1922): 57-9; A.G. Little, EHR 37 (January 1922): 116-20; T.F. Tout, SHR 19 (April 1922): 217-9; TABLET 171 (15 January 1938): 78-9; BLACK 19 (March 1938): 235; DR 56 (April 1938): 252.

The Jesuits

1022. Basset, Bernard, S.J. THE ENGLISH JESUITS FROM CAMPION TO MARTINDALE. London: Burns & Oates, 1967.

Follows the Society's struggle for acceptance in
England after its restoration by Pius VII in 1814.
Though Bishop Baines felt compelled to secure a
written order from Leo XII requiring his fellow
bishops to recognize the Society in their areas,
the anti-Jesuit recriminations continued through
much of the century; harshest among the critics was
Cardinal Manning, who labeled the group snobbish,
narrow-minded, and aristocratic. The latter charge
is refuted by Basset's survey of the membership,
showing that the Order drew its candidates from all
ranks of society. Includes brief biographies of
some of the more prominent English Jesuits.

See: Vincent Alan McClelland, CLR 53 (July 1968): 565-
       7; TLS, 1 August 1968: 830; John F. Broderick,
       AMER 119 (7 September 1968): 166; Wilfrid
       Passmore, DR 86 (October 1968): 419-23; Patrick
       McGrath, EHR 84 (July 1969): 612.

1023. Edwards, Francis, S.J. THE JESUITS IN ENGLAND: FROM
       1580 TO THE PRESENT DAY. Notre Dame: University
       of Notre Dame Press, 1985.

       An institutional, rather than a biographical,
       treatment of the English Jesuit Province. Chapters
       10 to 13 provide dates and data concerning the
       Society's houses, work, and problems during the
       nineteenth century. Three appendices offer an
       assessment of the relationship between Manning and
       the Order, a list of provincials, and an explanation
       of Jesuit internal organization.

       See: Edward R. Norman, TLS, 9 August 1985: 885;
              Kenneth Wilburn, BS 45 (March 1986): 465-6;
              John W. Padberg, S.J., AMER 154 (17 May
              1986): 405; John T. Ford, RSR 12 (July/
              October 1986): 305; John Jay Hughes, CH 55
              (December 1986): 530.

1024. Holt, Geoffrey, S.J. "The English Province: The Ex-
       Jesuits and the Restoration." AHSI 42 (July/
       December 1973): 288-311.

       Looks into the whereabouts and activities of the
       more than two hundred English members of the Society
       of Jesus during the period between the suppression

of 1773 and the restoration of 1814.

1025.   ————. "Joseph Dunn of Preston from His Corre-
         spondence." In CATHOLIC ENGLISHMEN: ESSAYS
         PRESENTED TO THE RT. REV. BRIAN CHARLES FOLEY,
         BISHOP OF LANCASTER (item 1077), 29-36.

   A brief portrait of one of the first Jesuits in
England to confront the social problems created by
the Industrial Revolution. For over half a century,
from 1776 to his death in 1827, Dunn contributed to
the Catholic revival not only in Preston but
throughout the country, by his establishment of
mission chapels. His enormous correspondence,
addressed as often to Anglicans as to Catholics,
showed his zeal for emancipating and propagating
the faith.

1026.   Pollen, J.H. "An Unobserved Centenary." MONTH OS
         115 (May 1910): 449-61.

   Reviews the events leading up to the almost secret
restoration of the English branch of the Jesuits in
1803. Evaluates the cautious Papal decrees of 1778
and 1796 reestablishing the Order's common life, and
that of 1803 permitting it to resume its vows and
formal religious life. For the Order's troubled
efforts to obtain the privileges of a religious
community, see item 1027.

1027.   ————. "The Restoration of the English Jesuits,
         1803-1817." MONTH OS 115 (June 1910): 585-97.

   Continued from item 1026. Highlights the post-
1803 debate over the issue of granting the English
Jesuits the privileges of a religious order.
Dramatizes the continuing conflict within the Curia
and among the Vicars Apostolic, as the Order was
given small concessions in 1813, 1814, 1816, and
1818, but always with reservations or conditions.
For the final Jesuit victory, see item 1028.

1028.   ————. "The Recognition of the Jesuits in England."
         MONTH OS 116 (July 1910): 23-36.

   Continued from item 1027. Accounts for the
reestablishment of the English Jesuits as a

religious order, over the opposition of the Vicars
Apostolic.

1029.   Whitehead, Maurice.   "The English Jesuits and
          Episcopal Authority: The Liverpool Test
          Case, 1840-43."   RH 18 (October 1986):   197-
          219.

          Documents the most serious flare-up in the long,
          tedious, and complex conflict between the Vicars
          Apostolic and the "Gentlemen of Stonyhurst," as the
          recently restored Jesuits were called.   When, in
          1839, a group of Stonyhurst alumni raised funds for
          the erection of a Jesuit-operated Poor School in
          Liverpool, the Vicars Apostolic, headed by Bishop
          Brown, petitioned Rome to prevent its construction.
          The in-fighting, which eventually involved Jesuit
          Superior-General Roothaan and Cardinal Acton of
          Propaganda, continued for four years.

                          The Oratorians

                             General

1030.   Addington, Raleigh.   THE IDEA OF THE ORATORY.
          London: Burns & Oates, 1966.

          Compares the different ideas of the Oratory held
          by Newman and Faber, the two great Oratorian
          personalities of nineteenth-century England.   For
          Newman, who introduced the Congregation to England
          in 1848, the Oratorian life meant a combination of
          activity and contemplation, capable of producing
          something positive for the needs of the time.
          Consequently, he encouraged a teaching and literary
          apostolate, and governed his Birmingham house in a
          remarkably democratic way.   For Faber, rector of the
          London branch after 1849, true spirituality precluded
          active involvement in the world; thus, he was
          reluctant to establish a school, despite Newman's
          urgings to do so; and in the interests of discipline,
          his rule was quite autocratic.

          See: John T. Wilkinson, LQHR 191 (October 1966):   327;

                    TLS, 10 November 1966: 1027.

1031.   Bushell, Patrick.   "The Centenary of the London
             Oratory."   CLR 32 (October 1949):   217-27.

             Highlights the reasons for, and vociferous
             Protestant opposition to, Newman's decision to
             establish a branch in London; Faber's "Roman"
             rules and organization; the diversity of the
             Oratorian apostolate; and the long-term effect
             of the Congregation's work in the capital.

1032.   Napier, Michael, and Laing, Alistair, eds.   THE
             LONDON ORATORY CENTENARY, 1884-1984.
             London: Trefoil Books, 1984.

             Celebrates the one-hundredth anniversary of Faber's
             church in Knightsbridge.   Lavishly illustrated with
             prints, sixteen of which are in color, including
             Herbert Gribble's scheme of 1878 for the decoration
             of the interior.

             See: John P. Marmion, CLR 70 (July 1985): 263-4.

                                Faber

1033.   Cassidy, James F.   THE LIFE OF FATHER FABER, PRIEST OF
             THE ORATORY OF ST. PHILIP NERI.   London: Sands,
             1946.

             A positive portrait of Faber's rich personality,
             short but crowded life, and impressive achievements
             in literature, liturgical music, and spirituality.

             See: CLR 26 (August 1946): 443-5; DR 64 (October
             1946): 315-7.

1034.   Chapman, Ronald.   "English Spiritual Writers: VIII.
             Father Faber."   CLR 44 (July 1959):   385-94.

             Goes beneath Faber's repetitive, sentimental,
             extravagant, and Italianate prose, to discover a
             highly individual mixture of theology, apologetics,
             and devotional literature.

1035.   ————. FATHER FABER. Westminster, Md.: Newman
        Press, 1961.

        Seeks to correct Faber's image as a clerical
        showman, a popularizer of excessive Italianate
        devotions, and a composer of mediocre hymns.
        Stresses the richness and complexity of his
        personality: his enormous energy and drive,
        important spiritual insights, and ability to
        inspire respect and resentment at the same time.
        Presents these characteristics within the
        diversity of his achievements as Oxford don,
        Tractarian, Anglican rector, and early Oratorian.

        See: E.E. Reynolds, WR 235 (Spring 1961): 89-91;
              J.J. Dwyer, CLR 46 (April 1961): 247-9; Dom
              Dunstan Pontifex, DR 79 (Summer 1961): 280;
              R.W. Greaves, VS 5 (September 1961): 82-3;
              Louis A. Arand, CHR 47 (October 1961): 384-
              7; Owen Chadwick, JTS 12 (October 1961): 391-
              3.

                    The Redemptorists

1036.   Hull, Lawrence, C.SS.R. "A Redemptorist Centenary."
        CLR 30 (September 1948): 166-72.

        Commemorates one hundred years of activity at the
        first permanent Redemptorist foundation in England,
        situated in Clapham.

1037.   Sharp, John. "The Redemptorists in the United
        Kingdom: The Early Years." CLR 67 (November
        1982): 383-92.

        Contrasts the deep disillusionment and internal
        pressures of the first seven years (1843-1850) with
        the amazing successes during the 1850s. As their
        spiritual courage faltered and their social isolation
        increased, the first Redemptorists became ever more
        dejected; by 1854, however, the year in which they
        established their Irish headquarters at Limerick,
        their future as retreat masters and seminary teachers
        was assured.

1038. Shepherd, Charles, C.SS.R. "A Forgotten Apostle: John
      Furniss, C.SS.R. (1809-1865)." CLR 63 (March
      1978): 99-104.

      Introduces a unique apostolate in nineteenth-century
      England. Between 1852 and 1862 Furniss preached 115
      missions throughout the country, all of which were
      directed exclusively to children. Using stories,
      music, and visual aids, from which children were to
      draw the appropriate moral conclusions, he emphasized
      the necessity of frequent Mass, confession, and
      communion.

The Passionists

General

1039. Dommersen, Harold, C.P. "Aston Hall and the Passion-
      ists." CLR 22 (September 1942): 400-7.

      Traces the origins and development of the first
      Passionist house in England, founded in 1842 by
      Dominic Barberi.

1040. Gwynn, Denis. "Fr. Paul Pakenham, Passionist." CLR
      42 (July 1957): 400-19.

      Lists the achievements of one of the most attractive
      converts of the entire "Second Spring." Not long after
      his conversion in 1850, Pakenham was named first rector
      of Mount Argus, Dublin, the initial Passionist foun-
      dation in Ireland. His short life--he died at the age
      of thirty-six, barely a year after taking over in
      Ireland--was a model of spiritual heroism and virtue.

1041. Smith, Joseph, C.P. PAUL MARY PAKENHAM, PASSIONIST.
      Edinburgh: Sands, 1915.

      Studies the process whereby Charles Reginald
      Pakenham (1821-1857), fourth son of the Irish
      Protestant Earl of Longford, became a Catholic
      and brought the first Passionist house to Ireland.
      Concentrates on his spiritual evolution as he
      discovered in turn the writings of the recently

converted Newman, Thomas à Kempis, and St. Alphonsus
Liguori. Includes a great amount of material on the
establishment at Mount Argus, Dublin.

See: AMER 15 (24 June 1916): 263; IER 8 (September
      1916): 260-1; CW 104 (October 1916): 114-5.

1042. Young, Urban, C.P. THE LIFE OF FATHER IGNATIUS
           SPENCER, C.P. London: Burns Oates & Washbourne,
           1933.

       Concentrates on Spencer's varied pastoral activity,
       including retreat and parish mission work. Son of
       the First Lord of the Admiralty, and a graduate of
       Eton and Cambridge, he became an Anglican priest in
       1823; seven years later, he converted and was ordained
       in the Roman Church. In 1838 he inaugurated the
       Crusade of Prayer for the conversion of England. His
       ever deepening involvement in the "Second Spring"
       inspired him to join the Passionists in 1846, under
       the supervision of Dominic Barberi.

       See: E.I. Watkin, DUBR 194 (January/February/March
             1934): 166-8; CLR 7 (February 1934): 166; IER
             44 (November 1934): 558-9.

                            Barberi

1043. Bulman, David, C.P. "Cardinal Newman and Venerable
           Dominic Barberi." In A NEWMAN SYMPOSIUM: REPORT
           ON THE TENTH ANNUAL MEETING OF THE CATHOLIC
           RENASCENCE SOCIETY AT THE COLLEGE OF THE HOLY
           CROSS, WORCESTER, MASS., APRIL 1952 (item 931),
           71-5.

       Sketches the life of the man who brought Newman
       into the Catholic Church. Goes beyond his baptism
       of Newman to assess his larger role within the
       "Second Spring."

1044. Carey, Kenan, C.P. THE APOSTOLE OF THE SECOND
           SPRING. New York: Paulist Press, 1945.

       A biographical sketch intended for the general
       reader. Concentrates on the Passionist tradition

within which Barberi's vocation was defined, and on the obstacles and tragedies which confronted him during his ministry in England.

1045. Gwynn, Denis. "Dominic Barberi and the 'Cambridge Converts.'" CLR 22 (June 1942): 241-9.

Recalls the relationship between Barberi, newly arrived in England, and young converts such as George Spencer and Ambrose Phillipps de Lisle, who encouraged his missionary activity and helped him to adapt to his adopted country.

1046. ————. FATHER DOMINIC BARBERI. London: Burns Oates, 1947.

Goes beyond the biographical data, to provide an in-depth treatment of the major religious person- alities and events in England during the years immediately before and after Barberi's reception of Newman into the Roman Church, in May 1845. Incorporates much of the material from Young (item 1050), but adds a good deal of supplementary information. Notes that Barberi's rapid disil- lusionment stemmed not only from Protestant bigotry, but from his readiness to believe his friends' view that all England was eager to convert to Catholicism.

See: Stephen McKenna, C.SS.R., BS 8 (15 May 1948): 53; COMMWL 48 (30 July 1948): 382-3; Joseph McSorley, CW 168 (November 1948): 173; Joseph J. Reilly, THOUGHT 23 (December 1948): 703-4.

1047. ————. "Heralds of the Second Spring: VI. Father Dominic Barberi." CLR 30 (September 1948): 176- 96.

An abridgement of item 1046, which emphasizes the continuing opposition and obstacles to his missionary activity.

1048. Mead, Jude, C.P. SHEPHERD OF THE SECOND SPRING: THE LIFE OF BLESSED DOMINIC BARBERI, C.P., 1792-1849. Paterson, N.J.: St. Anthony Guild Press, 1968.

The most recent study. Portrays Barberi as seen

by his contemporaries, both supporters and opponents.
Contains a detailed character analysis.

1049. Wilson, Alfred, C.P. BLESSED DOMINIC BARBERI: SUPER-
       NATURALIZED BRITON. London: Sands, 1967.

       Details the personality and activities of a well-
       intentioned man who constantly ran afoul of his
       contemporaries. Stresses the paradoxes of his
       religious position: an ecumenist in an age of
       bigotry, a mystic who felt easily at home in the
       minutiae of daily life, and an independent thinker
       who accepted the Catholic faith unquestioningly.
       Sheds new light on why Barberi was chosen to receive
       Newman into the Church. Based on a large amount of
       material never before translated into English.

       See: TLS, 20 July 1967: 645; Sister Blanche Marie,
             B.V.M., CER 65 (November 1967): 559-60; J.H.
             Whyte, CLR 52 (December 1967): 997-8.

1050. Young, Urban, C.P. LIFE AND LETTERS OF THE VENERABLE
       DOMINIC BARBERI, C.P. London: Burns Oates &
       Washbourne, 1926.

       A highly sympathetic biography, featuring large
       segments of Barberi's letters to Wiseman, Newman,
       Ignatius Spencer, and Ambrose Phillipps de Lisle,
       among others. Underscores the optimism and devotion
       he brought to his ministry in England. Three
       appendices consider his relationship with Anglicanism
       and chances for canonization.

       See: IER 29 (March 1927): 333-5.

                     Gentili and the Rosminians

1051. Catcheside, P.H. "Father Gentili and the Resto-
       ration of the Hierarchy: The Chastening Fruits
       of Some Recent Researches." TABLET 196 (23
       September 1950): 256-60.

       Attributes to Gentili a major role in the re-
       establishment of the English hierarchy. In a
       series of reports he convinced the Vatican that

unless the ecclesiastical situation in England were regularized, Catholicism there would progress no further.

1052. Gwynn, Denis. "Father Gentili (1801-1848)." IER 70 (September 1948): 769-84.

Presents Gentili's life and personality. A summary of the material presented in item 1053.

1053. ————. FATHER LUIGI GENTILI AND HIS MISSION, 1801-1848. Dublin: Clonmore and Reynolds, 1951.

A highly sympathetic, almost hagiographical, biography. Focuses on Gentili's years in England, 1835-1848, during which he introduced the Roman collar; prompted public devotions such as Marian processions, the Stations of the Cross, and exposition of the Blessed Sacrament; and supervised dozens of parish missions and retreats. His dislike of compromise or even moderation not only made him unpopular with the very people he sought to convert; it led him to overwork, and to an early death.

See: J.J. Dwyer, CLR 37 (March 1952): 183-4; Florence D. Cohalan, CHR 38 (July 1952): 190-1; IER 78 (July 1952): 78-9.

1054. Leetham, Claude. "Gentili's Reports to Rome." WR 237 (Winter 1963-4): 395-414.

Denies the claim of Bernard Ward (item 780) that Gentili was an intriguer whose unsolicited reports to Rome caused a great deal of difficulty for the Vicars Apostolic. Proves, by an examination of Gentili's hitherto unpublished letters to Propaganda, that his recommendations were always made at Rome's request and were far from being irresponsible or mischievous.

1055. ————. LUIGI GENTILI: A SOWER FOR THE SECOND SPRING. London: Burns & Oates, 1965.

Deals solely with Gentili's thirteen-year missionary activity. Offers a more positive picture of his sensitivity to the English religious situation of his day than that presented by Gwynn (item 1053).

See: TLS, 3 March 1966: 164; Dennis Cleary, DUBR
       240 (Spring 1966): 91-3; Wilfrid Passmore,
       DR 84 (July 1966): 335-9; J.J. Dwyer, CLR 52
       (February 1967): 158-9; John Tracy Ellis, CHR
       54 (April 1968): 185-7.

Orders and Congregations: Female

1056.   Battersby, W.J., F.S.C. "Educational Work of the
        Religious Orders of Women: 1850-1900." In THE
        ENGLISH CATHOLICS, 1850-1950: CENTENARY ESSAYS
        TO COMMEMORATE THE RESTORATION OF THE HIERARCHY
        (item 759), 337-64.

        Surveys the philosophies, institutional structures,
        and accomplishments of the more than twenty different
        orders of nuns engaged in educational ministry at
        every social level.

1057.   Eaton, Robert. THE BENEDICTINES OF COLWICH, 1829-
        1929: ENGLAND'S FIRST HOUSE OF PERPETUAL
        ADORATION. London: Sands, 1929.

        Details the daily life of the Benedictine nuns
        who, after fleeing Douai at the time of the French
        Revolution, eventually settled in 1835 at Colwich,
        near Stafford.

        See: DR 47 (May 1929): 174; BLACK 10 (October
               1929): 1409-10.

1058.   Hudson, George V. MOTHER GENEVIEVE DUPUIS, FOUNDRESS
        OF THE ENGLISH CONGREGATION OF THE SISTERS OF
        CHARITY OF ST. PAUL THE APOSTLE, 1813-1903.

        Relates the story of how the French-born Dupuis,
        also known as Sister Zoile, came to England in 1847
        to teach poor children at Dr. Tandy's mission at
        Banbury. By October 1848 she had four followers,
        attracted by her personal sanctity and energy; these
        formed the core of her new Congregation.

        See: IER 35 (June 1930): 670-1.

1059. LIFE OF MOTHER MARY AGNES AMHERST. Exeter: Catholic
Records Press, 1927.

Sees Mary Barbara Amherst as an integral part of
that heroic period of English Catholicism immediately
preceding the restoration of the hierarchy, a period
illuminated by the personalities and achievements of
Wiseman, Rosmini, Gentili, and de Lisle. Influenced
in early life by personal contact with Mother
Margaret Hallahan (item 1061) and Bishop Ullathorne,
the twenty-two-year-old Amherst entered the Institute
of Charity at Loughborough, eventually becoming its
leader.

See: DR 46 (January 1928): 91.

1060. Monahan, Maud. "Religious Communities of Women." In
CATHOLIC EMANCIPATION, 1829 TO 1929: ESSAYS BY
VARIOUS WRITERS (item 761), 201-21.

Analyzes the work of the Irish Sisters of Mercy,
Faithful Companions of Jesus, Congregation of Notre
Dame, Little Sisters of the Poor, Little Sisters of
the Assumption, and Congregation of the Holy Child.
For a parallel discussion of male orders, see item
1010.

1061. STEWARD OF SOULS: A PORTRAIT OF MOTHER MARGARET
HALLAHAN, BY S.M.C. OF THE ENGLISH DOMINICAN
CONGREGATION OF SAINT CATHERINE OF SIENA.
London: Longmans, Green, 1952.

Follows Hallahan's progress from her miserable and
virtually uneducated childhood in the London slums,
to her foundation and leadership of an important
branch of English Dominican life, which, like the
saint whose special patronage it invoked, sought to
combat clerical apathy. Provides along the way
character sketches of Gentili, Ullathorne, and
Newman, all of whom were supporters of this hard-
driving and courageous sister.

See: CLR 38 (June 1953): 379-80.

The Laity

General Works

1062.   Aveling, J.C.H.   THE HANDLE AND THE AXE: THE CATHOLIC
        RECUSANTS IN ENGLAND FROM REFORMATION TO EMANCI-
        PATION.   London: Blond & Briggs, 1976.

        Chapters 12-15 delineate various developments in
        English Catholicism during the first three decades
        of the nineteenth century, including the rapid
        decline of the Catholic landed gentry, and the
        reasons for it; the impressive rise of the Catholic
        middle class and "lower orders," along with their
        religious beliefs and activities; the clergy's
        struggle for survival, going on at the same time
        as its prestige was growing; and the defeat of
        Catholic liberalism, as the proponents of episcopal
        authoritarianism, led by Bishop Milner, gained the
        upper hand.

        See: ECON 262 (22 January 1977): 104; Claire Cross,
               TLS, 17 June 1977: 737; Christopher Haigh, HJ
               21 (March 1978): 181-2.

1063.   Bossy, John.   THE ENGLISH CATHOLIC COMMUNITY, 1570-
               1850.   London: Darton, Longman and Todd, 1975.

        Part 3 offers an integrated account of the social,
        organizational, and intellectual development of the
        Catholic community during the first half of the
        nineteenth century.   Shows how, to what degree, and
        with what modifications English Catholicism main-
        tained its continuity through fifty years of
        unprecedented upheaval.

        See: Christopher Hill, NST 91 (2 April 1976): 436-7;
               John Kenyon, OBS, 11 April 1976: 33; James
               Lees-Milne, LIST 95 (6 May 1976): 575; ECON 259
               (12 June 1976): 83; Eamon Duffy, JEH 27
               (October 1976): 447-50; Jeffrey L. Lant, AMER
               135 (30 October 1976): 283-4; Hugh Kearney, TLS,
               10 December 1976: 1537; John Miller, EHR 92
               (January 1977): 134-7; Lawrence Stone, NYRB 24
               (3 February 1977): 36-7; Thomas H. O'Connor,

AMER 136 (7 May 1977): 425-6; Norris Merchant,
COMMWL 104 (27 May 1977): 344; Nadia Lahutsky,
RSR 3 (October 1977): 249-50; James Hitchcock,
REVREL 37 (January 1978): 153-4; Christopher
Haigh, HJ 21 (March 1978): 181-6; Robert
Trisco, CH 47 (June 1978): 229-31; W.R. Ward,
JMH 50 (September 1978): 506-7; Arnold
Pritchard, AHR 85 (February 1980): 121-2.

1064. Fitzalan, Viscount. "Catholics in Public Life." In
CATHOLIC EMANCIPATION, 1829 TO 1929: ESSAYS BY
VARIOUS WRITERS (item 761), 141-58.

Scans the process whereby Catholics came forward
to serve in positions of public service (e.g., public
office and higher education).

1065. Fletcher, Margaret. "The Influence of Catholic
Laywomen." In CATHOLIC EMANCIPATION, 1829 TO
1929: ESSAYS BY VARIOUS WRITERS (item 761),
223-42.

Assesses the efforts by laywomen's groups to
protect and educate their less fortunate sisters.

1066. Gorman, W. Gordon, ed. CONVERTS TO ROME: A
BIOGRAPHICAL LIST OF THE MORE NOTABLE CONVERTS
TO THE CATHOLIC CHURCH IN THE UNITED KINGDOM
DURING THE LAST SIXTY YEARS. London: Sands,
1910.

Provides brief biographies of more than six
thousand aristocrats, Protestant clergymen,
diplomats, physicians, military leaders, barris-
ters, artists, composers, authors, and university
graduates who turned to Rome during the second
half of the nineteenth century. Each entry lists
the individual's most significant achievement,
date of conversion, and, where applicable, the
date and place of entry into Catholic religious
life.

1067. Hickey, John. URBAN CATHOLICS: URBAN CATHOLICISM IN
ENGLAND AND WALES FROM 1829 TO THE PRESENT DAY.
London: Geoffrey Chapman, 1967.

A historical and sociological study of the

relationship between urban Catholics as a group and
their neighbors. Accounts for the continuing
isolation of the former throughout the nineteenth
century.

See: J.H. Whyte, CLR 53 (July 1968): 567-9; Neville
       Masterman, THEO 71 (November 1968): 522;
       Richard J. Schiefen, JEH 20 (April 1969): 183-
       4; P. McKevitt, ITQ 36 (October 1969): 360-2.

1068. Inglis, K.S. CHURCHES AND THE WORKING CLASSES IN
       VICTORIAN ENGLAND. Toronto: University of
       Toronto Press, 1963.

       Chapter 3 enumerates the efforts by Catholic
       leaders to stop the large number of (primarily
       Irish immigrant) workers from falling away from
       the faith. Central to the hierarchy's campaign
       were the pastoral activity of the St. Vincent de
       Paul Society, which made its English debut in
       1844; and the organization of the laity through
       such groups as Edward Lucas' Catholic Association
       of 1891. Yet, even with all of this, the campaign's
       goals were not fully realized; wealthy Catholics
       refused to help their indigent coreligionists, and
       there were never enough facilities for direct
       spiritual instruction of the workers.

       See: Henry R. Winkler, HIS 26 (November 1963): 101-
              2; David Owen, AHR 69 (January 1964): 436-8;
              Bryan Wilson, ASR 29 (April 1964): 289-90;
              J.M. Main, HS 11 (April 1964): 285-6; I.G.
              Jones, HIST 49 (June 1964): 245-6; R.K. Webb,
              JMH 36 (June 1964): 210-1; John B. Morrall,
              PS 12 (June 1964): 281-2; Donald P. Gavin,
              CHR 50 (July 1964): 229-31; Jennifer Hart,
              ECHR 17 (August 1964): 169-72; D.A. Martin,
              BJS 15 (September 1964): 267-8; James Winter,
              CANHR 45 (September 1964): 239-40; Winthrop
              S. Hudson, CH 33 (September 1964): 368-9;
              J.H. Whyte, IHS 14 (September 1964): 196;
              Stanley Pierson, VS 8 (September 1964): 83-5;
              John Kent, EHR 80 (April 1965): 427-8; Werner
              Stock, SOCAN 26 (Winter 1965): 232-3.

1069. Leys, M.D.R. CATHOLICS IN ENGLAND, 1559-1829: A
       SOCIAL HISTORY. New York: Sheed & Ward, 1962.

Chapter 10 profiles the daily life, outlook, and aspirations of English Catholics during the final three decades before Emancipation. Chapters 11 to 14 include discussions of Catholic education, political activity, clergy, nobles, gentry, and commoners through the thirty-year period.

See: Martin J. Havran, CHR 48 (January 1963): 519-20; R.W. Greaves, HIST 48 (February 1963): 120-1.

1070. Mathew, David. "Old Catholics and Converts." In THE ENGLISH CATHOLICS, 1850-1950: ESSAYS TO COMMEMORATE THE RESTORATION OF THE HIERARCHY (item 759), 223-42.

Compares the backgrounds, daily lives, religious perspectives, and political outlooks of the "Old Catholics"--that is, those from families whose firm loyalty to Rome could be traced back through several persecuted generations--and nineteenth-century converts, most of whom turned to Rome as a result of Newman's influence.

Regional Studies

1071. Bolton, Charles A. SALFORD DIOCESE AND ITS CATHOLIC PAST: A SURVEY. Manchester: Diocese of Salford, 1950.

Chapters 8 to 11 follow nineteenth-century developments, including the evolution of diocesan administration under Bishops Turner, Vaughan, and Bilsborrow; the growth of parishes; and the activities of several "martyrs of charity," that is, priests who worked with the immigrants of Manchester and other urban centers, and ended up dying of typhus or cholera.

1072. Bossy, John. "Four Catholic Congregations in Rural Northumberland, 1750-1850." RH 9 (April 1967): 88-119.

Measures the size, topography, and religious and social behavior of the congregations at Hesleyside/

Bellingham, Biddlestone, Thropton, and Callaly. Uses
materials such as the religious census of 1851,
mission registers, and tax assessments on Catholic
estates, to suggest a number of similarities and
differences among the four groups.

1073.   ————. "More Northumbrian Congregations." RH 10
         (January 1969): 11-33.

         Employs the same statistical and sociological
         approach as in item 1072, applying it to the groups
         at Alnwick, Ellingham, Haggerston, Berrington, and
         Berwick.

1074.   Burgess, John. "The Roman Catholics and the Cumbrian
         Religious Censuses." RH 15 (May 1981): 372-8.

         Describes and explains the Catholic renaissance in
         Cumbria after 1851, along with the Protestant
         hostility which it engendered.

1075.   Burke, Thomas. CATHOLIC HISTORY OF LIVERPOOL.
         Liverpool: C. Tinling, 1910.

         A sometimes chronological, sometimes topical in-
         vestigation. Nineteenth-century developments begin
         in Chapter 2, with the enormous Irish influx of the
         1820s, and its diverse results: a wave of new church-
         building, to accommodate the large increase in Mass
         attendance; heightened agitation for Catholic
         emancipation; an enlargement of the Church's social
         ministry; and the foundation of protective groups
         like the Catholic Defense Society.

1076.   Elliott, Bernard. "A Leicestershire Recusant
         Family: The Nevills of Nevill Holt (III)."
         RH 18 (October 1986): 220-4.

         Illustrates how Catholic life in nineteenth-century
         England was reflected in the development of one
         prominent family.

1077.   Hilton, J.A., ed. CATHOLIC ENGLISHMEN: ESSAYS
         PRESENTED TO THE RT. REV. BRIAN CHARLES FOLEY,
         BISHOP OF LANCASTER. Wigan, Lancs.: North
         West Catholic History Society, 1984.

A collection of short pieces on the history of
Catholicism in Lancashire, three of which deal with
the nineteenth-century scene. Contains items 1009,
1025, and 1110.

See: John P. Marmion, CLR 70 (August 1985): 302;
       Stewart Foster, O.S.M., MONTH 2nd NS 19
       (September 1986): 245-6.

1078. Holt, T.G., S.J. "'An Establishment at
       Salisbury': Some Letters Concerning Catholicism
       in the City, 1795-1834." RH 18 (May 1986): 103-
       11.

       An overview of church-building and the Jesuit
       presence in early nineteenth-century Salisbury,
       drawn from contemporary correspondence preserved
       in the Clifton Diocesan Archives.

1079. McDonnell, K.G.T. "Roman Catholicism in London, 1850-
       1865." In STUDIES IN LONDON HISTORY PRESENTED TO
       PHILIP EDMUND JONES, edited by A.E.J. Hollaender
       and William Kellaway, 429-43. London: Hodder and
       Stoughton, 1969.

       Examines aspects of Catholic life in the capital
       during Wiseman's tenure as Archbishop. Focuses on
       parochial activity, the degree of religious ob-
       servance (e.g., Mass attendance), and the social
       composition of the laity (mostly poor, heavily
       immigrant).

See: TLS, 9 April 1970: 390; CHOICE 7 (November
       1970): 1289; Charles Pythian-Adams, EHR 86
       (October 1971): 892-3.

1080. Supple, Jennifer F. "The Role of the Catholic Laity
       in Yorkshire, 1850-1900." RH 18 (May 1987): 304-
       17.

       Points to the dynamism and diversity of lay
       activity in Yorkshire: beyond financial support for
       diocesan organizations and missions, the laity's
       contributions included charity work, involvement in
       social associations, and the defense of Catholic
       interests. Only in political agitation and spiritual
       affairs was its role limited, in the case of the

first, by its own choice, and in that of the second
by hierarchical decision.

1081. Ward, Bernard. CATHOLIC LONDON A CENTURY AGO.
       London: Catholic Truth Society, 1905.

       A detailed look at Catholic London in 1805.
       Balances a treatment of noteworthy personalities
       and events--for example, Bishop Douglass, Vicar
       Apostolic of the London District; the French
       émigré clergy; or the disagreement between
       Poynter and Milner over the Oath of Supremacy--with
       an imaginative tour of St. Edmund's College,
       existing chapels, religious houses, convents,
       schools, and charitable institutions.

       See: DUBR 138 (January 1906): 200-1.

The Irish Immigrants

1082. Connolly, Gerard. "Irish and Catholic: Myth or
       Reality? Another Sort of Irish and the Renewal
       of the Clerical Profession among Catholics in
       England, 1791-1918." In THE IRISH IN THE
       VICTORIAN CENTURY (item 1092), 225-54.

       Disputes the simple identification of "Irish"
       with "Catholic." Shows that at least half of
       pre-famine and famine emigrants from Ireland did
       not regularly attend Sunday Mass in their homeland.
       This trend continued during their years in England,
       where Irish Catholic rates of religious observance
       were often below those of their Protestant neighbors.

1083. Gilley, Sheridan. "Catholic Faith of the Irish
       Slums, London, 1840-70." In THE VICTORIAN
       CITY: IMAGES AND REALITIES, edited by H.J.
       Dyos and Michael Wolff, II, 837-53.
       London: Routledge & Kegan Paul, 1973.

       Analyzes the methods devised by Catholic parishes
       for the salvation of the souls of the Irish poor in
       the slums of Victorian London. Studies, among other
       expressions of missionary activity, self-help and
       friendly societies; public-house clubs; temperance

organizations; new devotional practices, patterned after continental, especially French and Italian, types, and seen as ultramontanist; and an emphasis on simpler church interiors. Credits Wiseman with much of the inspiration behind the "mission to the poor."

See: ECON 248 (1 September 1973): 89; Angus Wilson, OBS, 2 September 1973: 35; TLS, 7 September 1973: 1016; E.J. Hobsbawm, GW 109 (8 September 1973): 22; Marc Girouard, SPEC 231 (8 September 1973): 313-4; Rosalind Mitchison, LIST 90 (20 September 1973): 380-1; John Clive, NST 86 (5 October 1973): 486-7; Michael Greenho, HT 23 (November 1973): 819-20; Raymond Williams, NYTBR, 4 November 1973: 6; CHOICE 10 (February 1974): 1904; E.P. Hennock, ENC 42 (May 1974): 80-1; Frank Kermode, NYRB 21 (30 May 1974): 6; Neil Harris, JMH 46 (December 1974): 709-13; Robert L. Patten, CRITICISM 17 (Summer 1975): 276-85; P.J. Waller, EHR 91 (April 1976): 446-7; R.K. Webb, AHR 81 (December 1976): 1110-1.

1084. Gwynn, Denis. "The Famine and the Church in England." IER 69 (October 1947): 896-909.

Argues that the Irish immigrants brought a remarkable vitality and openness to a traditionally lethargic and isolated English Catholicism professed primarily by old landowning families who had come to regard the Church as their own personal trust and inheritance. Points to this phenomenon as the major cause of the deep resentment between the recently arrived Irish and the "Old Catholics."

1085. ————. GREAT BRITAIN: ENGLAND & WALES. A History of Irish Catholicism, edited by Patrick J. Corish, vol. 6, no. 1. Dublin: Gill and Son, 1968.

Explores diverse aspects of the interaction between English and Irish Catholics through both the pre- and post-famine periods. Details the quantitative and qualitative effects of the Irish immigration upon the Church in England.

1086. ————. "The Irish Immigration." In THE ENGLISH

CATHOLICS, 1850-1950: CENTENARY ESSAYS TO
COMMEMORATE THE RESTORATION OF THE HIERARCHY
(item 759), 265-90.

Discusses the major contributions made by
nineteenth-century Irish immigrants to the Catholic
revival in England. Though the transplanted Irish
clergy figured little in the ranks of the English
hierarchy, it inspired the lay activity which
produced scores of flourishing churches, schools,
and charitable institutions.

1087.   Jackson, John Archer. THE IRISH IN BRITAIN.
        London: Routledge and Kegan Paul/
        Cleveland: The Press of Western Reserve
        University, 1963.

Chapter 7 considers the English Church's efforts
to provide for the rapidly increasing population of
Catholics due to immigration. Looks at how the
leadership dealt with such problems as the insuf-
ficient number of clergymen and schools, the deep
differences between the English and Irish religious
outlooks, and the continuing drift of the recently
arrived working classes away from the faith.

See: TC 172 (Spring 1964): 58; E.R.R. Green, HT 14
     (April 1964): 291-3; Malcolm J.C. Calley,
     R&S 5 (April 1964): 99; Arnold Schrier, HIS
     26 (May 1964): 432-3; Howard Brotz, ASR 29
     (December 1964): 936-7; Alfred McClung Lee,
     AAAPSS 362 (November 1965): 204.

1088.   Lees, Lynn Hollen. EXILES OF ERIN: IRISH MIGRANTS
        IN VICTORIAN LONDON. Ithaca: Cornell University
        Press, 1979.

Devotes Chapter 7 to a treatment of the strategy
used by the English clergy to promote social and
cultural change among the incoming Irish. This
strategy--which included an emphasis on religious
schooling and on membership in self-help and
temperance societies--worked well, for it turned
the immigrants away from their rather inert rural
roots and toward participation in urban life.

See: Neil L. Kunze, HRNB 8 (November/December

1979): 40; Kenneth O. Morgan, TLS, 23 November
1979: 30; David Reeder, HT 29 (December
1979): 850-1; Michael Drake, AHR 85 (April
1980): 396-7; F.M.L. Thompson, JHG 6 (April
1980): 211-3; Anthony Sutcliffe, VS 24 (Autumn
1980): 124-5; Hugh McLeod, EHR 96 (October
1981): 922-3.

1089.   Lowe, W.J. "The Lancashire Irish and the Catholic
        Church, 1846-71: The Social Dimension." IHS 20
        (September 1976): 129-55.

        Charts the emergence of the Church in mid-nineteenth
        century Lancashire as an institution which gave the
        immigrant Irish there a valuable sense of community
        identity, constancy, and continuity. Indicates that
        across the Irish Sea and at the same time, Catholicism
        was providing a similar service for those Irish who
        had not emigrated.

1090.   Samuel, Raphael. "The Roman Catholic Church and the
        Irish Poor." In THE IRISH IN THE VICTORIAN CITY
        (item 1092), 267-300.

        Points to the special relationship between Irish
        slum-dwellers throughout Britain and their priests
        as the central feature of the immigrant religious
        experience.

1091.   Swift, Roger. "'Another Stafford Street Row': Law,
        Order and the Irish Presence in Mid-Victorian
        Wolverhampton." In THE IRISH IN THE VICTORIAN
        CITY (item 1092), 179-206.

        Suggests that the anti-Catholic disturbances of
        the 1850s and 60s, in which Irish Catholics stood
        firm against the presence of anti-Catholic speakers,
        may reflect, in contrast to the sporadic Irish
        protests of the 1840s, a new self-confidence in the
        Irish Catholic community, which in turn elicited a
        new and bitter Protestant response.

1092.   ————, and Gilley, Sheridan, eds. THE IRISH IN THE
        VICTORIAN CITY. London, Sydney, and Dover,
        N.H.: Croom Helm, 1985.

        Features thirteen essays covering every major

aspect of Irish life in Victorian Britain, including
the Roman Catholic connection. Includes, in addition
to national surveys, local studies of the immigrant
presence in Bristol, York, Wolverhampton, and Stockport. Contains items 1082, 1090, 1091, 1183, and
1309.

See: Charles Townsend, GW 134 (2 February 1986): 21;
      Kieran Flanagan, BBN, March 1986: 151; Dennis
      Clark, VS 30 (Winter 1987): 273-5; Alan D. Lane,
      RSR 13 (July 1987): 269.

Missionary Activity

1093. Birt, Dom Norbert. "The Australian Mission." DR 33
       (June 1914): 118-41.

       Recalls the contributions of individual Bene-
       dictines in the Australian mission field, from
       Ullathorne's work in 1833 to the elevation of
       Patrick Francis Moran to the Archbishopric of
       Sydney in 1884.

1094. ————. BENEDICTINE PIONEERS IN AUSTRALIA. St.
       Louis: B. Herder/London: Herbert & Daniel,
       1911. 2 vols.

       Features extremely detailed treatments of the
       extraordinary hardships faced by missionaries
       whose only previous experience of a Catholic
       environment was that of the "Second Spring."
       Certain themes reappear frequently through both
       volumes: the animosity between English and
       Irish Benedictines, and the problem of too much
       work, with too few men to do it.

       See: DR 30 (December 1911): 323-6.

1095. Scantlebury, R.E. "Australian Pioneers." CLR 32
       (August 1949): 79-90.

       Spotlights four English priests, all active in
       Australia during the first half of the nineteenth
       century: James Watkins (Tasmania, 1835-1836); John
       Joseph Therry (Tasmania, after 1838); Francis

Murphy (Adelaide, after 1844); and Christopher
Vincent Dowling, O.P. (the first missionary in
Australia, whose work began at Botany Bay in
1815).

Religious Thought

Science

1096. Lyon, John Joseph. THE REACTION OF ENGLISH CATHOLICS
       TO THE DEVELOPMENT IN THE EARTH AND LIFE SCIENCES,
       1825-64. Ph.D. dissertation. University of
       Pittsburgh, 1966.

       Describes the efforts by prominent English
       Catholics to reinterpret the meaning of Scripture
       in light of the theory of evolution. Among the
       individuals studied are Wiseman; Newman; Richard
       Simpson; Peter Le Page Renouf, the leading Catholic
       Egyptologist of the day; William Kirby Sullivan,
       principal science contributor to the *Home and
       Foreign Review*; and the converts John Moore Capes,
       founder of the *Rambler*, and Frederick Lucas, editor
       of *The Tablet.*

1097. Root, John D. CATHOLICS AND SCIENCE IN MID-VICTORIAN
       ENGLAND. Ph.D. dissertation. Indiana University,
       1974.

       Discusses the widely different reactions of
       English Catholic intellectuals to the challenges of
       nineteenth-century science, as represented by the
       theory of evolution. Maintains that the contest
       between pro- and anti-scientific forces reflected
       other, equally dramatic confrontations within the
       mid-Victorian Church, such as those between liberals
       and conservatives, infallibilists and anti-infalli-
       bilists, and a dogmatically rigid magisterium and
       intellectuals demanding freedom of Scriptural and
       theological inquiry.

1098. ————. "Catholicism and Science in Victorian
       England: I." CLR 66 (April 1981): 138-47.

Explores the multifarious dimensions of the
relationship between Roman Catholicism and science.
Outlines the debate over Darwinism in the Catholic
periodical press (e.g., *Dublin Review*, *Home and
Foreign Review*, *The Month*) and in Church-sponsored
literary, scientific, and philosophical societies
(e.g., the Accademia). Confirms the conclusions
of item 1096 concerning the scientific outlook of
Catholic notables like Wiseman and Simpson.
Continues in item 1099.

1099. ————. "Catholicism and Science in Victorian
        England: II." CLR 66 (May 1981): 162-70.

Carries the themes introduced in item 1098
through the last three decades of the century.
Covers a variety of issues: Newman's theoretical
discussions of the proper interaction between faith
and science, the effect of the Syllabus of Errors
and the declaration of papal infallibility on
Catholic scientists, Mivart's campaign to reconcile
Scripture and evolution, Ward's controversy with
Rev. William Roberts over the Galileo case, the
prominence of the Jesuits in scientific circles,
and the role of ultramontanism in the conflict
between freedom of thought and traditional Roman
authority.

1100. Windle, Sir Bertram C.A. "The Catholic Church and
        Science." In CATHOLIC EMANCIPATION, 1829 TO
        1929: ESSAYS BY VARIOUS WRITERS (item 761),
        103-20.

Details the English Catholic attitude toward
Darwinism and the newly emerging science of pre-
historic archeology.

Lingard

1101. Chinnici, Joseph P., O.F.M. THE ENGLISH CATHOLIC
        ENLIGHTENMENT: JOHN LINGARD AND THE CISALPINE
        MOVEMENT, 1780-1850. Shepherdstown, W.Va.: Patmos
        Press, 1980.

Rescues from neglect or misinterpretation the

efforts of Lingard and his followers to reconcile
traditional Catholicism and the Enlightenment.

See: CHOICE 18 (November 1980): 412; Nigel
      Abercrombie, MONTH 2nd NS 13 (December
      1980): 429-30; Donald F. Shea, AHR 86
      (February 1981): 133; John V. Crangle,
      JCS 23 (Spring 1981): 350-1; Gerald A.
      Largo, JAAR 49 (December 1981): 693-4;
      Leonard Swidler, RSR 8 (January 1982): 83;
      David M. Thompson, JEH 33 (April
      1982): 338; Josef L. Altholz, CH 51 (June
      1982): 231-2; Robert Trisco, CHR 68
      (October 1982): 638-40; Paul Misner, HRZNS
      10 (Spring 1983): 153.

1102. ————. "English Catholic Tradition and the Vatican
       II *Declaration on Religious Freedom*." CLR 60
       (August 1975): 487-97.

       Maintains that the *Declaration* has its roots in
Lingard's "Cisalpine" movement, which advocated full
religious freedom within a state and reconciliation
among the different branches of Christianity.

1103. Culkin, Gerard. "John Lingard and Ushaw." CLR 35
       (June 1951): 361-71.

       Examines Lingard's association with the College of
Douai (1782-1794) and its successor at Ushaw (1794-
1811). It was in France that Lingard discovered his
special vocation: to combat Protestant bigotry
through his historical writing. After the institution was removed to England, he worked constantly
to meet the demands of his unique apostolate.

1104. Fletcher, John. "John Lingard, D.D., F.R.S. (1771-
       1851)." DUBR 176 (January/February/March
       1925): 36-58.

       Focuses on Lingard's education and historical work.

1105. Gilley, Sheridan. "John Lingard and the Catholic
       Revival." In RENAISSANCE AND RENEWAL IN CHRISTIAN
       HISTORY: PAPERS READ AT THE FIFTEENTH SUMMER
       MEETING AND THE SIXTEENTH WINTER MEETING OF THE
       ECCLESIASTICAL HISTORY SOCIETY, edited by Derek

Baker, 313-28. Studies in Church History, vol. 14.
Oxford: Published for the Ecclesiastical History
Society by Basil Blackwell, 1977.

Specifies Lingard's twofold contribution to the
nineteenth-century Catholic revival in England: he
told the truth about his faith, but did so in a way
which persuaded rather than offended Protestants.
His historical work shows exactly how he was able
to strike this balance; though he hid his apologetic
purpose as far as possible, he was passionately
devoted to accuracy, detail, and fullness of
information.

See: TLS, 4 November 1977: 1293.

1106. Gwynn, Denis. "Lingard and Cardinal Wiseman." CLR
        35 (June 1951): 372-86.

Follows the course of their relationship, from
Wiseman's arrival at Ushaw in 1810 to Lingard's
death in 1851. Attributes their lack of closeness
to their very different personalities and religious
aims. Lingard, for example, disapproved of Wiseman's
vision of a grand Catholic revival in England.

1107. Haile, Martin, and Bonney, Edwin. LIFE AND LETTERS
        OF JOHN LINGARD, 1771-1851. St. Louis: B.
        Herder/London: Herbert & Daniel, n.d. [1912].

A view of the "Second Spring" filtered through the
diverse activities of one of its most influential
thinkers. Within the presentation of Lingard's life
and ideas are glimpses of the daily routine at the
College of Douai, the reigns of Pius VII and Leo
XII, the campaign for Catholic emancipation, the
English College in Rome, the Tractarians, and the
early years of both Pius IX and the *Rambler*.

See: CW 95 (May 1912): 246-7.

1108. Hegarty, W.J. "The Lingard Centenary (1851-1951)."
        IER 76 (November 1951): 386-98.

Labels Lingard the pioneer of scientific history
in England, the man whose work restored dignity to
a Catholic mentality too long repressed by

penal legislation.

1109.   ————. "Was Lingard a Cardinal?" IER 79 (February 1953): 81-93.

Gives reasons in favor of the theory that Lingard was created a cardinal *in petto* by Leo XII in 1826.

1110.   Hilton, J.A. "Lingard's Hornby." In CATHOLIC ENGLISHMEN: ESSAYS PRESENTED TO THE RT. REV. BRIAN CHARLES FOLEY, BISHOP OF LANCASTER (item 1077), 37-44.

Describes Lingard's four decades of service as the priest of a small and declining congregation in Lonsdale. Labels his ministry a failure, for he was unable to revive his parish, just as he found it impossible in the long run to prevent his Cisalpine movement from being swallowed up by ultramontanism.

1111.   Hollis, Christopher. "Lingard." HB 11 (May 1933): 71-2.

Combines an evaluation of Lingard's public achievements--including, most notably, his ability to steer a middle course between "Old Catholics" and converts in England--with anecdotes about his personal life.

1112.   Ryan, Edwin J. "Lingard (1771-1851)." In CHURCH HISTORIANS, INCLUDING PAPERS ON EUSEBIUS, OROSIUS, ST. BEDE THE VENERABLE, ORDERICUS VITALIS, LAS CASAS, BARONIUS, BOLLANDUS, MURATORI, MOEHLER, LINGARD, HERGENROETHER, JANSSEN, DENIFLE, LUDWIG VON PASTOR (item 266), 277-88.

Places Lingard within the context of early nineteenth-century historical scholarship.

1113.   Shea, Donald F. THE ENGLISH RANKE: JOHN LINGARD. New York: Humanities Press, 1969.

Hails Lingard not only as the founder of scientific history in England but also as one of the most effective promoters of the Catholic cause during the

first half of the century. Offers a balanced view of
his historical works, showing his anticipation of
Ranke's critical use of primary sources, on the one
side, and his oftentimes weak literary style and
organization, on the other. Even with these defects,
however, he was read by Protestants, for whom his
defense of Catholicism was at least worthy of
interest, if not acceptance.

See: Thomas P. Peardon, AHR 75 (October 1970): 1725;
      A.E. Firth, EHR 86 (October 1971): 865; Marvin
      R. O'Connell, CHR 59 (April 1973): 96-7.

The Oxford Movement

1114. Davies, Horton. WORSHIP AND THEOLOGY IN ENGLAND.
       Vol. 3: FROM WATTS AND WESLEY TO MAURICE, 1690-
       1850. Princeton: Princeton University Press,
       1961.

       Chapter 10 sketches the influence of Catholic
       thought upon the Oxford Movement.

       See: Kenneth Scott Latourette, VS 5 (September
             1961): 80-1; Richard Schlatter, AHR 67
             (October 1961): 110-1; John J. Murray,
             AAAPSS 338 (November 1961): 165-6; John T.
             Wilkinson, LQHR 187 (July 1962): 227;
             Lawrence L. Brown, WMQ 19 (July 1962): 475-
             7; Leonard W. Cowie, HIST 47 (October
             1962): 319.

1115. Donald, Gertrude. MEN WHO LEFT THE MOVEMENT: JOHN
       HENRY NEWMAN, THOMAS W. ALLIES, HENRY EDWARD
       MANNING, BASIL WILLIAM MATURIN. London: Burns
       Oates & Washbourne, 1933.

       Presents with great sympathy the spiritual and
       intellectual struggles of four Tractarians, for whom
       the logical and inevitable end of their journey was
       Rome. Counters Purcell's negative assessment of
       Manning's reasons for converting (item 863).

       See: CLR 5 (June 1933): 512; DR 51 (July 1933): 557-
             9; Michael Trappes-Lomax, DUBR 193

(July 1933): 143-6; Lancelot C. Sheppard,
THOUGHT 8 (December 1933): 490-1; Edwin Ryan,
CHR 20 (January 1935): 445-6.

1116. Dougherty, Charles T., and Welsh, Homer C. "Wiseman
      on the Oxford Movement: An Early Report to the
      Vatican." VS 2 (December 1958): 149-54.

      Investigates the Vatican's interest in the
      Tractarians, as piqued by Msgr. Wiseman's letter
      to Propaganda, 12 January 1839. Wiseman's
      favorable assessment, one he shared with the so-
      called "Romantic converts," the only Catholic
      group in England sympathetic to the Oxonians,
      prevailed in Rome; the Movement was viewed as a
      symbol of the Catholic resurgence becoming
      increasingly evident throughout the century.

1117. Leslie, Shane. THE OXFORD MOVEMENT, 1833-1933.
      Milwaukee: Bruce, 1933.

      Appendix 6 describes the English Catholic reaction
      to Tractarianism. Though many, if not most, "Old
      Catholics" branded the Movement insincere and even
      willfully hypocritical, Wiseman's conciliatory
      position won the day, although he himself lost touch
      with the Oxonians after his elevation to the
      cardinalate. For their part, the former High Church-
      men became the ultramontanist vanguard of the English
      Church, and encouraged and assisted the very "Old
      Catholics" who had once suspected them.

      See: DR 51 (October 1933): 747-8; CW 138 (November
            1933): 248; HB 12 (November 1933): 19; J.A.
            Muller, CH 2 (December 1933): 250-1; N.J.
            Abercrombie, DUBR 193 (December 1933): 306-8;
            Thomas F. Coakley, COMMWL 19 (22 December
            1933): 218-9; AMER 50 (30 December 1933): 306;
            Joseph T. Durkin, S.J., THOUGHT 9 (September
            1934): 326-7.

1118. Morris, Kevin L. "The Cambridge Converts and the
      Oxford Movement." RH 17 (October 1985): 386-98.

      Sketches the lives and spiritual development of
      Ambrose Phillipps de Lisle, George Spencer, and
      Kenelm Henry Digby. All three came from upper-class

backgrounds, attended Trinity College, Cambridge,
and converted within the same four-year period.
Their self-imposed mission to convert English
Protestants, combined with their intellectual
distinction, would later inspire the Tractarians.

1119. Morrison, John L. "The Oxford Movement and the
         British Periodicals." CHR 45 (July 1959): 137-
         60.

       Provides glimpses into the British public's
       perception of the role played by resurgent Roman
       Catholicism in the Oxford Movement.

                    Phillipps de Lisle

1120. Allen, Louis. "Ambrose Phillipps de Lisle, 1809-
         1878." CHR 40 (April 1954): 1-26.

       Justifies his honored place in nineteenth-century
       Catholic history on two grounds: (1) he was actively
       involved in a good deal of the most important
       religious activity of his day; and (2) his perception
       of situations was more often than not quite accurate.
       Looks at de Lisle's twentieth-century "biographical
       fate," life, and views (e.g., on corporate reunion,
       Anglican orders, and ecclesiastical politics).

1121. Purcell, Edmund Sheridan. LIFE AND LETTERS OF
         AMBROSE PHILLIPPS DE LISLE. London: Macmillan,
         1900. 2 vols.

       A detailed biography of a key layman of the
       English Catholic revival. A convert at fourteen,
       de Lisle devoted the rest of his life to the Church.
       Allied with Shrewsbury and Norfolk, the premier
       Catholic peers of the realm, he brought the Trappists
       to England, built monasteries and chapels throughout
       the country, and reintroduced primitive ecclesiastical
       chant. His correspondence with Montalembert, Newman,
       Gladstone, and Aubrey de Vere testifies to the degree
       of his commitment to promote Catholic interests. On
       the other hand, his work for the Association for the
       Promotion of the Unity of Christendom points to his
       equally strong ecumenical concern.

See: CW 70 (March 1900): 841-2; CW 71 (April
       1900): 131-6; J.H. Rigg, LQR 95 (April
       1901): 393-5; DUBR 130 (January 1902): 182-5.

The Wards

*   Eigelsbach, Jo Ann. "The Intellectual Dialogue of
       Friedrich von Hügel and Wilfrid Ward." Cited
       above as item 293.

1122. Hoppen, K. Theodore. "Church, State, and Ultra-
       montanism in Mid-Victorian England: The Case
       of William George Ward." JCS 18 (Spring
       1976): 289-309.

       Elucidates Ward's views on the proper theoretical
       relationship between Church and State. Explains why
       these views were popular among both the Victorian
       clergy and laity. Includes biographical background
       on Ward, showing his almost lifelong concern over the
       problems associated with the relationship between
       Rome and England.

1123. ————. "W.G. Ward and Liberal Catholicism." JEH 23
       (October 1972): 323-44.

       Demonstrates how necessary Ward's thought was to a
       sectarian situation in which English Catholic intel-
       lectual life still largely re-echoed the language,
       terms, and concerns of the Oxford Movement. As the
       foremost English ultramontane intellectual, Ward
       broadened Catholic horizons, appealing to ideas
       which, even if more often ignored than understood,
       won the general approval of most of the hierarchy.

*   Neill, Thomas P. "Wilfrid Ward." THEY LIVED THE
       FAITH (item 33), 325-48.

       Contends that Ward taught English Catholics the
       necessity of opening up to the world and assimilating
       modern developments into their outlook. In so doing,
       he won for the Church the respect of all thinking
       English people.

1124. Ward, Maisie. "W.G. Ward and Wilfrid Ward."

DUBR 198 (April/May/June 1936):   235-52.

Compares and contrasts father and son. Notes their
editorship of the *Dublin Review* (for W.G., 1862-1878;
for Wilfrid, 1906-1916). Stresses, however, two key
differences in outlook and interests: while the
father advocated a "fortress mentality" for the
English Church, and thus showed interest only in
theology and philosophy, the son opted for Catholic
openness to the world, and enjoined his coreligionists
to interest themselves in the widest possible range of
human activities.

1125.   ————.   THE WILFRID WARDS AND THE TRANSITION. New
        York: Sheed & Ward, 1934-7. 2 vols.

Fixes Ward's life within the leading developments
of English Catholicism between 1892 and 1916. Emphasizes his conservative views and deference to
authority, in order to counter lingering suspicions
of his strong modernist sympathies. Though written
by an admiring daughter, the two massive volumes
present a responsible assessment of his contributions
to the faith in England. In addition to his
biographies of W.G. Ward, Wiseman, and Newman, and
editorship of the *Dublin Review*, he urged Catholics
to fight agnosticism and scepticism by adapting to
changing philosophical and cultural contexts. At the
same time, he emphasized the need for ecclesiastical
reform of a type which would enrich, rather than
unsettle, people's spiritual lives. As he brought
his brand of Catholic intellectualism into the public
forum, he broadened the nation's interest in—and
admiration for—the faith of Rome.

See: (for vol. 1) Hugh Gray, BKMN 87 (December
        1934): 176; Joseph McSorley, CW (December
        1934): 367; Dom Fabian Pole, DR 53 (April
        1935): 153-63; William H. McCabe, AMER 53
        (27 April 1935): 67; Henry Tristram, Cong.
        Orat., DUBR 197 (April/May/June 1935): 292-
        303; CLR 10 (July 1935): 65-8; H.L. Stewart,
        DALR 15 (July 1935): 256-7; Anselm M.
        Townsend, O.P., CHR 21 (October 1935): 348-9.
        (for vol. 2) David Mathew, BLACK 19 (February
        1938): 151-3; Raymond Corrigan, S.J., HB
        16 (March 1938): 56; Joseph McSorley,

CW 147 (April 1938): 110-12; Dom Fabian Pole,
DR 56 (April 1938): 149-58; CLR 15 (September
1938): 269-72; Edward Hawks, CHR 24 (October
1938): 354-5; W.J. Williams, IHS 1 (March
1939): 317-8.

1126. Ward, Wilfrid. WILLIAM GEORGE WARD AND THE CATHOLIC
REVIVAL. London and New York: Macmillan, 1893.

Mixes biography and history. As the former, it
examines Ward's contentious personality, conservative
outlook, and stormy career. As the latter, it points
to selected key episodes of the revival in which Ward
played a part. A pendant to item 1127.

See: CW 57 (July 1893): 584-5; LQR 80 (July
1893): 378; NATION 57 (24 August 1893): 140-1;
LQR 81 (October 1893): 143-64; AMER 8 (25
January 1913): 379; CW 97 (September 1913): 827.

1127. ————. WILLIAM GEORGE WARD AND THE OXFORD MOVEMENT.
2nd ed. London and New York: Macmillan, 1890.

Less restrained in its interpretation than its
sister volume (item 1126). Seems to transfer
intellectual leadership of the Oxford Movement from
Newman to Ward, as it shows the future ultramontanist
in constant theological combat with opponents of
every stripe.

See: SPEC 62 (25 May 1889): 713-4; DUBR 105 (July
1889): 213-6; ACQR 14 (October 1889): 755-7;
LQR 73 (October 1889): 130-53; Margaret F.
Sullivan, CW 50 (November 1889): 155-63; CW
50 (December 1889): 405-10; CW 50 (February
1890): 597-606; DUBR 106 (April 1890): 467-8;
LQR 74 (April 1890): 183.

Gasquet

1128. Baer, Alban, O.S.B. "The Careers of Cardinal
Gasquet." ABR 5 (Summer 1954): 113-22.

A brief biography of the English prelate who most
faithfully and consistently symbolized all that was

best in the Church of his day. Enumerates his many
roles,--controversialist, apologist, friend of intellectuals, reviser of the Vulgate, and Abbot President
of the English Benedictines,--noting that although he
was not a natural leader, he was always in the
religious vanguard.

1129. Fowler, Abbot. "Cardinal Gasquet at Downside." DR
       47 (May 1929): 123-31.

       Recalls Gasquet's fifteen active years (1870-1885)
       at Downside, the final seven of which he spent as
       Conventual Prior. During that time he not only
       improved the educational facilities but also built a
       large portion of the monastic church.

1130. Knowles, Dom David. "Cardinal Gasquet as an
       Historian." In THE HISTORIAN AND CHARACTER, AND
       OTHER ESSAYS, 240-63. Cambridge: At the
       University Press, 1963.

       Maintains that while Gasquet neither founded a
       school nor initiated a new specialization, and
       though he proffered no germinal idea or interpre-
       tation, he did leave an enormous impact upon the
       study of medieval history, for it was he who in-
       spired the late nineteenth century's interest in
       Tudor monastic life.

       See: Oliver J.G. Welch, DUBR 231 (Winter 1957): 375-
             8; H.A. Cronne, HIST 49 (February 1964): 54-5;
             J.G. Rowe, CH 33 (March 1964): 99-100; Aubrey
             Gwynn, IHS 14 (March 1964): 93-5; Martin R.P.
             McGuire, CHR 50 (April 1964): 111; James Lea
             Cate, AHR 70 (January 1965): 420-2; R.W.
             Southern, EHR 80 (July 1965): 570-1.

1131. Kuypers, Dom Benedict. "Cardinal Gasquet in London."
       DR 47 (May 1929): 132-49.

       Outlines the nature and extent of Gasquet's
       historical research in the British Museum and
       Public Record Office, done at the request of
       Manning, who ordered the Prior of Downside to
       the capital in 1885, as a result of Leo XIII's
       encouragement of historical studies. Appends a
       list of Gasquet's publications from 1890 to 1912.

1132.   Leslie, Shane. CARDINAL GASQUET: A MEMOIR. New
        York: P.J. Kenedy & Sons, 1954.

        Not a full biography, but an outline of some of
        the many activities of a cleric who belongs with
        Wiseman, Manning, and Newman in any account of
        nineteenth-century English Catholicism. Using
        Gasquet's diaries, fragmentary autobiography, and
        enormous correspondence, Leslie touches on his
        achievements as monastic reformer, Prior of Down-
        side, Abbot President of the English Benedictines,
        historian, chairman of the Pontifical Commission
        for the revision of the Vulgate, curial cardinal,
        and Librarian and Archivist of the Holy Roman
        Church.

        See: CLR 39 (March 1954): 176-7; R.G.G. Price,
              PUNCH 226 (3 March 1954): 302; QR 292
              (April 1954): 269-70; Gerald Ellard, HB 32
              (May 1954): 234-5; Florence D. Cohalan,
              CHR 40 (July 1954): 206-7; J.J. Hennessey,
              THOUGHT 29 (Winter 1954-5): 632-3.

1133.   Morey, Adrian. "Cardinal Gasquet the Historian."
        CHR 15 (October 1929): 262-74.

        Discusses Gasquet's commitment to the writing of
        Church history, which he saw as a means of advancing
        religious belief and strengthening the Church.

                              Mivart

1134.   Gruber, Jacob W. A CONSCIENCE IN CONFLICT: THE LIFE
        OF ST. GEORGE JACKSON MIVART. New York: Columbia
        University Press, 1960.

        Recounts Mivart's struggle and eventual failure to
        unite the truths of Catholicism and Darwinism.
        Though not a pure Darwinist, for he accepted
        structural and physical, but not intellectual or
        spiritual, evolution, he attempted to convince his
        fellow Catholics of the respectability of biology;
        though not a born Catholic--he converted at seven-
        teen--he sought to persuade the Victorian scientific
        community of the Church's liberality. In the end,

neither side was convinced, despite Mivart's self-confidence; shortly before he died, he abjured the faith.

See: Shane Leslie, WR 235 (Spring 1961): 48-55; Joseph Allan Panuska, S.J., VS 4 (June 1961): 363-4; John J. O'Connor, CHR 47 (July 1961): 245-6; Bert James Loewenberg, ISIS 53 (December 1962): 538-40.

1135. Root, John D. "The Final Apostasy of St. George Jackson Mivart." CHR 71 (January 1985): 1-25.

Explains Mivart's sudden religious volte-face on his deathbed. Argues that his apostasy was quite real, an accurate expression of his theological outlook during the last years of his life.

1136. Windle, Bertram C.A. "Memories of St. George Mivart." DUBR 173 (July/August/September 1923): 70-85.

Examines Mivart's place in the Victorian scientific community, with special reference to his relationship with Darwin.

Other Thinkers

1137. Abercrombie, Nigel. THE LIFE AND WORK OF EDMUND BISHOP. London: Longmans, Green, 1959.

A heavily detailed study of one of late nineteenth-century England's most important liturgical scholars and historians of the medieval Church. Converted in 1867, he settled at Downside in 1885, but without ever joining the Benedictines. There he produced liturgical studies and corresponded with some of the leading Catholic intellectuals of the day, including Gasquet. Offers insights into daily life at Downside, as well as glimpses into larger events affecting the life and viewpoint of educated Catholics like Bishop.

See: E. Long, ITQ 27 (January 1960): 80-1; George Every, S.S.M., THEO 63 (February 1960): 75-7; Eric John, DUBR 234 (Spring 1960): 52-67; IER 93 (June 1960): 416-8; Dom Wilfrid Passmore,

DR 78 (Summer 1960): 247-51; Stephen J. Tonsor,
AHR 65 (July 1960): 957; R.J. Schoeck, VS 4
(September 1960): 79-81; E.E.Y. Hales, CHR 47
(April 1961): 36-8.

1138. Allies Mary H. THOMAS WILLIAM ALLIES. London: Burns
& Oates/New York: Benziger Brothers, 1907.

A biography by his daughter. Emphasizes his high
level of spirituality, which Allies cultivated after
discovering, upon his conversion, that his adopted
Church could find no official use for his talents.
His sole escape from obscurity came through his role
as secretary of the Catholic Poor School Commission
(1853-1890).

See: CW 86 (November 1907): 258-9.

1139. Barry, William. "William Samuel Lilly." DUBR 165
(October/November/December 1919): 192-208.

Sketches the life and career of a leading defender
of Catholicism in late nineteenth-century England.
Himself a convert, Lilly considered Rome the source
of all Christian history; Anglicanism, on the other
hand, was a sixteenth-century nationalistic sect.
His apologetic writings had an enormous impact upon
the average English Catholic.

1140. Hoskins, W.G. "George Oliver, D.D., 1781-1861." DR
79 (Autumn 1961): 334-48.

Concentrates not on Oliver's more than fifty years
as a priest, but rather on his historical works,
which studied the monasteries, churches, and great
Catholic families of Devonshire, as well as the city
of Exeter.

1141. Mathew, David. "English Spiritual Writers: VI.
Provost Husenbeth." CLR 44 (May 1959): 257-64.

Introduces the little-known work of John Frederick
Husenbeth (1797-1872), whose fourteen books included
the lives of various saints, biographies of Bishop
Milner and Msgr. Weedall, and a history of Sedgley
Park, the seminary-college to which he was tied
throughout his life.

Education

General

1142. Gilbert, Sir John. "The Catholic Church and Edu-
       cation." In CATHOLIC EMANCIPATION, 1829 TO
       1929: ESSAYS BY VARIOUS WRITERS (item 761),
       45-76.

       Emphasizes the political obstacles to nineteenth-
       century Catholic educational development in England.

1143. Murphy, James. CHURCH, STATE AND SCHOOLS IN BRITAIN,
       1800-1970. London: Routledge & Kegan Paul,
       1971.

       Specifies the Catholic role in the complex
       nineteenth-century evolution of the religious
       question in British education. Delineates the
       impact of the "Irish System" of 1831; the Catholic
       withdrawal from the Liverpool Corporation School
       Plan, 1842; the Catholic Poor School Committee's
       rejection of the first offer of state aid for
       religious institutions, 1847; and the laity's
       critical reaction to the Education Act of 1870.

       See: Gillian Sutherland, HIST 57 (October
             1972): 449.

                 Primary and Secondary Schools

1144. Battersby, W.J., F.S.C. "Secondary Education for
       Boys." In THE ENGLISH CATHOLICS, 1850-
       1870: CENTENARY ESSAYS TO COMMEMORATE THE
       RESTORATION OF THE HIERARCHY (item 759), 322-36.

       Traces the phenomenal growth and serious
       deficiencies of both the well-known "Old Schools,"
       covered in item 1151, and the smaller and less
       ambitious Catholic institutions, founded for the
       most part after 1840.

1145. Beales, A.C.F. "The Struggle for the Schools."

In THE ENGLISH CATHOLICS, 1850-1950: CENTENARY
ESSAYS TO COMMEMORATE THE RESTORATION OF THE
HIERARCHY (item 759), 365-409.

Relates the organizational, financial, and political
problems faced by the nineteenth-century bishops in
their efforts to establish primary education for the
average Catholic.

1146. Bland, Sister Joan, S.N.D. "The Impact of Government
on English Catholic Education, 1870-1902." CHR 62
(January 1976): 36-55.

Assesses the long-term impact of the Education Act
of 1870 on English Catholic education. Concludes that
the legislation led to the creation of more and better
religious schools, while at the same time showing that
the Church was willing to cooperate with the government on the issue of compulsory education.

1147. Gaine, Michael. "The Development of Official Roman
Catholic Educational Policy in England and Wales."
In RELIGIOUS EDUCATION: DRIFT OR DECISION?,
edited by Dom Philip Jebb, 137-64.
London: Darton, Longman and Todd, 1968.

Reconstructs the Catholic position in the struggle
over denominational education in Victorian England.
Before 1850, as seen in the Liverpool interdenomi-
national venture, not all English Catholics were
concerned about isolating their children from those
of their non-Catholic neighbors; after mid-century,
however, the outlook changed radically, as Catholic
schools were considered absolutely necessary to
safeguard the children's faith.

1148. McClelland, Vincent Alan. "The Liberal Training of
England's Catholic Youth: William Joseph Petre
(1847-93) and Educational Reform." VS 15 (March
1972): 257-77.

Investigates Petre's innovative school at Woburn
Park, its origins, philosophy, and ultimate failure.
Three years after his ordination, Petre published a
pamphlet denouncing Jesuit education for its
narrowness and harshness; there was absolutely no
individuality or freedom at an institution like

Stonyhurst. Woburn Park, opened in 1877, deemphasized
the classics, encouraged private study, and allowed
students to make decisions on important aspects of
academic life. The experiment lasted a mere five
years, for parents found it too novel, and refused to
send their children.

1149.   ————. "The Protestant Alliance and Roman Catholic
          Schools, 1872-74." VS 8 (December 1964): 173-82.

          Looks into the conflict between the violently anti-
          Catholic Protestant Alliance and the Catholic hierarchy
          over the latter's violation of the Education Act of
          1870. Portrays a conciliatory Manning, who ordered
          his clerics to comply strictly with the law's
          restrictions on the amount and type of religious
          training permitted in the classroom.

1150.   Murphy, James. THE RELIGIOUS PROBLEM IN ENGLISH
          EDUCATION: THE CRUCIAL EXPERIMENT.
          Liverpool: Liverpool University Press, 1959.

          The fullest treatment of the seven-year (1836-1842)
          Liverpool Corporation School Plan, an experiment to
          determine whether children of all faiths could be
          educated together in public elementary schools.
          Though initially successful, since it received the
          warm support of both Protestants and Catholics, the
          program broke down after the latter's withdrawal,
          in the wake of a change in rules which forbade the
          classroom use of any other Bible than the Authorized
          Version.

          See: P.J. Dowling, DUBR 233 (Autumn 1959): 281-3;
                Neville Masterman, HIST 45 (October 1960): 277-
                8; G.H. Bantock, VS 4 (December 1960): 167-70;
                John Whitney Evans, CHR 46 (January 1961): 487-
                9; W.H.G. Armytage, EHR 76 (April 1961): 369-
                70.

          Colleges, Universities, and Adult Education

1151.   Barnes, Arthur Stapylton. THE CATHOLIC SCHOOLS OF
          ENGLAND. London: Williams and Norgate, 1926.

Chapters 9 to 15 are short accounts of the nine
major Catholic institutions of higher learning in
the nineteenth century. Whether secular (Old Hall,
Ushaw, Oscott), Jesuit (Stonyhurst, Beaumont),
Benedictine (Downside, Ampleforth, Douai), or
Oratorian, each school is analyzed according to a
common set of criteria, which includes overall
facilities, church or chapel, library, daily
routine, teaching, recreational offerings,
theatrical activity, and discipline and punishments.

See: DR 45 (January 1927): 87-8.

1152. Beales, A.C.F. "Catholic Higher Institutes: The
       Historical Backlog." WR 236 (Spring 1962): 70-
       87.

       Surveys a number of English Catholic initiatives
       in the field of higher education during the
       nineteenth century, including Newman's Irish
       venture, various Jesuit projects, episcopal
       encouragement and support, and the Kensington
       scheme.

1153. Buscot, W. THE HISTORY OF COTTON COLLEGE: AT
       SEDGLEY PARK, 1763-1873; AT COTTON, 1873-.
       London: Burns Oates & Washbourne, 1940.

       Points to the College's central place in the
       history of nineteenth-century English Catholicism.
       Virtually every major personality and movement of
       the "Second Spring" had some association with this
       oldest of all Catholic schools in England: Shrews-
       bury bought Cotton Hall for the Church's use; Faber
       and his followers were among its first guests; it
       was the cradle of the Oratory and, for a time,
       Newman's home; and its chapel is Pugin in his
       most engaging simplicity.

       See: Philip Hughes, TABLET 176 (6 July 1940): 13;
             DUBR 207 (October 1940): 259-60.

1154. Coyne, John J. "A Forgotten Plan: The Leonine
       College." CLR 25 (January 1945): 6-15.

       Examines the frustrating and frustrated efforts of

the late 1890s to convert Oscott College into a central seminary for the dioceses of the Midlands and the South.

1155. Croft, William. HISTORICAL ACCOUNT OF LISBON COLLEGE, WITH A REGISTER COMPILED BY JOSEPH GILLOW, ESQ. Barnet: St. Andrew's Press, 1902.

Chapters 9 to 15 offer an anecdotal account of nineteenth-century developments. Stresses the crucial role of the Presidents in the realization of the College's goal, which was to train secular clergy for missionary work in England. The final one hundred pages of the book contain biographical data on alumni.

1156. Evennett, H.O. "Catholics and the Universities." In THE ENGLISH CATHOLICS, 1850-1950: CENTENARY ESSAYS TO COMMEMORATE THE RESTORATION OF THE HIERARCHY (item 759), 291-321.

Follows the mishandled attempts to found a Catholic University College during the later decades of the nineteenth century. Concentrates on Manning's ideas and initiatives--e.g., the Kensington scheme--and their redirection by Vaughan in 1895. Attributes the failure to create a national Catholic university to several factors, including, most notably, the comparative poverty of Catholic intellectual resources and the lack of coordination among them.

1157. Gasquet, F.A. A HISTORY OF THE VENERABLE ENGLISH COLLEGE, ROME: AN ACCOUNT OF ITS ORIGINS AND WORK FROM THE EARLIEST TIMES TO THE PRESENT DAY. London: Longmans, Green, 1920.

Chapters 11 and 12 sketch the College's history from its reopening in 1818, after twenty years of inactivity, through Wiseman's successful rectorate of 1828-1840. The Conclusion carries the story to the end of the century.

See: William Barry, DUBR 166 (April/May/June 1920): 235-55; George McN. Rushforth, EHR 35 (July 1920): 468-9; DR 39 (July 1921): 141-3.

1158. Holmes, J. Derek. "The Lisbon Letter-Books of

Edmund Winstanley, 1819-1852." CLR 60 (April 1975): 236-52.

Uses the large correspondence of the President of the English College, Lisbon, to detail the difficulties of administering an overseas seminary. Reveals a host of chronic problems, such as an understaffed and overworked faculty and severe financial shortages.

1159. McClelland, Vincent Alan. ENGLISH ROMAN CATHOLICS AND HIGHER EDUCATION, 1830-1903. Oxford: Clarendon Press, 1973.

Examines the struggle of English Roman Catholics to create a philosophy and structure of higher education which would enable them to come to terms with the larger society within which they had to function.

See: ECON 246 (13 January 1973): 78-9; TLS, 16 March 1973: 299; J.H. Whyte, CLR 58 (April 1973): 318-21; Michael P. Fogarty, ECSOR 4 (July 1973): 599-600; CHOICE 10 (September 1973): 1061-2; Edward Norman, JTS 24 (October 1973): 623-4; Sheldon Rothblatt, AHR 78 (December 1973): 1466-7; A.E. Firth, EHR 89 (April 1974): 454-5; J.S. Hurt, HIST 59 (June 1974): 290-1; Sheridan Gilley, VS 17 (June 1974): 443-5; Alfred Gilbey, AMPJ 79 (Summer 1974): 88-90; Richard J. Schiefen, CHR 63 (October 1977): 600-2; Eamon Duffy, JEH 29 (October 1978): 499-500.

1160. ————. "Wiseman, Manning, and the 'Accademia': An Experiment in English Adult Education." PH 11 (1971): 414-25.

Reviews the founding and development of an educational agency designed to bring converts, immigrant Irish, and "Old Catholics" more closely together by helping them to understand each other's point of view. Set up by Wiseman in 1861, and modelled after the Roman Accademia di Religione Cattolica, it not only sought to integrate Catholics more quickly and effectively into national life, but also served as a watchdog against scientific error. Under Manning the Accademia expanded its functions

to include the teaching of morals, politics, and
history.

1161. Milburn, David. A HISTORY OF USHAW COLLEGE: A STUDY
       OF THE ORIGIN, FOUNDATION AND DEVELOPMENT OF AN
       ENGLISH CATHOLIC SEMINARY WITH AN EPILOGUE, 1808-
       1962. Durham: Ushaw College, 1964.

       A survey of the College's Presidents, problems,
       conflicts, and achievements, all of which were
       overshadowed by its continuing identity crisis: was
       Ushaw primarily a perpetuation of Douai, a Tridentine
       seminary, or a diocesan seminary? Highlights
       Wiseman's and Manning's relationship with the school,
       and the latter's decision of 1884 to subordinate it
       to the collective authority of the northern bishops.

       See: Philip Hughes, CHR 50 (January 1965): 588-9;
             A.C.F. Beales, JEH 16 (April 1965): 116.

1162. Moriarty, Provost. "'Men of Little Showing'
       (7): Bishop Giles." CLR 2 (December
       1931): 513-20.

       A portrait of the Vice-Rector, and later Rector,
       of the English College in Rome (1867-1913). His
       total commitment to the College made him the prime
       representative in the very heart of Catholicism of
       all the best features of the English Church.

   *   Roche, J.S. A HISTORY OF PRIOR PARK COLLEGE AND ITS
       FOUNDER, BISHOP BAINES. Cited above as item 883.

       Describes the checkered development of the
       institution founded by Baines in 1830, sold by
       Archbishop Errington in 1856, repurchased and
       reopened by Bishop Clifford in 1866, and closed
       by Bishop Brownlow in 1894.

1163. Root, John D. "The 'Academia of the Catholic
       Religion': Catholic Intellectualism in
       Victorian England." VS 23 (Summer 1980): 461-
       78.

       Details the goals, membership, and educational
       services of the Academia, from its founding by
       Wiseman in 1861, to the establishment of its first

branch at Manchester in 1876. Maintains that rather than being a unifying force among English Catholic intellectuals, as both Wiseman and Manning had hoped, the Academia only hastened their division into (often hostile) parties.

1164. Villiers, Arthur. "'Men of Little Showing' (2): Provost Northcote, Rector of Oscott, 1860 to 1877." CLR 2 (July 1931): 38-46.

Demonstrates how almost singlehandedly, and by dint of hard work, zeal, and extraordinary talent, Dr. James Spencer Northcote resurrected Oscott, which had deteriorated both intellectually and physically. His complete overhaul of the educational system made the College the leading center of Catholic higher education in England.

1165. Whitehead, Maurice. "The Jesuit Contribution to Science and Technical Education in Late-Nineteenth-Century Liverpool." AS 43 (July 1986): 353-68.

Illustrates how the Jesuits of St. Francis Xavier College, Liverpool, adapted their curriculum during the last quarter of the nineteenth century to the demands of the major commercial and industrial center in which they taught. After critical examination of their teaching, they moved away rapidly from classical training, directing their efforts toward such areas as chemistry, physics, and manual instruction. So important a departure from the centuries-old RATIO STUDIORUM introduced a new era in the history of Jesuit education in England.

1166. Williams, Michael E. ST. ALBAN'S COLLEGE, VALLADOLID: FOUR CENTURIES OF ENGLISH CATHOLIC PRESENCE IN SPAIN. London: C. Hurst/New York: St. Martin's Press, 1986.

Chapters 8 to 10 relate the nineteenth-century problems and progress of the institution founded by the Jesuits in 1589 to train priests for the English mission. Analyzes the College's development from the viewpoint of its rectors or administrators, among whom John Guest (1846-1878) is singled out for his moderately successful efforts to establish a

closer and more formal relationship between the
College and the newly restored English hierarchy.
The appendices discuss student life and the
school's archival holdings.

See: Aidan Bellenger, DR 105 (July 1987): 245-6;
      Philip Caraman, S.J., THS 48 (December
      1987): 790.

1167. ————. THE VENERABLE ENGLISH COLLEGE, ROME: A
       HISTORY, 1579-1979. London: Associated Catholic
       Publications, 1979.

Chapters 4 to 7 offer a detailed account of the
College during the nineteenth century, set against
the twin backgrounds of Papal politics and English
Catholic life. Surveys developments within the
context of its nine rectors between the reopening
of 1818 and 1900. Singles out Wiseman (1828-1840)
for his success in rebuilding the institution's
fame, Robert Cornthwaite (1851-1857) for his
establishment of the Collegio Pio and renewal of
the link between the English College and the Jesuits
of the Roman College, and William Giles (1888-1913)
for his encouragement of a family atmosphere.

See: Adrian Morey, JEH 32 (October 1981): 557;
      J. O'Higgins, EHR 97 (April 1982): 420-1.

The Press

1168. Altholz, Josef L. *"The Month*, 1864-1900." VPR 14
       (Summer 1981): 70-2.

A sketch of one of Victorian England's most
successful Catholic periodicals. Founded in 1864
by Fanny Margaret Taylor, in an effort to provide
educated readers with a lighter and freer fare
than that usually found in the Catholic press, it
was taken over by the Jesuits in the following
year. The highly capable Jesuit editors dispensed
with the foundress' approach, bringing to the
reader an ever more serious tone, which caused it
to become involved in most of the significant
religious controversies during the last quarter

of the century.

1169. ———. "The Redaction of Catholic Periodicals." In
INNOVATORS AND PREACHERS: THE ROLE OF THE EDITOR
IN VICTORIAN ENGLAND, edited by Joel H. Wiener,
143-60. Contributions to the Study of Mass Media
and Communication, Number 5. Westport,
Conn.: Greenwood Press, 1985.

Follows the narrowing and growing profession-
alization of nineteenth-century English Catholic
editorial structures, as they passed from single-
handed management to control by several persons
and, finally, to the corporate staff.

See: Neil Berry, TLS, 20 June 1986: 688; R.T.
Van Arsdel, CHOICE 23 (July/August 1986): 1676;
Catherine Gallagher, AHR 92 (June 1987): 662-4;
Walter L. Arnstein, RSR 13 (July 1987): 269;
James J. Barnes, VS 30 (Winter 1987): 275-7.

1170. ———. "The *Tablet*, the *True Tablet*, and Nothing
but the *Tablet*." VPN 9 (June 1976): 68-72.

Follows the humorously complex and contention-
filled first decade of the journal which would
become in 1892 the official organ of the Archdiocese
of Westminster.

1171. Braybrooke, Neville. "Two Editors: Wilfrid Ward and
Wilfrid Meynell: Their Contribution to the
Catholic Literary Revival." DUBR 228 (Spring
1954): 46-52.

Considers Ward and Meynell the founders of the
Catholic periodical press in England. Praises their
ability to understand the climate of their age.

1172. Dwyer, J.J. "The Catholic Press, 1850-1950." In THE
ENGLISH CATHOLICS, 1850-1950: CENTENARY ESSAYS TO
COMMEMORATE THE RESTORATION OF THE HIERARCHY (item
759), 475-514.

Discusses the founding, aims, specialties, and
influence of the *Dublin Review*, the *Rambler*, *The
Month*, and other less prominent journals of
nineteenth-century origin.

1173. Fletcher, John R. "Early Catholic Periodicals in
        England." DUBR 198 (April/May/June 1936): 284-
        310.

        Includes an annotated listing of journals founded
        between 1801 and 1878. Provides useful information
        on founders and editors, title changes (if any), and
        statements of purpose.

1174. Gwynn, Denis. "The Centenary of the *Dublin Review*."
        CLR 11 (May 1936): 372-80.

        A brief narrative of the journal's origins,
        purpose, editors, and contributors.

1175. ———. "The *Dublin Review* and the Catholic Press."
        DUBR 198 (April/May/June 1936): 311-21.

        Places the *Review* in the larger contexts of
        Victorian England and the "Second Spring."

1176. ———. "Heralds of the Second Spring: VIII.
        Frederick Lucas." CLR 30 (November 1948): 310-
        27.

        Features the life and journalistic career of one
        of the most remarkable of all converts to play a role
        in the "Second Spring." In 1840, one year after his
        conversion from Quakerism, Lucas founded *The Tablet*,
        which quickly established a reputation for well-
        informed and dignified Catholic commentary upon the
        issues of the day.

1177. Holland, Mary Griset. THE BRITISH CATHOLIC PRESS AND
        THE EDUCATIONAL CONTROVERSY, 1847-1865. New
        York: Garland Publishing, 1987.

        Examines Catholic press coverage of the highly
        controversial question of state aid to Catholic
        schools. Focuses on the attitudes expressed by
        sixteen publications, to show that Catholics were
        quite concerned about and deeply divided by this
        issue. Concludes also that this controversy
        deepened already existing tensions between the
        press and the hierarchy, English and Irish Catholics
        in England, and liberals and ultramontanes.

* Horgan, John J. "Frederick Lucas, M.P.: The Founder
  of the *Tablet*." GREAT CATHOLIC LAYMEN (item 31),
  203-46.

  Evaluates Lucas' journalistic campaign to improve
  the Church's position in England. Praises his faith
  and perseverance in the midst of numerous setbacks
  in his public life.

* McElrath, Damian, O.F.M. "Richard Simpson and Count
  de Montalembert, the *Rambler* and the *Correspondant*."
  Cited above as item 473.

* ————. "Richard Simpson and John Henry Newman: The
  Rambler, Laymen, and Theology." Cited above as
  item 962.

1178. Ryan, Guy. "The Acton Circle and the *Chronicle*."
  VPN 7 (June 1974): 10-24.

  Profiles the short-lived but scholarly successor
  to the *Home and Foreign Review*, founded by Thomas
  Frederick Wetherell and other followers of Acton
  in 1867. Looks into the nature of its subject
  matter and its liberal perspective, which delighted
  secular critics but drew nothing but complaints from
  Manning, Newman, Ullathorne, and other clerics.
  Attributes its demise in February 1868 to a lack of
  subscribers and severe financial problems.

1179. Tristram, Henry, Cong. Orat. "Cardinal Newman and
  the *Dublin Review*." DUBR 198 (April/May/June
  1936): 221-34.

  Studies the ongoing relationship between the
  journal and the writer. Argues that it was the
  Dublin Review which forced the Anglican churchman
  to recognize and confront the issue of Catholicity,
  a confrontation which led him to Rome some nine
  years after the *Review* was founded. Sees Newman's
  contributions to the *Review*--e.g., his articles on
  papal infallibility and Catholic higher education--as
  some of his best work.

1180. Walsh, Leo J. WILLIAM G. WARD AND THE *DUBLIN REVIEW*.
  Ph.D. dissertation. Columbia University, 1962.

A biography, focusing on Ward's years as editor of
the *Dublin Review* (1863-1870). Describes how Ward,
one of the lay leaders of ultramontanism in England,
used the journal to thwart liberal Catholicism.
Includes material on his post-1870 activity, e.g.,
his opposition to Newman on papal infallibility, the
temporal power, and Catholic higher education; his
correspondence with Mill; and his literary campaign
against phenomenology.

Piety and Devotion

1181.   Champ, Judith F.   "Bishop Milner, Holywell and the
        Cure Tradition."   In THE CHURCH AND HEALING: PAPERS
        READ AT THE TWENTIETH SUMMER MEETING AND THE TWENTY-
        FIRST WINTER MEETING OF THE ECCLESIASTICAL HISTORY
        SOCIETY (item 28), 153-64.

        Analyzes the mounting popularity of the miraculous
        spring of Holywell through the nineteenth century.
        Though the site enjoyed a thaumaturgic reputation
        since the twelfth century, it was only after Winefrid
        White's dramatic cure in 1805 that it became "the
        English Lourdes."   Milner's investigation and
        verification of the miracle not only reinforced the
        Tridentine concept of a bishop actively involved in
        the affairs of his area, but also brought Catholicism
        back into English public awareness.

1182.   Charles, Conrad, C.P.   "The Origins of the Parish
        Mission in England and the Early Passionist
        Apostolate, 1840-1850."   JEH 15 (April 1964):   60-
        75.

        Reviews the Passionists' introduction of Forty
        Hours Devotion, the renewal of baptismal vows, and
        other religious practices into England.

1183.   Gilley, Sheridan.   "Vulgar Piety and the Brompton
        Oratory, 1850-1860."   In THE IRISH IN THE
        VICTORIAN CITY (item 1092), 255-66.

        Demonstrates how on a local pastoral level
        Catholicism was defined for the immigrant Irish
        community, using ultramontane forms of popular

devotion, introduced into England by Hutchinson,
Faber, and others.

1184.   Goodier, Alban, S.J. "The Catholic Church and the
        Spiritual Life." In CATHOLIC EMANCIPATION, 1829
        TO 1929: ESSAYS BY VARIOUS WRITERS (item 761),
        23-44.

        Looks at diverse aspects of nineteenth-century
        English Catholic spirituality.

   *   Pourrat, Pierre, S.S. "English Spirituality."
        CHRISTIAN SPIRITUALITY. Vol. 4: FROM
        JANSENISM TO MODERN TIMES (item 319), 435-67.

        Details the contributions of Wiseman, Ullathorne,
        Hedley, Newman, Faber, and Manning to the revival
        of spiritual devotion within nineteenth-century
        English Catholicism.

1185.   Sharp, John. "Juvenile Holiness: Catholic
        Revivalism among Children in Victorian Britain."
        JEH 35 (April 1984): 220-38.

        Details the apostolate of John Joseph Furniss
        (1809-1865), whose breakthroughs and setbacks were
        typical of those known by pioneers of large-scale
        Catholic revivalist work among Victorian youth.

                    The Liturgical Movement

1186.   Sandeman, Dame Frideswide, O.S.B. "Laurence
        Shepherd, 1825-85: Apostle of Guéranger."
        AMPJ 80 (Autumn 1975): 38-47.

        Presents the personality and work of the priest
        who introduced French liturgical reform and
        plainchant into the English Church. As a result of
        his almost yearly visits to Solesmes, Shepherd
        established a close friendship with Guéranger,
        following his advice on everything from the monastic
        life to theology, history, and patrology. In
        England, and as chaplain of a community of nuns at
        Stanbrook, he served as a conduit through which
        Guéranger's ideals spread throughout the country.

Social Catholicism

1187. Aspinwall, Bernard. "Before Manning: Some Aspects
       of British Social Concern before 1865." NB 61
       (March 1980): 113-27.

       Contends that Catholics showed considerable
       interest in social problems long before Manning
       launched his programs of social concern.
       Illustrates the diverse expressions of charity,
       from the traditional *noblesse oblige* of wealthy
       Catholic aristocrats, to the clergy's dedication
       to the urban Irish poor, to the construction of
       churches and educational facilities.

1188. ————. "Social Catholicism and Health: Dr. and
       Mrs. Thomas Low Nichols in Britain." In THE
       CHURCH AND HEALING: PAPERS READ AT THE
       TWENTIETH SUMMER MEETING AND THE TWENTY-FIRST
       WINTER MEETING OF THE ECCLESIASTICAL HISTORY
       SOCIETY (item 28), 249-70.

       A biography of a couple whose activities during
       the years 1860-1880 challenged the public's image
       of Catholics as reactionary and isolated. Discusses
       at length their extension of the theory and practice
       of social Catholicism, based on their belief that
       their involvement with the general welfare could
       lead to the acceptance of Catholics as full members
       of the English community. Highlights their campaigns
       for sex education, coeducational schools, vegetarian-
       ism, prison reform, the abolition of capital punish-
       ment, animal rights, and compulsory vaccination.

1189. Bennett, John. "The Care of the Poor." In THE
       ENGLISH CATHOLICS, 1850-1950: CENTENARY ESSAYS
       TO COMMEMORATE THE RESTORATION OF THE HIERARCHY
       (item 759), 559-84.

       Offers diverse examples of Catholic social
       activity in several nineteenth-century dioceses.

1190. ————. FATHER NUGENT OF LIVERPOOL.
       Liverpool: Liverpool Catholic Children's
       Protection Society, 1949.

Reconstructs the long life and extraordinary
accomplishments of Father John Nugent (1822-1905),
who spent his entire clerical career working among
the Irish immigrants in Liverpool. Realizing the
need for Catholics to be trained to take their
rightful place in the social and professional life
of the city, he pressured successfully for both a
middle school and an industrial school. His "Save
the Child" campaign of 1854 established shelters
for homeless children, while in 1863 he spearheaded
the Liverpool Catholic Reformatory Association. In
1865 he founded *The Catholic Times*, designed to
educate Catholics about their faith. His later
years were spent protecting destitute women and
children, and preaching in favor of temperance and
against abortion.

1191. The Bishop of Brentwood. "Catholics and Phi-
         lanthropy." In CATHOLIC EMANCIPATION, 1829
         TO 1929: ESSAYS BY VARIOUS WRITERS (item
         761), 159-75.

         Details the growth and operation of various
         Catholic charities, with emphasis on those
         religious and lay groups which sought to reduce
         misery in Ireland.

1192. Connolly, Gerard. "'No Law Would Be Granted
         Us': Institutional Protestantism and the
         Problem of Catholic Poverty in England." In
         PERSECUTION AND TOLERATION: PAPERS READ AT
         THE TWENTY-SECOND SUMMER MEETING AND THE
         TWENTY-THIRD WINTER MEETING OF THE
         ECCLESIASTICAL HISTORY SOCIETY, 1983 (item
         29), 303-16.

         Gauges the extent to which the Protestant English
         State provided assistance for a Catholic population
         growing disproportionately at a very low economic
         level. Using the welfare situation in Victorian
         Manchester and Salford as a sign of progress, or the
         lack of it, Connolly concludes that, contemporary
         and jaundiced Catholic perceptions notwithstanding,
         a case can be made for assistance having been dis-
         charged in an even-handed, proper, and unprejudiced
         way.

1193.   Donovan, Robert Kent. "The Denominational Character
        of English Catholic Charitable Effort, 1800-1865."
        CHR 62 (April 1976): 200-23.

        Criticizes the often unrealistic outlook of
        English Catholic philanthropists during the first
        half of the nineteenth century. Though initially
        optimistic, and hoping to build a great future on
        the basis of their good works, they retreated into
        a fortress mentality at the first sign of obstacles
        or hardships.

1194.   Elliott, Bernard. "Mount St. Bernard's Reformatory,
        Leicestershire, 1856-81." RH 15 (May 1979): 15-
        22.

        Outlines the constant problems faced by Abbot
        Bernard Burder and his successor, Bartholomew
        Anderson, in their operation of an agricultural
        colony for male juvenile delinquents. For a
        critique of this article, see item 1208.

1195.   ————. "Mount St. Bernard's Reformatory: A
        Reply." RH 15 (October 1980): 302-4.

        A rejoinder to item 1208. Reconfirms the
        interpretation presented in item 1194.

1196.   Feheney, J. Matthew, F.P.M. "Catholic Orphanages in
        the Nineteenth Century: I." CLR 67 (October
        1982): 355-61.

        Surveys the development of Catholic orphanages in
        Victorian London. Explains their slow growth in
        terms of the large and rapid Irish influx; Church
        leaders were ill-equipped psychologically and
        financially to handle the enormous increases in the
        number of parentless and abandoned children.
        Continued in item 1197.

1197.   ————. "Catholic Orphanages in the Nineteenth
        Century: II." CLR 67 (November 1982): 396-
        401.

        Uses as its point of departure the difficult
        situation described in item 1196. Investigates
        the rescue work done by religious orders and

lay groups.

1198. ————. "The Fruits of Inventiveness: Catholic Child
Care in Victorian London." CLR 70 (February
1985): 61-7.

Lists the means by which Catholic child care was
funded. Proclaims the entire enterprise a good
example of a successful combination of a central
authority--Wiseman, followed by Manning--defining
the task, and different voluntary groups taking
responsibility for financing the actual operation.
These groups used a number of highly innovative
schemes to raise money, including solicitation by
letter and door-to-door, pressure for special
collections at church services, sale of items made
by children, encouragement of sponsorship by private
individuals, and application for grants from the
Committee of the Council of Education.

1199. ————. "The London Catholic Ragged School: An
Experiment in Education for Irish Destitute
Children." AH 39 (1984): 32-44.

Examines the ten years (1851-1861) of an institution founded by Tractarian converts of the London
Oratory, in response to the Protestant Ragged School
Union, which was luring young Irish away from the
faith by offering them free soup, clothing, and
shelter at night. Traces its failure to its loose
organization and inability to gain the confidence
of the hierarchy.

1200. Gilley, Sheridan. "English Catholic Charity and the
Irish Poor in London. Part I: 1700-1840." RH
11 (January 1972): 179-95.

Disputes the charge that the cliquish and callous
English Catholic laity ignored the pressing economic
and spiritual needs of their newly arrived Irish coreligionists. Maintains, on the contrary, that
London Catholics, following a tradition of administrative ability and public service, established
several agencies to help the immigrants, including
the Association of Catholic Charities (1812) and the
Free Schools of Spicers St., Spitalfields (1827).
For post-1840 philanthropic efforts, see item 1201.

1201.   ———. "English Catholic Charity and the Irish Poor
         in London. Part II: 1840-1870." RH 11 (April
         1972): 253-69.

         Continued from item 1200. Emphasizes charitable
         institutions founded during the 1840s, including,
         most notably, the Society of St. Vincent de Paul,
         set up in 1843 to work with juvenile delinquents.
         Qualifies the term "lay involvement," in speaking
         of mid-nineteenth-century Catholic philanthropy in
         London, by pointing to a well-to-do minority at the
         center of these charitable efforts.

1202.   ———. "Heretic London, Holy Poverty and the Irish
         Poor, 1830-1870." DR 89 (January 1971): 64-89.

         Sees the English Catholic response to Irish
         immigration into England during the 1830s and
         40s as motivated by a specifically Catholic idea
         of a just society, which was developed as an
         anti-Protestant polemic during the 1830s and
         asserted ever more vigorously during the ultra-
         montane revival of the 1840s.

1203.   ———. "The Roman Catholic Mission to the Irish
         in London, 1840-1860." RH 10 (October 1969): 123-
         45.

         Describes the tactics used by London priests to
         handle the enormous influx of Irish immigrants.
         Concentrates on efforts to adapt pastoral care to a
         devout proletariat, and away from the "Old Catholic"
         gentry. Evaluates the clergy's attempt to bring
         together the English and the Irish, so widely
         separated by class, culture, and pious practice.

1204.   McEntee, Georgiana Putnam. THE SOCIAL CATHOLIC
         MOVEMENT IN GREAT BRITAIN. New York: Macmillan,
         1927.

         Stresses the consistently practical character of
         English social Catholicism, a character which,
         according to the author, came from Manning.
         Acknowledges the impact of lay, and especially female,
         participation in the movement.

         See: Francis A. Christie, AHR 33 (January 1928): 438-

9; C. Bruehl, CHR 13 (January 1928): 716-8;
Grace M. Quinlan, THOUGHT 4 (June 1929): 151-5.

1205. Marmion, John P. "The Beginnings of the Catholic
Poor Schools in England." RH 17 (May 1984): 67-
83.

Details the establishment of schools for socially
deprived Catholics during the Victorian period.
Focuses on the work of the Catholic Poor Schools
Committee, the role of the religious orders in
providing teachers, and early indications of growth.

1206. Ryan, Alvan S. "Catholic Social Thought and the
Great Victorians." THOUGHT 23 (December
1948): 641-56.

Summarizes the Catholic response to "the condition-
of-England Question," that is, nineteenth-century
socioeconomic problems. From Emancipation to the
publication of *Rerum Novarum*, a "siege mentality"
undeniably characterized the thought of many Catholics
who, in their desperation to fight back the advances
of secularism, failed to produce any positive social
programs. Moreover, the "Old Catholic"-convert and
ultramontane-liberal conflicts dissipated Catholic
energies which might have been more constructively
spent in the social area.

1207. Treble, J.H. "The Attitude of the Roman Catholic
Church towards Trade Unionism in the North of
Englnad, 1833-1842." NH 5 (1970): 93-113.

Attributes the northern English clergy's slow
acceptance of trade unions to its growing social
awareness and recognition that the organization
it once condemned as subversive was in fact a
potent agent of justice for the workers.

1208. Tucker, J.L.G. "Mount Saint Bernard Reformatory,
1856-81: A Correction." RH 15 (May 1980): 213-7.

Disagrees with three specific points raised in
item 1194. For Elliott's response to this correction,
see item 1195.

Architecture

1209. Clarke, Basil F.L. CHURCH BUILDERS OF THE NINETEENTH
CENTURY: A STUDY OF THE GOTHIC REVIVAL IN ENGLAND.
London: Society for Promoting Christian Knowledge,
1938.

Chapter 4 upbraids Pugin on three counts: his
designs, most of which were impossible to implement;
his attachment to the Gothic style, which did not
reflect the new social order of his time; and his
adherence to what Clarke calls "the ethical fallacy,"
that is, the belief that Catholics built honest and
noble structures, while non-Catholics did not.

1210. Gwynn, Denis. "A.W. Pugin's Centenary." CLR 37
(September 1952): 513-31.

Gives Pugin a key place in the "Second Spring."
Presents him, on the one hundredth anniversary of
his death, as a convert whose sincerity was always
suspect to some "Old Catholics," and an architect
whose innovative designs brought angry responses
from such prominent English Catholics as Bishop
Baines and Lingard.

1211. ———. "The Centenary of St. Chad's." CLR 20
(June 1941): 471-83.

Sketches the circumstances surrounding the
construction and dedication of St. Chad's,
Birmingham, the first Roman Catholic cathedral
built in England since the Reformation and one
of Pugin's major works. Sees the finished
product as one of the most important signals of
the nineteenth-century English Catholic revival.

1212. ———. "Heralds of the Second Spring: IV.
Augustus Welby Pugin." CLR 30 (July 1948): 39-
53.

A summary of Pugin's artistic outlook and work.
Emphasizes the importance of his collaboration with
Shrewsbury.

1213. ———. LORD SHREWSBURY, PUGIN AND THE CATHOLIC

REVIVAL. London: Hollis and Carter, 1946.

Details the efforts of a highly creative, energetic, and devout trio who set out to restore the prestige and dignity of the Church in England. If Ambrose Phillipps de Lisle provided the inspiration, and Pugin the architectural expertise, for the campaign of church-building, it was the Earl of Shrewsbury, one of England's most prominent peers, who financed it. Includes much anecdotal material about Pugin.

See: CLR 27 (February 1947): 136-8; Barry Byrne, THOUGHT 22 (September 1947): 511-2; Charles Frederick Harrold, MODPHILOL 45 (November 1947): 143-4; Joseph P. Bradley, CHR 34 (April 1948): 106-7.

1214. Little, Bryan. CATHOLIC CHURCHES SINCE 1623: A STUDY OF ROMAN CATHOLIC CHURCHES IN ENGLAND AND WALES FROM PENAL TIMES TO THE PRESENT DECADE. London: Robert Hale, 1966.

Chapters 3 to 10 survey the major nineteenth-century ecclesiastical styles, along with their diverse social and intellectual backgrounds. Features a large selection of excellent illustrations.

See: Edward Corbould, DR 85 (July 1967): 359-60; CHOICE 6 (January 1970): 1564; Richard J. Douaire, CHR 57 (January 1972): 655.

1215. Patrick, James. "Newman, Pugin, and Gothic." VS 24 (Winter 1981): 185-207.

Contends that Newman's lifelong emotional attachment to Gothic was as strong and as real as Pugin's, though it rested upon a totally different set of assumptions. Whereas Pugin believed that a true religion could only be expressed through a simple style, Newman maintained that truth knew no one style and could be expressed properly in a number of highly diverse ways.

1216. Stanton, Phoebe. PUGIN. New York: Viking Press, 1971.

Concentrates on Pugin's art and place in nineteenth-
century England. Introduces the principal characters
and events of his short career, while at the same time
analyzing the development of his practice, his
theories of religious architecture, and his talent as
a designer. Not only was Pugin the founder of that
type of Victorian Gothic which was universally
followed later in the century, but he was *the* Catholic
architect of his century. Building in the Gothic
style was for him, as for his friends Scott and
Ruskin, a spiritual vocation. Contains 168 illus-
trations--photographs and sketches--of his buildings.

See: R. Furneaux Jordan, OBS, 21 November 1971: 33;
       David Watkin, SPEC 227 (11 December 1971): 854-
       5; TLS, 14 January 1972: 42; CHOICE 9 (June
       1972): 501; Michael Landgren, LJ 97 (15 June
       1972): 2176-7; John Emerson, LIST 88 (24 August
       1972): 249.

1217. Trappes-Lomax, Michael. PUGIN: A MEDIAEVAL
       VICTORIAN. London: Sheed & Ward, 1932.

A sympathetic treatment of Pugin's ecclesiastical
work, intended to complement Benjamin Ferrey's much
earlier (1861) study of his secular designs. Praises
Pugin's brilliant mind for being the first to
consciously conceive of the idea of a rational
architecture which related form to purpose. Even
with his genius, however, Pugin never appealed to
most English, for whom his output was too closely
identified with Popery.

See: John Summerson, BKMN 83 (January 1933): 418;
       DR 51 (January 1933): 168-70; Donald Attwater,
       CLR 5 (March 1933): 250-3; Michael de la
       Bédoyère, DUBR 192 (April 1933): 316-7.

1218. Yarham, E.R. "Westminster Cathedral: Crowning Glory
       of English Catholicism." IER 84 (December
       1955): 402-5.

Describes the political and religious context in
which the Cathedral was conceived and built; the
vision of John Francis Bentley, its architect; and
some of its more interesting external and internal
architectural features.

Music

1219.   Oldmeadow, Ernest.   "The Catholic Church and Music."
        In CATHOLIC EMANCIPATION, 1829 TO 1929:   ESSAYS
        BY VARIOUS WRITERS (item 761), 121-40.

        Presents the work of some of the leading English
        Catholic composers of the nineteenth century.
        Describes the varieties of liturgical music
        commissioned by the hierarchy.

                          Literature

1220.   The Abbot of Downside.   "Literary Output of the
        Century."   DR 33 (June 1914):   181-96.

        A bibliography of the more important nineteenth-
        century religious works produced by members of the
        Downside community.   Includes the output of Gasquet
        and Ullathorne.

1221.   Cecil, Algernon.   "The Catholic Church and
        Literature."   In CATHOLIC EMANCIPATION, 1829 TO
        1929:   ESSAYS BY VARIOUS WRITERS (item 761),
        77-101.

        Focuses on Biblical criticism and ecclesiastical
        history produced by nineteenth-century English
        Catholics.

1222.   Hammerton, H.J.   "The Two Vocations of G.M. Hopkins."
        THEO 87 (May 1984):   186-9.

        Attributes Hopkins' depression, as seen in the
        "terrible sonnets" of his last years, to his in-
        ability to reconcile his poetic and priestly
        callings.

1223.   Hutton, Edward.   "Catholic English Literature, 1850-
        1950."   In THE ENGLISH CATHOLICS, 1850-
        1950:   CENTENARY ESSAYS TO COMMEMORATE THE
        RESTORATION OF THE HIERARCHY (item 759), 515-58.

        Divides the enormous literary achievements of

nineteenth-century English Catholics according to the
following areas, emphasizing the activities of the
major practitioners in each: history (Lingard, Acton,
Bishop, and Gasquet); biography (Wilfrid Ward, Faber);
poetry (Aubrey de Vere, Hopkins); essays, criticism,
and belles lettres (Lilly); fiction (Fullerton, Corvo,
Kavanagh); and religion (von Hügel, Dalgairns,
Hedley). Points to the overwhelming importance of
Wiseman and Newman, the outstanding place occupied by
the writers of Downside, and the leading role of
converts in the literary revival.

1224. Lahey, G.F., S.J. GERARD MANLEY HOPKINS.
        London: Oxford University Press, 1930.

        A study derived from a reading of his poetry.
        Chapter 3 sketches his long friendship with Newman,
        who became for Hopkins the symbol of great learning
        and deep holiness. Chapter 8 looks at Hopkins'
        personality, particularly as shaped by his Jesuit
        training.

        See: E.R.L. Gough, DR 48 (October 1930): 340-1.

1225. Leahy, Maurice. "A Priest-Poet: Father Gerard Manley
        Hopkins, S.J." IER 47 (April 1936): 355-68.

        Concentrates on his relationships with Newman,
        Pusey, and Henry Liddon, and the religious themes
        expressed in his poetry.

1226. Maison, Margaret M. THE VICTORIAN VISION: STUDIES IN
        THE RELIGIOUS NOVEL. New York: Sheed & Ward,
        1961.

        Published in England under the title, SEARCH YOUR
        SOUL, EUSTACE: A SURVEY OF THE RELIGIOUS NOVEL IN
        THE VICTORIAN AGE. Part 2 discusses and evaluates
        the small but impressive Catholic contribution to
        religious fiction. Passes from the work of Newman
        (LOSS AND GAIN, 1848; CALLISTA, 1856) to that of
        less celebrated converts (A.H. Edgar's JOHN BULL
        AND THE PAPISTS, 1846; Lady Georgiana Fullerton's
        MRS. GERALD'S NIECE, 1869) and lifelong Catholics
        like Wiseman (FABIOLA, 1854). Concludes with a
        consideration of the image of the wicked Jesuit in
        Victorian literature, an image inspired by the

widespread fear of Jesuitocracy and expressed most
eloquently by Charlotte Brontë and Charles Kingsley.

See: TLS, 9 March 1962: 154; Vivian Mercier, COMMWL
      76 (11 May 1962): 183-4; Horton Davies, VS 6
      (September 1962): 90-1; Joseph E. Baker, NCF 17
      (December 1962): 290-3.

1227. Phillipson, Dom Wulstan. "Gerard Hopkins, Priest."
       DR 56 (July 1938): 311-23.

       Salutes Hopkins as "the first of the moderns,"
       basing this verdict on an assessment of his person-
       ality, poetry, and clerical career. Believes that
       his faith was the central feature of his life, and
       was manifested through an extraordinary obedience,
       holiness, humility, and peacefulness.

1228. ————. "Gerard Manley Hopkins." DR 51 (April
       1933): 326-48.

       Follows Hopkins' progress toward Rome and the
       Jesuits, from his first experiences of monastic
       life at Glastonbury and Gloucester, to his con-
       version, ordination, and first years of ministry
       in Liverpool, London, and Ireland. Stresses his
       growing asceticism and literary ability through
       this process.

1229. Thomas, Alfred, S.J. "A Note on Gerard Manley
       Hopkins and His Superiors, 1868-77." IER 104
       (October/November 1965): 286-91.

       Highlights the relationship between Hopkins and
       his six religious superiors during his years of
       training in the Society of Jesus.

1230. ————. HOPKINS THE JESUIT: THE YEARS OF TRAINING.
       London: Oxford University Press, 1969.

       Reconstructs Hopkins' novitiate (1868-1882), based
       on previously unpublished journals kept by him during
       his time at Manresa House, Roehampton. A heavily
       detailed, almost day-to-day, account of his spiritual
       and literary formation.

See: Geoffrey Grigson, NST 78 (15 August 1969): 214-

5; TLS, 18 December 1969: 1455; William F.
Gleeson, THOUGHT 45 (Spring 1970): 136-8;
Judith M. Hazard, RES 21 (November 1970): 517-
9; G.A.M. Janssens, ES 53 (December 1972): 569-
70; W.R. Mundt, SOR 9 (Autumn 1973): 1032-4.

1231. Wolff, Robert Lee. GAINS AND LOSSES: NOVELS OF FAITH
        AND DOUBT IN VICTORIAN ENGLAND. New York and
        London: Garland Publishing, 1977.

Part 1 profiles Catholic novels or novels about
Catholicism, by author. Among the works considered
are Grace Kennedy's violently anti-Catholic FATHER
CLEMENT; A ROMAN CATHOLIC STORY (1823); Newman's
highly intellectual LOSS AND GAIN and CALLISTA;
Wiseman's FABIOLA (1854); and Lady Georgiana
Fullerton's popular ELLEN MIDDLETON (1844),
GRANTLEY MANOR (1847), LADYBIRD (1852), and MRS.
GERALD'S NIECE. Beyond biographies of the authors
and a summary and interpretation of plots, Wolff
traces the development of various general themes
in nineteenth-century English Catholic literature,
from the efforts of the earliest writers to show
that Catholics were not a threat to the social
order, to those of the fin-de-siècle polemicists,
who set out to persuade their materialistic and
immoral Protestant neighbors that true spiritual
peace could only come by submitting to Rome.

See: Edward Norman, TLS, 26 August 1977: 1022;
        CHOICE 14 (November 1977): 1218; Valentine
        Cunningham, VS 22 (Spring 1979): 321-34;
        Rolland Hein, CSN 9 (no. 2, 1979): 153;
        John Halperin, MFS 25 (Summer 1979): 300-3.

Special Challenges

Church and State

Anglo-Papal Relations

1232. Buschkühl, Matthias. GREAT BRITAIN AND THE HOLY SEE,
        1746-1870. Dublin: Irish Academic Press, 1983.

Hinges the development of nineteenth-century Anglo-Papal relations upon the complexities of the Irish Question and the threats to the Temporal Power. Highly favorable to Pius IX and ultramontanism; highly critical of misguided English liberal Catholics, the duplicitous Odo Russell, and those government leaders, both Tory and Whig, who tried to rule Ireland through Rome, and yet at the same time hoped for the overthrow of papal political power on the peninsula.

See: Frank MacDonald Spindler, HRNB 12 (February 1984): 74; Derek Beales, TLS, 23 March 1984: 297; Paul W. Schroeder, ALBION 16 (Summer 1984): 193-5; C.T. McIntire, CH 53 (September 1984): 401-2; Joseph P. Chinnici, AHR 89 (October 1984): 1068-9; James C. Holland, CHR 70 (October 1984): 590-2; Keith Robbins, JEH 36 (January 1985): 129-30.

1233. Gaselee, Sir Stephen. "British Diplomatic Relations with the Holy See." DUBR 204 (January/February/March 1939): 1-19.

Discusses three key instances of nineteenth-century Anglo-Papal relations: the negotiations over the selection of the Archbishop of Malta, 1816-1817; Canning's overtures to the Vatican, in the interests of European peace and order, 1823-1824; and the British government's proposal to accredit the Duke of Norfolk as special envoy to the Pope, 1887.

1234. Gwynn, Denis. "Heralds of the Second Spring: VII. Cardinal Acton." CLR 30 (October 1948): 248-65.

Sketches the outlook and activities of Charles Acton (1803-1848), the Pope's adviser on English affairs during the 1840s. Explains his opposition to giving the Vicars Apostolic the full powers of diocesan bishops and his reservations about the much-discussed restoration of the Roman hierarchy in England.

1235. Kelly, Nicholas J. "An Internuncio in England, 1830-31." DUBR 200 (April/May/June 1937): 265-81.

Recounts the eleven-month English visit of Msgr. Francesco Capaccini, the Internuncio at the Hague,

who came to London in October 1830 to represent papal
policy at the peace conference called to deal with
the problem of the Belgian revolution.

1236. Kerr, Donal A. PEEL, PRIESTS AND POLITICS: SIR
       ROBERT PEEL'S ADMINISTRATION AND THE ROMAN
       CATHOLIC CHURCH IN IRELAND, 1841-1846.
       Oxford: Oxford University Press, 1983.

Illustrates the effects of Peel's recognition that
the Irish Question would be solved as much in Rome as
in London and Ireland itself. Highlights the government's contacts with the Curia and with the powerful,
lively, and self-confident Irish Church.

See: R. Dudley Edwards, CLR 69 (January 1984): 35;
      Stanley H. Palmer, HRNB 12 (February 1984): 77;
      Donald H. Akenson, AHR 89 (April 1984): 449;
      Emmet Larkin, RSR 10 (April 1984): 185; John
      Whyte, IHS 24 (May 1984): 109-10; Oliver
      MacDonagh, VS 27 (Summer 1984): 526-7; Maurice
      R. O'Connell, CHR 70 (October 1984): 613;
      Boyd Hilton, JEH 35 (October 1984): 644-6;
      Mark Finnane, JRH 13 (December 1985): 453-4.

1237. McIntire, C.T. ENGLAND AGAINST THE PAPACY, 1858-
       1861: TORIES, LIBERALS, AND THE OVERTHROW OF
       PAPAL TEMPORAL POWER DURING THE ITALIAN
       RISORGIMENTO. New York: Cambridge University
       Press, 1983.

Details the interrelationship between the issue of
the Temporal Power and British foreign policy, from
the revolutions in the Romagna to the final annexation of the Marches and Umbria by Piedmont. Goes
beyond specific events to proffer insights into the
motivations of the leading players, including Pius
IX, Cardinal Antonelli, and the English government,
as it jockeyed against Austria, France, and Piedmont
for peninsular influence. Agrees with Buschkühl's
view (item 1232) of a strong anti-Catholicism shared
by Tories and Whigs, and expressed through opposition
to the continuation of papal secular rule.

See: Paul W. Schroeder, ALBION 16 (Summer 1984): 193-
      5; Thomas W. Davis, JCS 26 (Autumn 1984): 537-8;
      Joseph P. Chinnici, AHR 89 (October

1984): 1068-9; Keith Robbins, JEH 36 (January
1985): 129-30; Dale A. Johnson, CH 54 (March
1985): 137; Walter L. Arnstein, VS 28 (Spring
1985): 552-4; S. Morris Sider, CSN 14 (no. 3,
1985): 282-3; Ivan Scott, CHR 72 (April
1986): 324-5.

1238. Mooney, Gary, S.J. "British Diplomatic Relations
       with the Holy See, 1793-1830." RH 14 (May
       1978): 193-210.

       Divides the first three decades of nineteenth-
       century Anglo-Papal relations into two distinct
       phases. Before 1823 there was a gradual warming,
       culminating with the friendship between Castlereagh
       and Consalvi. Dialogue was prompted by London's
       need for Italian ports and for assistance in
       governing Irish, Maltese, and Canadian Catholics;
       Rome, for its part, sought British support against
       the recurring threat of revolution. After 1823
       relations, though continuing, were strained, as
       anti-Catholic opinion in England swelled after
       Canning's appointment as Foreign Secretary.

1239. Randall, Alec. "A British Agent at the Vatican: The
       Mission of Odo Russell." DUBR 233 (Spring
       1959): 37-57.

       Looks at Russell's twelve years (1858-1870) in
       Rome, his warm relationship with Pius IX, and,
       more importantly, his perceptions of the Papacy's
       mounting problems, as presented in his dispatches
       to Whitehall. Documents from an English viewpoint
       the decline and fall of the Temporal Power, the
       Pope's efforts to extend his spiritual and moral
       prerogatives, and the strengthening of the central
       authority of the Holy See.

1240. ————. "British Diplomacy and the Holy See, 1555-
       1925." DUBR 233 (Winter 1959-60): 291-303.

       Provides a list of British agents assigned to the
       Vatican during the nineteenth century. Considers
       efforts by Pius VII, Consalvi, and Castlereagh to
       establish formal relations.

1241. Reynolds, Julian. "Politics vs. Persuasion: The

Attempt to Establish Anglo-Roman Diplomatic
Relations in 1848." CHR 71 (July 1985): 372-93.

Uncovers the many complex issues surrounding the
defeat of Lord John Russell's proposal to establish
formal ties with the Holy See. Sees the stillborn
bill as a barometer of religious feeling as it
existed midway between the Maynooth Affair of 1845
and the "Papal Aggression" crisis of 1850, the two
greatest outbursts of Victorian anti-Catholic
opinion. Maintains that Pius IX's rejection of the
bill was not shared by most of the English public,
proving that fanatical anti-Catholicism was a dying
force, able to move only an ever diminishing number
of Protestants as the century proceeded.

1242.   Temperley, Harold. "George Canning, the Catholics
and the Holy See." DUBR 193 (July/August/
September 1933): 1-12.

Probes Canning's indirect attempts to ascertain
the Pope's views on the best practicable means of
reconciling English and Irish Catholics to the
Crown. In 1825, thirteen years after Canning's
proposal for Catholic relief was rejected by the
House of Lords, he sent Lord Burghersh, British
Minister to Tuscany, to Rome, with the goal of
sounding out the Curia.

1243.   Woods, C.J. "Ireland and Anglo-Papal Relations,
1880-85." IHS 18 (March 1972): 29-60.

Deals with George Errington's five-year term in
Rome, and his success in obtaining papal support for
British policies in Ireland. Himself a Catholic,
and though officially British Minister to Tuscany,
Errington was able to provoke papal intervention in
Irish episcopal affairs and to persuade the Curia of
the soundness of his government's view whenever
issues of episcopal succession or precedence arose.

The British Government and Vatican I

1244.   Adshead, S.A.M. "Odo Russell and the First Vatican
Council." JRH 2 (December 1963): 295-302.

Disputes Purcell's interpretation (item 863) of Russell's conduct in Rome during the early sessions of Vatican I. Uses papers not available to Purcell.

1245. Altholz, Josef L. "Gladstone and the Vatican Decrees." HIS 25 (May 1963): 312-24.

Clarifies Gladstone's motives in publishing his VATICAN DECREES IN THEIR BEARING ON CIVIL ALLEGIANCE (1874). Gladstone was convinced that there existed a "vast conspiracy" of Roman Catholic bishops, aimed at starting a continental war, with the idea of forcibly restoring the Temporal Power; the decrees of Vatican I would be a way of compelling English Catholics to use their influence on behalf of their spiritual leader. His denunciation, therefore, was an attempt to forestall this design; as its subtitle indicates, it was a political expostulation, not a religious tract.

1246. ————. "The Vatican Decrees Controversy, 1874-1875." CHR 57 (January 1972): 593-605.

Evaluates English public reaction to the decree on papal infallibility. Maintains that the lively controversy engendered by Vatican I's work actually marked the end of "no popery" as an overt issue in English politics.

1247. Bastable, James D. "Gladstone's *Expostulation* and Newman." In NEWMAN AND GLADSTONE: CENTENNIAL ESSAYS (item 1248), 9-25.

Contrasts Gladstone's THE VATICAN DECREES IN THEIR BEARING ON CIVIL ALLEGIANCE: A POLITICAL EXPOSTU-LATION (1874), a vehement and overstated attack born of personal political disappointment and a deep attachment to the Anglican idea of religious nationalism, with Newman's measured and wise response of 1875, A LETTER ADDRESSED TO HIS GRACE, THE DUKE OF NORFOLK, ON OCCASION OF MR. GLADSTONE'S RECENT EXPOSTULATION.

1248. ————, ed. NEWMAN AND GLADSTONE: CENTENNIAL ESSAYS. Dublin: Veritas, 1978.

A series of sixteen essays by English, Irish,

European, and American scholars, dealing with various
aspects of the confrontation between the churchman
and the politician over the issue of Catholic civil
allegiance in a post-Vatican I age. Contains items
114, 948, 1247, and 1249.

*   Johnson, Humphrey J.T. "The Controversy between
      Newman and Gladstone over the Question of Civil
      Allegiance." Cited above as item 949.

1249.   Nicholls, David. "Gladstone, Newman and the Politics
       of Pluralism." In NEWMAN AND GLADSTONE: CENTENNIAL
       ESSAYS (item 1248), 27-38.

Maintains that Gladstone's THE VATICAN DECREES was
not an attack on the concept of religious pluralism
in Britain, but rather a warning to his countrymen
about the dangerous way in which ultramontanes might
interpret the recent declaration of papal infallibility.

Political Leaders and Roman Catholicism

1250.   Clausson, Nils. "English Catholics and Roman
       Catholicism in Disraeli's Novels." NCF 33
       (March 1979): 454-74.

Presents Disraeli's literary ambivalence towards
his Catholic countrymen; while his earliest works
were strongly sympathetic to their Catholic
characters, his later efforts showed only mistrust
and suspicion. Argues that Disraeli always respected
those English Catholics who were for him a symbol of
his nation's highest ideals; however, he had no use
for the ultramontanes who followed a foreign creed
antithetical to English tradition.

1251.   Edwards, H.W.J. "Disraeli's Homage to Catholicism."
       IER 90 (September 1958): 158-72.

Presents Disraeli's ambivalent view of Catholicism.
On the one hand, he opposed Emancipation, branding it
the cause of "bustling hucksters," and was genuinely
alarmed by the "Second Spring." On the other, he
admired unreservedly the splendor and genius of the

Church, and may have had during his youth a brief
attack of "Roman fever," as he became absorbed in
the glories of medieval Christendom.

1252. Hegarty, W.J., P.P. "Gladstone's Attitude to
           Catholicism." IER 86 (July 1956): 26-42.

Dismisses the view that Gladstone considered
joining the Catholic Church, demonstrating, quite
to the contrary, that no man was more responsible
than he for the anti-papal feeling in England
during the reign of Pius IX.

1253. Herrick, Francis H. "Gladstone, Newman, and Ireland
           in 1881." CHR 47 (October 1961): 342-50.

Provides an in-depth look at Gladstone's perception
of post-1870 Roman Catholicism, within the context of
his appeal to Newman for help against the Land League
in Ireland.

1254. Holmes, J. Derek. "Gladstone and Newman." DUBR 241
           (Summer 1967): 141-53.

Displays an uneven friendship, in which Gladstone
admired and respected Newman, despite their widely
divergent religious beliefs.

1255. Matthew, H.C.G. "Gladstone, Vaticanism, and the
           Question of the East." In RELIGIOUS
           MOTIVATION: BIOGRAPHICAL AND SOCIOLOGICAL
           PROBLEMS FOR THE CHURCH HISTORIAN: PAPERS
           READ AT THE SIXTEENTH SUMMER MEETING AND THE
           SEVENTEENTH WINTER MEETING OF THE ECCLESIASTICAL
           HISTORY SOCIETY, edited by Derek Baker, 417-42.
           Studies in Church History, vol. 15.
           Oxford: Published for the Ecclesiastical History
           Society by Basil Blackwell, 1978.

Establishes a connection between Gladstone's
writings on Vatican I (1874) and on the Bulgarian
massacres (1876). Asserts that as the declaration
of papal infallibility convinced Gladstone once and
for all that the ultramontanism which he detested
was now supreme, he abandoned the hope of a Roman-
Anglican reconciliation, and turned toward the
Orthodox. His condemnation of the Turks thus served

two purposes: it showed support for an Orthodox
nation, and it enabled him to compare the ultramontanist Roman Church with the Turkish government,
which also sought to destroy any expression of
"religious nationality."

See: Edward R. Norman, EHR 96 (January 1981): 184-5.

1256. Painting, David E. "Disraeli and the Roman Catholic
       Church." QR 304 (January 1966): 17-25.

       Details Disraeli's lifelong fascination with Roman
Catholicism, one which survived even the strong anti-
Catholicism of his later novels.

1257. Sommerville, H. "Disraeli and Catholicism." MONTH
       OS 159 (February 1932): 114-24.

       Demonstrates how Disraeli used his novels to
illustrate both the most admirable convictions and
ideals of Roman Catholicism and the most admirable
Roman Catholics. Even in his Protestant-oriented
LOTHAIR, Disraeli pictured the Church as a bulwark
of civilization; in SYBIL he praised the model
clergyman Aubrey St. Lys, who was in fact Father
Faber, while in CONINGSBY, the virtuous Eustace Lyle
is Ambrose Phillipps de Lisle.

1258. Stephen, M.D. "Liberty, Church and State: Glad-
       stone's Relations with Manning and Acton, 1832-
       70." JRH 1 (December 1961): 217-32.

       Focuses on Gladstone's ongoing and oftentimes
very heated argument with Manning and Acton over
the nature of the proper relationship between
Church and State.

Catholic Political Activity

General

1259. Altholz, Josef L. "The Political Behavior of the
       English Catholics, 1850-1867." JBS 4 (November
       1964): 89-103.

Traces the assimilation of English Catholics into English political life, as they made a rather complex transition from a faction which maneuvered inconspicuously among the established parties in pursuit of their special interests, to a pressure group which resorted to meetings, petitions, and other tactics to gain their ends.

1260. Champ, Judith F. "Priesthood and Politics in the Nineteenth Century: The Turbulent Career of Thomas McDonnell." RH 18 (May 1987): 289-303.

Finds in the confused and contradictory ideas and activities of the resident secular priest of St. Peter's, Birmingham (1824-1841), a microcosm of the larger English Catholic community's stormy debate over the direction in which its revival should go. While McDonnell openly advertised his liberal politics, non-sectarian viewpoint, and independence of mind, his activities were a preview of the coming ultramontane clericalism, ecclesiastical authoritarianism, and sectarianism.

1261. Hoppen, K. Theodore. "Tories, Catholics, and the General Election of 1859." HJ 13 (March 1970): 48-67.

Assesses the impact of Disraeli's appeal for Catholic support in the election of 1859. Though the hitherto politically untapped Catholic community responded favorably to the Tories, giving them its support, this fragile alliance withered away soon after the election.

1262. Machin, G.I.T. POLITICS AND THE CHURCHES IN GREAT BRITAIN, 1869 TO 1921. Oxford: Clarendon Press, 1987.

A sequel to item 1263. Follows the growing political strength of Catholics during the decades after Irish disestablishment, and the ways in which that strength was both expressed (e.g., the Home Rule campaign of the 1880s and 90s) and challenged (e.g., the civil allegiance controversy of 1874-1875). Places this vitality within the ever diminishing role of religious issues in British politics.

See: Edward Norman, TLS, 23 October 1987: 1172.

1263. ───. POLITICS AND THE CHURCHES IN GREAT BRITAIN,
         1832 TO 1868. Oxford: Clarendon Press, 1977.

         Traces the growth of Catholic political agitation,
    as the large influx of Irish immigrants made the
    question of religious liberty more pressing than
    ever. Singles out along the way four situations in
    which the Church became involved, willingly or
    otherwise, in politics: Peel's Maynooth Grant and
    Academical Institutions Act (1845-1846), the
    Ecclesiastical Titles Bill (1851), the revival of
    the Maynooth controversy by ultra-Protestants (1852),
    and the campaign for the disestablishment of the
    Church of Ireland (the late 1860s). For developments
    after 1868, see item 1262.

    See: Edward R. Norman, TLS, 17 February 1978: 194;
          CHOICE 15 (September 1978): 893; A.R. Vidler,
          JEH 29 (October 1978): 503; W.R. Ward, JTS 29
          (October 1978): 607-8; D.W. Bebbington, HJ 21
          (December 1978): 1013-4; Norman Gash, EHR 94
          (January 1979): 142-4; Josef L. Altholz, AHR
          84 (February 1979): 162-3; William L. Sachs,
          CH 48 (June 1979): 227-8; J.B. Conacher, JMH
          51 (June 1979): 344-6; Gavin White, SJT 32
          (December 1979): 572-3; Standish Meacham, VS
          22 (Winter 1979): 209-10; John V. Crangle,
          JCS 22 (Winter 1980): 143-4.

1264. Rossi, John P. "Catholic Opinion on the Eastern
         Question, 1876-1878." CH 51 (March 1982): 54-
         70.

         Shows how the reactions of English Catholics to
    the Near Eastern crisis deepened their relationship
    with the Tories and, through Manning's use of the
    situation, represented another victory for ultra-
    montanism.

1265. ───. "English Catholics, the Liberal Party and
         the General Election of 1880." CHR 63 (July
         1977): 411-27.

         Documents the efforts of the Liberal Party to win
    over the badly fragmented Catholic community during

the campaign of 1880. Though the Liberal victory was won without Catholic votes, the fact remained that never before had Catholic support been considered worthy of attention by a major political party; this represented an enormous advance over the recent past, when Catholic votes had been either neglected or taken for granted.

The Politics of Emancipation

1266. Albion, Gordon. "Catholic Emancipation, 1829: A Reminder." CLR 64 (September 1979): 335-8.

Sketches the early nineteenth-century circumstances which necessitated a repeal of the penal laws against Catholics.

1267. Allen, W. Gore. "William IV and His Catholic Subjects." IER 88 (October 1957): 259-62.

Uncovers a little-known aspect of William IV's political and religious outlook, which accounted for his popularity among Catholics. In 1829, a year before his accession to the throne, he not only spoke before the Lords in favor of the Relief Bill, but added that it should have been passed a quarter-century earlier, as a simple matter of justice.

1268. Amherst, W.J., S.J. THE HISTORY OF CATHOLIC EMANCI-PATION AND THE PROGRESS OF THE CATHOLIC CHURCH IN THE BRITISH ISLES (CHIEFLY IN ENGLAND) FROM 1771 TO 1820. London: Kegan Paul, Trench, 1886. 2 vols.

Not a general account, but a study of specific aspects of the Emancipation process. Includes treatments of the veto question, the activities of Bishop Milner and his fellow Vicars Apostolic, and the opposition to Catholic pressure for civil equality.

See: CW 48 (November 1888): 287-8.

1269. Bennett, Scott. "Catholic Emancipation, the

'Quarterly Review,' and Britain's Constitutional
Revolution." VS 12 (March 1969): 283-304.

Describes the disagreement within the editorial
circle of the *Quarterly Review*, the Tory Party's
journal, over the issue of Catholic Emancipation.
Blames John Gibson Lockhart, editor of the *Review*,
for his failure to demand responsible rhetoric from
such fanatically anti-Catholic members of his staff
as Robert Southey, whose opposition to any relief
for Catholics neither represented nor advanced the
interests of the journal, its management, or its
Party.

1270. Butler, W.F. "What Catholic Emancipation Meant."
          DUBR 184 (April/May/June 1929): 194-205.

Hails the magnitude of O'Connell's achievement of
1829, by presenting the severe philosophy and
application of the Penal Laws repealed in that year.

1271. Dark, Sidney. "Emancipation and the Catholic
          Movement in the Church of England." DUBR 184
          (April/May/June 1929): 287-94.

Suggests that the Anglo-Catholic movement owed its
origins to Catholic Emancipation, for the freedom
gained in 1829 allowed a greater knowledge of Roman
teaching and devotion to spread throughout England,
a knowledge which influenced the Tractarians, in
spite of their well-known dislike of O'Connell and
his methods.

1272. Davis, R.W. "The Tories, the Whigs, and Catholic
          Emancipation, 1827-1829." EHR 97 (January
          1982): 89-98.

Clarifies a number of crucial facts about Emancipation which have been confusing from the very
beginning, among which are the timing of the
legislation and the terms on which the settlement was
made. However, for a response to this clarification,
see item 1282.

1273. Greaves, R.W. "Roman Catholic Relief and the
          Leicester Election of 1826." TRHS (Fourth
          Series) 22 (1940): 199-223.

Measures the degree to which the Tories' anti-
Emancipation agitation played a role in the Leicester
election of 1826. The Catholic Question occupied a
major role in the campaign, for it became a political
football in the conflict between the Leicester
Corporation, a traditionally Tory group, devoted to
Establishment and violently anti-Catholic, and its
opponents.

1274. Gwynn, Denis. THE STRUGGLE FOR CATHOLIC EMANCIPATION
(1750-1829). London: Longmans, Green, 1928.

Deals with the Emancipation process from an Irish,
rather than an English, viewpoint, though Gwynn
recognizes and credits English participation in the
movement. Contrasts the deplorable state of Catholic
affairs before 1829 with the more relaxed post-1829
situation, using a detailed account of Catholic
agitation as the bridge between them.

See: DR 47 (January 1929): 65-7; IER 33 (January
1929): 104-5; LQR 151 (January 1929): 125;
Robert H. Murray, THEO 18 (May 1929): 294-5;
A. Aspinall, HIST 14 (October 1929): 274.

1275. Henriques, Ursula. RELIGIOUS TOLERATION IN ENGLAND,
1787-1833. Toronto: University of Toronto Press,
1961.

Chapter 5 lists the major opponents and supporters
of Catholic Emancipation, along with their motives.
Among the most determined within the former were the
Irish Protestants, High Church clergy, and dissenters
(Methodists and Evangelicals). Among the latter, who
contested the stereotype of Catholics as idolaters
and traitors, were the "Liberal Tories" and the Whigs.

See: Carl B. Cone, CHR 48 (July 1962): 259-60;
Roger B. Manning, HIS 24 (August 1962): 507-8;
John Roach, HIST 47 (October 1962): 316-7;
Francis G. James, AHR 68 (January 1963): 431-
3; D.J. McDougall, CANHR 44 (December
1963): 355-6; E.P. Hennock, EHR 79 (January
1964): 188-9.

1276. Hexter, J.H. "The Protestant Revival and the Catholic
Question in England, 1778-1829." JMH 8

(September 1936):   297-319.

Underscores the growing complexity of the Catholic
Question after 1800, as it was tied not only to the
age-old problem of Ireland, but also to the resurgence
of anti-Catholicism brought about by the evangelical
revival.

1277. Holmes, J. Derek. "Catholics and Politics at the Time
       of Emancipation." NB 54 (August 1973): 365-73.

       Disputes the image of widespread Catholic indiffer-
       ence to the general campaign for civil rights during
       the Emancipation period. Maintains that even a
       cursory reading of contemporary periodicals shows a
       politically concerned and active Catholic population.

1278. Hughes, Philip. THE CATHOLIC QUESTION, 1688-1829: A
       STUDY IN POLITICAL HISTORY. New York: Benziger
       Brothers, 1929.

       Book 3 discusses the immediate background to the
       passage of Emancipation, placing it within the
       context of the British government's continuing
       political problems in Ireland. Follows the emergence
       of the Catholic Question through twelve years of
       foreign war and another fifteen years of internal
       agitation. Sees the Relief Act of 1829 as not only
       the vehicle by which "[O'Connell's] Church entered
       the Constitution," but also as the government's
       recognition of the ongoing Catholic revival.

1279. Lewis, Clyde J. "The Disintegration of the Tory-
       Anglican Alliance in the Struggle for Catholic
       Emancipation." CH 29 (March 1960): 25-43.

       Discusses the rift between Anglican clergymen and
       Tory political leaders during the controversy over
       the Emancipation legislation of 1828-1829. Concludes
       that Catholic Emancipation offered the first definite
       sign that some Anglican principles might be sacrificed
       by Tory politicians.

1280. Linker, R.W. "The English Roman Catholics and
       Emancipation: The Politics of Persuasion."
       JEH 27 (April 1976): 151-80.

Argues that far from being mere spectators during the struggle for Emancipation, English Catholics were active and even energetic participants.

1281. MacDonagh, Michael. "The Story of Catholic Emancipation. III--Emancipation." IER 32 (December 1928): 578-99.

Clarifies Peel's role in the Emancipation process. Details the reasons for his support of Catholic relief,--he was initially opposed to the idea,--his political activity on behalf of the bill, and the problems involved with obtaining royal approval of the legislation.

1282. Machin, G.I.T. "Canning, Wellington, and the Catholic Question, 1827-1829." EHR 99 (January 1984): 94-100.

A response to item 1272. Differs with Davis over the exact nature of the settlement of 1829.

1283. ————. "The Catholic Emancipation Crisis of 1825." EHR 78 (July 1963): 458-82.

Brings to light the most neglected crisis over Catholic Emancipation in the 1820s, that of 1825. During that year the progress of the question nearly drove the anti-Catholic Lord Liverpool to resign the Prime Ministership.

1284. ————. THE CATHOLIC QUESTION IN ENGLISH POLITICS, 1820 TO 1830. Oxford: Clarendon Press, 1964.

Explains why and how the question of Catholic Emancipation overshadowed all other political issues during most of the 1820s. Demonstrates how reaction to proposals for Emancipation cut across party lines; not all Whigs, for example, favored it, while a large number of Tories were pro-Catholic. Moreover, though the largely anti-Catholic English did not approve of the legislation of 1829, at the same time they refrained from displaying any fervent opposition to it.

See: E.W. Ives, PA 17 (Autumn 1964): 472-3; Wilfrid Passmore, DR 82 (October 1964): 375-6;

Josef L. Altholz, AHR 70 (January 1965): 528;
Georgiana McEntee, CHR 51 (April 1965): 118-9;
R.W. Greaves, HIST 50 (June 1965): 240; Olive
J. Brose, JMH 37 (June 1965): 256; Norman Gash,
EHR 80 (October 1965): 865-6; Gilbert A. Cahill,
CANHR 47 (March 1966): 77; Christopher Howard,
JEH 17 (April 1966): 133.

1285. ————. "The Duke of Wellington and Catholic Emancipation." JEH 14 (October 1963): 190-208.

Claims that Wellington was largely responsible for
the legislation of 1829. Instead of foolishly and
uselessly opposing the bill, he used his political
standing, skill, and popular reputation to secure its
passage. Emphasizes the fact that Wellington's actions
were motivated by practical domestic considerations,
and not by the pressure of O'Connell and his followers.

1286. Milne, Maurice. "J.G. Lockhart and the Catholic
Question." VPR 17 (Spring/Summer 1984): 49-51.

Illustrates the complexity of the Tory response to
Emancipation, by examining the attitude of John Gibson
Lockhart, editor of the Tory *Quarterly Review*, toward
the issue. On the one hand, Lockhart was openly pro-
Catholic; on the other, he permitted Robert Southey to
write violently anti-Catholic articles for the *Review*.
Complicating this situation is the recent attribution
of an anti-Catholic tirade in *Blackwood's Magazine* to
Lockhart, written slightly earlier than Southey's
first efforts.

*   Parsons, Reuben. "The Emancipation of the Catholics
in the English Dominions; Daniel O'Connell."
STUDIES IN CHURCH HISTORY, 5 (item 26), 159-236.

Sees fear as the sole motive of every Catholic
relief measure from the bill of 1774 to the Act of
1829. Places the Catholic agitation of the 1820s,
which it covers in great detail, within two key
contexts: (1) popular bigotry; and (2) conflict
within the English Church between Cisalpines and
Ultramontanes, with Bishop Milner as the pawn.

1287. Ronan, Myles V. "What Is Meant by Catholic Emancipation." CHR 15 (January 1930): 363-88.

A straightforward account of the Emancipation
process, with special reference to the pre-1829
penal restrictions upon Catholics and O'Connell's
successful campaign to eradicate them.

1288. Thomas, George Stephen. WORDSWORTH, SCOTT, COLERIDGE,
       SOUTHEY, AND DE QUINCEY ON CATHOLIC EMANCIPATION,
       1800-1829: THE CONSERVATIVE REACTION. Ph.D.
       dissertation. New York University, 1963.

Focuses on a group of prominent writers whose views
formed the hard core of resistance to Emancipation.
Spells out the bases of their conservatism: all, with
some qualifications for Scott and Coleridge, believed
that Catholic relief would lead to the demise of
Anglicanism, England, and even Protestantism itself.
Among them only Scott and Coleridge cited reasons for
acquiescing to Emancipation. For Scott, the measure
was expedient and practical; for Coleridge, England
had ways to protect herself from the religious and
political subversion which would result from granting
Catholics greater freedom.

1289. Whelan, Basil, O.S.B. "Behind the Scenes of Catholic
       Emancipation." DUBR 184 (April/May/June
       1929): 295-328.

Looks at Catholic Emancipation through the eyes of
Peel and the Duke of Buckingham and Chandos, Privy
Councillor and holder of several cabinet appointments.
From these two, according to Whelan, one can learn a
great deal about the religious outlook and motives of
the inner circle of the British government during the
late 1820s.

1290. Woollen, Wilfrid H. "Shelley and Catholic Emanci-
       pation." DR 44 (October 1926): 271-84.

Reconstructs Shelley's trip to Ireland in 1812,
made in the hope of furthering the cause of Catholic
relief. While there, he met the leaders of the
Catholic campaign and wrote his impassioned ADDRESS
TO THE IRISH PEOPLE, which demanded immediate emancipation and repeal of the Union as the first in a
lengthy series of reforms.

Anticlericalism and Anticatholicism

General

1291. Arlinghaus, Francis A. "British Public Opinion and
       the Kulturkampf in Germany, 1871-1875." CHR 34
       (January 1949): 385-413.

       Examines the assumption that the British public,
       because it was generally anti-papal during the years
       after 1870, was also automatically pro-German, pro-
       Bismarckian, and anti-Catholic in its view of the
       Kulturkampf. Uses journals and periodicals as a
       reflection of public opinion concerning the contest
       between Church and State on the continent.

1292. Arnstein, Walter L. PROTESTANT VERSUS CATHOLIC IN
       MID-VICTORIAN ENGLAND: MR. NEWDEGATE AND THE
       NUNS. Columbia: University of Missouri Press,
       1982.

       Studies the campaign of Charles Newdigate
       Newdegate, the M.P. for Warwickshire, to show
       that while the clauses of the Emancipation Act
       of 1829 guaranteeing Catholic political freedom
       had been regularly honored, other clauses--e.g.,
       provisions regarding the elimination of Jesuits
       from Britain and the suppression of certain
       convents and monasteries--had not been enforced.
       Correlates Newdegate's activity with the height
       of popular hostility against the declaration of
       papal infallibility.

       See: A.J.P. Taylor, OBS, 30 May 1982: 30; Edward
             Norman, TLS, 16 July 1982: 758; Christopher
             Kent, ALBION 14 (Fall/Winter 1982): 318-9;
             CHOICE 20 (October 1982): 283; Michael Moore,
             HRNB 11 (November/December 1982): 45; R.W.
             Davis, AHR 88 (February 1983): 113-4; Patrick
             V. O'Dea, VPR 16 (Spring 1983): 38-40; Josef
             L. Altholz, VS 26 (Spring 1983): 363-4; F.B.
             Smith, JRH 12 (June 1983): 340-1; M.B. McNamee,
             S.J., REVREL 42 (July/August 1983): 634-5;
             Daniel L. Pals, CH 53 (March 1984): 116-7;
             Frank M. Turner, JMH 56 (June 1984): 343-5;

A.D. Macintyre, JEH 35 (July 1984): 495-6; John
R. Griffin, CHR 70 (October 1984): 616-7; H.C.G.
Matthew, EHR 100 (January 1985): 202-3.

1293. Best, G.F.A. "Popular Protestantism in Victorian
Britain." In IDEAS AND INSTITUTIONS OF VICTORIAN
BRITAIN: ESSAYS IN HONOUR OF GEORGE KITSON CLARK,
edited by Robert Robson, 115-42. London: G. Bell
& Sons, 1967.

Explains the nature and effects of that Protestant
state of mind which believed that "Roman Catholics and
midnight assassins are synonymous terms." Identifies
anti-sacerdotalism as the central objection of
Protestants to the Roman faith; sacerdotalism meant a
large and complex variety of structures, ideas, and
practices. Catholics were perceived as followers of
a Papacy which threatened liberty and rejected the
idea of civil allegiance; obscurantists, who preached
casuistry and obeyed the Index; and practitioners of
an unmanly and unEnglish ritual. Concludes that these
perceptions, as expressed in novels and speeches, were
widespread throughout England from the mid-1830s to
the late 1870s, and affected the course of politics
and society.

See: Gareth Stedman Jones, NST 74 (21 July 1967): 92-
3; TLS, 26 October 1967: 1010; Norman Gash,
HIST 53 (February 1968): 142-3; Henry Pelling,
HJ 11 (no. 2, 1968): 390-2; CHOICE 5 (May
1968): 397-8; Donald Read, NH 3 (1968): 211-3;
Brian Harrison, EHR 84 (January 1969): 202-3;
H.J. Perkin, ECHR 22 (August 1969): 355-6.

1294. Cahill, Gilbert A. "Irish Catholicism and English
Toryism." RP 19 (January 1957): 62-76.

A précis of the material in item 1295.

1295. ————. IRISH CATHOLICISM AND ENGLISH TORYISM, 1832-
1848: A STUDY IN IDEOLOGY, Ph.D. dissertation.
State University of Iowa, 1954.

Analyzes the remarkable success of the ultra-
Tories in rallying anti-Irish, anti-Catholic feeling
during an allegedly liberal period in English history.

1296.   Collingwood, Cuthbert.   "The Catholic Truth Society."
        CLR 37 (November 1952):   641-58.

        Sketches the founding and early development of the
        CTS.   Established in 1884 by James Britten, in response
        to Protestant literary efforts to disparage Catho-
        licism, the Society grew rapidly.   Its two earliest
        stimuli were the active encouragement of Cardinal
        Vaughan and the expansion of its catalogue to
        accommodate the enormous number of periodicals and
        pamphlets it published during the controversy over
        Anglican orders.   In 1892 it opened its first branch
        office in Manchester.

1297.   Cooter, R.J.   "Lady Londonderry and the Irish Catholics
        of Seaham Harbour: 'No Popery' Out of Context."
        RH 13 (October 1976):   288-98.

        Demonstrates the non-religious, personal motiv-
        ations behind Victorian anti-Catholicism, by an in-
        vestigation of the three-year (1860-1862) confron-
        tation between the dowager Marchioness of Londonderry
        and the Irish Catholics of her town, whose request
        for a chapel she turned down.

1298.   Denholm, Anthony F.   "The Conversion of Lord Ripon in
        1874."   RH 10 (April 1969):   111-18.

        Describes the increase of popular anti-Catholicism
        following the news, in September 1874, of Lord
        Ripon's decision to become a Roman Catholic.   The
        hostility toward Rome was matched only by the shock
        of hearing that an evangelical Anglican, ex-Christian
        Socialist, and Grand Master of the English Freemasons
        had submitted to Rome.

1299.   Feheney, J. Matthew, F.P.M.   "Delinquency among Irish
        Catholic Children in Victorian London."   IHS 23
        (November 1983):   319-29.

        Disputes the connection between Catholicism and
        Irish juvenile crime, made not only by nineteenth-
        century ultra-Protestants, but also by some Roman
        Catholic priests.   Accuses the police of prejudice,
        and of frequently classifying destitute youth as
        delinquent, and then treating them accordingly.

1300.   ————. "The Poor Law Board August Order, 1859: A
        Case Study of Protestant-Catholic Conflict." RH
        17 (May 1984): 84-91.

        Analyzes the vigor and persistence with which
        Protestants campaigned to repeal the Poor Law
        Board order obliging masters of all workshops to
        provide for the religious instruction of the
        Catholic orphans in their employ.

1301.   Gilley, Sheridan. "The Garibaldi Riots of 1862."
        HJ 16 (December 1973): 697-732.

        Contends that these disorders may well be the
        strongest proof of the link between Irish immigrants
        and the development of Victorian "no popery." Dis-
        plays the dramatic contrast between English and
        Irish working-class loyalties: the Irish were
        unreservedly papalist, while the English were either
        patriotic, secularist, or republican.

1302.   ————. "Nationality and Liberty, Protestant and
        Catholic: Robert Southey's *Book of the Church*."
        In RELIGION AND NATIONAL IDENTITY: PAPERS READ
        AT THE NINETEENTH SUMMER MEETING AND THE
        TWENTIETH WINTER MEETING OF THE ECCLESIASTICAL
        HISTORY SOCIETY (item 25), 409-32.

        Considers two widely varying Catholic responses to
        Robert Southey's anti-Roman BOOK OF THE CHURCH (1824),
        written as a defense of Anglicanism against the
        growing Catholic political activity of the 1820s.
        As it became increasingly apparent after 1820 that
        English Catholics were determined to repeal the Test
        and Corporation Acts, and destroy the Anglican
        monopoly of government, education, and charity work,
        Southey warned against damaging the faith which had
        saved England from papal tyranny and superstition.
        In reply, the Gallican Charles Butler published his
        BOOK OF THE ROMAN CATHOLIC CHURCH (1825), and the
        ultramontanist Bishop Milner his STRICTURES ON THE
        ... BOOK OF THE CHURCH (1824), inspiring a controversy
        which would use the providentialist view of history
        on behalf of partisan positions.

1303.   ————. "Papists, Protestants and the Irish in
        London, 1835-70." In POPULAR BELIEF AND

PRACTICE: PAPERS READ AT THE NINTH SUMMER MEETING
AND THE TENTH WINTER MEETING OF THE ECCLESIASTICAL
HISTORY SOCIETY, edited by G.J. Cuming and Derek
Baker, 259-66. Studies in Church History, vol. 8.
Cambridge: At the University Press, 1972.

Details the intense competition between Roman
Catholics and Protestant Evangelicals in London
for the souls of the Irish immigrants. Gauges the
strengths and weaknesses of the rivals: the
Evangelicals were better equipped, numerically
stronger, and wealthier, but the Catholics drew on
a large body of Irish inherited loyalties.

See: TLS, 24 March 1972: 342; Scott H. Hendrix, JAAR
41 (December 1973): 636-7; H. Boone Porter, Jr.,
AHR 80 (April 1975): 369-70; Robert F. Scholz,
CH 44 (September 1975): 419-20.

1304.   ————. "Protestant London, No-Popery and the Irish
Poor, 1830-1860. Part I: 1830-1850." RH 10
(January 1970): 210-30.

Disputes the widely held theory that Victorian
anti-Catholicism was the outcome of growing Irish
immigration. Finds the motivations behind "No
Popery" agitation in other areas, and particularly
in the poisoned atmosphere created by evangelical
sermons and "no popery" societies (e.g., the
Protestant Association of 1836 and the Protestant
Alliance of 1851). Continued in item 1305.

1305.   ————. "Protestant London, No-Popery and the Irish
Poor, 1830-1860. Part II: 1850-1860." RH 11
(January 1971): 21-46.

A continuation of item 1304. Highlights the
specific measures taken by Protestants and Catholics
in their rivalry to win over the Irish immigrants.
Sets out the organization, diverse activities, and
effectiveness of Protestant societies and Catholic
missions.

1306.   ————. "Supernaturalised Culture: Catholic
Attitudes and Latin Lands." In THE MATERIALS,
SOURCES AND METHODS OF ECCLESIASTICAL
HISTORY: PAPERS READ AT THE TWELFTH SUMMER

MEETING AND THE THIRTEENTH WINTER MEETING OF THE
ECCLESIASTICAL HISTORY, edited by Derek Baker,
309-23. Studies in Church History, vol. 11.
Oxford: Published for the Ecclesiastical History
Society by Basil Blackwell, 1975.

Discusses the reactions of nineteenth-century
Catholics to their non-Catholic countrymen's
negative attitudes toward the Catholic cultures of
southern Europe. Emphasizes the mixed feelings of
Catholics as they attempted to defend Italy and
France. On the one hand, they were examples of the
glories of the Roman faith; on the other, their
moral and material backwardness was a great
embarrassment. Provides detailed examples of
Newman's and Faber's efforts to solve this dilemma;
as long as souls were being saved, argued the two
Oratorians, of what importance were material failings?

See: Paul Crunican, CHR 66 (July 1980): 434-5.

1307. Machin, G.I.T. "The No-Popery Movement in Britain
       in 1828-9." HJ 6 (no. 2, 1963): 193-211.

       Accounts for the failure of the ultra-Protestant
       campaign to defeat the Emancipation measures of 1829,
       in the name of the Protestant Constitution. For nine
       months before the passage of the legislation, the
       Dukes of Cumberland and Newcastle, Marquess of
       Chandos, and other peers sought to counter Irish
       Catholic political zeal by appealing to the tradition-
       al anti-Roman instincts of the general populace.
       Their fragmentary approach and lack of coordination
       doomed their efforts from the start.

1308. Meynell, Wilfrid. "The Marquis of Ripon." DUBR 170
       (January/February/March 1922): 95-110.

       Presents details of Ripon's background, public
       reaction to his conversion in 1874, and the advantages
       and disadvantages to English Catholicism in gaining so
       distinguished a follower.

1309. Millward, Pauline. "The Stockport Riots of 1852: A
       Study of Anti-Catholic and Anti-Irish Sentiment."
       In THE IRISH IN THE VICTORIAN CITY (item 1092),
       207-24.

Looks beyond the usual explanation for the dis-
orders of 28-30 June 1852, that they were a reaction
by English cotton workers against the incursions of
cheap immigrant Irish labor into the mills, to
discover more subtle workings: Anglican clergymen
and electorally weak Tory politicians, in a bid for
power, fanned the flames of anti-Catholicism by
exploiting the two-year-old issue of "Papal Aggression."

1310. Murphy, Martin. "Blanco White: An Anglicised
          Spaniard." HT 28 (January 1978): 40-6.

A biographical sketch of an anti-Catholic who never
found a comfortable home in any religious organization.

1311. ─────. "Blanco White's Evidence." RH 17 (May
          1985): 254-73.

Inquires into the credibility of White's notori-
ously anti-Catholic allegations, as found most
graphically in his PRACTICAL AND INTERNAL EVIDENCE
AGAINST CATHOLICISM (1825). Judges his ideas a
significant part of the rearguard action against
Catholic Emancipation.

1312. Norman, E.R. ANTI-CATHOLICISM IN VICTORIAN ENGLAND.
          New York: Barnes & Noble, 1968.

Offers insights into a ubiquitous state of mind,
by examining four specific episodes: the Maynooth
Grant question of 1845, the restoration of the
hierarchy in 1850, Gladstone's denunciation of the
Vatican Decrees in 1874, and the King case of 1890.
Supplements the text with excerpts from a number of
key documents related to the episodes.

See: Josef L. Altholz, AHR 74 (December 1968): 612-
        3; Dunstan Pontifex, DR 87 (April 1969): 235-
        6; Richard J. Schiefen, C.S.B., JEH 20 (April
        1969): 153-4; William J. Feeney, CW 209 (June
        1969): 134-5; W.R. Ward, EHR 85 (January
        1970): 196; B.A. Knox, JRH 6 (June 1970): 85-
        7; J.C. Beckett, IHS 17 (September 1970): 292-
        3; James C. Holland, CHR 57 (January
        1972): 688-9.

1313. O'Keefe, Timothy J. "*The Times* and the Roman
      Catholics, 1857." JCS 18 (Spring 1976): 253-
      72.

      Focuses on the first serious resurgence of anti-
Catholicism in England after the "No Popery"
agitation of 1850-1851. In 1857 Wiseman attacked
the English treatment of Catholics in India; *The
Times*, in the throes of a patriotic fervor then
sweeping Britain as a result of the Sepoy Mutiny,
appointed itself the standard-bearer of Protestant
and English civilization, and questioned Catholic
loyalty to the State. The ensuing war of words
soon brought in Cullen and even Veuillot. Within
a few months, however, the conflict was over, and
without a resolution, as the newspaper simply lost
interest in continuing it.

1314. O'Neill, James E. "The British Quarterlies and the
      Religious Question, 1802-1829." CHR 52 (October
      1966): 350-71.

      Compares the positions on Catholic Emancipation
taken by three of the most important pre-Victorian
periodicals, the *Edinburgh Review*, the *Quarterly
Review*, and the *Westminster Review*. Each reflected
a different point of view within the ruling class,
and thus they indicate the divergence of opinion
within the aristocracy of birth and wealth over the
issue of Catholic relief. The *Quarterly Review* was
opposed to any religious concessions which might
endanger the Established Church. The *Westminster
Review* advocated complete separation of Church and
State as a matter of principle, arguing for emancipation and disestablishment. The middle ground was
occupied by the *Edinburgh Review*, which favored
emancipation for practical reasons and the continuation of an established, albeit reformed, church.

1315. Paz, D.G. "Anti-Catholicism, Anti-Irish Stereo-
      typing, and Anti-Celtic Racism in Mid-Victorian
      Working Class Periodicals." ALBION 18 (Winter
      1986): 601-16.

      Submits that if nineteenth-century English workers
were anti-Catholic, it was because they viewed the
Roman faith as superstitious, idolatrous, and

intolerant and not, as sometimes held, because most
of its adherents in England were Irish.

1316.   ─────. THE PRIESTHOODS AND APOSTASIES OF PIERCE
         CONNELLY: A STUDY OF VICTORIAN CONVERSION AND
         ANTICATHOLICISM. Studies in American Religion,
         vol. 18. Lewiston, N.Y., and Queenston,
         Ont.: The Edwin Mellen Press, 1986.

         A biographical approach to Victorian anti-
         Catholicism. Reconstructs the erratic life and
         work of an apostate priest who validated all the
         worst Protestant suspicions concerning Roman
         practices and institutions. Born a Presbyterian,
         Connelly (1804-1883) became, in turn, an Episco-
         palian, and then a Roman Catholic, priest. Four
         years after his second ordination, in a celebrated
         trial of 1849-1850, he sued his wife Cornelia (see
         items 185-9), now a nun, for restitution of conjugal
         rights. His judicial defeat was followed by his
         abandonment of Catholicism, in favor of the under-
         world of anti-Catholic pamphleteering. Included
         among the appendices is the complete text of his
         REASONS FOR ABJURING ALLEGIANCE TO THE SEE OF ROME
         (1852).

         See: Walter L. Arnstein, ALBION 19 (Spring 1987): 111-
               3; Josef L. Altholz, AHR 92 (June 1987): 637;
               William L. Sachs, RSR 13 (October 1987): 355-6;
               G. Howard Miller, JSOH 53 (November 1987): 664-
               5; Mary Griset Holland, CHR 74 (April
               1988): 308-9; John Kent, JEH 39 (April
               1988): 319.

1317.   Pinnington, John. "Living with Catholic Emanci-
         pation: Some Anglican Reactions." DUBR 241
         (Summer 1967): 154-61.

         A survey of popular anti-Catholicism in England
         during the two decades following Emancipation.
         Points to the restoration of the hierarchy in 1850
         as the climax of the anti-Roman tensions which had
         been building for so long, fueled by misunderstanding
         and a stubborn refusal to negotiate.

1318.   Robbins, Keith. "Papal Progress." HT 32 (June
         1982): 12-17.

Links the widespread fear and hatred of the Papacy
in nineteenth-century England to the belief that
Protestant values and national values were inter-
twined and inseparable, and that a threat to one was
automatically an attack on the other. Accompanying
the text are several contemporary cartoons which
support this interpretation.

1319. Rossi, John P. "Lord Ripon's Resumption of Political
       Activity, 1878-1880." RH 11 (April 1971): 61-74.

       Shows how Ripon's distinguished political career
       in the years after his conversion helped to under-
       mine a deeply felt prejudice in English society
       against the appointment of Catholics to high state
       office.

1320. Usherwood, Stephen. "'No Popery' under Queen
       Victoria." HT 23 (April 1973): 274-9.

       Charts the progress of "Victoria hysteria" through
       the deepening anti-Catholic hostility evoked by the
       Oxford Movement and the various manifestations of the
       Catholic revival.

The "Papal Aggression" of 1850

1321. Albion, Gordon. "'Papal Aggression' on England."
       IER 74 (October 1950): 350-7.

       Outlines the problems involved in the restoration
       of the hierarchy in 1850: public hostility, the
       choice of titles and qualified candidates for the
       new sees, the appointment of the metropolitan, and
       the division of the London ecclesiastical juris-
       diction.

1322. Blass, Homer Harrison. POPULAR ANTI-CATHOLICISM IN
       ENGLAND AND THE ECCLESIASTICAL TITLES BILL OF
       1851. Ph.D. dissertation. University of
       Missouri, Columbia, 1981.

       Locates the roots of the "No Popery" agitation
       deep within that Victorian mentality which responded
       to the Roman aggression by passing the never enforced,

and soon repealed, Ecclesiastical Titles Act.

1323.   Klaus, Robert J. THE POPE, THE PROTESTANTS, AND THE
        IRISH: PAPAL AGGRESSION AND ANTI-CATHOLICISM IN
        MID-NINETEENTH CENTURY ENGLAND. New York and
        London: Garland Publishing, 1987.

        A study of the anti-Catholicism arising from the
        "Papal Aggression" of 1850. Sees the "no popery"
        campaign as more than just a reaction to the
        restoration of the Roman hierarchy in England; it
        was the confluence of several disparate themes
        brought together by an almost atavistic set of
        emotions inspired by Rome, Ireland, and Catholicism.
        Relates this anti-Catholicism to the development of
        Victorian politics, foreign policy, social institu-
        tions, and "xenophobic nationalism."

1324.   Paz, D.G. "Another Look at Lord John Russell and
        the Papal Aggression, 1850." HIS 45 (November
        1982): 47-64.

        Argues that Russell's "Papal Aggression" policy
        was not, as often thought, a conscious policy aimed
        against his religious enemies, but rather a thought-
        less and unpremeditated response which not only
        failed to achieve its goals, but also proved
        disastrous for his political fortunes.

1325.   ————. "Popular Anti-Catholicism in England, 1850-
        1851." ALBION 11 (Winter 1979): 331-59.

        Looks at the causes and expressions of the British
        public's vehement reaction to the restoration of the
        Roman hierarchy in 1850. Sees anti-Catholic senti-
        ment as motivated not simply by the papal action
        but also by fears over growing Irish immigration and
        the revitalization of Catholicism in England.

1326.   Ralls, Walter A. THE PAPAL AGGRESSION OF 1850: ITS
        BACKGROUND AND MEANING. Ph.D. dissertation.
        Columbia University, 1960.

        Examines the varied and complex causes of the
        great outburst of "no popery" in 1850. Places
        against a Catholic community deeply divided between
        "Old Catholics" and converts, the mounting English

irritation over Irish immigration, Wiseman's pompous-
ness, and Pius IX's reactionary stance, along with
widespread anxiety over a foundering Established
Church.

1327.   ————. "The Papal Aggression of 1850: A Study in
Victorian Anti-Catholicism." CH 43 (June
1974): 242-56.

Follows anti-Catholic agitation in England during
the six months prior to the opening of the Great
Exhibition, in an effort to understand how the
aroused bigots of November 1850 became the congenial,
progressive-minded citizens of the Crystal Palace
summer of 1851. Stresses the importance of religious
rhetoric in the press and pulpit on both sides.

Liberal Catholicism

General

1328.   Altholz, Josef L. THE LIBERAL CATHOLIC MOVEMENT IN
ENGLAND: THE "RAMBLER" AND ITS CONTRIBUTORS,
1848-1864. London: Burns & Oates, 1962.

Traces the progress of English liberal Catholicism
through the fortunes of the *Rambler*. Under the
direction of Simpson, Newman, and Acton, the review
sought to inform the laity of modern developments in
science, history, and politics; at the same time, it
promoted freedom of inquiry and an ecumenical outlook
which respected non-Catholic thought. Such progressive activities led to the periodical's break-up,
upon the hierarchy's order, in 1862. Its successor,
the *Home and Foreign Review*, ceased operation in
1864, after receiving episcopal censure. Liberal
Catholicism could not prosper without being given a
certain amount of freedom, or at least being
tolerated, by Church authorities.

See: Ronald Chapman, CLR 47 (December 1962): 762-4;
John Coulson, DR 81 (January 1963): 81-3;
Patrick J. Corish, IER 99 (January 1963): 69-
70; Wilbur S. Shepperson, HIS 25 (February

1963): 232-3; Damian McElrath, CHR 49 (April
1963): 121-3; Stephen J. Tonsor, VS 7
(December 1963): 197-9; Emmet Larkin, AHR 70
(October 1964): 126-7; Gertrude Himmelfarb,
JMH 36 (December 1964): 461-2.

1329. Bottino, Edward Joseph. THE *RAMBLER* CONTROVERSY: PO-
        SITIONS OF SIMPSON, NEWMAN AND ACTON, 1856-1862.
        Ph.D. dissertation. St. John's University, 1970.

        Documents the opposition faced by the editors of
        the *Rambler* in their campaign to bring English
        Catholicism into the mainstream of continental
        liberal Catholicism. Studies the effects of the
        controversy between liberal and "Old Catholics" on
        English Catholic life in general. Offers insights
        into the character and motives of the leading pro-
        tagonists on both sides, with special reference to
        Newman.

1330. Burtchaell, James Tunstead, C.S.C. "The Biblical
        Question and the English Liberal Catholics."
        RP 31 (January 1969): 108-20.

        Evaluates the scholarly, critical, and optimistic
        approach to Scriptural studies taken by Tractarian
        converts to liberal Catholicism. Emphasizes their
        use of the scientific method, in an effort to dis-
        credit fundamentalism, and their deference to
        established authority when faced with uncertainty.

1331. McElrath, Damian, O.F.M. RICHARD SIMPSON, 1820-
        1876: A STUDY IN XIXTH CENTURY ENGLISH LIBERAL
        CATHOLICISM. Bibliothèque de la Revue d'Histoire
        Ecclésiastique, vol. 55. Louvain: Publications
        Universitaires de Louvain, 1972.

        Follows, within a loose chronological structure,
        the major events and ideas of Simpson's life.
        Focuses on his membership in a small group of
        nineteenth-century Englishmen, dominated by Acton
        and preaching a variety of liberal Catholicism
        distinct in some important ways from its conti-
        nental counterpart.

        See: Bernard M.G. Reardon, AMPJ 79 (Spring
              1974): 9-16; Paul Misner, CH 43

(June 1974): 274-5; Alec R. Vidler, JEH 25
(July 1974): 349-50; William J. Schoenl, AHR
80 (February 1975): 111-2; David M. Thompson,
EHR 90 (July 1975): 665-6; Richard J. Schiefen,
CHR 62 (October 1976): 626-8.

1332. Roe, W.G. LAMENNAIS AND ENGLAND: THE RECEPTION OF
LAMENNAIS' RELIGIOUS IDEAS IN ENGLAND IN THE
NINETEENTH CENTURY. London: Oxford University
Press, 1966.

Establishes the relationship between Lamennais'
thought and the outlook of the liberal Catholic
movement in England.

See: TLS, 1 December 1966: 1131; The Abbot of Downside, DR 85 (April 1967): 231-4; A.R. Vidler,
JEH 18 (April 1967): 127-8; Martin E. Marty,
JR 47 (July 1967): 277-8; CHOICE 4 (September
1967): 694; John Ratté, AHR 73 (October
1967): 138; John Ratté, COMMWL 87 (6 October
1967): 26; A.E. Firth, EHR 83 (January
1968): 198-9; Neville C. Masterman, HIST 53
(February 1968): 141-2; E.D. Mackerness, MLR
63 (July 1968): 685-6; Josef L. Altholz, JMH
40 (December 1968): 617-8; Damian McElrath,
CHR 55 (July 1969): 199.

1333. Schoenl, William J. "The Reappearance of English
Liberal Catholicism in the Early 1890's." CLR
62 (March 1977): 92-105.

Illustrates the diversity of English liberal
Catholicism during the last decade of the nineteenth
century, placing Ward in the middle of the spectrum,
von Hügel at left center, Tyrrell at far left,
Gasquet at right center, and Bishop sometimes to the
left, and sometimes to the right, of Ward. Charts
their rising hopes that Rome would provide an
atmosphere within which scholars and thinkers would
be able to meet the challenge of modern culture;
these hopes would be destroyed not only by the
English bishops' pastoral condemning liberal
Catholicism (1900), but also by ever wider divisions
among the liberals themselves.

Acton

1334.   Barry, William. "Lord Acton: A Study." DUBR 162
        (January/February/March 1918): 1-24.

        Explores his immense correspondence, in an effort
        to understand how so devout a Catholic could be so
        critical of papal personalities and policies, and
        so friendly with Döllinger and Gladstone.

1335.   Chadwick, Owen. "Lord Acton at the First Vatican
        Council." JTS 28 (October 1977): 465-97.

        Explains why Acton succeeded in exerting so
        extraordinary an influence over the early delib-
        erations of Vatican I. Using his Roman diary of
        November 1869 to January 1870, Chadwick details
        Acton's leadership of an anti-infallibilist
        network.

1336.   Conzemius, J.V. "Lord Acton and the First Vatican
        Council." JEH 20 (October 1969): 267-94.

        Discusses the content and impact of Acton's
        lengthy eyewitness reports on the proceedings of
        Vatican I, sent to Gladstone and Döllinger. The
        latter published some of these letters in the
        Augsburger Allgemeine Zeitung, a prominent liberal
        newspaper, adding his own contributions under the
        name "Quirinus."

1337.   Dwyer, J.J. "Lord Acton." CLR 38 (April 1953): 202-
        14.

        Demonstrates the extent to which Acton's view of
        Church history was colored by his hatred of ultra-
        montanism and frustration over Vatican I and its
        proclamation of papal infallibility.

1338.   Himmelfarb, Gertrude. LORD ACTON: A STUDY IN
        CONSCIENCE AND POLITICS. London: Routledge &
        Kegan Paul, 1952.

        Follows the evolution of Acton's political and
        religious outlook. Reveals the full extent of his
        rupture with Döllinger, whose significance in

Acton's life is underscored.

See: George N. Shuster, COMM 15 (February 1953): 212-
      4; Golo Mann, PARR 20 (March/April 1953): 239-
      41; F.A. Hayek, FREE 3 (23 March 1953): 461-2;
      Duncan Forbes, EHR 68 (April 1953): 292-3; W.D.
      Nutting, RP 15 (April 1953): 257-8; Russell
      Kirk, YR 42 (June 1953): 600-3; Crane Brinton,
      AHR 58 (July 1953): 870-1; Peter Marshall, AR
      13 (September 1953): 406-9; Edward Gargan, CHR
      39 (October 1953): 329-30; Clarence L. Hohl,
      Jr., HB 33 (May 1955): 231-3; Sheldon S. Wolin,
      WPQ 8 (September 1955): 508-10.

1339. Hohl, Clarence L., Jr. "Lord Acton and the Vatican
       Council." HB 28 (November 1949): 7-11.

       Explains the motives behind Acton's pre-conciliar
       attacks on the idea of papal infallibility. His
       study of ecclesiastical history convinced him that a
       proclamation of infallibility would cause the Church
       to lose both prestige and power, for it was an
       erroneous doctrine which tied Catholicism to the
       varying (and perhaps unscrupulous) personalities of
       its pontiffs.

1340. Keating, Kathleen C. JOHN ACTON AND THE CHURCH OF
       PIUS IX. Ph.D. dissertation. Fordham University,
       1973.

       Considers the development of Acton's religious
       outlook up to 1870, in order to determine why he
       took so strong a stand against infalliblity. His
       lifelong ecclesiastical attitude was formed during
       his schooling in Munich, at the height of the
       German Catholic revival. Rooting his views in
       Church history, he saw Pius IX as the antithesis
       of the Catholic tradition of liberty, the leader
       who enslaved the Church through Roman absolutism
       and papal infallibility. Acton's deep faith,
       however, enabled him to transcend what he believed
       were only temporary aberrations; unlike Döllinger,
       he chose to remain within the Roman fold.

1341. MacDougall, Hugh. "The Later Acton: The Historian
       as Moralist." In BISHOPS AND WRITERS; ASPECTS
       OF THE EVOLUTION OF MODERN ENGLISH CATHOLICISM

(item 785), 35-49.

Sympathizes with Acton's post-1870 moral
dilemma: he was torn between instinctual loyalty
to the Church and devotion to a form of historical
thinking which made official statements like those
of Vatican I impossible to accept without numerous
qualifications. Points to his withdrawal from
issues affecting Catholicism during his later
years, in favor of a moralistic view of history,
which promoted a deeper understanding of human
society. Credits Acton with doing more than any
other nineteenth-century Englishman, except
Newman, to keep alive a spirit of intellectual
inquiry within English Catholicism.

1342. Marshall, Norma. "Lord Acton and the Writing of
        Religious History." JRH 10 (December 1979): 400-
        15.

Presents Acton's skillful reconciliation of his
religious beliefs and historical scholarship; his
dedication to impartiality was tempered by his
awareness that all great historians injected their
personalities into their work. Searches for the
major issues in Acton's intellectual development,
reconstructing his attempts to put these into
finished form.

1343. Mathew, David. LORD ACTON AND HIS TIMES.
        London: Eyre & Spottiswoode, 1968.

A panoramic treatment which recreates in depth
the environment in which Acton lived, thought, and
worked. Highly sympathetic to its subject, this
account includes sensitive character sketches of
Wiseman, Manning, Newman, Döllinger, and others
who played a significant role in Acton's life.

See: ECON 229 (9 November 1968): xxii; J.M. Cameron,
       OBS, 10 November 1968: 26; Archdale A. King,
       DUBR 242 (Winter 1968-9): 293-5; Robert Blake,
       SPEC 222 (14 February 1969): 213-4; Maurice
       Adelman, Jr., AMER 120 (15 March 1969): 310-2;
       Wilfrid Passmore, DR 87 (April 1969): 223-6;
       Asa Briggs, LIST 81 (10 April 1969): 502; R.T.
       Shannon, HIST 54 (June 1969): 306;

CHOICE 6 (July/August 1969): 696; Josef L.
Altholz, AHR 75 (October 1969): 124; YR 59
(October 1969): xviii-xxvi; R.J. Schoeck, VS
14 (December 1970): 212-3; H. Butterfield,
EHR 86 (April 1971): 433; Damian McElrath,
O.F.M., CHR 58 (April 1972): 92-4.

1344. Murphy, Terrence. "Lord Acton and the Free Church
Policy of Baron Ricasoli." JEH 32 (July
1981): 321-35.

Highlights Acton's growing anti-Roman sentiment
during the years 1864-1869, along with its major
cause, the Vatican's denunciation of the Free Church
Bill, which, according to Acton, was a sincere effort
by Italian liberals to give Italian Catholicism the
freedom it needed to continue its social mission.

1345. Watt, E.D. "Rome and Lord Acton: A Reinterpretation."
RP 28 (October 1966): 493-507.

Clarifies the relationship between Acton and the
Catholic hierarchy. Traces his anti-Roman stance to
a personal dislike of ecclesiastical centralization
as well as to his considered opinion that he need not
submit either to a doctrine not formally defined or
to any "private interpretation" which might extend
the scope of a formally defined doctrine.

Scotland

General Works

1346. Anson, Peter F. THE CATHOLIC CHURCH IN MODERN
SCOTLAND, 1560-1937. London: Burns & Washbourne,
1937.

Part 2 includes nineteenth-century developments
through the restoration of the hierarchy in 1878.
Features considerations of the vicariate system's
five districts, the final years of the penal laws,
and Catholic life during the early years of the
century. Part 3 contains accounts of the first
two decades of the six revived dioceses (St.

Andrews and Edinburgh, Aberdeen, Argyll and the
Isles, Dunkeld, Galloway, and Glasgow).   In the
Appendices are found statistics and lists of
Scottish religious orders, congregations, and
institutes.

See: CLR 14 (March 1938): 279-81; Dom Ninian Fair,
      DR 56 (April 1938): 232-3; DUBR 202 (April/
      May/June 1938): 375; Andrew B. Baird, CH 7
      (September 1938): 287-8.

1347.   ————.   UNDERGROUND CATHOLICISM IN SCOTLAND, 1622-
        1878. Montrose: Standard Press, 1970.

A revised and expanded version of the post-
Reformation section of item 1346. Chapters 6-10
survey nineteenth-century developments in the
vicariates (or Districts, after 1852), while
Chapter 11 outlines the restoration of the
hierarchy in 1878. Presents a minority striving
to maintain its own distinctive religious and
political loyalties, both of which were despised
by the majority.

See: TLS, 18 June 1971: 691; Ian A. Muirhead, SJT
      24 (November 1971): 504-5; David McRoberts,
      CLR 56 (December 1971): 996-8; Ian B. Cowan,
      HIST 57 (February 1972): 102-3; Patrick
      McGrath, EHR 87 (April 1972): 416-7; Mark
      Dilworth, O.S.B., AMPJ 77 (Spring 1972): 98-9;
      John Durkan, SHR 51 (October 1972): 204-6.

1348.   Aspinwall, Bernard. "The Second Spring in
        Scotland: I." CLR 66 (August 1981): 281-90.

Describes the nineteeth-century Catholic revival
in Scotland as carried out by converts of substance
and education, whose self-confidence and enthusiasm
enabled them to do for the Scottish Church what
middle-class converts had done for the English
Church during its "Second Spring." Continued in
item 1349.

1349.   ————. "The Second Spring in Scotland: II." CLR
        66 (September 1981): 312-19.

A continuation of item 1348. Assesses Scottish

Catholicism's diversified pastoral response to the
problems of urban poverty,--education, child care,
nursing, and preaching,--along with its establishment
of a popular press to present a reasonable statement
of Catholic attitudes and to inspire a sense of
Catholic community and cohesion.

1350.   ————. "Some Aspects of Scotland and the Catholic
         Revival in the Early Nineteenth Century." IR 26
         (Spring 1975): 3-19.

Discusses the impact of secular Scottish culture
upon the Catholic progress of the years 1780-1830.
Spurred on by Scott's glorification of the chivalric
Middle Ages, and Forbes' dissemination of Indian
religious thought, among other developments, the
Church rediscovered its historical identity, using
it as one of the bases for its religious offensive.

1351.   Bellesheim, Alphons. HISTORY OF THE CATHOLIC CHURCH
         OF SCOTLAND FROM THE INTRODUCTION OF CHRISTIANITY
         TO THE PRESENT DAY. Translated by D. Oswald
         Hunter Blair, O.S.B. Vol. 4: FROM THE ACCESSION
         OF CHARLES THE FIRST TO THE RESTORATION OF THE
         SCOTTISH HIERARCHY, A.D. 1625-1878. Edinburgh and
         London: William Blackwood and Sons, 1890.

Chapter 5 covers various aspects of Scottish
Catholic history from 1800 to 1878, including the
impact of the French clergy, the workings of the
vicariate system, the effects of Emancipation,
sketches of lay leaders, and the negotiations for
the restoration of the hierarchy. Chapter 6 details
Leo XIII's two bulls regularizing the position of
the Scottish Church: *Ex Supremo Apostolatus Apice*
(1878), which reestablished the hierarchy, and
Romanos Pontifices (1881), which specified the
rights and privileges of regular and secular clergy.

1352.   Cooney, John. SCOTLAND AND THE PAPACY.
         Edinburgh: Paul Harris, 1982.

A survey of developments in modern Scottish Roman
Catholicism, seen from the viewpoint of Scottish-
Papal relations. Chapter 2 follows the fortunes of
"no popery" agitation throughout the nineteenth
century. Chapter 4 looks into the effects of the

Irish immigration and the reestablishment of the
hierarchy. Chapter 5 explains the spread of
ultramontanism, while Chapter 6 considers the
devotional revolution, as expressed through church-
building and the introduction of such distinctly
Roman practices as Marian devotion, processions,
and the veneration of saints.

See: T. Corbett, ITQ 49 (no. 4, 1982): 313.

1353. Darragh, James. "The Catholic Population of Scotland,
       1878-1977." IR 29 (Autumn 1978): 211-47.

       Contains a detailed statistical evaluation of each
       of the newly created dioceses of 1878.

1354. Johnson, Christine. DEVELOPMENTS IN THE ROMAN
       CATHOLIC CHURCH IN SCOTLAND, 1789-1929.
       Edinburgh: John Donald, 1983.

       Places various aspects of Scottish Catholic
       progress within the larger national context.
       Chapters 19-27 examine nineteenth-century
       ecclesiastical structures, ritual and music,
       churches and chapels, clerical and lay life, and
       educational institutions and advances.

       See: E.D. Steele, BBN, April/May 1983: 352-3;
             Bernard Aspinwall, CLR 68 (July 1983): 264-
             5; CHOICE 21 (December 1983): 588; R.K. Browne,
             MONTH 2nd NS 17 (January 1984): 34-5; Maurice
             Lee, Jr., HRNB 12 (February 1984): 77-8; John
             Simpson, IR 35 (Spring 1984): 47-8; Sheridan
             Gilley, JEH 35 (April 1984): 286-8; Tom
             Gallagher, TLS, 6 July 1984: 765; Stewart J.
             Brown, CH 53 (September 1984): 403-4; Elmer
             H. Duncan, JCS 27 (Spring 1985): 346-7; Mark
             Finnane, JRH 13 (June 1985): 315-6; Vincent
             Alan McClelland, CHR 72 (April 1986): 290-1.

1355. McCaffrey, John F. "Roman Catholics in Scotland in
       the 19th and 20th Centuries." RSCHS 21
       (1985): 275-300.

       Sketches Scottish Catholic growth, concentrating
       on three key issues which provide insights into that
       growth, and suggesting areas of future inquiry.

Discusses the tension between Scottish priests and
Irish parishioners, the role of politics in causing
both conflict and assimilation, and educational
strategies, using sources drawn mainly from the
western part of Scotland.

The Hierarchy and Diocesan Organization

1356. Cunningham, John. "Church Administration and
Organization: 1878-1978." IR 29 (Spring
1978): 73-91.

Provides background on *Ex Supremo Apostolatus
Apice*, *Romanos Pontifices*, and Propaganda's decree
of 1883, on the subject of episcopal election.

1357. Darragh, James. THE CATHOLIC HIERARCHY OF
SCOTLAND: A BIOGRAPHICAL LIST, 1653-1985.
Glasgow: John S. Burns & Sons, 1986.

Includes brief *vitae* of the nineteenth-century
bishops. Indicates sources for all data, and why
in particular instances certain details are missing;
adds background material if necessary. An intro-
ductory essay clarifies the nature of the relationship between Rome and the Scottish episcopate.

See: Mark Dilworth, IR 37 (Autumn 1986): 106-7;
John McCaffrey, JEH 39 (April 1988): 312-3.

1358. McClelland, Vincent Alan. "Documents Relating to the
Appointment of a Delegate-Apostolic for Scotland,
1868." IR 8 (Spring 1957): 93-8.

Reconstructs from letters in the Errington file of
the Clifton Diocesan Archives, the complex negotiations of 1868 to establish George Errington,
Archbishop of Trebizond, as Vicar Apostolic of the
Western District of Scotland, with the responsibility
of restoring the Scottish hierarchy. Continued in
item 1359.

1359. ———. "A Hierarchy for Scotland, 1868-1878." CHR
56 (October 1970): 474-500.

A sequel to item 1358. Studies the mechanics of
the hierarchical restoration. Underscores the
difficult problems solved by Errington: the
partition of the new dioceses, the choice of a
metropolitan see, and the selection of a suitable
candidate for the see of Glasgow.

1360.   Macdonald, Roderick. "Bishop Scott and the West
        Highlands." IR 17 (Autumn 1966): 116-28.

Summarizes Bishop Andrew Scott's heroic ministry
in the Western Highlands. To an area notorious for
its clerical indifference Scott brought order and
discipline, building churches and sharing all the
hardships of his reformed priests.

1361.   McRoberts, David. "The Catholic Directory for
        Scotland, 1829-1975." IR 26 (Autumn 1975): 93-
        120.

A history of the oldest ecclesiastical yearbook
in the British Isles, founded by Father John
Macpherson in 1829.

1362.   ————. "The Restoration of the Scottish Catholic
        Hierarchy in 1878." IR 29 (Spring 1978): 3-29.

Sees the restoration as a logical and inevitable
product of the increasing dynamism and vitality of
Scottish Roman Catholicism after 1829. Analyzes
the pre-1878 vicariate system and the conditions
necessitating the reestablishment of territorial
bishoprics. Supplements the material in item 1359
on the negotiations over restoration, by emphasizing
for the first time the role of Cardinal Cullen.

Diocesan Clergy and Pastoral Activity

1363.   Aspinwall, Bernard. "A Glasgow Pastoral Plan, 1855-
        1860: Social and Spiritual Renewal." IR 35
        (Spring 1984): 33-6.

Assesses the reinvigoration of parochial life at
St. Mary's, Glasgow, under the leadership of Father
Peter Forbes. Over a five-year period, Forbes

introduced new devotional and liturgical practices,
including Benediction, the novena to the Sacred Heart,
and community singing at Mass; established a Sunday
school, as well as elementary and industrial schools;
and brought in the St. Vincent de Paul Society.
Points to a strong sense of religious identity and
cohesion created by Forbes against a background of
urban poverty and a predominantly non-Catholic
culture.

1364. Duffy, Timothy. "George A. Griffin: A Priest among
       Antiquaries." IR 27 (Autumn 1976): 127-61.

       Demonstrates the extent of Catholic clerical
participation in nineteenth-century Scottish
scholarship. Griffin (1810-1860) served as a
missionary at Strichen, Aberdeenshire, from 1834
to 1846; taught at St. Mary's College, Blairs,
from 1846 to 1852; and spent the last years of his
life at New Abbey, near Dumfries. His antiquari-
anism, which earned him universal respect, was
always expressed within the context of his priesthood, as his studies of Scottish ecclesiastical
history indicate.

1365. Forbes, F., and Anderson, W.J. "Clergy Lists of the
       Highland District, 1732-1828." IR 17 (Autumn
       1966): 129-84.

       Contains, in order of seniority, the names, ordi-
nation dates, and ministries of all Highland District
priests during the first three decades of the
nineteenth century.

1366. McCluskey, M. "The Early Life of Abbé Nicholas." IR
       15 (Autumn 1964): 187-8.

       Supplements item 1367, by providing material on a
phase of the abbé's life not discussed by McGloin.

1367. McGloin, James. "The Abbé Nicholas." IR 14 (Spring
       1963): 10-29.

       Presents the Scottish ministry of a French
refugee, whose dynamic personality and selfless
activity contributed enormously to breaking down
anti-Catholic prejudice during the first decade

of the nineteenth century. Focuses on his years
at Ayr Academy, using extensive passages from his
correspondence. For his youth and training in
France, see item 1366.

1368.   ————. "Some Refugee French Clerics and Laymen in
         Scotland, 1789-1814." IR 16 (Spring 1965): 27-
         55.

         Attempts to ascertain the number, location, and
         types of ministry of the French clergy in Scotland
         during the Revolutionary and Napoleonic era.
         Maintains that in marked contrast to the English
         experience (items 1001-4), Scotland gained a good
         deal from the French presence.

1369.   MacWilliam, Alexander S. "The Highland Seminary at
         Lismore, 1803-1828." IR 8 (Spring 1957): 30-8.

         An account of the institution's activities, from
         its founding by Bishop John Chisholm, Vicar Apostolic
         of the Highland District, to its amalgamation with
         its Lowland counterpart, to form the National
         Seminary at Blairs. Praises the Masters of Lismore,
         who fought against tremendous odds and the direst
         poverty, to train priests for the Scottish Church.

                     Orders and Congregations

1370.   Edmond, Louis, C.P. "Father Austin Edgar, C.P., the
         First Scottish Passionist." IR 16 (Autumn
         1965): 159-64.

         A biography and character sketch of the founder of
         the first Passionist house in Scotland (1865). In
         addition to his organizational work in Scotland,
         Edgar conducted numerous missions among the Irish in
         England.

The Laity

General

1371. Ross, Anthony, O.P. "The Development of the Scottish
Catholic Community, 1878-1978." IR 29 (Spring
1978): 30-55.

Concentrates on the two major challenges to
nineteenth-century Scottish Catholicism: the
divisions between the natives and Irish immigrants,
and between Highlanders and Lowlanders; and the
campaign to maintain, if not elevate, the moral
standards of urban Catholics, and particularly
those in areas of heavy industrialization like
Glasgow.

Regional Studies

1372. Aspinwall, Bernard. "The Formation of the Catholic
Community in the West of Scotland: Some
Preliminary Outlines." IR 33 (1982): 44-57.

Suggests that the various Scottish Catholic
responses to the Irish Catholic influx of the
mid-nineteenth century produced a remarkably
dynamic and durable framework within which
Catholic life flourished with its own special
ethos until the middle of the twentieth century.
Before the arrival of the Irish, there was no
infrastructure capable of promoting a vibrant
religious life.

1373. Macdonald, Roderick. "The Catholic Gaidhealtachd."
IR 29 (Spring 1978): 56-72.

Describes nineteenth-century efforts to Catholi-
cize the large, unabsorbed Gaelic section of Scotland.
Emphasizes the problems of reaching out to an area so
different from the rest of the country in language,
racial origins, political history, and social
conditions, as well as of the continuing and often
bitter rivalry among the missionaries themselves.

1374. MacWilliam, Alexander S. "Catholic Dundee: 1787 to
         1836." IR 18 (Autumn 1967):   75-87.

         Profiles the growth of Dundee's Catholic population
         and institutions over a fifty-year period. Over these
         five decades the number of Catholics rose from
         approximately thirty to more than eight thousand.

1375. Roberts, Alasdair. "Catholic Baptismal Registers in
         the City of Aberdeen, 1782-1876." IR 31 (Spring
         1980):   17-25.

         Uses baptismal registers for Aberdeen parishes to
         establish the incidence of illegitimacy among
         nineteenth-century Scottish Catholics.

The Irish Immigrants

1376. Handley, James E.   "The Famine and the Development of
         the Church in Scotland." IER 69 (October
         1947):   910-24.

         Details the negative impact of Irish immigration
         upon the religious life of Scottish Catholics. Not
         only did the influx lead to the rapid erection of
         churches and chapels in every industrial center,
         but the zealous Irish priests who accompanied their
         flock disrupted the prudent tenor of Scottish
         Catholicism by their enthusiastic piety and heavy
         political involvement. Small wonder that friction
         soon broke out between Scottish pastors and their
         recently arrived coreligionists.

1377. ————. GREAT BRITAIN: SCOTLAND. A History of
         Irish Catholicism, edited by Patrick J. Corish,
         vol. 6, no. 1. Dublin: Gill and Son, 1968.

         A brief survey of the interaction between Scottish
         and Irish Catholics in Scotland during the second
         half of the nineteenth century.

1378. ————. THE IRISH IN SCOTLAND, 1798-1845.
         Cork: Cork University Press, 1945.

         Chapters 4 and 8 identify the feelings which the

Irish Catholic influx evoked in Protestants, along with the steps--organized ruffianism, demonstrations, and pamphlet warfare--which those feelings inspired.

See: D.W. Brogan, ECHR 15 (nos. 1-2, 1945): 98-9; Thomas P. O'Neill, IHS 5 (March 1946): 102-3.

1379. Walker, W.M. "Irish Immigrants in Scotland: Their Priests, Politics and Parochial Life." HJ 15 (December 1972): 649-67.

Challenges Friedrich Engels' assertion of 1845 that the Irish immigrants represented an explosive force within British society, by examining Irish religious organization and life in Scotland as a whole, and in Dundee, in particular. Shows that the parochial structure, in the person of the venerated and powerful priest, taught the Irish docility and resignation to their state.

Education

1380. Dealy, Sister Mary Bonaventure, O.S.B. CATHOLIC SCHOOLS IN SCOTLAND. Washington, D.C.: Catholic University of America Press, 1945.

Chapter 4 evaluates the work of the voluntary schools, established in the wake of Emancipation and maintained through the efforts and oftentimes even at the personal expense of the bishops and clergy, aided by small fees paid by the pupils. Considers, at the same time, the state of seminaries, teacher training, and the governance of the entire system.

1381. Fitzpatrick, Thomas A. "Catholic Education in Glasgow, Lanarkshire and South-West Scotland before 1872." IR 36 (Autumn 1985): 86-96.

Traces the development of Catholic schools in three areas of Scotland during the years 1817-1872. Points to a growing recognition of the need for rudimentary religious education as the Catholic population increased ever more dramatically through the century. Highlights landmarks in the growth

process, including, most notably, the granting of
government assistance (1847) and the willingness of
several religious orders--e.g., the Sisters of Mercy,
Marists, Jesuits, and Vincentians--to teach in the
system.

1382. McGloin, James. "Catholic Education in Ayr, 1823-
         1918--Part One." IR 13 (Spring 1962): 77-103.

         Recreates the first twenty-three trouble-ridden
         years of Father William Thomson's elementary school
         (1856-1879), using extracts from the daily academic
         log. Maintains that Thomson's establishment reveals
         most clearly the problems with which all Scottish
         Catholic education had to struggle: poverty, mal-
         nutrition, disease, and public apathy. Post-1879
         development of the school if discussed in item 1383.

1383. ————. "Catholic Education in Ayr, 1823-
         1918--Part Two." IR 13 (Autumn 1962): 190-
         216.

         Continued from item 1382. Carries the account of
         the Thomson school's fight for survival through the
         end of the century. Emphasizes the continuing con-
         flict between the need for Catholic education and the
         hard economic facts of the times, which presented a
         powerful obstacle to the fulfillment of that need.

1384. Skinnider, Sister Martha, S.N.D. "Catholic
         Elementary Education in Glasgow, 1818-1918."
         In STUDIES IN THE HISTORY OF SCOTTISH EDUCATION,
         1872-1939, edited by T.R. Bone, 13-40.
         London: University of London Press, 1967.

         Follows the efforts of Glasgow's Catholic com-
         munity to establish a viable and effective system
         of elementary education, despite such serious
         century-long problems as the lack of qualified
         male teachers, widespread poverty, and the
         Education Act of 1872. These challenges notwith-
         standing, and by the end of the century, Catholic
         schools were able to match the educational standards
         of their government-sponsored counterparts.

1385. Treble, J.H. "The Development of Roman Catholic
         Education in Scotland, 1878-1978." IR

29 (Autumn 1978): 111-39.

Outlines the problems faced by late nineteenth-
century Church leaders in trying to erect a network
of elementary schools to meet the needs, especially
in the industrial western and central counties, of
an expanding Catholic population. Among the problems
underscored are the dearth of proper educational
facilities, the inability to find enough qualified
instructors, and the poverty of most of the families
for whom the network was established in the first
place.

The Press

1386.   Edwards, Owen Dudley. "The Catholic Press in
        Scotland since the Restoration of the
        Hierarchy." IR 29 (Autumn 1978): 156-82.

Examines efforts by the late nineteenth-century
Scottish Catholic periodicals to reinforce indigenous
religious traditions against intrusions by immigrants
(the Irish) and foreign cultures (whether English,
French, or Roman).

Social Catholicism

1387.   Aspinwall, Bernard. "David Urquhart, Robert Monteith
        and the Catholic Church: A Search for Justice and
        Peace." IR 31 (Autumn 1980): 57-70.

Studies the activities of Urquhart and Monteith on
behalf of social justice and peace. The much maligned
Urquhart was a Catholic radical; Monteith, a much
neglected figure in Scottish Catholic history, sought
to awaken the conscience of his coreligionists to
social questions.

1388.   ————. "Robert Monteith (1812-1884): A Scottish
        Layman and Modern Catholic Social Thought." CLR
        63 (July 1978): 265-72.

A portrait of a key personality of nineteenth-

century Scottish Catholic history. After his conversion in 1846, Monteith balanced his rich intellectual life with a practical social activism, the
latter leading him to pressure the Papacy and the
English hierarchy for a reassertion of the Law of
Nations, in which the idea of social welfare was
rooted. At the same time, he built a model church,
school, and hospital in Lanark. Through his
influence Catholic participation in democratic
politics and the ecumenical movement broadened
considerably.

1389.   ————. "The Welfare State within the State: The
         Saint Vincent de Paul Society in Glasgow, 1848-
         1920." In VOLUNTARY RELIGION: PAPERS READ AT
         THE 1985 SUMMER MEETING AND THE 1986 WINTER
         MEETING OF THE ECCLESIASTICAL HISTORY SOCIETY
         (item 30), 445-59.

         Measures the Society's importance, influence, and
         contribution to the protection, consolidation, and
         improvement of the new and mainly immigrant church in
         Glasgow. Credits the lay apostolate with several
         significant achievements: (1) it succeeded in
         preventing any serious penetration of the Catholic
         community by proselytism; (2) it helped to transmit,
         although unknowingly, the values of the host
         country--thrift, sobriety, and self-help--to the newly
         arrived Irish; (3) it provided the poor immigrant
         with cradle-to-grave support, which led to the
         formation of a Catholic mentality in favor of social
         reform; and (4) it taught its beneficiaries to take
         pride in the accomplishments, both past and present,
         of their community.

                         Special Challenges

                       Church and State

1390.   Moffat, Charles Gordon. SCOTLAND AND THE CATHOLIC
         EMANCIPATION QUESTION. Ph.D. dissertation.
         University of Tennessee, 1974.

         Shows that the Scots, unlike the English and the

Irish, had no great difficulty in accepting the
legislation of 1829. Displaying a noteworthy
political moderation, they saw no real danger in
Emancipation; on the contrary, many Scots hailed
it as an expression of the ideals of liberty and
equality to which they had been attached since
the time of the French Revolution. For an opposing
view, however, see items 1391 and 1392.

1391. Muirhead, Ian A. "Catholic Emancipation: Scottish
Reactions in 1829--Part One." IR 24 (Spring
1973): 26-42.

Disagrees with item 1390. Argues that although
the intensity of feelings concerning Emancipation
varied from one geographical area to another, and
as one moved down the social ladder, the majority
of Scots were definitely against any concessions
to Catholics. Highlights the agitation both for
and against the legislation. Continues in item
1392.

1392. ————. "Catholic Emancipation: The Debate and the
Aftermath--Part Two." IR 24 (Autumn 1973): 102-
20.

Continued from item 1391. Considers the specific
issues raised during the Emancipation agitation of
the 1820s, including the arguments used by opponents
and the replies proffered by supporters.

Catholic Political Activity

1393. McCaffrey, John F. "Politics and the Catholic
Community since 1878." IR 29 (Autumn 1978): 140-
55.

Charts the growing political consciousness and
confidence of Scottish Catholics during the 1880s
and 90s. Illustrates how parishes and individuals,
encouraged by the hierarchy, pressured the government to observe the provisions of the Education Act
of 1872 and to grant Irish Home Rule.

Anticlericalism and Anticatholicism

1394.   Aspinwall, Bernard.   "Popery in Scotland: Image and
           Reality, 1820-1920."   RSCHS 22 (1986):   235-57.

        Describes the main features of Scottish "No
   Popery," attributing their nineteenth-century
   strength among all classes of Protestants to an
   almost paranoid fear of Catholic-inspired moral
   decay and loss of Scottish identity.   Notes an
   important transatlantic connection, for the view
   of the Roman faith as oppressive and anachronistic
   found equal favor at the same time in the United
   States.   Concludes that anti-Catholicism, for all
   its negative aspects, did serve a useful social
   and religious purpose in Victorian Scotland.

1395.   Bruce, Steve.   NO POPE OF ROME: ANTI-CATHOLICISM IN
           MODERN SCOTLAND.   Edinburgh: Mainstream
           Publishing, 1985.

        Chapter 1 details the causes, geographical location,
   and social composition of nineteenth-century "No
   Popery" agitation.   Asserts that anti-Catholicism in
   Scotland was essentially a reaction against the Irish
   influx, for the simultaneous arrival of the immigrants
   and the first traces of the social problems caused by
   industrialization led the populace to believe that one
   caused the other.   Focuses on the "No Popery"
   campaigns of James Begg and his Protestant Institute
   of Scotland, John Hope, and Jacob Primmer.

   See: Tom Gallagher, IR 37 (Autumn 1986): 104-6.

                              Ireland

                           General Works

1396.   Corish, Patrick J.   "The Catholic Community in the
           Nineteenth Century."   AH 38 (1983):   26-33.

        Suggests several promising areas of inquiry into
   nineteenth-century Irish Catholic history.   Among

the subjects worthy of exploration are the quality of
catechesis, levels of religious observance, the
position of the clergy, the Catholic school system,
and the parish mission.

1397. ————. THE IRISH CATHOLIC EXPERIENCE: A HISTORICAL
SURVEY. Wilmington, Del.: Michael Glazier, 1985.

Not a conventional history, but a synthesis,
emphasizing social structures and economic considerations. Chapters 6 to 8 outline the nineteenth-
century Catholic revival as expressed in clerical life
and training, education, the situation of urban Catholics, the activities of Catholic writers and
booksellers, the debut of continental devotions and
liturgical practices, and the work of religious orders
and congregations. With Cullen as its master
architect and the local priest its chief agent, the
revival brought Ireland in line with Tridentine
Europe, though not quite completely.

See: Lawrence S. Cunningham, BS 46 (April 1986): 29-
30; C. Carlton, CHOICE 23 (June 1986): 1555;
Mark Tierney, O.S.B., CHR 73 (January
1987): 103-4; Aidan Bellenger, DR 105 (January
1987): 69-72; Edward Norman, CLR 62 (February
1987): 77; Lawrence J. McCaffrey, AHR 92
(April 1987): 424-5; Edmond Grace, AMER 156
(18 April 1987): 331.

1398. Keenan, Desmond J. THE CATHOLIC CHURCH IN NINETEENTH-
CENTURY IRELAND: A SOCIOLOGICAL STUDY.
Dublin: Gill and Macmillan, 1983.

Divides the century into two equal phases: a
period of innovation, characterized by construction
of churches, convents, and monasteries, and by a
dramatic increase in devotion; and a period of
consolidation, in which both clergy and laity
strove to maintain earlier achievements in religious
practice and education. Stresses the unchanging
self-image of the Irish Church as a persecuted
community.

See: Ian Hamnett, BBN, May 1984: 274; CHOICE 21
(May 1984): 1320; Vincent Alan McClelland,
MONTH 2nd NS 17 (August 1984): 275-6;

Sheridan Gilley, TLS, 3 August 1984: 874;
William J. Schoenl, VS 29 (Autumn 1985): 172-3.

1399. Larkin, Emmet. THE CONSOLIDATION OF THE ROMAN
        CATHOLIC CHURCH IN IRELAND, 1860-1870. Chapel
        Hill and London: University of North Carolina
        Press, 1987.

        Volume 4 of a projected ten-volume history of the
        Irish Church from 1780 to 1918. (See also items
        1401-4.) Shows that the unification of the Catholic
        Church in Ireland was a direct result of the ability
        of its bishops to maintain their corporate unity in
        the face of pastoral, educational, political, and
        constitutional challenges. As each new challenge
        arose--e.g., Fenianism, education, the issue of
        ecclesiastical governance, Irish disestablishment,
        the land question--the hierarchy crystallized its
        policy, thus reinforcing its solidarity as the body
        in full control of the Irish Church.

        See: R.A. Callaghan, CHOICE 25 (April 1988): 1297.

1400. ————. THE HISTORICAL DIMENSIONS OF IRISH
        CATHOLICISM. New York: Arno Press, 1976.

        Reprints items 1449, 1544, and 1582. Proposes,
        in a brief Introduction, major changes in the
        arguments of item 1449, dealing with the Church's
        role in the nineteenth-century Irish economy, and
        a minor revision of a statement made in item 1582,
        addressing the problem of Church-State relations
        during the 1880s.

        See: Lawrence J. McCaffrey, VS 22 (Summer
              1979): 453-4.

1401. ————. THE MAKING OF THE ROMAN CATHOLIC CHURCH IN
        IRELAND, 1850-1860. Chapel Hill: University of
        North Carolina Press, 1980.

        Volume 3 of the Larkin series (see item 1399).
        A behind-the-scenes look at the fierce hierarchical
        in-fighting over such crucial issues as education,
        Church-State relations, clerical politics, and
        ecclesiastical reform.

See: Alan O'Day, VS 24 (Spring 1981): 384-5; Donald
        H. Akenson, AHR 86 (April 1981): 399-400;
        Patrick J. Corish, RP 43 (April 1981): 306-8;
        Christine J. Reilly, RSR 7 (April 1981): 170;
        John H. Whyte, CHR 68 (October 1982): 668-9;
        Donal Kerr, EHR 97 (October 1982): 926-7;
        Peter Alter, JMH 57 (March 1985): 124-5.

1402.   ————. THE ROMAN CATHOLIC CHURCH AND THE CREATION OF
        THE MODERN IRISH STATE, 1878-1886. Dublin: Gill
        and Macmillan/Philadelphia: The American
        Philosophical Society, 1975.

        Volume 6 of the Larkin series (see item 1399).
        Maintains that through the period 1878-1886 the
        Irish hierarchy allied itself with Parnell's Home
        Rule Party, forming through that alliance the
        basis of the modern Irish State.

See: Joseph M. Curran, RP 38 (April 1976): 278-80;
        Andrew M. Greeley, NYTBR, 27 June 1976: 8;
        David W. Miller, IHS 20 (September 1976): 212-
        6; Josef L. Altholz, JMH 48 (September
        1976): 544-5; Patrick J. Corish, ITQ 43 (no. 4,
        1976): 296-7; John V. Kelleher, CH 45
        (December 1976): 538; Donald H. Akenson, AHR
        82 (February 1977): 113-4; J.C. Beckett, EHR
        92 (April 1977): 463-4; Jonathan Phillips, HJ
        20 (June 1977): 515-6; P.M.H. Bell, JEH 28
        (July 1977): 325-6; Lawrence J. McCaffrey,
        CHR 63 (October 1977): 606-7; Lawrence J.
        McCaffrey, VS 22 (Summer 1979): 454-5.

1403.   ————. THE ROMAN CATHOLIC CHURCH AND THE PLAN OF
        CAMPAIGN IN IRELAND, 1886-1888. Cork: Cork
        University Press, 1978.

        Volume 7 of the Larkin series (see item 1399).
        Delineates the complex circumstances under which
        the Irish bishops' participation in the Plan of
        Campaign was severely tested. In 1888 Leo XIII
        condemned the anti-landlord activity as immoral.
        This left the bishops in a great dilemma, for
        while they sought to remain loyal to Papal
        teaching, at the same time they did not want to
        lose their congregations. In the long run, they
        simply chose not to accept the condemnation,

arguing that it had misjudged the actual situation in
Ireland. Clearly, the clerical-Nationalist alliance
was stronger than the attachment to Rome.

See: Donald H. Akenson, VS 23 (Summer 1980): 507-8;
      Desmond Bowen, AHR 85 (October 1980): 893-4;
      John V. Kelleher, CH 49 (December 1980): 471-2;
      R.F. Foster, JMH 53 (June 1981): 326-9;
      Stanley H. Palmer, CHR 67 (July 1981): 443-4;
      Maurice R. O'Connell, EHR 97 (July 1982): 663-4.

1404. ————. THE ROMAN CATHOLIC CHURCH IN IRELAND AND THE
       FALL OF PARNELL, 1888-1891. Chapel Hill: Uni-
       versity of North Carolina Press, 1979.

Volume 8 of the Larkin series (see item 1399).
Develops the thesis of the preceding volumes,
tracing the roots of the later constitutional and
democratic Irish State to the late nineteenth-
century Liberal-Nationalist and clerical-Nationalist
alliances in which the clergy played so prominent a
role.

See: Margaretta D'Arcy, NST 99 (1 February 1980): 171-
      2; F.S.L. Lyons, TLS, 15 February 1980: 164;
      CHOICE 17 (March 1980): 128-9; F.S.L. Lyons, BBN,
      April 1980: 215; Paul Misner, RSR 6 (April
      1980): 153-4; Josef L. Altholz, ALBION 12
      (Summer 1980): 202-3; Donald H. Akenson, VS 23
      (Summer 1980): 508; Dennis Clark, HRZNS 7 (Fall
      1980): 151-2; Desmond Bowen, AHR 85 (October
      1980): 893-4; John V. Kelleher, CH 49 (December
      1980): 471-2; Michael V. Hazel, HIS 43 (February
      1981): 267-8; R.F. Foster, JMH 53 (June
      1981): 326-9; Donal Kerr, JEH 32 (July
      1981): 374-6; John H. Whyte, JAAR 49 (December
      1981): 694; John V. Crangle, JCS 23 (Winter
      1981): 354-5; K. Theodore Hoppen, EHR 97
      (January 1982): 216-7; Mark Tierney, O.S.B.,
      CHR 68 (October 1982): 687-8.

The Hierarchy and Diocesan Organization

General

1405.   Ahern, John. "The Plenary Synod of Thurles." IER 75
        (May 1951): 385-403.

        An account of the episcopal assembly of 1850.
        Focuses on the debates over the Colleges Bill,
        proposed by the government in 1845, in an effort
        to provide greater opportunities in higher edu-
        cation for Catholics, who at the time had nowhere
        else to go but Trinity College. Continues in item
        1406.

1406.   ————. "The Plenary Synod of Thurles—II." IER
        78 (July 1952): 1-20.

        A pendant to item 1405. Evaluates the manner in
        which the Synod dealt with both theoretical and
        practical problems, including its rejection of the
        Colleges Bill.

1407.   Barry, P.C., S.J. "The Legislation of the Synod of
        Thurles, 1850." ITQ 26 (no. 2, 1959): 131-66.

        Analyzes the enormous number of decrees passed
        by the Synod, decrees which set the foundation for
        the bishops' meetings of 1875 and 1900. Categorizes
        the 187 separate pieces of legislation according to
        eleven sections: faith (11 decrees), sacraments
        (58), private life of the clergy (24), life and
        duties of parish priests (27), assistant pastors
        (5), duties of bishops (28), ecclesiastical
        archives (4), ecclesiastical goods (9), the
        Queen's Colleges (9), national schools (10), and
        episcopal disagreements (2).

1408.   ————. "The National Synod of Thurles (1850): Con-
        temporary Accounts." IER 86 (August 1956): 73-82.

        Reconstructs the Synod out of material taken from
        Irish newspapers of the day. The meeting was
        reported at considerable length in all Irish
        periodicals, for it was considered a great event in

national history.

1409. Cannon, Sean, C.SS.R. IRISH EPISCOPAL MEETINGS, 1788-
       1882: A JURIDICO-HISTORICAL STUDY. Rome: Ponti-
       ficia Studiorum Universitas a S. Thoma Aq. in Urbe,
       1979.

       Follows the development of the national meetings of
       Irish bishops, showing how they acquired a "national"
       character around the beginning of the nineteenth
       century, as they dealt ever more frequently with
       pressing issues of nationwide importance.

       See: Patrick J. Corish, CHR 67 (October 1981): 679;
             Patrick J. Corish, IHS 23 (May 1982): 76-7.

1410. Cunningham, Terence P. THE CHURCH SINCE EMANCI-
       PATION: CHURCH REORGANIZATION. A History of
       Irish Catholicism, edited by Patrick J. Corish,
       vol. 5, no. 7. Dublin: Gill and Macmillan,
       1970.

       Sketches various aspects of nineteenth-century
       ecclesiastical structure and discipline. Discusses
       general lines of authority, the Church's legal status
       (as seen through the O'Keeffe case, 1869-1875),
       appointment to offices, administration of the
       sacraments, regulation of feasts and fasts, handling
       of problems and abuses, and supervision of devotional
       activity.

1411. Whyte, John H. "The Appointment of Catholic Bishops
       in Nineteenth-Century Ireland." CHR 48 (April
       1962): 12-32.

       Compares the different methods of selecting Irish
       bishops through the nineteenth century, demonstrating
       that they were determined more by accidents of
       personality than by an ongoing Roman strategy of
       ecclesiastical centralization.

                      Dublin and Its Bishops

1412. Bowen, Desmond. PAUL CARDINAL CULLEN AND THE SHAPING
       OF MODERN IRISH CATHOLICISM. Dublin: Gill and

Macmillan/Waterloo: Wilfrid Laurier University Press, 1983.

An unflattering portrait, relying almost exclusively on Roman sources, of a churchman whose campaign for religious and cultural ascendancy caused much sectarian hatred and conflict after his death, and whose nationalism was expedient rather than sincere.

See: CHOICE 21 (July/August 1984): 1623; Sheridan Gilley, TLS, 3 August 1984: 874; E.D. Steele, AHR 90 (June 1985): 683; Declan Dean, S.J., MONTH 2nd NS 18 (July/August 1985): 282-3; William Schoenl, VS 29 (Autumn 1985): 171-2; Lawrence J. McCaffrey, CHR 72 (April 1986): 317-8; Brian P. Clarke, CH 56 (September 1987): 416-7.

1413. Corish, Patrick J. "Cardinal Cullen and Archbishop MacHale." IER 91 (June 1959): 393-408.

Compares the lives, careers, and achievements of the two leading figures of the Irish Church during the greater part of the nineteenth century. Finds that despite their different personalities and positions, which often put them at odds, the two prelates shared one important trait: they both found certain political and ecclesiastical issues of the day very difficult to grasp.

1414. Leslie, Shane. "The Cullen Era." MONTH 1st NS 33 (April 1965): 230-8.

Summarizes Paul Cullen's dynamic if controversial career as Archbishop of Dublin (1852-1878) and the first Irish Cardinal. His fight against proselytism, mixed education, and secular colleges, added to his promotion of a strongly visible and decidedly ultramontane Catholic presence in Ireland, made him the leading, but not necessarily the most beloved, figure of mid-nineteenth-century Irish history.

* ————. "Irish Pages from the Postbags of Manning, Cullen and Gladstone." Cited above as item 849.

Analyzes the Cullen-Manning relationship between 1865 and 1873, showing, through the use of their

correspondence, that the anti-British Cullen never
discouraged Manning from intriguing for him at
Westminster.

1415. McCormack, Jim, C.M. "Paul Cullen and the Definition
        of Papal Infallibility at Vatican I." ITQ 51
        (no. 1, 1985): 52-62.

Challenges the widespread belief in the Irish
Church during the years following Vatican I that
the decisive influence in the definition of infallibility had been Cullen's. Maintains, on the contrary,
that it is impossible to attribute the final form of
Pastor Aeternus to any one individual, given its
constant redraftings and amendments during the
course of the sessions.

1416. MacSuibhne, Peadar. PAUL CULLEN AND HIS CONTEMPO-
        RARIES, WITH THEIR LETTERS FROM 1820 TO 1902.
        Naas: Leinster Leader, 1961-77. 5 vols.

Uses a mixture of biographical narrative and
previously unpublished correspondence to fix the
Cardinal's place in Irish as well as in Catholic
history. Occasionally hagiographical, as it works
out its underlying theme that Cullen was to mid-
nineteenth-century Irish Catholicism what Pius IX
was to the nineteenth-century universal Church.

See: IER 97 (April 1962): 278-9; Emmet Larkin, CHR
        48 (July 1962): 266-7; Patrick J. Corish, ITQ
        29 (no. 3, 1962): 265-6; J.H. Whyte, IHS 13
        (September 1962): 191-3; IER 99 (March
        1963): 188; J.H. Whyte, IHS 13 (March
        1963): 274-5; IER 104 (October/November
        1965): 318; E.D. Steele, IHS 19 (March
        1975): 356-7; P.K. Egan, ITQ 42 (no. 3,
        1975): 237-8; R.V. Comerford, IHS 20 (March
        1977): 362-3.

1417. Ronan, Myles, P.P. "Archbishop Murray (1768-1852)."
        IER 77 (April 1952): 241-9.

Focuses on Murray's phenomenal record of
accomplishments as Archbishop of Dublin (1823-1852).
Over three decades the saintly and highly capable
churchman co-founded the Irish Sisters of Charity

(items 175-6), introduced various teaching orders
into his diocese, and built a pro-Cathedral. At
the same time he was a leading participant in the
Synods of Maynooth (1831) and Thurles (1850), and
fought strenuously against such anti-Catholic
measures as the Ecclesiastical Titles Bill (1851).

1418. Steele, E.D. "Cardinal Cullen and Irish Nationality."
IHS 19 (March 1975): 239-60.

Disputes the attempts by some historians (e.g.,
item 1412) to portray Cullen as an enemy of, or
as indifferent to, Irish nationality. Argues
that neither his ultramontanism nor his vehement
criticism of the Fenians implied a lack of sympathy
for Irish grievances or an enthusiasm for the
British connection; moreover, as a one-time
O'Connellite, he never forbade his clergy to
participate actively in political life.

1419. Walsh, Patrick J. WILLIAM J. WALSH, ARCHBISHOP OF
DUBLIN. Dublin and Cork: Talbot Press, 1928.

A flattering treatment of the man who held the
metropolitan see of Dublin during the last three
decades of English rule in Ireland (1885-1921).
Highlights Walsh's responses to the major political
and religious issues troubling late nineteenth-
century Ireland (the agrarian question, Home Rule,
the Parnell Affair, educational opportunities for
Catholics). Though the British government tried to
scuttle his appointment, using every type of
backstairs diplomacy to discredit him in Rome, the
strongly nationalistic Walsh was vindicated, for
through his years in Dublin, and partly as a result
of his expertise in canon law, he was constantly
asked for advice by British public officials,
including more than one Prime Minister.

See: Cornelius P. Curran, COMMWL 9 (2 January
1929): 253-5; CHR 15 (April 1929): 105-6.

1420. Walsh, William J. O'CONNELL, ARCHBISHOP MURRAY, AND
THE BOARD OF CHARITABLE BEQUESTS: AN ALL BUT
FORGOTTEN INCIDENT IN THE ECCLESIASTICAL HISTORY
OF DUBLIN IN THE 19TH CENTURY. Dublin: Browne
and Nolan, 1916.

Defends Murray's support of Peel's Bequests Bill of 1844, a stand denounced by O'Connell as a surrender of the right of Catholics to give charity to whom and in whatever amounts they pleased.

See: IER 9 (February 1917): 170-1.

Tuam and Its Bishops

1421. Bane, Liam. "John MacHale and John MacEvilly: Conflict in the Nineteenth Century Catholic Hierarchy." AH 39 (1984): 45-52.

Looks into the tensions between MacHale, Archbishop of Tuam (1834-1881), and his successor, MacEvilly (1881-1902). Though of similar backgrounds, they were opposed on every major issue, including those on which they might have been expected to agree (e.g., Irish elections, papal infallibility). The antagonism can be traced to the fact that MacEvilly was a protégé of the ultramontane Cardinal Cullen, the foremost opponent of the Gallican MacHale during the 1850s and 60s.

1422. Bourke, Ulrick J. THE LIFE AND TIMES OF THE MOST REV. JOHN MAC HALE, ARCHBISHOP OF TUAM AND METROPOLITAN. 4th ed. New York: P.J. Kenedy, 1902.

A sympathetic biography of the faithful pastor and ardent patriot, written by a priest of Tuam.

1423. Burke, Oliver J. THE HISTORY OF THE CATHOLIC ARCHBISHOPS OF TUAM FROM THE FOUNDATION OF THE SEE TO THE DEATH OF THE MOST REV. JOHN MAC HALE, D.D., A.D. 1881. Dublin: Hodges, Figgis, 1882.

Surveys the lives and achievements of Edward Dillon (1798-1814), Oliver Kelly (1814-1834), and John MacHale (1834-1881), along with a brief mention of MacEvilly.

See: DUBR 93 (October 1883): 483-4.

1424. Costello, Nuala. JOHN MAC HALE, ARCHBISHOP OF TUAM. Dublin: The Talbot Press/London: Gerald

Duckworth, 1939.

Illustrates MacHale's attitudes toward the major political issues and events of his time.

1425. D'Alton, E.A. HISTORY OF THE ARCHDIOCESE OF TUAM. Dublin: Phoenix Publishing, 1928. 2 vols.

Volume 2 treats nineteenth-century diocesan developments as motivated by the personalities and policies of Archbishops Dillon, Kelly, MacHale, and MacEvilly. Of the four, MacHale is singled out for his role as the patriot-bishop.

See: IER 33 (March 1929): 325-6.

1426. O'Reilly, Bernard. JOHN MAC HALE, ARCHBISHOP OF TUAM: HIS LIFE, TIMES, AND CORRESPONDENCE. New York and Cincinnati: Fr. Pustet, 1890. 2 vols.

Places MacHale within the troubled context of nineteenth-century Irish history, indicating the great extent to which he was associated with all the major events--political, educational, and ecclesiastical--of his time. Praises his mental gifts and eloquence, both of which he dedicated to the service of an aggrieved country and a persecuted Church. Details his sixty years of ceaseless activity, including his role in O'Connell's movement, Young Ireland, the controversy over the Charitable Bequests Act and the Ecclesiastical Titles Bill, and the fight against proselytism and landlords, and for Home Rule.

See: ACQR 16 (January 1891): 218-20.

Other Bishops

1427. Boyle, Patrick, C.M. "Dr. Hussey, Bishop of Water-ford, and the Concordat of 1801." IER 5 (April 1915): 337-45.

Asserts that Hussey had a real, if not a principal, share in the negotiations over the Napoleonic Concordat of 1801.

1428. Kerr, Donal. "Charles McNally: O'Connellite Bishop--Reforming Pastor." AH 37 (1982): 11-20.

Concentrates on three aspects of the life and ministry of the little-remembered Bishop of Clogher (1844-1864): his social and intellectual roots, the evolution of his political outlook, and his pastoral and reforming concerns.

1429. Masterson, M.J. "Bishop O'Higgins (1794-1853)." IER 34 (November 1929): 465-72.

Sketches the remarkable career of William O'Higgins, Bishop of Ardagh and Clonmacnoise (1829-1853), and one of O'Connell's staunchest supporters within the Irish hierarchy.

1430. Tierney, Mark. CROKE OF CASHEL: THE LIFE OF ARCH-BISHOP THOMAS WILLIAM CROKE, 1823-1902. Dublin: Gill and Macmillan, 1976.

Deals primarily with Croke's ardent nationalism and its expressions. Contains little on his pastoral activity as ordinary of Cashel (1875-1902).

See: R.F. Foster, IHS 20 (September 1977): 519-21; Patrick J. Corish, CHR 64 (October 1978): 702-3.

Diocesan Clergy and Pastoral Activity

1431. Connolly, S.J. PRIESTS AND PEOPLE IN PRE-FAMINE IRELAND, 1780-1845. Dublin: Gill and Macmillan, 1982.

Analyzes the interaction between clergy and laity in specific situations during the first four decades of the nineteenth century. Demonstrates how cooperation between priests and their flocks could successfully obstruct local implementation of unpopular hierarchical policies.

See: Peter Hebblethwaite, TLS, 18 June 1982: 652;
       Gerard O'Brien, JEH 34 (January 1983): 143-4;
       William D. Griffin, HRNB 11 (March 1983): 120;
       Lawrence J. McCaffrey, AMER 148 (12 March
       1983): 199-200; Francis H. Touchet, JCS 25
       (Spring 1983): 364-6; Donald H. Akenson, AHR
       88 (April 1983): 400-1; Emmet Larkin, RSR 10
       (January 1984): 77; Edward Brynn, CH 53 (March
       1984): 115-6; David W. Miller, JSH 17 (Spring
       1984): 533-5; Walter L. Arnstein, HIS 46 (May
       1984): 442-3; James W. O'Neill, VS 27 (Summer
       1984): 523-4; Maurice R. O'Connell, CHR 70
       (October 1984): 589-90.

1432. Egan, Michael Joseph. LIFE OF DEAN O'BRIEN, FOUNDER
       OF THE C.Y.M.S. Dublin: M.H. Gill, 1949.

       A portrait of one of the many Irish priests who
       devoted their lives to building up the Church during
       the years immediately following Emancipation. Sees
       O'Brien's construction of a church and school, along
       with his unrelenting involvement in politics, as
       typical of the clerical activity of the time.
       Praises, however, his one atypical achievement: the
       establishment of the Catholic Young Men's Society.

       See: IER 71 (February 1949): 174.

1433. Kerr, Donal. "Peel and the Political Involvement of
       the Priests." AH 36 (1981): 16-25.

       Inquires into the motives behind Peel's decision
       of 1845 to force both the Maynooth grant and a
       series of other pro-Catholic measures through a
       hostile Parliament. Concludes that his awareness of
       the attendant political difficulties and dangers both
       to himself and to his party, was balanced by his
       desire to reconcile the Irish clergy, so as to wean
       it away from O'Connell's influence.

1434. Murphy, John A. "Priests and People in Modern Irish
       History." CR 23 (October 1969): 235-59.

       Offers the following reasons for the great respect
       enjoyed by priests in nineteenth-century Ireland: (1)
       there was no tradition of deep anticlericalism; on the
       contrary, respect for the cloth was inbred; and

(2) the priest was frequently among the leaders of the
ongoing campaign against political and social
oppression.

1435.   Reilly, A.J.   FATHER JOHN MURPHY, FAMINE PRIEST, 1796-
         1883.   Dublin: Clonmore and Reynolds, 1963.

         Outlines the extraordinary career of the unde-
         servedly forgotten cleric who worked among the
         famine-striken people of west Cork.   Before his
         ordination, Murphy, the son of a wealthy Cork
         merchant, had been a midshipman, fur trader, and
         Indian chief.

         See: IER 100 (December 1963): 404; K.A. Pearson,
                THEO 67 (February 1964): 78-9.

1436.   Ronan, Myles V.   AN APOSTLE OF CATHOLIC
         DUBLIN: FATHER HENRY YOUNG.   Dublin: Browne
         and Nolan, 1944.

         Provides a detailed look at an extraordinary
         clerical career.   Young (1786-1869) worked in the
         diocese of Dublin for fifty-five years, during which
         he founded several confraternities, introduced a
         number of religious devotions, and published books
         or booklets on temperance, worship, and the Papacy.
         Devotes much space to the environment within which
         Young operated, with special reference to the
         nineteenth-century development of Maynooth, religious
         orders, schools and charitable institutions,
         religious societies, the secular priesthood, and
         pastoral activity.

         See: IER 64 (November 1944): 355-6; Maureen
                MacGeehin, IHS 5 (March 1946): 103-5.

1437.   Taylor, Lawrence J.   "The Priest and the
         Agent: Social Drama and Class Consciousness
         in the West of Ireland."   CSSH 27 (October
         1985):   696-712.

         Gauges the extent to which priests, in their con-
         flict with estate agents, influenced the social
         structures and relationships of nineteenth-century
         Ireland.   Discusses the litigation between Father
         John Magroarty of Carrick and Arthur Brooke as a

case in point.

Orders and Congregations

1438. Concannon, Helena. THE POOR CLARES IN IRELAND
(A.D. 1629-A.D. 1929). Dublin: M.H. Gill
and Son, 1929.

Chapters 11 to 14 examine the Order's nineteenth-
century advances: the origins of a ministry to
orphans and the poor of Dublin, the establishment of
a convent north of the Boyne for the first time since
the Reformation, and the return of the Poor Clares
Colettines to the original rule of their foundress.

1439. EDMUND IGNATIUS RICE AND THE CHRISTIAN BROTHERS, BY
A CHRISTIAN BROTHER. Dublin: M.H. Gill and Son,
1926.

Combines a biography of the founder and first
Superior-General of the Irish Christian Brothers
with a history of the community's first four
decades. Founded in 1802, and approved by the
Holy See in 1820, the Order performed two key
ministries within their poor and uneducated
milieu: philanthropy and teaching.

1440. Kevin, Neil. THE CISTERCIANS IN IRELAND. Mellifont
Abbey: Privately printed, 1929.

Chapter 5 describes the post-1830 revival of Irish
Cistercian life at Scrahan Abbey, a foundation
affiliated with the Trappists of Mount Melleray.

1441. Luddy, Ailbe J., O. Cist. THE STORY OF MOUNT
MELLERAY. Dublin: M.H. Gill and Son, 1946.

A historical account of the first monastic
establishment in modern Ireland. Founded by the
Cistercians in 1832, Mount Melleray was raised to
the status of an abbey in 1835. Underscores the
obstacles faced by the founders, who were refugees
from France, and the daily rigors and deep spirituality for which the Abbey became justly famous by
the end of the century.

1442.   MacKenna, Lambert, S.J.   LIFE AND WORK OF REV. JAMES
        ALOYSIUS CULLEN, S.J.   London: Longmans, 1924.

        A biography of one of nineteenth-century Ireland's
        most colorful and energetic churchmen.   Focuses on
        his fifteen years (1866-1881) as Director of the
        Missionaries of the Blessed Sacrament at Enniscorthy,
        a group devoted to preaching parish missions and
        working among the poor of the Shannon district.
        Beyond his activity at the "House of Missions,"
        Cullen (1841-1921) was actively involved in the
        temperance movement (1876), served as Director of
        the Apostleship of Prayer for Ireland (1887), and
        worked in the South African missions during the
        1890s.

        See: P. Coffey, IER 24 (September 1924): 233-42.

1443.   Rushe, James P.   CARMEL IN IRELAND: A NARRATIVE OF
        THE IRISH PROVINCE OF TERESIAN, OR DISCALCED
        CARMELITES, A.D. 1625-1896.   Dublin: Sealy,
        Bryers and Walker/M.H. Gill and Son, 1903.

        Chapters 11 to 14 cover the importance of
        O'Connell's patronage, the reopening of the
        novitiate at the Abbey of Loughrea, the operation
        of the House of Studies at St. Mary's, and
        obituaries of Irish Teresians who died during the
        century.

        See: DUBR 133 (July 1903): 198-9.

1444.   Walsh, Kilian J., O.C.S.O.   DOM VINCENT OF MOUNT
        MELLERAY.   Dublin: M.H. Gill and Son, 1962.

        A biography of Waterford-born Michael Ryan (1788-
        1845), who, as Father Vincent de Paul, restored the
        Cistercian life to Ireland.   In 1832 he became the
        Abbot of Mount Melleray, the Order's first Irish
        establishment of the post-penal period, and the
        motherhouse of a rapidly spreading network of
        monasteries which eventually covered the entire
        country.

Social and Economic Influences

1445. Connell, K.H. "Catholicism and Marriage in the Century after the Famine." IRISH PEASANT SOCIETY: FOUR HISTORICAL ESSAYS, 113-61. Oxford: Clarendon Press, 1968.

Shows how Catholicism reinforced the economic factors which led the Irish peasant to marry much later than any of his continental counterparts, though before the 1840s he had married much earlier. The clergy's exaltation of virginity provided a supernatural sanction for late marriage.

See: TLS, 2 January 1969: 14; E.R.R. Green, IHS 16 (September 1969): 505-6; Miriam Daly, HIST 44 (October 1969): 432-3; Arnold Schrier, AHR 75 (December 1969): 506; Barbara L. Solow, JECH 29 (December 1969): 778-9; Trefor M. Owen, SOCIOL 4 (January 1970): 124; Arnold McClung Lee, AMANTH 72 (February 1970): 131; G.D. Ramsey, EHR 85 (April 1970): 375-6; Michael Drake, POPS 24 (July 1970): 295; David W. Miller, JMH 42 (September 1970): 387-9; J.W. Boyle, LH 11 (Winter 1970): 117-9; Angus Macintyre, ECHR 211 (May 1971): 292-4; David Doyle, CHR 58 (October 1972): 420-1.

1446. Connolly, S.J. "Catholicism in Ulster, 1800-50." In PLANTATION TO PARTITION: ESSAYS IN ULSTER HISTORY IN HONOUR OF J.L. MC CRACKEN, edited by Peter Roebuck, 157-71. Belfast: Blackstaff Press, 1981.

Examines the nature of Catholic life in a province set apart from the others by its large Protestant population and economic prosperity. Concludes that while Ulster Catholicism was not spiritually backward, it was rather poor and showed very little evidence of political consciousness.

See: J.L. McCracken, BBN, December 1981: 764; Paul Rose, CONR 239 (December 1981): 330-1; K. Theodore Hoppen, EHR 99 (January 1984): 186.

1447. Gilley, Sheridan. "The Roman Catholic Church and the
      Nineteenth-Century Irish Diaspora." JEH 35
      (April 1984): 188-207.

      Evaluates the role played by Roman Catholicism in
      helping Irish immigrants to preserve their national
      and ethnic identity. Balances those elements which
      held the highly scattered expatriate Irish Catholics
      together against those which tore them apart.

1448. Kennedy, Liam. "The Roman Catholic Church and
      Economic Growth in Nineteenth Century Ireland."
      ECSOR 10 (October 1978): 45-60.

      Disputes the logical, theoretical, and empirical
      bases of the claim that the Church, by absorbing
      large amounts of physical and human capital, inhibited
      the economic development of nineteenth-century Ireland.
      (See item 1449.) Argues, on the contrary, that
      Catholicism's role in the Irish economic context was
      a positive one.

1449. Larkin, Emmet. "Economic Growth, Capital Investment,
      and the Roman Catholic Church in Nineteenth-
      Century Ireland." AHR 72 (April 1967): 852-84.

      Maintains that the Church, by appropriating a
      significant amount of risk capital for its own uses,
      impeded the economic development of nineteenth-
      century Ireland. Sees the ecclesiastical establish-
      ment as non-productive, draining rather than
      contributing to the national resources. For an
      opposing assessment, however, see item 1448.
      Larkin's much later retraction of part of his thesis
      is found in item 1400.

1450. Lee, Joseph J. "Women and the Church since the
      Famine." In WOMEN IN IRISH SOCIETY: THE
      HISTORICAL DIMENSION, edited by Margaret
      MacCurtain and Donncha Ó Corráin, 37-45.
      Westport, Conn.: Greenwood Press, 1979.

      Criticizes Roman Catholicism for encouraging Irish
      women to accept an increasingly male-dominated
      society. An increasingly clerical, i.e., male,
      Church discouraged marriage, preaching sex as sinful;
      in so doing, it joined forces with the famine to

cause a serious deterioration in the social and
economic status of women.

See: CHOICE 16 (February 1980): 1636; Richard J.
Evans, JMH 52 (December 1980): 673-4.

1451. Livingstone, Peadar. THE MONAGHAN STORY: A
DOCUMENTED HISTORY OF THE COUNTY MONAGHAN
FROM THE EARLIEST TIMES TO 1976.
Enniskillen: Clogher Historical Society,
1980.

Chapter 12 considers local agitation on behalf of
Catholic Emancipation and the violent reaction it
provoked from the Orangemen. Chapter 16 evaluates
the Catholic revival in the county during the first
half of the century, with special reference to the
state of the laity, clergy, hierarchy, religious
orders, and church-building.

1452. MacDonagh, Oliver. "The Irish Catholic Clergy and
Emigration during the Great Famine." IHS 5
(September 1947): 287-302.

Contrasts the unofficial clerical attitudes
toward emigration as expressed before and after
the Famine. Before the 1840s, most churchmen,
fearing a loss of faith among the expatriates,
discouraged emigration; the Famine, however,
made relocation a matter of survival, and a
number of priests themselves accompanied their
flocks to America.

Relations with Other Churches

1453. Murphy, Ignatius. "Some Attitudes to Religious
Freedom and Ecumenism in Pre-Emancipation
Ireland." IER 105 (February 1966): 93-104.

Describes the sincere efforts on the part of a
number of early nineteenth-century Irish Catholics
and Protestants to induce their coreligionists to
abandon their religious bigotry and live together
in peace and cooperation.

1454. O'Connell, Philip. "A Dublin Convert Roll: The
       Diary of the Rev. P.E. O'Farrelly." IER 71
       (June 1949): 533-44.

       Offers information--names, ages, backgrounds,
       and other relevant data--on O'Farrelly's converts,
       culled from his parochial registers for the years
       1837-1853. Continues in item 1455.

1455. ————. "A Dublin Convert Roll: The Diary of the
       Rev. P.E. O'Farrelly (II)." IER 72 (July
       1949): 27-35.

       Carries on from item 1454, listing the tallies to
       1858. Over his twenty-one years of service, first
       as assistant at St. Andrew's, Westland Row, and then
       as chaplain for the South Dublin Union, O'Farrelly
       brought 768 individuals into the Church.

                    Religious Thought

1456. Corbett, Thomas. "Patrick Murray as Theologian."
       ITQ 49 (no. 4, 1982): 276-84.

       Analyzes the most important work of the foremost
       Irish theologian of the nineteenth century, the
       three-volume TRACTATUS DE ECCLESIA CHRISTI (1860-
       1866).

1457. Corkery, John. THE CHURCH SINCE EMANCIPATION: EC-
       CLESIASTICAL LEARNING. A History of Irish
       Catholicism, edited by Patrick J. Corish, vol. 5,
       no. 9. Dublin: Gill and Macmillan, 1970.

       Presents developments in theology, philosophy,
       exegesis, Church history, liturgical studies, and
       educational theory.

1458. Kerr, Donal. "Dr. Patrick Murray (1811-1882)." ITQ
       49 (no. 4, 1982): 229-50.

       A biography of Ireland's leading nineteenth-century
       theologian, placed within the framework of everyday
       life at Maynooth.

1459.   McNamara, Kevin.   "Patrick Murray: The Man and His
        Writings."   ITQ 49 (no. 4, 1982):   251-75.

        Reviews the personality, career, and publications
        of nineteenth-century Ireland's leading theologian.
        Starting out at Maynooth in 1838 as Professor of
        English and French letters, Murray was given the
        Chair of Dogmatics and Moral Theology in 1841.   An
        avid book collector and reader, he was passionately
        committed to knowledge, writing on a variety of
        topics, and always with precision, color, elegance,
        and a scrupulous concern for the truth.

1460.   Tynan, Michael.   CATHOLIC INSTRUCTION IN IRELAND,
        1720-1950:   THE O'REILLY/DONLEVY CATECHETICAL
        TRADITION.   Dublin: Four Courts Press, 1985.

        A critical treatment of the two major catechisms
        used in nineteenth-century Ireland, both of which
        taught a particularly strident form of Counter-
        Reformation Catholicism.

        See: Charles B. Paris, CH 56 (December 1987): 533-4.

1461.   Walsh, Katherine.   "The Opening of the Vatican
        Archives (1880-1881) and Irish Historical
        Research."   AH 36 (1981):   34-43.

        Examines the work of late nineteenth-century Irish
        scholars in the Vatican Archives, including, most
        notably, the investigation of the medieval Papacy by
        Michael A. Costello (1824-1906), a member of the
        Irish Dominican community of St. Clement's, Rome.

                            Education

                            General

1462.   Auchmuty, James Johnston.   IRISH EDUCATION: A
        HISTORICAL SURVEY.   Dublin: Hodges, Figgis/
        London: George G. Harrap, 1937.

        Chapter 4 details the activity of Sir Thomas Wyse
        (1791-1862), who did for Catholic educational

equality what O'Connell did for Catholic political
equality. As a member of Parliament for Tipperary
(1830-1832, 1835-1847), he used his influence to
agitate for mixed elementary and secondary education,
as well as for the establishment of a Catholic
university in Ireland. Chapter 5 studies the
progress of the Irish university question after
Wyse's retirement from Parliament.

See: W.J. Williams, IHS 1 (March 1938): 93-5.

Primary Schools

1463.   Murphy, Ignatius. THE CHURCH SINCE EMANCI-
        PATION: CATHOLIC EDUCATION--PRIMARY EDUCATION.
        A History of Irish Catholicism, edited by
        Patrick J. Corish, vol. 5, no. 6.
        Dublin: Gill and Macmillan, 1971.

        Deals mainly with nineteenth-century developments,
        including the agitation for a national system of
        elementary schools and the Protestant reaction to it,
        the increasing dissatisfaction with religious
        teaching during the years 1851-1870, and the slow
        but definite post-1890 moves toward *de facto*
        denominationalism.

Secondary Schools

1464.   Ó Raifeartaigh, T. "Mixed Education and the Synod of
        Ulster, 1831-40." IHS 9 (March 1955): 281-99.

        Reviews the ill-fated efforts by Irish Catholic
        leaders to involve their entire community in "mixed
        education" schools. At the Synod of Ulster (1840)
        the Irish bishops decided to withdraw from the mixed
        system, arguing that safeguards for Catholic children
        in the schools had been violated by the policies of
        Lord Stanley, Chief Secretary for Ireland, as
        expressed to the Duke of Leinster, President of the
        board charged with administering the system. Beyond
        their abandonment of mixed education, the bishops
        rejected shortly afterwards Peel's Colleges Bill,

thus committing themselves to a future of exclusively denominational institutions.

1465. Ó Súilleabháin, Séamus V., C.F.C. THE CHURCH SINCE EMANCIPATION: CATHOLIC EDUCATION--SECONDARY EDUCATION. A History of Irish Catholicism, edited by Patrick J. Corish, vol. 5, no. 6. Dublin: Gill and Macmillan, 1971.

Outlines the nineteenth-century "mixed education" controversy, the daily operation of the intermediate schools, and the provisions and effects of the Education Act of 1878.

1466. Towey, John, F.S.C. "Summerhill, 1880." AH 36 (1981): 26-33.

Follows the establishment and troubled life of the Summerhill Industrial School for orphans, the Christian Brothers' first Irish foundation, located near Athlone. Though the institution lasted only eighteen months,--it dissolved in a conflict of interests and personalities,--it was not a complete loss, for it gave the Brothers a foothold from which they would eventually build several permanent and successful settlements on the island.

The University Question

1467. Gwynn, Denis. "O'Connell, Davis and the Colleges Bill." IER 69 (July 1947): 561-72.

Part 1 of a six-part series concentrating on O'Connell as an educational reformer. Condemns the tendency among many historians to understate or belittle O'Connell's importance in many areas of the national history. Continues in item 1468.

1468. ————. "O'Connell, Davis and the Colleges Bill. II.--Davis and Catholic 'Bigotry.'" IER 69 (August 1947): 668-82.

Continued from item 1467. A portrait of Thomas Davis, the Irish Protestant champion whose violent anti-Catholicism led him to oppose any religious

teaching—but especially Catholic religious teaching,
which he called "bigotry"—in the universities.
Continues in item 1469.

1469.   ———. "O'Connell, Davis and the Colleges Bill.
         III.—The Demand for Provincial Colleges." IER
         69 (September 1947): 767-81.

         Continued from item 1468. Compares Catholic and
         Protestant attitudes toward the Tory government's
         proposal to establish provincial colleges in Ireland.
         Continues in item 1470.

1470.   ———. "O'Connell, Davis and the Colleges Bill.
         IV.—The 'Godless' Bill." IER 69 (November
         1947): 957-71.

         Continued from item 1469. Reverses the generally
         accepted verdict on O'Connell's treatment of Davis
         and the Young Irelanders over the Colleges Bill.
         Contends that far from playing politics, O'Connell
         opposed the Bill on sincere religious grounds; Davis,
         on the other hand, did play politics, in order to
         prevent a majority vote against the Bill. Continues
         item 1471.

1471.   ———. "O'Connell, Davis and the Colleges Bill.
         V.—The Quarrel in Conciliation Hall." IER 69
         (December 1947): 1051-65.

         Continued from item 1470. Qualifies the tra-
         ditional claim that the split between O'Connell
         and the Young Irelanders became permanent after
         their public debate of 26 May 1845 over the
         Colleges Bill. Demonstrates that in subsequent
         discussions over the proposed legislation, the
         two sides actually worked together in presenting
         a number of amendments. The results of this
         cooperation are discussed in item 1472.

1472.   ———. "O'Connell, Davis and the Colleges Bill.
         VI.—The Bill Goes Through." IER 70 (January
         1948): 17-32.

         Continued from item 1471. Reconstructs the final
         haggling over the Bill, including the last-minute
         modifications introduced by the Irish hierarchy,

educated lay opinion, O'Connell, and Davis. Reviews
the tactical and substantial disagreements between
the two protagonists, declaring Davis arrogant and
unknowingly self-righteous, and O'Connell self-
restrained and undeniably generous.

1473. Larkin, Emmet. "The Quarrel among the Roman Catholic
        Hierarchy over the National System of Education in
        Ireland, 1838-1841." In THE CELTIC CROSS: STUDIES
        IN IRISH CULTURE AND LITERATURE, edited by Ray B.
        Browne, William John Roscelli, and Richard Loftus,
        121-46. West Lafayette, Ind.: Purdue University
        Studies, 1964.

        Sheds light on the heated conflict between Arch-
        bishops Murray and MacHale over the national system
        of education in Ireland. In 1838, seven years after
        the Irish bishops accepted Lord Stanley's idea of
        nondenominational schooling, MacHale denounced the
        system, implicitly criticizing Murray, who sat on its
        governing board. As the two prelates came to open
        blows in the press, attempts were made to restore
        ecclesiastical peace; however, the annual meeting of
        the Irish bishops in 1839 failed to effect a
        reconciliation, and in 1841 Rome, to which both
        sides had appealed, announced its decision not to
        pass any judgement whatsoever. Following this essay
        is a reply by Gilbert A. Cahill (147-52).

        See: Eoin McKiernan, JAF 79 (July/September
              1966): 504.

1474. McCartney, Donal. "Lecky and the Irish University
        Question." IER 108 (August 1967): 102-12.

        Clarifies the anti-Catholic Lecky's motives in
        arguing against denominational education in Ireland,
        on the one hand, while proposing, on the other, that
        Trinity College be opened completely to Catholics,
        who could have their own separate campus and
        curriculum.

1475. McGrath, Fergal, S.J. THE CHURCH SINCE EMANCI-
        PATION: CATHOLIC EDUCATION--THE UNIVERSITY
        QUESTION. A History of Irish Catholicism,
        edited by Patrick J. Corish, vol. 5, no. 6.
        Dublin: Gill and Macmillan, 1971.

Includes treatments of the Irish hierarchy's
reaction to the Queen's Colleges proposal, the
foundation of the Catholic University and Newman's
rectorship, the campaign for a Catholic University
charter (1859), the Royal University (1879), and
post-1886 solutions to the problem of providing
higher education for large numbers of Irish
Catholics.

1476. McGrath, Thomas G. "Archbishop Slattery and the
      Episcopal Controversy on Irish National Education,
      1838-1841." AH 39 (1984): 13-31.

      Locates and evaluates the material available in
      Irish episcopal archives concerning the ten-year
      hierarchical split over national education. Pays
      special attention to the correspondence of Dr.
      Michael Slattery, Archbishop of Cashel and Emly,
      which expresses in a general way the hopes and
      fears of the Irish bishops about education and
      other issues during the 1840s.

1477. Moody, T.W. "The Irish University Question of the
      Nineteenth Century." HIST 53 (June 1958): 90-
      109.

      Divides the nineteenth-century development of the
      University Question into two distinct periods: 1845-
      1850, in which a number of Catholic and government
      proposals were hotly debated and rejected; and 1873-
      1882, during which the hierarchy, led by Cullen,
      agitated successfully for government aid to the
      moribund Catholic University, though the funds had
      to be given in a roundabout way.

1478. Morrissey, Thomas J. TOWARDS A NATIONAL
      UNIVERSITY: WILLIAM DELANY, S.J., 1835-1924;
      AN ERA OF INITIATIVE IN IRISH EDUCATION.
      Topics in Modern Irish History. Atlantic
      Highlands, N.J.: Humanities Press/Dublin: Wolf-
      hound Press, 1983.

      Demonstrates that the attachment of the University
      College, under the presidency of Delany, to the Royal
      University was an ineffective and unpopular compro-
      mise solution to the problem of providing higher
      education for an ever more prominent and powerful

Irish Catholic middle class. Moreover, as they compared the wealthy and prestigious Trinity College to their own poor and ramshackle establishment, Catholics began to question the wisdom of passing up the latter, in favor of the former.

See: Hugh F. Kearney, AHR 90 (April 1985): 420-1; Lawrence J. McCaffrey, CHR 72 (April 1986): 333-4.

1479. Pemberton, Sandy Macpherson. IMPLICATIONS OF DIS-ESTABLISHMENT FOR CATHOLIC OBJECTIVES IN HIGHER EDUCATION IN IRELAND, 1869-1879. Ph.D. dissertation. University of California, Berkeley, 1969.

Studies the various ways in which Catholic goals in higher education were affected by the principle of disestablishment during the decade following the passage of the Irish Church Act of 1869. Illustrates the close relationship among the ecclesiastical question, the land issue, and the Catholic University problem. Sympathetic to the Catholic position, which is characterized as just and equitable.

The Catholic University of Ireland

1480. Doolin, William. "The Catholic University School of Medicine (1855-1909)." In STRUGGLE WITH FORTUNE: A MISCELLANY FOR THE CENTENARY OF THE CATHOLIC UNIVERSITY OF IRELAND, 1854-1954 (item 1489), 1-18.

Charts the School's slow but steady growth, attributing the success to the contributions made by its remarkable administrators and faculty.

1481. Gwynn, Aubrey, S.J. "The Jesuit Fathers and University College." In STRUGGLE WITH FORTUNE: A MISCELLANY FOR THE CENTENARY OF THE CATHOLIC UNIVERSITY OF IRELAND, 1854-1954 (item 1489), 19-50.

Explains the reasons for the Jesuit takeover of University College in November 1883. Evaluates the

changes introduced during the presidencies of
William Delany (1883-1888, 1897-1909) and Robert
Carbery (1888-1897).

1482. Hayes, Charles. "Cullen, Newman and the Irish
       Catholic University." RH 15 (May 1980): 201-12.

       Traces the failure of the University to the
       attitudes and roles of Cullen, its builder, and
       Newman, its first rector. Newman could not function
       effectively with the inadequate financial and
       academic foundation provided by Cullen; consequently,
       from its very beginning, the enterprise was doomed to
       fail.

1483. Kerr, Donal, S.M. "Dr. Quinn's School and the
       Catholic University, 1850-1867." IER 108
       (August 1967): 89-101.

       Sketches the history of St. Lawrence O'Toole's
       Seminary and Catholic Day School, Harcourt Street,
       Dublin. Popularly referred to as Dr. Quinn's,
       after its first president, it was founded by Arch-
       bishop Murray as both a feeder school into the
       projected Catholic University of Ireland and a
       challenge to the proposal to establish a national
       system of mixed intermediate education.

1484. McKenna, L., S.J. "The Catholic University of
       Ireland (I)." IER 31 (March 1928): 225-45.

       First part of a series on the history of the
       University from its foundation in 1854 to the
       Jesuit takeover of 1883. Sympathizes with Newman's
       all but impossible task as first rector, given the
       two realities of Irish education: (1) most parents
       and secondary teachers had no concept whatsoever of
       the importance of higher education; and (2) the
       standards of secondary education were appallingly
       low. Continued in item 1485.

1485. ————. "The Catholic University of Ireland (II)."
       IER 31 (April 1928): 351-71.

       Continued from item 1484. Discusses Newman's
       increasing disillusionment with the University,
       his resignation in March 1857, and the appointment

in 1861 of Dr. Bartholomew Woodlock, the highly
energetic and talented President of All Hallows
College, as his successor. During Woodlock's
first two years in office the University prospered.
However, for post-1863 problems, see item 1486.

1486. ————. "The Catholic University of Ireland (III)."
IER 31 (May 1928): 482-90.

Continued from item 1485. Presents the steady
deterioration of the University after 1863, as its
finances were strained and its building program
came to a complete halt. Explains the reasons
behind the bishops' refusal either to close the
institution or to let it be absorbed by the
government-proposed Dublin University. Concludes
in item 1487.

1487. ————. "The Catholic University of Ireland (IV)."
IER 31 (June 1928): 589-605.

Continued from item 1486. An account of the
futile efforts after 1873 to keep the dying
University open. Points to the Royal University
Bill of 1879 as the crucial factor leading to the
assumption of control by the Jesuits in 1883.
Condemns the British government for not treating
the University fairly during its declining years.

1488. Tierney, Michael. "'A Weary Task': The Struggle
in Retrospect." In STRUGGLE WITH FORTUNE: A
MISCELLANY FOR THE CENTENARY OF THE CATHOLIC
UNIVERSITY OF IRELAND, 1854-1954 (item 1489),
1-18.

Looks at the complex series of events leading to
the establishment of the Catholic University of
Ireland, by examining various political, social, and
religious factors, each in itself highly complicated.

1489. ————, ed. STRUGGLE WITH FORTUNE: A MISCELLANY FOR
THE CENTENARY OF THE CATHOLIC UNIVERSITY OF
IRELAND, 1854-1954. Dublin: Browne & Nolan,
1954.

A series of essays by specialists on the origins,
development, and achievements of the Catholic

University of Ireland. A balanced approach,
recognizing mistakes and failures as well as
strengths and successes. Contains items 1480,
1481, and 1488.

1490. Vale, Mary D. "Origins of the Catholic University of
        Ireland, 1845-1854. I. Sir Robert Peel's Govern-
        ment and Higher Education for Irish Catholics,
        1841-45." IER 82 (July 1954): 1-16.

        First of a three-part series. Inquires into
        Peel's motives for introducing the Colleges Bill
        of 1845. Reveals that his plan for a group of
        provincial colleges to spread mixed, non-sectarian
        education among the upper and middle classes was
        motivated by his desire to make Irish Catholics
        independent of the clergy in political affairs,
        thus bringing them closer to the Irish executive.
        Continued in item 1491.

1491. ————. "Origins of the Catholic University of
        Ireland, 1845-1854. II. The Catholic Bishops
        and the Colleges Bill." IER 82 (September
        1954): 152-64.

        Continued from item 1490. Explores the diversity
        of episcopal opinions concerning the Colleges Bill.
        Though some bishops supported Peel's proposal, a
        papal rescript of October 1847 declared the schools
        "detrimental to religion," and ordered the Irish
        hierarchy to take no part in establishing or
        supporting them. Concludes in item 1492.

1492. ————. "Origins of the Catholic University of
        Ireland, 1845-1854. III. The Decision to Found
        the Catholic University." IER 82 (October
        1954): 226-41.

        Continued from item 1491. Sees the bishops'
        decision to create the Catholic University as one
        forced upon them by the government's introduction
        of the Colleges Bill. Since the University was
        conceived as essentially a defensive measure, its
        desirability and chances of success were questioned
        by many Catholics.

1493. Wall, Thomas. "The Catholic University of

Ireland: 'The Fewer Men, the Greater Share of
Honour.'" IER 82 (July 1954): 17-25.

Details the daily life of students during the years
of Newman's rectorship. Discusses the small enrollment and large expenses, the annual academic
competitions and curriculum, various recreations and
sports, and Newman's remoteness and aloofness from
his charges.

Maynooth College

1494. Brady, John. "The Lay College, Maynooth. I." IER
61 (June 1943): 385-8.

Supplements the material presented in Chapter 11
of item 1511. A sketch of the troubled seventeen
years during which lay students attended classes at
Maynooth, at first with the seminarians (1800-1802),
and then at their own separate facilities (1802-
1817). For further information on the Lay College,
see item 1495.

1495. ————. "The Lay College, Maynooth. II." IER 62
(August 1943): 94-7.

Complements item 1494. Biographies of the five
Presidents of the Lay College, all of whom were
priests: Patrick Coleman (1800-1802), William
Russell (1802-1805), Morgan (Pelagius) D'Arcy
(1805-1807), Paul Long (1807-1814), and Patrick
M'Nicholas (1815-1817). In 1817 the College closed
its doors, having become "an inconvenient appendage."

1496. ————. "The Oath of Allegiance at Maynooth." IER
94 (September 1960): 129-35.

An account of the continuing controversy at
Maynooth over the legal requirement that all staff
members and students make a solemn declaration
denying certain beliefs and opinions commonly
supposed to be held by Catholics. Gives the entire
text of the oath used from 1795 to 1868, when it
was finally abandoned.

1497. Corish, Patrick J. "Gallicanism at Maynooth: Arch-
       bishop Cullen and the Royal Visitation of 1853."
       In STUDIES IN IRISH HISTORY PRESENTED TO R. DUDLEY
       EDWARDS, edited by Art Cosgrove and Donal
       McCartney, 176-89. Dublin: University College,
       1979.

           Describes Cullen's crusade to turn Maynooth away
       from its traditional Gallicanism and toward Ultra-
       montanism. Inspired by the advice of Giovanni
       Perrone, S.J., Rector of the Collegio Romano, the
       Archbishop attempted to make several changes,
       including the introduction of new theology text-
       books and the placement of the theology faculty
       under the direct supervision of the school's
       president. In the long run, all that these reforms
       did was to cause bad blood between the College and
       the prelate, who went on to establish his own
       diocesan seminary, strongly linked to the Papacy,
       at Clonliffe (see item 1532).

1498. Flood, J.M. "Dr. Peter Flood: President of Maynooth,
       1798-1803." IER 70 (February 1948): 97-113.

           Sketches the life and educational activity of
       Maynooth's second President, who led the fledgling
       institution through uncertain years of hostile
       scrutiny and intense criticism. Hails his consistent-
       ly outstanding contributions as administrator,
       theologian, teacher, and political lobbyist.

1499. Gwynn, Denis. "Pugin and Maynooth." IER 78
       (September 1952): 161-78.

           Presents the many problems faced by Pugin as
       architect of Maynooth (1845-1852). Believing that
       his plans were not being followed properly, due to
       a shortage of funds and shoddy workmanship, he
       resigned from the project, but later withdrew his
       resignation.

1500. Hamell, Patrick J., P.P. "Maynooth Students and
       Ordinations, 1795-1895: Index." IER 108
       (December 1967): 353-71.

           Introduces an eleven-part (and unfinished) series
       featuring data on nineteenth-century students, drawn

from three sources: lists of ordinations and
academic awards (1795-1864), the College calendar
(1863-1903), and the matriculation register (1795-
1895). Provides the following information for each
ordinand: years of matriculation, diocese of
origin, major, and date of ordination. After
offering a brief history of the institution and its
role within Irish political and social development,
this part covers those priests whose last names
begin with *A*. Continues in item 1501.

1501.   ————. "Maynooth Students and Ordinations, 1795-
1895: Index (II)." IER 109 (January 1968): 28-
40.

Lists a total of 667 priests, repeating the *A*
names found in item 1500, and adding to them those
names beginning with *B*. Continued in item 1502.

1502.   ————. "Maynooth Students and Ordinations, 1795-
1895: Index (III)." IER 109 (February
1968): 122-34.

Continued from item 1501. Lists a total of 669
priests, whose names begin with *C*. Continued in
item 1503.

1503.   ————. "Maynooth Students and Ordinations, 1795-
1895: Index (IV)." IER 109 (March 1968): 196-
203.

Continued from item 1502. Lists a total of 451
priests *C* and *D*). Continued in item 1504.

1504.   ————. "Maynooth Students and Ordinations, 1795-
1895: Index (V)." IER 109 (April 1968): 256-64.

Continued from item 1503. Lists a total of 510
priests (letters *D* and *E*). Continued in item 1505.

1505.   ————. "Maynooth Students and Ordinations, 1795-
1895: Index (VI)." IER 109 (May 1968): 335-40.

Continued from item 1504. Lists a total of 326
priests (letters *E* and *F*). Continued in item 1506.

1506.   ————. "Maynooth Students and Ordinations, 1795-

1895:   Index (VII)."   IER 109 (June 1968):   407-16.

Continued from item 1505. Lists a total of 556
priests (letters *F* and *G*). Continued in item 1507.

1507.   ————. "Maynooth Students and Ordinations, 1795-
        1895: Index (VIII)." IER 110 (July/August
        1968): 84-99.

Continued from item 1506. Lists a total of 909
priests (letters *H*, *I*, *J*, and *K*). Continued in
item 1508.

1508.   ————. "Maynooth Students and Ordinations, 1795-
        1895: Index (IX)." IER 110 (September
        1968): 173-82.

Continued from item 1507. Lists a total of 564
priests (letters *K* and *L*). Continued in item 1509.

1509.   ————. "Maynooth Students and Ordinations, 1795-
        1895: Index (X)." IER 110 (October/November
        1968): 277-88.

Continued from item 1508. Lists a total of 668
priests (letters *L* and *Mc*). Concluded in item 1510.

1510.   ————. "Maynooth Students and Ordinations, 1795-
        1895: Index (XI)." IER 110 (December 1968):   381-
        6.

Continued from item 1509. Lists a total of 308
priests whose names begin with *Mc*.

1511. Healy, John. MAYNOOTH COLLEGE: ITS CENTENARY
       HISTORY, 1795-1895. Dublin: Browne and Nolan,
       1895.

Divides the College's first century into four
approximately equal periods, studying internal and
external developments during each: 1795-1820,
marked by uninterrupted state funding; 1820-1845,
at the end of which the annual grant was increased
significantly by Peel's government; 1845-1870, the
final years of government aid, for the grant was
withdrawn in 1870; and 1871-1895, an era of
financial self-sufficiency, made possible by a

dramatic rise in enrollment.

1512. Kevin, Neil. "Maynooth College, 1795-1945." DUBR
217 (July/August/September 1945): 57-67.

A brief history of the institution, with emphasis
on its foundation and early years. Looks at its
first group of faculty, and the means by which it
was selected; the establishment and eventual failure
of the Lay College (1801-1817; see items 1494-5);
government inspection; endowments; and the controversy over the grant of 1845.

1513. Macauley, Ambrose. "Charles William Russell, D.D.,
President of Maynooth, 1857-80." AH 38
(1983): 34-42.

A portrait of a thinker who brought great academic
distinction to Maynooth. As a friend of Wiseman,
Newman, Acton, Montalembert, and Döllinger, Russell
was committed to an intellectual apostolate, though
the obstacles to carrying it out--the College lacked,
among other things, a respectable library--were
enormous.

1514. ————. DR. RUSSELL OF MAYNOOTH. London: Darton,
Longman and Todd, 1983.

Follows Russell's professorial and presidential
days at Maynooth, but within the context of his life
as a scholar who without any help became one of the
most distinguished Catholic intellectuals of his day.
In an atmosphere indifferent, and sometimes even
hostile, to mental activity, he developed a profound
critical sense, using it to work tirelessly in
religious periodicals and on behalf of Catholic
education.

See: Sheridan Gilley, TLS, 3 August 1984: 874; E.D.
Steele, JEH 35 (October 1984): 650-2; David
Watson, CLR 69 (December 1984): 460-1; R.V.
Comerford, ITQ 52 (nos. 1-2, 1986): 157-8;
John Tracy Ellis, CHR 72 (April 1986): 318-20.

1515. Machin, G.I.T. "The Maynooth Grant, the Dissenters
and Disestablishment, 1845-1847." EHR 82
(January 1967): 61-85.

Focuses on the badly fragmented Conservative and
Nonconformist opposition to Peel's proposal of 1845
to increase and make permanent the annual grant to
Maynooth.

1516. McLaughlin, Eve. "Maynooth and Heralds of Darkness."
       IER 79 (May 1953): 356-9.

Investigates the attacks against Maynooth launched
by Dr. Dill, missionary agent to the Irish Presbyterian
Church, and made in his THE MYSTERY SOLVED, OR IRELAND'S
MISERIES, THEIR CAUSE AND CURE (1852). Rome, according
to Dill, was the main cause of Irish misery; its
priests brought every kind of misfortune, including the
potato blight. As Ireland's major clerical training
ground, Maynooth represented all that was sinister,
cunning, and deceitful. The only remedy was to starve
out the institution by discontinuing its grant.

1517. McLaughlin, P.J. NICHOLAS CALLAN: PRIEST-SCIENTIST,
       1799-1864. Dublin: Clonmore & Reynolds, 1965.

Chronicles daily life at nineteenth-century
Maynooth, as seen through the teaching and scientific
research of one of its professors of Natural Philosophy (1826-1864), a pioneer in electromagnetism and
high-tension electricity, and inventor of the
induction cell. Offers sidelights on his colleagues
and anecdotes about student life.

See: IER 103 (May 1965): 342-4; Hugh F. Kearney, IHS
      14 (September 1965): 381-2.

1518. Meehan, Denis. "Maynooth and the Missions." IER 66
       (September 1945): 224-37.

A list of nineteenth-century Maynooth graduates
who served as bishops and priests in North America,
Australia, Asia, and Africa.

1519. ————. WINDOW ON MAYNOOTH. Dublin: Clonmore and
       Reynolds, 1949.

Tells the history of the College through its
buildings and squares.

See: Hugh J. Nolan, CHR 36 (January 1951): 460-1.

1520. Newman, Jeremiah. MAYNOOTH AND GEORGIAN IRELAND.
Galway: Kenny's Bookshops and Art Galleries,
1979.

Not a formal or definitive history of the College,
but an attempt to give a human slant on the early
development of the school, its professors and
students. Offers a well-rounded picture of everyday
life, showing the unedifying, and even scandalous,
aspects, as well as the expected intellectual and
religious commitment. Supplements items 1511 and
1512.

1521. Norman, E.R. "The Maynooth Question of 1845." IHS
15 (September 1967): 407-37.

Shows that the Maynooth controversy of 1845 was
more than simply a dispute over government funding
of a Catholic institution. It included several
larger issues of unequal significance: the identity
and direction of British conservatives, the success
or failure of Peel's Irish policy, the future of
higher education and the Church-State relationship
in Ireland, and the continuing appeal of "no popery."

1522. Quigley, E.J., P.P. "Dr. Murray of Maynooth--I."
IER 15 (June 1920): 453-67.

First of a six-part series detailing the life and
achievements of Patrick Murray (1811-1882). Presents
his family background, early years, and education.
In 1841, twelve years after entering Maynooth as a
student, he was given a chair in theology, at a time
when Catholics were looking for scholars who would
stem the growing Protestant revival in Ireland.
Continues in item 1523.

1523. ————. "Dr. Murray of Maynooth--II." IER 16
(July 1920): 20-8.

Continued from item 1522. Assesses his more than
thirty years of contributions to the *Dublin Review*.
Admires his refined, polished, and readable style,
but judges his content too volatile and polemical at
times. Continues in item 1524.

1524.   ———. "Dr. Murray of Maynooth--III." IER 16
         (August 1920): 94-9.

         Continued from item 1523. Highlights Murray's
         contacts with Thackery (1843) and Carlyle (1849).
         Continues in item 1525.

1525.   ———. "Dr. Murray of Maynooth--IV." IER 16
         (September 1920): 194-202.

         Continued from item 1524. Evaluates Murray's
         teaching, preaching, and academic publications.
         Continues in item 1526.

1526.   ———. "Dr. Murray of Maynooth--V." IER 16
         (October 1920): 289-99.

         Continued from item 1525. Discusses Murray's
         connection with the Royal Commission founded in
         1856 to investigate Protestant charges of edu-
         cational abuses at Maynooth. Sketches his own
         active pamphleteering against anti-Catholic
         groups. Concludes in item 1527.

1527.   ———. "Dr. Murray of Maynooth--VI." IER 16
         (November 1920): 377-88.

         Continued from item 1526. Deals with Murray's
         DE ECCLESIA CHRISTI, a powerful response to the
         Dublin Review's contention that the religion
         taught at Maynooth was Gallican and Jansenist.
         Measures his influence on the development of
         nineteenth-century Irish Catholicism.

1528.   Turner, Michael. "The French Connection with Maynooth
         College, 1795-1855." STUDIES 70 (Spring
         1981): 77-87.

         Proves that the two charges made most frequently
         against Maynooth during the nineteenth century--that
         it was Gallican and Jansenist--were, at the very
         least, overexaggerated. A study of faculty and
         textbooks indicates that the College was Gallican
         only in the sense of adhering to the first propo-
         sition of the French Articles of 1682, which pro-
         claimed the state's independence of the Church.
         And though ecclesiastical rigorism was taught, it

was more Roman than French in inspiration, and did
not produce in either the school or the Irish Church
which it nurtured a servile subjection to British
authority.

All Hallows College

1529. Condon, Kevin, C.M. THE MISSIONARY COLLEGE OF ALL
       HALLOWS, 1842-1891. Dublin: All Hallows
       Publications, 1986.

       Describes the foundation and first fifty years of
       one of Ireland's most productive ecclesiastical
       institutions. Places its growth against the national
       background and the worldwide work of the more than
       one thousand missionaries it trained. Balances its
       positive features--e.g., its acceptance of poor as
       well as middle-class students--against such drawbacks
       as its weak and often undisciplined organization. As
       a result of the confusion created by the latter
       problem, control of the College was given to the
       Vincentians in 1891.

       See: Thomas J. Morrissey, S.J., CHR 73 (October
       1987): 653-5.

1530. Purcell, W., C.M. "Father Hand (1807-1846): Part I."
       IER 60 (November 1942): 336-47.

       Reviews Hand's life from his birth to his
       establishment of All Hallows College, Dublin, in
       1842. Concentrates on the elaborate preparations
       behind the institution's founding: the clarification
       of his early desire to start a college to train
       foreign missionaries; his seven-month stay in Paris
       to study missionary institutes; and his visit to
       Rome, to obtain official approval for his project.
       Continues in item 1531.

1531. ————. "Father Hand (1807-1846): Part II." IER
       60 (December 1942): 413-21.

       Continued from item 1530. Reconstructs the first
       four years of All Hallows and the last four years of
       Hand's life. Underscores his undying commitment to

the school and the resulting successes in the number
of ordinands and supporters.

Holy Cross College

1532. Sherry, Richard. "Holy Cross College, Clonliffe,
        1859-1959." IER 94 (October 1960): 193-203.

    Concentrates on the foundation and early years of
the College. Established by Cullen, with an initial
enrollment of thirty-four students, the institution
grew quietly and uneventfully, unlike its sister
schools at Maynooth, Carlow, Kilkenny, and Wexford.

The Press

1533. Wall, Thomas. "Catholic Periodicals of the Past.
        I. *The Catholic Penny Magazine*, 1834-1835."
        IER 101 (April 1964): 234-44.

    Outlines the history of the first really popular
Irish Catholic magazine, founded by William Joseph
Battersby of Dublin's Catholic Book Society.
Nowhere else can the exhilaration following Emanci-
pation be felt in so profound a way. Continues in
item 1534.

1534. ———. "Catholic Periodicals of the Past. II. The
        Catholic Book Society and the *Irish Catholic
        Magazine*." IER 101 (May 1964): 289-303.

    Continued from item 1533. Details the aims and
early activity of the Irish Catholic Society for
the Diffusion of Useful Knowledge, also known as
the Catholic Book Society, established by James
Warren Doyle, Bishop of Kildare and Leighlin, in
1827. Emphasizes the limited impact of its chief
organ, the rather dull *Irish Catholic Magazine*, in
reanimating the Church in Ireland and fighting
militant Protestantism. Continues in item 1535.

1535. ———. "Catholic Periodicals of the Past. III.

Philip Barron's *Ancient Ireland,* 1835." IER 101 (June 1964): 375-88.

Continued from item 1534. Looks at a hierarchy-supported journal dedicated to the restoration of the Irish language through the collection and publication of manuscripts, records, and traditional folklore. Continues in item 1536.

1536. ————. "Catholic Periodicals of the Past. IV. *The Catholic Luminary,* 1840-1841." IER 102 (June 1964): 17-27.

Continued from item 1535. Follows the twelve-month existence of *The Catholic Luminary and Ecclesiastical Repertory,* a digest featuring the texts of important sermons, excerpts from recently published religious books, and summaries or analyses of Catholic news from all over the world. The uneven quality of its reporting and its frequent errata irritated many of its readers, both clerical and lay, and undoubtedly contributed to its early demise. Continues in item 1537.

1537. ————. "Catholic Periodicals of the Past. V. Duffy's *Irish Catholic Magazine,* 1847-1848." IER 102 (August 1964): 86-100.

Continued from item 1536. Describes the twenty-three months of the reinvigorated *Irish Catholic Magazine.* Through famine and national epidemic James Duffy, with the help of Charles Patrick Meehan and James Clarence Mangan, succeeded in providing a creative and entertaining periodical which proffered a wide range of subjects, including, most prominently, poetry. Continues in item 1538.

1538. ————. "Catholic Periodicals of the Past. VI. Duffy's *Irish Catholic Magazine,* 1847-1848. Part II." IER 102 (September 1964): 129-47.

Continued from item 1537. Pinpoints the contributions to Duffy's journal made by Maynooth professors through the year 1848. Illustrates the use of the *Magazine* to popularize the Gothic revival in Ireland and to defend Maynooth against various critics. Concludes in item 1539.

1539. ────. "Catholic Periodicals of the Past. VII.
        The *Catholic University Gazette*, 1854-1856."
        IER 102 (October 1964): 206-23.

        Continued from item 1538. A survey of Newman's
        journalistic attempt to arouse and maintain public
        interest in the idea of an Irish Catholic university.
        Published by James Duffy and edited by Newman himself,
        the *Gazette* gave the impression of unceasing academic
        activity, as it filled its front page with lists of
        new appointments, prizes and awards, examination
        results, lectures given and gifts received, and
        distinguished faculty.

1540. ────. "The *Irish Ecclesiastical Record* and
        Maynooth." IER 66 (November 1945): 322-30.

        Compares the origins, aims, and fortunes of
        Cullen's *IER* (1864-1876) with those of the Maynooth-
        directed *IER*, revived by Archbishop Walsh, Cullen's
        successor, in 1880.

                        Piety and Devotion

1541. Boyle, Patrick, C.M. "The Irish Pulpit in the
        Nineteenth Century." IER 3 (April 1914): 344-57.

        Recalls some of the more prominent Irish preachers
        of the nineteenth century, along with the types of
        speaking through which they demonstrated their elo-
        quence. The best of the homilists were Archbishop
        Murray of Dublin and Bishop Doyle of Kildare and
        Leighlin. Most skillful at controversial dis-
        cussions--i.e., debates with Protestants--was Daniel
        William Cahill. Parochial missions were most
        effectively preached by Newman, Bishop Moriarty of
        Kerry, and Thomas N. Burke, O.P.

1542. Burke-Savage, Roland, S.J. "The Growth of Devotion
        to the Sacred Heart in Ireland." IER 110
        (October/November 1968): 185-208.

        Traces the rise and expansion of the most popular
        Irish religious devotion of the nineteenth century.
        In 1831 Gregory XVI gave the bishops of Ireland the

right to celebrate the feast of the Sacred Heart. Through the spread of St. Margaret Mary's writings and Jesuit-sponsored confraternities and novenas, the cult grew quickly, climaxing in Ireland's public consecration to the Sacred Heart in March 1873.

1543.   Kerr, Donal, S.M.   "The Early Nineteenth Century: Patterns of Change." In IRISH SPIRITUALITY, edited by Michael Maher, 135-44. Dublin: Veritas, 1981.

Summarizes the Irish hierarchy's successful campaign to discipline popular piety. From a Gaelic spirituality, rife with superstition and excessive merrymaking at religious festivals, the faith was transformed into a respectable system of belief, controlled by the printed prayer-book in English, parish missions, and devotion to the Sacred Heart.

1544.   Larkin, Emmet.   "The Devotional Revolution in Ireland, 1850-1875." AHR 77 (June 1972): 625-52.

Attributes the dramatic change in nineteenth-century Irish popular piety to Cullen's determined leadership. Details the process by which the Archbishop of Dublin turned a worldly, largely indifferent, poorly organized, and strongly Gallican pre-Famine Church into a highly disciplined, devout, and Romanized religious unit, whose missionaries carried these new emphases throughout the world.

1545.   Miller, David W.   "Irish Catholicism and the Great Famine." JSH 9 (Fall 1975): 81-98.

Contends that Irish peasants in the Famine-inspired process of rural modernization became more rather than less religious, if the degree of participation in formal observance is a valid criterion. Labels this rise in rural piety a real devotional revolution.

1546.   Murphy, James H.   "The Role of Vincentian Parish Missions in the 'Irish Counter-Reformation' of the Mid-Nineteenth Century." IHS 24 (November 1984): 152-71.

Disputes the claim (e.g., item 1416) that Cullen
deserves all the credit for the tightening and
disciplining of devotion within the nineteenth-
century Irish Church, by pointing to the impact of
Vincentian parochial activity between 1840 and 1860.
Finds the stimulus for the missions in the surprisingly successful Irish Anglican attempts to
attract Roman Catholics.

Social Catholicism

1547. Gildea, Denis. MOTHER MARY ARSENIUS OF FOXFORD.
       London: Burns Oates & Washbourne, 1936.

Recalls the unprecedented achievements of one of
nineteenth-century Ireland's greatest practitioners
of social Catholicism. Born in England, Agnes
Morrogh Bernard (1842-1932) entered the Irish
Sisters of Charity in 1854, and was put in charge
of their school in Dublin. During her years there
she introduced training colleges for nuns teaching
in convent schools throughout Ireland. In 1877,
and as rectress of a new foundation at Ballaghadereen,
County Mayo, she established Foxford, a veritable
Catholic village, building a convent, school,
dispensary, and woolen mills, so as to alleviate by
care and employment the area's deep suffering and
poverty.

See: DR 54 (October 1936): 597-9.

1548. Maire, Elie. MOTHER PATRICK OF PARIS: AN IRISH
       MOTHER OF THE BLIND. Adapted from the French
       by Africanus. Dublin: Gill, 1949.

Praises the faith and courage of Brigid Devin,
who left her native Drogheda, entered a Parisian
convent, and spent the final three decades of her
life ministering to the blind.

See: IER 73 (May 1950): 472.

1549. O'Neill, Timothy P. "The Catholic Church and Relief
       of the Poor, 1815-45." AH 31 (1973): 132-45.

Assesses the role played by Catholics, both
clerical and lay, in relieving the suffering of
thousands of Irish laid low by the famines or
epidemics of 1815-1845. Describes the many
different sources of Catholic aid, from the
Saint Vincent de Paul Society and new religious
orders, to bishops' relief committees and
priests who successfully solicited help from
their congregations. Concludes that the Church's
efforts were extremely generous and far-reaching.

Temperance

1550. Father Augustine, O.F.M. Cap. FOOTPRINTS OF FATHER
MATHEW, O.F.M. CAP., APOSTLE OF TEMPERANCE.
Dublin: M.H. Gill and Son, 1947.

Places his temperance crusade within the larger
context of his work as a preacher, confessor, and
social worker who, notwithstanding his apolitical
stance, was frequently misunderstood and criticized.
Offers a vivid account of his administration of the
pledge in all parts of Ireland.

See: IER 70 (February 1948): 181-2; James A.
Reynolds, CHR 35 (January 1950): 443-5.

1551. Gwynn, Denis. "Father Mathew's Centenary." CLR 41
(December 1956): 705-19.

Centers on his achievements in the areas of
temperance and aid to the poor.

1552. Lucey, Cornelius. "Father Theobald Mathew." IER 86
(December 1956): 369-76.

Investigates the forerunners, meteoric rise, and
gradual decline of Mathew's movement. As early as
1817, the Society of Total Abstinence was organized
at Skibberren; it was followed in 1829 by the Ulster
Temperance Society, headquartered in Belfast. In
spite of initial government distrust, Mathew's
crusade grew rapidly, due to its vivid dramatization
of the worst evils of excessive drinking. Ironically,
its demise after 1842 was brought about by a

stultifying preoccupation with the evils of intemperance.

1553. Malcolm, Elizabeth. "The Catholic Church and the Irish Temperance Movement, 1838-1901." IHS 23 (May 1982): 1-16.

Clarifies the reasons behind the Irish hierarchy's hostility to the anti-drink movement, as it developed during the period between the Mathew crusade of the 1840s and Father James A. Cullen's Pioneer Total Abstinence League of the Sacred Heart, in the 1890s.

1554. Mathew, David. "Father Theobald Mathew." IER 87 (February 1957): 81-90.

A character study. Hails Mathew's humanitarianism, selflessness, and courage.

1555. Father Matthew, O.F.M. Cap. "Theobald Mathew, O.F.M. Cap.: A Centenary Tribute." IER 86 (December 1956): 377-89.

Emphasizes the many sides of the temperance movement and the serious obstacles to their effective operation. Points to Mathew's other, non-temperance-related achievements, including his establishment of Catholic youth groups and his service as Provincial of the Irish Capuchins.

1556. Rogers, Patrick. FATHER THEOBALD MATHEW: APOSTLE OF TEMPERANCE. Dublin: Browne and Nolan, 1943.

A detailed biography of the priest whose non-interference in politics lost him the support of those Catholics who resorted to physical force in 1848, and whose cooperation with Protestants in the fight against alcoholism earned him the antipathy of the Irish hierarchy.

See: IER 63 (March 1944): 210; A. Aspinall, EHR 60 (May 1945): 283; SSR 19 (June 1945): 280; J. Joseph Ryan, CHR 31 (July 1945): 193-5; Thomas P. Neill, IHS 4 (September 1945): 372-4; F.P. Donnelly, THOUGHT 20 (September 1945): 542-3.

1557. Rowe, John G. "The 'Father Mathew' Temperance
      Movement Centenary." CLR 15 (October 1938): 315-
      25.

      Focuses on Mathew's anti-drink campaign among the
      poor.

The Fine Arts

1558. Kennedy, Thomas P. THE CHURCH SINCE EMANCI-
      PATION: CHURCH BUILDING. A History of
      Irish Catholicism, edited by Patrick J.
      Corish, vol. 5, no. 8. Dublin: Gill and
      Macmillan, 1970.

      A brief survey of ecclesiastical design and
      decoration in nineteenth-century Ireland. Features
      a list of prominent architects, along with their
      principal works, and illustrations of building
      plans, stained glass, statuary, and other furnish-
      ings.

Missionary Activity

1559. Cooke, Colm. "The Modern Irish Missionary Movement."
      AH 35 (1980): 234-46.

      Surveys the origins and extent of the nineteenth-
      century Irish missionary movement, from the earliest
      days of immigration to the post-1850 targeting of
      specific areas--e.g., Africa and Asia--for Christiani-
      zation by religious orders and diocesan clergy.

1560. Duffy, T. Gavan. "An Irish Missionary Episode: The
      Bishops Fennelly." IER 17 (May 1921): 464-84.

      A case study of nineteenth-century Irish
      missionary activity at its best and worst.
      Relates the experiences in India of the Fennelly
      brothers, John (1805-1868) and Stephen (1816-
      1880). John, the newly appointed Vicar Apostolic
      of Madras, arrived in 1842; Stephen came two years
      later, to serve as his assistant. Despite their

problems in dealing with a radically different culture, a poverty-striken city, and a continuing lack of interest by Irish ecclesiastical authorities, they made a highly effective team. Stephen succeeded his brother as Bishop of Madras in 1868.

1561.   Finegan, Francis, S.J. "Irish Missionaries in Bengal, 1834-59." IER 99 (March 1963): 157-69.

Salutes the achievements of two pioneering Vicars Apostolic during the mid-nineteenth century, Thomas Olliffe of Cork and Patrick Joseph Carew of Waterford.

1562.   McGlade, Joseph. THE MISSIONS: AFRICA & THE ORIENT. A History of Irish Catholicism, edited by Patrick J. Corish, vol. 6, no. 8. Dublin: Gill and Son, 1967.

Devotes most of this brief introduction to considerations of mission organization and of the work done in Africa, the Far East, and Oceania by Irish religious orders.

1563.   Needham, Ciaran, S.P.S. "Irish Missions to Africa." IER 95 (March 1961): 167-75.

Details Irish missionary activity at the Cape, divided into the dioceses of Capetown and Port Elizabeth, and throughout the English-speaking areas of the continent, in which the Holy Ghost Fathers and the Society of African Missions made significant advances.

Special Challenges

Church and State

Irish-Papal Relations

*   Broderick, John F., S.J. THE HOLY SEE AND THE IRISH MOVEMENT FOR THE REPEAL OF THE UNION WITH ENGLAND, 1829-1847. Cited above as item 77.

*   Parsons, Reuben. "Pope Leo XIII and the Home Rule
       Movement in Ireland." STUDIES IN CHURCH HISTORY,
       6 (item 27), 216-24.

       Measures the extent and impact of Papal inter-
       vention in late nineteenth-century Irish political
       affairs, asserting that Leo XIII never condemned
       either the Land League or the principle of Home
       Rule; he opposed only the practice of boycotting
       and the Plan of Campaign, neither of which was
       ever officially accepted by the national organi-
       zation, Parnell, or Gladstone.

1564. Rhodes, Anthony. "Missions to Ireland: The Persico
       Papers." ENC 54 (February 1980): 7-19.

       Details the six-month visit to Ireland by Msgr.
       Ignazio Persico, who was charged by Leo XIII to
       assess the role played by the clergy in the
       violence caused by "agrarian agitation." Persico,
       a former bishop of Savannah, Georgia, and one of
       the Vatican's ablest diplomats, submitted his
       report in December 1887, heavily implicating much
       of the clergy and even a few bishops in the
       ubiquitous violence. Based on Persico's conclusion,
       Leo condemned the movement and ordered immediate
       clerical withdrawal from it.

       ## The British Government and the Irish Church

1565. Brady, John. "Ireland and the Ecclesiastical Titles
       Bill." IER 74 (October 1950): 338-49.

       Describes the Irish hierarchy's reaction to the
       anti-Catholic legislation of 1851. For the twenty
       years of the Act's existence,--it was repealed in
       1871,--Archbishop MacHale urged his colleagues to
       defy its ban on the use of the title of Archbishop
       by Roman Catholic prelates.

1566. McDougall, Donald J. "George III, Pitt, and the
       Irish Catholics, 1801-1805." CHR 31 (October
       1945): 255-81.

       Presents the details of a lost opportunity to

settle the question of Catholic Emancipation under the most favorable conditions, by including it in the political package which brought about the union of Great Britain and Ireland. Blames George III's stubbornness and Pitt's inconstancy for the continuing virulence of the religious struggle, which dragged on until 1829.

1567. Reynolds, James A.   THE CATHOLIC EMANCIPATION CRISIS IN IRELAND, 1823-29.   Yale Historical Publications, Miscellany vol. 60.   New Haven: Yale University Press, 1954.

Delineates the activities of a small group of lawyers, tradesmen, and journalists who headed the Catholic Association, but without losing sight of the two contexts within which they operated: the larger national organization and the Church. Bases its findings on extensive use of government and private collections in the Irish State Paper Office and the Dublin Archdiocesan Archives.

See: John E. Pomfret, AHR 60 (April 1955): 652-3; Edmund J. Murray, CHR 41 (April 1955): 32-3; David Thomson, HIST 40 (October 1955): 347-8; Norman Gash, EHR 71 (January 1956): 170-1; Maureen Wall, IHS 10 (March 1956): 112-4; Raymond G. Cowherd, JMH 28 (June 1956): 185-6; T.A. Birrell, DUBR 232 (Summer 1958): 189-91.

Catholic Political Activity

1568. Altholz, Josef L.   "Daniel O'Connell and the *Dublin Review*."   CHR 74 (January 1988):   1-12.

Delineates O'Connell's role in the founding and survival of the *Dublin Review*. Claims that the most significant aspect of his connection with the journal was not his willingness to be one of its proprietors, or even his financing of its third issue, but rather his promise to keep it totally apolitical and devoted solely to the interests of the Church.

1569. Biggs-Davison, John, and Chowdharay-Best, George.

THE CROSS OF ST. PATRICK: THE CATHOLIC UNIONIST
TRADITION IN IRELAND. Bourne End, Bucks.: Kensal
Press, 1984.

Examines the differences among nineteenth-century
Irish Catholics over the way in which their political
affairs should be handled. Indicates a split not
only between unionists and nationalists, but also
among the unionists themselves, over the proper
extent of British control. Contends that the
popularity of the British royal family in Ireland
was not as strong as once thought.

See: Denis Faul, MONTH 2nd NS 19 (June 1986): 214;
Edward Norman, TLS, 27 September 1985: 1051;
Laurence Tanner, CONR 249 (July 1986): 51-2.

1570. Corish, Patrick J. "Catholic Ireland, 1864." IER
102 (October 1964): 196-205.

Traces the origins of the National Association of
Ireland, founded in 1864 by an unenthusiastic
Cardinal Cullen, with the purpose of countering
Fenianism by organizing public support for Catholic
education, disestablishment, and land reform.
Paints, by way of introduction, a broad picture of
Irish Catholic political frustration during the
1850s and early 1860s.

1571. ————. POLITICAL PROBLEMS, 1860-1878. A History of
Irish Catholicism, edited by Patrick J. Corish,
vol. 5, no. 3. Dublin and Melbourne: Gill and
Son, 1967.

Looks at the hierarchy's relationship with the
Fenians, the goals and activities of the National
Association of Ireland, and the first stirrings of
the Home Rule movement.

1572. Fogarty, L. FATHER JOHN KENYON: A PATRIOT PRIEST OF
FORTY-EIGHT. Dublin: Mahon's Printing Works,
n.d.

Examines the life, character, and ministry of the
parish priest of Templederry, County Tipperary, who
during the years immediately preceding 1848 tried to
convince the rural Irish that physical force and

moral force were mutually exclusive terms. Though
accused of cowardice, of having retired to the
seclusion of Templederry when the hour for action
came, Kenyon (1812-1869) clung to his ideal of
peaceful resistance, which for him was a central
feature of his "holy patriotism." Reproduces many
of his letters, speeches, and poems *in extenso*.

1573. Gwynn, Denis. "Father Kenyon and Young Ireland--I."
      IER 71 (March 1949): 226-46.

      Explains why Kenyon, who had done so much to
      instigate the uprising of 1848, took no active
      part in it. Shows that the "Patriot Priest"
      never gave the Young Ireland movement any reason
      to believe that he would live up to their expec-
      tations by taking charge of the insurrection in
      the area between Cashel and Limerick. Concludes
      in item 1574.

1574. ———. "Father Kenyon and Young Ireland--II."
      IER 71 (June 1949): 508-32.

      Continued from item 1573. Follows Kenyon's
      activities between May and July 1848, during
      which time he decided against participation in
      the imminent uprising, and sought to discourage
      his friends from becoming involved in it.

1575. ———. "The Priests and Young Ireland in 1848."
      IER 70 (July 1948): 590-609.

      Accounts for the growing rift between the clergy
      and the Young Ireland movement during the months
      immediately preceding the uprising of 1848. Most
      priests opposed the idea of armed insurrection as
      unjustifiable and futile; moreover, they questioned
      the character of revolutionaries such as Duffy,
      Doheny, and Meagher.

1576. Hill, Jacqueline R. "Nationalism and the Catholic
      Church in the 1840s: Views of Dublin Repealers."
      IHS 19 (September 1975): 371-95.

      Discusses the reactions of the lay, middle-class
      members of O'Connell's Repeal Association to three
      issues of the 1840s, all of which had some

implication, whether direct or indirect, for the role of the Church in Irish society: (1) the Charitable Bequests Act of 1844; (2) the Queen's Colleges Bill of 1845; and (3) the so-called "defamation of the Catholic priesthood" case of 1848.

1577. Horgan, David Thomas. THE IRISH CATHOLIC WHIGS IN PARLIAMENT, 1847-1874. Ph.D. dissertation. University of Minnesota, Minneapolis, 1975.

A socio-political analysis of the major Irish parliamentary grouping during the period between O'Connell's death and the rise of Home Rule agitation. Composed of well-to-do individuals, the sixty-nine Whigs who sat at Westminster through the twenty-seven years argued for complete equality of opportunity and responsibility in Britain's international ventures. Unfortunately, their program had no great leader to support it, and by 1868 the Fenians had captured the popular imagination in Ireland.

* Horgan, John J. "Daniel O'Connell: The Man." GREAT CATHOLIC LAYMEN (item 31), 335-88.

Portrays O'Connell as a sincere and devout Catholic, ever anxious to defend and glorify the Church.

1578. Jenkins, Hilary. "The Irish Dimension of the British *Kulturkampf*: Vaticanism and Civil Allegiance, 1870-1875." JEH 30 (July 1979): 353-77.

Measures the degree to which the hotly debated question of religious education in Ireland exacerbated the controversy of the early 1870s over whether the Liberal State could in the long run successfully reconcile individual liberty and the freedom of the Roman Church, and the claims of papal supremacy and the requirements of allegiance to the Queen. Relates this controversy to contemporary anti-Catholic initiatives taken by the German and French governments.

1579. Jupp, P.J. "Irish Parliamentary Elections and the Influence of the Catholic Vote, 1801-1820." HJ 10 (no. 2, 1967) · 183-96.

Traces the evolution of a distinct Catholic
electoral program, demonstrating that the political
aims of Catholics during the first two decades of
the nineteenth century were essentially moderate.
Outlines the strategies and organizations used by
clergy and laity to return supporters of Catholic
Emancipation to Parliament, years before O'Connell
created his movement to mobilize his coreligionists'
political power.

1580.   Kennedy, Liam. "The Early Response of the Irish
        Catholic Clergy to the Co-Operative Movement."
        IHS 21 (March 1978): 55-74.

Discovers three main clerical reactions to the
development of agricultural cooperatives during
the 1890s: (1) either reserve or outright opposition; (2) active encouragement; and (3) qualified
and selective promotion. Highlights the specific
pastoral, ideological, and economic motives behind
the various positions, displaying the clergy as a
distinct social category with connections both
within and beyond the rural community.

*   Kerr, Donal A. PEEL, PRIESTS AND POLITICS: SIR
        ROBERT PEEL'S ADMINISTRATION AND THE ROMAN
        CATHOLIC CHURCH IN IRELAND, 1841-1846. Cited
        above as item 1236.

Reconstructs in great detail the Irish hierarchy's
responses to a triad of reforms proposed by Peel's
government: the Charitable Bequests Act, the
increase of the Maynooth grant, and the Queen's
Colleges Bill.

1581.   Larkin, Emmet. "Church and State in Ireland in the
        Nineteenth Century." CH 31 (September
        1962): 294-306.

Uses four examples of clerical correspondence from
Propaganda archives to illustrate the very complicated
history of Church-State relations in nineteenth-
century Ireland. Concludes that throughout the
century two churches, the Roman and the Irish,
confronted two states, the British and the Irish,
within the same country, creating a highly complex
and inevitably troubled relationship.

1582. ————. "Church, State, and Nation in Modern
Ireland." AHR 80 (December 1975): 1244-76.

Features within a broad treatment of the relationship between Catholicism and nationalism in
nineteenth-century Ireland, a consideration of the
O'Connell-MacHale combination of the 1840s, whereby
the Archbishop supported the movement to repeal the
Union, in return for the politician's endorsement
of government-funded Church schools. Claims that
Catholicism had a beneficial impact on Irish
nationalism throughout the century, steering it
away from a variety of excesses.

1583. ————. "The Roman Catholic Hierarchy and the Fall
of Parnell." VS 4 (June 1961): 315-36.

Focuses on the role played by the Irish bishops
in one of the great turning points of modern Irish
history. As a result of Parnell's fall in 1890, and
for the first time, the two dominant forces of
nationalism and Catholicism parted company,
beginning a long struggle for political ascendancy.

1584. McCartney, Donal. "The Church and the Fenians." In
FENIANS AND FENIANISM: CENTENARY ESSAYS, edited
by Maurice Harmon, 11-23. Dublin: Scepter, 1968.

Lists the reasons for Cullen's condemnation of
Fenianism in a pastoral of October 1865. Forming
the rationale for the censure, which was shared by
most of the Irish hierarchy, were three
arguments: (1) the Papacy had consistently
condemned "occult," that is, secret, societies;
(2) the Fenian newspaper, *Irish People*, preached
socialism and disrespect for ecclesiastical
authority; and (3) the movement was dedicated to
violence. The Fenian reply was the cry, "no
priests in politics." Underscores the idea that
the controversy was fueled by continuing misun-
derstanding on both sides.

1585. ————. "The Churches and Secret Societies." In
SECRET SOCIETIES IN IRELAND, edited by T. Desmond
Williams, 68-78. Dublin: Gill and Macmillan/
New York: Barnes & Noble, 1973.

Similar in content to the author's earlier analysis
of Fenianism (item 1584). Emphasizes, however, the
hierarchy's denunciation of the Fenians' secrecy, a
denunciation which created a conflict of loyalties
for many Irish, including, most notably, Father
Lavelle, the fanatically pro-Fenian Archdeacon of
Tuam.

See: CHOICE 10 (December 1973): 1619; Martin J.
Waters, AHR 79 (June 1974): 787-8.

1586. MacDonagh, Oliver. "The Politicization of the Irish
Catholic Bishops, 1800-1850." HJ 18 (March
1975): 37-53.

Describes how and why clerical influence in Irish
politics grew through the first half of the nineteenth
century. Sees O'Connell, working in three phases
(1801-1815, 1824-1829, and 1839-1843), as the main
agent responsible for bringing the bishops and priests
into secular politics, by harnessing them, along with
their influence and prestige, to the nationalist
agitation.

* Neill, Thomas P. "Daniel O'Connell." THEY LIVED
THE FAITH (item 33), 22-46.

Credits O'Connell with having roused nineteenth-
century Catholics from a tragic apathy to a realization of their political power. In so doing, he
was the first layman of his time to help the Church
in adjusting to the modern secular state.

1587. Norman, E.R. THE CATHOLIC CHURCH AND IRELAND IN THE
AGE OF REBELLION, 1859 TO 1873. Ithaca: Cornell
University Press, 1965.

Deals with the efforts of the Irish bishops to
convince the British government of the urgent
necessity of drastic and far-reaching reforms,
given the rise of Fenian violence.

See: Robert Rhodes James, SPEC 214 (5 February
1965): 172; TLS, 4 March 1965: 164; Shane
Leslie, MONTH 1st NS 33 (April 1965): 237-8;
IER 103 (May 1965): 345-7; Lawrence J.
McCaffrey, AHR 71 (October 1965): 197-8;

CHOICE 2 (October 1965): 520; Michael Hurst,
HJ (no. 1, 1966): 144-9; Nicholas Mansergh,
JEH 17 (April 1966): 124-5; John H. Whyte,
EHR 81 (July 1966): 572-4; Robert E.
Burns, CH 35 (September 1966): 371-2; Harry F.
Snapp, JCS 8 (Autumn 1966): 482-4; Galen Broeker, JMH
38 (December 1966): 440; Donald McCartney, IHS
15 (March 1967): 325-7; D.J. McDougall, CHR 54
(April 1968): 195-8.

1588.   ———. THE CATHOLIC CHURCH AND IRISH POLITICS IN
         THE EIGHTEEN SIXTIES. Dundalk: Published for
         the Dublin Historical Association by Dundalgan
         Press, 1965.

         Concentrates on the hierarchy's political
         activities within three main areas of long-
         standing grievances: Protestant Establishment,
         the Land Laws, and the education question. Fixes
         the crucial steps of the episcopal campaign
         between the years 1864, in which the National
         Association was founded, and 1869, when dises-
         tablishment became a reality.

1589.   Newsinger, John. "Revolution and Catholicism in
         Ireland, 1848-1923." ESR 9 (October 1979): 457-
         80.

         Attempts to unravel the central paradox of modern
         Irish history, whereby a country which witnessed
         continuous revolutionary activity throughout most of
         the nineteenth century, was at the same time the
         most profoundly Catholic and clerical country in
         Europe. Gauges the extent to which the Irish
         revolutionary movement was suffused with Catholic
         ideals and sentiments.

1590.   O'Ferrall, Fergus. CATHOLIC EMANCIPATION: DANIEL
         O'CONNELL AND THE BIRTH OF IRISH DEMOCRACY,
         1820-1830. Dublin: Gill and Macmillan/
         Atlantic Highlands, N.J.: Humanities Press
         International, 1985.

         The most recent and fullest account of the
         campaign for Emancipation. Stresses the campaign's
         importance as the first non-violent mass movement
         in European history, ono which foreshadowed modern

democratic parties and broadened the scope of
parliamentary politics.

See: C.W. Woods, Jr., CHOICE 23 (February 1986): 915;
       Roy Foster, TLS, 2 May 1986: 466; K. Theodore
       Hoppen, ALBION 19 (Spring 1987): 152-5; Maurice
       R. O'Connell, CHR 73 (October 1987): 652-3.

1591. ————. "'The Only Lever ...'? The Catholic Priest
       in Irish Politics, 1823-29." STUDIES 70 (Winter
       1981): 308-24.

       Examines the degree to which priests were involved
       in the Emancipation campaign as local political
       leaders, concluding that while they may have been the
       only "natural lever" readily available to the
       O'Connellites, the real power was exercised by the
       lay leadership of the National Association. Dismisses
       as Tory propaganda the contention that it was their
       Maynooth background which explained the propensity of
       so many priests to become activists.

1592. Ó Fiaich, Tomás. "The Clergy and Fenianism, 1860-
       1870." IER 109 (February 1968): 81-103.

       Challenges the traditional assumption that the
       Irish clergy was unanimously opposed to Fenianism.
       Provides evidence of substantial differences in
       clerical attitudes from diocese to diocese, order
       to order, college to college, and between older
       and younger priests. Presents several instances
       in which clergymen took a stand opposite to the
       hierarchy's official position.

1593. O'Shea, James. PRIESTS, POLITICS AND SOCIETY IN
       POST-FAMINE IRELAND: A STUDY OF COUNTY TIPPERARY,
       1850-1891. Atlantic Highlands, N.J.: Humanities
       Press/Dublin: Wolfhound Press, 1983.

       Points to the high level of political activity by
       Irish priests during the second half of the
       nineteenth century. Of 575 priests ministering in
       County Tipperary from 1850 to 1891, 77% were heavily
       involved in such efforts as selecting parliamentary
       candidates, escorting voters to polling places,
       speaking at gatherings, and writing letters to local
       and national newspapers. Outlines the priests'

stance on the major issues emerging during these
turbulent four decades.

See: C.W. Wood, Jr., CHOICE 22 (September 1984): 176;
Emmet Larkin, RSR 10 (October 1984): 403-4;
John Whyte, CHR 72 (April 1986): 316-7.

1594. Whyte, John H. "The Influence of the Catholic Clergy
on Elections in Nineteenth-Century Ireland." EHR
75 (April 1960): 239-59.

Displays the Irish clergy's increasing willingness
to become actively involved in political activity
over the course of the nineteenth century. Necessitated at first by the Emancipation question, strong
clerical intervention in politics was evident in
every election from 1829 to 1900, and challenged the
power of the Protestant landlords, who had controlled
Irish politics up to the 1820s.

1595. ————. POLITICAL PROBLEMS, 1850-1860. A History of
Irish Catholicism, edited by Patrick J. Corish,
vol. 5, no. 2. Dublin and Melbourne: Gill and
Son, 1967.

Sketches the hierarchy's reactions to four of the
major issues affecting Irish life during the
1850s: the Queen's Colleges, the Tenant League,
"priests in politics," and a national education
system.

1596. Woods, C.J. "The General Election of 1892: The
Catholic Clergy and the Defeat of the Parnellites."
In IRELAND UNDER THE UNION: VARIETIES OF TENSION;
ESSAYS IN HONOUR OF T.W. MOODY, edited by F.S.L.
Lyons and R.A.J. Hawkins, 289-319.
Oxford: Clarendon Press, 1980.

Denies the Parnellites' claim that their defeat in
1892 was due to clerical electioneering, and
especially to the influence wielded by priests over
timid or illiterate voters. Shows, using quantitative techniques, that the clergy had little if
anything to do with the electoral results; for the
most part, public opinion was formed without
ecclesiastical direction.

See: Donald H. Akenson, HRNB 9 (February 1981): 105;
      K. Theodore Hoppen, EHR 97 (July 1982): 655-6;
      Desmond Bowen, VS 26 (Autumn 1982): 97-9; David
      W. Miller, CHR 68 (October 1982): 647-8.

Anticlericalism and Anticatholicism

1597. Bowen, Desmond. THE PROTESTANT CRUSADE IN IRELAND,
       1800-70: A STUDY OF PROTESTANT-CATHOLIC
       RELATIONS BETWEEN THE ACT OF UNION AND DIS-
       ESTABLISHMENT. Dublin: Gill and Macmillan/
       Montreal: McGill-Queen's University Press, 1978.

       Charts the growing hostility between militant
       evangelical Protestants and aggressive Catholics,
       climaxing in the latter's disestablishment campaign
       of the 1850s and 60s. Demonstrates how Protestant
       attacks laid the foundation for the identification
       of the Catholic community with Irish nationalism, a
       bond which held fast until the victory of 1869.

       See: ECON 266 (18 March 1978): 122; Oliver
             MacDonagh, TLS, 4 August 1978: 885; CHOICE 15
             (October 1978): 1069-70; James Hennesey, AMER
             139 (11 November 1978): 335; Donald H. Akenson,
             AHR 84 (February 1979): 174-5; Lawrence J.
             McCaffrey, VS 22 (Summer 1979): 455-6; K.
             Theodore Hoppen, EHR 94 (July 1979): 656-7;
             Alan O'Day, JEH 30 (October 1979): 502;
             Charles B. Paris, CH 50 (June 1981): 221-2.

1598. ————. SOUPERISM: MYTH OR REALITY; A STUDY IN
       SOUPERISM. Cork: Mercier Press, 1970.

       Maintains that Souperism--proselytism featuring
       material inducements such as soup in times of
       famine, to Catholics who would change their religious
       allegiance--was a tactic used by very few nineteenth-
       century Protestants in Ireland. Probes the mentality
       and impact of the small minority who practiced it, in
       the hope of starting a second Reformation.

       See: E.R.R. Green, IHS 17 (September 1971): 586-7;
             E.R. Norman, HIST 57 (June 1972): 288-9;
             Robert Stewart, CJH 7 (September 1972): 190-2;

John W. Boyle, CANHR 53 (December 1972): 464-5;
F.S.L. Lyons, EHR 88 (January 1973): 206.

1599. Cahill, Gilbert A. "The Protestant Association and
the Anti-Maynooth Agitation of 1845." CHR 43
(October 1957): 273-308.

Describes the nature and effects of the Protestant
Association's "No Popery" campaign of 1845, instigated
by Peel's proposal for government funding of Maynooth
(items 1515 and 1521). The Association, founded in
1835 by ultra-Tories, had successfully intimidated
Melbourne's ministry; Peel, however, was not cowed,
and his continued support for the funding split the
Conservative Party for the second time, one year
before the repeal of the Corn Laws.

1600. McNamee, Brian, O.M.I. "The 'Second Reformation' in
Ireland." ITQ 33 (January 1966): 39-64.

Measures the impact of the Church of Ireland's
early nineteenth-century campaign to win over
Catholics. Concludes that the Protestant prose-
lytizing heightened religious tensions, while not
fulfilling the initial expectation of large numbers
of converts.

1601. O'Neill, Thomas. "Sidelights on Souperism." IER 71
(January 1949): 50-64.

Details the diversity of Catholic reactions--pro-
test meetings, pamphlets, and boycotting of
converts--to the unscrupulous proselytism of
Protestants. Explains why few nineteenth-century
Irish Catholics were liable to shift their religious
allegiance in return for food, clothing, and housing.

Poland

*   Parsons, Reuben. "Polish Catholicity and Russian
'Orthodoxy.'" STUDIES IN CHURCH HISTORY, 5
(item 26), 72-144.

A detailed survey of the nineteenth-century
treatment of Polish Catholics by the Russian

government. The tolerant administration of Alexander
I gave way to persecutions under Nicholas I and
Alexander II; under Alexander III, tensions subsided,
though the intense Russian hatred of the Roman faith
remained as strong as ever.

1602. Zoltowski, Adam. "Catholicism and Christian Democracy
in Polish Catholicism." In CHURCH AND
SOCIETY: CATHOLIC SOCIAL AND POLITICAL THOUGHT
AND MOVEMENTS, 1789-1950 (item 308), 587-600.

Describes the different ways in which the Church
played a dominant role in the political and social
life of nineteenth-century Poland. Traces the
powerful clerical influence to the popular identification of Catholicism with Polish nationalism during
a time when Poland was under Russian control.

Russia

1603. Barratt, Glynn. M.S. LUNIN: CATHOLIC DECEMBRIST.
The Hague: Mouton, 1976.

Links Lunin's liberalism and Catholicism, the
products of a Jesuit education in Paris and a
stay in Warsaw after 1822. Underscores his rather
tenuous connection with the Decembrists; he disapproved of open revolution, and did not participate
in the uprising of 1825.

See: Deborah Hardy, AHR 82 (April 1977): 401-2.

1604. Dirscherl, Denis, S.J. DOSTOEVSKY AND THE CATHOLIC
CHURCH. Chicago: Loyola University Press, 1986.

Analyzes Dostoevsky's lifelong animosity against
Catholicism, which he considered authoritarian,
devious, and spiritually negative. Illustrates how
this most poignant of all anti-Roman writers in
Russia used his "cruel talent" to castigate the
Papacy and the Jesuits for belittling the faith by
imprisoning it within a power-hungry structure and
false theological concepts.

See: A. Klimoff, CHOICE 24 (March 1987): 1074;

David Rooney, NATR 39 (22 May 1987): 54.

1605. Flynn, James T. "The Role of the Jesuits in the
Politics of Russian Education, 1801-1820."
CHR 56 (July 1970): 249-65.

Contends that one of the major reasons for the
expulsion of the Jesuits from Russia in 1820 was
the success of their schools, which idealized
Western values and were therefore considered
dangerous by conservatives.

1606. Fortescue, Adrian. "The Latin Church in Russia."
DUBR 162 (January/February/March 1918): 41-70.

The only survey of nineteenth-century Russian
Catholicism in the English language. Presents the
Church's development as extremely uneven, from the
religious respite under Alexander I and the outright
persecution by Nicholas I, to the subtle oppression
under Alexander II and the Concordat of 1882 with
Alexander III, who saw in Rome a powerful ally
against the threat of revolution. Only under
Nicholas II, during the closing years of the
century, was a semblance of religious equilibrium
restored.

1607. Lencyk, Wasyl. THE EASTERN CATHOLIC CHURCH AND CZAR
NICHOLAS I. Rome, N.Y.: Ukrainian Catholic
University Press, 1966.

An account of Nicholas I's liquidation of the
Uniate, or Eastern, Catholic Church during the
period 1825-1839. Denounces the traitorous
Metropolitan Joseph Semashko, Assessor of the
Uniate College in St. Petersburg, under whose
supervision the Uniates were transferred from
papal jurisdiction to that of the Czar and the
Holy Synod. Shortly after the transfer, which
occurred in 1839, Gregory XVI condemned the
imperial government for its underhanded tactics
and continuing persecution of resisters.

See: Roman Smal-Stocki, CHR 55 (July 1969): 196-7.

* Parsons, Reuben. "The Martyrdom of the Nuns of

Minsk."   STUDIES IN CHURCH HISTORY, 5 (item 26),
145-58.

Dramatizes the harsh treatment of the Basilian nuns
of Minsk by Nicholas I's government during the years
1838-1844. Despite the tenacity of Abbess Makrena,
their leader, the members of the order died off
gradually. Few remained by the time Makrena arrived
in Rome, in October 1845, to tell her story to
Gregory XVI.

*   ————. "Pope Leo XIII and the Russian Empire."
STUDIES IN CHURCH HISTORY, 6 (item 27), 283-90.

Centers on Papal overtures of the 1880s--e.g.,
diplomacy and encyclicals--to obtain religious
freedom for Polish Catholics, while simultaneously
attempting to rid the Russians of their anti-
Catholicism. Disdains Russian Orthodoxy, which is
deemed primitive, brutal, and one of the Roman
Church's mortal enemies.

1608.   Schlafly, Daniel Lyons, Jr. THE ROSTOPCHINS AND
ROMAN CATHOLICISM IN EARLY NINETEENTH CENTURY
RUSSIA. Ph.D. dissertation. Columbia University,
1972.

Explores the strong attraction to Roman Catholicism
among certain circles of high society in Alexander I's
Russia, by detailing the life of the Rostopchins. The
entire family, except for Feodor Vasil'evich, its
head and the Governor-General of Moscow, converted,
and through the succeeding two generations religious
questions dominated its everyday existence.

1609.   Zatko, James J. "The Catholic Church and Russian
Statistics, 1804-1917." PR 5 (Winter 1960): 35-
52.

Discusses the drawbacks in attempting to produce a
history of nineteenth-century Catholicism in Russia
based simply or primarily on official statistics.
Shows, despite the questionable validity of the
figures, the constant decline in the Church's
numerical strength through the entire country,
attributing it to a series of highly effective
persecutions.

The Ottoman Empire

1610. Frazee, Charles A. CATHOLICS AND SULTANS: THE CHURCH
AND THE OTTOMAN EMPIRE, 1453-1923. London: Cambridge University Press, 1983.

Part 4 (Chapters 15-22) covers various aspects of
the nineteenth-century situation: the status of
Catholics in Constantinople before and after the
Tanzimat of 1839; the efforts of Pius IX and Leo
XIII to incorporate Eastern Catholics more fully
into the Roman structure; the persecution of the
Balkan and Armenian Catholic communities; and the
problems of Catholicism in Syria, the Holy Land, and
Egypt.

See: Joseph Gill, SOB 6 (no. 2, 1984): 83-4;
Benjamin Braude, AHR 89 (October 1984): 1127;
Elizabeth A. Zachariadou, RSR 10 (October
1984): 408; Stephen K. Batalden, CH 54
(March 1985): 107-8; Stafford Poole, C.M.,
CHR 72 (January 1986): 159-60; Colin Imber,
EHR 101 (January 1986): 225-6.

1611. O'Connor, R.F. "The Capuchin Mission in Bulgaria and
Reunion with Rome." ACQR 43 (April 1918): 205-
27.

Reviews the first twenty years (1841-1860) of
Capuchin activity in Bulgaria. Contrasts the
initial opposition from Orthodox bishops and
Turkish officials with the successful passage of
the Act of Union (1860), by which the Bulgarian
Orthodox Church accepted Roman jurisdiction.

1612. Skendi, Stavro. "Crypto-Christianity in the Balkan
Area under the Ottomans." SR 26 (June 1967): 227-
46.

Inquires into the extent to which Albanian, Bosnian,
Serbian, and Cypriot Catholics practiced their faith
in concealment.

1613. Walter, Christopher. "Raphael Popov, Bulgarian
Uniate Bishop: Problems of Uniatism and
Autocephaly." SOB 6 (no. 1, 1984): 46-60.

Uses the two thousand pages of correspondence by
Father Victorin Galabert, first Assumptionist
Superior in Bulgaria and councillor to Popov, to
reconstruct Popov's episcopate (1863-1876), its
challenges and significance within the history of
Bulgarian Uniatism. Places the twenty-three years
within a larger ecclesiastical context, highlighting
the two crucial issues confronted by Popov: autocephaly (i.e., separation from the Orthodox Church)
and the movement toward Rome by the Slavic peoples.

AUTHOR INDEX

(Numbers refer to items)